THE
AMERICAN
THEATRE
READER

THE
AMERICAN
THEATRE
READER

ESSAYS AND CONVERSATIONS FROM
AMERICAN THEATRE MAGAZINE

EDITED BY THE STAFF OF **AMERICAN THEATRE** MAGAZINE
FOREWORD BY PAULA VOGEL
PREFACE BY JIM O'QUINN

THEATRE COMMUNICATIONS GROUP
NEW YORK
2009

The American Theatre Reader is published by Theatre Communications Group, Inc., 520 Eighth Avenue, 24th Floor, New York, NY 10018-4156

Specific credits for the individual articles published herein are referenced with the text of each article.

Notes on the magazine images used on the cover are on page 617.

This publication is made possible in part with public funds from the New York State Council on the Arts, a State Agency.

TCG books are exclusively distributed to the book trade by Consortium Book Sale and Distribution.

LIBRARY OF CONGRESS CATALOGING-IN-PUBLICATION DATA

The American theatre reader : Essays and conversations from American theatre magazine / foreword by Paula Vogel ; edited by the staff of American theatre.
p. cm.
Includes bibliographical references and index.
ISBN 978-1-55936-346-4 (alk. paper)
1. Theater—United States—History—20th century. 2. Theater—United States—History—21st century. I. Vogel, Paula. II. American theatre.
PN2266.5.A44 2009
792.0973"0904—dc22
2009009563

Text design and composition by Lisa Govan
Cover design by Kitty Suen Spennato

First Printing, April 2009

CONTENTS

PREFACE

By Jim O'Quinn

I'd love to be able to say that *American Theatre* magazine was my idea, but it wasn't. That distinction belongs to Peter Zeisler and Lindy Zesch, the inimitable executive team that led Theatre Communications Group, the multipronged national theatre service organization that is the magazine's publisher, for two eventful decades. Zeisler and Zesch (the Zs, in staff shorthand) kept TCG on a carefully modulated and purposeful track through the 1970s and '80s into the '90s—years during which the not-for-profit resident theatre movement that had taken root in the cultural upheavals of the '60s continued its unprecedented expansion in cities, towns and communities across America. More than anything, it was this burgeoning of ambitious new theatre organizations in far-flung parts of the country, distant from the art form's traditional East Coast capital, that made the advent of a national general-circulation magazine devoted to theatre not only a logical development but a virtually inevitable one. The question was who would take on the task. Lots of people thought about it, including a coalition of New York producers (who engineered a full-color prototype of such a magazine in the early '80s, complete with fake ads and a photo of impresario Joseph Papp on the cover) and a loose alliance of California academics (who never got that far). The Zs actually did it.

Opera, dance, classical music, even poetry—there have been viable publications devoted to these arts disciplines through the best and the worst of times. But, remarkably, when the first issue of *American Theatre* appeared in April '84, with an insouciant Sam Shepard squinting from beneath the brim of a straw cowboy hat on its cover, there hadn't been a monthly magazine about the theatre on American newsstands for more than 20 years—since January '64, the month before the final edition of *Theatre Arts Magazine* was published. (The final number of that iconic and fondly remembered publication rolled off the presses that February but was never distributed.) *American Theatre* has some similarities to its historic predecessor, which, over the course of its 48-year run, published the scripts of important new plays and provided a forum for artists' points of view. *Theatre Arts* had made gestures, as times changed, toward broadening its locus of coverage beyond Broadway and the road, but its essential identity was so tied to the theatre's commercial heritage that the occasional column datelined "Denver" or "Seattle" couldn't suffice to bring its identity in sync with the momentous changes that were underway. *Theatre Arts* succumbed. The changes kept coming.

I got in on the action when the Zs, with the seeds of a magazine project germinating in their heads, hired me out of the graduate performance studies department at New York University in early 1982 to edit TCG publications, including its spiffy, limited-circulation monthly newsletter, *Theatre Communications*. Six months later I was joined by a new publications director, a New Yorker–turned–San Franciscan named Terry Nemeth, who came back east to become my closest collaborator in documenting an era of American theatrical life in print. In the years that we have worked side by side, Terry has steered the book division of TCG to its current berth as the largest independent trade publisher of dramatic literature in North America, with a booklist that boasts 250 playwrights, 11 of them Pulitzer Prize winners. The book you're holding in your hands was not my idea either—it was Terry's.

Part of my job at TCG, I learned in short order, was to draw upon my journalism background (as a former city-desk reporter in New Orleans, publisher of an award-winning small-town weekly paper, managing editor of the NYU-based *TDR: The Drama Review*, and after-hours arts reporter for any of the Manhattan alternative publications that would have me) to lay the groundwork for a full-scale national theatre magazine. On that score, I was green, but the Zs handed me, Terry, and my fresh-out-of-Yale associate editor Laura Ross over to an advisory committee that would have dazzled any theatre journalist in America: Such idols of mine as the critics Richard Gilman and Robert Brustein proffered opinions about what the magazine should and should not be; the great anthropologist and author Joseph Campbell blessed the project with his enthusiasm; legendary directors Alan Schneider and John Hirsch pitched in with ideas for essays and articles; John Houseman lent his august presence to our meetings; Zelda Fichandler and Gordon Davidson, pioneers of the regional theatre movement, offered perspectives that I value to this day.

The magazine that debuted in April '84—some 25 years and 260 issues ago—was the product of discussion and debate among these and other guiding spirits. Its typography and layout were stiff, by today's media standards, but the writing and the ideas were authoritative and adventurous from the beginning, as any number of early pieces reproduced in this volume will verify. Those several members of the original advisory committee who did not get to follow *American Theatre*'s progress over the full course of its first quarter-century would be pleased to note, I like to believe, how the magazine's personality has continued to evolve along with that of the variegated and ever-expanding theatre scene under its purview.

That evolution in the magazine's character has been driven in no small part by an astonishing roster of writers and editors who have shared its masthead. Jan Stuart, who went on to be the longtime theatre and film critic of *Newsday*, and Kathleen Hulser, now the public historian at the New-York Historical Society, were early additions to the *American Theatre* staff, as were crack-shot theatre writers Janice Paran and, later, Steven Drukman. Stephen Nunns, who currently heads the graduate theatre program at Towson University, kept tabs on the arts and politics through the years of the culture wars. The unglamorous but oh-so-essential second-in-command position (variously called associate or managing editor) belonged over the years to Marc Robinson and Catherine Sheehy, now prominent figures at Yale School of Drama, as well as to my brilliant comrade Todd London; the ingenious James Oseland, now editor-in-chief of *Saveur*; dramaturg and translator Douglas Langworthy; small-town newspaperman Jack Savage, who devoted a stint in the big city to the magazine; artists-at-heart Michele Pearce and Stephanie Coen; journalist and critic extraordinaire Celia Wren; and the currently indispensable Sarah Hart. Randy Gener, recipient of the 2007–08 George Jean Nathan Award for Dramatic Criticism, continues to do the magazine proud as senior editor and head writer. Many of the stalwart freelance writers who have contributed to *American Theatre* year after year are represented in this collection; others are not, but the magazine's authority and readability have depended upon their knowledge, writerly skills and willingness to work for ridiculous, next-to-nothing fees.

If Zeisler and Zesch were the magazine's original master-builders, subsequent leaders of TCG had architectural adjustments to offer. With Ben Cameron at the helm and a savvy advisory board to assist us, we undertook a rigorous, cover-to-cover re-evaluation of the magazine's mission, a process that enlivened and sharpened its content and led to the classy, full-color redesign (by TCG creative director Kitty Suen) that distinguishes *American Theatre* today. Already, more than a year into Teresa Eyring's executive tenure, the magazine is finding new ways to advance best practices and innovative management models for arts organizations, matters she has prioritized for the field.

Funders as well as executive directors have strengthened the magazine's ability to cover the waterfront, particularly the Jerome Foundation, whose pioneering National Theatre Criticism/Affiliated Writers program has hooked us up with the nation's best and brightest emerging theatre writers since 1989; the Irvine Foundation, which underwrote a similar writer-development effort for several years in its home state of California; and the Hewlett Foundation, currently playing matchmaker between the magazine and established arts commentators in the theatre-rich Bay Area.

Twenty-five years is a long stretch, but thumbing through the manuscript pages of this book, it doesn't seem so: I remember each of these 80 articles, essays and interviews vividly, as if they were yesterday's projects. It should be noted that, for all its abundance, this volume bears only partial witness to the significant writing *American*

Theatre has generated. The limits of space mean that some of my own favorite pieces didn't make the cut: Todd London's series of much-discussed essays that view the relationships of critics, theatre professionals and audiences through a psychological lens; critic Eileen Blumenthal's essential commentaries on puppets and puppeteers; scholar Elinor Fuchs's dazzling observations on postmodernism and the theatrics of U.S. politics; Jonathan Kalb's encounters with Heiner Müller, Richard Foreman and other theatrical outlaws; the great James Leverett's early columns on opera, dance and Robert Wilson; Marian Seldes on acting Albee. Other pieces I particularly prize are key items in this collection—Robert Coe's definitive rendering of the Cornerstone Theater Company experience; Don Shewey's ode to the erotics of acting; Anne Bogart and Kristin Linklater arguing about language in the theatre; August Wilson's milestone speech on the politics of black theatre. Notice how these pieces, solid and eloquent in their autonomy, benefit from the frisson of their proximity to related material.

This is a book you can read sequentially, as an impressionistic history of theatre in our time, or dip into for reasons of your own. The artists, critics and commentators who rub shoulders in these pages are just a few of the thousands of theatre folk who have lent form and substance to *American Theatre* magazine. May the art form that animates them endure and prosper.

Sarah Hart led the staff effort in planning and editing *The American Theatre Reader* and following it through to publication, with the assistance of Nicole Estvanik Taylor. Randy Gener, Eliza Bent, Kathy Sova and Tiffany Mischeshin offered counsel and research assistance. Kitty Suen Spennato designed the cover, and Lisa Govan designed the interior. Special thanks go to *American Theatre* intern Suzy Evans, who over the course of several months completed the transformation of these 80 articles and interviews from magazine form into book form.

FOREWORD

By Paula Vogel

When I was in my teens, I would comfort myself with a romanticized vision of living on the plains in the early 20th century in a farmhouse. I envisioned spending long, bleak winter months doing schoolwork at the kitchen table; as a reward when my homework was finished, I imagined thumbing through the family treasure: the Sears, Roebuck catalog.

At the time of this fantasy, my family was moving, almost yearly, into the blank canvases of slightly seedy rental apartments in the sagging inner suburbs of Washington, D.C.—apartments long past their prime. We often chose "custodial" apartments—i.e., for $10 less a month, our windows fronted the ground level and were sunken into a sub-basement where we might watch the legs of our neighbors mount the front steps.

These apartment complexes had sylvan names: Maryland Farms, Oakridge, Willowbrook. They were perched beside or behind sagging strip malls and fast food chains, alongside traffic arteries where people sped past on their way to the city, never looking at the apartments whose balconies overlooked cars or trash dumpsters. As junior high school led to senior high, we moved further and further to the outskirts in search of cheaper rent—beyond the strip malls, beyond the bus lines, beyond everything but suburban cheap housing sprawling across what had once been farmland.

And so, in the midst of essays and algebra, I would dream of that kitchen table in the midst of a farmhouse in the midst of a prairie. I wondered what it felt like to be a schoolgirl far removed from the cities at a time when the ugliness of suburbs had not yet been invented.

What marvels in the catalog! At your fingertips, washing machines, clothing, bicycles, furniture, gramophones—even houses. Every comfort that a bustling American mercantile life could offer could be delivered, upon a payment schedule, to one's own solitary farmhouse. And if one could not afford the price, one could still own it on the page.

At the same time that I was dreaming of farmhouses and unending plains, I also dreamt of theatres that I thought I would never see from my sub-basement apartments—theatres that perched on wharves in Provincetown or San Francisco; small black boxes in the Village in New York; magnificent structures of civic pride in Minneapolis, Houston, and, most impossible of all, Washington, D.C. However could I afford a ticket—much less the price of transportation to the theatre itself?

Parallel to my prairie fantasy, this urban fantasy was equally remote.

I had no idea how to find those dreamscapes—the lobbies and dazzling cocktail parties, the pioneering women and men who boldly made their own dreamscapes into urban realities stretching across the country: the American regional theatre. So I worked odd jobs through the next decade. I struggled through school, reading plays as hungrily as I might the Sears, Roebuck catalog. Almost all of those plays were written by men who were household names; the books from my public library described their legendary loves and lives and whetted the appetite of my theatrical voyeurism.

It took another decade more before I became emboldened enough to admit to writing. The farmhouse and the theatre lobby were not, I felt, within my reach. I thought of theatre as history, not as a living reality—not, certainly, as a field, a business, a career or a calling. I assumed it required legacy—that you were born into posh apartments overlooking the Hudson (with witty maids and butlers from a Philip Barry or Noël Coward play), that you were bottle fed during rehearsals, that you were teething during previews, and that you read reviews by the time you got your long pants (or stockings). Surely you learned clever conversation for cocktail parties from your parents.

I think these presumed 1930s-'40s prerequisites for a theatrical career remain with us today. It's remarkable how often I talk to young people who despairingly tell me that they won't be able to follow their passion into theatre: "I'm not very good at cocktail parties," they all say. Neither am I. I have nothing to wear, and I never will have, and witty epigrams à la Dorothy Parker only occur to me 24 hours after the party's over.

Then suddenly it appeared—my theatrical Sears, Roebuck catalog: *American Theatre* magazine. I heard about this entity called Theatre Communications Group. I became aware that there would be a magazine filled with names of theatres, from plains to coasts; filled with articles about productions across the country; filled with interviews of people I wanted desperately to meet. In my head I argued, discussed and disagreed with people in the field; I spent hours composing the passionate love letters of a young fan (but never sent them). I would run each month to the library in the days when I could ill afford a subscription and pester the librarian with the same impatience ("Is it in yet?") that 19th-century Americans possessed on the docks of New York, waiting for the next installment of Dickens's *The Old Curiosity Shop* ("Is Little Nell dead?").

When at last the latest issue came in, I would retreat to a quiet corner, not to be rushed, and immerse myself in the words, the plays, the thoughts of Joseph Papp, Bill Rauch, Sam Shepard, Maria Irene Fornes, Stephen Sondheim, Naomi Wallace, Adrienne Kennedy, Anne Bogart—what marvels in these issues! Although I would never meet them, I conversed with Arthur Miller, Eva Le Gallienne and Alan Schneider. I hung on every word of the argument between Robert Brustein and August Wilson over multiculturalism, theatre and race. Even if we could not be at that Town Hall meeting the night these two theatrical heavyweights met on stage, we could read the debate on the page. The winner of the debate (and of every debate in every issue) is theatre itself, for the subtext of every article is that theatre is vital to American life—and no, it's not ridiculous to love theatre so much that you devote your life to it, or that you tap your foot waiting for the latest issue of *American Theatre*.

I had thought that by the time I reached my current age I would get over the tongue-tied, high-school-girl infatuation that agonizes me whenever I do get a chance to meet one of my theatrical heroines/heroes. I have now had the chance to meet many of the people I first read about on these pages. I am still tongue-tied. I love what so many of you have given me in the theatre that I can barely speak to you in public: I stammer, and my cheeks go red. It seems that stage fright gets worse with age.

The isolation of my younger days has changed, too, though I've exchanged the possibility of seeing work around the country for the great excitement of seeing new work by the playwrights I work with here at home in New England. Now when my homework (reading new plays; writing memos, letters and e-mails) is finished, I reward myself at my kitchen table in my house perched by the side of northern bays, and thumb through the latest issue. I am still talking in my head to artists I may never meet as I turn the pages of *American Theatre*. If I can't be by the side of all of these rising artists who are transforming our theatre, I can at least accompany them on the page.

I will never get any better at going to those cocktail parties. But thanks to Theatre Communications Group, we are all invited to the party in every issue.

THE ESSAYS

PURGING THE CITADEL

By W. McNeil Lowry

October 1984

Those who came of age in the '60s and '70s have seen both the most rapid and the widest expansion of theatre institutions in our history. What is more interesting is that the youngest in this field are—or at least seem to be—unaware of that phenomenon. They take the burgeoning of audiences, the proliferation of companies and groups, for granted. They are of course right to start from where they are, from their own generational vantage point.

But there are reasons for keeping the evolution clear in our minds, and the reasons are perhaps critical. Unless we understand the sweep of the past 25 years, we shall not easily identify the roots of some of the most acute issues threatening performing arts groups. For many of them are the direct results of the rapid growth of institutions, in some part perhaps the penalty of success.

If we think of institutions in their maturity, what are the differences over the past generation?

Twenty-five years ago artistic directors and actors were more or less on the same side, if I may put it that way. If there were ever a referee involved, it was Equity, and only sporadically. If there was a manager who was more than part time, he or she was the right hand of the artistic director rather than of the board. It was the creative head—the artistic director—who both expressed and symbolized the short- and long-range goals of the group.

The sources of financial support beyond the box office were fewer in number, chiefly private individual patrons and the private foundations just beginning to act more nationally in the arts. This was both bad and good; good only because it was easier for patrons and foundations to respond directly to the artistic personality. Already, perhaps, a few private patrons reacted because they wanted "good theatre" in their city, but most hopefully wanted a particular company to be good and match its professed aims with developing standards.

The proliferation of the '60s and '70s, we are all aware, had manifold effects on theatre. What I should like to observe is that the most telling of these were experienced through seismic shifts or even tremors in the structure of companies. Though institutional crises often seemed to be crises in funding, or at least to begin that way, they were actually crises in governance and motivation. (Parenthetically, if our subject were dance, symphony, the art museum, we would find this equally true.)

I suppose it is in most general terms positive that membership on the board of a theatre group has come to confer prestige, either in one community or more nationally. This obviously is another sign of a changed national climate for the arts. But what climate it is changing to we may not yet have fully encountered. Already, however, we have often seen dilution of leadership within the enterprise, sometimes to the clear deterioration of standards.

The use of performing arts trusteeships for personal status might be affordable in and of itself. It is when interlocked with other more tangible changes—economic, social, political—that governance and motivation become the central problems, the authority of the artistic director abridged, and new tensions felt between the artists and the company. One of these changes of course was the advent of governmental support. The National Endowment for the Arts may never have approached the categorical and long-range commitments made by the Ford Foundation to many key groups, but in its dispersal of financial resources, the Endowment was unparalleled.

The reading given to this by boards of directors changed many signals and many motivations, particularly after the possibility of challenge grants appeared. And the first shoots of corporate support visible in the '70s contributed to additional strains on relations within a performing arts company and on its governance. Public funds in the arts made the arts look more like other agencies in the community perhaps. And if corporations were ever to share significantly in contributed income to theatre (even to date they have been fairly slow to do so), then the manager might be more than equal to the artistic director, and the businessman on the board superior to both.

At the very least, in contrast to the scene in the '60s, the manager has become the right hand not of the artistic director but of the board. In a few instances, as in some museums and many orchestras, a paid lay president is brought into the structure with a strong delegation from the board over both management and art. Artistic directors are in that event consultants to the president, in the illusion that in times when fundraising is a full-time pursuit and chancy, the business of theatre is business.

I do not want to suggest that we can never tamper with relationships between the board and the artistic leadership. But never can this be done without anticipating carefully the consequences, the many cans of worms that can be opened, the clash of self-serving positions. All these take both an artistic and emotional toll. Slowly you may discover that the institution exists only for itself, that even artistic directors and actors begin to lose contact with it, can no longer feel where it is or whether it has a focus.

Somewhere in the analysis of this shifting scene, there arises the obvious question of whether the business or corporate leaders in the community are really the best acquisitions for the board. In the '40s and '50s, few of these had been strongly recruited, unless as thousand-dollar annual givers to a symphony or opera company. Trustees were chiefly private patrons or professional men in the community, people with some education or exposure in the arts, who understood, as President Kennedy said he did, that "far from being an interruption, a distraction in the life of a nation, art is very close to the center of a nation's purpose."

I assure you I am not anti-business in my commitment to strengthening artistic and academic resources. Indeed, I have to confess, because there are many who could testify to it, that I often worked personally, one-on-one, to help convince individual businessmen to commit themselves to the goals of a significant performing company. My only defense is that at the time the individual businessman professed to be responding to one artistic personality and a collective of performers sharing a personal vision.

The onslaught of the Reagan Administration on the motivation for government participation in the pluralistic support mechanism for the arts has been more injurious than that Administration's largely unsuccessful efforts to halve the level of government arts budgets. When Rep. Sidney Yates and his allies in Congress frustrated the budgetary slashes, the Administration created a special commission to push voluntarism, chiefly by corporate officers or their staffs, as a substitute for official support. Thus the illusion that business is the business of theatre is superseded by the delusion that voluntarism is for free when in truth everybody's business becomes nobody's. In this country, founded and nurtured on the dualism of public and private, official and voluntary, "not-for-profit" has perversely been twisted into a pejorative. In the '70s, looking at the conflicts over governance, we felt a growing fear that the tail might begin to wag the dog. But as a museum director said recently, already too often the tail *is* the dog.

It is all too reminiscent of a far earlier time when actors and directors were thought of as feckless artistic types indulging themselves so long as someone else paid the freight, when one of the most influential trustees of a large and commanding institution asked Alan Schneider one night: "What do you people do in real life?"

There are always new problems. Frequently they arise on top of or out of our greatest achievements. There may well be a time for shaking down in the next 10 years. But I shall risk the prediction that the struggle for survival will not be largely financial. Survival will go to those willing to bring the most focus to bear. If there is a Gresham's law in money, that bad money drives out good, there is not one in art or in ideas. Bad theatre does not drive out good; it ends only by exposing itself.

My proposal is that however bitter and disruptive the toll, creative leaders in theatre reassert control of their own institutions, purging the citadel of its enemies, whether they be inside or outside the gates; yes, even of those who come making promises and bearing gifts.

W. McNeil Lowry, who died in 1993, worked at the Ford Foundation from 1953–74, serving from 1964 till his retirement as its vice president for the humanities and the arts. Lincoln Kirstein, a co-founder of the New York City Ballet, called him "the single most influential patron of the performing arts that the American democratic system has produced." For this article, adapted from remarks delivered at a Dance/USA national conference in San Francisco, the author substituted "theatre" for "dance" in an argument which Lowry believed applied equally to both fields.

HOW FREE IS TOO FREE?

By Eric Bentley

November 1985

A great deal has been published lately about translation in the theatre. So, in all this literature, I ought not to have been surprised to come upon a not wholly favorable reference to my own work—"the often inspired (if at times too free) Brecht texts of Eric Bentley."

Too free for whom? Just this critic? Everyone? Too free just here and there? Everywhere? Let me open up some broader questions. The first is that of inevitable imperfection. Your perfect translation could only be made by God—because only He would know both languages perfectly and have a perfect gift of expression in the language translated into, so that everything in the translation would work on readers or spectators exactly as the original worked on them. Such is the ideal goal—though to reach it, God might have to perform other miracles, since, in transferring a work from one country to another, and/or from one era to another, there are problems other than the purely linguistic . . . .

The merely human translator is seldom even fully bilingual. If, for example, he has been brought up in the one country and has then moved to another, the way he knows the second language will be very different from the way he knows the first. The second language will carry no childhood associations, nor will it carry the signs of having been learned in the natural, organic way in which infants learn languages. As for the first language, he will probably speak it as it was spoken by the previous generation. He will lose contact with its development and thus with its living reality at the later moment.

Of course, there are millions of people in the world who habitually use two languages. It is another question whether they use either of them well—and, even if they do, they may still not make good translators. Familiar as they are with the language translated into, they may not write it well, either in a general sense or—which is our interest here—in a theatrical sense. For the stage, one must translate into language that passes (what used to be) the footlights. One must be able to create what Jean Cocteau called poetry *of*, as against poetry merely *in*, the theatre. One must have a histrionic sensibility.

The language translated into. I stress *that* language, because of the two languages in question, that is, for the translator, the more important one. He is writer first, scholar-linguist second. This is clearest in the theatre. If the play is not in the language it's supposed to be in, there's no play. That the translator may have perpetrated some howlers is a secondary matter. All the best people perpetrate howlers. Those who believe the English Bible was written by God must believe that even God perpetrates howlers, because there are quite a few in the only really great translation, the King James version. I am told that the same is true of Florio's *Montaigne*. Are the best translations perhaps the ones with the most mistakes? No reason why not. The primary criterion is what a text amounts to in the language it is (now) in. Florio and King James's clergymen made great books—as well as lots of mistakes. We have translators today who make few mistakes, perhaps none, and who make bad books, bad plays.

It's always a matter of what a given context needs. At a certain point, a scene in a play may be in desperate need of a joke. The audience has to be made to laugh at all costs. Good. The playwright has brought it off. What shall the poor translator do when he finds his accurate rendering isn't funny? Give a little lecture on the obligation of accuracy? Shall all those years of study go in vain? They'd better. At this moment, he has to be Woody Allen, not Ralph Manheim.

But humor is only the extreme case. What applies to the funny applies also to the beautiful—or, for that matter, the ugly. No use to come up with what the dictionary, backed by the Académie Française, says is exact. What you have to come up with is the quality that has the desired effect. Make the audience laugh. Make them cry. Make them see a point clearly. Make them see stars. Make them feel good. Make them feel sick. But make them.

In his Molière translations, the poet Richard Wilbur has come close to producing (so far as I can judge) the same effect that the French produces on a Frenchman. But even he can't get all the way there. Language itself imposes barriers no human can overleap. Take rhyme. Poets in both French and English have used rhymes. The problem lies in the fact that English poets have used rhymes differently. It was, I think, impossible for Wilbur to write all those rhymes without making most of them sound clever. "Why, he's even funnier than Molière," I have heard offered him as a compliment, whereas the fact is that rhyming couplets, in English, not in French, have wit built into them. Yes, I know a vast attempt was made at one time to write Heroic Tragedies in English rhyming couplets. It failed. Failing to be funny, those couplets just sound silly, and thus it comes about that while Wilbur can be surprisingly close to Molière, he is often unsurprisingly closer to W.S. Gilbert.

A perfect translation of a work of art cannot be made by human hands because one language does not offer exact aesthetic equivalents of another. You can translate science, but you can't translate poetry.

Poetry is (Frost said it) *what gets lost in the translation,* and under the heading "poetry" I'm placing the whole aesthetic dimension: everything that makes for "effect," an effect of beauty, ugliness, delicacy, indelicacy, funniness, lugubriousness . . . and on and on. Rhythm alone erects terrible barriers. Rhythmically, Shakespeare in English can sound rather like Shakespeare in German—but in French? I enjoyed Jean-Louis Barrault's *Hamlet* very much. It was probably the first time I could follow what was going on. That was because it was not Shakespeare but Gide.

Still, we try, we translators, and we are proud if we think we do even half as well as, say, King James's clergymen, for surely the Bible has been enjoyed as literature by persons with no Hebrew and Greek and we can't give all the credit to the translators. Stubbornly we insist on assuming that some of the beauty of those Psalms has come through from the original, and that Robert Frost must have been partly wrong.

Which is not to deny that there may also be works in which a major part of the poetic labor has been done by the translator. Scholars who know Persian tell us that there's more Fitzgerald than Omar in that famous *Rubaiyat.* In which case, we should count it a great English poem, not a great translation.

Is that what Robert Lowell meant by "imitation"—Fitzgerald's being a Victorian "imitation" of an original one could not get really close to?

Finally, then, I come to the liberties I've (sometimes) taken with Brecht. Did I have an acceptable alternative? Other translations I've read do not always convince me that I had. In the theatre, we meet with at least four different phenomena all called (by someone or other) translations:

1. The rendering that is so meanly literal that Arthur Miller has used the expression "Pidgin English" to describe its vocabulary and style. (Translations made in language classes to show the teacher one has used the dictionary properly are in this territory.)
2. The rendering that is in correct and cogent English but otherwise sticks as close to the original as possible.
3. The adaptation that can have number 2 as its basis but then takes such liberties as making cuts, making interpolations and deliberately changing the style and/or tone.
4. The variation that verges on an original play merely "based on" a foreign one. But I have introduced the term "variation" to describe such plays of my own when part of their point is an interplay between the old conception and the new. The *thing* existed long before I used the term as the title of my *Kleist Variations. Threepenny Opera* is a variation of *Beggar's Opera.* (Unconsciously perhaps, Fitzgerald's poem is a variation of Omar's.) Peter Brook's *Carmen* of two seasons ago is not, as has been claimed, a return to Mérimée's story: It is Peter Brook's variation on the Bizet opera.

Let me report one or two of my experiences with Brecht. A discovery I made was that not all his plays lend themselves to the same kind of treatment at the hands of a translator. In my view, *The Caucasian Chalk Circle* lends itself to close translation 2 but *Good Woman of Setzuan* does not—and therefore some of the expedients of 3 become allowable, if not mandatory. I can't imagine anybody finds me too free in my treatment of the one, but I know some find me guilty of that in my treatment of the other. Let me give my side.

In the library you can find two word-for-word translations of *Good Woman*. My name is on one of them, so perhaps that entitles me to say without undue competitiveness that neither of them reads well in English. And what reads badly plays even worse. German is often wordier (lengthier) than English and, especially in *Good Woman*, Brecht seems to me to have given way to a kind of verbosity (volubility?) which is possible in one language but not in another. After having worked with a colleague on a "literal" version (published by the University of Minnesota in 1948), I later went back to the German on my own and made a much shorter text. The original intention was not to abridge, though eventually whole passages did get left out. The intention was to say everything as snappily as we'd say it in English, not as elaborately as many things are said by many persons in German. A three-hour play thereby became something like a two-hour play, and I would argue that this happened organically, and on an aesthetic principle, not because we had to fit a two-hour schedule or were fearful that our audience had a short attention span. Critics may, of course, question either my premise or the merit of the result, or both, but I was dependent on my own judgment, that of my colleagues, and, of course, on experience with audiences.

Sooner or later, someone is going to compare the lyrics in three established versions of *Threepenny*: mine, Marc Blitzstein's and the Willett-Manheim. For they represent three distinct approaches. Take your pick:

A. Willett-Manheim—unfree, get everything in, never mind if it's a good lyric.
B. Blitzstein—very free, leave out what's not easy or politic to leave in, make it a good Blitzstein lyric.
C. Bentley—middle of the road, not too strict, not too free, trying to make a lyric that sounds good with the music and that sounds Brechtian.

I naturally think there's a case for C; I also think there is a case for B; in practice, there wasn't much of a case for A as you couldn't tell what the hell the performers were singing about and had to look it up in the book. (If you don't believe me, try to figure out the words in the recorded version of the Lincoln Center production.)

Blitzstein and I used to quarrel. There was sibling rivalry, and both the brothers wanted to own Dad (BB). But we agreed on a fundamental point, and I recommend it *an die Nachgeborenen*, to those who come after. We agreed that the place to translate Brecht songs is at the piano. The translator has to sing them—with their accompaniment. It's the only way—the only way known to Blitzstein and Bentley anyhow—to get them right. According to Goethe, it was the only way to get *his* songs right.

Anyone who looks up my early critical writings will find I used to attack all the freer translations, especially the Broadway adaptations I was called on to review. I still loathe such an effort as S.N. Behrman's free version of one of my favorite French plays, *Amphytrion 38*. This was why I led off with Brecht translations, in the '40s, which stuck close to the originals. The freedoms my critics speak of are all of later date—post-1960, in fact. It began with *A Man's a Man*. Those of us who were putting it on in the America of the Cuban missile crisis wanted to update it somewhat. As theatre people we also wanted more songs in it. We could perhaps have imported songs from other Brecht plays. I took the more arrogant step of writing in some lyrics of my own. The fact was that my interest was spreading out from translating to other things, notably songwriting and playwriting. I'll add that I did not continue to make Brecht the victim of my venturesomeness. From *A Man's a Man* on 42nd Street, I went to *Orpheus in the Underworld* at City Center, keeping all the old music but writing a new libretto—a free adaptation or, if I may be permitted, a "variation" of the old one . . . .

Let me make a suggestion. Any foreign play that's worth the trouble should be around in more than one form: specifically, in a reasonably close, strict, scholarly translation that leaves no passages out and writes no passages in; and in at least one freer version with certain more ambitious ends in view—in one case, to get at certain subtleties in the original that are missed in the more literal text; in another to make a text more theatrical and "public"; in yet another actually to add something in significant counterpoint to what was there before. I have already made it clear that a reader who finds my later version of *Good Woman* too free can hunt up the earlier, "unfree" version in the library. I was also at pains to bring out *A Man's a Man* in two different versions, one close to the German, one less close. Couldn't this procedure be adopted more often? (The publishers' answer is, "No, it costs too much." I tested this recently when the University of Minnesota Press asked me to endorse a very free adaptation of *Brand*. I said, "I will, if you print a literal version on opposite pages, so the reader can see what your poet added and subtracted." They wouldn't; so I didn't.)

Incidentally, the literal version I wanted printed on opposite pages was the text the adaptation had been made from. Another topic that's been under discussion lately: translating from languages one doesn't know. I wanted readers of *Brand* to see how this works to the extent that they can do so without also knowing Dano-Norwegian. I'm afraid that even a university press does not wish its readers to be aware of such problems; and perhaps the adapter didn't either. For my part, I couldn't ask students to read such an adaptation at all if there was no way in which they could check it against either the original or a closer translation. Natually, I apply this principle to my own work. Students of Kleist cannot find what they need in my *Kleist Variations*: They must read either the German original or close translation thereof.

Let me end with a comment on skullduggery in this field. A producer who wants to avoid paying royalties to translators goes to the library, takes out five versions of an Ibsen or a Chekhov, and puts them, as it were, in the blender. Some producers have been known to claim credit as translator and/or adapter and even to pay themselves royalties. The Ibsen scholar Rold Fjelde calls this abuse: larceny by pastiche. It cannot be stopped by the police, nor can the law courts render any service if the translations ransacked are in the public domain. The skullduggery will end only when producers cease to regard the translator as an eminently removable middle man and accept him as the peer of other artists in the theatre.

To have recourse to earlier translations is not, by the way, something an artist must refuse to do. Artists-translators of the Bible have done it ever since the 16th century. The offense in "larceny by pastiche" is the assumption that a good version of a play can be knocked together by a non-artist whose concentration is on a) hiding his sources and b) saving money.

Eric Bentley is a playwright, critic and scholar. He was drama critic for the *New Republic* for four years. His plays include *Lord Alfred's Lover* and *Are You Now or Have You Ever Been*. His critical works include *The Playwright as Thinker, What Is Theatre?*, which has been steadily in print for half a century, and *The Life of the Drama*, which began as the Norton Lectures at Harvard. He was inducted into the Theater Hall of Fame in 1997. A slightly different version of this article appears in *Thinking About the Playwright* (Northwestern University Press, 1987).

WHO'S AFRAID?

By Alan Schneider

February 1986

One day in the late spring of 1962, I sat at one end of producer Richard Barr's kitchen in his apartment just off Eighth Street, with Richard at the other end, both of us reading a new play by Edward Albee with a mysterious title, *Who's Afraid of Virginia Woolf?* It was the same untitled play whose first scene I had read and worked on almost a year earlier; and I still thought it might be about someone who wanted a room of her own. As we sat there, with Richard handing me a few pages at a time of what seemed to be an endless collection, I soon discovered otherwise.

I remember vividly the hand-to-hand passage and piling-up of those papers in that steadily darkening room, page after page of Edward's lightning—like words exploding in my brain. How many pages? Could it last? I felt as though I were being hit over the head with a succession of concrete blocks, and yet I didn't want them to stop hitting me. I had a headache, and yet I wanted to stand up and shout out the window. At that time, I had never seen or read Strindberg's *Dance of Death*, yet somehow it was Strindberg of whom I kept thinking. Strindberg and O'Neill—and Edward Albee, who was piercing the darkness with these unexpected, pulsating flashes of light. Those two marriage partners, Martha and George, were like dinosaurs battling on the cliff of emotional survival. When all the pages had been gathered, George and Martha huddled close in their pain, Richard and I tiptoed out to his living room, sat down, and could hardly say anything. Richard had already called the play "remarkable." Maybe too remarkable, he added, for Broadway. Now I thought, all too ruefully, he might be right. After a while I called Edward to tell him that I had read his new play and loved it.

Some of the notes I later wrote for myself in my director's script evoke the play's basic texture: "A dark legend of truth and illusion." "A modern parable, with musical structure and rhythms." "A portrait of people drowning and grasping for straws of awareness, of understanding, of communication." They are all hurt. Martha is hurt and wants to lash out to hurt back. George is hurt and has to fight back in order to survive. Nick wants to hurt others before they hurt him—he's out to get all he can. And Honey just tries not to get hurt any more. In rehearsal, I would tell the actors that they were not in a realistic play—otherwise they'd all be flat on the floor. "Try to make the largest possible choices," I would say. "These are not little people but giants battling on the cliff."

All that spring and summer, the fate of the new play remained as inscrutable as its title (which, I was eventually to learn, had come from Edward's seeing the question scrawled on a bathroom wall in a Village bar). Edward had just become involved, actively and enthusiastically, with the Actors Studio. The Studio, then at the height of its glamour period, with such superstars as Marilyn Monroe, Robert Redford and Paul Newman regularly in residence and with international visitors like Laurence Olivier and John Gielgud, was about to launch itself as a producing theatre. This was a step that the Studio's artistic director, Lee Strasberg, had always avoided, the memory of the Group Theatre's fall remaining too strongly fixed. But the pressures were strong, from both within and without, and Lee had finally given in.

Besides, he now had a play of prime quality and plenty of actors to play each of its four roles. *The Zoo Story* had had its first showing there, and then gone on to success outside. This time Edward's new play would be done, and done right, by the one organization best equipped with talent and understanding to bring his work to the world. Geraldine Page was selected—by Lee—to play Martha, and Eli Wallach, George. Evidently, I was going to direct it—although no one ever told me directly or talked to me about whether I approved of the casting. (I did.) There was talk about Lou Antonio or Ben Piazza for Nick, and a young Studio actress unknown elsewhere, Lane Bradbury, would play Honey. Since Gerry Page was pregnant, we couldn't go into rehearsal until the following January.

As usual, there's many a slip . . . . The Studio, about to embark on production, had just persuaded that optimistic Broadway impresario Roger L. Stevens to serve as fundraiser. Producer Cheryl Crawford, an old colleague of Lee's, had also come aboard to organize and manage. Lee was a terrific apostle of "the Method" but a totally inept administrator. Fate's Mona Lisa smile soon made itself evident. Cheryl did not particularly admire Edward's new play; besides, she said, it had too many dirty words in it—although I had some difficulty then, as I still do, in finding them. And Roger, after his initial reading of the script, called it "a dull, whiny play without a laugh in it." Roger is well known for having produced more successful plays than any man alive, but not necessarily for having read them. So Lee remained the only one of the Studio's ruling triumvirate who wanted to produce Edward's play.

When the chips were down, Lee could have insisted that the Studio put on the play even though both Roger and Cheryl demurred. He was, after all, not only artistic director but the Studio's guru, god and godfather. But Lee's Achilles heel, here as always, was that he wanted success and feared failure. His colleagues' negative vibrations rubbing off on him, he began to question his own judgment. In the crunch, he made the decision to back off—eventually settling on a less adventurous and safer revival of O'Neill's *Strange Interlude* for the Actors Studio Theatre's postponed debut. The membership's reaction—except for Gerry Page, who had never been enthusiastic about the play—was one of shock and dismay. In the hallways there were mutterings of meetings, petitions, even outright revolt; but Lee's psychological and moral hold on us was too strong. I often ruminate on the difference both for the Studio itself and for the entire American theatre had Lee, in the particular case of *Virginia Woolf,* had the courage of his own taste. Might we have had, back in 1962, a real permanent "theatre" in New York City?

Once the play came back to him, Richard Barr was not himself sure that Broadway was ready to accept its outsized intensity and shock value. He and his new partner, Clinton Wilder, a wealthy young theatre buff but no relation to Thornton, toyed with various ideas. One was simply to do the play Off Broadway—but then, it would be harder to get top actors for the cast. Another idea was to do simultaneous productions Off Broadway and on. If one didn't succeed, perhaps the other might. This alternative soon succumbed to several practical realities, chief among them the problem of getting a theatre. Only Billy Rose, persuaded by a perceptive production assistant, Malcolm Wells, offered us his theatre, only if we would agree to approach major stars to play Martha and George. Someone like, say, Katharine Hepburn and Henry Fonda.

All of us, from Edward to myself, had been talking only of Uta Hagen and Richard Burton. Uta wasn't sure, after her recent Broadway experience with *A Month in the Country*, that she wanted to work again in the commercial theatre—ever. Burton was not available. Katharine Hepburn was not a bad idea, though Uta was a much better one. We dispatched a script to La Hepburn in Hollywood. She read it immediately, returned it forthwith with thanks, saying that she wasn't good enough, bless her. Henry Fonda worried us; after we had gone through a list of about 50 unavailable, uninteresting or un-something-else names, we sent the script to his agent, name unmentionable. The unmentionable read it, decided that it was too dreadful even to submit to his client for a reading, and never forwarded it to Fonda. "Hank" later fired the agent. And he subsequently stated, orally and in a letter to me, that his single greatest artistic regret was that "I never got to play George." He would have been fine.

Somewhat off the hook with Billy, we applied pressure on Uta. I was selected to woo her back from her self-imposed exile as a successful acting teacher at the Bank Street studio of her husband, director Herbert Berghof, during the week, and an active gardener around their Montauk house on weekends. She finally consented to read the script—out there.

Richard telephoned Uta out in Montauk one day; and I spent, I think, about five hours talking her into accepting. She had evidently had a bad time with one of her directors, Michael Redgrave; quite apart from my previous "entanglements" with her husband, whatever she had heard about my methods and personality had not entirely reassured her that I wouldn't be equally impossible. At one point, she asked me it I carried a riding crop at rehearsals (evidently Redgrave did), or had ever hurt an actress physically. I explained that no matter how difficult I might be, the only whip I ever carried to rehearsals was a verbal one. And besides, my only course of action in this particular case would be to love, honor and obey her at all times. She was a great actress. She was ideal for the part. I had seen her in everything from *The Seagull* through *Othello* and *Saint Joan*, and there was no one in the world at this specific moment who was more "right" for Martha than Uta was. At the end of our conversation, having really wanted to play the part after she had read the first four pages of Edward's script, Uta took a deep breath and agreed. Richard and I did a little dance around the phone, and then went back to casting George.

We had gone through every actor in the United States and England who was even remotely possible, starting with Richard Burton and ending up with Robert Flemyng. Flemyng, at one point in our long-distance negotiations, accepted, but at the last minute—luckily for us, as matters turned out—changed his mind. We were desperate.

Somewhere, from the depths of my subconscious, I remembered an actor named Arthur Hill who had played the father in the James Agee/Tad Mosel *All the Way Home*. He didn't seem ideal for us, but he was around 50, male, with male strengths and weaknesses, and available. We sent him the script and, after the usual period of nail-biting silence, the word came back that he had accepted. No one was exorbitantly enthusiastic, notably Billy Rose, but we had our George.

For Honey, we went back to our original Actors Studio cast for Lane Bradbury, a sweet-faced and attractive brunette, whose work I had seen only in class. And for Nick, Edward's suggestion was another Studio actor then beginning to "make it," Robert Lansing. Interestingly enough, we lost Lansing almost at once in a disagreement over billing. I have never, I think, lost an actor because of salary problems but have done so many times when a question of billing could not be resolved. Actors, it seems, care more for their status than for their pocketbooks. I suppose in a world where image is more important than reality, it's hard to blame them.

From the first time I had read *Virginia Woolf*, George Grizzard had seemed to me ideal for Nick—except that he was not the hefty bruiser suggested by Edward's description. After we lost Bob Lansing, I once more brought up George's name to Edward, explaining that I was not sure if he was either interested or available; that was always the ploy to make an actor seem more desirable. In Edward's opinion, George was too lightweight, too small physically. The text spoke of a fullback, and that's what Edward wanted. I suggested that George was handsome, tough, aggressive; he might be able to do something more subtle with the role. "Why couldn't Nick be, after all, a halfback?" Richard and Clinton seemed to concur, especially since the horizon was not teem-

ing with fullbacks who could act. Edward finally gave in on one end—
and George, not too enthusiastically, on the other. I'll never forget the
way Edward looked at me when he finally said yes.

"You'd better be right, Alan!"

Which meant that if George didn't deliver, it would be my scalp.
As usual. Or Arthur. Or anybody. Casting is a large part of a director's
job, it has been said, and I agree. Fifty percent, or eighty percent, or
more. If you have a good script and you cast it well, it'll be good on stage.
If you don't, it won't. You're a director and not a magician, I always say to
myself as to the cast. "Dear George, please, please deliver! Dear Arthur!
Dear Everybody!"

Our "Evening Company" set, we proceeded to put together our
"Matinee Company." This was mainly Uta's idea. She felt that since
Virginia Woolf was almost four hours long, and the role of Martha
required such physical and vocal strength, she would not be able to
play two performances in one day. We were fortunate enough to get
Shepperd Strudwick, who had played George in the original television
scene the year before, and Kate Reid, the noted Canadian actress.

That matinee business had a fascinating sidelight. Evidently Uta,
deciding she didn't want to share the matinees with another major
actress, at some point told Richard she wanted to play all eight performances. When Richard—explaining that he'd already hired another
actress, spent a lot of money on publicity and had grown fond of the
idea—told her she couldn't, Uta went to Equity. Equity ruled that an
actress had the right to play all eight performances if she wanted to.
Everyone got angry and stuck to his or her guns. The impasse was settled only when Richard agreed to give Uta a share of the production's
profits, which of course have gone on for years and years, in fact are still
doing so (although I never got any part of them). In effect, Uta got paid
more for playing less. Bertolt Brecht, if not Karl Marx, might smile.

All these shenanigans were forgotten once I was safely back from
the West. Even before leaving, I had met with designer Bill Ritman to
discuss the setting and costumes. And while I was away, Edward had
contributed a few thoughts, some of which Bill had passed on to me.
When I got back, I discovered that one or two of my ideas had survived. I wanted the set, for example, to be less realistic than more;
Edward and Richard—then as generally always—wanted the opposite.
Bill, a quiet and congenial fellow with nerves of steel, managed to give
us a realistic set which suggested both a cave and a womb. And I was
able, ultimately, to fill George's professional living quarters with a few
specific artifacts of my own. Never liking the fake "spines" that passed
for books on most Broadway sets, I brought a suitcase full of books
from my own study to each rehearsal. My wife Jean's father's metal
newspaper rack, with a space for each day's paper, also came in handy.
It proved so suitable that the prop man built an exact copy.

We held our first reading in Uta's comfortable old-world apartment off Washington Square, which seemed an apt setting for a play
about academic life. It was very low key, not at all like a Broadway
rehearsal. Edward welcomed everyone and told them how happy he

was that they were all there. I gave them my usual spiel about a great play and a good cast making a good director; I told everyone to ask me whatever they wanted to even if I couldn't answer at the moment, never to take me literally, and not to worry if I changed my mind on something once in a while. I said that no matter what, critics and audiences would have to respect the material. Then we read it.

That was the first time I had heard Edward's words read aloud since an afternoon some months earlier, when Edward and Richard and a couple of actors had read through it at Edward's house—putting half the listeners to sleep with its seemingly interminable speeches, and making me think favorably of going off to Harold Pinter. This time it was a blockbuster. With four real actors really acting it, the play exploded like a sudden storm, one stroke of lightning, one thunder clap after another.

Moments later, I found myself alongside Uta in her kitchen as she was pouring coffee. "It's a disaster," she murmured, out of the corner of her mouth, without looking in my direction.

"Who? What? What was a disaster?"

She looked at me, amazed. "He's a disaster," she said, gesturing towards the living room and Arthur Hill, her costar.

I was as stunned as I was bewildered. I had thought that Arthur had proven amazingly effective, especially considering his state of nerves and his obvious exhaustion. Uta felt otherwise from the time she first set eyes on him. By the time we broke up that day, she had told everyone except Arthur that he was impossible and that we should replace him immediately with her own real-life husband, Herbert Berghof. Herbert was a fine character actor whom all of us knew, but he was all wrong for George, too old, too strange, and the possessor of a strong Viennese accent.

We were certainly not going to replace Arthur with anyone—he was doing too well. But a few days into rehearsals, we did have to make a change. Edward, along with the rest of us, came to the conclusion that we'd made a bad mistake with Lane Bradbury. Lane was a lovely actress but her quality was all wrong for Honey. I hated changing someone so soon in so small a cast—any cast—and tried to rationalize Lane's seeming colorlessness. Edward insisted, taking all the blame. When we began to explore the possibilities—and we knew we had very little time—I thought of a young actress whom I considered the most talented and exciting personality I knew: Melinda Dillon. Melinda had decided to leave the Arena Stage and was rattling around New York, not getting past many doors. Luckily, however, Richard had seen her in my production of *The Caucasian Chalk Circle*; he thought she was great.

No sooner were we all applauding ourselves on our new milk-fed Honey than I got a message to call George Grizzard at home. Late one night, calling from a public phone booth in Shubert Alley, I finally reached an angry George, who informed us he was leaving the show. Why? What was wrong? Everything was going so well; Edward had forgotten all about his original fullback image; Uta adored him. How could he possibly want to quit?

At first, George didn't want to tell me; but, finally, the truth came out. Bitterly, feeling betrayed by us all, me especially, he poured out the nature of that betrayal: We had changed our Honey without asking or even telling him, and to compound our felony had gotten someone several inches taller than himself. He was now the shortest person on that stage.

I had forgotten how sensitive George had always been about his height. From the moment he gave himself to the theatre, he had wanted to be a leading man, he saw himself as a leading man; and he wound up playing character roles. The romantic sexy leading man he saw himself as could not stand having a mate towering over him. I spent endless hours—in that lonely, isolated phone booth, pouring in dime after dime—talking George back into staying with us. I coaxed, cajoled, flattered, pleaded. We'd even get him a pair of Adler's elevated shoes. Fortunately for us, he probably wanted to be talked back. So he came back—to complain, almost without stop, about his role being unwritten, his sentences never completed, no logical reason why Nick would stay in Martha's house to take all those insults. As well as to give a wonderfully skillful and modulated performance—using every one of those dots he hated so much—and to grow more than fond of Melinda Dillon in spite of her being so tall.

Right up to our first preview, Uta never relented in her campaign to replace Arthur, a campaign that we were terrified might even register with him. He and Uta were at opposite poles of the acting spectrum. Uta worked from inside, but with exceptional control of her physical self. She always knew exactly what she was doing on stage and what effect it was having on the audience—even as she never lost hold of her inner impulses and instinctive grasp of the moment's truth. Arthur, on the other hand, was what Method-trained actors always contemptuously term "a technical actor." Each move, each gesture, came from outside, studied and deliberate. Yet his own sense of reality was so strong and so sincere that whatever he chose to do, no matter how externally imposed, seemed real and organic to his audience.

Our rehearsal period being inordinately short, we spent every legal minute of our daily seven hours working, and lots of nonlegal ones in the bar next door to the Billy Rose going over the notes that my redoubtable assistant, Joy Small, had managed to write legibly in the darkness. Counting the first two days of readings, we had less than three weeks prior to our first preview.

Edward and I followed the same pattern we had set in *The American Dream*. He let me stage each scene without being around. Then he would come in, fresh, to look at it and give me his thoughts. Prior to rehearsals, or course, we had spent many hours and days together, with me asking him dozens of questions, sometimes not even to get the answers but to start him talking or thinking. We had already made a few small cuts; more were to follow during rehearsals.

Most people think that a director is always making a writer cut out something he doesn't want to. In our case, I can take credit for persuading the author not to cut George's "Bergin" speech about the pain

of growing up even though Edward confessed he wasn't sure what specific relevance it had in the particular scene. I told him it was too good
to cut, regardless of its relevance. There was another speech of
George's at the end, summing up the meaning of the evening, which
I hated to see go; but this time I agreed with Edward that it held up the
last scene too much. The largest cut we made was some 11 pages at the
very beginning of Act 3, a long scene between George and Honey, which
was interesting and funny but obviously delayed the action. Edward came
in one day and presented us with a new opening which cut right to
Martha's entrance. Everyone except Melinda was very happy. Arthur didn't
mind having 11 fewer pages to memorize.

I'll never forget the day I'd finished staging the first act, and we
were showing it to Edward and the producers. Richard, bless him, shot
up from his seat, beaming. "I think it's excellent work," he said.
Clinton was noncommittal but smiling, as usual. We all looked over at a
slightly nervous Edward Albee, in baggy sweater and dirty tennis
shoes, roaming around the back of the auditorium all by himself. After
a few unspoken dots, his head slightly turned, he said: "Well . . . it's not
all the way I had seen it."

I turned pale, inside as well as out. "What was wrong?"

"I'm not sure. It's all different."

Richard, bless him, came in with, "Well, I loved it!"

"Okay," I persisted. "What's different? What's one thing different?
What don't you like?"

Edward prowled up and down the aisle a moment. "Well, I think
Honey and Nick sit down too soon. I didn't see them sitting down that
soon."

"Oh," I said, "I think I can handle that. What else?"

"I don't know," Edward replied, looking away. "I'll think about it."

Through all this council-of-theatre, the actors were milling about
on stage, pretending nothing was happening, Richard smiled up at them,
as a good producer should (but doesn't always). "Edward," I whispered
between my teeth, "for Chrissakes, go up there and say something nice
to the actors. Anything. You don't have to mean it. They need it." Which
he proceeded to do, bounding up onto the stage like a cat and spreading
enthusiasm, like butter, onto their expectant, imploring selves.

Afterwards, having told everyone how well everything went and
how much Edward had loved it, I asked Nick to spend a little more
time admiring the abstract painting over the fireplace before he and
Honey sat down. Grizzard liked the idea. So did Edward the next time
he saw Act 1. "You changed the whole thing," he said. There's the difference between directors and playwrights, right there.

And so it went. Act 2 seemed reasonably "there" to Edward when
he saw it a few days later. I was especially pleased with my "chess game"
between George and Nick, but Edward took the whole scene, an
extremely subtle and difficult one to build, for granted. Act 3 was more
troublesome, especially in Uta's deepening struggle to hold on to the
imaginary child which George insisted on killing. Uta just would not
go far enough in opening herself up. Only once, in a preview, after

Edward and I had spent an hour with her in her dressing room imploring her not to hold back, did she let her insides really spill out. Her emotion was so strong, the scene was electric. We rushed back to tell her, but she refused even to talk to us. Nor did she ever play the scene with such intensity again. Months later we discovered that Uta had once lost a child. She could not suffer the pain of revealing herself that openly night after night.

Almost 20 years later, at a Dramatists Guild symposium, Uta blamed me publicly for never solving her problem of how to deal with that imaginary child. I'm sure she was right. And wrong. I told her at the start of rehearsals that George and Martha were not insane; they were always aware of their fantasy. Nor did they keep toys around, something she said she would have wanted. The child was, in Edward's own words, a "beanbag" for them to throw at each other, a way of getting at each other indirectly. Many of our critics later refused to accept the device. They could not believe that two intelligent adults, one of them a professor, could come to depend on such unreality to give meaning to their lives.

But life, as always, fools us. Years later, I heard—though I have no way of being sure—that Alfred Lunt and Lynn Fontanne had made up an imaginary child just as the two people in Edward's play had done. I wondered if there were any toys in their house in Genessee Depot, Wisconsin.

All during those rehearsals, I thought that I was at least doing tolerably well with Uta. She responded to most of my suggestions, beginning with the business I gave her in the first scene of cleaning up the place while carrying on her conversation about the guests with George. We improvised and improvised until a pattern that she could cope with emerged. She seemed to like most of my staging ideas, and carried them out beautifully. Wherever she didn't agree or felt uncomfortable, I always looked for and sometimes found an alternative. Where she felt strongly about a piece of business or a move of her own, I rarely challenged her.

I have often said that never have I worked with anyone more talented than Uta Hagen, or more capable of greatness. In any other theatrical society she would have been not just a star but a great lady of the theatre. In the last 20 years of our own theatrical miasma, she has played only a handful of roles, never coming near her accomplishment in *Virginia Woolf*. That is a pity. And, speaking personally, it is also a pity that after 20 years she still seems to harbor a grudge not only against the author of the play in which she was able to give so striking a performance, but against the director who, at the very least, did not get in the way of her being able to give it.

Arthur posed for me exactly the opposite problem to Uta's. He begged for help, he demanded help, he needed help. I spent hours in and out of rehearsal guiding him, encouraging him, making him feel that he was a match for Uta. I would drill him over and over in his moves until they became part of his motor mechanism. He was always willing to do anything I asked him, logical or crazy, right or wrong. And for that willingness I admired him and treasured his presence among us.

Interestingly enough, Arthur—for entirely different reasons—has also never been able to equal his *Virginia Woolf* achievement. A family man first and foremost, he left New York soon afterward, taking his family out of the theatre's unsettled rhythms to the regularity of Hollywood's films and television. That pram in the hallway does indeed remain the enemy of art.

The audience at our first invited preview (of which we had five) consisted mainly of actors and theatre people, the ones normally kept away at all costs for fear of their spreading unfavorable word. From the time the curtain went up, their reactions convinced us that we had, in Richard's words, "something interesting and original," and that all would be well once we opened. We had had practically no advance sale. By the time we got to our five low-priced public previews—Billy Rose took out an ad inviting secretaries and telling them to suggest that their bosses stay at home—there was hardly a seat to be had.

Opening night, Saturday, Oct. 13, 1962, was the most exciting night I've ever had in the theatre. The audience seemed to have a sixth sense that they were in for something special. With Uta's "Jesus H. Christ" entrance, I felt them fused into rapt attention, punctuated by machine-gun bursts of New York laughter. Whatever happened tomorrow or the next day, that audience was as one, absorbing Edward's "dark legend of truth and illusion" into their blood and bones. It was absolutely terrific to be part of that communal experience, to watch and listen and feel 1,100 people transported and transformed, knowing that it was their own guts that were being kicked around on that stage. When the last curtain finally came down, three-and-a-half hours—or three eons—later, I waited for the applause to end, which it wouldn't, then tore backstage through the pass door to congratulate or rather just hug everybody. On the way, I passed someone with a worried look, a middle-aged Gluyas Williams character telling his Helen Hokinson companion not to be fooled by the audience response: "I wish I could get out of my investment." Even though I'd made it a rule never to invest in any show I'm directing—or any show I'm not directing—I almost stopped in my tracks to tell him I'd be glad to take whatever he had.

After any opening, it's bad enough to wait up four or five hours for the notices, usually pretending to enjoy the company and the drinks, at Sardi's. Opening on Saturday night—which we did for some now-forgotten reason—meant that we had to wait for almost 24. Nor were there any television reviews at that time to serve as poisoned hors d'oeuvres. I opened Edward's opening night present, a newspaper headline stating "SCHNEIDER ESSENTIAL TO STAGE TRUTH—E.A." His accompanying card explained, in Edward's scrawl, "The enclosed sentiment is no shit." (A prized possession, it now hangs in my bathroom.)

Next morning, I slept into the afternoon, pretended to read the Sunday *Times*, kept my eyes on every clock in the house hoping one might conceivably get ahead of the others, and drove back into the city. Jean and I had been invited to Clinton Wilder's elegant townhouse on the Upper East Side to gather at about six o'clock with Richard and Clinton and Edward and Bill Ritman and Howard Atlee, our always-calm press agent, to wait for the Monday morning reviews to trickle in Sunday night. Billy Rose, who had somehow traced our whereabouts, joined us.

Just after seven, Howard was able to get to his spy at the *Daily News* and was about to write down the review in longhand as it was read to him via Alexander Graham Bell's boon to the theatre. At which convenient point, Richard said to Billy, "You used to be the champion shorthand writer in the world. Get on the phone and do your job!" Billy grabbed the receiver and a pencil and started to take down John Chapman's not ordinarily immortal words. I remember Billy's face, somber enough in normal repose, getting sadder and sadder, his mouth clamped around a huge cigar which kept drooping further and further earthward. It was clear not only that Mr. Chapman did not like us, but he did not like us in six figures. When Billy read us Chapman's headline, "For Dirty Minded Females Only" we knew the rest. Robert Coleman's verdict, in that other bastion of middle-class morality, the *Daily Mirror*, was even worse: "No red-blooded American would bring his wife to this shocking play."

The atmosphere in Clinton's warm living room suddenly became extremely chilly, Billy's cigar even more acrobatic. "I told you guys that furniture was lousy," he scowled. "You can't have a hit with that no-good furniture." We looked at each other.

Somehow, we all survived to read Kerr in the *Tribune* and Taubman in the *Times* the very moment our ubiquitous Howard Atlee brought them through the door. Neither wrote exactly what we would call a rave. But they seemed positive enough to keep us breathing. The rest of the reviews, which we read the next day, were more favorable. And even the ones that had reservations of one sort or another, managed to say enough to get people interested in buying tickets. People who wouldn't come to see *Who's Afraid of Virginia Woolf?* as a play of ideas about the failure of American marriage, or a philosophical drama dealing with the ambiguous conflict between truth and illusion, came to see us because we were a "dirty" play or because someone told them there were sexy scenes, Uta Hagen touching the inside of George Grizzard's thigh. I remember how carefully we worked on that one.

On Monday morning, I journeyed down to 41st Street to discover a line stretching out a fair distance from the Billy Rose Theatre, and Sam Zolotow, the *Times*'s inevitable leg-man and super sleuth, noting down the size of the line as well as my lurking presence. I decided that, in spite of both Mr. Chapman and Mr. Coleman, a lot of red-blooded American males and some non-dirty-minded females were going to be in our audiences for weeks or maybe months or perhaps even years to come. Suddenly, I realized that I was 44 years old, almost 45, and I was finally going to make a living in the theatre. Or if not a living, at least a temporary killing, which my playwright friend Bob Anderson had told me was easier.

Alan Schneider, who died in 1984, was known as the foremost American direc-tor of Samuel Beckett's plays, and noted for his work on plays by Albee, Pinter, Brecht and others. This article is an excerpt from Schneider's posthumously published 1986 memoir *Entrances: An American Director's Journey*.

FOR WHITES ONLY?

By Douglas Turner Ward

November 1986

A double bill of one-act plays by Douglas Turner Ward debuted Off Broadway in 1966, and the *New York Times* marked the occasion by printing his article "American Theatre: For Whites Only?"—a ringing call for a fully autonomous black theatre company wherein black artists could oversee their own creative destinies. The article captured the attention and subsequent support of the Ford Foundation, and led to the emergence the following year of the Negro Ensemble Company. Ward's clear-eyed assessment of the state of black theatre art in America brings into sharp relief the myriad accomplishments—and the aspirations still unfulfilled—of the nation's minority artists over the two decades between this essay's original publication and its reprinting in *American Theatre*.

During the last decade—coinciding with the explosion of Negro civil rights movements into public consciousness—a number of Negro playwrights have gained considerable notice. Louis Peterson, Lorraine Hansberry, Ossie Davis, James Baldwin, LeRoi Jones, and others . . . collectors of awards and honors . . . a few catapulted into international fame and dramatic prominence . . . critical barometers and Geiger counters whipped out to gauge possible winds, trends and resulting fallout.

However, this flurry of attention has tended to misrepresent the real status of Negro playwrights. Despite an eminent handful, Negro dramatists remain sparse in number, productions sporadic at most, and scripts too few to indicate discernible trends. Moreover, even when deemed successful—the critical and financial rewards reaped by *A Raisin in the Sun* excepted, and on a smaller scale, LeRoi Jones's *Dutchman*—few productions have managed to recoup capitalization. No, the millennium has not been reached.

Many factors contribute to this situation, but, surveying the total landscape of American theatre, results could hardly be otherwise.

The legitimate theatre, that fabulous invalid which, compared to its electronic bedpartner, is still dreamed of as the repository of high culture and artistic achievement in America, hardly qualifies when examined from a Negro viewpoint.

Tirelessly, predictably, almost repetitiously on cue, theatre critics and other Jeremiahs deplore rampant commercialism, the monopoly of escapist musicals, the dominance of brittle, frothy comedies and the inadequacy of experimental ventures. They also leave the impression that a little minor surgery would work wonders, that palliatives could restore health. But the patient is sicker than even the most pessimistic diagnosis suggests. No matter how severe their prognosis, pundits seldom question the basic structures or assumptions of their theatre.

With rare exceptions—an occasional native play of quality, or intermittent foreign infusions—American legit theatre, even at its most ambitious seriousness, is essentially a theatre of the Bourgeois, by the Bourgeois, about the Bourgeois, and for the Bourgeois. A pretentious theatre elevating the narrow preoccupations of restricted class interests to inflated universal significance, tacitly assuming that its middle-class, affluent-oriented absorptions are central to the dominant human condition. A theatre rarely embracing broader frames of reference or more inclusive concerns. A theatre—even if it tried—incapable of engaging the attention of anyone not so fortunate as to possess a college diploma or five-figure salary.

More specifically, a theatre in its lofty-modern niche—Broadway, Off Broadway, Off-Off Broadway, Happenings-land, wherever—overwhelmingly riddled with works of in-group concerns, *belles-lettres* pomposity, instant despair, stultifying boredom, humorless humor, hasty-pudding hijinks and pseudo-absurdity.

A Theatre of Diversion—a diversionary theatre, whose main problem is not that it's too safe, but that it is surpassingly irrelevant.

Occasional productions of stature and significance must usually display a cachet of foreign authorship and reputation to justify presentation.

Maybe this is all as it should be: Computer consensus—as yet—doesn't spawn meaningful plays; the most powerful country in the Western world doesn't necessarily usher in a golden age of drama.

It is not surprising that the Negro playwright and the power of his potential fit only peripherally into this spectrum. By his mere historical placement in American society, the Negro exists as a disturbing presence, an embarrassment to majority comfort, an actuality deflating pretenses, an implicit witness and cogent critic too immediate for attention.

Also, just as in real life, a black playwright—sight unseen, play unheard—is soothsaid as too bothersome, a prod to the sleeping conscience of numerical superiors. The stage establishment, like Hollywood, consigns even the most innocuous Negro subject matter to an ogre-category of problem drama. Even sympathetic advisers constantly bug the dark craftsman to shun racial themes and aspire to that pantheon of Olympian universality which all white playwrights, ironically enough, can enter by merely getting themselves born. As one naïve, well-meaning, but frighteningly boorish scribe put it—"No longer Negro playwright, just playwright." Whoever heard of batting an eyelash of lower-caste condescension when Sean O'Casey is mentioned as an Irish playwright?

That the Negro playwright is more or less excluded from legit boulevards is not a revelation for concern. More important is the fact that, even when produced within this environment, the very essence of his creative function is jeopardized. His plays stand to be witnessed and assessed by a majority least equipped to understand his intentions, woefully apathetic or anesthetized to his experience, often prone to distort his purpose. Spectators who, though afflicted with self-imposed ignorance, demand to be taught ABCs at the very moment when the writer is impatient to explore the algebra of his thematic equations. Observers, even when most sympathetic, whose attitudes have been repeatedly shaped by preconceptions and misconceptions, warped by superficial clichés and platitudes—liberal, conservative or radical though they may be. Catering to such insistence presages barren results. With imagination short-circuited, valuable time is wasted clueing in, exposition is demanded when action should be unfolding, the obvious must be overillustrated, and fantasy literalized.

Finally, when the curtain descends, whether the writer has pampered illusions, lectured ignorance, comforted fears, shouted for attention or flagellated consciences, probability dictates his defeat and the victory of customers—triumphantly intact in their limitations. With tears dried, the shouting quieted or the aches of the cat-o'-nine-tails subsided, the writer has been neatly appropriated, usurped, his creativity subverted. For those Negro playwrights eager to volunteer for this function, there's no advice to offer. They know the rules, they play the game and take their chances.

But for a Negro playwright committed to examining the contours, contexts and depths of his experiences from an unfettered, imaginative Negro angle of vision, the screaming need is for a sufficient audience of other Negroes, better informed through commonly shared experience to readily understand, debate, confirm or reject the truth or falsity of his creative explorations. Not necessarily an all-black audience to the exclusion of whites but, for the playwright, certainly his primary audience, the first persons of his address, potentially the most advanced, the most responsive or most critical. Only through their initial and continuous participation can his intent and purpose be best perceived by others.

The validity of this premise has been borne out previously in other productions and, most recently, during the current run of my own plays, *Happy Ending* and *Day of Absence*, two works of satirical content written from an unapologetic Negro viewpoint. Throughout the run, Negro attendance has averaged close to 50 percent—hundreds witnessing a professional play for the first time. Besides contributing immeasurably to the longevity of the run, the freshness of their response, immediacy of involvement, and spontaneity of participation have significantly underscored the essence of the works themselves and provided crucial illuminations for others. With Negroes responding all around, white spectators, congenitally uneasy in the presence of Negro satire, at least can't fail to get the message.

Any future hope for the Negro playwright depends upon whether or not this minuscule, singular, all-too-infrequent experience can be extended, multiplied and made permanent. As long as the Negro playwright remains totally dependent on existing outlets, he stands to continue as a pauper begging sustenance, never knowing from day to day, year to year, whether a few scraps will be tossed his way. Even burgeoning, tax-supported, privately endowed repertory companies are beyond the reach of his ambition (imagine rushing to present *Day of Absence* or any other work which would require jobbing in 15 Negro actors when your roster only allows for two or three at most—often tokens at that).

Eventually, an all-embracing, all-encompassing theatre of Negro identity, organized as an adjunct of some Negro community, might ideally solve the Negro dramatists' dilemma, but such a development—to me—must arise as part of a massive effort to reconstruct the urban ghetto. Small-scale cultural islands in the midst of the ghettos, separate and apart from a committed program of social and economic revitalization of slums, are doomed to exotic isolation.

Meanwhile, potential talent ready for exercise cannot wait. Without engagement, it lies dormant, stillborn. Time passes, aging proceeds. The talent withers and eventually dies of nonuse. If any hope, outside of chance individual fortune, exists for Negro playwrights as a group—or, for that matter, Negro actors and other theatre craftsmen—the most immediate, pressing, practical, absolutely minimally essential active first step is the development of a permanent Negro repertory company of at least Off-Broadway size and dimension. Not in the future, but now.

A theatre evolving not out of negative need, but positive potential; better equipped to employ existing talents and spur the development of future ones. A theatre whose justification is not the gap it fills, but the achievement it aspires toward—no less high than any other comparable theatre company of present or past world fame.

A theatre concentrating primarily on themes of Negro life, but also resilient enough to incorporate and interpret the best of world drama—whatever the source. A theatre of permanence, continuity and consistency, providing the necessary home base for the Negro artist to launch a campaign to win his ignored brothers and sisters as constant witnesses to his endeavors.

This is not a plea for either.

This is not a plea for either a segregated theatre or a separatist one. Negroes constitute a numerical minority, but Negro experience from slavery to civil rights has always been of crucial importance to America's existence. There's no reason why whites could not participate in a theatre dedicated to exploring and illuminating that experience if they found inspiration in the purpose.

Also, just as the intrusion of lower-middle-class and working-class voices reinvigorated polite, effete English drama, so might the Negro, a most potential agent of vitality, infuse life into the moribund corpus of American theatre.

Douglas Turner Ward began his career as a journalist. He studied playwriting at the Paul Mann Workshop in New York City and, in 1956, acted in Eugene O'Neill's *The Iceman Cometh*. He went on to perform and understudy in *A Raisin in the Sun*. In 1965, Ward, Robert Hooks and Gerald Krone formed the Negro Ensemble Company. Ward made his playwriting debut that same year with *Happy Ending* and *Day of Absence*. In 1967, the Negro Ensemble Company was officially opened with Ward serving as artistic director.

ON REPERTORY AND AUDIENCES

By Eva Le Gallienne

November 1986

The virtues and drawbacks of repertory are still hotly debated, but few thea-tre figures have explored its possibilities with more commitment than Eva Le Gallienne. In 1926, when she was at the height of her stardom on Broadway, the actress took over the old, battered but still-standing 14th Street Theatre in downtown Manhattan, established a permanent company of actors and apprentices, produced Shakespeare, Chekhov, Molière and Ibsen and sold sea-son memberships for a dollar a year to make her plays available to everyone. It was at Civic Repertory Theatre that she first staged her memorable adap-tation of Lewis Carroll's *Alice in Wonderland*, herself playing the White Queen. By 1933, worn down by financial difficulties and eroding audience support in the dark days of the Depression, she ended the experiment, which in many ways presaged a changing role for the theatre a generation in advance.

Le Gallienne struck a second blow for the cause of repertory in 1946, founding (with Cheryl Crawford, Margaret Webster and the support of the theatre establishment, if not the critics or the theatrical unions) an American Repertory Theatre on Broadway. When the company was forced to close its doors after a single, six-production season, Le Gallienne wrote, "There can be no doubt that the failure of the ART will discourage any other similar efforts for a long time to come. Its fate is also conclusive evidence of the impossibil-ity of establishing a permanent repertory theatre in this country without the aid of subsidy."

In her 1953 autobiography *With a Quiet Heart* (the Viking Press), Le Gallienne offers this analysis of the challenges of repertory.

After the appearance in this country of some foreign acting compa-ny, whether it be the Moscow Art Theatre, the Abbey Players, the Old Vic or that of Louis Jouvet, the critics are prone to bewail at great length the lack of similar companies here at home, and roundly scold us theatre people for making no attempt to provide the United States with comparable organizations. They neglect to take into account cer-tain primary facts:

1. These companies have had the opportunity of working together consistently for many years, thus achieving a confidence, a versatility and a smoothness of ensemble that only such long association can provide.
2. The endurance of such foreign organizations was made possible by subsidy of various kinds, which enabled the players to continue in their work and gradually achieve the perfection that makes them famous.
3. In the rare instances where such companies are not subsidized, the labor conditions in their respective countries are such as not to deprive them, by unreasonable demands and handicaps, of the possibility of survival.
4. The public in these foreign lands is definitely theatre-minded; it is accustomed to the repertory system and looks upon the theatre in the same way that we look upon music, opera, ballet and the fine arts. The theatre is not, with this public, limited to show business. In order to develop similar feelings in our own audiences, time is above all necessary. The public cannot be expected immediately to respond to something it has never known. It must have time to discover and enjoy the advantages of a repertory theatre, to become familiar with its aims and functions.

My long fight for the establishment of classical repertory theatres has often been misunderstood. I have been accused of having a contempt for the great popular shows, of gazing with lofty disdain at the best-sellers of Broadway. Nothing could be further from the truth. No one enjoys a good show more than I do, and I look with pride and wholehearted admiration on the skill and imagination that make our entertainment industry the finest in the world. But I see no reason why our theatre should be limited to that one facet. There should be room not only for classical repertories but for children's theatres and, very importantly, for the type of experimental playhouses known in France as *théâtres d'avant-garde*. None of these would be in competition with show business and should receive quite different treatment at the hands of the craft unions and the critics.

There exists in this country a large group of people that might well be called "the forgotten public." These are the people who have reluctantly given up theatregoing, not only because their means are usually limited, but because they find little there to satisfy their tastes. They represent perhaps the most enlightened and cultivated section of our population, yet they are almost completely ignored by those who control all branches of our entertainment world. These are the people that the kind of theatres I have in mind would serve. They are unquestionably a minority group—though perhaps not to the extent generally believed—but a group large enough to be important, and it is wrong that their needs should be denied. I feel this situation to be a great, a tragic pity. But of course if the theatre, along with its mechanical offspring, is considered solely as a means of getting the most money out of the public, and all thought of service and desire for giv-ing is brushed aside as so much nonsense, that is the logical procedure.

As an actor, Eva Le Gallienne came to prominence in Ferenc Molnár's *Liliom* on Broadway in 1921 at the age of 22. She went on to be known as a producer, director and translator, especially as an interpreter of Ibsen. She died in 1991.

A FRUITFUL UNION

By Tyrone Guthrie

November 1986

While most regional theatres began as seedlings, tended with love, care and hard work by their organizers, one of the largest and most influential sprang full-grown from its creators' heads in 1963. Oliver Rea and Peter Zeisler, both living and working in New York, wanted to start a regional theatre devoted to the classics in a hospitable American city. They enlisted the aid of the eminent British director Tyrone Guthrie, who joined as a partner in the enterprise. After four-and-a-half years of fundraising and planning and meetings in seven U.S. cities, the triumvirate settled in Minneapolis to bring forth what Guthrie called "an institution, something more permanent and more serious in aim than a commercial theatre can ever be." In the concluding chapter of his 1964 book *A New Theatre* (McGraw-Hill), Guthrie sums up the aspirations of the fledgling Guthrie Theater and, by extension, of the movement for which it became a potent symbol.

Our theatre has been called into being to serve the community of the Twin Cities. It is our belief that this service can best be rendered, for reasons which have been discussed, by a classical program; but a classical program which includes representation of American plays which have not had time to stand the test of survival, but which now seem at least possible candidates for classical status.

All these plays will be given a fully professional performance at the highest standard which we can achieve.

In time, it is our hope that the Minnesota Theatre Company may develop a distinctively Minnesotan style. This cannot come about quickly. It may take 10 years or even 20. The progress will, we hope, be aided by the inclusion in each season's company of a group of graduate students from the University of Minnesota. This is our taproot into the soil.

It will be our aim not to uplift or to instruct, but to entertain, to delight. A good performance of a great play cannot, in our view, fail to instruct. But this should not be the conscious aim of its interpreters, any more than it has been that of its authors.

It is our belief that a program of this character should not, and need not, be aimed at a cultural minority. It demands a considerably greater effort on the part of the audience than is demanded by a program of "pop" music or by the average commercial movie, which is deliberately and condescendingly aimed by its makers and promoters at a hypothetical intellectual and emotional level lower than their own. This kind of condescension, though it is often necessary, leads, in our view, to artistic death. An artist is entitled to assume that his public is less interested and less sophisticated than himself in his particular field. He is not entitled to assume that his public is, in general, less intelligent or sensitive than himself; or that well-off, well-educated people are more intelligent and sensitive than others who have not enjoyed the same advantages.

An experiment of this kind simply cannot be judged in short term. It is essentially an attempt to apply longer-term policies and a more serious, though not I hope on that account pompous, approach to the theatre than is implicit in the frantic pursuit of the Smash Hit.

Naturally, this does not mean that every member of every audience is not entitled to a severely critical attitude to every performance, as well as to our whole policy. Without such an attitude a theatre can be killed by kindness, like an overstuffed pet dog. But criticism of particular faults can be made with a patient and favorable attitude to the whole endeavor. This project is something more than the sum of a number of disparate productions and performances, more than the expression of a group of particular personalities. It is an attempt to relate a theatre to its supporting community. If such an alliance is to be fully fruitful, then patience, tolerance and forbearance are going to be demanded of all parties.

In America particularly, but increasingly in the whole modern world, an apparently (though not, I think, really) accelerating pace of change creates a demand for quick results. Every institution, like every animal or plant, has its own normal rate of growth. Good results are constantly being frustrated by the silly impatience of people who want to accelerate the natural pace. A theatrical institution can only be created very slowly. Many errors will be committed, many misdirections will be followed. The character of the institution will only form very slowly, and far more by a process of spontaneous growth than by the fulfillment of the conscious intentions of its founders.

Nonetheless, there must be such conscious intentions. This project has come into being through four years of hopes, which then became intentions, which then became practical decisions. Until, at last, a theatre was built, a company assembled, performances given. Finally, an audience came to see these performances and gave many signs of enjoying them very much.

It is our hope that gradually, as audience and management become mutually better acquainted, the audience will begin to create the sort of theatre which it wants, which will be an expression of itself.

Only thus can the intention of this project be fully realized. It is much more than merely building a theatre and creating a series of productions. The ultimate aim is to attract a creative audience.

The three greatest periods in the history of the theatre—the Athenian stage of Aeschylus, Sophocles and Euripides; the Elizabethan stage in England which produced Marlowe, Shakespeare, Ben Jonson and half a dozen lesser but significant poets; the French stage of Racine, Corneille and Molière—all these could not have happened if the writers, actors and craftsmen had not been fortunate enough to live in an age and place where a highly intelligent, lively and demanding audience had helped to create a theatre which was far more than a commercial business and far more than a frivolous pastime. Neither the artists and craftsmen nor the audience can do this alone. It is a shared process of creation, a fruitful union.

In sum, our project is to set up conditions where such a union may eventually be possible. No one can predict exactly how this new kind of theatre will develop. We must all keep open, but not therefore empty, minds; it is all too easy for those who work in a theatre to be disproportionately puffed up by success and cast down by failure; and, as a result, to pursue too eagerly a popularity which is ephemeral and often achieved at the cost of eventual reputation. It is all too easy for the audience of a theatre to take an irresponsible view of its share in the creation of standards; to assume that "support" is enough, without regard to the quality of the support.

That attitude belongs to an era when the theatre was organized as a business and the public had no more responsibility than a purchaser of merchandise. Those days are ending. If a particular public wants to have a serious theatre it must undertake the responsibility not merely of a customer but of a patron. That involves the exercise of Taste.

The development of taste is not just a matter of sensibility. Taste is formed by experience. That is why at Minneapolis we are starting with a classical program: to enable an audience to form its taste by contact with what the best minds of several generations have agreed to regard as important expressions of human spirit.

Later on, when both the management and the audience know better what we can and ought to attempt, and also what we can and ought to afford, then we may take the risk of producing, and possibly commissioning, new work.

The greatest works of art have, almost without exception, been created to please intelligent and sophisticated patrons. The greatest works of drama have, almost without exception, been written with a particular theatre or particular public, and a particular group of actors, in mind.

When, and if, our theatre can offer the right kind of conditions to a writer, or a group of writers, then we may begin to expect interesting and contemporary results. Meantime we believe that we can slowly begin to create such conditions.

Our policy may seem to many people more conservative than they would like. We must risk their disapproval; we must creep before we can walk. If our progress seems too deliberate, let me ask you to recall the result of the celebrated sporting event when the Hare raced the Tortoise.

Sir Tyrone Guthrie was the founding artistic director of the Stratford Shakespeare Festival of Canada from 1953 to 1955. He led the Guthrie Theater as artistic director from 1963 to 1966 and returned to direct each year until 1969. He died in 1971.

THE THEATRE AND ITS TROUBLE

By Lee Breuer

November 1986

"Nobody wants to wait for poetry," asserts writer/director Lee Breuer as he assesses the contemporary theatre scene in his own jive-lyrical narrative style. (Any resemblance to Brecht's *A Short Organum* is strictly intentional.) For a number of years, in theatre pieces he labels "performance poetry," Breuer has been forcing audiences to wait for the poetry. He blends cultural idioms helter-skelter, merging the driving rhythms of rock and reggae, the imagery of hotels and drive-ins and the language of the street, with the lyricism of dreams, memory and fairy-tale fantasy. *The Theatre and Its Trouble* is excerpted from his running commentary accompanying the first collection of his works, *Sister Suzie Cinema: Poems and Performances*, published by TCG Books in 1986.

1. If a fact falls in the forest and you hear it not—is it a fact at all? Might it not have been your fancy? The theatre, in fact, originated. I'm sure there was a time and a place. But I didn't have a ticket. And no one sent me the reviews. I'll content myself with the truth according to the fanciful. (For only fancy, the soul of fact, rings true.) And the truth is—it started with the wolves.

2. Moon! Mountain! Snow blanket; snow pillow; snow sheet. The bed is coldly made; the table is savagely laid—for a howling. Look! It is the moment of the turning around. *The turning around*—first initiated in the theatre of the wolves.

3. Sing, O wolves, of wolfish mysteries. Why does one wolf turn around? Is one chosen? Does one sing better than the rest? Is one inspired by the wolf ghosts of wolf ancestors? Does one preach the wolfish word? We hear! We echo! We howl! We harmonize—we wolves.

4. Sing! Dance! Paint your faces! Don't ask an actor why. Ask a singing bird. Ask a prancing peacock. Ask a fish who changes colors. Applaud the *mie* of Hideyoshi Danziburo! Applaud the postures of lions.

5. Read your program. It is a genetic program.

6. Performance is the method of natural selection adopted by culture. Culture is society's DNA. Performance is fashion. Survival of the fashionable. That's what it's all about.

7. What is acting? Acting is the moment when, after *performance* turns around to the front, it turns back to the side.

8. And half facing you is half assing you. And that's the theatre and its trouble.

9. Can you play poetry?

10. In order to better understand the problems of poetry in the theatre, I suggest you take a little standard shift out onto the FDR and head uptown at about 4:45. When you pass under the Queensborough Bridge, shift into neutral and put your foot down on the accelerator hard. You glide to a halt. The motor whines. There it is—that surge. There it is—that stillness. And there it is—that Cadillac riding up your bumper; the mob ready to tear you limb from limb. There it is, the straitjacket and the little white coats and the black leather jackets with the badges, saying "Hey man, let me see your license!"

11. What can you say. You can say, "Doctors! Officers! And Peers! I have no driver's license. I have a poetic license." Making poetry in the theatre is like learning to drive a standard shift. The key to not stalling is the foot on the clutch. The foot on the clutch downshifts you from high-speed dramas with their actions, their characterizations, their suspense, their plot, their psychology—shifts you down through the gears of language—down, down, down to poetry. The motor revs higher and time goes slower and the power is greater and you use a hell of a lot more gas. And then you get to the poem itself. You get to that great gear of art called neutral, where the motor mind can rev to infinite tach, where pistons have fantasies of a thousand miles an hour before they throw their rods and blow their gaskets, and the vehicle of time never moves at all. And right about there they book you. You really are illegal. The charge is spiritual sodomy.

    You're fucking with God.

12. Now this is nothing other than sad. The theatre and its trouble is that nobody wants to wait for poetry. Now, this vital neutral, this permission to subjectivize, has, on occasion, been extended with great good will. I've seen it at the dance; I've seen it at the gallery; I've seen it extended by tourists to scenic overlooks in the Smokies. But theatre has places to go and people to see and it cannot wait for poetry any more than life can wait for dreaming. You have to trick it.

13. Poetics is the foreplay of science.

14. *Ham's Law* or the *First Law of Thespodynamics* states that in the case of the one or several facing another one or several, the *fewer* are the more meaningful than the greater in inverse proportion to the square of the remainder of the lesser number from the greater of the two. (Corollary to this law is the implied reduction of the ratio

to a point where one faces everyone else and is, by inverse implication, the greatest.) In the language of Thespodynamics, the
greaters are known as the *hearers* and the lessers as the *sayers*—and
the process as *hearsay*—except in the special case of a reduction to
one—in which case the lesser is known as the *ham*.

15. (When the unions are involved the process is known as *gainsaying*.)
16. There follows from this a second law. The distance between the
hearers and the sayers—(the whole configuration known as size of
house)—is governed by the interaction of the forces between
them. There are weak forces and strong forces and gravities and
electromagnetics—all that shit is involved—but it's all twofold—
that's the point—it resolves into two. The force of the saying both
attracts and repels all who hear it. And the act of the hearing itself
can repel and attract what is said. And in this interaction, a fixed distance is found where the tension is in that terrifying balance called
suspense. And the suspense is the observing of an entr'acte of God.
The name of the first force is the *killer* force, as in *Kill'em dead, man*;
the name of the second force is the lover force and this force cries
bravo and *weeps*. The killer and the lover forces are volatile. Alone
they burn. Mixed they explode. And that ain't hay. That's Hegel.
17. The theatre and its trouble is its misappropriated dialectics.
18. Brecht! Marx! Science! Ha! What a laugh.
19. We are ensconced in the foreplay of science. We are a study in
dialectical dematerialism.
20. Theatre is a special case of performance concerned with demonstration in profile (see #8; characters are behaviorist profiles and
they know it. Try and look one in the eye).
21. What does theatre demonstrate?
22. The world according to illusion played out against a scrim of the
world according to the void. And one would hope that through
this scrim, dialectical light plays.
23. "So you want to be an actress!" (This is known as Boleslavski's
camp and there are various versions. If you've put the right name
by the right camp your matching quiz should read like this):

Stand on your head	Grotowski
Do what I tell you	Reinhardt
Get a little distance	Brecht
Dream	Richardson
Feel now, show later	Stanislavsky
Be cruel	Artaud
Don't be cruel, be a flower	Zeami
Take it off	Judith and Julian
Put it on	R. Foreman
Acting is semiotics	Delsarte
Acting is biological mechanics	Meyerhold
I am the truth	Strasberg
No! I am the truth	Bobby Lewis
Read one of my books	Pick a critic, any critic

24. If poetry is pork where theatre is concerned, then science must be kosher.

25. Descartes had an idea that you could account for everything mathematically. Art too! O how the equations flew. More recently we've seen scientific materialism turn its dialectics right into particle physics while turning left into epic theatre. And Stanislavsky had a nice equation too. Acting equals Freud times Pavlov not so squared.

26. You could be your own rat and Skinner too. Emotions were enticed by controlled stimuli (improvisations, stage business, actions and objectives—each salivation in the script needed its bell). Emotions triggered electrochemical responses which elicited changes in muscle tensions. These reactions manifested themselves as facial expression and characterizations of the body and voice. Actors were able to be other than they were by simulating the conditions of the otherness and responding thereto. Then the emotions of the viewers were triggered according to biological laws—laws no different for us than for the Stickleback. Truth in acting was a biological program. Science!

27. In the late '60s Grotowski spoke of "personalization." It was an idea about representing character and emotion by re-creating and remixing parts of yourself (your "self" being a Proustian entity of selves piled upon one another in remembered time). Characterization was persona recombinant. Under sexual tension, you mix parts of yourself and, like the DNA in mieosis, out comes the illusion of a new human being. Voila! Science! Take it or leave it.

28. If you want to leave it you can always account for a great performance as voodoo. You can account for acting by saying that if you pray to the Lua, and if the drums speak the right language, the God understands and comes down and rides. You are the horse of God. You are mounted. You dance. A horse of God dances. And where you will be ridden by God, called here inspiration, no one knows. Sometimes it is dangerous.

29. Art, the gift, is sometimes dangerous but even so, I wouldn't put Descartes before de horse.

Lee Breuer is a founding member of Mabou Mines Theatre Company, a MacArthur Fellow, stage director, author (*The Warrior Ant, Ecco Porco* and *La Divina Caricatura*), lyricist and co-creator of theatre productions such as *The Gospel at Colonus, Peter and Wendy* and *Mabou Mines DollHouse*.

PUPPETRY AND POLITICS

By Peter Schumann

November 1986

The fusion of American theatre and politics comes in many forms, none more aesthetically adventurous or genuinely revolutionary than the work of Bread and Puppet Theatre. Founded at the beginning of the '60s by German-born puppeteer and choreographer Peter Schumann, the troupe emerged from the New York theatre underground with such early works as *Fire*, inspired by the self-immolation of several Americans in protest against U.S. involvement in Vietnam, and awed audiences with its combined use of massive puppets with sometimes grotesque, sometimes noble countenances, tiny rod puppets and human figures, often masked. The company's spectacular processions and peace demonstration plays continue to freely mix rude humor, lyric gentleness and almost archetypal violence.

In his introduction to *Bread and Puppet: Stories of Struggle & Faith from Central America* (Green Valley Film and Art, 1986), Schumann evokes the theatrical life the company has forged for itself and its audiences on a Vermont farm during the years since 1970, and gives voice to the profound impulse that reconnects theatre art to the natural world.

Puppetry is a form of ecstasy, just as music is. It is caused by an overflow of muscle-power and brain-activity and by an urgent happiness that can't be held back, that has to manifest itself.

The most evident fact of our life is: We are surrounded by sky, wrapped in weather. Stones speak, hills laugh, worms sing. The great beauty of the universe makes us dizzy.

Puppetry is a simplification-device to make these incomprehensible riches accessible. Or, puppetry is a form-giving technique that makes it possible to respond to creation.

So why do we talk about Central America? Why don't we stick to the jolly practices of our trade?

In the early days, when we couldn't stand the grandeur of our Great-great-great-grandmother Nature anymore, we built boxes with tiny little windows to live in. The purpose of the boxes was to shut out a lot and just leave an understandable, controllable little bit. We used up whole thousand-year-long civilizations for the refinement of such boxes with windows, culminating in the invention of downtown Manhattan, where all windows face each other and all we see is our own selves mixed with a few square inches of dirty sky. Because of that sickening self-indulgent situation, we then progressed to our greatest achievement yet: a miniature box which easily fits into a corner of our living-room box and is equipped with a magical window which broadcasts the whole wide world painlessly into our hearts. We love it and hate it and call it affectionately the idiot box. And now the confusing universe and beloved chaos of the total world arrive at our senses so heavily processed and mangled by this box that we are left untouched. While our receptive organs shrink and wither, our yearning for the true ingredient grows.

Obviously the shamans-musicians-puppeteers have greater tasks now than ever before; it's their job to communicate the suffering, muddled reality. If this is the holy job of puppetry, why do we talk about Central America? What is that good for?

The truth is, we don't know what good it does. Political theatre tends to be slogan theatre that bores the equally-minded and offends precisely those customers whose hearts it wants to win. Our Bread and Puppet shows are not above that; we fall into the same trap. But we try to voice our concerns anyway, with or without success, simply because we have to.

When we moved from New York City to Vermont in 1970, it became necessary to see and learn and listen in a new way, to invent animals and to understand how to move in a landscape in order to become part of it. We thought that we could produce a cyclic event that would be representative of life in general and of our distinct political environment in particular. We called this event Our Domestic Resurrection Circus and have performed it almost every year since then.

These presentations with tree-sized puppets and herds of wild and domesticated papier-mâché beasts depend entirely on good will: Volunteers come from many towns in Vermont and from many states of the Union; some come from Canada, Eastern and Western Europe and Central America. Up to 200 women, men and children perform the Pageant. Scores of hard-working students, artists, farmers, professors, mothers, bicyclists, hardhats, grandfathers, typists and bakers do the daily chores of clay-kneading, armature-building, papier-mâché-molding, flag-printing and costume-sewing. Every summer, hundreds of masks, figures and props are made, and the biggest puppets that get built are burned in a great bonfire which ends the Pageant.

Starting with the first Pageant a few formal devices were established for these events: 1) There is always a creation-piece, not the re-telling of any creation myth, but rather a thank-you show singing the praises of the world. 2) There is always a more or less specialized representation of the world through the treatment of some specific aspect of history, a historical personality or an overall political theme. 3) The final part of the cycle is always a resurrection-piece, presenting either a logical resurrection growing out of the context of the defeat and death of the preceding part of the show, or an unreasonable resurrection, a reminder of the possibility of resurrection.

The arts are the privilege of the rich. Only wealthy individuals and wealthy societies can afford them. Their functions are to fill out leisure time and to decorate dull spaces. That's the reality. But in spirit the arts are gods: They heal, revolutionize, fulfill, perfect. They can do all these things that we never dare to dream as possible, and they are dead serious about it: They pursue their high-minded visions with passion, love and intelligence. And they are always ready to break out of their damned confinement. Compared to the functions which are considered essential to society, they don't have a function. They are meant to do nothing, to affect nothing, even in the face of the most horrible violations of the sense, beauty and dignity of the world.

Right now our Western Civilization, which provides so well for us, not only violates in very real ways the sense, beauty and dignity of the world while professing Christian ideals of neighborly love and compassion and while advocating human rights, it at the same time also teaches torture and exports torture to many parts of its sphere of influence, and openly assists the massacres of indigenous people in order to maintain its own disgusting wealth.

The arts are political, whether they like it or not. If they stay in their own realm, preoccupied with their proper problems, the arts support the status quo, which in itself is highly political. Or they scream and kick and participate in our century's struggle for liberation in whatever haphazard way they can, probably at the expense of some of their sensitive craftsmanship, but definitely for their own souls' sake.

Bread and Puppet Theatre performed the Domestic Resurrection Circus until 1998, and has continued to present smaller circuses in the summer. Peter Schumann has presented two art series on the subject of the Israel-Palestine conflict, "Independence Paintings: Inspired by Four Stories" (2007) and "The University of Majd: The Story of a Palestinian Youth" (2008).

THE CRITICAL INSTINCT

By Julius Novick

July/August 1987

This article was originally delivered as the keynote address at the 1986 Northern California Theatre Critics Conference.

Wilfred Sheed, the novelist and essayist, once said that "Whenever a good writer uses words, literature is a possibility." Now this of course is terrifying. "Literature . . ." I can hear you thinking, "I've just been reviewing the Carriage House Players in *The Star Spangled Girl* and some bozo is talking about literature."

I think we need to set that as our standard, however, even while we forgive ourselves for not meeting it. I figure that my own failure record at that standard is somewhere between 97 and 100 percent, and yet I think it's important that we continue to remember that what we are trying to do is make something beautiful and shapely out of words, the shape of which helps us to express some valuable meaning. This is possible to do in theatre criticism. Since it's possible, if we don't do it the responsibility is ultimately ours.

We need to set that standard for ourselves because under ordinary circumstances nobody's going to do it for us. There are so many expressed and implied demands on us to keep our standards down.

From editors, for instance. Find an editor whom you can trust—there are some around; the late Seymour Peck of the *New York Times* was my editorial mentor and I learned a great deal from him—and if you can find such an editor, for God's sake cleave to him or her. Remember, however, that editors, even arts editors, are not always chosen for their love and knowledge of the arts. Editors must sell papers—is that at the top of your agenda? Keep an eye on your editor.

We are also subjected to pressures from artists, who have their own vested interests, of ego as well as economics. Only athletes, politicians and artists are subject to being humiliated in public print as part of the ordinary course of their job. You never read in the paper that Dr. Butcher performed a distinctly uninspired appendectomy yesterday at

County Hospital. No wonder that in the attitudes of actors, play-wrights, directors and designers toward critics there is a certain dis-comfort, a certain defensiveness, a certain prickliness, a certain resent-ment. The wonder is how much respect and goodwill are mixed in with the resentments and defensiveness.

The problem is that artists need us too much to be safe guides for us. In the thousand or so panel discussions I've attended where artists talk about the responsibility of the critics, I've heard endlessly about the need for "constructive" criticism, "helpful" criticism. But sometimes it's dishon-est to be constructive and helpful—even to the extent that "constructive" and "helpful" are not code words meaning "praise me, praise me." Some-times the work you see is stupid, cheap, insulting or just basically ill-advised. This machine will never fly. There is no hope for it. The critic has to be free to say so, if he thinks so. And can any artist stand to hear that?

Bernard Shaw says (he seems to me still alive), "The cardinal guar-antee for a critic's integrity is simply the force of the critical instinct itself . . . . If my own father were an actor-manager, and his life depended on his getting favorable notices of his performance, I should orphan myself without an instant's hesitation if he acted badly. I am by no means the willing victim of this instinct. I am keenly susceptible to contrary influences—to private friendship and even acquaintanceship, to the pleasure of giving pleasure and the pain of giving pain, to con-sideration for people's circumstances and prospects . . . but the critical instinct gets the better of them all."

Most of us don't need to suppress that instinct. I think most of us need to cultivate that instinct. What it really means is the instinct to tell the truth as fully as we can tell it. That is our responsibility to artists and editors and everybody.

Above all, it's our responsibility to our readers who, like artists and editors, can mislead us from doing what it is that we are most deeply there to do. Readers often want us to be consumer guides, and this is a worthy function. But to be merely a consumer guide seems to me an unnecessarily humble ambition. Don't you want to be read by, don't you want to talk to, people who aren't in a position to buy tickets for whatever is on at the County Center this week? Don't you want what you write to be worth reading even after the show is closed? Don't you want what you write to be worth reading even after your own particu-lar show has permanently closed and you're no longer around? And more immediately, is it ultimately fair to your readers to be governed by that least common denominator standard of "Tell me if you liked it and then don't bother me"? Shouldn't you be expanding your readers' horizons rather than letting them contract yours? Presumably you've got something to tell them. If not, why are you wasting ink?

As with editors, compromise with your readers may very well be necessary. But if you make compromises, know you're making them. In some places, writing real criticism is more difficult than in other places. But you can sneak it in.

Okay then: Suppose we do preserve our independence from the demands of editors, of artists, even of readers? What is this "literature"

I seem to be claiming that we're supposed to be trying and mostly honorably failing to write? How do we go about writing it?

I think our analogy is with the work of the artist. We're writers first of all and what writers do, and other artists do, is take an experience, real or imagined, and render it in such a way as to bring out, pleasurably, some underlying significance that otherwise people might miss. The critic starts with the experience of the production seen last night. And the critic has an obligation to report that production accurately, to report *what happened*, an obligation that the writers of fiction do not have. But the critic too, if he's writing well, will be doing what the fiction writer does and finding general significance in the particular event. Our job is to help people understand human life—that's what writers do. Beginning in our case with the particular piece of human life that happened at the Shubert or the Geary or the Magic Theatre last night.

How do we do that? Robert Penn Warren once said in an interview, about writing poetry, "Everything starts from an observed fact of life and then the search begins for the issue—the ethical or dramatic issue—in the fact." The issue is in the fact. I find this idea to be crucially helpful in my writing. For the critic, the fact is the performance of *Hamlet* or *Up in Mabel's Room* that he saw last night. The issue is, what was really important about that experience? What does the production have to do with the art form of which it's an example? With the world which, however humbly, or even dishonestly, no production can keep from interpreting? What about this production matters even to someone who can't or won't see the play?

The most important act in writing a critical review is to take in the experience of the production as fully as possible. But right behind it in importance is the search for the answers to those questions, is the discovery of a significant issue in the fact. What I'm talking about is not merely idealistic, but eminently practical. In a good review the issue in the fact determines your lead, determines your structure, becomes the handle by which you pick the whole experience up. Of course, it's easier to discover a significant issue in the fact when the play is *Hamlet* than when the play is *Up in Mabel's Room*. But the issue is always there if you can find it.

There's a wonderful review by Max Beerbohm in which he doesn't mention the play until the last paragraph, at which point he says, "Meanwhile I do not propose to criticize *The Chief of Staff*. It is a rigamarole which shows off Mr. Waller [the leading actor] personally. This is all one needs to say of it." And he spends the rest of the review talking about the relationship between Waller and the audience, talking about what that audience is like, those silly girls who have made him a sex symbol instead of an actor, with his willing collaboration.

Now, you can imagine how the ordinary review of this production would take shape. "Lewis Waller returned to the stage last night in *The Chief of Staff* in which he plays . . ." or "Lewis Waller's newest vehicle, *The Chief of Staff*, is a rickety conveyance unlikely to carry him for a long run. In it he plays . . ." But Max could see that this time, what the play was about was irrelevant. What the occasion was about was a good actor prostituting himself to a public that didn't want his real talent. The power at that evening's performance was held by the public. Therefore the decision almost to ignore the play, to write about that public, was not a perverse decision to show off, but a true comment on what was really happening that night. And incidentally it also provided all the consumer guidance an intelligent reader would ever need.

Max wrote that review for the *Saturday Review* of Feb. 6, 1909. Lewis Waller is dead. When did you last hear about a revival of *The Chief of Staff*? But somebody is still reading the review. And what that production becomes a symbol of in that review—a talented artist who sells out by subjecting himself to the taste of an unworthy public—is that unknown today or is that as near as your television set? Even in a totally second-rate, transitory, star vehicle you can find something worth talking about if you're keen-eyed enough.

Is there danger in this of ignoring or scanting the immediate experience, the play itself? You bet there is, but only if you don't do it right. The issue is *in* the fact, the general is in the particular. By finding some general significance in what you're writing about, if you're doing it right, you will also be writing more keenly, not less, about the immediate experience, about what really happened. And your writing will be vivified, your discussion of the particularities will be vivified, because you'll have an impelling reason to write about them. You'll need those particularities to make a point. You won't just be mentioning the lighting designer in the next-to-last paragraph. The best critic is the one who puts what he sees into the largest possible context while re-creating most vividly the immediate experience.

Now by speaking of *the* issue in *the* fact, I don't mean to imply that there's just one issue per fact, just one matter worth really talking about per production. The fact is not just the production, it's *your* experience of the production, your collision, confrontation, transaction, with it. The best way to the issue in the fact is through yourself as the perceiver. Oscar Wilde says criticism is the sincerest form of autobiography. I think that's true. Art works on the subjectivity of the spectator, the viewer, the listener, the reader. How can you say anything worthwhile about it if you leave your subjectivity out of your account? As Jan Kott says, "To my mind, a deep limitation of the American critic is that he does not write as a man who has a political, sexual, emotional and national life."

To write as yourself is not arrogance, as it's sometimes thought. It's honesty. You have *your* eyes to see with, you have *your* ears to hear with, *your* feelings to feel with, *your* experience to respond through. Admit it. It's true anyway. For me to pretend I am "the critic" or "the *Village Voice*"—*that* would be arrogant. To write as yourself, to keep the reader aware that it's one individual writing, who may or may not be coming from where the reader's coming from, that's honesty. To own up to your own subjectivity is to give the reader what he or she needs truly to make up his or her mind.

Which is why it seems to me that the review that says "rush to the box office" is always an impertinence. *Who* should rush to the box office? Not everybody is the same. Not everybody is the same as the critic. It seems to me that by acknowledging our own individuality, we acknowledge that. The critic is in fact not God, not a computer, not a measurer by abstract standards—he's a human being. And if he can't make his humanity in some way interesting to his readers, he's not going to be interesting in any other way either.

Is there a danger that subjectivity will become self-indulgence, that the rampant critical ego will get between the reader and the production being reviewed? You bet there is. It's one of the temptations that we have to fight. But the way to fight it is not by denying your own subjectivity, because it's going to be there anyway; it's going to be working on you, it's going to be working on your reader. We have to learn to be objective about our own subjectivity. To analyze it as keenly as we analyze the interaction of the artists who collaborate on a production.

A disciplined critic, I think, needs to develop a double consciousness. Without diminishing the power to feel, to be moved, to be swept away by emotion, a good critic watches himself feeling, studies himself being swept away or, equally effectively, is swept away at the moment, and then afterwards studies the process of being swept away. This is not as hard as it may sound. Every spectator, however moved, knows that he's in a theatre, not seeing the real thing, but being manipulated by skilled artists, manipulated in the best sense. The actor more than anyone has this double consciousness, feeling and watching himself feel, carried away, yet not so carried away that he doesn't remember that that's Miss Smith and not Desdemona, and he's not supposed to strangle her in earnest. The critic's double consciousness, I think, parallels the actor's, enabling a good critic to be emotionally free, yet intellectually in control.

I spend a lot of time leading workshops in criticism, teaching classes, working with the critic fellows at the National Critics Institute at the O'Neill Theater Center, working with professional critics as well as college students. And more and more, I'm impressed with the similarity between learning to be a critic and learning to be an actor. In both cases, people come to learn the formula, to learn how to do it, and the first thing to learn is to let go of the formula.

We all know the basic reviewing formula: Put a snappy generalization about the production in your lead, then you have a paragraph of plot summary, do your little checklist—writing, acting, directing and miscellaneous, then you have a tag that restates the lead, also snappy if possible, and then you get to go home. Now that may be reviewing, TV reviewing most likely, but it isn't criticism.

Like the actor, the critic must learn to be fresh every night, which isn't easy—he must learn to be open, honest, flexible, not to get in the way of his own responses. Both the actor and the critic need to learn to let the encounter between himself and the material determine the shape of what he creates.

The word that's been chiming through what I've been saying is honesty. Honesty is essentially what Shaw means by "the critical instinct." What the good critic, like the good actor, discovers is that honesty isn't easy. Honesty needs to be worked for—it's not just a matter of not being consciously *dis*honest. To be truly honest is to be engaged in a never-ending fight against a never-ending human capacity for self-deception. Nobody wins that fight all the time, but a good critic is constantly pressing himself to discover what he really thinks and feels, what's really going on.

Now, not all the results of this process of self-examination are relevant to the task at hand of writing the review, or, if you're an actor, of giving the performance. Nobody wants sloppy confessional criticism any more than sloppy confessional acting. Nevertheless, the good critic, like the good actor, has to be willing to go out on a limb, to make the chance of self-exposure. Randall Jarrell, the poet-critic, says, "Taking the chance of making a complete fool of himself—and sometimes, doing so—is the first demand that is made upon any real critic: He must stick his neck out just as the artist does, if he is to be of any real use to art." Those of you who have studied acting or worked as actors knows how vital that is. To take that chance.

This honesty is dangerous, it's frightening. As Federico Fellini says about *being* criticized, "If you show yourself naked to others, you have to accept that some won't like your body." Are you afraid that you really have nothing worth saying? So am I. So is everybody. But you'll never know that you do have something worth saying unless you seek it in yourself.

If you're honest and open, you may still be a terrible critic. But the chance is worth taking because the careful, self-protecting critic is *always* a dull critic. If you're honest, you have a chance. If you're dishonest, if you put yourself off with manufactured reasons, you will never be any good. And you'll never have any fun. Because this honesty—dangerous and uneasy-making as it can be—is where the fun is. I always forget whether it's Gwendolen or Cecily in *The Importance of Being Earnest* who says that there are times when speaking one's mind is not only a duty, but a pleasure. And it's the central duty and the central pleasure of our profession. Why are we critics, if not for the delight of speaking our minds, of telling the best and deepest truths we can discover about a given experience, and telling these truths as well and deeply as possible? God knows we're not in it for the money.

Henrik Ibsen once said, "If I cannot be myself in what I write, then my work would be nothing but lies and humbug, and our country has had enough of that." I think that's true of critics as well as playwrights.

The 1981–82 winner of the George Jean Nathan Award for Dramatic Criticism, Julius Novick has served as theatre critic for the *Village Voice*, the *New York Observer* and *New York Newsday*. He is the author of *Beyond Broadway: The Quest for Permanent Theatres* and *Beyond the Golden Door: Jewish American Drama and Jewish American Experience*. He is professor emeritus of drama studies at Purchase College of the State University of New York. This address was first printed in the Theatre Bay Area publication *Call Board*.

BECOMING A PLAYWRIGHT

By Adrienne Kennedy

February 1988

NEW YORK, 1962: Edward Albee was wearing a tweed suit and seemed shy and frightened. In a muted voice he read from his notes about what our playwriting class was to consist of. Each person was required to have a play done in workshop. The class was upstairs over the theatre at Circle in the Square on Bleecker Street. Outside the wind blew the Circle in the Square sign which still hangs there today. He invited the class to a rehearsal of *The Sandbox* at the Cherry Lane. During the rehearsal he went up on the stage and quietly spoke to the actors. There was a hole in his sweater, which gave him the air of a struggling writer.

Michael Kahn was the Circle's brilliant young director. It was his job to cast the workshop productions. My play was to be in April. Michael had mentioned the possible casting of Diana Sands, Yaphet Kotto and others. But during the winter I became frightened. My play seemed far too revealing.

I sat in the bedroom of our Park West Village apartment and carefully edited out the word "nigger" from *Funnyhouse of a Negro*, the word that Sarah used to define her own self-hatred. Before the next class I took the new edited script up to the office above the Circle and asked for my original script back. I thought it was settled.

When it was time for me to have my meeting with Michael Kahn about my workshop production I discovered he had other copies of my original script and had somehow not received the edited one. I said I would drop out of the class if they used my original script. "Don't worry," he said, "I'll tell Edward Albee you want the new version done." I arrived early at the next class to tell Albee I wanted the edited version of *Funnyhouse* done, unaware that this pattern I had clung to for a decade—editing out the darkness and violence in my work, in this case Sarah's self-hatred—had very often destroyed my work. It was a problem too big to handle.

Albee was in the theatre alone.

"Mr. Albee," I said, "I've decided to drop the class." He stared straight into my face. "Oh," he said. "It's your decision. But don't you want to see your play performed? It is a chance to see your characters on the stage."

"My play is too revealing," I said. "I'm embarrassed to have it done. The other plays so far are not so revealing."

He stuck his hands into his pockets, came closer to me and stared. His gaze was hypnotic.

"Do you see that stage?" he said, glancing at Circle's theatre in the round.

"Yes."

"Well, do you know what a playwright is? A playwright is someone who lets his guts out on the stage and that's what you've done in this play." I didn't know what to say. That was the point. I didn't want my guts let out in front of the whole class. I stepped back and started toward the door.

"It's your decision," he said.

I remained in the class. For the first time, the anguish that most often I had carefully blotted out in the second and third drafts of my work was revealed, first to my director, then to the actors, Diana Sands, Yaphet Kotto, Andre Gregory, Lynne Hamilton and Fran Bennett, and finally the writers in the workshop. I still wasn't sure I had done the right thing.

When the play was performed at Circle in the Square in April it was so controversial that Michael, who was a member of the Actors Studio, decided to do it as his project there the following week. While we rehearsed *Funnyhouse*, as now everyone called it, Michael told me that several theatre people would be there to see it: Rip Torn, Geraldine Page, Harold Clurman.

Although Michael was many years younger than I, he was experienced in the theatre and attempted to be reassuring. The idea of doing a play that these theatre people were coming to see—and were going to comment on afterwards while I sat on a single chair in front of the entire Playwrights Unit and explained what I was trying to say—made me sick. During one of the last rehearsals I felt so frightened that I ran outside and sat on the steps.

It was on one of those days that I asked Michael why people were suddenly calling me "Miss Kennedy." He explained it was somehow theatrical. I had heard that after the play it was the practice of the Unit members to demolish the playwright. Although I was totally demolished (despite a final suggestion that the play might have a deep charm and be "important") I was asked to join the Unit.

By now I had forgotten all about Brando and Kazan. I was too frightened. The next week as I was waiting in the lobby of Circle to go to our last class, Albee came in and stopped and asked me would I be going to the Actors Studio every Tuesday. I expressed uncertainty.

"Tennessee Williams sometimes goes," he said and turned and walked away.

I went for a while.

People now started to refer to me as a playwright.

Even after years of attending playwriting workshops I still wondered how that could be. Shakespeare was a playwright; Miller, Williams, Langston Hughes, Ionesco. A playwright was Sartre standing in a raincoat in a street in Paris.

Adrienne Kennedy's *Funnyhouse of a Negro* **won an Obie Award in 1964 and has since been translated into several languages. She earned a second Obie in 1996 for** *June and Jean in Concert* **and** *Sleep Deprivation Chamber,* **which premiered as part of Signature Theatre Company's season devoted to her. Her other works include** *The Ohio State Murders, A Movie Star Has to Star in Black and White, A Rat's Mass, The Owl Answers, Motherhood 2000, She Talks to Beethoven, An Evening with Dead Essex, A Lesson in Dead Language,* **and** *The Lennon Play.* **In 2008 she co-authored the play** *Mom, How Did You Meet the Beatles?* **with her son, Adam Kennedy.**

THE SOVIET DIARY

By Harold Clurman

Edited and introduced by Joan Ungaro

March 1988

The Group Theatre was in its fifth year when it finally encountered box-office success in 1935 with three Clifford Odets plays—*Awake and Sing!*, *Waiting for Lefty* and *Till the Day I Die*. The windfall gave two of the Group's three directors enough time and money to travel to the U.S.S.R. for a look at Soviet theatre. On April 26, 1935, Harold Clurman and Cheryl Crawford embarked on a five-week visit. (The year before, Sidney Kingsley's *Men in White* had helped fund a tantalizing two-week Soviet trip for Clurman, Lee Strasberg and Stella Adler.) In 35 days Clurman and Crawford saw 35 plays; as Clurman later noted, that amounted to not half of what was available. It would have taken six months to see everything! Neither American spoke Russian, which was of course the primary language employed on the Soviet stage, even for the numerous Shakespeare productions that enjoyed popularity at the time. French sufficed for their conversations with the leading figures of the Russian theatre: Stanislavsky and Meyerhold, Nemirovich-Dantchenko and Sergei Eisenstein, among others.

The two Group directors were not the only visiting artists in Moscow at the time. Other outsiders were Bertolt Brecht, Gordon Craig, Edmund Wilson, Jay Leyda and Paul Strand (both long-standing Group friends) and Joseph Losey (as a reporter for the *Moscow Daily News*). Clurman saw them all. During the trip he took notes in a leather-bound book given to him by his colleagues at the Group. He called the notes *Soviet Diary 1935*. What happened to the actual hand-written journal I do not know; someone typed it for him at some point, and he gave me a photocopy in the mid-'70s. What follows is an excerpted version. He did not think of it as a book, so we have retained his shortened, diary-style phrasings.

The purpose of the trip seems to have been to observe and gather information with which to instruct, encourage and motivate the Group, which counted among its members Luther Adler, Kermit Bloomgarden, J. Edward Bromberg, Morris Carnovsky, Elia Kazan,

Robert Lewis, Sanford Meisner, William Saroyan and Irwin Shaw, among others. The diary mentions many people at work in the Soviet theatre who are relatively unknown here today, and much of that material I have deleted; the notes on meetings with Stanislavsky and Meyerhold are included in large part; material on the Group, its problems and achievements, is selectively excerpted.

In returning to the diaries, I have been struck again by the personality of Harold Clurman himself: How little he seems to have changed in the 40 years between the time he wrote what follows here and the times that I went regularly to the theatre with him in New York in the '70s—and read his criticism in the magazine I worked for, the *Nation*. He always combined his aesthetic, intellectual and moral approach to things theatrical with a forthright interest in everyday affairs—notice below his mention of Moscow's new subway and a cigarette factory in the midst of rather complex theatrical discussions. The diary reflects his deep interest in scenic design and body movement—in fact, his orientation may have been more visual in Russia because of not knowing the language. His notes on Russian actors such as Mikhoels and Shchukin reinforce his abiding concern with the creative process of acting, which he never slighted even when directing on Broadway.

On his return, Clurman read these notes at two sessions with the Group; Crawford described outstanding productions in detail at a third. Group members—actors, playwrights and directors—were invited, as were friends of the Group and other artists. Nothing came of the meetings; the diary was never published. Until now.

—*J. Ungaro, November 1987*

Moscow, April 29

In the evening went to see *King Lear* at the Jewish Kamerny Theatre. Hopes were high. First act seemed interesting and charming (almost piquant) due to a certain clarity in the business. The fluency of the play, the originality of the set: It was a miniature that had a kind of sharpness about it, a little grotesque like certain engravings I have seen that were "fantastic"—bizarre—yet clear. The second act began to lose its quality. I hesitate to condemn the whole thing, as these Russian productions have a way of growing on one. The American habit of judging a production as soon as one has seen it does not fit here. Yet, despite Gordon Craig's statement that this was the first production that made *Lear* clear to him, this was a strange interpretation that portrays Lear as a madman from the very beginning. (Mikhoels plays Lear without a beard; a small, skinny old man with an impish quality that changes: at times to a crazy roaring that reminds me of a caricature I have seen somewhere of an old-time actor gone cuckoo.) I think, on further reflection, that what I liked best in this production was its wildness. Considering the sanguinary extravagance of most of Shakespeare's plays, nearly every American production I have ever seen has been as fitting as a Maxfield Parrish painting would be to illustrate the Book of Job.

April 30

At night saw *The Forest* at the Meyerhold Theatre. It began raggedly (the company was sort of a second company) and my hopes began to waver. But soon I found myself admiring it very much, and then knowing for a certainty that Meyerhold is a genius. Only two or three of the performances were adequate. Yet the shape of the production—its form, its idea—are such that the *creation* that it is comes out clearly, nonetheless. I have seen shows that I have enjoyed more (the raggedness and lack of distinction in many roles made complete enjoyment impossible), but very few that have impressed me more for sheer originality, inventiveness and a new kind of theatricality.

Meyerhold, I have discovered, is a kind of romantic (despite a certain coldness in his temperament), a romantic very much in love with the glamorous theatre, often even with the things that were colorful in the decayed societies of the past. But there is nothing decayed in this production: It is fresh and sound all through. What I learned might be summarized in one phrase: "Do anything you want in the theatre." This is a very dangerous maxim unless one also realizes that to do anything one wants in the theatre, study and work are necessary in order for you to do it so that other people *want* what you do.

After the show, Moscow, on the eve of May Day, was a blaze of glory. The whole town was aglow in red. Banners all over, slogans, portraits, electric lights proclaimed the holidays. When I look around and see how Moscow has grown in one year, and at the people who are building it with love and enthusiasm—rough people—it all seems like a miracle come true. It revives one's belief in man: in his ability to dream, to suffer, to fight, to sustain misfortune and still through great strength (which is fundamentally the *desire to live* and a love of life), to build and create.

May 2

In the afternoon, [the critic, editor and translator] Jay Leyda and I went to an exhibition of scenic design covering the past 17 years in the Soviet theatre. It was the most interesting exhibition of this sort I had ever seen. I do not speak of the quality of the design—though of course many of the models were amongst the best work in this field in the modern theatre—but of the variety, the individuality, the daring and, above all, the freedom. It is difficult to give any idea of how far a Soviet scene designer can go when he wants to "experiment." He demands what would be technically and economically impossible in America. The stage pictures of the Soviet theatre are therefore nearly always entertaining.

Of course this liberty has certain disadvantages. The settings can become a matter of display merely—and this may extend beyond the setting to the direction and even to the acting. A merely formalistic element enters into the theatre—the temptation simply to play with the medium—with a resulting emptiness. Even the subtlest effects in art—those wrought with the greatest technical and intellectual competence—can become dead and useless things if they have no roots in a sincere, humanly *necessary* desire to express a real experience. Naturally for us in America with our monotonous and technically inelastic theatre, the

Soviet theatre is very stimulating and highly instructive, but our whole problem is to learn how to use the formal achievements of the Soviet theatre together with our own organic message (in which regard we have little to learn and much to give) in relation to our American audience.

Theatre-for-theatre's sake (and despite the revolutionary themes of the plays, I detect a good deal of this in the productions) is almost as bad as theatre-for-money's sake. And in *no* theatre—I can say this confidently now that I have really looked around—in *no* theatre today has the theoretical and practical basis been so established for this linking of theatre and life as in the Group. In other theatres, a clearer political line has been laid down, but this is rarely organic: It simply means that a director or board of directors has announced a political program affecting plays and the organization of audiences. It does not mean that the theatre expresses through its work—which includes the development of its directors, actors and audience—the very process of attaining political clarity, the moving toward greater understanding of social issues through the medium of the theatre as an artform.

In the late afternoon Cheryl and I, accompanied by Jay Leyda, went to see Eisenstein. He lives in one room—this world-famous artist—surrounded by books of every description in an apartment that includes many other one-room apartments. If he were an American movie director, would he have a yacht, a mansion, a Hispano-Suiza and a well-publicized affair with a continental actress?

At night we went to see an act-and-a-half of a play called *The Prelude or Introduction* at the Meyerhold Theatre. We were told that only one act of this play was worth seeing, being the least successful of Meyerhold's productions, although by now I feel that one should see *all* of Meyerhold's work because technically he has the most to teach in the theatre. The act we saw was not particularly distinguished.

This play, like *The Final Conflict*, seemed very bad. In fact, it was probably no play at all. But this may be partly due to Meyerhold's treatment of his scripts, which consists, it appears, of taking episodes and scenes from a play and presenting them as theatrical bits when he as a director can make them interesting and vivid. Thus, from a literary standpoint, and perhaps from a general artistic standpoint, havoc is wrought with character development as we generally understand it. (I cannot be absolutely sure of this without knowing the lines.) I am afraid this might lead to a strengthening of theatrical craft but to a weakening of the playwright's technique as an artist. Certainly if any of us tried to do to our plays what Meyerhold and some of the other Soviet directors do to theirs, the playwrights would sue us and proclaim to the world that we were the enemies of art.

May 4

At 3 o'clock we have an appointment with Madame Toumansova, Stanislavsky's secretary. We find out first that Stanislavsky is in Moscow and that he works very hard. He is 72 and he is busy for seven or eight hours a day. He is directing Bulgakov's *Molière* as well as the opera studio and a school, and is finishing his book. He directs at home. The government, we are also informed, offered him a new, more spacious apartment where he would have greater facility for his rehearsals but he prefers to stay where he is . . . . Another bit of information: When we remarked that the Moscow Art seemed the busiest theatre in Moscow, Madame Toumansova said, "Yes, we have 1,086 people employed in our theatre and 240 of them are actors. I suppose this is the largest dramatic company in the world." "What would the Group be like," Cheryl muses to me, "if it had 240 actors?"

Madame Toumansova arranged for all our tickets for the Moscow Art performances. So in the evening we see *Night Lodging* [Gorky's *The Lower Depths*] with Moskvin and Katchalov in their original parts. Moskvin is so relaxed, so simple, so real that he does not seem to be playing at all. But he is acting and his acting is an object lesson in concentration, listening, talking and true emotion borne without effort from these premises.

Here is an important difference between the Moscow Art Theatre today and the Meyerhold—at the Moscow Art it is the little things that are still good; at the Meyerhold the big things are good. In all such minor details as the actors really taking a new character in as he enters, really listening, watching, being at home in the environment of the play, the Moscow Art is still unmatched. Yet the whole performance (of this play at least) is very weak as a creation. Thus, we learn that a good technique, a repertory system, good actors and a very good play, all of them are not sufficient to make good theatre. What is needed in addition—and what is needed fundamentally—is a true production idea, a theatre idea, animated by the personal participation and effort of all the actors in the cast in bringing this idea to life within the scope of their part.

May 5

Last night's performance made my purpose in coming to the Soviet Union clearer than ever before. I have come to realize all the possibilities of the theatre—since all of them find an expression here. There are formal theatres, aesthetic theatres, naturalistic theatres, experimental theatres, fantastic realistic theatres, revolutionary theatres and every sort of theatre—right and left. Out of all this I want to see what can be done with each of these methods so that we in the Group may learn to apply them if we wish to. The problem resolves itself to one of artistic choice, which is based, of course, on the exact content one wishes to express and the effect one wishes to make on the audience. This, in turn, depends on the sense of one's own role in the theatre and what one aspires to be and the function of our own theatre from a general point of view. Certainly, one should be capable at least of doing anything.

May 6

At night we saw the Moscow Art production of Gogol's *Dead Souls*, one of its more recent productions. There were excellent scenes in this and two or three superb characterizations in small parts. Nearly all of it had the usual Moscow Art maturity of acting which is very satisfying—almost like a lesson. Yet I did not feel that it was important: I shall not think of it as much as I have about some of Meyerhold's poor productions. One sees these Moscow Art productions as one picks up a well-bound classic sometimes: one reads a little, one says "this is first-class stuff" and stifles a yawn. There was no *drive* in this production, no creative fire. One did not feel as if all the actors were saying or the director had thought, "With this production I want to achieve something and say something that it is impossible to say in just this production alone, that it may take all our lives to say and to achieve." One does not sense *some other world* outside the frame of the production to which the actors belong and which they are making every effort to express.

One organizational element that interested me in the production of *Dead Souls*, however, was the fact that a good many important actors were playing bits in the large cast.

May 9

I saw the last two acts of *Carmen*—a new production and Stanislavsky's latest work. This interested me for two reasons. First, it proved once again that producing an opera as a real play is not only possible but actually desirable. Second, the staging of this opera with its action and speech necessarily slower than in a play gave me a good picture of Stanislavsky's new emphasis in his direction of acting. The acting in this opera—despite its passionate melodramatic story and the "big emotions" it requires—was as easy as A-B-C. This is instructive. For while Stanislavsky finds physical equivalents that are natural and sensible, which makes the acting a little too workaday; the principle of the physical equivalent for each action carried out continuously and completely will give you a certain element of that external theatricality (without the loss of truth) which we in the Group are seeking. What limits Stanislavsky, of course, is his realistic bias on the one hand, and a certain lack of truly general ideas on the other. (When more closely analyzed, these two faults will be seen to be almost inseparable and also to explain why in the realm of the deeper meaning of the conception implied in the term ensemble the Moscow Art Theatre is really not very strong.)

May 10

Got up early to meet [the photographer] Paul Strand. Saw him to the hotel and then had to rush off to a *biomechanics* class at the Meyerhold Theatre. I had seen funny pictures and had heard abstruse explanations of the theory of biomechanics, neither of which had interested me particularly. But this class, for which the teacher apologized continually, interested me greatly. To put it bluntly, this was the best body work for the actor I had ever seen. After seeing this (though other Soviet theatres do not use biomechanics exactly, they do use related systems or body training) I could understand why Russian actors are so fluent and graceful on the stage compared to our own Group actors, who as individuals have just as strong and muscular bodies.

The difference is in the *kind* of body training the Russians get. The biomechanics exercises are not only excellent in the purely physical elements for training the muscles through tension and relaxation, movement and the stopping of movement, but remarkable for the dramatic elements (without any artiness), for each of these exercises is a kind of play, with two characters generally in conflict—so that the movement is always related to a partner and demands a constant adjustment of person to person—most often of a man to a woman. One can see at once that these exercises have been devised by a person with a profound sense of theatre. They demand agility and poise, feeling and physical freedom: They are actually a pleasure to see and they must be even a greater pleasure to perform.

Some of the things the students are able to do are extraordinary: A man jumps on another's chest while his partner stands erect; the first man slides off him, slowly, his feet never touching the ground till he gets down on the floor. Besides biomechanics—done three times a week—the Meyerhold actors also do acrobatics. Acrobatics, of course, are recommended by Stanislavsky as training for the actor.

At night was supposed to see *Pickwick Club* at the Moscow Art but went instead to see Strand show his photographs to Eisenstein. Eisenstein was really impressed . . . . I felt that this was a little victory for American art.

May 12

I went to see a matinee of *Cherry Orchard* rather reluctantly. I was beginning to be bored by the Moscow Art routine. But I was very glad later that I had gone—this was the best production of all those we saw at this theatre. In *The Cherry Orchard* the reality is personal, immediate, everyday, normal and, as Lee [Strasberg] once put it, "like bread." The main point is that in this production the realism is carried to perfection. This is the cream of the bourgeois art. It is not exalted or very intense but it has no vulgarity: It is decent, homely, tender and satisfying. The end of the play was the only time thus far in Moscow that tears came to my eyes at the end of a theatrical performance.

May 15

Got up early to visit a cigarette factory. It was not especially exciting although I find myself always fascinated when I go to a place where things are in the making. Work in the Group has had a subtle influence on me in this respect: Nowadays I am fascinated in the development of an object from the state of a plan to its conversion into materials that soon begins to function for an audience in an aesthetic way. Middle-class people and especially middle-class intellectuals have been spiritually impoverished by taking all the objects they use for granted. They have no sense of the rough material, the human labor, the energy and fatigue that go into the making of anything they use. Gorky has put this thought admirably: "The social and cultural development of people proceeds normally only when the hands teach the head and, having become wiser, the head in turn teaches the hands."

At night went to see *Love and Intrigue* by Schiller at the Vakhtangov Theatre. The chief charm of this production is visual—but it is not a matter of just pretty sets. These were by Akimov and they were amongst the most original, the most imaginative, the most beautiful I have ever seen. Yet despite great daring—they resembled nothing I knew from any stage—they were really quite simple. Certainly there was perfect coordination of the visual with the other elements. The actors had the proper "removal" for a romantic play, their background was rich and bright (the tin-foil took the light so that every scene had a different quality) and yet the eye was never distracted. The general characteristic of these settings was their freedom. The final moment, in idea, placement, lighting, etc., was a masterpiece—a *theatrical* creation.

I have always maintained, generally speaking, a play in the theatre was only what we *see* and *hear* on the stage and that therefore the essential artistic creation, while composed of the interrelation of all the elements, would sometimes rest predominantly on one of them. But I had never been able to think of an example of a set which made the *art* of a play (most sets are merely accessories, even when they are good). Akimov's *Love and Intrigue* is such a set—though of course even this set could not function without the actors and other elements of the play. (In fact, without them the sets would not be comprehensible at all, since they don't look *like* anything.) Designers should be sent to the Soviet Union to see it. Also painters.

A curious thing at this performance was my increasing absorption with the *play* while the *plot* became increasingly unintelligible. But I had no desire to inform myself about it: I was enjoying it fully, simply by looking . . . . Schiller's play was unimportant, some of the acting was mediocre and some of the casting as far as type was quite wrong and yet the *play* I *saw* (the play we *see*, I repeat, is the *only play* in the theatre) was magnificent.

There is a lesson—or rather symbolic value—in this. The lesson for designers, of course, is obvious. The lesson for theatre critics and theatricians is equally clear. The symbol for theatre people generally is this: A production of a play, if sufficiently thought out and creatively imagined, may become a true work of art—completely organic, completely integrated, and absolutely right from moment to moment (despite the literary limitations of the script and even the limitations of the actors) to the extent of seeming as *pure* an expression as a good piece of music or a fine bit of architecture.

I must confess that, allowing for the flaws noted, this evening at the Vakhtangov was the nearest thing to what might be described as an "art-for-art's sake" experience I have had in the Soviet theatre.

May 16

Went to see *Yegor Bulichev* again at the Vakhtangov Theatre. Last year I was impressed by the element of stylishness in this production, because it was much freer in its treatment of a realistic play than we are accustomed to in America. But this time I was impressed with the *realness* of the production: the observation, the concrete detail, the quiet truth. Everything is done lovingly, cleanly and clearly: Nothing is missed, nothing is overstressed, nothing neglected. Shchukin as Bulichev is still superb. He dominates the play by his part and his personality (which is vigorous and young without a trace of coarseness or vulgarity) and yet he brings a perfect ensemble feeling to the stage. His spiritual attitude in the performance (and this counts a great deal in the first impression created by an actor on the audience) breathes dignity, simplicity and a masculine sweetness. He is universally loved by audiences and fellow actors. And because I know he is no miracle man but an honest theatre worker of talent who by force of a real desire to grow (he was an illiterate boy and is almost completely self-educated) has risen to the point of his present performance, I feel closer to him. I love him as an actor more than any I know. One does not sink to one's knees in admiring him, one feels like embracing him and working by his side.

There are great men in the theatre from whom we can learn little; from Shchukin and the Vakhtangov Theatre much can be learned: We are akin. The difference between us is not one of talent. It has to do with a certain kind of theatrical conscience or devotion, and a certain discipline.

May 17

I took the Metro—the new subway—which had just been opened to the public. I wonder what the opening of the subway in New York was like. This particular achievement really deserves the wonder and acclaim it is getting. When one buys one's ticket (50 kopeks) one has the feeling that one is buying opera seats. To see the workers who built this subway with their rough clothes, their still untamed bodies and their untutored earthy ways crowd into the decorative, modernistic halls of their creation is to realize once again the inspiring contradiction, the unparalleled and glorious paradox of the Soviet Union.

At night we went to see *Romeo and Juliet* at the Theatre of the Revolution. And indeed this production is brilliant. First of all, the sets have a sweep, a variety, a largeness, a colorfulness that are beyond anything I have ever seen in a classic production in America. In fact, I explained to people during intermission that we were too poor in America to put on Shakespeare this way. The production cost for us would be over $100,000 surely—not to mention the fact that the production was rehearsed for over a year. [*Editor's note:* $100,000 in 1935 would be close to $820,000 in 1987; in 1935, *Waiting for Lefty* cost $5,000.] The lavishness was overwhelming, as was the way the stage was used.

The first scene—the fight—was one of the most exciting theatrical moments you can imagine. Here the body training—the ease of movement, the ability to fence, to run, to jump—was used to the full with an effect that was Shakespearean in its energy, breadth, fluency and strength. What came through was not the romantic tragedy of love but the general colorfulness and splendor of the period: the physical dynamics. At last, a virile Shakespeare instead of the literary sissy, the drooping, swooning, lisping namby-pamby son of a professional bore that he is in every American production I have seen.

In the midst of all this we find very spirited and technically expert acting. But on the whole, it is characteristic of a general defect in production here that they treat the actors much too instrumentally. An actor directed externally only, howsoever brilliantly, remains slightly *untheatrical.* In other words, true theatricality does not reside only in business, in visually interesting or pictorially dramatic movement, in general stage colors, dances, leaps, etc.—it resides also and perhaps even to a greater extent in the inner life, in the emotion, in the spirit (to put it boldly) of the actor.

May 18

In the evening we saw *Revizor* (*Inspector General*) at the Meyerhold. A very brilliant production. It is harder, more complex, trickier and less revolutionary than *The Forest*. (Less revolutionary in the sense that it seems like an amazing picture of the past by someone who was very much part of it rather than the fresh breathing of new air that one gets from *The Forest*.) But it is full of a specifically theatrical genius: cultivated, inventive, incisive and profound in craftsmanship. A strange feeling comes from this production: It is very funny and it is tomblike. It has a definitely macabre quality—cold, beautiful, grimacing, distorted and graceful. The production ends with the actors running off stage laughing while on the stage we see their prototypes, who are puppets. Meyerhold's *Revizor* is a masterpiece, but somehow not a warming one: It leaves one slightly uncomfortable.

May 21

Quite suddenly came the announcement that Stanislavsky would see us. At 3:30 we were told we could visit him at 4:15. I brought him Stella Adler's gift and he shook my hand for it. And then I began asking questions—not too many, however.

"Miss Adler wants to know what you meant by inner clichés."

"Actors of experience often have certain emotional tricks by which they indicate sorrow, anger, etc. These are not pieces of business, physical things, but inner processes over which they have control and which they can use to indicate deep feeling. But they have little to do with life: They are born of the theatre. They do not derive from *action* but from representation (from performance). The way to overcome it is for the actor to say to himself or for the director to ask, 'What were you *doing* at that moment? Were you *doing* anything?' If the actor senses that he was only *feeling* (or trying to feel) but not doing (carrying out an action) he will be able to rid himself of the inner clichés."

Cheryl asked, "Do you set the problem for the actor or do you make him set it for himself?"

"I would like the actor to set the problem for himself. But the actor is lazy so I set the problem for him."

"Your actors are lazy!" I exclaimed in genuine astonishment.

"Oh, they know how to work," Stanislavsky replied, "but they don't unless you push them to it. They are willing to work as hard as you please on physical problems, position, etc., but on the other and more important things—yes, they are lazy."

He later spoke about body work. "Acrobatics are very useful. But even more for the soul than for the body." We smiled at this paradox. "Yes, acrobatics train you not to be afraid in the big moments of your part. Because these moments—they may not be physical—are equivalent to a difficult jump. If you hesitate you are lost. Acrobatics prepare you for them."

The conversation turned to other aspects of the theatre. Stanislavsky tells us about his difficulties with a playwright. "We tell him a certain scene or speech has to be put into the play and he answers, 'The actor will do it.' And then the actor says, 'I can't do it. I need a speech.' Finally, there is no acting and no speech."

Immediately after our Stanislavsky visit we had a date to see Meyerhold. He also received us in his apartment, composed of large pleasant rooms—by no means luxurious or ornate in any way. Meyerhold is utterly simple and direct in conversation. I found him sympathetic and charming. "Your productions," I began, "are built differently from anyone else's. Have you a special conception of dramaturgy?"

"Yes, I believe that plays should be written differently for the new theatre than they have been up to now. Because of this I have had constant conflicts with my playwrights. I have therefore become a director-author.

"I believe it would be useful to have a school for playwrights in the theatre. When I direct a play I can do nothing else, even write a letter. I think of nothing else, I see nothing else. And I can't work with assistants who might relieve me in my direction. [*Editor's note:* Sergei Eisenstein was one of two laboratory assistants to Meyerhold in *Tarelkin's Death* (1917), and also worked on a design for *Heartbreak House*, a production that Meyerhold never completed.] Yes, the problem of the dramatist is now our most important problem. That and the problem of a new theatre architecture. The two problems are related."

"Do you work on your productions much before you go into rehearsal?"

"I thought about *Revizor* for 10 years before I produced it. I always knew I would do it. I always wanted to do it. But I was not ready and kept on thinking about it. There are plays about which I say to myself, 'This play I will do in three years or in five years.'"

"Do you write down your thoughts about your productions—your plans for the staging, etc.?"

"I used to when I was young, but now I am able to keep everything quite clearly in my head. Anyhow, I am likely to stage a scene one way and 10 days later come to rehearsal and change the staging completely. For me every rehearsal is a sketch. The actors do not write down that they must move here or there, because they know I am likely to change the staging at the very next rehearsal."

We then mentioned this biomechanics class we had seen and told him how much we liked it. "Yes," he said, "it is a theatrical method of body training for the actor. Each exercise is a melodrama. Each movement gives the actor a sense of performing on the stage."

"How long," Cheryl wanted to know, "would it take a person to learn it, so that he or she might teach it to American actors?"

"One winter," Meyerhold answered. "It is not very complicated. In fact, it is simple."

Cheryl and I both decided to try to find someone to learn it here in Moscow who would return and teach it to the Group. [*Editor's note:*

Like Clurman's idea of having a Group restaurant and a Group magazine, this remained an expression of hope and intent only.]

May 22

In the evening we saw *The Magnificent Cuckold,* a typical Meyerhold production of the "wild," "constructivist," "modernistic" period (around 1924)—another Meyerhold masterpiece. I enjoyed it immensely and was deeply impressed with Meyerhold's extraordinary theatrical genius. Strangely enough, instead of finding this wild farce quite formalistic as a production, it seemed to me that this play could not and should not be done in any other way. I had seen it done realistically in 1921 in Paris, and while it was extravagant in idea, it was strained and repellent to see. There is no pathology in Meyerhold's production: All its extravagance and sickness is worked off in brilliant physical exercises that are made part of the play, in stage-business composed of amazing acrobatic hokum, in a theatrical freedom and imaginativeness that shows how strong stage illusion can be with a minimum of means. But not only is the gymnastic splendor of the actors demonstrated here—all this ultra-stylization expresses a real content, a content that one feels could not be communicated any other way.

And though this production of *The Magnificent Cuckold* is considered "experimental," to me it is no experiment at all. First, it is completely successful; second, it is truly creative in the sense that it embodies something quite personal to the author (Meyerhold himself) and third, it fits the spirit of the time for which it was made—a hungry, stark time when, despite physical deprivation and amidst all the grimness and hunger, people wanted to laugh and be boisterous. *The Magnificent Cuckold* to me is one of the big achievements of the modern theatre: and the fact that it depends on biomechanic expertness (without it the actors would break their necks) makes it keep its form better than Meyerhold's more recent productions such as *La Dame aux Camelias.*

The Forest, Revizor and this, together with the *Habima Dybbuk*—and, on quite another level, *Carmencita* and *The Soldier*—are the finest productions I have seen in the nonrealistic theatre. One should see these productions—or as many of them as possible—to be glad once again that we belong to this beautiful, lively art. Let no one speak lightly of Meyerhold: He is one of the really great men in the theatre of the world.

May 24

In the evening went to see the first performance in Moscow of the Vakhtangov Theatre's production of *The Aristocrats* directed by Zachava. After the first act I thought, "This is the nearest thing to an American production I have seen in Moscow." But Cheryl put it more precisely by saying, "This reminds me of a dress rehearsal back on 52nd Street." All in all, an undistinguished production.

Leningrad, May 26

At night (with the accidental aid of Edmund Wilson) we got to see *Pique Dame,* produced by Meyerhold this year at the Little Opera

Theatre, popularly known as the Michailowsky. I found the score very captivating in its romanticism, and the production itself, with a new specially written libretto, unusually good-looking, in Meyerhold's most tasteful and luxurious manner. The production has something of a nostalgia for grandiose, romantic gloom, a sense of mighty yet decorative oppression which fits this opera very well, and which is characteristic of one side of Meyerhold.

As I sat in the theatre I remembered Meyerhold's face as he sat laughing in his apartment, and, in retrospect, I recognized in it the look of a very old, very cultured nobleman who was secretly sorcerer, part ballet master—an intellectual Dr. Caligari of the theatre.

May 27

During the last two days of our stay Cheryl and I began to talk about what we had learned from our trip. We were taking stock. An attitude of firmness and faith, coupled with the sentiment that the strong must use their strength to protect the weak so that the latter may also become strong, is the great human characteristic of the Soviet Union today. This attitude has infinite importance for us in America, particularly in organizations such as the Group. It must form the basis of the personal discipline we need. The theatrical discipline concerns the absolute necessity of every actor to do his utmost to correct every technical fault he may have, to work continually (apart from rehearsals as well as in rehearsal) to increase his professional proficiency and to complete himself as an artistic instrument.

Russian actors are not more talented or necessarily more intelligent than we are, but they are indisputably on a higher technical level—merely because of concentrated, systematic work. They make up better than we do, they have better voices, there are absolutely never any complaints of inaudibility (though almost all their theatres are larger), their bodies are freer. They do not neglect anything that has to do with their jobs as theatre workers. This is the most important part of their lives. We shall never make great progress unless we begin at once to imitate them.

In this alone do we have to think of emulation. We must learn through ourselves by daring to work in our way. Nothing important can come from people who merely attempt to follow in the path of a master—however great. And last, we see the necessity of understanding our social-organizational-financial situation very realistically so that we never lose contact with all the facts of our immediate world—with the facts that we must forever cope with if we are to function successfully—which means continuously—as a collective group in the New York and the American theatre.

On the boat Cheryl and I confessed to one another how badly we needed the Group, how painfully we missed it and how damned anxious we were to be with it again.

Director Harold Clurman co-founded New York's legendary Group Theatre in 1931, and from 1953 until his death in 1980 was a drama critic for the *Nation*.

Joan Ungaro is a New York–based theatre artist and critic.

WHAT IS A SHAKESPEARE?

By Peter Brook

October 1988

I think that one of the things that is very little understood about Shakespeare is that he is not only of a different quality, he is also different in kind.

So long as one thinks that Shakespeare is just Ionesco but better, Beckett but richer, Brecht but more human, Chekhov with crowds, and so on, one is not touching what it's all about. If you can talk about cats and a bull, one sees that these are different species. In modern scientific analysis you would beware of the dangers of mixing categories, and talking about a person in category A as though he really belonged to category B. I think that this is what happens with Shakespeare in relation to other playwrights, and so I'd like to dwell for a moment on what this particular phenomenon is.

To me, this phenomenon is very simple. It is that authorship as we understand it in almost all other fields—in the way that one talks about the authorship of a book or poem, and today the authorship of a film when directors are called authors of their films, and so on—almost invariably means "personal expression." And therefore the finished work bears the marks of the author's own way of seeing life. It's a cliché of criticism that one comes across very often, "his world," "the world of this author." Now it's not for nothing that scholars who have tried so hard to find autobiographical traces in Shakespeare have had so little success. It doesn't matter in fact who wrote the plays and what biographical traces there are. The fact is that there is singularly little of the author's point of view—and his personality seems to be very hard to seize—throughout 37 or 38 plays.

If one takes those 37 plays with all the radar lines of the different viewpoints of the different characters, one comes out with a field of incredible density and complexity; and eventually one goes a step further, and one finds that what happened, what passed through this man called Shakespeare and came into existence on sheets of paper, is something quite different from any other author's work. It's not Shakespeare's view of the world, it's something which actually resembles reality. A sign of this is that any single word, line, character or event has not only a large number of interpretations, but an unlimited number. Which is the characteristic of reality. I could say that is the characteristic of any action in the real world—say, the action you're doing now, at this moment, as we are talking together, of putting your hand against your head. An artist may try to capture and reflect your action, but actually he interprets it—so that a naturalistic painting, a Picasso painting, a photograph, are all interpretations. But in itself, the action of one man touching his head is open to unlimited understanding and interpretation. In reality, that is. What Shakespeare wrote carries that characteristic. What he wrote is not interpretation: It is the thing itself.

And if we're very bold, and think not in very constricting verbal terms, "He's an author, he wrote plays, the plays have scenes," and so on, but think much more broadly and say, "This creator created an enormous skein of interrelated words," and if we think of a chain of several hundred thousand words unfolding in a certain order, the whole making an extraordinary fabric, I think that then one begins to see the essential point. It is that his fabric reaches us today, not as a series of messages, which is what authorship almost always produces, but as a series of impulses that can produce many understandings. This is something quite different. It is like tea leaves in a cup. Think of the chance arrangement of tea leaves in a cup—the act of interpretation is a reflection of what is brought to the cup by the person looking at it. The whole act of interpreting tea leaves—or the fall of a sparrow, for that matter—is the unique meeting, at one point in time, between an event and the perceiver of the event.

I think two things come out of this. On the one hand, it is obvious that every interpretation of this material is a subjective act—what else could it be?—and that each person, whether it's a scholar writing, an actor acting, a director directing or a designer designing, brings to it— and always has and always will—his subjectivity. Which means that even if he tries to bridge the ages and say, "I leave myself and my century behind, and I'm looking at it with the eyes of its own period," this is impossible. A costume designer tries to interpret one period and at the same time he reflects his own epoch—so he produces a double image. We look at photographs of, say, Granville-Barker's productions—or we look at any production anywhere—and the double image is always there.

This is an unavoidable human fact. Each person brings what he is; there's no one walking around this world who has somehow dropped his personality. How you use your personality is the question. You can willfully and blindly give your ego free rein, or you can put your ego into play in a way that can help a truth to appear. For instance, the history of leading acting. The actor who's crude, bombastic, self-inflated, seizes on Shakespeare's plays because he sees, in their million facets, the facets which are food for his "me." He certainly gets a powerful energy out of what he finds, and the demonstration may be dazzling. But the play has gone, and the finer content, and many other levels of meaning are steam-rollered out of existence.

Of course, the theatre artist's relations with his material are basically affective, they come out of a love for and affinity with what he's doing. Doing a play as a solemn duty, with the highest level of respect, won't work. The mysterious and essential creative channel will not be opened by respect alone. So obviously for a director as for an actor the decision to do a certain play is purely instinctive and affective.

On the other hand, the danger that also has to be watched is when any of the artists or scholars dealing with a play by Shakespeare allow their love and excitement and enthusiasm to blind them to the fact that their interpretation can never be complete. There's an enormous danger that takes very precise form and leads to a form of acting that one's seen over many years, a form of directing, a form of designing, which proudly presents very subjective versions of the play without a glimmer of awareness that they might be diminishing the play—on the contrary, a vain belief that this is the play and more . . . not only Shakespeare's play, but Shakespeare's play as made into sense by such-and-such an individual. And that's where the virtue of having a feeling of love and enthusiasm has to be tempered by a cool sense that anybody's personal view of the play is bound to be less than the play itself.

I saw the other day an interview on French television with Orson Welles, on Shakespeare, where he started by saying something like, "We all betray Shakespeare." The history of the plays shows them constantly being reinterpreted and reinterpreted, and yet remaining untouched and intact. Therefore they are always more than the last interpretation trying to say the last word on something on which the last word can't be said.

One of the first productions of Shakespeare that I did was *Love's Labor's Lost*, and at that point I felt and believed the work of a director was to have a vision of a play and to "express" it. I thought that's what a director was for. I was 19 or 20. I had always wanted to direct films, and in fact I started in films before going into the theatre. A film director shows his pictures to the world, and I thought a stage director did the same in another way. Even before I did *Love's Labor's Lost*, when I was up at Oxford I terribly wanted to do *Coriolanus*, and I remember very strongly that my way of wanting to do *Coriolanus* was sitting at a table and drawing pictures. I drew images of *Coriolanus*, which is the film director's way of wanting to bring into life a personal picture one has, a picture of Coriolanus walking away in brilliant sunlight—things like that.

When I did *Love's Labor's Lost*, I had a set of images in mind which I wanted to bring to life, just like making a film. So *Love's Labor's Lost* was a very visual, very romantic set of stage pictures. And I remember that from then all the way through to *Measure for Measure* my conviction was that the director's job, having found an affinity between himself and the play, was to find the images that he believed in and through them make the play live for a contemporary audience. In an image-conscious time, I believed designing and directing to be inseparable. A good industrial designer has to sense just what the shapes are for a particular moment, and therefore he produces the right car body, and so on. In exactly the same way I understood that a director studies deeply, is as in tune with the play as he can be, but that his real work is the making of a new set of images for it.

Since then, my view has changed, evolved, through a growing awareness that the overall unifying image was much less than the play itself. And eventually, as I worked more and more outside proscenium theatres and in forms of theatre where the overall image proved to be less and less necessary and important, it became clear that a play of Shakespeare, and therefore a production of Shakespeare, could go far beyond the unity that one man's imagination could give, beyond that of the director and designer. And it was only through discovering that there was far more to it than that that my interest moved from just liking the play, and therefore showing my own image of the play, to another process, which starts always with the instinctive feeling that the play needs to be done, now.

This is a big change of attitude: Without thinking consciously or analytically, there is this sense that this play is meaningful in many ways at this moment which opens a new awareness. It's not only that it's meaningful for me autobiographically at this moment. At certain points in one's life one can identify with and wish to do a youthful play, a bitter play, a tragic play. This is fine, but one can then go beyond to see how a whole area of living experience that seems close to one's own concerns is also close to the concerns of the people in the world around one. When these elements come together, then is the time to do that play, and not another.

Fortunately, I've never been in the position of having to do lots of plays systematically. I think it's always destructive to have to do plays in this way. For years I wanted to do *Lear*, I wanted to do *Antony and Cleopatra*, and I did them. I never wanted to do a *Twelfth Night*. These are purely personal things. I think that every director has them that way, plays he's more drawn to, and every actor too. But I would now say that that's our loss: Choosing plays is a Rorschach test by which you can tell the openness and blinkeredness of each individual. Because if I could sympathize and empathize with every one of Shakespeare's plays, and every one of his characters, I would be that much the richer, and I think that goes for any actor. And if a theatre were to take on the task of doing the entire work of Shakespeare, out of an absolute conviction that this is the greatest school of life that they know, that group would be an astonishing group in human terms.

A fuller attitude begins to shape itself when we have not only a response to what we like and dislike, but when we respond to what we can discover through working on the play. This is a very big step, because as long as one's in the first instinct, "I like this, I want to do it," one is most likely within the closed circle of wishing to illustrate what one likes. "I like it, and I'll show you why I like it." The next step is, "I like it, because it parallels all that I need to know about the world." If I spend three months on a play, at the end of that time my wish to understand will have taken me further into its complexity, and it will do the same for an audience. So personal expression ceases to be an aim and we go toward shared discovery.

British director Peter Brook is the founder of the International Centre of Theatre Research, based at the Théâtre des Bouffes du Nord in Paris. He is the author of the classic theatre text *The Empty Space*, as well as *The Shifting Point* (HarperCollins, 1987; now published by TCG Books), from which this essay is reprinted by permission.

THE MISSING EYE

By Ross Wetzsteon

March 1989

For two years I served on the five-member Pulitzer Prize panel for criticism, sifting through the 150 or so submissions to choose the three we'd send on to the Pulitzer board for its final selection. Thirty to forty of the entries each year came from theatre critics, presumably representing the very best work being done in American journalism, yet only a handful seemed worth publishing, let alone honoring. Gee-whiz community-service flattery alternated with condescending one-liner putdowns, in either case revealing ignorance of both the process of theatre making and the history of dramatic literature.

Why is the level of theatre criticism in this country so superficial, so ill-informed, so illiterate, a couple of the judges wondered during a brief break. Are talented young writers turning to film and popular music instead? (The quality of the entries in those fields was markedly superior.) Many newspapers still send novice reporters to cover drama, one of the panelists suggested gloomily, and another blamed the con-sumer-guide mentality of most editors.

But looking over the list of entrants back in the panel office, I noticed something nearly as discouraging—out of the half-dozen or so submissions that surfaced out of the sea of mediocrity, almost all of them came from the New York area. Now the single most significant development in the American theatre in the past 20 years, as readers of this magazine know all too well, has been decentralization—how demeaning the word "regional" has come to seem—yet at the same time that a national theatre has taken root, criticism remains as New York–centric as ever. Stimulating theatres have emerged in dozens of cities, provocative playwrights and directors, skilled performers and designers, sophisticated funding sources and audiences—yet reading the critics in most of these cities makes you feel you're back in the days when the highlight of the season was the road company of *Hello, Dolly!* Criticism, in short, has simply not kept pace with the theatre it claims to evaluate.

It's tempting to suggest that this can hardly be an accident, that perhaps a thriving theatre needs the attention of critics to the same degree that a healthy tree needs the ministrations of a full-bladdered dog. Is it even possible that the increasing hegemony of New York criticism goes hand in hand with the decline of New York's theatrical power? Given the temperament and tone of many New York critics, a good argument could be made that this is the case. The smugly philistine superciliousness of the leading critic of one of our leading newspapers threatens to thwart the potential of the very art form he purports to serve, while the sadistically gleeful hostility of another New York critic has made him the shame of the very profession he presumes to deride. When Diaghilev said "astonish me," he was eager to be pleased, but too many of our "major" critics make the demand in a tone of aggressively bored superiority.

But there's no need to single out such inquisitorial criticism—a kind of cultural barbarism carried out in the name of "high standards"—when the entire critical profession so often seems so lacking in respect for theatre and its practitioners. By "respect," I should make clear, I don't mean the kind of parietal "they've all worked so hard" encouragement that doesn't do anybody any good, but simply a sense of mutual commitment to enhancing the theatre, a sense of alliance, however uneasy, in a common cause. Far from being incompatible with "high standards," this attitude provides their very basis.

Critics should not regard themselves as caretakers of taste or proprietors of culture—allowing some to enter the temple and keeping others out—but as guides who help point the way. This kind of detached, independent, but judiciously supportive eye is precisely what is most missing from today's national theatre. And operating on the assumption that everyone in the theatre recognizes the need for astute analysis and informed perspective, it seems to me imperative that the members of the American theatre community develop some mechanism for *demanding* it.

As Robert Brustein has observed, when black people or women respond to racist or sexist remarks they're regarded as responding on behalf of all black people and women, but when theatre artists respond to ignorant or malicious reviews they're seen as thin-skinned and self-interested. Overcoming this injustice seems to me one of the preeminent priorities of our theatre, and the traditionally passive, defensive, silently embittered posture on the part of theatre workers, while understandable, can only exacerbate the situation.

Properly perceived, criticism is a part of a dialogue in which both parties learn, but at present only one voice can be heard. Critics worth reading want dialogue more than they want power, and would welcome the same kind of evaluation they try to exemplify. So people in the theatre must find ways to speak up, to encourage accountability, to demand responsibility—at the very least they can serve as models by embodying the same respect for others they want for themselves. We're all involved in a common enterprise, and we critics need to hear your voices as much as you need to hear ours.

Ross Wetzsteon was a longtime editor at the *Village Voice* who helped build the Obie Awards into major theatrical accolades for Off and Off-Off Broadway. He is the author of *Republic of Dreams: An Intellectual History of Greenwich Village*. He died in 1998.

VERONA, MISSISSIPPI

By Robert Coe

May 1989

> *The rest of America don't mean jackshit. You in Mississippi now.*
> —The Sheriff of Neshoba County, *Mississippi Burning*

On Main Street in old Port Gibson, Miss. (pop. 2,371)—"the town too beautiful to burn," Ulysses S. Grant called it—the neon–lit marquee of the Trace Theater glows in the mist like shelter from a threatening sky. Angry gray-black storm clouds, thunder and lightning are rolling east across the Mississippi River and the mighty nuclear power station at Grand Gulf, through the mossy pine forests and hilly pastures of Claiborne County midway between Natchez and Vicksburg, and into town, enveloping the copper-covered roof of the antebellum county courthouse and Confederate War Memorial three blocks north. Outside the Trace, a steady stream of local actors, singers and musicians—a school music teacher, a town election commissioner, a surgical nurse, a nuclear-power information officer, a Shakespeare professor from nearby Alcorn State University, a physical therapist, a lawyer, a housewife, a few dozen students—pass under the deco marquee and the scrutiny of the good ol' boys at the half-century-old gas station on a side street. Just a week ago, on Valentine's Day, a white woman hugged a black teenager outside the theatre. "That's shitty," one of the men said later. "White girl, black boy. I don't know where you folks are from, but I hope nobody gets hurt."

Tonight, Monday, is the first run-through before the opening three days away, and for many participants, hopes run high. For most of the past three months, an ensemble of 11 young professional theatre artists calling themselves Cornerstone Theater have been living and working in Port Gibson, collaborating with more than 70 Claiborne County residents on a production of *Romeo and Juliet*, keyed to local realities. Romeo will be played by an 18-year-old black Port Gibson High School distance runner; Juliet, by a 24-year-old Harvard-educated white woman from Glastonbury, Conn. Up North this is High Concept, but in a county where the descendents of black slaves outnumber whites three-to-one and an all-but-black public school system and a private, all-but-white military academy help preserve a substantially segregated lifestyle, racial passions are never far below the surface: Port Gibson is less than two decades away from a bitterly disputed black boycott resolved seven years ago by a U.S. Supreme Court decision, and faces the possibility of another boycott in three months' time. Enter a bunch of white, middle-class, Harvard-educated Northerners—celebrated on the pages of the *Wall Street Journal*, *People*, *Newsweek* and the *New Yorker*, featured on "The Today Show," "The CBS Evening News" and "West 57th," the inspiration behind an upcoming Robert Benton film at 20th Century Fox—reimagining the Montagues as the former leaders of a civic boycott, the source of the ancient family enmity. Not surprisingly, many white citizens of Port Gibson are made anxious and adrenalized by this approaching collision of fictional and historical reality; additional rumors about the production's use of racial epithets, prolonged hot kissing and partial nudity have inspired a number of white cast members' families and friends to plan not to attend what will in all likelihood be the most provocative integrated cultural event in the town's history.

"This is the greatest thing that has happened to Claiborne County in a long, long time," says Arnette Nash, a local welder, school board member and founding member of the Bells of Heaven, a local gospel group. Nash is reclining on plush red seats with the rest of the company in the recently renovated black-owned cinema, facing an airy pinewood set with a hanamichi reaching to the rear wall. Following time-honored custom, blacks are sitting in the rear of the house, whites in front, but the mood is respectful and friendly.

"Hi everybody!"

"Hey Bill!" Twenty-six-year-old Bill Rauch, Harvard '84, stands on stage in his customary baggy gray clothes holding his customary scrawled yellow notepad, promising to dispense hundreds of actors' notes in the dressing rooms. A former assistant director at the American National Theater in Washington, D.C., Rauch is unflappably kind and cheerful, combining the perfectionist instincts of a theatre professional with the patience of Job. His strongest oath in public may be "Goodness gracious!" but he knows how to keep three dozen balls in the air. He lets Edret Brinston, Port Gibson's Romeo, call roll. "Where's Earl?"—Earl Wilson, Claiborne County's high school Benvolio.

"His parents won't let him come because of the tornado watch," someone answers. "Could someone call his parents and tell them that the tornado watch is in the next county and that we need him here, please?" Bill proceeds to explain how a technical run-through is a kind of dress rehearsal; unfortunately too many cast members have left their costumes at home to make it one. Tonight's performance is vital for continuity but may have to be stopped occasionally because lighting designer Mary Ann Greanier is still writing cues. Everything is coming in under the wire, as usual with Cornerstone, only this time there is a better than ever chance that the show won't be ready.

The run-through begins. A massive black woman dressed in mourning black rises from a centerstage staircase as the Chorus, singing in rolling gospel cadence. Time: the Present. Place: Verona, Mississippi, a town remarkably similar to Port Gibson itself. A black teenager provokes a fight with a white boy not by "biting his thumb" but by "shooting his finger." Stylized by a visiting Baton Rouge fight director, a slo-mo riot is halted not by a Prince but by a black female mayor, played by a local fire dispatcher and election commissioner, Mary Curry.

Booming church voices from a loft at the rear of the house plead with people to forgive their enemies—in the mode of the 19th-century traveling Shakespeare companies, Cornerstone has added 14 songs by resident composer David Reiffel, with additional music by locals Jerome Williams and Larry Davis. The singing is powerful, but the majority of the locals have never acted on stage before; their line readings are stiff and often difficult to understand. Romeo raps about his love-sickness, accompanied by the Montague boys' bouncing basketball and rhythmic beat; three white cheerleaders underscore Juliet's response to her mother's inquiry about the banker, Paris. Mercutio's Queen Mab has been reconceived as slasher-film phantom Freddy Krueger in a theatre where *Nightmare on Elm Street—Part IV* was playing not two months ago—and in the middle of the speech comes Queen Mab's Revenge: every light in the Trace goes down. A power blackout—during storms they can come block by block in old Port Gibson.

"Everyone relax and stay where you are," Rauch calls out in the pitch darkness. I grope my way to a side door and open it for the streetlight—to see that the Mississippi sky has opened, sending torrents through the gutters that will raise the river five feet by morning. Rauch has commandeered a flashlight: "I want everyone to move slowly into the lobby. We're going to continue the run-through."

The storm and the blackout alter the course of Cornerstone's Port Gibson residency. Protected by darkness in the overcrowded lobby, with thunder and lightning crashing in the street outside, a new intimacy moves behind the words; freed from blocking, actors drop some of their Southern formality for Southern warmth, a sense of injured family pride and hot young blood. "My only love, sprung from my only hate?" cries Juliet, just as a sizeable chunk of damp plaster falls from the lobby ceiling on the back of her hoop skirt. Confronting adversity again makes Cornerstone magic, but at some cost: two hours of lost tech and run-through before dress rehearsals begin. But Cornerstone has chosen its lot: to reinvent America's community theatre, to give a new direction for the avant-garde of the '90s. Some Harvard friends still think they're wasting their time, but in less than two-and-a-half years Cornerstone has managed to create a national experimental community theatre network as one alternative to work in established nonprofit institutions and urban isolation; they have rediscovered connections between professionalism and amateurism which have inspired theatrical alternatives since the little theatre movements of the teens and '20s, the trade union theatre of the '30s, the Living Theatre of the

'50s, the '60s theatre of personal liberation, and the performance art of the '70s and '80s.

What it is that matters most about theatre is obviously not the exclusive property of professionals, but how that spirit will play here in Port Gibson—where even "The Cosby Show" is larded with 15-second commercials on Mississippi togetherness without a single black face—is anybody's guess. There are folks here who will tell you that there are no racial problems in Claiborne County: Whites go their way, blacks go theirs, and never the twain shall meet. But with the Klan operating out of nearby Vicksburg and Natchez, and with a former Grand Wizard ending a triumphant election campaign for the state legislature across the river, these statements are not to be believed. In Mississippi two societies, both alike in dignity, once separated by law, remain separated by custom and prejudice. And if 12 performances of a play written over 350 years ago are to make any difference at all, they will have to renew a faith in interracial harmony that time and history have never allowed to stand.

Port Gibson gives its name to a nearby Civil War battlefield where the fate of Vicksburg and the entire Confederacy were sealed back in 1863; within living memory black people were paid 50 cents for hand-picking a hundred pounds of cotton. The 1963 civil rights summer of *Mississippi Burning* failed to reach this southwest portion of the state, but two years later Charles Evers arrived in Claiborne County to begin the dangerous process of registering voters. Local police disrupted many of these early meetings; tensions in Claiborne County continued to build toward a historic 1969 consumer boycott of white businesses. White community leaders initially agreed to some black demands, including equal access to the town medical clinic, employment and political office; the right to courtesy titles such as "Mr." and "Mrs."; the right to maintain places in shopping lines in the presence of white people. Community leaders refused, however, to integrate public toilets or employ blacks on cash registers.

The resulting boycott lasted two years, becoming a national cause célèbre, with black leaders accused of physical intimidation and white provocateurs reportedly paying blacks to cross picket lines and provoke fights. As more and more businesses went bankrupt, local merchants filed an improbable lawsuit against the NAACP and black property owners, winning more than $1 million in damages from a local chancery court; the NAACP and labor groups responded by raising an appeal bond of more than $1 million, continuing litigation until July '82, when the Supreme Court voted 8-0 to uphold the right of individual citizens to stage nonviolent political boycotts and spend their money as they pleased.

With the end of the boycott in 1971, changes came swiftly to Claiborne County: Today blacks and whites mingle casually in restaurants and nearly all places of business. With their demographic superiority, blacks have come to dominate the local courts, the sheriff's office, the fire department and county government. Culturally, however, segregation continues nearly as strongly as ever, with churches and schools the major cultural divisions. Faced with mandatory school desegregation in 1969, white families transferred their children to the private Chamberlain-Hunt Academy, a military reform school established in 1879. Nothing divides a town more painfully than school segregation: Racially divided schools socialize parents and kids, magnify differences into oppositions, and produce a racially divided community. A second and more recent source of tension is the Grand Gulf Nuclear Power Station, a 20-year-old project which has transformed one of Mississippi's poorest counties into one of its richest, increasing the tax-base thirtyfold. To hear most whites tell it, much of that money was stolen by a corrupt black board of education president through sweetheart construction deals and valueless educational programs, resulting only in a loss of state accreditation at Port Gibson High. With black juries unwilling to convict a black elected official, white leaders decided to play their cards at the state level: They pushed through a constitutional amendment which divides the Grand Gulf money, taking half away from Claiborne County and giving substantial new revenues to the city of Port Gibson. Most of Claiborne County's white population lives in town, where the mayor and three of five city aldermen are white. The same white attorney represented both city and county during these political battles, exercising what most local blacks consider a shameful conflict of interest.

"Mississippi is still Mississippi, and Mississippi is still burning," says Claiborne County tax assessor Evan Doss. If the city and county attorney isn't dismissed by May 1, Port Gibson will face another consumer boycott, although Doss and other black leaders are holding open the possibility of more discussion.

Cultural apartheid; racially motivated battles over tax money; the prospect of renewing the town's most bitter human conflict: This is the hot water into which Cornerstone was lowering itself, assisted by the only multiracial cultural organization in Claiborne County. "Mississippi: Cultural Cross Roads" is the 10-year-old creation of a petite white woman from Chicago named Patty Crosby, who constantly searches for politically neutral ground on which blacks and whites might build trust. The Mississippi Arts Commission recommended her to Cornerstone, and Cornerstone phoned; she paid little attention until she heard that all Port Gibson had to provide was housing and a theatre for a four-month company residency.

Crosby took the idea to the Port Gibson Chamber of Commerce for support; the white community responded well to the prospect of returning theatre to a town which long ago enjoyed visits from Joe Jefferson and blackface musical troupes, in a state with a long and lively history of segregated community theatre. Cornerstone's original production idea was *The Good Person of Setzuan*, but this sounded arcane; Patty Crosby's husband David, a Shakespeare professor, suggested *Romeo and Juliet* without giving a thought to any possible racial implications. Both parties simply assumed that the integrated casting would be racially blind—Cornerstone's progressive approach since Harvard days. The Chamber of Commerce, Claiborne County's Board of Supervisors, even Mississippi Power & Light, proprietors of Grand Gulf, all produced small grants to help bring Shakespeare to Port Gibson.

A few weeks before moving South, Cornerstone members drove east from Oregon, where they had just experienced their first taste of social controversy: During a fall 1988 residency in Long Creek (pop. 265), a timber and ranching community in Oregon's eastern outback, Brecht's *Good Person* had hinged on issues of what goodness meant to a town largely populated by fundamentalist Christians. In Mississippi social backlash was already in progress: An offer to perform in an historic former Jewish synagogue had been withdrawn when the owner discovered that the production was interracial. For a time the show was transferred to a shoe store presently occupied by courthouse facilities, but when the antebellum courthouse's renovations weren't completed in time, Cornerstone was once again homeless. Finally the company settled on its natural venue, the town's only movie-house, which was far from neutral territory: The owner of the Trace was William Dowery, a former black boycott leader viewed with suspicion in Port Gibson's white business community, largely because he conducts most of his business in cash.

On principle, Cornerstone had no desire to inflame a county: Its members work with good cheer to reconceive the classics, to absorb and reflect the nature of community, town, locale. But this time the group decided to select a racially specific cast—white Capulets, black Montagues. "We wanted to create a world in which race was the major factor," says Rauch. "What had initially seemed too obvious seemed right for Mississippi." Cornerstone's first Deep South production, the largest it had ever done anywhere, was to be about interracial hatred, sex, marriage and murder—and with Montagues as boycott leaders. In a sense, this *Romeo and Juliet* was throwing a gauntlet into a community as symbolically divided as fair Verona. Over dinner Patty and David Crosby tried to change Rauch and Cornerstone co-founder Alison Carey's minds but finally relented—though not without trepidation.

"We've only got one world," says Patty Crosby. "We've only got one community and we've got to figure out how to live in it together or the kids will go elsewhere. And to my way of thinking, the best way to be together is to work together."

Arriving in Port Gibson on Nov. 5, Cornerstone settled into William Dowery's drafty and dilapidated two-story boarding house on U.S. Highway 61, the main drag through town, and launched into its usual first order of business: seducing a community with a good mind to resist. Five performances at the local public and private schools, at nearby Alcorn State and at the Trace, revived three works: the company's adaptation of *A Midsummer Night's Dream*, an original school-age piece called *I Can't Pay the Rent* and a musical revue with slides of selected Cornerstone works. Company members visited churches— Presbyterian, Methodist, Episcopalian, Catholic, several varieties of Baptist, Evangelical and Pentecostal, even the local African Methodist Episcopal Ministry—and rose in each to address the congregation. PSAs on local radio stations and newspaper ads appealed for actors, singers and musicians; Cornerstone members went door to door, stopped motorists at stoplights, even pulled kids off bicycles to tell them about auditions over two weekends in mid-November.

The company's double-barreled nightmare was the possibility that whites would stay away because the Trace was black (despite being the only movie-house in town) and that blacks would stay away because Cornerstone was an all-white company. On at least one occasion black citizens walked into the Trace, saw whites auditioning, and walked out; Carey literally ran out after them, and when she couldn't find them cruised the streets in her car until she did. "I'm sick of culture being for the elite," said one man, who returned to audition for the chorus with a Sarah Vaughan standard, then announced, "I'm schizophrenic." A core group of five-to-ten local black alcoholics began hanging out regularly around the theatre, including one 35-year-old veteran who claimed to have been a bodybag sorter in Vietnam. The best reader in town, he won the role of Montague. Seventy people auditioned in all, from drunken illiterates to pillars of the community. Forty-seven won parts, an extra-large cast which would mean heavier work for everyone. "We don't like to leave anyone out," says Rauch. Cornerstone actors filled the parts of Juliet, Mercutio, Tybalt and Friar Lawrence, but the rest came from a remarkably diverse cross-section of town, forging the kind of art-life correspondences that characterize the postwar avant-garde. Cornerstone's *Romeo and Juliet* would help the town see itself for what it was.

The wife of the mayor, Joan Beasley, became one of the "Mint Julep Belles" who attends the Capulets' Antebellum Plantation Fest dressed in the ball gown of a daughter of the Confederacy. So did Linda Headley, the daughter-in-law of the recently defeated former white sheriff, who wept during her moving improvised audition about teenage suicide. One of the town's leading lawyers, 39-year-old Melvin McFatter, limping permanently with a cane as the result of a hunting accident, took the role of Paris. As usual, Cornerstone failed to produce enough community men: "There I was," recalls a laughing Amy Brenneman, Cornerstone's Juliet, "chasing the manager of the local Piggly Wiggly around the tomatoes, saying, 'Don't you want me to be your daughter?' Afterwards I walked out saying to myself, 'Is this what I want to be doing with the rest of my life? I am very confused.'" In the end Rauch reconceived the Capulet clan as a matriarchy, with Kay Bilbro, a former elementary school principal and currently a nuclear information officer at Grand Gulf, cast as Mamaw Capulet, Juliet's grandmother and stern leader of the Capulets; Kathy Ellis, a local dentist's wife and a physical therapist by profession, became a very feminine Mrs. Capulet. Bobbi Jean Young, a rotund music and elementary school teacher, was cast as Juliet's black Nurse—the term "Mammy" was never used. To attract young men for the Montague clan, Cornerstone had to ask Port Gibson High School's principal to summon some students to the school auditorium to audition; for a time the leading candidate for Romeo was a one-armed town alcoholic and drug-addict named Julius, but at the high school one day Carey heard a voice calling, "Hey, I want to be Romeo!"

Edret Brinston had been a troublemaker until his track coach got him in line. A handsome 18-year-old raised by his grandmother in a small, wood-heated shack in the nearby town of Pattison, Brinston grew up with an iron will, a cool gaze and a strong physical presence. He became the most important of a dozen or so public high school students in the cast, many of them from Patty Crosby's local Peanut Butter and Jelly Theater—including the Schaufnagel girls, Dana and Darcy, two of only three whites enrolled at Port Gibson High. Three students were cast from Chamberlain-Hunt Academy, and two from the private elementary school. The sole black student at CHA, a sad and inexpressive victim of regular beatings and at least one cross-burning incident outside his dorm room, was specially invited to audition. He averted his eyes, saying only, "I'm booked."

With a cast in place, a welcoming supper was held at a local Catholic recreation hall, black and white educators, clergy, politicians and business people eyeing one another over fried chicken from the Piggly Wiggly. The mayor's wife rose to speak of "a new beginning for Port Gibson." "I assumed it was sincere," Rauch says. "It was hard to tell how much of a first this was, this coming-together of the two sides of town. We could definitely feel a lot of politics going on beneath the surface that we knew nothing about. But the fact is that the patterns for our residencies are always the same: During the first weeks we meet people we never see again. The cast becomes our contact with the community."

The first read-through of Shakespeare's script was painfully slow; Brinston reads with difficulty, and at certain points older black cast members leapt in to help with Romeo's lines. Port Gibson's adaptation would be written during the three weeks before Christmas, with Rauch and Carey seated at the boarding house word processor, "guided by our aesthetic—working for clarity, and for the audience," says Rauch. "We're the first to admit that we lose some of the poetry, but we hope we gain another kind of poetry." Some of the rewriting was guided by local high school students approached during classes taught by all 11 Cornerstone members on a grant from the Mississippi Humanities Council. Asked to describe a spirit that comes in your sleep, Claiborne County schoolchildren of all ages invariably cited Freddy Krueger; what seemed corny to Harvard graduates had universal meaning here, and so Queen Mab was pushed aside by Hollywood's dream time master. The decision to change Juliet's balcony fantasy so that Romeo would deny not his "name" but the color of his skin was Cornerstone's. Consequently, Tybalt's taunt, "Thou art a villain," had only one obvious rewrite, but rather than present "Thou art a nigger" to unsuspecting cast members, Carey and Rauch decided to leave the offending word a blank. When the new script was read before Christmas, everyone in the cast agreed that there was only one appropriate epithet. Cornerstone broke for the holidays on a positive note, organizing a Christmas show that brought together choirs from black and white churches for the first time in Claiborne County's history. Around their own production, however, the controversy had barely begun.

Most of Cornerstone's membership now believes that the month-long holiday break was a mistake, and not simply because their 15-person van was stolen during the interim. Returning on Jan. 16 left only six weeks to assemble a massive musical-dramatic production with a very amateur cast. In the best of cases, "a Cornerstone residency is a very weird psychological beast," Carey tells me two days before the opening, seated with Rauch near the gas heater in the chilly boarding house living room. The cold weather has continued; six feet away from the heater's open flame, the room is 40 degrees. Cornerstone is a warm, civil, close-knit group, difficult for outsiders to penetrate but completely aboveboard.

"Each time we go into a community it's a little like reinventing the wheel, which of course is no way to live," Carey continues. "For one thing, we're in the position of always have to be 'nice,' both among ourselves and with the community. We're forced as outsiders to dis-cover everything, and in most instances there's nothing fueling us but bravado—'Well, we've done it before, we'll do it again.' People are being asked to work mind-numbingly long hours just on our promise that they won't make fools of themselves."

"The Mississippi cast is probably the warmest we've ever worked with," Rauch adds, "but that hasn't meant a constant round of parties. People have little concept of how hard we work and for no money. Most people find that odd."

Rehearsals were held at the Trace, and on one occasion at the pub-lic high school, where many white cast members had never set foot. Gradually the cast shrank from 47 to 38, due to the demand on time and constant schedule changes. Twice the Vietnam vet playing Montague showed up at rehearsals too drunk to work; he finally with-drew from the production. Bells of Heaven singer Arnette Nash moved from the chorus to replace him. But more serious problems arose among white cast members: The mayor's wife, who had promised a new beginning for Port Gibson, quit, saying simply that she was too busy. Rumors persisted that her husband's political differ-ences with Trace owner Dowery were behind the move.

"If it was Mayor Beasley's daughter playing Juliet, maybe he wouldn't even allow the play," Curry told me. "His wife was in it, now she's gone. Maybe she's too good to be around black people." Rauch was taken out to lunch by another one of the Mint Julep Belles, who told him that Romeo and Juliet were kissing with a bit too much enthusiasm; that whites wouldn't come see the show. "She felt that a shy little kiss would be okay in Port Gibson," says Rauch, "but that they seemed to be enjoying it." Another white participant complained that with such goings-on, she wouldn't be able to bring her children. A chorus member objected to Mercutio's dying curse, "A plague on both your races." And worse: At work someone told Kay Bilbro that if she embraced a black man on stage, as she did in Mamaw Capulet's concil-iation with Montague at the end of the play, then the recent unsolved sex murders in Port Gibson's black community might well cross racial lines. Bilbro telephoned Rauch to tell him privately that she'd rather not do it anymore, and Rauch relented—without telling Montague the reason. "The closer we came to production," Patty Crosby later remarked, "the more I was saying to myself, 'Goodness, girl, what have you done?'"

Curry believes she understands the reasons for white resistance: "I suppose the idea is that it might give black boys the initiative, show that white girls are no longer forbidden fruit—you know, 'He kissed her, so we can go get us one.'" Curry was unafraid of any serious white backlash—"Racists don't want to make the blacks mad"—but black members of the cast were unaware that the good ol' boys at the gas station across the street were waving the red flag of interracial fraternizing around town. Cornerstoners were labeled immoral pot smoking hippies by one CHA instructor; when its members visited the nuclear power station, rumor had it that they'd chained themselves to the door. Gratefully, the KKK was nowhere in evidence, but the town's former sheriff reportedly joked that "the Klan was probably figuring how big a bomb it would take to torch the place." Such dark humor cut both ways: "He's got a lot of bodies in his backyard," muttered one black cast member.

Given these unpleasant conflicts and innuendos, attorney McFatter persisted in his belief that "the community would have been better served by a play with an integrated cast which did not have racial strife and interracial sex and marriage as its central themes." Whatever the case, Cornerstone worked to moderate the flames their drama fanned; their steady good cheer and unpatronizing warmth was richly returned by Claiborne County cast members of both races. "We're theatre artists, not social workers," says Rauch; indeed, Cornerstone members were not above rolling their eyes at bad acting or joking among themselves about the cast member who wondered aloud whether he had to attend all the performances or not. Cornerstone staff and performers continued to work without snobbery or condescension, willing to make allowances, eager to assist the uninformed, the ungifted, and draw out the best colors in everyone. Certainly Cornerstone had its own problems to deal with: While the prospect of a cinema had prepared them for working with no wings, no flies and no backstage space, Rauch and designer Lynn Jeffries went through four different set designs after discovering that they couldn't tie into the walls or ceilings. The building's bricks were crumbling and wouldn't bear weight; the original two-story structure, along with most of Rauch's early blocking and staging ideas, went out the window. Cornerstone actors received little directorial help because of the need to focus on community members; Bilbro as Mamaw Capulet, for instance, had to understand that there was no "right" way for her to say her lines—that understanding her own freedom was the beginning of her portrayal. Although Brinston's Romeo tended to drop most of his final consonants—"Nigh's can'les are blown out," "I am too bol', t's no't' me she speak'"—Rauch decided to let the accent stand. Neither missionaries nor cultural imperialists, Cornerstone chose to transcend cultural and racial differences for the rich and complicated business of putting on a drama. A week before opening, the cast feeling of us and them, whether black or white, began to wane somewhat; with the introduction of costumes and a make-up artist from out of town, suddenly a payoff was in sight.

Strange and wondrous things had begun to happen: A CHA student with the improbably white Southern name of Graven Bilbo was actually hanging out with Briston, Earl Wilson and Walter Mays—kids roughly the same age, kids who'd grown up in the same hometown without ever having met before. Three nights before the opening the huge storm and a blackout caused a company breakthrough. Theatre was once again exercising its magical ability to bring people together in community.

"It's not Broadway," Patty Crosby told her husband. "Yes," David Crosby answered. "But it's hard to believe it's Port Gibson."

An hour before the opening night performance, a crowd has already gathered under the neon glow of the marquee; *Romeo and Juliet*'s competition tonight is the regional championship game of the Port Gibson Wavettes, a girl's basketball team ranked fourth in the nation by *USA Today*. In the lobby Carey is pouring Mercutio's bloodbags; Brenneman is laughing with a group of young black children from the cast—hugging, kissing, rubbing each other's faces, a mutual fan club. In the theatre Rauch is on stage directing the Montague gang—"You guys be talking together as you go"—while Ashby Semple, Cornerstone's female Tybalt, in a jacket with a Confederate flag on the back, tries to summon a curdling rebel yell for Mercutio's death blow. In the house the rest of the cast gathers for notes. Excitement has been stirred by a flattering front page story in the *New Orleans Times-Picayune*. For the first time cast seating is more or less colorblind; black and whites share every row.

"This is the hardest I've ever worked for no scratch," Kay Bilbro is saying, rubbing fingers together.

One of the Mint Julep Belles pronounces the word "hair" with three syllables: "I'm gonna have to get me a little fall for my hay-eh-er . . . . If I'd done this right, I coulda lost a lot of weight."

In one of the rear rows Juliet's Nurse announces in a booming voice, "People are comin' to see Miss Bobbi Jean Young!"

"I told my father-in-law it's great to be working with professionals," says Mint Julep Belle Headley. "He said, 'If they're that good, why aren't they on TV?'"

Curry assumes a country voice to describe her son's response to the show. "He say, 'Mama, why you be hollerin'?' I say, 'I'm in the play, honey. Do I be scarin' you?' He say, 'Nah . . . .'"

"Hi everybody!"

"Hey Bill!"

As boyishly as ever, Rauch again promises to circulate some of the hundreds of individual notes he's taken. "That young man is going places," murmurs Ron Temple, the local star of Cornerstone's Kansas production *Tartoof*, who has driven from Norcatur for tonight. One of Rauch's final group notes is odd: "Everybody should chew gum in the final scene, when the corpses are discovered in the county morgue."

"And why are we supposed to do that?" asks a flabbergasted McFatter.

"You never asked why before," says Bill, and gets a good laugh, although the Belles continue to grumble that no Southern lady would ever chew gum in public—not even in a mausoleum.

Bill closes by wishing everyone a great show, even chokes up a little, saying, "You're all part of the Cornerstone family now." I glance into the aisle and watch Port Gibson's Romeo crawl on all fours as a gag towards the dressing room. In the early going Brinston was Joe Cool, even skipping an entire rehearsal once; it took three weeks before he would let Brenneman into his house, and he still keeps her away from girlfriends. Brinston has risen to his challenge; he has overcome his reading problem and learned his part down cold. One Cornerstone member remarked that this was probably the first time in his life that anyone had ever taken him seriously for his mind.

When the doors open at quarter to seven, the opening night audience is notable for the absolute absence of the town elite, black and white. Less than a quarter of the crowd is Caucasian; nearly all of the white people are middle-aged, affluent, with a couple of kids; a large contingent of black high schoolers includes Brinston's track team, dressed to the nines. Admission to the theatre is free, but the older black audience members, seeing a donation box by the door, drop in a buck or two, good churchgoers all. Carey and Rauch pace the lobby, as tense as if they were opening a $6-million musical. Outside, 25 people have to be turned away from the 123-seat house as the doors are closing, when a voice cries out, "It's me! It's me! Hattie Turnipseed!" The seamstress who sewed Juliet's costume is one of the last people admitted.

Anyone who attended opening night of Cornerstone at the Trace is not likely to forget the scene: When the brawl starts between the black dudes and the white kids in the uniforms of Chamberlain-Hunt Academy, the younger black contingent in the packed house erupts in wild whoops and hollers. The audience is suddenly electrified; no one had anticipated such a visceral response, but the tone of the evening is set. When the Montagues burst into the Plantation Fest in Freddy Krueger masks, Tybalt calls out, "Fetch me my shotgun!" For a moment I think seats are going to be pulled out of the floor. "Give me my sin again!" says a black Romeo in high-tops to a gorgeous white woman in a strapless evening gown, and Brinston's friends almost drown in tears of their own hilarity. "Henceforth, I'll never be black," says Romeo, producing snorts and howls of derision, which at least shows they're listening.

The Trace Theater is out of control, a vision straight out of Mark Twain or some 19th-century riverboat Shakespeare company; somehow Brinston is unaffected, handling his first public appearance on stage with absolute aplomb. Father Lawrence, reconceived by Cornerstone actor Peter Howard as a Boston liberal Catholic priest, exposes a Martin Luther King T-shirt under his jacket, to more laughter; when Mercutio turns his back to the audience and exposes himself to Tybalt, saying "Here's my Confederacy!" the riot reaches its peak.

Tybalt's taunt, "Thou art a nigger," draws a collective "uh-oh," segueing after Mercutio's death into cheers and triumphant shouts as Romeo plugs his White Supremacist slanderer five or six times with a handgun. A small black boy, not more than four or five years old, races up the aisle from the stage in terror, hot tears streaming down his cheeks; one of four little girls seated in front of me fetches him to her seat, where all four pat his back, saying, "Hush now, Jefferson, it's all pretend." Father Lawrence offers Romeo a vision of a lynch mob, Romeo flees, and the first act, blessedly, is over.

Very light applause; kids bolt up the aisles towards the popcorn stand; little intermission talk among the adults. A very pasty-looking Rauch passes me with a mortified smile and a cold shudder. The three-and-a-half-hour performance is only half over, but despite the pandemonium some of its deeper meanings are coming through. Cornerstone and Port Gibson are offering a *Romeo and Juliet* driven by an irrational, unexamined belief in the twining power of sex and death. There is no sense of natural rightness in *Romeo and Juliet*'s passion; issues of education and class are completely avoided here in Claiborne County, where there is no earthly reason for this Romeo and Juliet to be together. The mechanisms of love are unexplained, but the raw impact of black and white lovers, kissing long and hard, he shirtless, she in a T-shirt and panties, is undeniable; their defiance of bigotry feels courageous and true.

Rauch pounds home the theme of death at every opportunity: At the top of the second act, Juliet sings a beautiful song repeating Shakespeare's image of Romeo's dead body cut up in little stars, then absorbs her Nurse's faulty news of Romeo's death with instant acceptance. By mid-act the teenagers have stopped changing seats and seem to settle a little. They watch quietly while Romeo lies atop Juliet's slumbering body in the morgue; they snicker when Romeo ODs with a needle, laugh nervously when Juliet blows her brains out with a pistol, then roar when poor Montague bursts into tears at the sight of Romeo's corpse. For me, the single most moving image in the production is Mamaw's refusal to embrace the grieving Montague—a chilling image of white Southern rectitude released when Lady Capulet embraces him instead. After one of the more legato death scenes in the history of Shakespeare's Verona, the Mayor declaims, "Never . . . was a story . . . of more woe . . . than this . . . of Juliet . . . and her Romeo."

Curtain call for the entire cast of 38; light applause, as if a movie has just ended. The high school jerk-offs in the front row stand to cheer—they have been making kissing noises to Juliet throughout the show—but the rest of the house remains dazed, glued to their seats. Three teenage girls in the audience are sobbing. In the turbulent lobby, families gather to greet friends, sons, daughters, husbands and wives dribbling down from the upstairs dressing rooms. Brinston arrives looking customarily cool and unperturbed, greeted by friends who, when all is said and done, seem impressed.

With the exception of actor Howard, who goes home to bed depressed, the Cornerstone people are unfazed by the wildly indelicate response of their opening night audience. Rauch gradually waxes philosophical: In the boarding house kitchen where he's heating up a pizza, we decide that the art/social service dichotomy thrown Cornerstone's way is false—that in theatre, art and social service are identical. Port Gibson's *R & J* is no artistic triumph, but judgments of good and bad which have crippled the American theatre at large seem irrelevant here; an RSC production in Port Gibson wouldn't have meant as much. For Rauch the real work of the show, the real contact with the community begins now, and he's convinced that the deeper meanings of the play will out—that audiences will understand the work subliminally—which is to say, that they will understand that love is a force to overcome even the bitterest enmity.

Friday morning the Trace Theater office is swamped with phone calls, a madhouse: *Romeo and Juliet* is a hit, a palpable hit. Chris Moore's Mercutio is the overnight sensation of Port Gibson High—a white man who gets himself killed defending the honor of a black man who's been called a nigger. Friday's audience makes a sharp contrast to the opening: attentive, almost demure, with only a few choice comments hurled from the peanut gallery. Several black teenagers rap along with Romeo and Benvolio—a sure sign that a cult is building. In the green room at the beginning of Act 2, there's a party going on that will continue through every night of the run: Juliet's song speeding Phoebus's fiery wheels is piped over the intercom and sets everyone on their feet, blacks and whites dancing together on the linoleum, under the harsh fluorescence. "Get down, Juliet!!"

A bigger problem is where to continue partying after the show: The conflict arises when Cornerstone's Semple wants to bring two public high school boys to Buddy's, the local redneck roadhouse. "I never had to feel white before," Ashby tells me. Blacks can go to Buddy's for dinner, but not late-night dancing—certainly not interracial dancing. Blacks go to Zanzibar and the Diamond Lounge, where white newcomers are approached to buy drugs, then left alone—unless they try to dance with a black woman. After the Saturday night show, with the first days off in nearly two weeks looming, everybody wants to blow off steam—but no one wants to divide the cast along racial lines. The solution, at least for the teenagers in the company and Cornerstone, is a spontaneous party on the street outside the Trace.

Under the neon marquee, Briston, Wilson and Mays turn up Ice-T on the boom box to show Cornerstone's Howard a few steps. Four or five Academy girls join in for a soul-train line, and Cornerstone's technical director Benajah Cobb comes from the theatre with a rectangular piece of plywood, which he plunks on the sidewalk to breakdance, spinning on his knees like a New York street kid. Now as many as 15 blacks and whites are boogeying off the curb, Bobby Brown is on the box, and Wilson is doing his fresh thing; suddenly a County Sheriff's squad car cruises by, slows, checks out the scene—and drives on. The face behind the wheel is black. Then a station wagon cruises by; one of the Academy girls squeals and tries to hide, but Mom has caught her, 90 minutes past her curfew. "Oh god! I'm *grounded*!"

White girls and black boys dancing together on the streets of Port Gibson at half past midnight: impossible. Unfortunately, just like in *Romeo and Juliet*, the adults are a bit slower in getting together. I called Mayor Jimmy Beasley for a statement: "I don't have any problem with it," he told me. "What do you want me to say? Everything I heard about it sounds okay." Will you be attending soon? "I suspect I'll see it, but I'm a pretty busy guy." Rauch sends a personal invitation by mail, but the mayor will never show—nor will his wife, although rumor has it that she wants to attend. Over the next two weeks, blacks will continue to outnumber whites in the audience roughly two or three to one, as they do in the county; blacks will consistently cite the racial themes as the best part of the play. To whites, it's the worst. One audience questionnaire respondent notes that interracial marriages are "Biblically forbidden."

In the Old South, a real-life black Romeo might have been lynched; in the New South, he would probably be let off by an all-black jury, says McFatter during a Thursday Humanities meeting addressed by a number of Mississippi Shakespearean scholars. There are grounds for that statement; these and other issues explode during an in-company discussion of the play's themes and issues following Friday's performance, provoked by the Thursday meeting. The cast, which has decided that when all is said and done the production was worth the work, presents Cornerstone members with Port Gibson T-shirts and a plaque, before launching into a rare, often angry and sometimes tearful open discussion of the future of Claiborne County.

Mary Curry rises to say that her son Allan and another 10-year-old cast member, Athena Hynum, an Academy girl, may be playing together now, but as soon as the show is over everything will return to normal—whites will once again pass black people in the streets without so much as a hello. Cast members of both races are extremely upset by these remarks and say so, sometimes in the presence of their children; as Allan Curry dolefully tells Rauch, "The past brings out a lot of pain in people." Much of the discussion hinges on specific issues of public education, made especially urgent by the financial instability of Chamberlain-Hunt, temporarily kept alive by a recent $100,000 gift from an anonymous local citizen. Everyone agrees that the public schools must be reintegrated; given the public high school's loss of accreditation and its all-black faculty, the question is how. From the discussion it is clear that the end of racism won't solve black and white problems, it will only make solutions possible. But solutions are necessary; if they are not forthcoming, Claiborne County risks the fate of its neighboring Jefferson County, which saw a white exodus and an economic depression when blacks assumed power. As Mississippi's rural agrarian past continues to recede into memory, the worst strangleholds of racism will surely ease as well; what is amazing to me is that a bunch of Northerners barely out of Harvard figured out how to use theatre to advance society's ends.

The 12th and final performance of *Romeo and Juliet* had a waiting list of 230 people, more than a tenth of the town's population. The show runs 15 minutes longer than usual because Brinston is savoring his words for the first and possibly the last time. Afterwards Cornerstone presents a $500 check to Arnette Nash and Patty Crosby—seed money for a new community theatre that will continue the interracial spirit Cornerstone and Crosby's Cross Roads organization began. Semple and Greanier will stay in town for a week past closing to help organize this future company, which will begin by doing a fully integrated, colorblind play—one definitely not about racial tension, thank you very much. The rest of Cornerstone has plans to take to the four winds for its first annual "Scatter Project," a visit to the community theatres left behind in every town they've visited except Prince George, Va., and Miami—a project temporarily curtailed when Rauch and Carey, along with two-thirds of the student body at CHA, come down with the flu. Borrowing a page from the Federal Theater Project of the '30s, Rauch has hopes that on Feb. 1, 1990, all eight Cornerstone-inspired theatres will present regionally specific productions of an as-yet-unnamed one-act play, simultaneously with Cornerstone's own production in a new home theatre.

After this year's Scatter Project and a two-month break, Cornerstone will move on for a West Virginia Ibsen and a Maine O'Neill; they would also like to work in the Soviet Union, but glasnost has produced no thaw for them as yet. Then, in the summer of 1991, an alumni show will bring together the most talented people they've met from around the country—European, African, Latin and Native Americans—for a truly national tour. An Asian-American project can't be far behind.

As the Free Southern Theater and others demonstrated in the '60s, as Kentucky's Roadside Theater, California's Los Angeles Poverty Department and Nebraska's Magic Theater demonstrate today, theatres that redefine risk in social as well as aesthetic terms release vital energy into an art form stagnating in the backwaters of the culture industry, recycling itself for the sake of its own institutional survival. With Cornerstone the emphasis is on art, but this has been precisely the basis for its social achievement: Urging a renewed faith in that infinite moment of connection between the stage and the world, Cornerstone creates singular communities that ripple outward through a playwright's vision like pebbles tossed in a pond. Director Peter Sellars views Cornerstone as part of a new vision for the theatre of the '90s: "Instead of pontificating about what the public wants, Cornerstone has gone out and met that public—indeed, has found out what it is. It's a new generation discovering theatre on its own terms, not believing what theatre is supposed to be, but discovering it from scratch."

Or as Nash put it, Cornerstone in Claiborne County demonstrated "that people can work together without consideration of race when their efforts and energy are used to make a project successful." No one knows if its spirit will last, but no one believed it could ever happen in Port Gibson, Miss. And there it was.

Robert Coe is a screenwriter, playwright and journalist living in New Jersey.

THE (R)EVOLUTION OF BLACK THEATRE

By Paul Carter Harrison

October 1989

Black theatre was born in the crucible of the Civil Rights Movement of the '60s. Its mood of insurrection was galvanized by the Cuban revolution and the specter of global liberation in North and West Africa. The apotheosis of the Civil Rights Movement was not the riots but the 1963 march on Washington—it was showtime, an almost ritualistic diffusion of rage into a massive spectacle of restraint in the face of rising passions for direct confrontation.

Before that, there was only the Negro in the American theatre. The Negro as subject matter was largely created in the minds of Euro-Americans starting as far back as the American Revolution; by the mid-19th century, a paucity of realistic character traits had degenerated into gross caricature in the process of developing minstrelsy, the only theatrical form created in America. The vision of the Negro theatre artist was guided by the gratuitous standards dictated by the social expectation and tastes of Euro Americans. Irrespective of what quarter the patronage of black entertainment came from—the artistic Left or the commercial conservatives—the result was the same old sad song: beautifully sung, but sad and socially hollow. The presentation of black life that appealed to the sympathy of white patrons invariably produced language and images reflecting the biases of the patronizing audience. The black experience became mired in an appropriation of the more exotic aspects of black life (*Porgy and Bess* being one popular example) which satisfied the voyeuristic expectations of the patron.

During the '40s and '50s, mimicking the dramaturgy of Social Realism was not difficult to accomplish, given that blacks had been acculturated to be Euro Americans despite a dubious assimilation into American society. Even today, in spite of the enlightenment of the Civil Rights Movement, it may come as a surprise for those who live outside the black experience that an African-American culture exists, not as a sub-culture but as a psycho-spiritual repository of African retention in the socializing process of 30 million African Americans.

This culture's linguistic and social styles have had a seminal influence on the evolvement of American culture for many generations. While most students of theatre are advised to study the European classics, such as Shakespeare and Molière, few blacks (and almost no whites at all) will be advised to study the linguistic stylization of the Yoruba classical tales, or the social symbology of the Nigerian storyteller Amos Tutuola or the cosmic wisdom of the Dogon. Such a study of ideas leads to a new formulation of aesthetics and dramaturgical logic.

The emergence of the black theatre movement in the '60s created the demise of the Negro in the American theatre. No longer would the black experience be defined from without, but from within the parameters of African-American culture. The standards of excellence would not be gauged by how well the artistic product articulated the collective objectives of the black identity. At the core of this new self-approbation was a renewed sense of Afro-centric identity. This identity released artists from the constraints of Euro-centric socialization and freed them from the ambivalences of a dual-consciousness. Such duality of consciousness between Africa and Europe was nowhere more hauntingly explored than in Adrienne Kennedy's 1964 play *Funnyhouse of a Negro.*

Kennedy's abstract ritual, produced at Edward Albee's Playwrights Unit in New York's Greenwich Village, examines the impact of European acculturation on the "Negro," who, being neither European nor African—being perhaps a mere pigment of the imagination—is tormented by the schism of personality. It is a work dredged up from the memory of when we were "Negroes," or, as the poet Amiri Baraka would anathematize, impotent "knee-grows" wearing the masks of an alien culture, closing our minds to the humiliation and "terribleness" of the slaves' journey through the Middle Passage while extolling the virtues of our oppressors and expressing contempt for all remnants of the African genius. No slice-of-life here for Kennedy. *Funnyhouse* is an introspective surrealistic excursion into the mind of the protagonist Clara, whose efforts to grapple with the contradictions of her identity precipitate madness, despair and a predictably nihilistic violence.

Early in the development of the American theatre, African Americans found acclaim, for the most part, as singers, dancers and comedians. In the early 19th century, the African Grove Theatre—a black company based in Greenwich Village—dedicated itself to performing Shakespeare, only to be greeted with resistance and ridicule. One of its leading actors, Ira Aldridge, moved on to England and became a highly acclaimed tragedian, performing throughout Europe. In the 1920s, black intellectuals such as W.E.B. DuBois tried to encourage blacks to abandon Broadway—particularly its aimless musicals—and concentrate on excavating black folk culture for the development of serious theatrical exercises. At the time, DuBois was responding to the cultural revitalization known as the "Harlem Renaissance," which, not unlike the Black Arts Movement of the '60s, generated a wealth of poetry, literature, theatre and music reflecting the ethnocentric sensibilities of African Americans. DuBois's vision of a more ethnocentric art was echoed and refined in the '60s by the poet Larry Neal, who is credited with bringing into focus the aesthetic relationship between art and politics in his now famous manifesto, which appeared in a 1968 issue of the *Drama Review*:

"The Black Arts Movement is radically opposed to any concept of the artist that alienates him from his community," Neal wrote. "Black Art is the aesthetic and spiritual sister of the Black Power concept. As such, it envisions an art that speaks directly to the needs and aspirations of Black America. In order to perform this task, the Black Arts Movement proposes a radical reordering of the western cultural aesthetic. It proposes a separate symbolism, mythology, critique and iconology. The Black Arts and the Black Power concepts both relate broadly to the Afro-American's desire for self-determination and nationhood."

Self-determination was by no means a call for the ghettoization of the African-American culture. It simply meant that the creative process should advance artworks informed by the African-American point of view. While the black experience may produce its own evaluation of social and political reality, or invent imagery based upon its worldview, the Euro American will invariably be included due to the very intimacy whites share with blacks in the formation of American history. However, Neal's new orthodoxy of cultural nationalism eschewed the black reality portrayed in adaptations of white classics such as Joseph Papp's New York Shakespeare Festival production of an all-black *Cherry Orchard* or the Richard Allen Center's black production of *Long Day's Journey into Night*. The new orthodoxy demanded a sovereignty of ethnocentric values and a new rigor in the evaluation of the black experience. Implicit in such demands was the belief that universal truth resides in the black experience for the enlightenment of all Americans.

Still, the integration, however meager, of blacks into the mainstream of American theatre might seem less threatening than notions of self-appraisal and self-identification, since the dominant culture had always been the sole arbiter of the appropriate representation of black images or black life. August Wilson, winner of the 1985 Pulitzer Prize for his play *Fences*, recalls that his high school teacher would often complain that his poems were too preoccupied with black characters as opposed to "more universal themes." In order to accommodate his teacher's admonishment, Wilson abandoned black characters for a while and turned his attention to nature. Few black writers have been able to escape such abrasive insensitivity to African-American cultural identity. It is not uncommon for those of the dominant culture—or even counterculture—to arrogate a smug sense of cultural hegemony when judging the artistic expression of their black students or peers. Rarely has the dominant culture been able to accept that black exploration of African-American culture is no less myopic or parochial or lacking in universal truths than the illumination of Irish culture by James Joyce, Russian culture by Chekhov, French culture by André Gide, German culture by Goethe or the Jewish-American experience by Philip Roth. Self-determination, then, is an effort to shed the Emperor's robes in order to assert the sovereignty of personal and collective ethnocentric aspirations.

Ethnic kinship invites spiritual renewal. The preoccupation with African symbology in the '60s was not simply a case of nostalgia for the past. It was, rather, a reaffirmation of the continuity of African culture in the American experience, albeit transformed by intimacy with Euro-American culture. Revival of a collective African memory had a chastening effect which urged the contemporary artist beyond an ambivalent identification to a more vigorous expression of ethnic ethos.

The 1963 civil rights march on Washington did not remedy the manifold social contradictions in American democracy, nor did it alter the status of second-class citizenship for African Americans. Rebellion against the agencies of oppression continued. The theatre served the rebellion, mounting works that addressed the community's particular inquiry about social justice in America. It became a source of communication where the enactment of social conflicts both informed the community and at times provided an opportunity for a volatile build-up of rage to find catharsis. It was the didactic, often agitprop quality of these initial theatrical effects that led to the characterization of the black theatre movement as parochial and militant. The movement's vituperation probably served to buttress the animosity shared by most blacks against Euro Americans.

Ironically, the play that is credited with first awakening the possibilities of artistically conceived political and social discourse was Jean Genet's *The Blacks*, which appeared at New York's St. Mark's Playhouse in 1961. The play, which did not do well in France, had enormous success Off Broadway largely because its theme, the liberation of blacks from French colonial oppression, had great emotional resonance in racist America and galvanized the performance of the cast to an enlightened urgency. Several members of that cast—among them Cicely Tyson, James Earl Jones, Louis Gossett Jr., Billie Dee Williams and Maya Angelou—have become household names in mainstream American entertainment.

Amiri Baraka (LeRoi Jones) had never intended to become mainstream. Baraka, whose poetic voice would influence two generations of poets and awaken the communal spirit in many black readers, was perhaps the most outspoken recanter of Western culture and the evils of Euro-American oppression on black life. The 1964 production of Baraka's incendiary play *Dutchman*—also produced by Edward Albee's Playwrights Unit—introduced the poet to the American stage as a dramatist. Stylistically, *Dutchman*, like *Funnyhouse*, makes the leap from social realism to a symbolist dramaturgy, using language to excavate rather than explicate sexual and racial aggression. Unlike *Funnyhouse*, the symbols in *Dutchman* are not obscured by interior abstractions; the events provoke an immediate visceral response.

Riding the subway is Clay, a young "Negro" dressed benignly in a three-button, Ivy League suit—the Emperor's robes. He encounters Lulu, a white "bitch-goddess" who stalks the underground in search of young black men who are disconnected from their racial identity. Clay feels self-assured, leaving himself vulnerable to Lulu. When she finally strips away the mask of the young "Negro," she reveals, much to Clay's own surprise, a festering hostility against whites, residing deep in the recesses of his ancestral memory.

Clay's dilemma brings to mind what I would call the "Othello syndrome." Until recently, most black male actors have felt it imperative to play Othello, despite the Elizabethan biases inherent in the character. Like these actors, Othello must embroider his ethnic qualities with a kind of lofty language uncharacteristic of a Moor. His performance serves to deflect the court's skepticism away from his external properties to his basic humanity. Without kingdoms of his own to rule, Othello, like Clay, is an illusion, a self-conceit that ends in the precipitous rage of sexual and racial violence. Baraka might see the slayings of Desdemona and Lulu as liberating—the desecration of the oppressors' prize possessions—but in both cases self-illumination also ends in self-destruction. Othello and Clay come to their demises because they accept the illusion of the Emperor's robes and are, in hostile lands, unable to draw on the continuity of their own ethnic experiences.

In 1965 Baraka left Greenwich Village and formed the Black Arts Repertory Theatre in Harlem, where he was able to commit his energies to the uncompromising development of theatre pieces designed to raise black consciousness to the heights of social action, even revolution. Baraka, however, was not alone uptown; the mid-'60s witnessed a plethora of theatre groups in Harlem with a diversity of artistic and political objectives. Most notable were Ernie McClintock's teaching/ performance group, the Afro-American Studio Theatre; the ritual work at the National Black Theatre, inspired by Barbara Ann Teer's African and Black Church; and Robert Macbeth's revolutionary-ritual exercises at the New Lafayette Theatre, which boasted the dramaturgical talents of Ed Bullins and Richard Wesley.

Still, the most important institutional development for black theatre emerged in the East Village with the 1967 formation of the Negro Ensemble Company at St. Mark's Playhouse, the same theatre that had housed *The Blacks* at the beginning of the decade. St. Mark's had also been the home for *Happy Ending* and *Day of Absence*, two seminal plays written by actor/director Douglas Turner Ward that led to the organization of the NEC under his leadership. After opening its inaugural season with *The Song of the Lusitanian Bogey*, a work by the German playwright Peter Weiss that showcased the company's ensemble style, Ward set the company's objectives toward the development and promotion of new African-American playwrights. Irrespective of the many actors who have benefited from exposure with the company and moved into the mainstream of American entertainment, the NEC clearly became a writer's theatre. Over the past 20 years, Ward has been responsible for developing the works of several award-winning playwrights, such as Lonnie Elder III's *Ceremonies in Dark Old Men*, Joseph Walker's *The River Niger*, Derek Walcott's *Dream on Monkey Mountain*, Phillip Hayes Dean's *The Sty of the Blind Pig*, Samm-Art Williams's *Home*, Leslie Lee's *First Breeze of Summer*, Charles Fuller's *A Soldier's Play* and my own ritual-drama, *The Great MacDaddy*.

By 1970, Woodie King Jr. picked up the slack in the production of works by new black playwrights through the formation of the New Federal Theatre at the Henry Street Settlement on the Lower East Side. Operating as both an independent producer and the director of an institution, King has produced more black works for the commercial theatre than any other single individual, and perhaps as many as the NEC produced as a nonprofit institution. A special arrangement between King and Papp allowed the New Federal to maximize the exposure of its plays by showcasing productions in subsequent runs at the New York Shakespeare Festival's Public Theater. A few of the beneficiaries included Ed Bullins's *The Taking of Miss Janie*, Ntozake Shange's *for colored girls who have considered suicide / when the rainbow is enuf* and Ron Milner's *What the Winesellers Buy*. Papp successfully mounted the original production of Charles Gordone's *No Place to Be Somebody*, which was awarded the 1970 Pulitzer Prize, the first to go to a black dramatist. Along with Stella Holt, who produced at the Village Mews Theatre during the '50s, and Wynn Handman, director of New York's American Place Theatre, Papp was among the few white institutional theatre directors to regularly produce black playwrights.

During the '80s, black theatre became a prominent aspect of the American cultural scene as black students demanded more ethnic specificity in their theatre training, and new theatres—such as the ambitious Crossroads Theatre Company in New Brunswick, N.J., which produced the original production of George Wolfe's *The Colored Museum*, Atlanta's Jomandi Productions and Just Us Theatre Company, Oakland Ensemble Theatre and Bullins's Memorial Theatre in California and the Penumbra Theatre Company of St. Paul, Minn.—have been organized throughout the country. While most contemporary theatre experiences are no longer insulated by nationalistic ideology, they still remain committed to the resurrection of folk values and the perpetuation of a black worldview that has sociopolitical consequences for all Americans. Having demonstrated its resiliency through the '80s as a legitimate cultural resource in America, black theatre enters the '90s with a dramaturgical preference for expressionistic works, such as the nonlinear, testimonial style of Wolfe's *Colored Museum* or the narrative techniques used in August Wilson's 20th-century cycle, which bridges realism with the nonreal, parabolic wisdom of African-American folk mythology.

The plays of Wilson's cycle—each one deals with a decade in African-American life—represent the culmination of political, social and aesthetic objectives presaged by the Harlem Renaissance of the '20s and the Black Arts Movement of the '60s. In *Ma Rainey's Black Bottom*, *Joe Turner's Come and Gone* and *The Piano Lesson*, Wilson reclaims the blues voice—dredged up from the oral and musical tradition of black life—as the vehicle for folk narratives, stories rooted in the mythic sediments of reality, as opposed to being simply "folksy." Like the blues, folk language wryly points to the ironies of life, especially to the existence of good and evil as a noncontradictory moral experience. Apprehension of such a reality depends upon the characteristic rhythms and repetitions of black speech, which invest the narrative with the heightened quality of poetry. Safely ensconced within the oral tradition, Wilson has been able to explore the icons and cosmic sensibilities of folk culture. He examines the impact of the spirit world on corporeal life—the interaction between the physical and the metaphysical—without trivializing the experience or reducing such revelations to superstitious encounters with ghosts.

Wilson has also managed to demonstrate the healing effect of self-empowerment that occurs when a person reestablished bonds with his ancestry. Such bonding stimulates personal renewal and collective liberation from oppression. The very authenticity of Wilson's voice has become a welcome model for African-American dramaturgy in the future.

Institutionally, black theatre in the '90s will be positioned to reach out to a nationwide audience by means of new promotional strategies which take into account the growing influence of the regional theatre markets. The shift in thinking that has resulted from the decentralizing of black theatre out of New York is evident in the growing emphasis on audience development, marketing and institution-building—as well as the role of black theatre in the economic development of African-American communities. These concerns were reflected on the agenda of the recent Black Theatre Network Conference at the 1989 National Black Theatre Festival, hosted in August by the North Carolina Black Repertory Company in Winston-Salem.

Given these developments and the maturing vision of artists like August Wilson, black theatre can never again be considered an insignificant celebration of ethnic chauvinism. Just as the psychic commitment of blacks toward social change brought a new energy into the world during the '60s that would be universally validated two decades later in such remote corners of the world as South Africa, Poland and China, the aesthetic and humanistic strategies of black theatre in the '90s will surely continue to gain new ground as a cultural option within the mainstream of American culture.

Paul Carter Harrison, a playwright and director, has had a long association with the Negro Ensemble Company. He is the author of a book of essays, *The Drama of Nommo*, and has edited several books, including *Black Theatre: Ritual Performance in the African Diaspora* and the play anthologies *Kuntu Drama, Totem Voices* and *Classical Plays of the Negro Ensemble Company*. He is a professor emeritus at Chicago's Columbia College.

50 OBSERVATIONS ON ACTING

By Charles Ludlam

October 1990

Charles Ludlam seems to have been a consummate actor from the first, but he stood out from other actors because of his great theatricality—overacting, some said. He needed his own company, he claimed, to accommodate acting others might find "pasty." Thus, for the 20 years prior to his death in May of 1987 at age 44, he was the leading actor as well as principal writer and guiding spirit of the New York–based Ridiculous Theatrical Company. His acting style may have come naturally, but his restless intelligence forced him to try to understand and explain it, as in these fragmentary notes and excerpts from interviews.

1. At the heart of the dramatic event lies the spirit of masochism. In the boxing ring or at a tragedy it is the delight in conflict and the illusion of opposition that enthralls. The primary desire of the audience is to witness suffering. The actor willingly undergoes the ordeal of passing through various states of physical and mental torture. Could the theatre ever become a place of profound security?
2. There should be a balance of elements. Even a balance between successful scenes and unsuccessful, a balance between good acting and bad.
3. If you tell people the truth you'd better make them laugh or they'll kill you.
4. When I was in conventional theatre, even when I was going to school, people thought my acting was too broad, too pasty. So I had to create a theatre where I could exist. I had to create, for my own survival, a world where I could take advantage of my talents.
5. Artaud was almost a springing off point for me. The idea that actors could be hieroglyphic symbols. A character is an embodiment of a concept made of flesh and blood, and I think that is something that gives tremendous strength.
6. Naturalistic theatre is a very recent innovation, a corrective device, and it wasn't the end of anything. It was a fashion to do things nat-

urally. You can't really perform an unnatural act, unless you claim to have supernatural powers. So the whole idea of something being natural becomes a very oppressive concept; it's shallow. Gradually, through training with Stanislavsky teachers, I realized that they wanted me to behave in a civilized manner in a room, and not do anything extraordinary. But everything I'm interested in is extraordinary.

7. I think I'm terribly Geraldine Page and Kim Stanley. Don't you? Whenever I feel the least bit dried up, I think of them and a whole new life comes over me. Those funny little nervous twitches and so forth.

8. I'm really a very impressionable person and I've always absorbed a lot of influences; not so much stylistic influences as psychological, working with actors in ways which allow them to perform in different styles. I'm known for kinky casting and I discover people— sometimes on the street, and sometimes they are old friends. I also draw on a pool of rather extraordinary actors out of the avant-garde.

9. When the actor becomes a primary creator he is totally responsible for who he is on stage.

10. [Creating a role] is terrifying to most actors. It's like having nothing to go on but yourself, an immediate situation and your co-workers. The actor creates the role in a primary way—from his own imagination, wish-fulfillment and fantasy life. It's your creation; it's more daring. There's a lot invested, and the risks are great.

11. In our company, there is virtually no risk, though, because we all work that way. Since we share this way of working, there's something going on that makes it possible to be free.

12. Finally, the most profound theme of the theatre is this business of role-play—roles are interchangeable, personality is an artifice in life, and it can be changed or interchanged. When each actor is working, partially through wish-fulfillment or whatever, to project his idea of what the character will be, we begin to find the "play" in these characters.

13. You know you can't ask an actor to make a moral judgment about the character he's playing.

14. You *can* do it, I mean, Brecht said you should, and all that. But I think when it comes to getting into the role, there is some reason why you want to play the role. A lot of time it's something that you wouldn't exactly want to admit, and a lot of time it goes unspoken . . . why would I want to play this nasty character who beats people up?

15. I read this little pamphlet, the Mao Zedong line on Stanislavsky. It was attacking Stanislavsky because Stanislavsky had the "seed" theory which was that each person has the seeds of any kind of character in him and all he has to do is to find those seeds or those germs and cultivate them, and he can become the character. Well, Mao was very upset about that . . . . The Party didn't like it because they said that some characters were heroic, who should be showing what people should aspire to—it's idealist theatre—and not show people as they are. Some people—like the working class—

are heroes and don't have the seeds of being filthy capitalists or exploiters.

16. I think that actors can take more control of their destinies, their stage lives, if there's a wholehearted kind of communication, if they're not just passive.

17. I do think of myself as part of a viable tradition in theatre. The romance of the theatre gives me energy and inspiration: Molière acting in his own plays, with his wife and his two brothers-in-law; Shakespeare playing a lead in Ben Jonson's *Every Man in His Humour*; Marlowe and Kyd sharing a room in London. I feel a part of all that.

18. To me there's something miraculous about the theatrical mask— the mask that is the actor. Through sheer force of will, I can look handsome on stage, or ugly.

19. When I was in college, I just happened to find, browsing in the library, a copy of *The Art of Acting*, by the French actor Coquelin, who originated the role of Cyrano. He wrote that, before he even learned a line of a play, he would go to the costume room and dress up as the character, put on the full makeup. When he looked in the mirror and saw the character staring back at him, then he was ready to begin. That impressed me tremendously.

20. In school, of course, there was all that emphasis on the Method, and feeling your way into the part, and it was always sort of schizophrenic for me; there were too many different things to juggle.

21. But now I think I'm really a Stanislavsky actor par excellence. I go into a sort of trance on stage and believe in my role completely.

22. Of course, I also know I'm on stage and people are watching—I'm admitting I'm acting—but on another plane my belief is total.

23. People talk about great performances, most of which are luck— the right role coming along at the right time for an actor. But I'm seeing to it that I get the role. I've created it, written it, directed it. My immersion is total!

24. What has influenced me, for one thing, is that I'm an actor. Throughout history, playwrights generally were actors. Shakespeare. Molière acted in all his plays. Shakespeare retired from acting. In music there's the tradition that Bach and Mozart were virtuoso performers who needed material to play so they wrote their own scores. The director as a separate entity started with Stanislavsky at the end of the 19th century.

25. In modern times, we've had to deal with something actors have never dealt with before, which is the long run. If you play it every day, give or take 50 days, you've got close to 300 performances a year, even more.

26. This means that [actors] must perform the same way over and over again. This encourages predictable habits rather than experimentation and growth.

27. A true artist, on the other hand, must dare to try something new.

28. Something that gets a laugh once, and you know it's good, may never get a laugh again during rehearsal, because the surprise is gone, or people have seen you do it so many times. There's a ten-

dency to drop it before opening night, forgetting how funny it was the first time. That's a problem—keeping things in; instinct reminds the actor that something was good, that it worked and that it will be funny again for people who haven't seen it yet.

29. I think all forms of acting should be played side by side. Some of my actors do a type of acting that tips the audience, with a stylistic wink, that this or that is supposed to be funny. But others perform deadpan or ambiguous acting that gets a laugh only when they do or say something that is actually funny. So, there's a lot of confusion in my audience as to whether something is funny. I savor that because it makes the audience make a judgment, commit themselves, and I appear more inscrutable and my work takes on more levels of meaning.

30. In naturalism there is always the tendency to be less than you are, to be more specific and less, and that is always a terrible danger. It certainly didn't work for me.

31. If Clive Barnes thinks the Royal Shakespeare Company's acting is exemplary, where does that leave me? Out in the cold, because that stuff is dead as a doornail. They direct all their lines to the audience.

32. Some people say our style is so broad, but I think of what we do as extremely realistic acting.

33. Sometimes a reviewer will call our performances "amateurish," but what he doesn't understand is that our so-called amateurish style has been consciously, purposefully arrived at. We don't want to be slick like Broadway performers because we don't want our acting to belie the effort that goes into a production.

34. After all, it's the awareness of effort that makes a live production, such as a concert, more exciting than a recording, or a Navajo rug more interesting than a factory-made one.

35. The mistakes in handmade rugs and live productions might show more than they would in slicker, highly edited art forms, but so do the triumphs.

36. Furthermore, the conventions of commercial acting just aren't broad enough to encompass the variety of human life that you see right here on the streets of New York. At the Ridiculous Theatrical Company we want to create vivid, memorable characters, and the mannerisms used by many commercial actors are simply inadequate to the task.

37. First, many Broadway actors tend to shout at moments of high emotional intensity. And they all shout at the same pitch! That drives me up the wall.

38. There's the habit male actors have of sitting with their legs a mile apart when they want to indicate their masculinity. It has become such a cliché, and not even a valid one. European men don't sit that way.

39. One more annoying mannerism: Many commercial actors wander around the stage too much. They walk and turn, walk and turn for no reason except that they fear the show will be dull if they stand in one place.

40. I'm the most constantly employed actor in New York. I'm the hardest working man in the American theatre . . . . And I'm very vain about myself.

41. Really great artists who know they're the best have trouble remaining tactful.

42. I do my own bravos by ventriloquism.

43. Lately I've been thinking about Lady Sneerwell in *School for Scandal*.

44. I'm very interested in Judith Anderson. Her Medea. I've always loved that. That's one of those rare performances that's had so much impact on me, like Garbo's Camille. But Medea is for a more mature woman. I'll have to wait until I've seasoned.

45. I hate *Macbeth*.

46. [About his dressing room] There are three mirrors in here. One in which I look unbelievably gorgeous. One in which I look unbelievably ugly. And one I never look in. I never know which one to believe.

47. Acting is a daily chore that I do. It's the physical work of the theatre. It's very satisfying physically and emotionally. It's difficult. It's frustrating and it's very demanding, and it's from this that one must rest because you can get really tired. It's like running a marathon.

48. I feel that, as an artist, as an entertainer, your basic job is to create something of interest for others. But what happens is that you can get so caught up in a part in a play that you never think about whether anything is of interest to your "other," more real self. You're so busy being interesting on stage that you can sometimes forget to be interested in the so-called real world.

49. I think artists whose lives are about *being interesting to others* have to take rests, which means time to be boring and not being of any interest to others. This may not have publicity value. It's just something for you. You must find the time.

50. All actors, you'll notice, wanted to be marine biologists.

THE ACTOR AS OBJECT OF DESIRE

By Don Shewey

October 1990

1.

You are just my type. Blond, blue eyes, balding. I have watched you play a cowboy, an angel, a man alone in a room. You are the epitome of what one famous director describes as his favorite kind of actor: "a guy who looks like he's got secrets in his pockets." You have plenty of secrets.

You wear your characters lightly. The mask you wear is transparent. I can see your own face under the mask. Often I can understand what your mask is doing but not your face. Your voice is a mask, too. You hesitate when you speak. Your speech is soft, but there's anger and violence in the jagged pauses. You have an interior life on stage that bothers me, that gives me pause, that makes me ask questions and make up my own answers.

Through my advocacy, you've won your first acting award. I've described you in print as "beautiful." Then it turns out we go to the same health club. You occupy the next lounger on the sun deck. You dress in the same row of lockers. We shower together. We talk. You are friendly and guarded. You come to my house for dinner. I drink a beer; you refuse one. You tell me the story of your life: your unusual family, your juvenile delinquency, the time you spent working as a day laborer on an oil rig in Louisiana. We speak about our personal lives. You are seeing "someone," gender unspecified. We talk about New York City. You describe a scary encounter, a macho cockfight on the Bowery in which a knife suddenly appears and you are stabbed.

"Do you want to see the scar?" Before I can say anything you take off your shirt. Your chest and arms are powerful from working out on the punching bags. They're covered with blond fur. You are standing in the doorway of my kitchen with your shirt off, showing me your scar.

I am an arm's length away. Here is my chance to enter the movie, to do the dreamed-of thing, to touch the scar and maybe more.

I can't. I don't want to break the spell you cast when you exhibit your power on stage. I want to keep guessing. I stay put. I admire from afar.

In the theatre my desire is ardent, unchecked. In the distance between actor and spectator, desire can run rampant. Intimacy pulls the plug.

2.

Any balletomane who's being honest will cheerfully admit that one of the primary pleasures of going to the ballet is looking at the dancers' bodies—beautiful, sleek, idealized bodies. Theatre holds the same allure, but we tend not to talk about it, because we can pretend to "higher" matters; the play, after all, is the thing. So why do I spend 20 minutes absorbed in the sweat that pours off of Tom Hulce's face? How long do I tune out while I sit mesmerized by Elizabeth Ashley brushing her hair and stretching her sinewy body across the bed? Why does a hush fall over the audience every time Alec Baldwin takes his shirt off? What playwright's lines could compete with the line of hair that descends from Alec Baldwin's muscular chest over his paunch and disappears into his boxer shorts?

3.

I'll come no more behind your scenes, David; for the silk stockings and white bosoms of your actresses excite my amorous propensities.
—Samuel Johnson

Ogling actors is a guilty pleasure, an ancient one. The persecution of actors throughout history stems almost entirely from the perception of the actor as object of desire.

In ancient Rome, a third-generation descendant of an actor was not allowed to marry a third-generation descendant of a senator, lest he pollute noble Roman blood. In Imperial China, descendants of actors were not eligible to take the examination that opened the way to a career in public service. In France, not alone among Christian countries, actors were not allowed to be buried in consecrated ground until the revolution.

At heart, of course, objections to the theatre boiled down to a morbid obsession on the part of clergymen and puritanical social leaders with the hopeless task of controlling the sexuality of the populace. Or as French scholar Moses Barras piquantly put it, the church fathers feared "especially the effect of actresses upon the male members of the audience."

4.

You manipulate time like a lover. You slow down, you stretch your neck, you speak softly so I have to lean forward to hear you. You make me shift in my seat. You display yourself. You keep still, you say nothing, you hang back, you conceal yourself. You stalk me, you seduce me. You say things, but that's only the beginning. You want me to know what the words mean, and you want me to guess what you're not saying. You want to impress me with your eloquence, your sense of humor, your deep emotion. You hope I don't notice the surgical scar above your collarbone or the burn on your leg. You do want me to look at your ass. But you don't want to be cheap about it. Oh, go ahead. Be cheap. You're an actor. We expect it of you.

We expect actors to be pretty. To be easy on the eyes. The hero should have clear skin and broad shoulders. The heroine should have good hair and nice legs. We will be looking at you continuously for an hour or two. We want to relax in your beauty. Your beauty is at once a gift from God for all humanity to share and your link to us. We look at you and see our inner selves, the people we know ourselves to be really, underneath our workaday clothes and our potbellies and our fear and our anger.

No wonder directors and casting agents tend to hire actors who are younger, prettier, thinner (not to mention whiter) than the characters they're supposed to play. It's understandable, if not exactly excusable. But beauty takes many forms. What are the lines from Stephen Sondheim's *Sunday in the Park with George*? "Pretty isn't beautiful / Pretty is what changes / What the eye arranges / Is beautiful."

5.

To what extent is my desire for you welcome and to what extent threatening?

6.

"What we love that we have," writes Emerson, "but by desire we bereave ourselves of the love." In other words, desire signifies separation from the beloved—or, from another angle, we desire what we don't have. Aside from the erotic desire aroused by performers we find sexually attractive, our desire is provoked by a curiosity about people very different from ourselves. Sometimes they are our mirror, sometimes we are theirs. We try on their attributes; we imagine looking like them. Watching actors is a form of human window-shopping.

Watching Jesse Borrego dance on stage alone to Marvin Gaye's "Ain't That Peculiar" in JoAnne Akalaitis's production of Len Jenkin's *American Notes*, I want to have his streetwise gracefulness. Watching Roc Dutton curse God ("Turn your back on me, motherfucker!") in August Wilson's *Ma Rainey's Black Bottom*, I crave his ability to express blistering anger. Howie Seago used to be a leading actor with the National Theatre of the Deaf; I'd like to have his poetic hands. I don't know what kind of ethnic cocktail Kevin Gray is, but seeing him in the Off-Broadway revival of *Pacific Overtures* makes me dream of possessing such quintessentially Asian, definitively masculine beauty. Watching Colleen Dewhurst, I don't know which I'd rather have—her amazing, raspy, O'Neill-meets-Janis-Joplin voice or those sunken blue eyes burning out of a face crinkly with life and laughter.

Sometimes I think that if I could swap my short hairy Portuguese body with that of any actor, I'd like to be Danitra Vance. If only I could have her expressive eyes, her rich chocolate-colored skin, her comic timing, the way she wears a hat.

7.

You think I'm admiring your technique, but I'm studying your torso. You think I'm enthralled with your interpretation, but I'm examining your legs. You think I'm listening to the words you're saying. I'm listening, I'm listening. But I'm also following your line of vision, to see whose eyes you're looking into. I want to make contact with your eyes. Laurie Anderson: "Your eyes / It's a day's work just looking into them."

8.

The erotic relationship between actor and spectator can only exist in live theatre, when there are breathing creatures in proximity. Desire for actors on the screen is more pornographic: a one-way sensation. I once watched Richard Gere shoot a scene from a movie. The scene required no acting, and got none, but it had a lot of erotic presence. He sat in the cab of a pickup truck while a bank of electric lights set up on the frosty lawn of an Iowa farmhouse simulated the lonely moon. To observe Gere in repose is to understand the objectness of movie stars. He is the perfect example of the actor as a beautiful surface. Just the lighting falling on his cleanly shaved cheek and jaw is haunting.

Actors can be sensual in a movie or on television but not consensual. That's when actor-as-object gets dangerous. Ask Jodie Foster. Ask Theresa Saldana.

9.

Like most very successful actresses, Miss Fayne was not beautiful. That is, she possessed few of the attributes which the adolescent taste of America usually demands of its beauties. She had a broad free brow, eyes set well apart and slightly protuberant, high cheekbones, and a wide scarlet mouth like a venomous flower. The effect of all this was arresting—even startling. So her great following, baffled by this mask which gave the effect of beauty without actually being beautiful, *fell back on the trite word 'glamorous' and clung to it.*
    —Edna Ferber, "Glamour" [Emphasis added.]

10.

One of the most interesting volumes of theatre history I've ever read is Mendel Kohansky's *The Disreputable Profession: The Actor in Society*, which deals at length with the public perception (part disapproving, part envious) of actors as prostitutes and sexual libertines. This age-old fantasy picked up steam when it became acceptable in the second half of the 16th century for women to take their place on stage. Kohansky writes, "In times when modesty was regarded as one of woman's chief virtues, the home and hearth her sole province, it was naturally assumed, and much of the time with some degree of truth, that a woman who exhibits herself in public, be her attire as decorous as a nun's and may she confront her male partner at a distance only, was a woman of loose morals, and she was treated accordingly."

Is it such an insult for actors to be compared to whores? After all, they are paid to give pleasure, to satisfy desire. Even those who condemn actors on moral grounds sometimes acknowledge the hypocrisy of society's excluding from the privileges of citizenship the people who entertain them. Female Roman street mimes and actresses in commedia dell'arte were considered to be no better than common whores because they enacted bawdy scenes of adultery with the penchant for realism that the audience demanded. As second-century Roman theologian Tertullian pointed out, "What perversity! They love whom they lower; they despise whom they applaud; the art they glorify, the artist they disgrace."

It's true, of course, that in many cases there was a fine line between women who wore revealing garments in public in service of a playwright's intentions and those who were trying to attract paying customers. Actresses in Restoration theatre, with few exceptions, came from the lowest strata of society, some directly from the brothels. Highly undisciplined, most with little talent, they had only their good looks and self-confidence to offer; many didn't even pretend to separate their work on the stage from more lucrative pursuits in the boudoir. In 19th-century Russia, actresses were assumed to be available as bedmates to noblemen. Turn-of-the-century British streetwalkers picked up by police officers frequently gave their occupation as actress, since many had trodden the boards at one time or another. One of the first great French actresses, Adrienne Lecouvreur, maintained a luxurious household not through her work in the theatre but as courtesan to a number of rich, aristocratic lovers. And the term *demi-monde* arose to describe the mid-19th century theatre scene in Paris when women who made a living as prostitutes also performed on stage in plays about women who made a living as prostitutes.

The twilight overlapping of acting and prostitution had its squalid aspects—gentlemen often enjoyed free access to backstage areas while the actresses were dressing—but the theatre nonetheless offered social mobility as well as economic and sexual independence to women. Nell Gwynn was brought up in a brothel, started out in the theatre as an "orange girl" (serving as go-between for illicit lovers), began playing bit parts, and eventually became a star—Dryden's favorite actress—and then the king's mistress. Her epitaph read: "Here Nelly lies, who, though she lived a slattern / Yet dies a Princess acting in St. Cattrin."

11.

You remind me of my sister, with your flippy brown hair and your funny southern accent. I've seen you play a goofy teenage orphan, a lesbian folksinger's tomboy sidekick, a high-strung suburban wife, not to mention your movie breakthroughs, the comic kidnapper and the TV executive. You toss your hair a lot. Your vitality alone makes people laugh and feel happy.

Here you are playing a character with badly dyed hair, twirling a baton in your living room, front and center on a major theatre's tiny second stage. Suddenly my anatomy registers your presence: a sparky young actress with gorgeous breasts standing a few feet away, wearing nothing but a frilly slip, in the throes of thespian passion. Your body is telling my body something that hadn't occurred to my mind. This desire takes me by surprise, and I feel unexpectedly vulnerable. You're the first woman who's given me an erection in years. I feel like an adolescent.

Does this mean we have to get married?

12.

Why do eyes, mouth, nose and brow transfix us, when they have so little relation to the sexual prowess and bodily perfection of their bearer? The answer is simple: The face is the primary expression of consciousness, and to see in the face the object of sexual attraction is to find the focus which all attraction requires—the focus on another's existence, as a being who can be aware of me.

Much has been written about the glance of love, which seems so imperiously to single out its object and so peremptorily to confront him with an intolerable choice. In truth, however, it is the glance of sexual interest that precipitates the movement of the soul, whereby two people come to stand outside the multitude in which they are presently moving, bound by a knowledge that cannot be expressed in words, and offering to each other a silent communication that ignores everything but themselves.

—Roger Scruton, *Sexual Desire:*
A Moral Philosophy of the Erotic (The Free Press, 1986)

13.

What's the difference between an attractive person on the street and an attractive person on stage? You're permitted to stare at the person on stage. In fact, it's required. And actors know it. That's why they're on stage, to be looked at. "An actor," Milan Kundera writes, "is someone who in early childhood consents to exhibit himself for the rest of his life to an anonymous public. Without that basic consent, which has nothing to do with talent, which goes deeper than talent, no one can become an actor."

He's talking about vanity, and can I just put in a word in praise of vanity? Vanity is a public service. Most of us have neither the time nor the raw materials to indulge in personal vanity. Yet we love, enjoy, crave witnessing beautiful human beings. Smooth, perfect beauty. Ragged, zesty, carnal beauty. We drink it in. It makes our souls feel big. We understand and appreciate the human body, God's taste.

My preference is for as little vanity as it takes to convince an actor to show his or her work. Is it logic and practical experience or some kind of snobbery that makes me believe stage actors are better equipped for great performances than film actors? Actors in films who have no stage experience often have nothing to go on *but* vanity, the indeed rare ability to exhibit oneself, especially if one has extraordinary good looks. Acting for the camera is, after all, measured in seconds at a time. Actors on stage must act continuously for minutes, an hour, sometimes several hours. That takes talent, training, stamina, more than vanity. (I'm not saying film acting doesn't require stamina—it certainly does. But it's the stamina to fight the boredom of the slow pace of moviemaking, not the stamina required of exercising your art over a period of time.) The fact of the matter is that in film, talent is secondary. Vanity is often sufficient. Look at Kim Basinger.

14.

Choreographer William Forsythe recalls skipping high school classes in Long Island to go to musical comedy auditions in New York, even though he didn't have a union card: "They let me in—probably liked my butt or something."

15.

The public celebration of men as erotic objects is a phenomenon that could only occur in periods when women had gained a measure of social equality. The late 19th century saw the emergence of the matinee idol, an actor whose looks and personality especially appealed to female audiences. "The matinees were patronized by women who would never have ventured out of the house alone in the evening, lest their reputation be soiled," explains Mendel Kohansky. "Moreover, when the lady went to the theatre in the evening, properly chaperoned by husband or parents, she had to maintain a demure stance, while at the matinee, surrounded by other women, she could give vent to her desire to shout, blow kisses, even swoon at the sight of her idol making love to the lucky woman on the stage." Hundreds of women used to gather at the stage door waiting for the arrival of Harry Montague, America's first matinee idol. When he died young, thousands of women walked around with black ribbons across their chests and built huge altars in front of the theatre where he had appeared with his initials spelled out in red carnations.

Idolatry of male performers is an ancient tradition, though. Pliny the Younger describes a wealthy, high-ranking Roman woman named Ummidia Quadratilla, who had in her employ a troupe of male mimes who performed both at parties and in her boudoir. And Caesar Augustus once ordered the Roman comedian Stephanio flogged on three consecutive nights after a lady of senatorial rank, disguised as a boy, was found waiting for the actor at the stage door.

16.

Receding hairlines I have known and loved: Paul McCrane. Dan Butler. Ed Harris. Peter Friedman. John Malkovich. Will Patton. Jessica Tandy. John Pankow.

17.

Stagy acting used to be the epitome of bad acting in movies; selling it to the balcony looks repulsive in close-up. That's the main reason Broadway legends such as Ethel Merman, Zero Mostel and Carol Channing never made the leap to Hollywood success. For anyone who wishes to check it out, the old scream-shout-wave-your-arms style of American stage acting has been captured for posterity, with all its energy and excessiveness intact, by Sidney Lumet in movies such as *Bye Bye Braverman* and *Just Tell Me What You Want*. But American theatre has changed, and so has American acting. When Broadway entered its dinosaur era sometime in the '50s, the art part of theatre began to develop Off Broadway in theatres much cozier than those that sustained the great American stage actors of previous generations. The current ranks of 40-ish stage-trained American movie stars—Meryl Streep, William Hurt, Glenn Close, Kevin Kline, John Malkovich, etc.—all spent their formative years working out only a few feet from most people in the audience. No wonder they were able to move into film acting without transition. Their acting style had always been an intimate one. If anything, now the pendulum has swung in the opposite direction—the theatre is short on flamboyant, tempestuous, showoffy performers who can electrify a 1,500-seat house and long on subtle, superbly detailed, technically polished performers whose mortal fear is to be accused of overacting.

18.

The connection between eros and theatre goes very deep. Scratch the surface of ancient Greek theatre and you uncover phallic worship. The very art of acting, the practice of representing someone other than oneself, grew out of the religious rapture of Dionysiac devotees who, drunk on wine and frenzied from dancing in the mountains to flutes and drums, believed themselves to be satyrs and maenads, the fertility god's sacred herd making visible to others the ecstasy they experienced in their devotion. These rituals served a serious function in primitive society, whose members genuinely believed their sexual self-expression magically made the crops grow. When the science of agriculture revealed that things grew by other means than sexual magic, the ruling class would have liked to get rid of the Dionysiac rituals, but the peasantry clung to them as a release from the inhibitions of social repression.

The Dionysian drama festivals took their form directly from this social tension. The middle class sought to refine the intellectual content of the drama and remove it from direct contact with reality; thus evolved tragedy. Meanwhile, to satisfy the taste of the peasantry and the proletariat for the obscene and riotous behavior of primitive rituals, a satyr play—a burlesque variation on classic heroic tales—always accompanied the tragedies at festival time.

In the Greek imagination, satyrs are *daimones*, immortal beings with superhuman wisdom, yet at the same time they are wild creatures of the forest full of uninhibited desires. They are part beast and part god, mythological tributes to the phenomenon of sexuality no less celebrated than deities representing other human traits. Whenever in history theatre has been attacked or suppressed, it's usually been true that the prevailing culture viewed sexuality not as a joyous aspect of human life but as demonic, diabolical, the opposite of godliness, the antithesis of spirituality.

St. John Chrysostom condemned fifth-century Roman theatre as "naught but fornication, adultery, courtesan women, men pretending to be women, and soft-limbed boys." Clergyman John Northbrooke attacked Elizabethan theatre using the argument that it teaches people "howe to bee false and deceyve your husbandes, or husbandes their wives . . . to move to lustes, to ransacke and spoyle cities and townes, to bee ydle, to blaspheme, to sing filthie songes of love, to speak filthily, to be prowde, howe to mocke, scoffe and deryde any nation . . . ." In his famous 1697 pamphlet *A Short View of the Immorality and Profaneness of the English Stage*, the Rev. Jeremy Collier made the classic case for theatre not as an open-eyed reflection of human behavior but as a vehicle for moral tales whose business "is to recommend Vertue, and discountenance of Vice." Not content with holding the theatre responsible for the ills of society, Collier later blamed the theatre for causing a natural disaster, a two-day violent storm in 1703 that took lives and destroyed property.

This attitude has had some of its most virulent proponents in the United States. In the early 1800s, Yale president Timothy Dwight called actors "a nuisance in the earth, the very offal of society." Today, artists whose work deals with homoeroticism are publicly accused by televangelist Pat Robertson of using federal funds to teach taxpayers' "sons how to sodomize one another." And performance artist Karen Finley, whose shamanistic performances express feminist outrage at violence against women, has been reduced in public discourse to being described as "a nude, chocolate-smeared woman."

19.

The word "theatre" comes from the Greek work "theatron," meaning "a place for seeing." Heroic fantasies, spiritual visions, glimpses of the truth—these are what we hope to see. But what we actually see is the actor, the body that gives life to those visions we desire.

A theatre is among other things a temple of Eros, and when I enter I am looking for YOU.

20.

My desire for you (inevitably?) produces shame. I want to possess you, and I know I cannot, and I feel the violence of my passions rise within me. The taking of photographs and the use of recording devices can be hazardous for the performers and is prohibited by law in many states. Still, I want to take snapshots. I'm trying to possess your image while you're trying to move through a transcendent action. I feel guilty about this. I feel I am blaspheming your art. But I can't help myself.

Years later, when I see you in a play or on the street, I get a sharp feeling in my heart thinking of the first time I ever saw you. It was your first play in New York. You were still in high school. I remember the scene where you washed your mother's hair, and when you stood under a stark spotlight singing a fragment of a song. It always surprises me to hear you sing. You have a beautiful voice.

Maybe I feel guilty, too, because I don't tell you enough. If by some chance I'm in the lobby when you leave or someone introduces us,

I shake your hand and deliver my all-purpose benediction to actors: "Good work." To say more would be embarrassing; but to say so little feels like a betrayal, of myself and of you, of my appreciation and of my desire.

This desire between us must always be frustrated. You are the actor. I am the spectator. You play for me. I witness. That is the exchange. I go home, and my heart aches where you sliced it, with your performance, your intelligence, or your beauty, or your face, or the curve of your buttocks. You take off your makeup, you wash your face. If you're lucky, you have a mate to cling to or a fellow actor who shared your passion tonight. But maybe you, too, leave the theatre with an emptiness, a longing to complete the connection you made with me tonight.

But you don't know who I am.

Journalist and critic Don Shewey lives in New York City. He has published three books about theatre. His articles and essays have appeared in publications including the *New York Times*, the *Village Voice*, *Esquire* and *Rolling Stone*, as well as anthologies such as *The Politics of Manhood* and *Best Gay Erotica 2000*.

SCENES FROM A CENSORED LIFE

By Athol Fugard

November 1990

I am sure you will understand what I mean when I talk about that extremely significant moment when a writer discovers his own voice. About 27 years ago, when I was 30 years old, I had written only two apprenticeship works. I call them apprenticeship works because, like a good apprentice, I started off trying to master my craft by imitating masters. I followed those two plays with *Blood Knot*, which was one of the really major events in my career as a playwright—major in the sense that it was the end of my apprenticeship. I had discovered *what* I wanted to talk about and *how* I wanted to talk about it.

The actor Zakes Mokae and I started off in a little garret, a little space in Johannesburg, and put the play together. We sat our audience down on upturned fruit boxes to give *Blood Knot* its first life.

As it turned out, that play also gave Zakes and me the courage to believe we could, in fact, earn our livings in the theatre. Although it met with a lot of opposition in South Africa, disturbed a lot of people and brought a lot of fury down on our heads, it was a success. For months, it provided us with a living, and then it took us both out of the country. Eventually, I ended up back in my hometown, Port Elizabeth, ensconced in a little apartment on Bird Street and ready to start writing the next play.

One night there was a knock on my door. I ushered in a group of about six black men and women from New Brighton, the black township that is attached to Port Elizabeth. They had heard about the success of *Blood Knot* and knew it had involved a black man and a white man together on a theatre stage for the first time in South Africa.

They had come around to ask me if I would help them start a drama group. I groaned. I'm very selfish; I think all artists, in some way or the other, most probably are.

Being very jealous of my time and energy and resentful of anything that takes me away from what I want to do, I saw this appeal to my generosity as a sort of imposition. To pass on my knowledge to these people who could obviously only work in an amateur context, because there is no such thing as theatre in Port Elizabeth—there still isn't—was going to take time and energy away from the writing I wanted to do.

But being a good, guilty liberal, I agreed. That encounter led to the formation of Serpent Players—the group that is mentioned sometimes in my bios—and through them, I have been witness to the most extraordinary thing you can see if you are a practitioner of the spoken word. A people who had been silenced and gagged—who had endured throttles of every conceivable form, legal and physical, from prison cells and banning orders to legislation on statute books—discovered a voice through theatre. They discovered a way of speaking about the world in which they lived, and found that theatre offered them—sometimes at considerable cost—the opportunity to talk aloud instead of whisper secretly to each other.

Bertolt Brecht says that a human being conquers his fate the moment he starts to make a noise about it. And obviously, the most supreme noise a human being can make is the spoken word. After the crying comes the word, the articulated word.

As regards the politics of South Africa, I had sort of muddled through instinctively during the years prior to the night that the knock came on my door. My ideas were half-formed; my sense of responsibility still only vaguely developed. I was groping for clarity when I started with the Serpent Players. Three of the men in the company, because of their work in the theatre, ended up imprisoned on Robin Island with Nelson Mandela for part of their lives. Whatever morality I have finally acquired, whatever responsibility informs my work in theatre, comes from the realization that we were at the center of a historical event of extraordinary importance.

When I started with *Blood Knot*, apartheid wasn't the defined philosophic and legal structure it eventually became. It wasn't the chamber of horrors—no, the mansion of horrors—which we are now in the process of dismantling. At that point, there was no legal structure. There was, however, a clearly defined traditional South African way of life which had built into it all that was evil and awful in terms of segregating people into different categories—preferred, lesser preferred and despised—on the basis of skin color.

Even in that context, censorship was there, but it was loosely defined. As successive nationalist party governments laid down the foundations and defined apartheid in legal terms, censorship became more concrete. We eventually ended up with a very strict and powerful legal censorship system that made it possible for virtually anybody to stop a show. All the authorities needed was for one member of the public who had seen a play, viewed an exhibition of paintings, read a book or watched a film to lodge a protest with the publications control board. The board would then put that play or that exhibition or that book into a sort of limbo—close it to the public—while it was examined by a duly appointed censorship board. That board would then decide whether or not it was fit for public consumption.

If the work was found unfit, it was closed down permanently. Even under those circumstances, the niceties were observed; you were allowed to appeal to higher authorities. In some remarkable cases, appeals were successful. Even in the darkest times of South African history, the highest level of our judiciary has enjoyed a degree of independence.

It was in this way, for example, that plays of mine like *"Master Harold"... and the boys*—a recent work which was banned outright initially—was finally allowed to go into production. We appealed successfully—we had better lawyers than they did! There were other ways to get around censorship as well. I refused to put *Sizwe Bansi Is Dead* down on paper for the first six months of its life. The actors, John Kani and Winston Ntshona, and I memorized it. When the government asked for a copy of the script, I said there wasn't one. They would have put us out of business. I believe that dissident writers in the U.S.S.R. have resorted to memory as a way of keeping certain texts alive. But I shouldn't draw comparisons, because every form of Hell is unique in its own way.

The reality of censorship under which we operated was three-pronged: Ideas of a political nature were obviously dangerous. But in some senses, the control over political content paled in comparison to the absolute frothing at the mouth and rabid detestation of anything that was—as they defined it—blasphemous or pornographic. In the final analysis, I think I ran into more trouble because of deliberate crudities in language and my questioning of the Calvinist religious ethics of my country than I did for the political content of my plays.

And then finally, there were also the double standards. I'm a bastard white South African, meaning I had a mother who was an Afrikaner and a father who was an English-speaking South African, as we call them. I'm at home in both languages, but I instinctively chose at a very early point to write in English because I think it is the more powerful instrument. I couldn't write now in the Afrikaans language if I wanted to. In that sense, my identity is an English-speaking writer, although I know my soul is that of an Afrikaner.

Under the censorship laws of the past, the board of control was much harder on Afrikaners than it was on English-speaking writers. And that is understandable; the traitor from within is always infinitely more dangerous than the enemy on the outside, particularly to the old-style Afrikaner with his closed, wagons-pulled-in-a-circle mentality. By comparison, the black writer was even more severely dealt with than the white writer.

I recognize that on a lot of scores, I had a relatively easy time of it as a writer in South Africa. But even so, the question of censorship remained. I knew we would be in trouble if we tried to do our plays publicly. That was certainly the case with *Sizwe Bansi*. For a couple of years, our performances in South Africa of this play were all underground, even though John Kani and Winston Ntshona had played on Broadway stages in America and West End theatres in London.

Coming back to South Africa from New York and London, we were still too scared for quite a long time to take our plays out and make them public. We eventually felt—and as it turned out, we were right—that the reputation the work had acquired overseas afforded us a degree of protection.

One of the first areas in which South Africa felt the wind of change was in theatre and the arts, generally. The arts were regarded as so innocuous in the overall South African situation that the government decided to let artists have a measure of freedom. The truth of the matter is that for the past six or seven years there has been no segregation in audiences and no segregation on stages. I think this was as an attempt at window dressing—an effort to persuade the outside world that our society had started to change significantly.

In South Africa, art through the dark years was a survival kit. It kept alive a sense of decency. It kept alive a few ideas which the system was trying its best to obliterate. Our battle with censorship over the past 30 years might have some relevance to the very serious situation that I understand American theatre is facing at this point.

The forms of censorship that threaten and already exist in your country are infinitely more sophisticated than those I faced. In talking to young American writers, I have discovered that they envy the simplicity of the South African confrontation. Standing up and being counted in that society if you choose to do so is very brutally simple— there are no gray areas.

Let's use the big word—that powerful word that Martin Luther King Jr. used—vision. An extraordinary vision was defined by America quite a way back. And I have a sense that your society has arrived at an extremely critical moment in its life when yet another explosion and enlargement of that vision must take place. There are pent-up forces in your society as dark and dangerous as any that have threatened my country. Artists need to exercise a high degree of vigilance to make sure that nothing compromises their work.

Which brings me to another real danger—self-censorship. I became most aware of this danger when I started to write *Boseman and Lena*. At that point, the South African government had taken my passport away and refused to allow me to leave the country—which was actually their way, I think, of trying to get me to leave the country permanently on a one-way ticket. I was made aware of the consequences of saying things. And I became aware that I was watching the hand that was putting down the words, and that sometimes that hand paused.

I also realized, thank God, that if I ever allowed that moment of hesitation to lead to the self-censoring of a thought or an idea, then, as a writer, I would be as good as dead. If there was one area of my life in which I had to operate in context of total freedom, it had to be when I was writing.

Having exercised that freedom to its maximum, I could leave the director and the actor to deal with its consequences. It's a different story when a text—which has hopefully come out of a context of total personal freedom and frank self-confrontation—moves first into a rehearsal room and then onto a stage to confront audiences. When you are writing for yourself at your desk, you can say anything you like. You will never offend yourself—it's impossible, a contradiction in terms. But when you start to put your work on stage, you've made a commitment to an act of communication *with others.*

And it's a freedom that's not just unique to writers. The actor also needs that freedom in confronting himself in that very private inner-dialogue as he prepares for a role. The director and designer, for that matter, need as great a freedom as a writer. The moment of freedom when we deal with ourselves—that attempt to be free of all forms of self-censorship—is critical in all creative endeavors.

I've had a couple of disturbing experiences in the course of writing and presenting my most recent play, *My Children! My Africa!* I hope that they don't reflect anything more than just a passing phase, but I would be dishonest if I didn't share them with you. In the course of writing, I suddenly realized that my pen—and I'm not being metaphorical, I do write with a pen—had paused, was hesitating, once again. But this time it had paused not because I was frightened of what the government was going to say to me; but because I was wondering what the radical left was going to say.

I realized as I wrote I was on the point of saying things that might be resented by The Struggle, exactly as in the old days when I was saying things that might be resented by the government. As it turned out, I again got rid of my pausing and went on to write the play just as I wanted.

Ultimately, there has been a very powerful response from my people—white, black, brown—to *My Children! My Africa!* I know how it has spoken to my people, and I realize I shouldn't have paused.

Another moment came when I handed an early draft to John Kani, whom I wanted to play one of the roles. I asked him to read the play and tell me if he wanted to do it.

By way of his extraordinary talent and the enormous success he has had in South Africa itself and overseas, John has become a role model and hero to a lot of young South Africans, black and white. When John and Winston Ntshona came to the Serpent Players, John had been working on the assembly line of a Ford factory, and Winston was a laborer in another factory. They came to me and said, "We want to earn our livings in the theatre." I laughed—you had to know South Africa to fully realize the degree of stupidity that statement involved— but they persisted. The degree of stupidity turned out to be mine. Within three years, they were indeed earning their living as actors because we had established an underground circuit, eventually gone overseas, and were making money. From those beginnings, John went on to become a Tony Award–winner.

I offered John the role of Mr. M., the schoolteacher in *My Children! My Africa!*, a character who in an act of tragic desperation becomes a police informer. Being a good actor, he smelled the role of his lifetime. But he had reservations. How could he—a hero of the people—play a government collaborator? He asked his children to sit down at the table, told them what I wanted him to do, and asked how they would feel if they saw their father on stage as a man who goes to the police and informs on his people.

I'm not qualified to explore John's psychology in terms of the way he cleared his various hurdles. All 1 know is that he tells of how it all came to a burning focus one night. Having read the play again and again, he put the script at his bedside, turned off the light, and went to sleep.

When he opened his eyes the next morning, the sun was shining outside his window. He woke up and said, "Good morning, Mr. M." In the course of that night's sleep—that night's journey of his subconscious—he had come to terms with something and made his commitment. His doubts and anxieties helped him bring great depth to the soul of a character who comes out of an appalling dilemma and makes a tragic mistake. In confronting the psychological hurdles which he had to clear in order to embrace the character, I think John ended up giving the kind of compassionate performance that could not have been achieved had there not been an enormous personal conflict to overcome in order to make the commitment.

I'm sure you understand what I'm getting at. Conflict generates passion that leads to a depth of commitment in performing or writing. John's fears were groundless. My fears were groundless. But they were indicative of a danger that is present in any society that is going through a process of radical change.

I personally could never accept any limitation to my freedom as a writer. I would like to believe that is true for all artists of any sort.

I have been told that as a white man, I cannot fully comprehend or appreciate what the black reality is. My plays have earned me a degree of anger and resentment, both inside South Africa and out, because I have on occasions been described as a spokesman for black South Africa. And I try to make a very clear and coherent response to that. First, I have tried to be nobody's spokesman. I have never assumed that I have the authority to stand up and speak politically for any other human being, or certainly for any group of human beings.

I *have* gone about the business of telling stories, and I have trusted that whatever political animal I am would emerge in the course of telling those stories which come out of my response to South Africa— feelings of love, anger, outrage and pity. I never start off writing a play thinking, "Now if there's *one* message that society needs at this moment . . . ." The situation in South Africa is so highly politicized that the notion of South African stories without political consequence or resonance is a contradiction in terms. Even if told willy-nilly, the story will end up revealing and expressing whatever political convictions and whatever political profile I have as a *human being*.

I can't separate Fugard from South Africa. Because I've mastered the code of one time and place, I can stand on a street corner in Port Elizabeth—even to a certain extent in Johannesburg or Cape Town— and put together the stories of the people I see. That barefoot black lady with the shopping bag and the shoes sticking out? I know where she comes from and where she's probably going. That businessman in the motor car? I know him, too. I've cracked the code.

To write about another man's reality if he's got a black skin is no greater a challenge to my imagination than to write about a woman's reality. Surely the differences that separate me as a man (and part of me as a male chauvinist) from the reality of what it means to be a woman requires as great a leap for my imagination as do those barriers between white and black that I am confronted with daily in South Africa.

People who judge me in any other way are dismissing my work because of the color of my skin, not the quality of my imagination. I do examine myself very ruthlessly on this score. My final belief is that my work *must* be judged on the quality of my imagination. And I claim it is my right as an artist to try to make the leap in any direction I choose.

You can tell me that I failed. But don't tell me that I can't make that leap.

South African playwright Athol Fugard's work has been widely produced in South Africa and London, on Broadway and across the United States. *The New Yorker* **has called him "a rare playwright who could be a primary candidate for either the Nobel Prize in Literature or the Nobel Peace Prize." This article is based on Fugard's presentation at Theatre Communications Group's National Conference, held in June '90 at Smith College in Northampton, Mass.**

FACING THE MUSIC

By Harold Prince as told to Ira Weitzman

February 1991

Today, most people are accustomed to the craft of modern musical theatre. When I first saw shows as a kid, however, Broadway was far more primitive—and far more popular. I hated musicals. I thought they were mindless. I liked the music—it was jolly—but the books were damned foolishness. Perhaps I felt that way because I had been weaned on intensely theatrical productions. My first experiences with live theatre were Orson Welles's Mercury Theatre production of *Julius Caesar* and Maxwell Anderson's *Winterset*.

In the musicals that I was taken to see on Saturday afternoons, the books were there just to string together a lot of swell songs. The lyrics of these songs were written for popular purposes, not to advance the story or dig psychologically into the characters who were singing them.

I vividly remember a 1939 show called *Too Many Girls*. It was a George Abbott musical in which—just to give you an idea of the depth of plots in those days—the heroine came out wearing a little beanie. At the end of the first act, half of the girls on stage wore them, half didn't.

Somebody, probably Desi Arnaz, turned to Van Johnson and said, "Why is she wearing a beanie and they're not?" The answer was, "Well, she's a virgin." The audience fell on the floor. I was a little kid and I have been told—although I don't remember it—that I asked in a loud voice, "What's a virgin?" They got a second laugh they weren't expecting.

You can figure out the rest of the plot of that show easily. In the second act, the heroine came out without her beanie and the audience went to pieces.

There was also a wartime musical called *Something for the Boys*. In that show, Ethel Merman got graphite in her teeth and was able to pick up radio messages from spies through her mouth. That was its plot.

Surprisingly, I no longer ridicule these shows. As a matter of fact, as I grow older, I find I'm trading in a little of my persistent no-fun-at-all seriousness for a little foolishness. Times do change.

Along with their very lightweight libretti and wonderful songs, those early shows starred performers who sang and/or danced, but rarely both. There were exceptions, of course, such as Gertrude Lawrence, who didn't do either terribly well but had enormous charm, stage presence and charisma.

Then there was the chorus: either a singing chorus or a dancing chorus, about 14 of each. At that time you could afford people just to dance or sing while the book waited in the wings. When you finished with a production number, you always closed the traveler, and the conductor raised his arms and played what we called utility music. The audience patiently and happily sat there listening to "Lady Be Good!" or whatever while the scenery was changed upstage—sometimes rather noisily.

It was a different and more innocent time, and these musicals were the only ball game in town. When did it all start to change?

It's been said that the acerbic tone for the books of musicals was set with *Pal Joey* in 1941. But surely the first modern musical was 1927's *Show Boat*. On the other hand, the minute you accept *Show Boat* as such, you're making a connection with Vienna and the great operettas. (Musical comedies, operettas and operas are not so easy to pigeonhole.)

I believe the most dramatic change in musical stagecraft came in 1949 with *South Pacific*. Joshua Logan invented the continuous musical. I happened to be lucky enough to be there on opening night. I had just gotten a job as an office boy in George Abbott's office, and he was there as well. The next morning I went to work with a grin on my face and said, "Wasn't that something?" Abbott said, "Just remember that what you saw last night was epoch-making."

What Logan had done was to devise scrim travelers that went all the way across the stage. They were two deep, so that he was able to continue the story in front of one traveler, work simultaneously between the two, and change the scenery behind the second. That was innovative—all those sailors and marines crossing the stage, keeping the plot on course. Modern musicals were on their way.

When *My Fair Lady* opened in 1956, for example, there were old-fashioned stage waits with utility music. However, some years later when it was revised, they kept the action continuous.

Until the '50s, chorus people were singers or dancers. Then it was demanded they begin to cross over. By the time *West Side Story* was in rehearsal in '57, Jerome Robbins insisted that everyone do everything. Principal singers danced and dancing principals sang and everyone tried to act.

So, what emerged with the knowledge of all this craft was the seamless musical. Ironically, perhaps, we suffer today from too many people knowing how to do it seamlessly and not enough with anything on their minds. To further complicate things, there are many people out there (critics included) who long for the mindless musical. I submit that if we consciously set out to create mindless musicals, we would have to fail. History has changed the way we look at the musical. Today we expect songs to be motivated and books to have substance as well as structure.

Each of us defines substance differently. I've read enough about how I've taken away the fun in musicals. Perhaps. But my idea of fun is getting involved—staying awake in the damn theatre, for one thing! Simply put, you get mindless entertainment elsewhere, and you get it free.

What makes the popular musical unique? Well, not technology, that's for sure. Certainly not high-tech effects or mixed media. Remember holography and lasers? That was supposed to be the wave of the future.

The black box, the empty space that links the audience and the stage in collaboration, and simple stagecraft—at the right moment—can create a profound effect. Among the best reactions I've ever gotten in a show is in *Phantom of the Opera* when the young lover jumps from a bridge into a hole in the stage. Audiences have gasped from the first moment it happened. Why? The story's good! And his jumping from a bridge comes at a moment of palpable tension. Thirty-four people jumping simultaneously into holes in the stage wouldn't do a thing for the audience if the story didn't hold.

So musicals have gotten more and more finely crafted and at the same time soulless—accomplished and soulless.

Directors have had to fill a void in the musical's development, and I don't feel good about this. The word remains the most important element; but it is very difficult to find good writers willing to write musicals. To get a serious, accomplished playwright into the musical theatre is a neat trick. I have invited a lot of them over many years and more often than not have failed to hook them.

Hugh Wheeler was one of the exceptions. He had written two or three wonderful dramas which had failed at the box office and perhaps 150 detective novels. By the time we met, he was more than ready to make a living in the theatre writing libretti. It must have bothered him that as good as his book for a musical was, if the production wasn't up to par, he was the one who took the brickbats. Only those of us working on musicals know how important books are.

My preferred way of working is to start a project rather than come into the process after the book has been written or the score composed. It's much better starting with the idea. Once the authors have an outline for perhaps the better part of the first act, I assign a choreographer and a designer. I think one of my strongest contributions as a director is defining the motor of a show, how it moves, what its energy level will be. And that has a great deal to do with the production scheme as well.

Take *Company*, for example. It's a show defined by space. By looking at Boris Aronson's set, reading the script and listening to the score, you can see how important an influence space had on the behavior of the piece. Boris was fond of saying about his sets that they didn't exist without people on them.

The idea for *Follies* developed in a different way. Originally, the show was called *The Girls Upstairs*. It had been conceived and written by Jim Goldman and Stephen Sondheim as a realistic study of a group of people gathering for a reunion in the theatre. There were to have been some tables and chairs, waiters and waitresses, food and drink during a party that was to last the length of the play, perhaps two-and-a-half hours. Four principals were to get drunk, re-examine their marriages, consider the failure in their lives and then either accept compromise and reunite or separate.

The energetic moment in the musical was a fight between the two husbands carrying stage-prop spears when they were drunk. For me, that was all too realistic. I felt no compassion for the people, and I didn't want to spend an evening with them. It needed a larger canvas, a metaphor. It needed to be hallucinatory, absurdist, surrealistic. I suggested that the leading characters were more interesting when they were young than in the present; that perhaps the way to develop compassion for them was to see them before the disenchantment set in, before they'd developed a protective coating, before the bitterness. So we decided to animate their alter egos, which Jim and Steve did brilliantly. The juxtaposition of the past and present became the motor of the show, and co-director Michael Bennett and I took full advantage of it.

I was as proud of *Follies* as anything I have ever been a part of. Yet *Follies* lost all of its investment—which didn't matter a damn. There was a time when you could make a life in the theatre on Broadway, fail on Broadway and learn on Broadway. You were given a first-class production to show off your words, your performance and your direction. And if that production failed, you did another until you got it right. Kander and Ebb's first show was a disaster, their second a hit. I produced both of them. Sondheim's first show failed; his second succeeded.

The other day, sitting on a committee examining the future of the musical, a colleague referred to a new writer as "awfully young." "How old is awfully young?" I asked. "Twenty-six," he replied. I pointed out that Betty Comden, Leonard Bernstein and Jerome Robbins were 26 when they created *On the Town*; that Sondheim was 26 when he wrote the lyrics for *West Side Story*. I was 26 when I co-produced *The Pajama Game*. It used to be the right age to get started. But not anymore.

The economic crunch is such that we can't fight it. If you have to raise $5 or 6 million to make a mistake, you're going to be allowed only one mistake.

For example, I directed *Roza* at CENTERSTAGE in Baltimore and then at the Mark Taper Forum in Los Angeles. I was interested in the problems presented by a musical that takes place on four floors of a tenement. I remember on the first days of rehearsal repeating to the authors that it was not a Broadway show—that it was an audience show, but would never get past the critics. That wasn't important to me, and furthermore, maybe the copyright would be worth something even if it didn't play on Broadway. After all, it was a one-set musical with a small cast and no chorus.

We opened in Baltimore and sold out every performance. In Los Angeles, the run was extended from six to nine weeks. There were production contracts for Germany, Scandinavia and Paris. Flushed with the success on the road, we came to Broadway after all . . . and closed, possibly with the worst set of reviews I never read. The foreign contracts were canceled, and as of this moment, the copyright has no value.

Similarly, had I worked on Broadway for popular success, there would have been no *Pacific Overtures*. A musical about the acculturation of the Japanese with an all Japanese cast and in the kabuki style isn't going to run three years!

Of course there were advantages to moving *Pacific Overtures* to Broadway, even for only five-and-a-half months. After all, Broadway remains our window for the rest of the world. And because it was seen on Broadway, there have been other productions. Last year it was in the repertory of the English National Opera.

Don't get me wrong, I'm an optimist; you have to be to work in the musical theatre. But you also have to be a realist, and no one in his right mind thinks that the future of the American musical lies on Broadway or in the West End. Today the conventional route to Broadway for non-musical theatre has been Off Broadway or the regional theatre, and some chamber-sized musicals have followed the same path. But how many regional theatres are equipped to produce full-scale musicals?

I worry that because of the success of Lynn Ahrens and Stephen Flaherty's *Once on This Island* and William Finn's *Falsettoland*, the accepted agenda on the part of the press and many commercial producers and theatre owners will be that all musicals can be initially produced on postage stamp–sized stages and on a shoestring, which in my opinion brings us back to the workshopping mentality. This year's big hit, *City of Angels*, could not have been produced in such an environment, nor could *Les Misérables*.

It is depressing to redefine an art form because of the strictures imposed on it by economics.

It is one thing to curtail the size of a cast from 50 to 30; it is another to cut it to 14. And cutting an orchestra of 26 to 14 can be savaging. We have an obligation to release Sondheim and artists like him from the confinements of a chamber musical, to restore 35 people to the stage and 26 musicians to the pit.

It is time to create institutions across this country equipped to do full-scale musicals.

These things that concern me should concern theatre owners who exercise an unhealthy control over the Broadway theatre. They keep lamenting the "lack of product." The average Broadway musical of my youth may have been primitive, less ambitious, but at least it was never called product.

Director and producer Harold Prince has won 20 Tony Awards, including a lifetime achievement award in 2006, and received the National Medal of Arts in 2000 from President Clinton. As a director, he premiered the musicals *She Loves Me*, *Cabaret*, *Company*, *Follies*, *Candide*, *Pacific Overtures*, *A Little Night Music*, *Sweeney Todd*, *Evita*, *The Phantom of the Opera*, *Parade*, *Bounce* and *LoveMusik*. Among the plays he has directed are *Hollywood Arms*, *The Visit*, *The Great God Brown*, *End of the World*, *Play Memory* and his own play, *Grandchild of Kings*.

Ira Weitzman is currently the musical theatre associate producer for Lincoln Center Theater. This article is based on an April '89 interview and appears in longer form in the winter '91 issue of the *Journal*, a publication of the Stage Directors and Choreographers Foundation.

ISLANDS IN THE MAINSTREAM

By David Henry Hwang

October 1991

One impression I took away from last summer's *Miss Saigon* contro-versy, which centered on British producer Cameron Mackintosh's casting of the Welsh actor Jonathan Pryce as a character of "Eurasian" descent, is of the confusion and anger which permeate our nation today. I, along with many others, argued for the casting of an Asian American. When Actors' Equity denied Pryce's application for American employment, Mackintosh canceled the show, and the op-ed pieces and letters roared in. That a relatively esoteric dispute about minority casting should end up making headlines all the way to Moscow is in itself amazing. Certain issues, however, become lightning rods for larger tensions in society, and I believe that this accounts partly for the debate's intense, if momentary, hold on the American psyche. For ours is a nation struggling towards a radical redefinition of self, born of demographics and the faceless jottings of census-takers.

By now, we are all aware that America is rapidly evolving into a country with no single racial majority. Some call it the birth of the first "one-world" nation. Others refer to the "Balkanization" of society, and foresee the coming of a "New Tribalism." There is certainly as much fear and anger as hope, and even optimists like me are slowly realizing this will be no easy transition. Against such a backdrop, the idea of "multiculturalism," once used to advocate the inclusion of diverse voices into the cultural landscape, may be worth re-examining. For it is no longer a question of whether this nation will become multicultural; statistical inevitability tells us as much. Rather, the focus of the debate could more profitably shift to how these multiple voices might best come to interact with one another. And, the manner in which our art and artists relate to multiculturalism may well reflect and even prefig-ure the workings of society as a whole.

Our examinations must first recognize the fact that there does exist a vocal group who feel particularly threatened by the notion of previously disenfranchised groups gaining real power, artistic or otherwise. This faction is indulging a sentimental attachment to the mono-cultural past, while attempting to give their very human insecurities intellectual credibility by styling themselves into advocates of "stan-dards." To these apostles of Cultural Correctness (or C.C.), multicul-turalism threatens artistic excellence by demanding that theatres pro-duce works of inferior quality simply to satisfy some affirmative action agenda. Many state openly that the greatness of this society is built upon Western ideals, and this invasion of other perspectives threatens our future. Still others suggest that writers who choose to concentrate on characters of one ethnic group are somehow limited.

The stridency of the advocates of C.C. saddens me, because I feel that theirs is a philosophy which ultimately devalues the potential for human growth. In academia, for instance, some object to Stanford University's new world-cultures requirement, which adds to the cur-riculum courses on non-Western history and civilizations; detractors argue this will force students to absorb works and ideas of lesser quality. How cynical to regard learning as a pie of fixed size, where knowledge in one area detracts from some other. The same individuals who might easily agree that travel is a broadening experience seem to revert to petty provincialism when this same principle is applied to intellectual and artistic journeys.

If August Wilson is limited as a playwright because he focuses on African-American culture, then so too must be George Bernard Shaw, Tennessee Williams, Harold Pinter and others who draw from the soil of some particular society. Surely the artistic principle that universality derives from the skillful observation of specifics must apply to all human beings, regardless of race. If not, then the promoters of C.C. are advocating a kind of artistic apartheid, where access to institutions is limited to a shrinking white population on the basis of some self-defined inherent superiority. I first experienced Cultural Correctness as a young boy: Friends of my parents argued the 5,000-year-old Chinese civilization was superior to all others. Even at the time, I suggested that such myopia probably contributed to China's decline as a world power, which did not endear me to them. Now, I see the current batch of C.C. proponents as American reincarnations of the old Manchu emperors, who ruined a nation in order to preserve its standards.

That the motivations of the Culturally Correct are rooted in fear and insecurity does not preclude them from making some valid obser-vations. Many had a field day during the *Miss Saigon* ruckus, holding up the controversy as a battle between artistic freedom and minorities seeking to legislate affirmative action. I was surprised by how quickly the spark of debate raged into a fire, with camps hardened against one another and little opportunity for meaningful dialogue. That the imag-ination of the larger public seized upon the issue testifies to barely hid-den currents of anger and resentment that run through many segments of society. For about two weeks, I felt I had become a character in *The Bonfire of the Vanities*. From this vantage point, I came to realize that, simply put, virtually everyone feels "ripped off." Minorities know in their hearts that their opportunities have been circumscribed by racism, while many Anglos know deep in theirs that they have become the current victims of racism in the form of affirmative action. To call this a recipe for unrest is to understate the obvious.

In such a volatile climate, opportunities for a sensitive exchange about the complexities of minority casting, for constructive acknowledgment of the fully 90 percent of stage productions in this country which still employ all-Anglo casts, all became impossible. An us-versus-them mentality developed, fueled by the fact that many groups in our country neither trust nor understand one another. One year later, upon reflection, I also indict myself, feeling that my own frustrations as an Asian American manifested themselves in a belligerent tone in my early statements, which fed the general bunker mentality. I have become shy to take a legislative attitude which says to any actor, "No, you cannot play this part." Rather, I'd prefer an approach in which both sides recognize that producers have the right to cast whomever they want, but those who don't like it have the right to protest as loudly as they want and expect a responsible hearing. And, under such conditions, I yearn for a mode of dialogue which will bypass the defensiveness and anger represented by symbols of race.

In order to begin such a dialogue, we must start to build bridges of trust and understanding. This, I believe, is where the very art about which we argue can serve as a path to some solution. For what better way to attempt an exchange of the often painful views we hold of one another than through the creation of a new world together? It is more intimate today to hold a frank discussion about race with someone of different ethnicity than to sleep with that person. We need to search for some slim reeds of trust on which to initiate an act of communication. Perhaps respect for one another as artists can serve as that fragile beginning.

I hope to see a growth in cross-cultural explorations which will expand our personal, political and artistic boundaries. As an Asian, I've read enough bad haiku poetry in English to know that the form of an attempt does not in itself lead to deeper understanding. As a man, I look at some of my own failed attempts at women characters and realize that I have often fallen short in making those leaps of understanding necessary to comprehend the "other." On the occasions when I have succeeded, however, through sensitivity and openness and a willingness to learn, I have grown not only as an artist, but also as a human being.

The works that excite me most today are those that try, with greater or lesser success, to transcend racial boundaries. Spike Lee's ability to empathize with both sides of a war between African Americans and Italian Americans, or John Guare grappling with a clash of class and culture in *Six Degrees of Separation*, represent attempts to go beyond traditional definitions of multiculturalism into a sort of interculturalism that recognizes both our differences and the essential oneness of our evolving national partnership. I would like to see commissions awarded for collaborations between people of different backgrounds, whose artistic spirits recognize an innate kinship.

Granted, the attempt to write about or create with members of other races will be fraught with difficulty and false starts. Many writers,

I believe, refrain from tackling "ethnic" characters for fear they will inadvertently discover stereotypes they may not have even realized existed somewhere in their minds. There will be criticism and charges of racism, but out of all this may come some excellent work. In general, it has been easier for members of minority groups to write about Euro-Americans than the reverse, simply because people of color have had to understand the Anglo power structure just to survive. As this traditional system of dominance breaks down, the burden of sensitivity will have to become more equally distributed; the arts are an excellent place to begin such a transition.

When I attended college in the late 1970s, "assimilation" was a dirty word. To assimilate meant to cast aside one's own ethnic identity and pathetically mimic the white man. While this objection had much to recommend it, it always sidestepped an important reality—mainstream American culture had already become inseparably linked with all of the ethnic communities. For example, there exists no such thing as a "pure" Asian-American culture divorced from the context of its wider American influences. Nonetheless, it was useful for minorities to emphasize their differences with Anglos so as not to aspire toward cultural models they could never truly become. In an intercultural age, however, we can aim for a Dynamic Assimilation, whereby all ethnic groups influence one another with equal authority. Under such conditions, the mainstream would continue to change us, but we would more actively be reshaping the mainstream in our own images. In this way, America might slowly evolve something new: a world culture, inclusive of all the diverse peoples of this nation.

If the interculturalism I am proposing sounds little more than a New Age version of those "love one another" clichés from the Pollyanna 1960s, I acknowledge the similarities, but beg one important difference. In order for interculturalism to be constructive, it must be preceded by genuine multiculturalism. One weakness of '60s liberalism lay in the inability of Euro-America to ultimately cede control over the political agenda. Only as people of color in this country start to gain real power, as minorities collectively become the majority, as race becomes as painful an issue for Anglos as it has always been for the rest of us, only then will an equality of needs develop which will force us to discover our essential commonality.

Against such a backdrop, the current diatribes of the Culturally Correct ring especially hollow. As they cloak themselves in rhetoric about freedom of speech and expression, they sidestep the question of whether or not the monocultural society they remember so fondly was actually such a beacon of liberty. When accusing minorities of denigrating freedom, they are in effect demanding that we exercise our new and limited powers more responsibly than Euro-America did its old monopoly.

What did I learn from the *Miss Saigon* controversy? In a nation where artistic life has so often been seen as escapist or out of touch with the concerns of the populace, ordinary people can indeed become passionate about aesthetic issues. Witness the popular debate that swirls around the films *Jungle Fever* and *Thelma and Louise*, around photographer Robert Mapplethorpe and the National Endowment for the Arts, around Sinead O'Connor and the rap group N.W.A.—and realize that the political and the personal have unambiguously come together. It is sometimes said that artists in America have enjoyed so much freedom because they have never been taken seriously. Both these assumptions are now open to question. An evolving America is struggling for redefinition, and one role of the artist has always been to give a culture its names. As we move together into the next century, perhaps the current vogue for multiculturalism will give birth to an interculturalism which will help us see ourselves anew.

David Henry Hwang's 2007 play *Yellow Face* is a mock documentary of his experience following the *Miss Saigon* controversy. He is the author of *M. Butterfly*, *Golden Child* and *FOB*, among other plays, and the book writer for the musicals *Tarzan*, *Aida* and the revised *Flower Drum Song*. His opera libretti include three works by composer Philip Glass, *1000 Airplanes on the Roof*, *The Voyage* and *The Sound of a Voice*.

WILSON, DANTON AND ME

By Richard Thomas

July/August 1993

At the Alley Theatre in Houston, Robert Wilson loosed his imagination on *Danton's Death*, Georg Büchner's brilliant descant on morality, meaning and meaninglessness. Set during the French Revolution's Reign of Terror, the play sets up an impassioned debate between the hedonistic reformer Danton and his nemesis, the fanatically rational Robespierre. For the role of Danton, Wilson cast Richard Thomas. His physical dissimilarity to the large bullish historical Danton, and his experience in the roles of Hamlet and Peer Gynt, made Thomas an interesting choice for the project. After the production, Thomas worked with Alley dramaturg Christopher Baker to record his reflections of the play, the production and working with Robert Wilson.

The actor's work on *Danton's Death* began in June '92, in a three-week workshop that Wilson labeled Phase B. At the end of the workshop the company spent two days on stage, where a full-scale mock-up of the set was installed for the bauprobe, or scenic rehearsal. Phase A—the design conferences held in April—resulted in a series of storyboard sketches, a "visual book," which would serve as the foundation for all of the work to follow. These sketches covered one wall of the rehearsal room during the workshop and rehearsal process and provided an architectural and spatial scheme for the entire play. The actors knew, for instance, the play of light and dark in a scene, whether the space was open or closed, and an indication of where the objects and even the actors might be in that space.

Before coming to Houston, I began trying to find ways into the role. I thought of Danton as a kind of "Natural Man" among the Revolution's politicians, idealists and dogmatists. He has been called a passive character, but I did not—could not—think of him that way. He is, rather, trapped between a nihilistic worldview and a passionate love of life—one moment letting go, surrendering to the tidal wave of history, and the next engaged and fighting. Never still, he is continually changing, at times even in a matter of lines, of words.

Danton faces a great contemporary dilemma between private identity and social identity, between what he wants as a human being and what he does as an icon of the Revolution. We have this dilemma in our own lives. Of course this tension between the private individual and the individual in society has existed throughout history. It produces an isolation, an aloneness. In the opening scene Danton's wife says, "You know me, don't you Danton?" And he replies, "I know I've touched you many times. I've tried to reach into you, to rub through your skin, but our skins are so thick and in the end we're as lonely as ever."

So in June we came together to work on this fragmented, disjointed (and very wordy) play. Most of us had never worked with Bob before. We had certain notions of what the production would be like, but not the process. After reading through the play, we immediately got "on our feet." For each scene, Bob worked with the actors to create the movements, usually with an idea of how many moves it should contain or how long it should be. We worked without the text, adhering to all the requirements of the scene—who enters, who leaves, how many are in the room, what is happening—but the creation of this movement was not generated by specific lines. We created more or less an abstract movement sequence that had its own life, its own rhythms.

After these movements were created they were numbered and learned, as one would learn a dance. Then we spoke the text while doing the movements. Sometimes the words and gestures reinforced each other, sometimes they had nothing to do with one another, and sometimes the pairings revealed something new and extraordinary, some third idea between gesture and text.

What Bob wants to avoid is illustration, the movements being secondary to the text. He often said that what is seen should stand on its own in the same way that the text does. We didn't rely on psychology and emotional response to provide the "appropriate" or "required" gestures. Working within the framework of this new pairing of text and movement, we made adjustments, alterations, and eventually began to make sense of how these words and gestures went together. The pairing could not seem arbitrary. We very much had to "suit the action to the word and the word to the action," but not in a behaviorally realistic relationship, since the actions were not generated by the words.

The wonderful and surprising thing about this method is that I felt a great freedom as well as a great sense of purpose. I had the movements and the text—separately created and equally important—and I was in the middle, required to perform a kind of alchemy to bond them together and eventually transform them into something else completely.

It was, also surprisingly, a very relaxed process. Many of the things an actor usually has to work out—How do I come in? How do I leave? What am I thinking as I do all these things?—were approached in purely theatrical, often utilitarian, terms. We spent time working on the technical aspects of walking, or entering—finding the correct placement of body weight, or the exact number of steps required to arrive in the same place every time.

This method of working was new to most of us, but because we worked pretty much the same way on each scene, we always knew how to begin. There was no question of mental or artistic blocks. We could look at the sketches to see what the space looked like. Within that framework we would continually adjust our moves, our line-readings, our gestures. We tried something, and if it seemed right it stayed and if not we changed it. And if it was too soon to tell, it was too soon to tell; we didn't worry about it. Bob had very clear ideas about some things, but he also relied on input from the entire company. The actors always had a voice, always had a vote, sometimes literally: "How many of you like the box in this position? How many in the other?"

The most challenging aspect of the work was trying to figure out what Bob was looking for while at the same time having my own experience of the play and the role. I never knew how I stood in relation to "Wilsonian theatre." "Is this too real?" I would ask myself. Then: "Is this too Robert Wilson?" Eventually I just had to figure out where this character is in this production, how to play the performance and, ultimately, truly make it my own.

When Bob directs or choreographs a scene for the first time, or when he imagines a sequence, I believe he sees himself as the performer. This may be especially true since he had worked with so few of us before. He's a performer. It's beautiful to watch him demonstrate a move or explain—verbally and physically—the way a line should be read. Part of what occurs in rehearsal is a shift of the characters moving from him to the performers.

When we finally moved out of the rehearsal hall and onto the stage, the focus shifted to the technical aspects of the piece. The composer and sound designer were with us in almost every rehearsal, and Bob was thinking about light from the beginning, but there was still much work to do. The technical rehearsals were a slow meticulous process. Nothing is an "extra" or secondary element. Everything is important.

During the previews Bob told us: "Make the piece yours. This is not my play anymore now. You know the form is boring. It's how you embody the form that counts." An actor who had worked with him before turned to me and said, "I've never heard him talk like this."

Once in performance, the production continued on that course that all plays take; rhythms change, people relax in certain scenes where they haven't been able to relax, people take little chances that they were not able to take before. The evolutionary process continued, as with any other production. It might not have been as noticeable because the form was so strict, but it was happening. It may have been most evident in the tribunal scenes. But for me, the last prison scene, right before Danton's execution, was the most changed. It became clearer and clearer. All of the elements were the same—the lines, the lights, the sound, certainly the gestures—but somehow it had evolved. Something was different. The form was becoming filled, the alchemy was working.

An actor never really knows what the experience of the audience is. In *Danton's Death*, however, each element of the production has a structure of its own. Amidst these many different—and autonomous—structures it was almost impossible to know how much of the experience of the play was being conveyed by the performers.

Of course, the experience of a production is always created by all the elements. But in playing Hamlet, for instance, I had a sense that all the other elements were supporting me—especially the text. In this production I never had that sense. Sometimes the sound and lights supported the scenes, and sometimes they didn't. Like the pairing of movement and text, all the elements were brought together to make one thing, but without sacrificing their autonomy. I always had the feeling that the production was communicating on many levels simultaneously, and my performance was one of those equally important levels.

Bob's idea is to keep from imposing an interpretation—his or the actors'—on an audience and to allow them space to enter into the production. For an audience that goes in with a more conventional idea of theatre, expecting to be told what to think and how to follow the play, the production can seem impenetrable. They just can't find a way into the piece. But people having that response doesn't mean Bob doesn't think about the audience. Not only is he attempting to let interpretation rest with the audience, to let them make up their own minds, but he is also thinking about them in the rehearsal process, as he shapes the piece.

Wilson is a theatre craftsman and a pragmatist—he likes a good show. In rehearsals, he makes himself a part of the audience. In many ways he becomes the audience member that should never go to a Robert Wilson production. He'll become impatient. "This is too boring. This is too slow. This isn't working. Things have to be linked more, we need more bridges. I can't understand what the main points of this speech are." And he is so meticulous because he doesn't want things to be muddled. He wants each part, each level, to be clear. That is thinking about the audience.

I heard a lot of praise for the production and I, of course, heard a lot of criticism. On the one hand there were those people who found it too avant-garde: "There is no point in producing a great play," they say, "if you're not going to do the play."

On the other hand there were some Wilson aficionados who felt that it was too conventional! They thought the elements were not autonomous enough, that the lights and sound, did, in fact, serve too much to support the text.

But with this production, Wilson was directing a play—a play written by someone else and with a long production history. He's only recently started doing that. There was no mistaking this was a Robert Wilson production, and the "visual book" of the piece was a Robert Wilson creation; but the production also did a service to the play, to Büchner's text in Bob Auletta's adaptation.

If audiences feel free to have a nonjudgmental approach, to "experience" the play, they will see things they love, things they hate, things that confuse them and things that make perfect sense. Pretty much like life.

Richard Thomas has performed on Broadway and at theatres around the country, including Primary Stages, Second Stage, Lincoln Center Theater, Circle Repertory, Hartford Stage, the Shakespeare Theatre Company, Center Theatre Group, the Kennedy Center and the Alley Theatre, where *Danton's Death* was produced. He has also appeared in several films and television series, and received an Emmy for his TV role in "The Waltons."

LIVING FOR DESIGN: A FRAGMENT OF A SCREENPLAY

By Marjorie Bradley Kellogg

October 1993

Scene One: THE COLLABORATION BEGINS. FADE IN. INT. DAY.

> *CLOSE UP of white field crossed with parallel rule, adjustable triangle and a hand with pencil, painstakingly drafting an elaborate column cap.*

DESIGNER [**V.O.**]: No, not at all. Just sitting here scribbling.

> *PULL BACK to see DESIGNER perched on stool at drafting board, drawing with cordless phone cradled tightly under chin.*

DIRECTOR [**V.O. ON PHONE**]: It's so great we finally get to do this together. Sorry it had to be so last minute. Is everything all set on the business end?

DESIGNER: (*still drafting*) Contracts went back this morning, so I guess it's really going to happen.

DIRECTOR: I'd have had you out here sooner, but you're always so busy.

> *PAN around DESIGNER's studio. Shelves crowded with books and supplies. Two ASSISTANTS working, models and drawings scattered everywhere.*

DIRECTOR: And trying to get you at the same time as those OTHER two . . . and my composer! Phew!

DESIGNER: (*laughs*) Feast or famine . . . you know how it is in the mad rush to make a living. I have considered suggesting production meetings in the air. But I hear you spend as much time these days in other people's theatres as you do in your own.

DIRECTOR: Oh, they're so much nicer to guest directors, how can I resist? Listen, I know there's the meeting out here next week with the other designers and all, but with time so tight, I thought we might just . . . ?

DESIGNER: Sure. Why not?

Gives up on drawing with a silent sigh.

DESIGNER: If this is a good time for you, let's go ahead and talk now.
DIRECTOR: Great. Did you get a chance to look at the script?

DESIGNER searches for and grabs the relevant script out from under piles of books and research. It is open to a spot 10 pages from the end.

DESIGNER: (*quickly skimming final pages*) Yup, sure did.
DIRECTOR: What'd you think?
DESIGNER: Really enjoyed it. I'd forgotten how much I like this piece. It's going to be just right for your space.
DIRECTOR: Great. I think so, too. So—you got it all designed already?
DESIGNER: (*laughing, still reading*) There are people out there who expect that.
DIRECTOR: Tell me about it. A finished production the first day of rehearsal. But seriously, folks . . . what'd you have in mind?
DESIGNER: (*laughs again, stops reading*) I think that's what I'm supposed to ask you.
DIRECTOR: (*theatrically pathetic*) Oh, God, you're actually going to make me WORK on this one . . . .
DESIGNER: Hey, you know . . . it always seems a good idea to hear just a little from a director . . . like, before I go charging off on some wild and irresponsible tangent.
DIRECTOR: We might as well charge off irresponsibly together.
DESIGNER: Since there are so many ways you could go with this piece, and I know you really do your homework . . . .
DIRECTOR: (*wryly*) Well, I did have a thought or two . . . .
DESIGNER: Although, you know . . . I, um . . . I did have one really strong response.
DIRECTOR: Ah ha! So let's hear it.
DESIGNER: (*Picks up pencil and scrap paper, starts to doodle*) It was about the relationship of the play to the space, how it could sort of mirror the characters' relationships to each other . . . about using the long axis as the focal point . . . ?
DIRECTOR: (*mystified*) Uh-hunh . . . .
DESIGNER: (*sketching now*) Something about distance and perspective. About length, moving away from the audience, rather than lateral . . . ?
DIRECTOR: Right. Yeah. Sounds right, all right.

You can hear in the voice that the DIRECTOR is suddenly glad this play is not a comedy. DESIGNER hears it too, throws down pencil, shoves paper away, shifts phone to other ear and opens up script again.

DESIGNER: Well, that's all a little cold and abstract. I'll rough it out for you, show you on paper. I want to start with ground plan. Ground plan's going to be the key here, I think.

DIRECTOR: (*relieved*) In this space? Absolutely.

DESIGNER: So I'll send you a bunch of stuff to look at before next week. You mind being inundated with research?

DIRECTOR: Never. You have my fax number?

DESIGNER swivels on stool. CLOSE UP of big wall calendar beside drafting board. It is a maze of due dates, rehearsal and tech schedules, and scrawled phone numbers.

DESIGNER: Probably I'll FedEx it. Tomorrow, maybe Thursday. Your theatre shouldn't be crammed onto a greasy 8 x 10. Now, what about period? Are we doing it in period? How do you feel about working on a rake?

DIRECTOR: Mmmm . . . possible. Maybe. But shallow. I need to be able to move the furniture around in rehearsal.

DESIGNER: Do you expect there'll be a lot of furniture?

DIRECTOR: Well, you know—stuff. I just gotta keep it loose for the first couple of weeks. A rake, hunh? Let me think about it. And I think we should pretty much stick to the period but give it, you know, a solid contemporary feel.

DESIGNER: And kind of . . . urban?

DIRECTOR: Yes. But not the usual trash-and-graffiti urban.

DESIGNER: No. Metallic urban.

DIRECTOR: Exactly.

DESIGNER: Good, good. We can really have fun with that. Kind of gritty and lyrical. After all, these big-city problems haven't changed that much since then.

DIRECTOR: Hardly at all—and I really want to make that connection for the audience.

DESIGNER'S ASSISTANT comes into frame, holding out a half-done model piece for DESIGNER'S inspection. DESIGNER squints at it silently.

DESIGNER: Yeah, it's really important. I was thinking it would be really great if we . . . .

DIRECTOR: Damn, that's my other line. Sorry. I'm at home this morning, waiting on some casting news. I go into rehearsal in four days, and I just lost my Undershaft to a pilot. Hold on, I'll be right back to you.

DESIGNER shrugs phone tighter under chin, takes model piece in both hands. CLOSE UP of model from DESIGNER's P.O.V.

DESIGNER: (*V.O. to ASSISTANT*) It's fine but you're going to have to work this detail out a little better. Can't this be shorter? I need it shorter.

PULL BACK to see DESIGNER tweaking and bending part of model while ASSISTANT looks on anxiously.

DIRECTOR: I'm back. It was my damn plumber. Where were we?
DESIGNER: Well, let's see . . . how do you feel about windows and doors?
DIRECTOR: (*laughs*) Probably oughta have some . . . .
DESIGNER: (*rolls eyes at ASSISTANT*) Oh. Okay.

ASSISTANT grins, takes model, goes away shaking her head.

DIRECTOR: They don't have to be REAL doors.
DESIGNER: The idea of doors . . . .
DIRECTOR: Right.
DESIGNER: Oh, good.

FADEOUT

Scenic designer Marjorie Bradley Kellogg's Broadway credits include *Any Given Day*, the George C. Scott revival of *On Borrowed Time*, *Lucifer's Child* starring Julie Harris, *American Buffalo* with Al Pacino, *Da*, *Requiem for a Heavyweight*, *A Day in the Death of Joe Egg*, *Steaming* and *The Best Little Whorehouse in Texas*. Kellogg has worked for a wide range of not-for-profit theatres and has taught at Princeton University and Columbia University, and has been associate professor of design at Colgate University since 1995.

DON'T CALL THE POST-MOD SQUAD

By Roger Copeland

November 1993

> *The framework tells you what it is: A cow in a concert hall is a musician, a cow in a barn is a cow.*
> —Allan Kaprow

> *I did a picture of a guy with his finger up a cock. I think that for what it is, it's a perfect picture, because the hand gestures are beautiful. I know most people couldn't see the hand gestures, but compositionally I think it works. I think the hand gesture is beautiful. What it happens to be doing, it happens to be doing, but that's an aside.*
> —Robert Mapplethorpe, interviewed by Janet Kardon, 1987

Three years ago, Dennis Barrie, then the director of Cincinnati's Contemporary Arts Center, was indicted for "pandering obscenity" when his museum exhibited a touring exhibition of photographs by the late Robert Mapplethorpe. Since then, censoriousness of one sort or another has been so much in the news that the Barrie trial may seem like ancient history. But the "lesson" of Cincinnati is worth recalling, especially now that the religious Right is focusing more and more of its energy on the local level (with its "San Diego" strategy for electing candidates to school boards and its unceasing activity on behalf of anti-gay legislations akin to Colorado Amendment 2).

Assuming that Jane Alexander, Bill Clinton's appointee to head the National Endowment for the Arts, steadfastly refuses to play the role of decency czar, those who favor "content-based" restrictions on the arts will redouble their efforts on behalf of censorship. Groups such as Pat Robertson's Christian Coalition and Donald Wildmon's American Family Association may well begin to pressure local prosecutors into declaring open season on "pornographic panderers" posing as artists. You know their names . . . . Round up the usual suspects: Karen Finley, Holly Hughes, photographers whose work resembles Mapplethorpe's. (Indeed, in the unlikely event that Finley or Tim Miller receive an invitation to perform in Cobb County, Ga., they should probably fear entrapment.)

These are the very same artists whose concern with the politics of gender and "transgressive" forms of sexuality endear them to so-called postmodern cultural critics. But there's a terrible, if largely unacknowledged, irony at work here. And that is: The critics most eager to come to the defense of artists like Finley and Mapplethorpe (the postmodern critics who sing their praises in the pages of *Artforum* or the *Village Voice*) are the very people least able to mount an intellectually coherent—and logically consistent—*legal* defense.

The problem is that the postmodernists tend to deemphasize the very values, the formal and compositional values that most easily distinguish the photographs of someone like Mapplethorpe from other images that can be branded as legally obscene.

But there's a more basic problem with the postmodernist embrace of artists like Mapplethorpe; and it's a complicated problem, so bear with me as I attempt to unravel it. Put glibly, postmodernists tend to equate modernism with formalism and formalism with a variety of escapism. (Finley, Hughes and Mapplethorpe are admired by postmodernists in part because their work deals with highly charged subject matter; it isn't "abstract" or concerned with purely "aesthetic" issues such as "line," "form," "color," "texture," etc.) Holly Hughes's monologue, *World Without End*, launches a frontal assault on the presumed insularity of formalist art. Listen to what Hughes's alter ego has to say about art school: "Oh I tried to learn how to lie, in art school, and I learned to believe in the universality of art, that art transcends the grubby artless ghettos of gender and race and sexual preference, that art is abstract and never gets blood on his clothes even when witnessing a murder, oh, no! Art turns the other way and looks out the window."

A few pages (or minutes) later, she adds: "Oh I know the difference between politics and art! I went to art school . . . and the first thing they said when they saw me coming through the door was: 'Holly, don't hit them over the head. Art is not supposed to hit them over the head!' Well, neither are fathers. And when Joel Steinberg hit his daughter so hard she died I read in the paper the next day a columnist, Pete Hamill, saying it was worse morally for Hedda Nussbaum to not intervene than it was for Joel Steinberg to kill her in the first place. That's when I gave up on my macramé career."

Several years ago, the Whitney Museum in New York mounted a certifiably postmodern exhibition called "The Image World." No abstract exercises in visual formalism. No color field paintings. Holly Hughes would have approved. The featured artists, who included Barbara Kruger, Cindy Sherman, Jenny Holzer, Jeff Koons and Richard Prince, all drew their images from the world of advertising and media. An introductory wall placard greeted each visitor with the following words of warning: "Those looking to art as a refuge from the outside world will not find comfort here."

Those who regard formalist art as a "refuge from the outside world" have, in my opinion, greatly misunderstood the nature and purpose of formalism. But let's assume, for the sake of argument, that the postmodernists are correct. What they forget (or else choose to ignore) is that "a refuge from the outside world" can also mean a safe haven, a defense against censoriousness, philistinism and narrow-minded community standards. Modernism—now so widely and unfairly reviled as an attempt to isolate artists from social reality—was also a declaration of independence for art, the creation of a special zone (traditionally known as "the art context") in which the artwork is granted protections that would not pertain to its "content" alone if that content weren't framed in a specifically "aesthetic" way (and left to the not-so-tender mercies of the vice squad in a city like Cincinnati). An obvious example: nudity in the context of a play performed on a stage is presumably protected. If, by contrast, a member of the audience disrobes, he or she can be arrested for indecent exposure.

But the postmodernists don't want to claim any special privileges for "high culture." (That would be "elitist"—one of the ultimate sins in the postmodern moral universe.) For postmodernists, there's no fundamental distinction between a Rembrandt and a LeRoy Neiman. High Culture, Middlebrow Culture, Mass Culture—they're all instances of "cultural production." Forget about the sort of connoisseurship that would enable you to distinguish the formal achievements of a Piet Mondrian from a Peter Max. What matters are the social networks or systems of exhibition, distribution, interpretation and marketing. Seen from this postmodern vantage point, the modernist heritage is viewed as a cool, highly cerebral affair, myopically (indeed, autistically) focused on the internal properties of the artist's medium rather than on the external features of the Real World. Modernism thus stands accused of celebrating the distance that separates art from daily life and of segregating art into a frame, a gallery or museum—at the very least, a special aesthetic zone or "art context."

But without this venerable *modernist* notion of the "art context," it becomes almost impossible to defend the photos of someone like Mapplethorpe against charges of obscenity in a city like Cincinnati. Cincinnati, by the way, is a very special place: Under its obscenity laws (which have survived constitutional challenges) the town fathers have done their darnedest to take the sin out of Cincinnati. Prosecutors have successfully closed down all adult bookstores, peepshows, massage parlors and bars that feature nude dancing.

Right-wing Evangelical groups didn't need to protest against Martin Scorsese's film *The Last Temptation of Christ* in Cincinnati—no theatre owner was willing to show it. A few months before the Mapplethorpe exhibition hit town, a production of Peter Shaffer's *Equus* was forced to stage a special preview for the vice squad before being allowed to open.

In March of 1990, gearing up for the High Noon showdown with Dennis Barrie and the Mapplethorpe photos, Monty Lobb, the president of an anti-porn organization called "Citizens for Community Values," told the *New York Times*, "We don't selectively enforce murder laws, so we can't selectively enforce pornography laws. Whether it's in a porno store or an art gallery, we have a right to speak up." In other words, no "art context." But give the devil his due. Mr. Lobb is nothing if not consistent. In fact, he's downright egalitarian., (If you can't buy sadomasochistic images of gay men in an adult bookstore, why should you be able to look at them in a museum?)

I doubt that Mr. Lobb would knowingly want to associate himself with the more academic varieties of "postmodern" discourse. But, *mutatis mutandis*, what he's expressing is merely postmodernism by another name: He's denying the sanctity of the art context. Rather than blurring the distinction between Rembrandt and LeRoy Neiman, he's deemphasizing the differences between Mapplethorpe photos and the images in gay S&M magazines (or to put a slightly different spin on it, between Karen Finley's unclothed body smeared in chocolate and the bodies of naked female mud wrestlers). In Mr. Lobb's neighborhood, community values, old-time philistinism and postmodernism find common ground. It's here that we encounter the ultimate conflating of high and low culture, the ultimate denial of elite privileges to some special category of experience the Eastern Liberal Establishment calls art. Alas, the Cincinnati vice squad could easily be mistaken for the Post Mod Squad.

Well, Dennis Barrie, thank goodness, was acquitted. And I don't deny that the verdict in the Barrie trial was a triumph for the First Amendment as well as for common sense, the basic decency and tolerance of the average Midwesterners who made up the jury, etc. But— and this is what hasn't been fully enough appreciated—it was also a triumph for the cardinal principle of modernism that the postmodernists dismiss so cavalierly: the notion of aesthetic autonomy.

It may or may not be a coincidence that the first and most important philosophical treatise defending this notion of the aesthetic an "autonomous" realm, Immanuel Kant's "Critique of Judgment," is exactly contemporaneous with our Bill of Rights. Kant's great work was published in 1790. The ratification process for the first 10 amendments to the U.S. Constitution began in 1789 and was successfully completed in 1791. Kant lays the groundwork for the philosophy that would later be called "art for art's sake." The "autonomy" of art is a powerful model for the inalienable rights that our Constitution confers upon the individual. For Kant, aesthetic experience is unburdened by any sort of utility. It is complete unto itself and serves no end beyond itself. It exhibits what he calls "purposiveness without purpose"; the perceiver experiences it in a state of mind Kant called "disinterestedness." Not *un*interestedness—which implies aloofness and indifference—but *dis*interestedness, meaning that the work can't be pressed into serving anyone's (especially not the state's) immediate self-interest.

That helps to explain why totalitarian governments of both the Left and the Right have so often repressed aesthetic "formalism." Such work can't easily be made to serve the ends of propaganda. It resists the intrusion of the state and refuses to place political aims above more purely aesthetic ones.

Of course, "purposiveness without purpose" doesn't mean that art can't influence life. But its effect is much less direct than the yelling of "fire" in a crowded theatre. In fact, to the extent that it treats even the hottest sort of subject matter in a "disinterested" way, to the extent that it places such subject matter in a frame or in quotes, the result is actually more like yelling "Theatre!" in a crowded fire. As W.H. Auden put it in his elegy for Yeats, "Poetry makes nothing happen. It survives in the valley of its saying." William O. Douglas, the great Supreme Court Justice and civil libertarian, consistently maintained that "[for] speech to be punishable [it] must have some relation to action which could be penalized by government." The Kantian frame precludes any "causal" relationship between art and action. (Of course, there's also an important avant-garde tradition that plays with and relocates the frame in ways that undermine one's sometimes comforting sense of aesthetic distance.) But those postmodernists who yearn to enlist art in the service of social activism dislike the Kantian argument that aesthetic experience is non-utilitarian. To some, this may seem a very great sacrifice indeed. But what art loses in efficacy, it gains in protection. The very same boundary or frame that prevents art from engaging life in a directly utilitarian way also prevents the long, censorious arm of the law from encroaching upon the "autonomy" of art.

Here we encounter the unfortunate practical consequences of claiming—as many postmodernists do—that "all art is political." The "defunded four"—Karen Finley, Holly Hughes, John Fleck and Tim Miller—accused John Frohnmayer of denying them funding for purely political reasons. But if art is always political, then it's merely a question of whose politics prevail. The doctrine of aesthetic autonomy, by contrast, assumes that determinations of artistic excellence will be arrived at without resorting to political considerations.

The quintessential formulation of this notion comes from the writings of the modernist painter Ad Reinhardt, who once declared, "The frame should isolate and protect the painting from its surroundings." For Reinhardt, the art context (or the frame) radically transforms the artwork's content. What happens "inside the frame" should not be confused with similar-looking content or activity outside the frame.

"The meaning of art," writes Reinhardt, "is not meaning. The morality of art is not morality . . . . Humanism in art is not humanism. Dehumanism in art is not dehumanism." Applied to Mapplethorpe, Serrano, Finley, et al., these aphorisms can be amended to read, "Pornography in art is not pornography. Blasphemy in art in not blasphemy. Chocolate-covered nudity in art is not . . . etc." This, of course, is not to suggest that no work of art has ever been racist, sexist or imperialist. It's difficult to imagine a responsible reading of D.W. Griffith's great film *The Birth of a Nation* that would fail to address its glorification of the Klan. But in any certifiable work of art, there are always other values to be considered alongside the objections that one (rightly) registers to the work's offending content. And it's these other values (formal values) that offer the work legal protection no matter how objectionable the content may be. The town fathers in Cincinnati would be quick to disagree. And so, I fear, would the postmodernists.

Luckily for Barrie, Mapplethorpe and those of us who care about artistic freedom and freedom of expression more generally, the defense strategy in the Cincinnati trial was quintessentially and unapologetically modernist and formalist. The first and most important witness for the defense was the art historian Janet Kardon, who organized the touring Mapplethorpe exhibition when she was director of the Institute for Contemporary Art in Philadelphia. She began by using the "F" word, formalism. She told the jury, "Mapplethorpe was one of the most important photographers working in the '80s in a formalist mode." The subject matter of the seven offending photographs included images of one man urinating into the mouth of another and images in which the rectum and penis of various male models were penetrated by an assortment of exotic objects. But Kardon's analysis focused on the formal and compositional values ("opposing diagonals," "the centrality of the forearm," etc.) In other words, she emphasized the values that distinguish these photos from images that one might find in an X-rated bookstore.

The art critic Robert Hughes, in his recent book *The Culture of Complaint*, ridiculed Kardon's analysis, particularly the claim she makes in the published catalogue for the exhibition that the formal arrangement of subject matter in Mapplethorpe's photos "purifies, even cancels, the prurient elements." He dismissed her analysis as "the kind of exhausted and literally de-moralized aestheticism that would find no basic difference between a Nuremberg rally and Busby Berkeley spectacular, since both, after all, are examples of Art Deco choreography." Granted, Kardon's eminently modernist defense may have been motivated by expediency, but I believe that in the final analysis, it proved both appropriate and correct. No one—not Kardon, certainly not Mapplethorpe—would want to deny the very real differences between his photographs of a calla lily and the portrait of himself with a bullwhip protruding from his rectum; but that doesn't negate the fact that both the lilies and the self-portraits exude the same formal, highly studied, compositional values.

For me, Mapplethorpe's photos—yes, even those in the notorious X portfolio—have more in common with the painting we know by the sentimentalized title of "Whistler's Mother" than with the pornographic images one finds in an adult bookstore. The *actual* title that Whistler gave his painting is *Arrangement in Black and Gray: The Artist's Mother*. Note his priorities: black and gray first, mom second. The painting is first and foremost an exploration of color and shape, and only secondarily a portrait of a real person (let alone the artist's mother). I take Whistler at his word when he said of his paintings, "[they are] an arrangement of line, forms and color first; and I make use of any incident of it which shall bring about a symmetrical result."

Mapplethorpe made many similar declarations. And regardless of where his photos are displayed (museum, bedroom, sex shop), their formal dimension will always place their subject matter in an "art context," and will always guarantee that they possess the "artistic value" needed to differentiate them from prosecutable modes of "obscene" image-making (*Miller v. California*, 1973). Indeed, when the modernist concept of the "art context" is functioning fully, the successful prosecution of a figure like Mapplethorpe becomes a contradiction in terms.

But—as we've already seen—no "vestige" of high modernism has been more consistently attacked in the postmodern era than the idea that the art context should afford artists a special degree of protection. In fact, one can trace the transition from modern to postmodern values by chronicling the steady erosion of this concept over the past two decades.

A convenient barometer for gauging this change in the aesthetic and political weather is the (now largely forgotten) "Donald" affair of the late '70s: A New York artist named Donald Newman had titled an exhibition of his visual art "The Nigger Drawings." (None of these drawings dealt with issues of race in any readily recognizable way.) Convinced that his use of the word "Nigger" amounted to a mean-spirited and gratuitous bid for attention (and they were probably right), Carl Andre, Sol LeWitt, Leon Golub and 21 other artists and critics sent a letter of protest to the *Village Voice* complaining of "a peculiar blind spot in art-world thinking which cultivates the habit of detaching art from any human meanings. In other words, many in the art community lull themselves into believing that in an art context, racism isn't racism: it's art."

Without explicitly mentioning Ad Reinhardt, the signatories to this letter were announcing loud and clear that they no longer accept his defense of the inviolability of the "art context." When the frame ceases "to protect and isolate the painting from its surroundings," not only has high modernist orthodoxy come to an end, so has the sort of legal defense that prevents the Cincinnati prosecutors from locking up Dennis Barrie.

Perhaps it's a politically correct form of poetic justice that one of Donald Newman's critics, Sol LeWitt, has himself recently fallen victim to the new passion—so visible at both ends of the political spectrum—for placing content-based restrictions on art. Two summers ago, Elizabeth Broun, the director of the National Museum of American Art in Washington, tried to remove from an exhibition a work of LeWitt's (created in 1964!) called *Muybridge 1*, a minimalist black box with 10 apertures through which the viewer sees images of a naked woman coming progressively closer. Ms. Broun felt that the image "objectified" women and therefore, in her words, "degraded" them.

Perhaps Ms. Broun or the signatories of the above-mentioned letter would even endorse the following attempt to prevent federal monies from being used to "promote, disseminate or produce . . . material which denigrates, debases or reviles a person, group or class of citizens on the basis of race, creed, sex, handicap, age or national origin." It certainly sounds like the sort of language they'd want to be associated with. But maybe they'd reconsider upon learning that those words are an excerpt from the notorious Helms Amendment, which would have prohibited federal support not only for the affiances listed above, but also for "obscene or indecent materials, including but not limited to depictions of sadomasochism, homoeroticism, the exploitation of children, or individuals engaged in sex acts."

There is, of course, a way to protect the Mapplethorpes and the Dennis Barries of this world without having to grant special protections to certifiable works of art. And I'll confess that as a longtime card-carrying member of the ACLU, it's the solution I prefer: Eliminate the anti-obscenity laws. Grant the same sort of protection to adult bookstores, strippers and nude dancers that you grant to Robert Mapplethorpe. But given the current cultural climate in this country, that's not likely to happen. Just last year, the high court ruled that nude dancing is not a constitutionally protected form of "free expression." (Ironically, this opinion was handed down by the very same set of justices who defended the constitutionality of cross-burning,)

Campaigns against freedom of expression have become so commonplace in recent years that it may seem arbitrary to single any of them out for special comment. But I would like to mention three such enterprises that pose a clear and present danger to artistic expression. First, the tireless efforts of Michigan law professor Catherine MacKinnon on behalf of legislation that would ban images she regards as pornographic. What many people in the arts community don't realize is that MacKinnon isn't just targeting the sort of stomach-churning stuff one finds in *Hustler* magazine. In fact, MacKinnon makes a point of not creating any special exemptions for redeeming "artistic value." ("If a woman is subjected, why should it matter that the work has other value?" asks MacKinnon.) MacKinnon's writings, by the way, were cited in briefs on behalf of the Indiana law that prohibits nude dancing in bars and clubs.

At the opposing end of the political spectrum, Robert Bork and other like-minded legal theorists also deserve a special place in this hall of shame. Bork recently attacked those advocates of free expression that he calls "First Amendment voluptuaries." The arts, he went on to argue, enjoy an unreasonable immunity from the moral "cost-benefit analysis" that society applies in all other domains when placing limits on liberty.

But when it comes to questioning the very concept, indeed the desirability, of free expression, no one outdoes Stanley Fish and his colleagues on what might be called the "post-structuralist left." In a recent essay with the provocative title "There's No Such Thing As Free Speech, and It's a Good Thing, Too," Fish comes to the defense of content-based restrictions on "hate speech." For utilitarians like Fish, free speech is never an end in itself (the First Amendment equivalent of aesthetic formalism!), but is merely a means to an end (such as social justice). And if that "end" can be better achieved by suppressing speech, so be it. "Speech, in short," notes Fish, "is never and could not be an independent value, but is always asserted against a background of some assumed conception of the good to which it must yield in the event of conflict."

Those are but a few of the reasons why we can't do without the *cordon sanitaire* provided by the modernist notion of "the art context."

Unless, that is, we're willing to do without the many artworks that local prosecutors in places like Cincinnati will continue to regard as obscene, blasphemous or otherwise at odds with culturally conservative "community standards."

So if, like Dennis Barrie, you find yourself indicted for "pandering obscenity" when you display sexually explicit artworks, how best to defend yourself? My advice is simple: If your defense attorney's initials turn out to be "P.M.," you'd better hope those letters stand for Perry Mason rather than Post-Modernism. The "lesson" of Cincinnati is that when push comes to shove, it's modernism—not postmodernism—that's most likely to get you off the legal hook.

Roger Copeland is a professor of theatre and dance at Oberlin College in Ohio and has published essays in a wide variety of publications including the *New York Times*, the *New Republic*, the *Village Voice*, *Partisan Review* and *Dance Theatre Journal*. His books include *What is Dance?* and *Merce Cunningham and the Modernizing of Modern Dance*. He has also worked as a consultant for the National Endowment for the Arts, the "Dance in America" series on PBS, Brooklyn Academy of Music's Next Wave Festival and the eight-part television series "Dancing."

THE ESSENTIAL MING CHO LEE

By Mel Gussow

April 1995

Ming Cho Lee peered inside the scale model of a stage, fixing a Gulliver-like eye on the miniaturized theatrical world. The model was a set design for an imaginary production of *Othello*, the current assignment in the designer's first-year class at the Yale University Graduate School of Drama. Working in tandem with student directors, student designers had been encouraged to be freely creative in their choices of a Shakespearean setting. As usual, Lee's instruction came not through criticism but through questions. Will the set work for both the outdoor and indoor scenes? Does the set serve the play?

As he moved from model to model offering comments, Lee noticed that in one set the bed on which Desdemona would be slain was floating in the center of an otherwise empty stage. He asked a purely practical question: "How is Emilia going to knock on the door?" To a student who had situated the play in Washington, D.C., he said, "If it's Washington or not, it's the seat of power. What icon says it's the seat of power?"

Another had transplanted *Othello* to Vietnam. Looking at the mock-up of a Saigon street, Lee said, "You've researched Southeast Asia, but how are you going to do the bedroom scene?" And studying a model that was overflowing with scenery: "So you're going to do *Sunset Boulevard*, flying in the whole set?" Occasionally, and very politely, he admitted, "I just don't understand."

When teaching, his approach is akin to that of a psychoanalyst. Quietly he leads students to clarify their thoughts and explain their choices. He does not impose his opinions. Asked a question, he prefers to answer obliquely. That, he says, is the secret of teaching.

The dean of American scenic designers, Lee is a master of his art in theatre, dance and opera. Through his work and through his teaching, he has become one of the most influential people in his field. During his 25 years at the Yale School of Drama, 20 of them as cochairman of the design department, he has trained scores of successful designers (including John Lee Beatty, Heidi Landesman, Tony Straiges and Michael Yeargan). In so doing, he is carrying on the tradition established by designers reaching back to Robert Edmond Jones. Theatre design is that rare art that continues to operate through the apprentice system, as established designers pass on their knowledge and techniques to younger designers.

Lee teaches, at least partly, by example. His own designs illuminate changes in his profession and in the wider world of art. Currently, through May, there is a comprehensive retrospective of his work at the New York Public Library for the Performing Arts at Lincoln Center. Some 40 exhibits have been carefully culled from the hundreds of shows, dances and operas he has designed during the past 40 years, including sets he created for Joseph Papp's New York Shakespeare Festival and for the Martha Graham Dance Company.

Lee also helps to perpetuate his profession through his Stage Design Portfolio Review. Commonly known as "Ming's clambake" (because it is his invention and his show), the Portfolio Review is an annual spring exhibition and informal colloquy at Lincoln Center of the works of student designers from universities across the country. Designers and directors act as respondents, meetings may lead to job offers—and Ming takes everyone to lunch. He spends a large part of his time and energy (and, in the case of the clambake, his own money) giving something back to those who will become his colleagues and successors.

In his own designing, Lee is the enemy of decoration, of effects, of anything that detracts or distracts from the drama. The idea that theatregoers might actually applaud a set offends his scenic sensibility. Listening to him talk about design, one might conclude that he does not actually like scenery. He does not like excessive or useless scenery, scenery that makes its own architectural statement and does not complement the play.

When he teaches, he begins with contextual analysis. The students read the play, discuss it, draft a portrait gallery of the characters and consult with their directors before beginning any project. Gradually, and from a firm intellectual base, they work their way into the physical properties that will enhance the telling of the story. As he says, "We hardly talk about design, and then only in the context of the play."

In the case of *Othello*, one in a series of design projects for the class, he could call upon his past experience with the play at the New York Shakespeare Festival and the recent production he designed for the Stratford Festival in Canada. On the latter occasion, as he and his director Brian Bedford were looking at Lee's scale model, a wall in the model tipped forward. The tipped wall "looked terrific," but Lee realized that it would "interfere with the actors and the action." It was a case in which design would have taken precedence over performance. Lee decided that the play came first, and used a straight bare wall as backdrop.

Lee's work draws upon his two cultures, his childhood in China and his subsequent immersion in American art. He was born in

Shanghai on Oct. 3, 1930, and studied landscape painting before coming to the U.S. at the age of 19. At Occidental College in Los Angeles, he majored in speech and acted in student plays. He says that at the first lecture he attended he could not understand one word. He learned English quickly; he is now one of the most voluble of men.

In his junior year, Lee studied design, continuing that interest at UCLA. With the encouragement of Edward Kook, the lighting expert, he came to New York, where he apprenticed with Jo Mielziner, at the time the dean of his profession. The first show of Mielziner's in which the young Lee played an active role was *Cat on a Hot Tin Roof* in 1955. Subsequently he was an assistant to Rouben Ter-Arutunian and Boris Aronson. He was influenced by each of them, and also by Brechtian theatre, which led him to take a "formalistic and spatial" approach. Eventually he developed his own more sculptural style and found self-definition in the clean bold line of his stage work.

Throughout his career, Lee has been a freelance designer, a life that can be as precarious as that of an actor. With remembered pessimism, he says, "If you don't get any calls, you don't do any work." Periods without work made him nervous and made him question his own viability as a designer: Was he keeping up with the times? Of course he was, and in his career he has discovered a wide range of opportunity, working for many regional theatres as well as for major dance and opera companies. His steadiest employment was as a principal designer for the New York Shakespeare Festival. In 11 years, he did 22 Shakespearean productions as well as many contemporary plays, including *Hair* in 1967 and *for colored girls who have considered suicide / when the rainbow is enuf* in 1976. His adventurousness in new works is exemplified by the striking background he designed for Jack MacGowran's one-man evening from the works of Samuel Beckett. With its cloudlike swirls, the set looked like a close-up section of a Turner painting.

Because of his Shakespeare designs for the Delacorte Theater in Central Park, Lee became identified with vertical sets. Often he used stairs, metal piping and scaffolding, an approach that was particularly suited to the Delacorte sightlines, but one that he felt was not necessarily conducive to other stages. When he was asked to duplicate his Central Park design for the Broadway and touring versions of the musical adaptation of *Two Gentlemen of Verona*, he felt "so demoralized that it almost drove me away from doing theatre." Lee remains his most demanding critic.

At the New York Shakespeare Festival and Arena Stage in Washington, D.C., he took an innovative approach to thrust and arena-style stages. But he refused to be trapped into specializing in a single stage configuration. At the same time, he has refused to design in isolation, insisting that designers should be aware of and affected by what is happening in related arts. In the 1960s, Lee was influenced by Abstract Expressionism, which is one reason he worked so well with Martha Graham. Later in that decade, in some of his work he adapted himself to Pop Art, which, along with Op Art, carried him through the

1970s. That was followed by explorations of postmodernism, in architecture and other fields. "We're now thinking about installations," he said. "With installations, the space to do it in becomes as important as the work itself." All these various styles have been amalgamated into the language of his design.

Lee's work has also been affected by what was happening in the world outside the arts. Increasingly he has been able to demonstrate that stage design can express social relevance, as in his design for Berkeley Repertory Theatre's large-scale 1993 dramatization of Maxine Hong Kingston's *The Woman Warrior*. He is in fact a man of strong political convictions. In a recent discussion with an undergraduate class in theatre arts at Yale, Lee began with a post-election analysis, announcing that he was an "incurable liberal, and very proud of it." He was extremely critical of those students in his design class who had not voted. From his perspective, a designer should be a responsible citizen as well as a polymath. He added that art deserved public support and expressed his outrage that artistic directors of theatres had to "go through life with a tin cup in their hands." Art is "ambiguous and dangerous; it offers no absolute truth." The important thing for emerging artists is, of course, to find their own voices.

Considering the austerity of his best designs, it comes as a surprise to see Lee in his apartment (also his studio) on Manhattan's Upper East Side. It is a cluttered environment, with books and papers piled high over sketches and notes for projects. For other designers, however, this jumble probably would be nothing unusual. As Donald Oenslager once said, "Few designers are good housekeepers," and "most are not preservationists."

Ming and his wife Betsy (who handles the business side of her husband's career) have lived here for more than 30 years, and when their three sons were young, it was of course even more crowded. Every morning the Lees converted their bedroom into Ming's studio. With their sons grown up—each is involved in the arts, one as a composer, another as a theatrical carpenter, the third as a gaffer in films—the Lees have spread out. But there is still no apparent filing system. Things proliferate and research relies on memory; he and his wife would prefer it if the work were safe in a central design museum, if one existed.

During a recent visit, Lee's models were still in the process of being packed up and transported to Lincoln Center for his one-man exhibition. In every room there were elements of designs past, some wrapped in plastic prepared for removal. To the chagrin of his two assistants, he undid the wrapping on several models in order to explain the idea behind the concept. He began with a set for a production of *Romeo and Juliet* that he did this season for Jon Jory at Actors Theatre of Louisville.

While thinking about the possibilities of the director's choice of period—fascism and the time of Mussolini—he considered having "a cold neoclassic space." Then he noticed a book entitled *Inside Rome*, opened to a double-page spread of a photograph of a 19th-century

Roman arcade. On the spot, he decided his design would be an adaptation of that picture. He made a color Xerox and sent it to Jory in Louisville. It was, he said, "the easiest set I have ever done," and one of the few with which he seemed entirely pleased. More difficult, though also satisfying, was a set he did for *Nine Songs*, a dance for the Cloud Gate Dance Theater of Taipei. It involved lotus blossoms, which faded and died in the course of the performance. That dance is scheduled to be presented in this season's Next Wave Festival at the Brooklyn Academy of Music.

Explaining the changes in techniques over the years, he said that most designers no longer made finished sketches, but preferred to build three-dimensional scale models, at first quarter-inch models, then half-inch. "People still think of set design as flatwork." They want to buy scenic drawings as if they are paintings, "and we really don't work that way anymore." In his case and others, the models are often supplemented by rough sketches and storyboards, in which he synchronizes the setting with the action. To illustrate the point, he looked around his studio for his storyboard for Terrence McNally's *A Perfect Ganesh*, which he had designed the previous season for Manhattan Theatre Club. Because neither he nor his assistants could find the storyboard, he brought out the Ganesh scale model. It was a long, low-lying set of sliding screens, a resplendent environment for the panoramic Asian travels of the leading characters.

Over lunch—dim sum, gathered by his wife on a trip to Chinatown—he talked about the state of design. He is a watchful observer of the design scene, especially so this season when he is a nominator for the Tony awards. Traditionally, the most elaborate sets, especially those for musicals, are those that are nominated. He would like to see a change in attitude. His conversation was filled with outspoken opinions, sometimes censored after the fact when he realized that he was caught criticizing colleagues. While praising the set for *Sunset Boulevard*, he expressed his dismay about the design of the musical *A Christmas Carol* at the Paramount Theater. The set was so busy that "half the time you can't see Scrooge. It's a theme park." He wondered, "Is the theme park going to be the ultimate achievement in our life? The show made me think I was locked in a shopping mall." One design he liked so far this season was for the short-lived Broadway production of Donald Margulies's *What's Wrong with This Picture?*—a household interior set free in a cloud-lined environment.

In Lee's diverse and distinguished career, most of his work has been away from Broadway, and he has won only one Tony award, in 1983, for the imposing mountain he designed for Patrick Meyers's *K2*. That design is not in the Lincoln Center exhibition; it is not one of Lee's favorites. It was explicit, overpowering and in the New York production of the play, it depended too much on surprising the audience. When the play was first presented at Arena Stage, the mountain faced theatregoers when they arrived in the theatre. By the time the play began, "they could concentrate on the two characters on stage." On Broadway, the curtain rose on the set, and the two-character play "became a spectacle about scenery." Since then, partly in reaction to *K2*, Lee has often created low horizontal designs.

His teaching has enriched his own work. For one thing, he began to think about plays "in a much more directorial way." Now he concludes that the most edifying part of designing is "working with the director, when words are transformed into imagery or a physical environment." But in contrast to some of his colleagues, like John Conklin and Jennifer Tipton, he says he has no directorial instincts himself. He prefers to be a conduit of another's artistic expression.

When the subject turned to fine art, he said provocatively that he no longer liked to go to museums to look at art as objects. "I hate to scrutinize things like that," he said. "I like to look at things in the context of a way of living. If I look at paintings in a book and they're connected with a person and a time, somehow that's more satisfying than going to a museum. Looking at a Frank Lloyd Wright room is exciting, but to look at miles and miles of furniture drives me up a wall." Lee himself helped design the Chinese garden in the Astor Court at the Metropolitan Museum of Art.

For him, design is a process of distillation. Repeatedly he says to himself, as he does to his students, "You don't need it." The search is often for "an icon," a single object, perhaps a hanging, to represent the central theme. When the set is finally in place, "the people who are living the life on stage are paramount. The design is to create a world in which that event can take place. But when the image becomes so overwhelming that the action is not needed, then I have a problem doing it. I don't know how to design for an audience. I have to design for the work."

Mel Gussow wrote thousands of theatre-related articles and reviews for the *New York Times* before his death in 2005. He was the author of eight books, including a *Conversations with . . .* series featuring the playwrights Samuel Beckett, Arthur Miller, Harold Pinter and Tom Stoppard.

THE GROUND ON WHICH I STAND

By August Wilson

September 1996

This address was delivered at the 1996 TCG National Conference, held at Princeton University. Wilson's remarks sparked a debate with Robert Brustein that played out in the pages of *American Theatre* and is excerpted in the two articles following this one. The conversation culminated in a discussion at New York City's Town Hall, moderated by Anna Deavere Smith, in 1997.

I have come here today to make a testimony, to talk about the ground on which I stand and all the many grounds on which I and my ancestors have toiled, and the ground of theatre on which my fellow artists and I have labored to bring forth its fruits, its daring and its sometimes lacerating, and often healing, truths.

I wish to make it clear from the outset, however, that I do not have a mandate to speak for anyone. There are many intelligent blacks working in the American theatre who speak in loud and articulate voices. It would be the greatest of presumptions to say I speak for them. I speak only for myself and those who may think as I do.

In one guise, the ground I stand on has been pioneered by the Greek dramatists—by Euripides, Aeschylus and Sophocles—by William Shakespeare, by Shaw and Ibsen, and by the American dramatists Eugene O'Neill, Arthur Miller and Tennessee Williams. In another guise, the ground that I stand on has been pioneered by my grandfather, by Nat Turner, by Denmark Vesey, by Martin Delaney, Marcus Garvey and the Honorable Elijah Muhammad. That is the ground of the affirmation of the value of one being, an affirmation of his worth in the face of society's urgent and sometimes profound denial. It was this ground as a young man coming into manhood searching for something to which to dedicate my life that I discovered the Black Power Movement of the '60s. I felt it a duty and an honor to participate in that historic moment, as the people who had arrived in America chained and malnourished in the hold of a 350-foot Portuguese, Dutch or English sailing ship were now seeking ways to alter their relationship to the society in which they lived—and, perhaps more important, searching for ways to alter the shared expectations of themselves as a community of people.

The Black Power Movement of the '60s: I find it curious but no small accident that I seldom hear those words "Black Power" spoken, and when mention is made of that part of black history in America, whether in the press or in conversation, reference is made to the Civil Rights Movement as though the Black Power Movement—an important social movement by America's ex-slaves—had in fact never happened. But the Black Power Movement of the '60s was a reality; it was the kiln in which I was fired, and has much to do with the person I am today and the ideas and attitudes that I carry as part of my consciousness.

I mention this because it is difficult to disassociate my concerns with theatre from the concerns of my life as a black man, and it is difficult to disassociate one part of my life from another. I have strived to live it all seamless . . . art and life together, inseparable and indistinguishable. The ideas I discovered and embraced in my youth when my idealism was full blown I have not abandoned in middle age when idealism is something less than blooming, but wisdom is starting to bud. The ideas of self-determination, self-respect and self-defense that governed my life in the '60s I find just as valid and self-urging in 1996. The need to alter our relationship to society and to alter the shared expectations of ourselves as a racial group I find of greater urgency now than it was then.

I am what is known, at least among the followers and supporters of the ideas of Marcus Garvey, as a "race man." That is simply that I believe that race matters—that is the largest, most identifiable and most important part of our personality. It is the largest category of identification because it is the one that most influences your perception of yourself, and it is the one to which others in the world of men most respond. Race is also an important part of the American landscape, as America is made up of an amalgamation of races from all parts of the globe. Race is also the product of a shared gene pool that allows for group identification, and it is an organizing principle around which cultures are formed. When I say culture I am speaking about the behavior patterns, arts, beliefs, institutions and all other products of human work and thought as expressed in a particular community of people.

There are some people who will say that black Americans do not have a culture—that cultures are reserved for other people, most notably Europeans of various ethnic groupings, and that black Americans make up a sub-group of American culture that is derived from the European origins of its majority population. But black Americans are Africans, and there are many histories and many cultures on the African continent. Those who would deny black Americans their culture would also deny them their history and the inherent values that are a part of all human life.

Growing up in my mother's house at 1727 Bedford Ave. in Pittsburgh, Pa., I learned the language, the eating habits, the religious beliefs, the gestures, the notions of common sense, attitudes towards sex, concepts of beauty and justice, and the responses to pleasure and pain, that my mother had learned from her mother, and which you could trace back to the first African who set foot on the continent. It is this culture that stands solidly on these shores today as a testament to the resiliency of the African-American spirit.

The term black or African American not only denotes race, it denotes condition, and carries with it the vestige of slavery and the social segregation and abuse of opportunity so vivid in our memory. That this abuse of opportunity and truncation of possibility is continuing and is so pervasive in our society in 1996 says much about who we are and much about the work that is necessary to alter our perceptions of each other and to effect meaningful prosperity for all.

The problematic nature of the relationship between white and black for too long led us astray from the fulfillment of our possibilities as a society. We stare at each other across a divide of economics and privilege that has become an encumbrance on black Americans' ability to prosper and on the collective will and spirit of our national purpose.

In terms of economics and privilege, one significant fact affects us all in the American theatre: Of the 66 LORT theatres, there is only one that can be considered black. [*Editor's note:* As of 2009, there were 77 LORT theatres, with none devoted specifically to African-American culture.] From this it could be falsely assumed that there aren't sufficient numbers of blacks working in the American theatre to sustain and support more theatres.

If you do not know, I will tell you that black theatre in America is alive . . . it is vibrant . . . it is vital . . . it just isn't funded. Black theatre doesn't share in the economics that would allow it to support its artists and supply them with meaningful avenues to develop their talent and broadcast and disseminate ideas crucial to its growth. The economics are reserved as privilege to the overwhelming abundance of institutions that preserve, promote and perpetuate white culture.

That is not a complaint. That is an advertisement. Since the funding sources, both public and private, do not publicly carry avowed missions of exclusion and segregated support, this is obviously either a glaring case of oversight, or we the proponents of black theatre have not made our presence or our needs known. I hope here tonight to correct that.

I do not have the time in this short talk to reiterate the long and distinguished history of black theatre—often accomplished amid adverse and hostile conditions—but I would like to take the time to mark a few high points.

There are and have always been two distinct and parallel traditions in black art: that is, art that is conceived and designed to entertain white society, and art that feeds the spirit and celebrates the life of black America by designing its strategies for survival and prosperity.

An important part of black theatre that is often ignored but is seminal to its tradition is its origins on the slave plantations of the South. Summoned to the "big house" to entertain the slave owner and his guests, the slave began a tradition of theatre as entertainment for whites that reached its pinnacle in the heyday of the Harlem Renaissance. This entertainment for whites consisted of whatever the slave imagined or knew that his master wanted to see and hear. This tradition has its present life counterpart in the crossover artists that slant their material for white consumption.

The second tradition occurred when the African in the confines of the slave quarters sought to invest his spirit with the strength of his ancestors by conceiving in his art, in his song and dance, a world in which he was the spiritual center and his existence was a manifest act of the creator from whom life flowed. He then could create art that was functional and furnished him with a spiritual temperament necessary for his survival as property and the dehumanizing status that was attendant to that.

I stand myself and my art squarely on the self-defining ground of the slave quarters, and find the ground to be hallowed and made fertile by the blood and bones of the men and women who can be described as warriors on the cultural battlefield that affirmed their self-worth. As there is no idea that cannot be contained by black life, these men and women found themselves to be sufficient and secure in their art and their instructions.

It was this high ground of self-definition that the black playwrights of the '60s marked out for themselves. Ron Milner, Ed Bullins, Philip Hayes Dean, Richard Wesley, Lonne Elder III, Sonia Sanchez, Barbara Ann Teer and Amiri Baraka were among those playwrights who were particularly vocal and we remain indebted to them for their brave and courageous forays into an area that is marked with land mines and the shadows of snipers—those who would reserve the territory of arts and letters and the American theatre as their own special province and point blacks toward the ball fields and the bandstands.

That black theatre today comes under such assaults should surprise no one, as we are on the verge of reclaiming and reexamining the purpose and pillars of our art and laying out new directions for its expansion. As such we make a target for cultural imperialists who seek to empower and propagate their ideas about the world as the only valid ideas, and see blacks as woefully deficient not only in arts and letters but in the abundant gifts of humanity.

In the 19th century, the lack of education, the lack of contact with different cultures, the expensive and slow methods of travel and communication fostered such ideas, and the breeding ground of ignorance and racial intolerance promoted them.

The King's English and the lexicon of a people given to such ignorance and intolerance did not do much to dispel such obvious misconceptions, but provided them with a home. I cite Webster's *Third New International Dictionary*:

"BLACK: outrageously wicked, dishonorable, connected with the devil, menacing, sullen, hostile, unqualified, illicit, illegal, violators of public regulations, affected by some undesirable condition, etc.

"WHITE: free from blemish, moral stain or impurity; outstandingly righteous, innocent, not marked by malignant influence, notably auspicious, fortunate, decent, a sterling man."

Such is the linguistic environment that informs the distance that separates blacks and whites in America and which the cultural imperialist, who cannot imagine a life existing and flourishing outside his benevolent control, embraces.

Robert Brustein, writing in an article/review titled "Unity from Diversity" [*The New Republic*, July 19–26, 1993] is apparently disturbed that "there is a tremendous outpouring of work by minority artists" which he attributes to cultural diversity. He writes that the practice of extending invitations to a national banquet from which a lot of hungry people have long been excluded is a practice that can lead to confused standards. He goes on to establish a presumption of inferiority of the work of minority artists: "Funding agencies have started substituting sociological criteria for aesthetic criteria in their grant procedures, indicating that 'elitist' notions like quality and excellence are no longer functional." He goes on to say, "It's disarming in all senses of the word to say that we don't share common experiences that are measurable by common standards. But the growing number of truly talented artists with more universal interests suggests that we may soon be in a position to return to a single value system."

Brustein's surprisingly sophomoric assumption that this tremendous outpouring of work by minority artists leads to confusing standards and that funding agencies have started substituting sociological for aesthetic criteria, leaving aside notions like quality and excellence, shows him to be a victim of 19th-century thinking and the linguistic environment that posits blacks as unqualified. Quite possibly this tremendous outpouring of works by minority artists may lead to a raising of standards and a raising of the levels of excellence, but Mr. Brustein cannot allow that possibility.

To suggest that funding agencies are rewarding inferior work by pursuing sociological criteria only serves to call into question the tremendous outpouring of plays by white playwrights who benefit from funding given to the 66 LORT theatres.

Are those theatres funded on sociological or aesthetic criteria? Do we have 66 excellent theatres? Or do those theatres benefit from the sociological advantage that they are run by whites and cater to largely white audiences?

The truth is that often where there are aesthetic criteria of excellence, there are also sociological criteria that have traditionally excluded blacks. I say raise the standards and remove the sociological consideration of race as privilege, and we will meet you at the crossroads, in equal numbers, prepared to do the work of extending and developing the common ground of the American theatre.

We are capable of work of the highest order; we can answer to the high standards of world-class art. Anyone who doubts our capabilities at this late stage is being intellectually dishonest.

We can meet on the common ground of theatre as a field of work and endeavor. But we cannot meet on the common ground of experience.

Where is the common ground in the horrifics of lynching? Where is the common ground in the maim of a policeman's bullet? Where is the common ground in the hull of a slave ship or the deck of a slave ship with its refreshments of air and expanse?

We will not be denied our history.

We have voice and we have temper. We are too far along this road from the loss of our political will, we are too far along the road of reassembling ourselves, too far along the road to regaining spiritual health to allow such transgression of our history to go unchallenged.

The commonalities we share are the commonalities of culture. We decorate our houses. That is something we do in common. We do it differently because we value different things. We have different manners and different values of social intercourse. We have different ideas of what a party is.

There are some commonalities to our different ideas. We both offer food and drink to our guests, but because we have different culinary values, different culinary histories, we offer different food and drink. In our culinary history, we have learned to make do with the feet and ears and tails and intestines of the pig rather than the loin and the ham and the bacon. Because of our different histories with the same animal, we have different culinary ideas. But we share a common experience with the pig as opposed to say Muslims and Jews, who do not share that experience.

We can meet on the common ground of the American theatre.

We cannot share a single value system if that value system consists of the values of white Americans based on their European ancestors. We reject that as Cultural Imperialism. We need a value system that includes our contributions as Africans in America. Our agendas are as valid as yours. We may disagree, we may forever be on opposite sides of aesthetics, but we can only share a value system that is inclusive of all Americans and recognizes their unique and valuable contributions.

The ground together: We must develop the ground together. We reject the idea of equality among equals, but we say rather the equality of all men.

The common values of the American theatre that we can share are plot . . . dialogue . . . characterization . . . design. How we both make use of them will be determined by who we are—what ground we are standing on and what our cultural values are.

Theatre is part of art history in terms of its craft and dramaturgy, but it is part of social history in terms of how it is financed and governed. By making money available to theatres willing to support colorblind casting, the financiers and governors have signaled not only their unwillingness to support black theatre but their willingness to fund dangerous and divisive assaults against it. Colorblind casting is an aberrant idea that has never had any validity other than as a tool of the Cultural Imperialists who view American culture, rooted in the icons of European culture, as beyond reproach in its perfection. It is inconceivable to them that life could be lived and enriched without knowing Shakespeare or Mozart. Their gods, their manners, their being, are the only true and correct representations of humankind. They refuse to recognize black conduct and manners as part of a system that is fueled by its own philosophy, mythology, history, creative motif, social organization and ethos. The idea that blacks have their own way of responding to the world, their own values, style, linguistics, religion and aesthetics, is unacceptable to them.

For a black actor to stand on the stage as part of a social milieu that has denied him his gods, his culture, his humanity, his mores, his ideas of himself and the world he lives in, is to be in league with a thousand naysayers who wish to corrupt the vigor and spirit of his heart.

To cast us in the role of mimics is to deny us our own competence.

Our manners, our style, our approach to language, our gestures, and our bodies are not for rent. The history of our bodies—the maimings . . . the lashings . . . the lynchings . . . the body that is capable of inspiring profound rage and pungent cruelty—is not for rent.

To mount an all-black production of a *Death of a Salesman* or any other play conceived for white actors as an investigation of the human condition through the specifics of white culture is to deny us our own humanity, our own history, and the need to make our own investigations from the cultural ground on which we stand as black Americans. It is an assault on our presence, our difficult but honorable history in America; it is an insult to our intelligence, our playwrights, and our many and varied contributions to the society and the world at large.

The idea of colorblind casting is the same idea of assimilation that black Americans have been rejecting for the past 380 years. For the record, we reject it again. We reject any attempt to blot us out, to reinvent history and ignore our presence or to maim our spiritual product. We must not continue to meet on this path. We will not deny our history, and we will not allow it to be made to be of little consequence, to be ignored or misinterpreted.

In an effort to spare us the burden of being "affected by an undesirable condition" and as a gesture of benevolence, many whites (like the proponents of colorblind casting) say, "Oh, I don't see color." We want you to see us. We are black and beautiful. We are not patrons of the linguistic environment that has us as "unqualified, and violators of public regulations." We are not a menace to society. We are not ashamed. We have an honorable history in the world of men. We come from a long line of honorable people with complex codes of ethics and social discourse, people who devised myths and systems of cosmology and systems of economics. We are not ashamed, and do not need you to be ashamed for us. Nor do we need the recognition of our blackness to be couched in abstract phases like "artist of color." Who are you talking about? A Japanese artist? An Eskimo? A Filipino? A Mexican? A Cambodian? A Nigerian? An African American? Are we to suppose that if you put a white person on one side of the scale and the rest of humanity lumped together as nondescript "people of color" on the other side, that it would balance out? That whites carry that much spiritual weight? We reject that. We are unique, and we are specific.

We do not need colorblind casting; we need some theatres to develop our playwrights. We need those misguided financial resources to be put to better use. We cannot develop our playwrights with the meager resources at our disposal. Why is it difficult to imagine 9 black theatres but not 66 white ones? Without theatres we cannot develop our talents. If we cannot develop our talents, then everyone suffers: our writers; the theatre; the audience. Actors are deprived of material, and our communities are deprived of the jobs in support of the art—the company manager, the press coordinator, the electricians, the carpenters, the concessionaires, the people that work in wardrobe, the box-office staff, the ushers and the janitors. We need some theatres. We cannot continue like this. We have only one life to develop our talent, to fulfill our potential as artists. One life, and it is short, and the lack of the means to develop our talent is an encumbrance on that life.

We did not sit on the sidelines while the immigrants of Europe, through hard work, skill, cunning, guile and opportunity, built America into an industrial giant of the 20th century. It was our labor that provided the capital. It was our labor in the shipyards and the stockyards and the coal mines and the steel mills. Our labor built the roads and the railroads. And when America was challenged, we strode on the battlefield, our boots strapped on and our blood left to soak into the soil of places whose names we could not pronounce, against an enemy whose only crime was ideology. We left our blood in France and Korea and the Philippines and Vietnam, and our only reward has been the deprivation of possibility and the denial of our moral personality.

It cannot continue. The ground together: The American ground on which I stand and which my ancestors purchased with their perseverance, with their survival, with their manners and with their faith.

It cannot continue, as other assaults upon our presence and our history cannot continue: When the *New York Times* publishes an article on pop singer Michael Bolton and lists as his influences four white singers, then as an afterthought tosses in the phrase "and the great black rhythm and blues singers," it cannot be anything but purposeful with intent to maim. These great black rhythm and blues singers are reduced to an afterthought on the edge of oblivion—one stroke of the editor's pen and the history of American music is revised, and Otis Redding, Jerry Butler and Rufus Thomas are consigned to the dustbin of history while Joe Cocker, Mick Jagger and Rod Stewart are elevated to the status of the originators and creators of a vital art that is a product of our spiritual travails; the history of music becomes a fabrication, a blatant forgery which under the hallowed auspices of the *New York Times* is presented as the genuine article.

We cannot accept these assaults. We must defend and protect our spiritual fruits. To ignore these assaults would be to be derelict in our duties. We cannot accept them. Our political capital will not permit them.

So much of what makes this country rich in art and all manners of spiritual life is the contributions that we as African-Americans have made. We cannot allow others to have authority over our cultural and spiritual products. We reject, without reservation, any attempts by anyone to rewrite our history so as to deny us the rewards of our spiritual labors, and to become the cultural custodians of our art, our literature and our lives. To give expression to the spirit that has been shaped and fashioned by our history is of necessity to give voice and vent to the history itself.

It must remain for us a history of triumph.

The time has come for black playwrights to confer with one another, to come together to meet each other face to face, to address questions of aesthetics and ways to defend ourselves from the naysayers who would trumpet our talents as insufficient to warrant the same manner of investigation and exploration as the majority. We need to develop guidelines for the protection of our cultural property, our contributions and the influence they accrue. It is time we took responsibility for our talents in our own hands. We cannot depend on others. We cannot depend on the directors, the managers or the actors to do the work we should be doing for ourselves. It is our lives and the pursuit of our fulfillment that are being encumbered by false ideas and perceptions.

It is time to embrace the political dictates of our history and answer the challenge to our duties. I further think we should confer in a city in our ancestral homeland in the southern part of the United States in 1998, so that we may enter the millennium united and prepared for a long future of prosperity.

From the hull of a ship to self-determining, self-respecting people. That is the journey we are making.

We are robust in spirit, we are bright with laughter, and we are bold in imagination. Our blood is soaked into the soil and our bones lie scattered the whole way across the Atlantic Ocean, as Hansel's crumbs, to mark the way back home.

We are no longer in the House of Bondage, and soon we will no longer be victims of the counting houses who hold from us ways to develop and support our talents and our expressions of life and its varied meanings. Assaults upon the body politic that demean and ridicule and depress the value and worth of our existence, that seek to render it immobile and to extinguish the flame of freedom lit eons ago by our ancestors upon another continent—these must be met with a fierce and uncompromising defense.

If you are willing to accept it, it is your duty to affirm and urge that defense, that respect and that determination.

I must mention here, with all due respect to W.E.B. DuBois, that the concept of a "talented tenth" creates an artificial superiority. It is a fallacy and a dangerous idea that only serves to divide us further. I am not willing to throw away as untalented 90 percent of my blood; I am not willing to dismiss the sons and daughters of those people who gave more than lip service to the will to live and made it a duty to prosper in spirit, if not in provision. All God's children got talent. It is a dangerous idea to set one part of the populace above and aside from the other. We do a grave disservice to ourselves not to seek out and embrace and enable all of our human resources as a people. All blacks in America, with very few exceptions—no matter what our status, no matter the size of our bank accounts, no matter how many and what kind of academic degrees we can place beside our names, no matter the furnishings and square footage of our homes, the length of our closets and the quality of the wool and cotton that hangs there—we all in America originated from the same place: the slave plantations of the South. We all share a common past, and despite how some of us might think and how it might look, we all share a common present and will share a common future.

We can make a difference. Artists, playwrights, actors—we can be the spearhead of a movement to reignite and reunite our people's positive energy for a political and social change that is reflective of our spiritual truths rather than economic fallacies. Our talents, our truth, our belief in ourselves is all in our hands. What we make of it will emerge as a baptismal spray that names and defines. What we do now becomes history by which our grandchildren will judge us.

We are not off on a tangent. The foundation of the American theatre is the foundation of European theatre that begins with the great Greek dramatists; it is based on the proscenium stage and the poetics of Aristotle. This is the theatre that we have chosen to work in. We embrace the values of that theatre but reserve the right to amend, to explore, to add our African consciousness and our African aesthetic to the art we produce.

To pursue our cultural expression does not separate us. We are not separatists, as Mr. Brustein asserts. We are Americans trying to fulfill our talents. We are not the servants at the party. We are not apprentices in the kitchens. We are not the stableboys to the King's huntsmen. We are Africans. We are Americans. The irreversible sweep of history has decreed that. We are artists who seek to develop our talents and give expression to our personalities. We bring advantage to the common ground that is the American theatre.

All theatres depend on an audience for their dialogue. To the American theatre, subscription audiences are its life blood. But the subscription audience holds the seats of our theatres hostage to the mediocrity of its tastes, and serves to impede the further development of an audience for the work that we do. While intentional or not, it serves to keep blacks out of the theatre where they suffer no illusion of welcome anyway. A subscription thus becomes not a support system but makes the patrons members of a club to which the theatre serves as a clubhouse. It is an irony that the people who can most afford a full-price ticket get discounts for subscribing, while the single-ticket buyer who cannot afford a subscription is charged the additional burden of support to offset the subscription-buyer's discount. It is a system that is in need of overhaul to provide not only a more equitable access to tickets but access to influence as well.

I look for and challenge students of arts management to be bold in their exploration of new systems of funding theatres, including profit-making institutions and ventures, and I challenge black artists and audiences to scale the walls erected by theatre subscriptions to gain access to this vital area of spiritual enlightenment and enrichment that is the theatre.

All theatregoers have opinions about the work they witness. Critics have an informed opinion. Sometimes it may be necessary for them to gather more information to become more informed. As playwrights grow and develop, as the theatre changes, the critic has an important responsibility to guide and encourage that growth. However, in the discharge of their duties, it may be necessary for them to also grow and develop. A stagnant body of critics, operating from the critical criteria of 40 years ago, makes for a stagnant theatre without the fresh and abiding influence of contemporary ideas. It is the critics who should be in the forefront of developing new tools for analysis necessary to understand new influences.

The critic who can recognize a German neo-romantic influence should also be able to recognize an American influence from blues or black church rituals, or any other contemporary American influence.

The true critic does not sit in judgment. Rather he seeks to inform his reader, instead of adopting a posture of self-conscious importance in which he sees himself a judge and final arbiter of a work's importance or value.

We stand on the verge of an explosion of playwriting talent that will challenge our critics. As American playwrights absorb the influence of television and use new avenues of approach to the practice of their craft, they will prove to be wildly inventive and imaginative in creating dramas that will guide and influence contemporary life for years to come.

Theatre can do that. It can disseminate ideas, it can educate even the miseducated, because it is art—and all art reaches across that divide that makes order out of chaos, and embraces the truth that overwhelms with its presence, and connects man to something larger than himself and his imagination.

Theatre asserts that all of human life is universal. Love, Honor, Duty, Betrayal belong and pertain to every culture or race. The way they are acted out on the playing field may be different, but betrayal is betrayal whether you are a South Sea Islander, a Mississippi farmer or an English baron. All of human life is universal, and it is theatre that illuminates and confers upon the universal the ability to speak for all men.

The ground together: We have to do it together. We cannot permit our lives to waste away, our talents unchallenged. We cannot permit a failure to our duty. We are brave and we are boisterous, our mettle is proven, and we are dedicated.

The ground together: the ground of the American theatre on which I am proud to stand . . . the ground which our artistic ancestors purchased with their endeavors . . . with their pursuit of the American spirit and its ideals.

I believe in the American theatre. I believe in its power to inform about the human condition, its power to heal, its power to hold the mirror as 'twere up to nature, its power to uncover the truths we wrestle from uncertain and sometimes unyielding realities. All of art is a search for ways of being, of living life more fully. We who are capable of those noble pursuits should challenge the melancholy and barbaric, to bring the light of angelic grace, peace, prosperity and the unencumbered pursuit of happiness to the ground on which we all stand.

August Wilson is the two-time Pulitzer Prize–winning author of *Gem of the Ocean, Joe Turner's Come and Gone, Ma Rainey's Black Bottom, The Piano Lesson, Seven Guitars, Fences, Two Trains Running, Jitney, King Hedley II* and *Radio Golf*, a 10-play cycle exploring the African-American experience through the 20th century. In 2003, he made his professional stage debut in his one-man show *How I Learned What I Learned*. Broadway's August Wilson Theatre was named for the playwright after his death in October '05.

SUBSIDIZED SEPARATISM

By Robert Brustein

October 1996

August Wilson's keynote address at the TCG Conference in late June, later published in these pages as "The Ground on Which I Stand," was greeted with a standing ovation by the various resident theatre people attending, though some found it divisive and disturbing. Since I was not present at the conference, I was hardly in a position to express my own reactions, though word leaked back to me that chief among the malefactors identified in Wilson's broadside—his "snipers" and "naysayers" and "cultural imperialists"—was myself. I frame this reply not just to defend and clarify a personal position which I believe to have been misrepresented but also to debate some of the more troubling general issues raised in his speech.

Wilson's rambling jeremiad is essentially an effort to accentuate the achievements of black theatre, which he claims to be supreme today though "often accomplished amid adverse and hostile conditions." "Black theatre is alive, it is vibrant, it is vital," he says. But not all its practitioners are worthy of praise. In the same speech, Wilson manages to express his disdain for black "crossover artists" who, "like house slaves entertaining the white master and his guests," manage to "slant their material for white consumption." He rebukes white foundations for failing to create and subsidize black theatre companies. And he characterizes the idea of "colorblind casting" as "a tool of the Cultural Imperialists"—"the same idea of assimilation that black Americans have been rejecting for the past 300 years."

If you hear echoes in this of 1960s radicalism, particularly the language of Black Nationalism, your ears are not deceiving you. And Wilson is hardly reluctant to admit his militant inheritance. Testifying that the Black Power Movement was "the kiln in which I was fired," he proclaims that its concern with "self-determination, self-respect and self-defense" are the values that govern his life. He claims that "I am what is known, at least among the followers and supporters of Marcus Garvey, as a 'race man.'" He announces that the ground on which he stands was pioneered "by Nat Turner, by Denmark Vesey, by Martin Delaney, Marcus Garvey and the Honorable Elijah Muhammad"— rebels or separatists all, some proponents of a return in Africa. Conspicuous by its absence is the name of Martin Luther King, among many other honored black Americans for whom the idea of integration has not been considered anathema.

The foundation of this long tirade is Wilson's insistence on black culture, particularly black theatre, not only as an unparalleled achievement but also a singular and discrete experience of life. It is an experience that cannot be fully absorbed or understood by white people, much less criticized by them: "We cannot allow others to have authority over our cultural and spiritual products," he says. "We need to develop guidelines for the protection of our cultural property, our contributions and influence they accrue." Whites and blacks can occupy the same country, but they cannot occupy the same ground. "Where is the common ground in the horrifics of lynching? Where is the common ground in the hull or the deck of a slave ship . . . ?" He describes: "black conduct and manners as part of a system that is fueled by its own philosophy, mythology, history, creative motif, social organization and ethos." He deplores the presence of a black actor in a non-black play, standing on the stage "as part of a social milieu that has denied him his gods, his humanity, his mores, his ideas of himself and the world he lives in . . . ." Indeed, he considers the very idea of an all-black production of *Death of a Salesman* to be "an assault on our presence . . . an insult to our intelligence."

This is the language of self-segregation. At times, it is true, Wilson is willing to concede that blacks and whites breathe the same air and partake of certain "commonalities" of culture. Among these "commonalities" he mentions food, though even that admission is weirdly exclusionary. Black people have had to be satisfied with the leavings of the pig. Yet, blacks and whites "share a common experience with the pig as opposed to say Muslims and Jews, who do not share that experience." (Black Muslims? Reform Jews?) It is also true that, in the rolling cadences that bring his speech to its climax, Wilson concedes the American theatre's power to "inform about the human condition, its power to heal, its power to hold the mirror as "'twere up to nature, its power to uncover the truths we wrestle from uncertain and sometimes unyielding realities." Even this boilerplate rhetoric, however, for all its afterthought references to the unifying nature of the theatre, fails to compensate for the divisive nature of his remarks. Perhaps some future student of syntax will analyze how Wilson's vacillating use of the word "we" in the same paragraph (first inclusive: "We have to do it together," then exclusive: "We are brave and we are boisterous") betrays his ambivalent sense of American identity. This ambivalence makes for some confusing assertions. "We are black and beautiful . . . . We are not separatists . . . . We are Africans. We are Americans."

Furthermore, Wilson's insistence on the strength and uniqueness of a proud black culture is oddly inconsistent with his notion that blacks are "victims of the counting houses who hold from us ways to develop and support our talents." This inconsistency grows more glaring when Wilson directs his biblical fury towards some of these "counting houses" (that is, the funding agencies) and concludes that "the economics are reserved as privilege to the overwhelming abundance of institutions that promote and perpetuate white culture." He notes that of the 66 LORT theatres only one can be considered black. And in an impassioned if curious appeal for subsidized separatism, he sees no contradiction in demanding the white foundations take the responsibility for founding as well as funding black theatres, as if theatre companies were the creation of philanthropic agencies rather than the indigenous outgrowths of dedicated artists and supporting communities.

I'm not at all certain anymore what constitutes a "black" or "white" theatre. Both the now-defunct Negro Ensemble Company and the thriving Crossroads Theatre fit Wilson's exclusive definition clearly enough. But how does one describe New York's Public Theater and Atlanta's Alliance Theatre under the black artists George C. Wolfe and Kenny Leon? Or Yale Repertory Theatre and Syracuse Stage when they were led by such black directors as Lloyd Richards and Tazewell Thompson? Most American theatres today, like many American cities—indeed like many Americans—are racially mixed. Are black actors now to perform only black parts written by black playwrights? Will James Earl Jones no longer have a chance to play Judge Brack or Darth Vader? Must we bar Andre Braugher and Denzel Washington from enacting the Shakespearean monarchs? Is Othello not to be an acceptable opportunity for Morgan Freeman or Laurence Fishburne? Will Athol Fugard be told he cannot take a colored role in his own plays? No more *Voodoo Macbeth*s or all-black *Godot*s? No more efforts on behalf of nontraditional casting and integrated theatre companies? Must history be rolled back to the days of segregated theatres?

I fear Wilson is displaying a failure of memory—I hesitate to say a failure of gratitude—when he charges nonprofit resident theatres with using "sociological criteria" in choosing seasons that "traditionally exclude blacks." All of his own plays were originated and produced by a large consortium of mainstream institutions, including Yale Repertory Theatre, the Huntington, American Conservatory Theater, the Goodman, the Mark Taper, and so on. Wilson's pervasive tone of victimization, in fact, is oddly inappropriate for a playwright whose six LORT-generated plays, after completing the resident theatre circuit, all found their way to Broadway, where they won two Pulitzer Prizes, five New York Drama Critics' Circle awards, and I don't know how many Tonys, besides generating enormous box-office income for the playwright (from white and black audiences alike). Is a man who has garnered such extraordinary media attention (not to mention every conceivable playwriting fellowship) really in a position to say that blacks are being excluded from the American theatre or that these institutions only "preserve, promote and perpetuate white culture?" Has he read any foundation reports lately? Does he have any idea of the proportion of grants, both public and private, that are exclusively reserved for inner-city audience development and multicultural activities in resident theatres?

I am the only villain identified by name in Wilson's speech. He makes reference to my article "Diversity and Unity," but there are also hidden allusions to what I wrote in "The Options of Multiculturalism," my unfavorable review of his play, *The Piano Lesson*, and my *Times* op-ed piece on coercive foundation funding. Wilson specifically attacks what he calls my "surprisingly sophomoric assumption" that the present funding climate is characterized by confused standards and sociological rather than aesthetic criteria. I confess to believing that most foundations (by their own admission) no longer make artistic quality their primary consideration. But I categorically deny I ever said that "the practice of extending invitations to a national banquet from which a lot of hungry people have been excluded" (my phrase, uncredited) establishes (his phrase) "a presumption of inferiority of the work of minority artists."

Wilson's charge, with its nasty imputations of racism, is intended to characterize a review of two minority playwrights who, in my estimation, met the highest standards and without being exclusionary. "Drenched in their own cultural juices," I wrote, "they are nevertheless capable of telling stories that include us all, thus proving again that the theatre works best as a unifying rather than a segregating medium." I was talking about transcendence, about recognizing that the greatest art embraces a common humanity. Although Wilson might dismiss such playwrights—the younger generation of black writers like Anna Deavere Smith and OyamO and Suzan-Lori Parks—as "crossover artists" entertaining the slave owner and his guests, my article was a plea to minority playwrights like himself to acknowledge, without any loss of racial consciousness, that they belong as artists to the same human family as everyone else.

Some people may remember that, almost alone among white critics, I have expressed reservations about Wilson's plays. This was an aesthetic judgment, not a racial one. While I admire Wilson's control of character and dialogue, a lot of his writing has seemed to me weakly structured, badly edited, prosaic and overwritten. Consider, for instance, *Seven Guitars*, which I didn't review (I left after four guitars). I don't think it exposes the "values of white Americans based on their European ancestors" to believe that a conventionally realistic play needs an animating event, and that, however colorful its subject matter, it cannot ramble willy-nilly for two-and-a-half hours before establishing a line of action. My less technical objection has been that, by choosing to chronicle the oppression of black people through each of the decades, Wilson has fallen into a monotonous tone of victimization which happens to be the leitmotif of his TCG speech.

I am also disturbed by other attitudes reflected in that speech, notably that only the black experience inspires the work of black artists. In "The Options of Multiculturalism," I suggested that, while Wilson has announced he will never allow a white director to stage his plays, a backyard drama like *Fences* shows the considerable influence of white playwrights, particularly Arthur Miller and his *All My Sons*. (It may be that Wilson's anger over this conjecture ricochets into his ferocious attack on the *New York Times* for allegedly underplaying the influence of black singers on Michael Bolton—something he calls an "intent to maim.")

It is perfectly possible that I am wrong in my assessments. And I can understand how a playwright, no matter how highly praised by mainstream critics, can smart under adverse criticism, even in a relatively small-circulation periodical such as the *New Republic*. But that is no justification for wheeling out the creaky juggernaut of Black Power to roll over any critic who makes a negative judgment on his plays. Indeed, Wilson seems to suggest occasionally that the only true critical function is boosterism. For at the same time that Wilson is questioning the very idea of critical opinions ("The true critic does not sit in judgment . . . the critic has an important responsibility to guide and encourage . . . growth"), he is announcing that every African American, contrary to DuBois's idea of "the talented tenth," is artistically gifted: "All God's children got talent." This is progressive-school nonsense. The greatest tribute that a critic can pay to a playwright such as Wilson is to judge and analyze his work by the same criteria as anybody else's work.

Wilson writes: "I stand myself and my art squarely on the self-defining ground of the slave quarter." Isn't it time to acknowledge that, for all the grim uncompleted racial business in this country, those quarters have long been razed to the ground? Isn't there some kind of statute of limitation on white guilt and white reparations? Isn't it possible to recognize that there is a difference between losing your freedom and losing a Tony, between toting a bale of cotton and carrying around an unfavorable review? To say that whites can't understand black culture because their ancestors were not enslaved is almost as problematical as saying that Wilson can't understand the writings of a Jew because he hasn't experience life under the Pharaohs. Many brilliant black artists and intellectuals—Albert Murray, Ralph Ellison, Henry Louis Gates, Shelby Steele and others—have repudiated the "ethnographic fallacy" that one writer's peculiar experiences can represent a whole social category. This tribalist approach, as Diane Ravitch has written, "confuses race with culture, as though everyone with the same skin color had the same culture and history."

August Wilson is more comfortable writing plays than apostolic decrees. His speech is melancholy testimony to the rabid identity politics and poisonous racial consciousness that have been infecting our country in recent years. Although Wilson would deny it, such sentiments represent a reverse form of the old politics of division, an appeal for socially approved and foundation-funded separatism. I don't think Martin Luther King ever imagined an America where playwrights such as August Wilson would be demanding, under the pretense of calling for healing and unity, an entirely separate stage for black theatre artists. What next? Separate schools? Separate washrooms? Separate drinking fountains?

Robert Brustein was the founding director of Yale Repertory Theatre in New Haven, Conn., and American Repertory Theatre in Cambridge, Mass. He is the author of numerous adaptations and full-length plays and more than a dozen books, is a former dean of the Yale School of Drama, and since 1959 has served as the theatre critic for the *New Republic*, in which a version of this essay previously appeared.

A RESPONSE TO BRUSTEIN

By August Wilson

October 1996

Truth is not an individual perception. There are 66 LORT theatres strung like pearls across this country from Maine to Alaska. Only one of them is dedicated to preserving and promoting black culture. This gives us a theatre not only skewed toward whites and the so-called classical values of European theatre, but one that impedes the development of a truly American theatre and ignores the contributions being made by others of various ethnic and racial backgrounds.

The American theatre is not the property of any one race or culture. To have a theatre that promotes the values of black Americans, our hard-won survival and prosperity, that addresses ways of life that are peculiar to us, that investigates our personalities and social intercourse and philosophical thought, is not to be outside of the American theatre or Western theatre any more than Ibsen and Chekhov's explorations of Norwegian and Russian culture make them outsiders—or David Mamet's insightful and provocative explorations of white American culture make him an outsider.

Yet the influence and contributions of black Americans are not recognized by any gain in material culture that would allow us to further develop our arts and establish control over their dissemination. We are being strangled by our well-meaning friends. Money spent "diversifying" the American theatre, developing black audiences for white institutions, developing ideas of colorblind casting, only strengthens and solidifies this stranglehold by making our artists subject to the paternalistic notions of white institutions that dominate and control the art.

Doing a black play or allowing blacks to have roles not written for them does not change the nature of the institution or its mission. Blacks come and go and the institution remains dedicated to its ideas of "preserving culture and promoting thought." Our visitor pass expires and we never have a permanent place to hang our hat, to develop our own ideas, and to provide our community with a sense of cultural worth and self-sufficiency. The damage this does to our present institutions and our already debilitated communities is evident and significant.

It is true, as Robert Brustein asserts, that theatres are the indigenous outgrowths of dedicated artists and supporting communities. No one knows that better than the people involved in black theatre. Most of the time all they have to make theatre with is their passionate dedication and loving, supporting communities. The funding is reserved as the privilege of sociological criteria for white theatres and *their* dedicated individuals and supporting communities.

When Brustein trumpets as universal artists those whose "perceptions go beyond racial and sectarian agendas," he is denying those artists who explore and investigate their lives as African Americans the right to occupy the ground of universality because they have values other than his, and he sees no value to their agendas. His bias blinds him to the fact that being a black artist isn't "limiting" any more than being a white artist is limiting, and that being a black artist does not mean you have to disengage yourself from the world and your concerns as a global citizen or from the ideas of love, honor, duty, betrayal, etc., that are the concerns of all great art.

Brustein also demonstrates an irresponsibility of language, makes false and spurious accusations, categorically denies factual information (see the *New Republic*, July 19–26, 1993, p. 29, col. 1, line 10), mis-titles his own essay and makes large and erroneous assumptions. At the very least he need not invent things for me to say. I have never said I consider black theatre "supreme." That is not my word or my belief or my attitude.

Furthermore, I have never said I wouldn't allow a white director to direct my plays. Having worked with Bill Partlan and Amy Saltz and Steve Robman at the O'Neill National Playwrights Conference on five separate occasions, I have had nothing but the highest praise for their work; likewise Irene Lewis's stirring production of *Joe Turner's Come and Gone* at CENTERSTAGE in Baltimore, and Howard Davies's splendid staging of *Ma Rainey's Black Bottom* at the National Theatre in London. I approved of both those directors. What I did say about white directors is known or available to any attentive reader.

To suggest that I owe a debt of gratitude to the theatres that have done my work is to suggest my plays are without sufficient merit to warrant their production other than as an act of benevolence. I reject that, as well I am sure the artistic leadership of the theatres in which I have worked would reject such blighted thought.

Brustein has no way of knowing what I think of the work of OyamO, Anna Deavere Smith, Suzan-Lori Parks or anyone else. I would take exception to his characterization of their work as "crossover," and he is emphatically wrong in saying I hold them in "disdain." While I do believe I am correct in the two parallel traditions of black art as defined in my talk, I would never be so arrogant as to tell any artists what kind of work they should be doing.

My criticism of DuBois's concept of a talented tenth was that it was divisive among blacks, as it set up a hierarchy that allowed its enemies to drive a wedge between the talented and untalented and obscure their assaults on the body politic of black America. Obviously, everyone is not artistically talented, but there are kinds of talent other than artistic, and here in America everyone deserves the opportunity to develop whatever talent they have to its fullest.

Brustein confuses the role of the critic with "authority," and sees my call for the control and dissemination of black art, our spiritual product, as an attack on critics. I don't see critics as authority, and was actually talking about others who set themselves up as custodian of the black experience and who exercise real control of the dissemination of its products. For the record: We do not ask, we do not seek, nor do we want special treatment. Inasmuch as we are part of Western Theatre, work should be judged on those terms and principles as outlined by Aristotle in his *Poetics*. We have never asked to stand outside of that or to have our work treated differently or judged by different standards or criteria because we are black. We have never said that white reviewers cannot understand black theatre—if you can understand Duke Ellington and Ray Charles, you can understand black theatre. We *have* said that critics have a valuable and important role to play in the continuing development of theatre, but we do recognize not all critics are valuable and important.

Finally, Martin Luther King Jr. was an honorable man who died on the battlefield while challenging America to live up to the meaning of her creed so as not to make a mockery of her ideals. Before Brustein gets so carried away in invoking the name of King in service of the status quo, let us remember that it is Brustein's failure to imagine a theatre broad enough and secure enough in its traditions to absorb and make use of all manners and cultures of American life that contributes to the failure of the American spirit that permits King's challenge to go unmet. We issue the challenge again. We cannot afford to fail.

August Wilson is the two-time Pulitzer Prize—winning author of *Gem of the Ocean, Joe Turner's Come and Gone, Ma Rainey's Black Bottom, The Piano Lesson, Seven Guitars, Fences, Two Trains Running, Jitney, King Hedley II* and *Radio Golf*, a 10-play cycle exploring the African-American experience through the 20th century. In 2003, he made his professional stage debut in his one-man show *How I Learned What I Learned*. Broadway's August Wilson Theatre was named for the playwright after his death in October '05.

WHO NEEDS ARTISTS?

By Robert MacNeil

April 1997

A merica is creative or it is nothing. Americans created a nation and have been re-creating it ever since. American creativity in the arts and sciences may conceivably outlive the nation, but in the present it is as essential to the nation's re-creation and its constant reinvigoration as it is to the refreshment of us all as individuals. To conceive of American creativity at risk is to imagine this country losing its dynamic force, its ability to imagine the future and the desire to shape it.

In a practical sense, sustaining American creativity is particularly important in our newly competitive world, where American pre-eminence will be continuously tested. We started with huge advantages—vast natural resources and a population self-selected to be bold risk-takers, impatient of an unsatisfactory status quo. Our advantages have eroded as nations who lack them (witness Japan) have managed to catch up by using intelligence, ingenuity, imagination.

That situation justifies the concern that we identify and invest in the best brains in science and technology; keeping us competitive and innovative translates into jobs and prosperity, and that the average American easily understands. But he understands less easily why it is important to invest in creative minds in the arts. That need is less obvious, because it is more abstract.

A document recently prepared for the American Assembly at Columbia University gives the following statistics: The number of Americans calling themselves artists increased from 400,000 in 1950 to 1.7 million in 1990. An estimated 3.2 million—2.7 percent of all U.S. workers—are employed in profit and nonprofit cultural work. Over the past 25 years, the number of artists tripled; the number of symphony orchestras grew from 58 to 230; professional theatres increased from 22 to 420; dance companies from 37 to 250, and opera companies from 27 to 120.

This means we are feeding in the arts a much bigger animal than in the past, and now government, corporations, foundations and Americans as individuals seem eager to put this beast on a diet.

In doing so, what, precisely, is at risk? Take music: It is widely noted that the audience for classical music is declining. Much of the rock generation is hostile or indifferent, and soon that generation will be pushing the rest of us over the hill with our Beethoven quartets and Mozart concertos. But audiences are not creative, nor are the orchestras they come to hear. They are interpretive artists and consumers, both part of the cultural matrix or infrastructure which may inspire new composers to create works, however modern, that are grounded in the classical tradition. But do you need to worry about subsidizing the composer, or subsidizing the orchestra or the audience—not only the artist but the cultural infrastructure that he composes to, the cultural milieu which can inspire and then appreciate new work? And do you then work to restore some musical education to public schools, to create new audiences? In Japan, I read, in a typical elementary school, half the children study piano or violin. In many American public schools, music and art have been abandoned as unnecessary frills.

It is a lot easier to dismiss art as a frill in a time when budget-cutting is good politics and many social needs cry out for funding priority. But hostility to the arts is also good politics, particularly in the eyes of the Christian Right and those who curry favor with it. In work that deliberately stretches the moral boundaries of the time, it is always easy to find materials that offend conventional morality and paint them as evidence of corruption, filth or pornography. It is an old charge, fought to an enlightened conclusion 60 years ago over James Joyce, fated to be re-fought to a less enlightened conclusion in our time over Robert Mapplethorpe.

But current political hostility is part of a larger picture. It plays on emotions raised by anxiety about the American standard of living; by the painful dislocations in many lives forced by the third industrial revolution caused by the computer, that world-altering example of American creativity. Happy assumptions that our standard of living was destined by God always to rise—that our children would always be better off than we are—have crashed. But so have the moral codes: Millions of Americans see a moral collapse in this society as momentous, if not as instantaneous, as the Wall Street crash that started the Great Depression. They see in one generation wholesale abandonment and mockery of values they thought sacred: a hateful permissiveness about adultery, divorce, abortion, births out of wedlock, homosexuality, sexual promiscuity and so on.

As the Chicago historian William H. McNeill has noted, fundamentalism all over the world is born in fear of change, particularly changes in morality that are forced when people of traditional beliefs collide with the moral relativism of sophisticated urban life. Today American fundamentalists feel in collision with such relativism through the unavoidable mass communications of our culture, and they resent it. Bob Dole attempted to tap that resentment and failed, but it has a growing hold on the Republican Party for the future. And it will be the rare congressman, state legislator, endowment executive, corporate donor or foundation grantmaker who will not have one ear tuned to that resentment.

Beyond fundamentalism, the great majority of Americans are probably benignly indifferent to what we call The Arts, and do not see the gap between the commercial marketplace for culture and individual artists as important.

Even if they are sympathetic, people know that almost everyone has a struggle in life: Self-fulfillment does not come easily to most people, why should the artist be an exception? Artists have always struggled; they have chosen a life apart; they scorn our grimy toil for money; they have made their bed, and in our puritan ethic, perhaps we feel that self-denial and struggle will produce better artists; out of that annealing fire will come the searing genius.

But I see other reasons for alienation of ordinary people from The Arts, or at least alienation from the distant respect average Americans traditionally paid to great art. One is the turn Modernism took at the beginning of this century: away from the representative, the figurative, the world recognizable to Everyman, into a private vision so abstract, so unrecognizable that it excluded everyone who did not have special knowledge. The painting, the music, the poetry, the prose literature of that period are still shocking, perhaps annoying, to the uninitiated, the subject of endless ridicule, suspicions of fakery or hoax. Morley Safer's exposé on "60 Minutes" of abstract painting probably struck a responsive chord in millions.

Second: Even the authorities differ on what is great art. The advance of multiculturalism has reduced the hitherto unquestioned prestige of the great white Western male names of the past, and introduced confusing claims from Asia, Africa and Native Americans.

Third: I think a new, democratic mass culture has replaced the prestige classics to which even the masses used to pay some reverence. In the past, the canon was the canon.

Brilliantly eclectic, the mass culture dips into the classics and all the fine arts just enough to make it unnecessary for busy people without special motivation to address the real thing. Even for the motivated, the real thing (opera, ballet, orchestras, theatre) grows prohibitively expensive, despite the subsidies. As for special motivation: Thousands of young Americans privileged to go to a university get through on little more than CliffsNotes and will enter a world of consumerdom where great art is similarly absorbed. We are surrounded by Impressionist and Fauvist images that revolutionized painting a century ago— on our coffee mugs, our sheets, our shower curtains. Who needs to do the museum when you can do the museum shop?

Such merchandized appropriation of art certainly improves the visible taste environment, but our society has made it almost unnecessary for people, especially young people, to be exposed to good graphic art, literature or music except as cultural background noise, elevator music; merchandisers, who appropriate snatches of these arts, clearly rank high in the hierarchy of American creative genius.

We have displaced any reverence for art by a whole new culture cunningly targeted to age groups that can be assembled around certain icons in entertainment and advertising. Starting with the rock generation, the time when children became serious consumers, Americans now grow up in a culture created for them—food, clothing, transportation, sports and entertainment, all consumable and self-contained. They don't need to aspire to musty stuff people used to consider great. They can go through life in their own cultural bubble.

At its best, this new culture can be fresh and highly creative, employing all the skills of the artists we are here to support. At its worst, and more commonly, it is a triumph of marketing over content, art produced with an attitude film critic Pauline Kael nailed years ago as "the audience is a jerk"—contempt for the customer. The question is what will sell, what the customer can be persuaded to buy if you hype it enough. If you're big enough you *can* hype it plenty, and producers are getting plenty big. Hence the Disneyfication, the Time-Warnering, the Murdochization of content, all now conveniently reducible to one digital language, flung around the world by satellite—books, rap music, newspapers, movies, television sitcoms, TV news—everything a commodity, bearing on, or failing to bear on, some megacorporate bottom line.

Where does this leave the creative artist today? Or, as it has come to be called in foundation-speak, the "originating artist"? That term says a great deal about the appropriating nature of our cultural product. I guess Vincent Van Gogh was the "originating artist" in the huge industry that now exploits his images. Sunflowers, adapted by, redeveloped by, produced by, designed by, enhanced by (and in tiny letters) from an original concept by Van Gogh. The more artistic product is a commodity affecting the bottom line of big corporations, the less it will ever be the work of one brain, one talent. It must be worked, shaped, edited, sent back for rewrites, brainstormed by concept artists, market artists and merchandising artists, run up the flagpole, market-tested, focus-grouped, trashed, redesigned, reconfigured. Or in the nonprofit world, it must be first defined in a proposal for funding, evaluated by a panel, examined for relevance to the funder's mission description, subjected to ascertainment for political correctness and multicultural values. I don't care that "originating artist" has legal and copyright implications; it has a dismissive connotation, making it seem (like the writer in Hollywood) the least important figure in the creative food chain, the lower species that gets eaten by everyone higher up the chain.

If we are going to truly honor creativity and recognize that some rare individuals have ideas the rest of us—however deserving we may be in this egalitarian land—do not have, ideas which soar above the commonplace, if we believe such creativity is both the glory of a great nation and seriously at risk, then we had better stop condescending to those with true gifts with expressions like "originating artist."

So, why does a great nation, which bestrides the world as no colossus ever did, need artists: not just the arrived, the Jasper Johns of today, but the hundreds of men and women painting in obscurity this evening, or writing poems or novels, or composing music; all of them knowing that what they are doing is too different to be marketable now, may never be marketable, but yet for each contains something that fills its creator with pleasure? Why does America need them?

America needs them to continue telling the country its story, its unfolding narrative and what it means. A person is not mentally healthy who does not command his own coherent personal narrative. By analogy, a people needs to have its own evolution in mind. In pre-literate, tribal cultures, a shaman or medicine man used ritual occasions to pass on and reinforce the received myths of their people and to interpret them to fit current experience. In our (almost post-literate) culture today, the creative artist serves that function, to delve into our history, to humanize it, when necessary to demystify it. America needs its artists to help it metabolize rapid changes in mores, in manners, in attitudes to gender, in the coming changes in our very appearance, the racial complexion of the nation. In a nation as heterogeneous, as diverse as this, the need may be greater than in the older, more homogenous nations of Europe and Asia, to mediate tensions by portraying them and by revealing the common humanity underlying the differences.

America needs its artists to sharpen its moral conscience, as James Joyce's Stephen Dedalus vowed, "to forge in the smithy of (his) soul the uncreated conscience of (his) race." In a country so hooked on mobility and change as this, with so many dreams unfulfilled, with such disparities in wealth, that conscience needs constant reforging; and the smithy needs to be kept continuously alight.

America needs its artists to gratify the non-material spirit in this land of unprecedented material appetites and satisfactions, where so much genius is applied to stimulating them; the thirst for spiritual meaning beyond the consolations of affluence.

America needs its artists to restore our frayed sense of community, of fellow identity, when our embrace of such transforming technology as cars, television, now the Internet, make it ever easier for isolated individuals to help only themselves.

America needs its artists to stimulate our sensitivity to beauty not evaluated only by its market worth, ratings, sales. But in doing so, those artists may feed the imaginations of those who produce the products of popular culture; many serious artists, like Stephen Sondheim, exist at the junction between the two. In fact, no society has tested more strenuously what is art, what is art today and won't be tomorrow, and vice-versa. America needs its artists to reconcile Americans to their place in the New World Order, where old assumptions of a superiority, both moral and material, as though ordained by divine providence (that other providence), no longer wash.

America needs its artists, as well as its religious figures, in Milton's phrase, to "justify the ways of God to men," at the end of a century when for many, God died, but for many others, God lives even more imperatively. At the end of a century of the most inhuman human behavior, we need artists to help us understand our species. We need artists to help us know our place in the cosmos, in a time where the universe seems to be growing more infinite while our planet feels correspondingly more finite.

In short, America needs its artists to help it obey that most ancient of humanist admonitions, to know thyself. Artists lead us to know ourselves better as a people, and as individual human beings.

Robert MacNeil was executive director and co-anchor of public television's "The MacNeil/Lehrer NewsHour" (originally "The MacNeil/Lehrer Report") for 20 years before leaving that post in October '95 to devote his time to writing books. This article is adapted from a speech he delivered to the "American Creativity at Risk" conference at Brown University in November '96.

A MODEST PROPOSAL

By Tony Kushner

January 1998

These remarks were delivered as a keynote address to the Association of Theatre in Higher Education's annual conference in Chicago in August '98.

America, the country which last year spent less than 20 cents per citizen on federal funding for the arts, and is now led by a Congress the lower half of which has voted to eliminate all federal funding for the arts, has in the same year authorized an expenditure of $250 million, around one dollar per citizen, in federal grants to states to encourage teenagers not to have sex. And this money has been allocated in the form of matching grants: It's attached to the Welfare Reform Bill, the lousiest piece of legislation since the Fugitive Slave Act. *Every* state in the United States has agreed to accept the money and to match it, so eventually we're talking about nearly a half-billion dollars spent trying to convince teenagers not to have sex.

This is extremely unwise: With the NEA gone and almost no arts programs available, into what, exactly, will these horny teenagers channel their frustrated, pent-up, unspent orgone? Outbreaks of acne are to be anticipated. The manufacturers of pimple cream are probably behind the whole idea. Even if this is not true you should put it on the Internet and start a big rumor. I furthermore predict a sharp decline in teenage manners, more pierced body parts, more tragic haircuts, more gunnysack/war-trauma clothing, and quite possibly an upswing in adolescent crime rates. If this money is effective, and teenagers give up sex, I hope incredible teenage anger will follow, and a wave of muggings, of mostly Republican victims—who will then insist even more loudly that criminal kids should be prosecuted as adults. The rise in our already world-record inmate population will help justify the big boom in federal and state-funded prison construction. And then we can spend money trying to get inmates to stop having sex. Except, oh yeah, if they have unprotected sex because we don't allow them condoms, they relieve the state of the burden of incarcerating them by dying before their sentences run out. So it all works out in the end.

No one is certain how the half-billion anti-sex dollars are going to be spent. And there's some concern about this on Capitol Hill, though not nearly as much concern as there was over faggot artists getting federal grants. Each state will receive something in the neighborhood of four to five million anti-sex dollars, which it will match on a three-to-four ratio. No one will supervise how the states spend the money. Now something that isn't often discussed in the Age of Newt, when all power is flowing back to the states (as great Americans like Jefferson Davis, George Wallace and David Duke have always dreamed it would) is that it's easier to become a state legislator than it is to do the Macarena! It's easier to be a state legislator than it is to buy an assault rifle in Texas! It takes many zillions of bucks and a severe personality disorder to become president; you apparently have to sell your soul to the Devil and be a major shareholder in Hell to become a senator and very few Americans are sleazy, dumb *and* rich enough to become a House freshman; but to be a state legislator, all you have to be, basically, is sleazy and dumb. It doesn't cost all that much. You can't be poor, of course, the poor were disenfranchised last year. But if you have a credit card—and these days household pets have credit cards (thank *God* we're about to eliminate the deficit) you can charge enough to make an independent film, or to become a state legislator. If you choose the latter option, probably you were unpopular in high school and have a secret vendetta against everyone in your county. *Anyone* in this great nation of ours can be a state legislator, and pretty much anyone is: madmen, bagmen, con-men, Book of Revelations–reading Eschatologists. My home-state legislature, in Louisiana, just passed a law creating the option of marriage in which divorce is *not permitted*. Just so the kids who haven't had sex as teenagers will have something to look forward to.

So once these state lawmakers get a hold of those grants, we can look forward to all sorts of creative ideas. Chastity belts, hair-shirts, electro-shock, Prozac, lobotomies, anti-sex ads featuring the singers the young people love, like, oh, I dunno, Zamfir? LENGTHY homework assignments featuring Bill Bennett's Monster Morality Readers. Everything *except* safe-sex education and condom distribution. Gertrude Himmelfarb is going to be made the Ayatollah of Sex in Indiana—it's a new position they made up. She will peddle her appealing message—BRING BACK SHAME!—to all Hoosier teens! *Really*, I read this somewhere, I'm not making it up! Gertrude Himmelfarb! In mufti! Okay, I *am* making it up, but it's a good idea, and any closet case in the Indiana State Legislature who secretly reads the *Advocate* is welcome to use it.

When I was a teenager I was years ahead of my time. I had no sex. Okay, it's because I was gay and I would have been killed, probably, if I'd asked anyone, or at least I believed I would. I *love* the idea that now straight teenagers will have to see what it's like, being lonely and ashamed. I think it's the first fair thing the GOP has proposed since the

Emancipation Proclamation. We hold this truth to be self-evident: All are created equally frustrated. But I do worry about the lack of venues for sublimation, and so I recommend increasing the NEA's budget. Hey kids! When masturbation becomes insufficient, try art! It worked for me! It still does!

I'm not in the best of heads to be speaking to you tonight, though I'm really very honored to have been asked and I hope you don't hate me for what I'm about to say. I hope my speech doesn't occasion a purging of the Keynote Speaker Selection Committee and call for the question "Who invited this creep?" to be flung about by executive board members in varying tones of vituperation, acrimony and ire. I hope that what I say tonight doesn't cause coronaries and apoplexy and eventuate the disbanding of this august institution. Though the speaker's fee is generous, I don't think you've paid me enough to expect all that.

And it's improbable that any non-alcoholic playwright not in his or her cups could cause such a stir. And American playwrights as a whole seem to me to be drinking and taking controlled substances with far less enthusiastic abandon than our tradition and heritage dictates. Hence, playwrights are probably better behaved, more presentable in public, and this must be a disappointment to us all. I agree with what the great Pier Paolo Pasolini said: "To give scandal is a duty, to be scandalized is a pleasure and to refuse to be scandalized is moralism."

I'm not in the best of heads tonight, because I'm in the middle of writing a play and as I've noticed time and again throughout the 17 years I've been playwriting, something happens to my surety of opinion the minute I start writing a play. Basically it goes out the window, I become fuzzy and tremulous and hesitant, unless I am speaking in the name of a character other than myself; the dialectical floodgates open, and when that happens one's overarching view of life and the world and all subjects appropriately keynotarian becomes unforgivably maddeningly *balanced* and relativistic. This state of mind is a painful thing for a thunderously opinionated person such as myself to reveal in public. I will therefore overcompensate for any momentary work-related wishy-washiness by *posing* as a thunderously opinionated person; and this pose will be, as any pose must be, exaggerated—but not unrecognizably so.

Here is my opinion, then, the nominal topic of my keynote address, and if you don't hear the thunder, well, I tried: I think we should abolish all undergraduate arts majors.

If any of you heard thunder when I said that—let me repeat it: I think we should abolish all undergraduate arts majors—the thunder probably sounded like this: UNEMPLOYMENT! And you are probably thinking, "Danger! Danger! This asshole is dissing me! He wants me to lose my not-terribly-remunerative-but-absolutely-irreplaceable job!" This or something like it is what Marx and all sorts of other people would call "enlightened self-interest" and, to the extent that you constitute a class, and you do, it is class-consciousness. I share in your apprehensiveness. I too teach, and also I imagine, having said "I think we should abolish all undergraduate arts majors" not once but twice, I hear the sound of *Angels in America* being vindictively stricken from the syllabi of several hundred courses in modern drama. It's only fair.

But of course we should all breathe a sigh of relief in recalling that university administrators, too, form a class with their own class-consciousness and self-interestedness, and since there are such a great number of undergraduate arts majors paying such a great deal of money in tuition, I can say this appalling thing—that we should abolish all undergraduate arts majors (I will repeat it many times tonight as a kind of desensitization process. And also it's fun to say, like burping after drinking bicarbonate of soda, a relief!)—since the undergraduate arts majors mill is almost as profitable for cash-strapped institutions of higher learning as pesticide development and biochemical warfare research, certainly considerably more profitable than liberal arts departments. Since it's so very lucrative, I can say let's get rid of it and we don't have to worry that anything will actually happen.

So my speech is rather like theatre in this regard, and this frees us to consider the validity of my proposal—that we should abolish all under-graduate arts majors—as a pure abstraction ultimately productive of nothing more unpleasant than a spasm of conscience and perhaps something as pleasant as a whiff of scandal and a flicker of ire. Let the purging of the committees begin! I will testify at the show trials. I will admit the error of my chosen path. Someone can shoot me in the back of my head. Then I can stop worrying about deadlines and drama critics.

Two points of clarification: 1) When I say we should abolish all undergraduate arts majors, I mean we should abolish the administrative, metaphysical, ontological, epistemological category Under-graduate Arts Major. I am not advising the wholesale slaughter of young people interested in the arts. I have no doubt that will be a plank in the next Republican Party Platform. But I am not espousing it. I *like* kids. I carry baby pictures of my new niece. Kids are cool, I am down with kids, I really enjoy teaching them.

2) Nor do I mean that we should abolish the teaching of the arts for undergraduates. There should be lots and lots and lots of fine arts *elective classes*, taught by competent and brilliant and responsible and caring and handsome and tasteful arts educators, such as ourselves. What I am proposing is that any college or university worth its salt tell its undergraduate students that henceforth they cannot major in theatre, the visual arts, writing, filmmaking, photography or musical composition. Seventeen-year-old dancers and seventeen-year-old per-forming musicians, singers and oboists, and the like, should go to good conservatories. All others must prepare to spend the next four years of their lives in the Purgatory of the Liberal Arts; after matriculation from which, of course, all sorts of lovely graduate programs in the arts, conservatories and training programs, writers' workshops and film schools will receive the most talented and determined among them with open arms.

I am in fact such a Grinch that I would be very happy to see this atmosphere of purification extend to the liberal arts themselves, where, making sure that *no one* leaves the auditorium tonight without taking offense, I would be very, very happy to see the elimination of all undergraduate degrees in speech and communication as well.

Two disclaimers: 1) I went to Columbia College for my undergraduate studies, and there were no arts majors, so what I am doing really is revealing how rigid I am and how little I have changed since I was 17, and how I want all children to suffer as I have suffered, though in this regard I suppose I'm no different from most of the people in this room.

2) Though I have recently started teaching on the full-time faculty at New York University, and have been teaching off and on for years, I know absolutely nothing about educational theory or the status of the debate regarding any of these issues; I am the wrong choice to make this speech, and again I urge the public execution, or at least humiliation, of the persons responsible for inviting me.

I come from a family of working artists. My father and mother were musicians. I earn my living as an artist. So do my siblings. I don't think you have to earn your income as an artist to be an artist. But if you are an artist, then artist is what you do, whether or not you're paid for doing it; it is what you do, not what you are. I regard *artist* not as a description of temperament but as a category of profession, of vocation. What we call education in the arts is mostly *training*; it is, in fact *vocational training*. And vocational training is not what I mean when I talk about education.

Don't get me wrong: Vocational training is a great thing. The technicians at a major computer superstore in New York, just yesterday, in the process of doing a memory upgrade on my desktop computer, "accidentally" erased all the data on the hard disk—every play, essay, screenplay, poem, letter I've ever written—and then they "accidentally" erased the backup tape. And I think the Almighty might have dragged me through this remarkably hideous experience (which perhaps accounts for my bilious mood tonight) just to remind me that I shouldn't be too dismissive of the advantages of *truly effective* vocational training, of which the technicians at this computer superstore have obviously not had the benefit.

Education, as opposed to training, I think, addresses not what you do, or will do, or will be able to do in the world. Education addresses who you are, or will be, or will be able to be. In your early years the processes of education and of training go hand in hand and are mostly indistinguishable. Practical, useful knowledge *and* the burgeoning of the imagination and the sowing of the seedbeds of moral integrity, communal responsibility and individual courage and daring all transpire more or less simultaneously in the very young, all can be learned by the stacking of blocks and the tying of shoelaces and the learning of multiplication tables and the successful manipulation of art supplies— and I'd better stop before I turn into Robert Fulghum. I think you know what I'm saying. After kindergarten, with the commencement of one's formal education, following grade school and up until one has reached young adulthood (which in my book starts at 21 years of age, or thereabouts): In the grand dialectic of life, in the dialectic between thought and action, one's formal education ought to speak more to the thesis, thought, than to its antithesis, action.

I think this is so because I have so many women friends who have just given birth and they tell me it really, really hurts to have to squeeze that huge head with its tremendous brain through the birth canal, and I believe them, and it seems to me all that suffering shouldn't be for naught. If my friends are going to go through such misery to introduce new Homo sapiens into the world, someone ought to see to it that these newcomers earn their fancy binomial nomenclature and become as sapient as possible. Someone ought to make sure their massive craniums are crammed as full as possible, otherwise I suggest the purchasing of household pets as a more pleasant alternative to seven hours of labor or a c-section. I think we should make sure these big-headed hominids become, as a result of being brilliantly educated, as deeply confused, conflicted, complicated, contrary, contemplative and circumspect as only years and years of sustained thought can make them.

While children still, before the end of latency and the onslaught of sexuality sets in at puberty, they should be sheltered from everything except joy, love, admiration, nutrition and shelter, math, books, and great art—*Where the Wild Things Are*, *The Wizard of Oz*, Burl Ives records (or a more contemporary equivalent, but not, God help us, Kermit the Frog)—and for an entirely salutary taste of the tragic and the unjust, for the best possible religious instruction in the caprices of the Deity, they should all be assigned to really tough sixth-grade grammar teachers. They must be protected from all forms of abuse including nearly everything Hollywood and the networks produce, the repulsive sexualization of public spaces, Channel 1, the learning of bad taste, racism, sexism and homophobia through Walt Disney cartoons.

At puberty, while they are being driven mad with hormones, between ages 13 to 17, all that can be done is to pray that their table manners aren't irretrievably lost, and otherwise they must be remanded to the newly funded anti-sex instructors, who will, I am sure, do all sorts of effective counseling against sex. I only wish I could be there to witness it.

At 17, until they are 21, these big-headed hominids should be forced into an atmosphere of the utmost rarification and isolation from life—because by now they have grown large and potentially dangerous, or potentially magnificent, and before they enter the world stage as Actor, capable of God knows what sorts of mischief, they need really good Actor training: Think of the liberal arts, in other words, as meta–Acting Training for Life.

Ours is a world which does not like nor protect its children. Ours is a world in which $250 million is allocated to teaching kids to stop having sex in the selfsame bill which terminated a 70-year-old commitment to protect children from poverty. Ours is a world in which millions and millions of children live in conditions of revolting, physically and mentally destructive poverty, in which children are exploited, abused, exposed to toxic chemicals and toxic art and toxic ideologies. Ours is a world in which adults, having failed to grow up, cling frantically to childhood, avenge themselves with impunity on children, on the young. Ours is a world in which no one ever admits to being middle-aged or old, while real children are stripped of the protections of child-hood as soon as is convenient, cost-effective and pleasing to vengeful adults. Hence the new opinion polls that reveal an all-time high in the dislike older generations feel toward the young. Hence the mania for prosecuting 15-year-old offenders as adults. Hence the repulsive mer-chandising of children. Hence the eagerness to transmogrify higher education into vocational training.

It goes so much against the world's common sense to suggest that all children, between the ages of 17 and 21, should be given a real lib-eral arts education, this trip to the moon on gossamer wings. In a world in which mad, out-of-control profiteering and record disparities in wealth in the midst of catastrophic environmental despoliation is called "downsizing" and "growth" in "a robust economy"; in a world in which imbalanced budgets are accorded far more moral indignation than a dearth of affordable health care; in a world in which the refugee and the immigrant are nowhere welcomed and the stranger is despised and barbaric nationalism is recrudescent because the apparently com-plete ideological dominance of the free market teaches everyone to behave as if he or she lived in a starvation economy, regardless of the manifestly gigantic wealth of nations; in such a world, children arrive at the age of 17 about as secure, about as open-minded, about as curi-ous, about as full of the love of life that is the birthright of youth as the bound Isaac watching his daddy hoist up the sacrificing knife, as Little Orphan Annie come to stay for a weekend visit with the parents of JonBenet Ramsey. These children with the tremendous brains, they aren't stupid—they know roadkill when they see it. To paraphrase the immortal Pogo: They have met the enemy and it is them. That's why they dress so abominably, in hobo clothes. Theirs is a world of preda-tors, and their only hope, lacking a social resistance movement, is to skunk the velociraptors away.

And capitalism isn't stupid, either. The great social revolution that was the '60s was birthed, in substantial measure, by a generation of children whose parents had the wealth to suckle their prodigy luxuri-ously, and to send them to the four-year summer camps of useless information for the mighty brain that is a liberal arts education. Many of these bright, beautifully educated pampered brats were excused (horrors!) from military service in Vietnam; and these brainy brats read Marcuse, and Paul Goodman, and Simone de Beauvoir, and Simone Weil, and Trotsky, and W.E.B. DuBois, and the rest—the rest is the '60s, inspiring history to many of us, and a nightmare that weighs on the brains of the neo-cons and neo-libs and Reaganite counterrevolutionaries and Gingrich ego anarchist radicals and even draft-dodgin', pot-smokin', Fleetwood Mac–listenin' Bill "Bipartisan Compromise" Clinton.

Just as the attack on public elementary and secondary education, in the form of the school voucher, and the attack on affirmative action are intended to defeat what's left of the African-American Civil Rights Movement, and the slow whittling away at reproductive rights is intended to defeat what's left of the women's movement, and the Defense of Marriage Act and 36 anti-rights initiatives at the state level are intended to defeat what's left of the lesbian-and-gay-rights movement—and in every instance there's a great deal left—the transmogrification of liberal arts education into vocational training is, I think, intended to destroy any possibility of a troublesome, restive student population. Not *intended* as in someone on the National Security Council sat around and planned it (though remembering COINTELPRO and Iran-Contra, I wouldn't want to bet a lot of money that hasn't happened), but largely this lamentable state of affairs has come to pass through what Althusser calls "Ideological State Apparatuses." The fact that many of your students wouldn't know what an Ideological State Apparatus is, or what ideology means, and the fact that this general incomprehension is a rather recent development, is *precisely* what I am talking about. We are being dumbed down. We are being trained, but not trained to think; we are becoming more efficient, by which I mean more exploitable and cooperative laborers, but we are becoming less smart than we can afford to be. Too much action, too little thought: It's not just the formula for an Arnold Schwarzenegger summer blockbuster; it's the formula for what we used to call surplus labor, and for the lumpenproletariat, before we all forgot what words like that meant.

I seem to have recovered my opinions. I seem in fact to have become something of a pill. The vocationalization of the liberal arts undergraduate education echoes the loss in the world at large of interest in the grand dialectic of life, in all dialectics, in breadth, in depth, in thinking as a necessary luxury, in the Utopian. The vocationalization of undergraduate education is, I think, akin to all sorts of social malaises, all of which commenced or burgeoned simultaneously with the death of Utopia as a place about which serious adults devote serious thought; and its replacement by corporate-sponsored Never-Never Land, a place in the name of which Peter Pans and Inner Children, instead of reading, devote serious shopping time.

My point being that it is not multiculturalism which has catalyzed the crisis in education, as William Bennett and his ilk tell us over and over and over again, but rather the budget-slashing this motley crew has either championed or complacently accepted and its concomitant ideology of starvation-based pragmatics. It is not progressive politics nor the left, such as it is, which benefits from the degradation of liberal arts education; the notion that indoctrination by left-wing teachers (and sitcoms starring lesbians) has "sold" the country on the legitimacy of the multi-frontal campaign for social and economic justice, is predicated on the belief that justice is a matter of as much indifference to the majority of people as it is to the ruling classes.

I know how deeply unfashionable it is to speak of the ruling classes—I sound like Clifford Odets on a toot. But there *are* ruling classes, aren't there? I mean there are people who have bajillions more in the bank than you or I—isn't that so?—and there are fewer of them and more of us, instead of the other way around (which is the way it's supposed to be going), and one way or another we work for these people, and they have gotten richer than anyone in history and we . . . well, we haven't. And if the Fortune 500 doesn't behave like a class, preserving the concentration of wealth, if there isn't a multinational corporate culture and an ethos created by the robber baronetcy, created by Nike and Disney and Capital Cities and Rupert Murdoch, if there is no such thing as Reaganism or Thatcherism, if these things aren't so, I will eat the first hat proffered to me.

The death of the debate that used to make it possible to talk about "the ruling classes" without sounding like a cartoon, that's what frightens me most. That's the greatest political achievement of, well, of the ruling classes, goddammit. And it is their vision of society, not mine, best served by the vocationalization of education.

The left is not lacking in culpability: There are those for whom multiculturalism has become a new kind of exclusionism, there are those who seek to eliminate the teachings of Plato instead of insisting on the inclusion of C.L.R. James; those who seek to eliminate the study of Melville instead of insisting upon the inclusion of Toni Morrison; those who, in concluding that one must study *either* Mozart or Miles Davis, rather than both, have bought into the logic of the starvation economy. Only so much time to go around, and to whom is it to be apportioned? Mark Twain or Zora Neale Hurston? There are those who have surrendered the all-important fight for integrated education. But these are few and far between, and overreported by the *Wall Street Journal*'s hysterical editorial board. What really threatens education in this country is when we decide we need more money to go into schools because the Japanese factory workers are (we are told) more diligent, more skilled and less demanding than their American counterparts. The vision of a better world is not served by the death of liberal arts education.

I am a playwright who wants an audience of overeducated dilettantes and wannabe intellectuals—people like me, in other words. I want an audience of people who want to be students *forever*, who hate it that the world *ever* tapped them on the shoulder and said, "You have to go to work now and earn money," right in the middle of some great book they were reading or painting they were analyzing or argument they were having that consumed the entire night. How are you going to know that you want to be a student forever (and what possible better audience can there be for the theatre than an audience of real honest-to-god hungry, cantankerous impatient students?) if you were never a student in the first place, if you were never allowed to be, never allowed yourself to be? If all of life is McDonald's and you have always been either only a slacker or a junior trainee, how am I going to get you to sit through one of my interminable plays? Or, for that matter, speeches?

Entirely too much time has passed without sounding my keynote: We should abolish all undergraduate arts majors. I travel around the country doing lectures—after tonight I expect the invitations to dry up—and I am generally tremendously impressed with the students I meet and talk with, and generally unimpressed with what they know, and among these impressive and impressively undereducated students the worst, I am sorry to say, are the arts majors. And it isn't simply that they seem remarkably non-conversant with the pillars of Western thought, with the political struggles of the day, with what has been written up in the morning's paper—these arts majors know shockingly little about the arts. Forget literature. How many theatre majors do you know who could tell you, at the drop of a hat, which plays are by Aeschylus, which by Sophocles and which by Euripides? Or the dates of any of those writers? How many undergraduate playwriting majors, for instance, know even a single sentence of ancient Greek, just to have the sound of it in their ears and the feel of it in their mouths? How many really know what iambic pentameter is? How about alexandrines? How about who wrote what in alexandrines? How many know the names of a single Chinese playwright, or play? Or of more than one or two African playwrights? How many have read Heiner Müller? Suzan-Lori Parks? How many have read more than one play by either of these writers? How many have never heard of them? How many know who Lessing was, or why we should care? How many have read, I mean really read and absorbed, *The Poetics*? *A Short Organum*?

And even if your students *can* tell you what iambic pentameter is and can tell you why anyone who ever sets foot on any stage in the known universe should know the answer to that and should be able to scan a line of pentameter in their sleep, how many think that "materialism" means that you own too many clothes, and "idealism" means that you volunteer to work in a soup kitchen? And why should we care? When I first started teaching at NYU, I also did a class at Columbia College, and none of my students, graduate or undergraduate (and almost all the graduate students were undergraduate arts majors—and for the past 10 years Columbia has had undergraduate arts majors), none of them, at NYU or Columbia, knew what I might mean by the idealism/materialism split in Western thought. I was so alarmed that I called a philosophy teacher friend of mine to ask her if something had happened while I was off in rehearsal, if the idealism/materialism split had become passé. She responded that it had been deconstructed, of course, but it's still useful, especially for any sort of political philosophy. By not having even a nodding acquaintance with the tradition I refer to, I submit that my students are incapable of really understanding *anything* written for the stage in the West, and for that matter in much of the rest of the world, just as they are incapable of reading Plato, Aristotle, Hegel, Marx, Kristeva, Judith Butler and a huge amount of literature and poetry. They have, in essence, been excluded from some of the best their civilization has produced, and are terribly susceptible, I would submit, to the worst it has to offer.

What I would hope you might consider doing is tricking your undergraduate arts major students. Let them think they've arrived for vocational training and then pull a switcheroo. Instead of doing improv rehearsals, make them read *The Death of Ivan Ilych* and find some reason why this was necessary in learning improv. They're gullible and adoring; they'll believe you. And then at least you'll know that when you die and go to the judgment seat you can say, "But I made 20 kids read Tolstoy!" and this, I believe, will count much to your credit. And if you are anything like me, you'll need all the credits you can cadge together.

You are probably unqualified to teach Tolstoy, Kant or Althusser. I am completely unqualified. I am a dilettante, but more or less unapologetic (this is necessary if one is going to be a playwright) and my playwriting students, who spend their time with me reading books, led by a fraud, are being cheated, because there are dozens of people in the NYU system who could teach the material better than I. I must remember that misreading and misunderstanding Kant made Heinrich von Kleist kill himself, so well-intentioned dilettantism can be a dangerous thing. But reading Kant also helped make Kleist a very, very, very great playwright, full of wondrous uncertainty and dazzling irony, and who knows, maybe one of my students will be similarly gobsmacked. Anyone can teach Kant, and I submit to you that we'd all better learn how.

Another presumptuous suggestion: We should turn our students, and ourselves, into activists clamoring for the preservation, restoration and expansion of the NEA. This, too, is enlightened self-interest. Last year a group of students at NYU tried to start a national movement with precisely those aims. It culminated in the smallest demonstration Washington, D.C., has ever seen. But there is far, far more honor in their attempt than in the safe and dignified and disgraceful inertia and inaction of most of the rest of the arts community. Most of us know as much about activism as we know about Kant. But we have no choice in this sink-or-swim world but to make an attempt, and to risk everything in doing so.

I think we should abolish all undergraduate arts majors. I think while we're at it we should give a half billion dollars every year to the NEA. I think Jocelyn Elders should be put in charge of the anti-sex campaign. I think Lani Guinier should be the next President of the United States. I think I should be vice president. We should have democratic socialism, clean air, clean water, clean food. Our children, *all* our children, should feel safe—should, in fact, *be* safe. The Messiah should come, or should come again, whichever you prefer. Until then, and to hasten his or her arrival, we must teach undergraduate theatre majors how to read Kant.

Even if that means we have to learn how to read Kant ourselves.

Tony Kushner is best known for his two-part *Angels in America,* **also a six-hour television event produced by HBO. His other plays include** *Homebody/Kabul, A Bright Room Called Day* **and** *Slavs!;* **as well as adaptations of Corneille's** *The Illusion,* **Ansky's** *The Dybbuk* **and Brecht's** *The Good Person of Setzuan* **and** *Mother Courage and Her Children.* **He wrote the book for the musical** *Caroline, or Change* **and the screenplay for Steven Spielberg's film** *Munich.* **The Guthrie Theater of Minneapolis will premiere** *The Intelligent Homosexual's Guide to Capitalism and Socialism with a Key to the Scriptures* **in May '09.**

WOMEN'S WORK:
WHITE GLOVES OR BARE HANDS?

By Tina Howe

September 1998

When my friend, Honor Moore—the poet, biographer and feminist—produced my first play, *The Nest*, in 1970, she used to ask me, "Which are you first, a woman or a writer?"

"A writer!" I answered without thinking twice.

"Are you sure?" she pressed.

"Absolutely! I grew up in a family of writers."

And growing up, I didn't particularly like women. In fact, I was terrified of them. My mother towered over my father, who was only five-foot-six. With her upsweep hairdo, wiglet and hat adorned with feathers and plastic fruits, she was six feet tall and given to excess in speech and behavior. She was what's known as a character. You never knew what was going to come out of her mouth next: a greeting as loud as a bullhorn or a thoughtless comment that would bring the room to a standstill.

And then there were the punishing little girls I went to school with as a child. Those privileged Brearley and Chapin girls who were so cruel to me. Like my mother I was tall, almost six feet by the time I was in fifth grade. To make matters worse, my front teeth had been knocked out in the playground, so I had a lisp.

"Say scissors," they'd taunt.

"Thithers," I'd respond.

"Again, again!" they'd cry, screaming with laughter.

"Thithers, thithers, thithers . . . ."

I was so exhilarated to be the center of attention, I'd say it over and over until the halls rang with their derision.

Years later, in 1972, I actually joined a women's group when we were living in upstate New York. My husband was teaching American history at the state university in Albany and we lived in a farmhouse in Kinderhook, 30 miles south. Women's groups were sprouting up all over the place, so I joined one in Hudson.

I can't tell you how uncomfortable I felt. The room was filled with young mothers like me. One by one, they revealed how overwhelmed and isolated they felt. When it was my turn to identify myself, I told them I was a playwright. The minute they heard "writer," their eyes narrowed with suspicion.

"I get it," one of them said. "You're here to appropriate our pain for your plays. You don't care about sharing, you're just here to use us."

I was stung to the quick. It was the old "scissors" routine. Once again I was the outsider who'd never be part of the group. They'd completely misread me. I found their confessions heartbreaking. It was just that my concerns were different. Because I have such an understanding husband, I didn't feel their pain and isolation; my problems were more about how to balance work and motherhood. But once I was identified as a writer, the die was cast. I was not welcome. So, I left after two sessions and started a writing group closer to home, and this time men were invited. We met every two weeks to read our work. This was clearly where I belonged.

Now that I've lived through 10 productions of my plays, I finally understand Honor's question. I'm most definitely a woman first. My gender defines my work and its reception. I'm always identified as a woman playwright. One never makes such a distinction with the fellas—Shepard and Mamet are simply playwrights. But not us. I remember all those lethal "Women's Playwriting" panels of the '80s, how all the Wendys and I would be asked, "Can you write if you have your period?" "Can you write and nurse at the same time?" As if we are mere leaking sacks of milk and blood, ruled by the phases of the moon—Macbeth's three witches incanting over vats of newts and frogs. I'd like to see a panel of male playwrights questioned about their work in terms of their sperm counts or enlarged prostate glands.

I remember what an anomaly I was when *Museum* was produced at the Public Theater in 1977. All the women in the cast were a good 15 years younger than I. They were all in the throes of affairs with dashing men and each other. I was the one who had to race home to put the children to bed.

"Put the children to bed?" they'd say, wide-eyed. "You have children?"

It was as if I were from Mars. Times have changed. Now there are more working mothers in the theatre. Or are there?

The question I'm asked most frequently is, "Can you have a family and write for the theatre?" The answer is "Yes." You just have to be made of steel and have a partner who's behind you 150 percent. Making a living as a playwright is almost impossible, regardless of your gender.

Let me tell you about *The Nest*. It had its first production at the Act IV Theater in Provincetown in the summer of 1969. It was about three female friends competing for husbands. The action takes place during a dinner party they give for two male friends. Their anxiety about luring the men into marriage reaches such a fever pitch that dinner ends with the arrival of an eight-foot wedding cake—hint, hint.

By the second act, things spin so out of control that the most desperate of the three takes off all her clothes and plunges head first into the cake, to be licked clean by one of the delighted men. If Ionesco could present a male teacher ritualistically raping and murdering his female student, why couldn't I present a woman ritualistically raping a man? All's fair in love and war, right?

Wrong.

The New York critics were appalled. When the play moved to Manhattan's Mercury Theatre, Clive Barnes said of the 10 worst plays he'd seen in his life, *The Nest* was at the top of the list. He was sure we'd never hear from Tina Howe again.

My first review. Thank God I wasn't around to read it. I gave birth to my second child the week it appeared. What I found so puzzling about the experience, given the critics' dismay, was how much the audience loved it—they were rapturous.

Needless to say, we closed the following day.

Because I come from New England stock, which is drawn to self-flagellation, the play's closure didn't dampen my spirit—it emboldened it. I've always maintained it's much easier to begin a career getting bad reviews because then you don't expect anything. Pity the playwrights who come out of the gate a winner the first time. Then they covet good reviews, but as we all know, you're only as good as your last play. To be wildly praised and then suddenly attacked must seem such a betrayal. But I was attacked for so long, I never expected to succeed. I was always in a defensive position. Which is the only position to be in, if you ask me.

So, what did I do for my second play? I whipped up even more mayhem and wrote *Birth and After Birth*, a piece about how women compete over fertility. Even though I married at 23, I didn't have children for five years. This was in the early '60s, when women blindly marched to the altar right after college. I can't tell you how many women harassed me for being childless for so long.

"You're not a woman until you have children!" they'd intone, wagging their fingers at me. "What do you know about femaleness when you're denying yourself the most basic experience a woman can have?"

How dare they? I deeply resented these attacks. To this day, there's a tyranny of women who have children versus those that don't. I find their zeal arrogant and hurtful. I may rejoice in my two kids, but I'd never tell another woman how to live her life. Our biology and choices are too complex. They say women can have it all now, though I'm not entirely convinced. Back in the late '60s, there really was a divide between women who had children and those who didn't. It seemed a thrilling subject for a play.

If *The Nest* was a shocker, *Birth and After Birth* left audiences speechless. It was about Sandy and Bill Apple celebrating the birthday of their four-year-old son, Nicky—played by a large, hairy man. Sandy has invited her first cousin, Jeffrey, over to celebrate. Like his wife Mia, Jeffrey is an anthropologist who studies children from primitive societies. Jeffrey and Mia don't have kids because they're so wrapped up in their careers. Sandy's determined to change their minds. The first act shows her and Bill vainly trying to discipline Nicky, who's in such a fever of excitement over his birthday, he destroys the house.

Jeffrey and Mia show up in the second act and Sandy puts her plan into action. She and Bill literally force Mia to the floor and convince her she's going through labor. Mia tries to resist but eventually goes along with the charade after telling a gruesome story about the Whan See, a mythical tribe of monkey people who live in trees in the Australian bush: The moment a baby is born in this culture, it's stuffed back into its mother's womb. Successful birthing involves enduring at least 10 reinsertions. As Mia recounts witnessing this ghastly ritual, she realizes she was the one pushing the baby back in.

"You know what it felt like?" she asks. "Stuffing a turkey. Stuffing a 50-pound turkey with some little . . . hamster or guinea pig."

You can imagine the response. No self-respecting theatre would touch the play. My agent at the time fired me because he got so dispirited with all the rejection letters. It wasn't until 1995 that the play finally saw the light of day—it only took 23 years. It was done at the Wilma Theater in Philadelphia and then at Woolly Mammoth Theatre Company in Washington, D.C.

How was it received? The audience loved it and the critics were appalled. "What is this self-indulgent throwback to Absurdism?" they complained. It's one thing for men to take on questions of power and identity, but for a woman to approach the sacred cows of courtship and motherhood is just not done. We can write "issue" plays, but the moment we try to penetrate the mystery of the bedroom or nursery, the critics run screaming. The fellas get to work with their bare hands, but we have to don white gloves.

After my first two disasters, I knew I'd have to change course. I may be into self-flagellation, but at some point one has to cry, "Enough!" I desperately wanted a career in the theatre. So I looked around to see what sort of plays were succeeding. The year was 1974. The big hits were *Seascape*, *Travesties*, *The Changing Room* and *A Chorus Line*. Audiences clearly wanted spectacle and escape. They wanted to be transported to beaches, locker rooms and rehearsal studios. I could do that. So I wrote *Museum*, set in a contemporary art museum filled with eerie sculptures and gigantic white paintings. It had 44 characters. What did I care if I was creating a casting nightmare? My muse was calling.

Amazingly enough, the play was produced—with a cast of 55. The Los Angeles Actors Theater did it in 1976, back in the days when it was a free theatre. The actors weren't paid and neither was I. The audience got in for free. Needless to say, there were performances when there were more people on stage than in the house, but the play was a hit. Joe Papp remounted it at the Public Theater a year later with a cast of 18 doubling and tripling their roles.

How was it received? Once again the audience was rhapsodic, but the critics were mystified. Forty-four characters going berserk in an art museum? What sort of play was this? Pirandello, Ionesco and Stoppard were allowed such excesses, why not me?

Because women don't do this sort of thing.

Theatre is a conservative art form by its very nature—a play needs immediate acceptance in order to run. It's all about money: Because we're so dependent on a healthy box office, we can't get too far ahead of the audience or the critics. Women have more room to experiment in literature and the visual arts because those operating costs aren't as high. Not that it's easy for any of us these days. Look where our national priorities are: The federal government spends more money maintaining military bands than supporting the arts. That's why I go to galleries when I need to be inspired. The work is invariably so much more radical and surprising.

All playwrights suffer from the economics of the business. Very few of us can make a living at it, but women have it twice as hard because the theatre is still largely a male bastion. You can count the number of important female critics and artistic directors on one hand. This has a tremendous impact on what and how we're allowed to write.

I didn't get my first good review until *Painting Churches*—a white-glove play if ever there was one. Not that it didn't contain a few primal screams, but the setting was elegant and non-threatening. Everyone heaved a huge sigh of relief because finally I could be pigeonholed, just as all women writers are pigeonholed. Some of us write comedies, others write political plays. Some of us write about gender and others about race. We all have our niche. But what if we want to expand? Or, God forbid, change?

Every time I see a play by a woman that's been commercially produced, I'm painfully aware of the subterfuge she's had to adopt—the artful structure, the cautious handling of dangerous themes. The reason I'm so sensitive to these ploys is because I use them myself.

Take my new play, *Pride's Crossing*. I wanted to write about the passion of old ladies. When men age, they just get old, but when we age, we become very powerful. The membranes between what we should do and what we want to do get thinner and thinner. There's no rage like old-lady rage, just as there's no tenderness like old-lady tenderness.

As the century comes to a close, I wanted to celebrate the life of women who lived through most of it, and who better than the thwarted women from my mother's background and generation? They came from a stultified strata of Boston society that was all about exclusivity, fear and privilege. I wanted to articulate the howl they could never muster, but I had to be careful. I didn't want everyone bolting for the nearest exit. So I decided to open it out of town. Premiering a play in New York has just gotten too risky—for women as well as men.

The white-gloves-or-bare-hands dilemma exists on two levels. We wear gloves to protect our hands, but we also wear them to protect what we handle—food, photographs, rare manuscripts. So when I ask whether we should wear gloves to do our work, I'm not just talking about appearances. I'm also trying to figure out what we have to wear to protect our work. Because the percentage of women who have their plays produced is so low, our plays by their very nature are rare. It's not because we're less creative than men—look at the literary output of Emily Dickinson, Virginia Woolf, Doris Lessing and the other long-ball hitters. We're just as prolific as the fellas. Just not in the theatre, for the reasons I've already mentioned.

We have to wear gloves to protect ourselves and our work. What I'm really railing against is that we're not allowed more of a selection—

boxing gloves, surgical gloves, riding gloves, driving gloves, welding gloves, the list goes on and on. So I thought I'd add another pair to your wardrobe. They're double duty, inexpensive and mold right to the hand. They'll allow you to handle comedy, tragedy and everything in between. [*At which point Ms. Howe flings 150 pairs of latex gloves into the audience.*]

Tina Howe heads the graduate playwriting program at Hunter College in Manhattan. Her other plays include *Coastal Disturbances,* **which won a Tony Award in 1987,** *such small hands, Chasing Manet* **and translations of Ionesco's** *The Bald Soprano* **and** *The Lesson.* **This piece was excerpted from a keynote speech she gave at the 20th anniversary Women's Project conference in November '97 in New York City.**

WHAT MYTHS MAY COME

By Naomi Iizuka

September 1999

Let's start here. Let's say myth is memory. Let's say making theatre is the act of remembering.

Myths are condensed particles of cultural memory—cautionary tales, magic spells, incantations to raise the dead. They are volatile pieces of a larger puzzle, human riddles we return to.

> *Myth is absolute truth spoken in a dead language.*
>
> —Erik Ehn

In kabuki, the actors stomp on the floorboards. In classical French theatre, they knock three times before beginning. The conventions have everything to do with waking the dead. In theatre, the dead are always in the room. The dead have a lot to say. Myth is the language they speak. It behooves us to strive for fluency, even though fluency is impossible.

Learn the language. You will never learn the language.

Myth is a lesson in paradox.

Myth is a funhouse mirror. Myth is the vital organs, the slick, glistening arteries underneath the skin. Myth is a swim in a giant ocean. You dive into the choppy waters. You bring your oxygen, a camera, a spear. In the murk, you glimpse an alien universe—translucent fish, electric eels, whole cities made of coral. And then your lungs begin to ache, and you swim back toward the light.

Myth is a crash course in metaphor.

> *I think of mythology as the homeland of the muses, the inspirers of art, the inspirers of poetry. To see life as a poem and yourself participating in a poem is what myth does for you.*
>
> —Joseph Campbell

Enter Joseph Campbell. He sits at the head of a long table. A feast is laid out before him. It's a banquet. Everybody you've ever heard of is there. Campbell is the guest of honor. Enter Roland Barthes. He's smoking a cigarette. He's full of irony. He speaks in French. He says: "Ladies and gentlemen, the food is poisoned."

Myth is a poison, too. It's the sleeping potion, the Mickey Finn. Myth is the invisible assumption.

We are sleeping beauties, all of us. We live in a culture saturated by myth—myths about what's normal and what's freakish, what's appropriate and what's obscene. The myths we know by heart are the most dangerous. The ones embedded in our flesh, in the habitual dance step of our lives, the thing that seems most natural, in the stories whispered by the voices closest to home, a mother, a father, a television set.

Theatre is not immune. Theatre has its myths aplenty. The thrall of the fourth wall. The ghost of Aristotle. The bits and pieces of Stanislavsky we stumble across in the rehearsal room, fragments from an ancient urn.

> *The miniaturization or Americanization of the Stanislavsky method has become like the air we breathe, and like the air we breathe, we are rarely aware of its omnipresence.*
>
> —Anne Bogart

Some myths need to be ripped apart or, at the very least, stretched. If they're hardy they'll survive. If not, not.

Not just Ovid and Sophocles and Euripides.

Not just true or false. True *and* false.

> *Myths explain things that logic cannot.*
>
> —Migdalia Cruz

Myths contain truths about the known (and unknown) universe. But they're ultimately fabrications. By definition, they condense, omit, distort in the retelling. The question is not whether they will, but how. Myths are sly bullies. They have their blind spots and agendas. They are constructed to persuade, to seduce, to silence the competition in the moment of the telling. They say: This is the story I want you to believe.

Myth is the spitting image of something you used to know. We hear the first few lines of the story, and we feel the tickle of déjà vu. We say: "I know the myth of Persephone, La Llorona, Saint Cecilia, the Monkey King. I know you."

That's the tricky thing. Myths always seem familiar. They're populated by archetypes we recognize—absent parents, brutal children, petty gods. We get the message (or think we do)—the violence of love, the logic of fate. But myth is ultimately an alien life form. In structure and in syntax, in the way meaning is articulated in what is said and left unsaid, it is a mysterious language. Myth reminds us of the unknown in the quotidian, the seed of the unfamiliar buried in the everyday.

> *Myth is what sex is to a virgin. Sex is what myth is to a writer— useful, complicated, as bitter as life.*
>
> —Erik Ehn

We think we know what sex is. We think we know what myth is. And then we get a taste of the really good wine, and the walls crack open, and the ceiling blows away, and we find ourselves standing on an open plain, a strange lunar landscape we don't recognize, we didn't know was there.

Myth is strong and slippery and quick. It's always the one that got away.

Myth is metaphor. I said it before. I'm saying it again. Myth is repetition. Theatre is, too. Repetition with the hope that in repeating, you remember something you forgot. Or maybe you think of something new.

Though I have my doubts about the word new, I think newness is another kind of myth.

Myth is never new. Not really. It's been around the block. It's old and it looks like hell, and sometimes it has a bone to pick with somebody in the room. And that seems a lot more honest and interesting than being a virgin, or pretending to be.

> *On the Easter album, Patti Smith shouts that she doesn't fuck much with the past, but that she fucks plenty with the future. Now I love me some Patti Smith, but that's pure gringo arrogance, because there is no way to forge a future without laying claim to a past. Not The Past, all official and closed off to me and mine. But a past harvested for new meanings, relit, so it complements new players, fresh from years spent waiting in the wings, now taking central stage.*
> —Jorge Cortiñas

The theatre artists who are working in the most exciting ways are creating new fusions or hybrids from old material. They sing old songs in their own strange, wild, utterly singular voices. Imagine Tom Waits singing a Mozart aria. Imagine Diamanda Galás singing Gershwin. They spin out new yarns with old thread. I can think of few skills more useful in the times in which we live.

Myth makes an art of recycling.

Myth is a story we tell. So is history. So is science. The story determines our perception of reality. Which is to say: The story determines our reality.

Enter Richard Rorty. He says: "There is no Platonic ideal. There are only stories. The stories shape and define our reality. Change the stories, and you begin to change the reality." He demonstrates. He sings a song about fire. As he sings, real sparks fly. His singing is the flint that makes it so.

I'm talking about a kind of magic.

> *In redescribing our inherited assumptions, new truths are realized.*
> —Anne Bogart

Or, if you don't believe in magic, look to physics for your metaphors: The universe is unstable. The truths about our universe are *Rashomon*-like. They change depending on the spatial and temporal angle from which we look. New solar systems appear in what we thought was a void. Celestial bodies surprise us when we get up close.

The stories we tell ourselves and our children are always up for grabs. If myth teaches us nothing else, it teaches us this.

> *I believe in mythology versus pathology. That's the creed of the Medea Project. We who survive in a world that says we shouldn't survive, we are the mythological creatures, the phoenixes rising from the flames.*
>
> —Rhodessa Jones

We have a choice of how to tell the story. We have a choice of whom to make the hero, how to name the demon, how to chart the journey. And the choice matters more than I can say.

When you make a myth the necessary conduit for telling your story, when your relationship to that particular song is visceral and urgent, when it's the only song you can sing—then you're onto something interesting.

Clever is not interesting. A clever restaging is not interesting. Concepts and gimmicks are not interesting.

> *It's not about drawing a moustache on the original. It's not about anachronism. The most interesting approach to this kind of work is one that doesn't elbow you in the ribs and constantly remind you of the classic status of the story that's being hijacked, but rather casually appropriates that story in the way a writer cops material from a half-forgotten TV show or a conversation overheard in a restaurant.*
>
> —Matt Wilder

The most vital theatrical explorations of myth are not about *about*. They're not commentaries on, or analyses of. If you're working with myth, don't be dainty. Don't hold back. Whether you're working with the story of Medea or the story of how Changó fell in love with Yemaya or the story of Genesis, handle it with strong hands.

Make it your own. Swallow it whole.

> *I started to imagine that myths were already embedded in my veins, already swimming the blood lakes of my head, sleeping, reproducing, metamorphosing recklessly. All I had to do was put the fucking books down, close my eyes and listen for the noises. Listen to the memories of my culture. Listen to the stories recorded on the fragile tape of my child's recollections, those told by abuelas and godfathers and second cousins from Newark, New Jersey, those stored in the clothing my father wore, the Virgin Mary statues guarding the sacred, private spaces on my mother's bureau. Listen to beats in the music. The spices in the pasteles and wondrous plates of bacalao. The hips of dancers, echoing the palm trees tossed by indifferent hurricanes . . . . Once I started to really listen, the noises and cries and howls were impossible to silence. Myth became actual. Myth became Living Material.*
>
> —José Rivera

Myth is food. Say grace. Devour it. Share.

But then I have my doubts. They chatter in the background. They raise a giant ruckus.

Is there truth in this metaphor? Can you honestly say myth is food? Is it really a necessity? Does it feed you? Does it feed others? Or is it incidental and beside the point? A quaint curiosity, a relic from the past? Substitute the word "theatre" for the word "myth." Ask the same questions. Don't settle for easy answers. Grapple with your doubts.

Let the doubts keep you up nights. Let the doubts make your work stronger and sharper. Let the doubts burn off the dross.

Myth is a kind of fire.

> *Myth is unwelcome simplicity when complexity is called for. Myth is unwelcome simplicity . . . on which all our joy depends.*
> —Erik Ehn

Bare bones. What do you love? What do you need?

Joseph Campbell lobbied hard for the continuing relevance of myth in our contemporary lives. He said essentially this: "You need myth. With it, your life will be better. Without it, you'll be missing out." He was selling maps by the side of the road. Or maybe knives. It was a classic sales pitch. It was much more than that, but it worked on that level, too.

Myth is a map to navigate the unknown.

New shapes. New maps. Old legends. Getting to the inside, getting to the meat. Myth is a knife to cut through the skin.

> *Why we need myths is the same to me as why we need prayers.*
> —Migdalia Cruz

It's 1999. We prognosticate. We look for signs. We seesaw between optimism and anxiety. On good days, we're happy astronauts, euphoric in our little metal spaceships. On bad days, we're Charlton Heston in *Soylent Green*, bellowing our indignation and running for our lives.

It's 1999. No wonder *The Power of Myth* sells so many copies. Find a need. Fill it. Along the way, be humane. Be idealistic. Genuinely embrace diversity. Avoid ironic posturing. Don't mistake cynicism for sophistication. You could do a lot worse than casting Joseph Campbell as the hero in this drama.

It's 1999. I'm not reading science fiction these days. I have a yen to look at old photo albums. I want to read Chekhov all over again. And Dickinson and Stein. I want to drink some mind-blowing old wine.

> *Myth and theatre are inseparable. As theatre artists, we are myth-makers.*
> —Chay Yew

Theatre is the act of remembering. Remember repetition. Listen carefully.

Remembering means listening carefully. Turning the earth up again and again, until you spot the glint of buried gold.

It's 1999. And we suffer from a kind of temporal arrogance on account of it. We think our unknowns are somehow grander and more terrifying than those of our predecessors. We forget what it was like for our ancestors setting off in their papyrus boats or trekking across a tundra towards the horizon line. We forget the pain of birth and the constancy of death. The experience of facing the unknown, how we name it, how we face it, is an ancient thing.

Myth reminds us of a simple fact. There were those who came before. They are our kin. We are more like them than not.

It's like finding old pictures of people you love, or used to love, who aren't there anymore.
—Erin Cressida Wilson

Pictures of your family. People to whom you bear a striking resemblance, people whose names you barely can remember. They were ancient the day you were born. You search the pictures for clues of who they really were, the smell of their skin, their innermost thoughts.

We enact the play in order to remember the question.
—Anne Bogart

What are we trying to remember?

Make a list. What do you love? What do you need?

Two years ago, I had a miscarriage. To feel life thrive and then wither inside you is an incomprehensibly dark feeling. My mother told me it was because God needed an angel. When I became a maker of angels, I felt a part of the greater scheme of creation—even when my body could not sustain that singular human life. This made my despair tolerable, even understandable somewhere in my heart.

"Two weeks ago, I had a baby. When she was handed to me, I thought, 'What a miracle! Surely, something so beautiful, so alive, and trusting, couldn't be meant for me.' But for me she was. We birth angels whether they emerge from our wombs or slip away to another, more spiritual place. This child I will write about—as I have written about so many other children. But this time she is a part of my flesh. A part of my personal myth. What else is there to write about? What is more important? More interesting? More human?
—Migdalia Cruz

Myths ask basic questions, as simple as they are necessary, as necessary as they are hard. Our hearts crack open in the asking.

How do we comprehend the most human parts of ourselves—the fleshiest parts, the sex, the guts, the human heart? How do we comprehend the mysteries of our parents, our lovers, our loneliness? How do we make sense of our appetites and longings, the fact of catastrophe, the abrupt disappearance, the inevitable ending?

Because this is about the human body. It has always been about the human body. In theatre and in myth, we recall the flesh, the sweat, the timbre of a human voice. The silence and the breathing. The human body moors us to the real, reminds us what's at stake.

At its best, theatre does what myths do. It asks these basic questions. It asks them compulsively, again and again.

> *Myths are living, electric patterns: the ferocious menagerie of voices. Noises, memories, ideas, dreams, hallucinations, overheard dialogue, found objects, blood stains, semen stains, tear stains, adrenaline, hungers.*
>
> —José Rivera

What do you love? What do you need? Whose face do you see at the end of the day? Which loss haunts you? Which loss sears your soul? Where is the place you call home? How do you find your way back? Who do you take with you? What do you save? What do you let burn?

Make a list. Make a list before you go.

> *We are between myths . . . . We need new shapes for our present ambiguities.*
>
> —Anne Bogart

What will those shapes be? How do we recycle the pieces of our past and also our present to make something astonishing and beautiful, something necessary and new?

The answers are as multiplicitous as the people in the room. There are many, many people in the room. Some of them are just beginning to speak.

> *I want to honor the past, but not let it write my future for me. I want a hand in that. I want to push it. I want to fuck with the future, and I'm going to raid my photo album to do it. I'm going to raid ghost stories, my nightmares, movies I saw when I was a kid, stuff I drove past, and things my grandmother told me before she passed away.*
>
> —Jorge Cortiñas

Who we were and are. Who we want to become.

We all have our photo albums, our ghost stories, our songs and memories. We share our great, dusty books. We share the things our grandmothers said. We share our magic spells.

This is about a kind of magic.

If you find the right words, if you say them in just the right way, you make the air electric with ghosts. That is a powerful and worthwhile thing. The ghosts have a lot to say. They bring us solace and illumination. They help us remember. They give us inklings of what lies ahead.

If the theatre were a verb, it would be to remember . . . . We are the living conduits of something humanity is trying to remember.
—Anne Bogart

What are we trying to remember?

That's the starting point. It will always be the starting point. Where we go from there is a postcard to posterity.

So let's start again. Let's say myth is memory. Let's say making theatre is the act of remembering, remembering again and again. This is how we make and remake theatre. This is how we honor the dead. This is how we make sense. This is how we find our way. This is how we give gifts. This is how we stake our claim. This is how we conjure anew.

Naomi Iizuka is the author of *Polaroid Stories*; *36 Views*; *Aloha, Say the Pretty Girls*; *War of the Worlds*; *Language of Angels*; *Skin*; *Tattoo Girl*; *Anon(ymous)* and other plays. She heads the playwriting program at University of California–San Diego.

THE IMMATERIAL THEATRE

By W. David Hancock

September 1999

The Theatre of the Future exists only in my imagination. It is a movement I invented because I felt despair about my own playwriting. If I hadn't become a practitioner of the Theatre of the Future, I would have stopped being a playwright a long time ago. If theatre is a calling—and I'm a bit suspicious when people try to convince me it is—but if theatre is a calling, then it is the future, and not the past or present, that calls me to it.

The past called the Greeks, I think. Their essential question was, I believe, "to repeat or not to repeat." The present called Shakespeare, and so for him the question was "to be or not to be." But today television and film—not theatre—entertain the masses. Today, playwriting faces a crisis of action that is more crippling than Hamlet's. As I prepare to enter the new millennium, the existential question that I consider daily is "to become or not to become."

Each day I am faced with the distinct possibility of becoming something besides a playwright. Theatre is so insignificant to our popular culture—everyone knows it is impossible to make a living writing plays—that I am constantly tempted to become a teacher, to become a lawyer, to become a screenwriter instead. Along with this temptation from without, there is also an insidious temptation from within: to become a cynic. I find it much easier to sneer at what others are doing than to say what I mean in front of an audience. I am afraid to say what I mean because I am afraid that what I mean isn't new, isn't important.

Thankfully, I came to the realization a number of years ago that my role as a playwright was to accept this place of doubt and to write myself out of it. I discovered that it is exactly my doubt about the relevance of playwriting that makes this time such a potentially fertile one for me to be writing plays. Doubt is a precious gift because it is during times of intense doubt that I am able to reinvent my faith in the unknown. If I don't fall prey to my own cynicism, there is the possibility that faith will appear to me in all its glory, as it must have appeared when I was a child—unencumbered by plot.

We're a society obsessed with plot. Religious and artistic epiphanies have been replaced by marketplace epiphanies. The stock market runs on plot, elections run on plot, even wars run on plot. Plot creates anxieties that only a new product or a new politician or a new defense system can ease. These false epiphanies—both the highs and the lows—suck us into materialism. It is no accident that television news programs, sporting events and situation comedies all create the most anxiety or elation right before they cut to commercials. I feel happy, I feel anxious, and so I buy.

Sadly, even when I write plays, I am stuck with the anxieties and fears that come from worrying about what comes next. I write a play, but worry about whether it will be produced. When it is produced, I worry about whether it will be reviewed. When it is reviewed, I worry about whether it will be a good review. When I get a good review, I worry about whether certain important people have seen the review. When these important people begin to recognize my work, I worry that I'm no longer writing important plays. So I try to write a new one, but worry about whether it will be produced.

To deal with my highs and lows while on this treadmill, I succumb to the distractions of the material world. I find sitting for hours in front of the blank page unbearable, so I go out and buy a new computer. I'm elated at winning an award, so I go on a trip. And after I have indulged myself in all there is to avoid writing, I return to the blank page not refreshed, but ashamed, tired and lonely.

Instead of worrying about what will happen next, maybe I should be asking myself why things are the way they are. Theatre should, after all, be one place that isn't consumed by plot. In fact, in the noncommercial theatre in this country there are very few external market forces telling us what to say or how to say it. The theatres that produce my plays don't require me to have commercial breaks. I don't have to sell products for them. And yet, I am still afraid to say what I mean in front of an audience, and to deaden the fear I attempt to create for myself a professional environment that models itself after business—that measures its success in business standards. How can I make art when the very language of my playwriting has become infected with the language of the marketplace: payoff, investment, production, process, material, development, workshop? And this is why I finally had to invent the Theatre of the Future for myself, because I knew that if I wanted to continue to be a playwright, I had to find a way to escape this inevitability of materialism. For me, making theatre has become a journey towards an unknown future. I may still fear it, but in writing towards it, I constantly have to project meaning into the world, rather than constantly deriving my meaning from it.

My theatre becomes materialistic when I allow my plays to have an intrinsic meaning outside the theatrical event. I may charge people to witness the events I create, but if my script can be bought and sold as property—if I assign my plays a value separate from their existence in performance—then I am in danger of making the audience irrelevant to my art form. I believe audiences shy away from theatre when they sense, intuitively, that they are unimportant to the play. How many times have I gone to the theatre and seen a piece that I know would be performed no differently to an empty house?

It is only when my plays are presented in front of an audience that they transform from the material into the immaterial. Each night I try to make an event that can't be sold because it can never be reproduced exactly. My play can take place only in this space on this particular evening and—most significantly—with this particular audience. If you see one of my plays, I hope you get the feeling that you are essential to the piece, that the event unfolds as it does only because you are in attendance tonight. For this reason, my plays are never better than the way they are performed by these particular actors under these particular circumstances. If my work fails, as it often does, I create no theoretical parallel universe where it doesn't fail. To say that a perfect version of my play exists in my head or in an ideal production with somebody else in the lead role—this is simply delusion. In fact, if I have no play performed tonight, then I don't even consider myself a playwright. I may write for eight hours today, but what I am writing is not a play. It is merely the groundwork that ensures my possibility of being a playwright some night in the future.

One of the grave consequences of materialism has been the loss of free will in our society. I believe you give away a little of your free will each time you dip into the world for meaning. For some of us, the only choices left in life are the false choices of the Pepsi or Coke variety. Along with the loss of free will comes a sameness that spills over from popular culture into the arts. Audiences flock to *The Lion King* because they know the show will be the same tonight as it was last night. Your kid can have the same experience as my kid and every other kid on the planet.

Unlike materialistic theatre, the Theatre of the Future has the potential to uncover the lost free will in the audience. It allows for plays that are different each night. It allows you to have an experience that is different from my experience, and is based upon your particular imagination. The Theatre of the Future allows for us to be individuals and yet to be together in one room. When I write for the Theatre of the Future, I try to create theatrical events to which the audience must actively give their own meanings—give their own experiences, history and beliefs. I try to write plays where the audience is expected to project into the work what *they* mean—along with the actors, the director and the designer. I try to bring the audience out of its current malaise by reminding them of the possibility for transformation through chance, accident and grace.

The difficulty is that I must present my plays to an audience that often enters the theatre bogged down by the day-to-day. Sometimes I think my work is transformational, but other times the relationship between my plays and the audience seems more like the scene in *Frankenstein* where the monster meets the blind guy. My play is the monster, of course, befriended by an audience who—by and large—has forgotten how to watch theatre. And I am Igor, opening graves and using other people's remains to cobble together a play. I'm not making anything new. I have stolen most of my good ideas, snatched them from dead playwrights in the middle of the night, hoping none of you will notice. And in order to make my monster live, I know that some force has to animate it from far outside my own worldly experience. This animating force—this lightning strike—comes suddenly out of the darkness of the future. It comes from the place that is past my own death, past my doubts. It comes from the faith of chance. It comes from the grace of awkwardness. It comes from the gut of uncertainty. It comes from writing about that which I can't possibly understand.

In school I was taught that writers must only tell what they know. But the Theatre of the Future forces me to tell what I don't know, what I can never be certain of. It is no longer enough for me to try to articulate some ancient notions about the human experience. If I am going to write plays for tomorrow, I know that I must be prepared to reinvent for myself what it means to be human. If I don't hurry to reinvent myself through a life of theatre, then my new meanings will be determined for me by the computer software people, by the genetic determinists, by the Fundamentalists. For me, the Theatre of the Future offers hope that the future will still hold the possibility of community, of human contact, of freedom, of free will, of artistic integrity, of accountability, of many distinct voices speaking together in one room. It is only because of theatre that I can envision a future in which we don't stare at screens all day, but instead sit around campfires together and share our ghost stories. I know that unless I have the courage to write toward the Theatre of the Future, that there will be for me only a Theatre of the Present. I will continue to act as if *Waiting for Godot* is the last play ever written, and even the writers I admire most will simply be filling in the blanks between Shakespeare and Beckett.

W. David Hancock's plays include *The Race of the Ark Tattoo*, *The Convention of Cartography*, *Ordering Seconds*, *The Incubus Archives*, *Deviant Craft*, *The Ghost Canister* and *The Sisters of Eve*.

TOWN IN A MIRROR

By Don Shewey

May/June 2000

Moisés Kaufman had a hunch. When news reports started emerging from Laramie, Wyo., in October of 1998 that a gay college student named Matthew Shepard had been savagely beaten, tied to a fence on the edge of town and left to die by two local roofers he met in a bar, Kaufman sensed that this was no fleeting news event. The Venezuela-born, New York–based writer and director, who'd scored an enormous theatrical triumph in 1997 with his play *Gross Indecency: The Three Trials of Oscar Wilde*, saw that people all over the world were being emotionally affected by the symbolism and the brutality of Shepard's death.

In Kaufman's hands, *Gross Indecency* clearly dramatized how Oscar Wilde's prosecution and imprisonment for homosexual behavior became a public referendum on Victorian England's attitudes about sex, gender, money, class and education. Now Kaufman wondered if the lethal gay-bashing of Matthew Shepard might be a similarly resonant turning point for American culture—a moment around which a socially conscious piece of theatre might be created.

"What I read in the press about Matthew Shepard told me that the crime captured people's imaginations," he recalled recently. "How did it do that? And how do we deal with it in the theatre? Before this, did anyone in Laramie ever have to talk publicly about these questions? I wanted to hear what they were saying among themselves." So in November, barely a month after the murder, Kaufman flew to Laramie with nine members of his company, the Tectonic Theater Project, to interview as many people as they could about reactions to the crime.

Fifteen months, five more trips and four workshops later, the company presented the world premiere of *The Laramie Project* at the Denver Center Theatre Company. The Feb. 26 opening night performance was extraordinarily emotional, partly because the audience included several Laramie residents who were characters in the play, and partly because the company had managed to create a powerful and evocative work of art. Eight actors played dozens of characters (including themselves) based on some 200 interviews.

Although the play factually recounts the events that took place on the night of Shepard's beating, the three-day vigil before he died and the trials of his assailants, *The Laramie Project* is not primarily a re-enactment of the crime but a portrait of a small town—think of an *Our Town 2000*. Its form—open stage, minimal sets, direct address—harkens back to Greek tragedy, in which the outcome is known from the beginning and the play provides an opportunity for the community to talk about things that are on its mind. After a well-received six-week run in Denver, the play transferred directly to the Union Square Theatre in New York in April for an open-ended Off-Broadway run.

This gratifying result was never a foregone conclusion. As Kaufman puts it, "I had a panic attack on the plane to Laramie. I thought, 'What the fuck are we doing?' I was terrified."

From the beginning, *The Laramie Project* was an unusual experiment in collective creation. Among those who accompanied Kaufman on the first trip to Laramie were not only three actors from the original cast of *Gross Indecency* (Michael Emerson, who played Wilde, Andy Paris and Greg Pierotti) but also its set designer, Sarah Lambert. Others on the trip had longer associations with Kaufman and Tectonic, including Kaufman's assistant director Leigh Fondakowski, writer and actor Maude Mitchell, and the company's managing director, Jeff LaHoste, who has been Kaufman's partner for 11 years.

It was the success of *Gross Indecency*, whose 18-month run Off Broadway spawned companies in San Francisco, Los Angeles, Toronto and London, that gave Tectonic the financial luxury of funding its first round of research on *The Laramie Project*. "To take 10 people to Laramie for a week cost $20,000," says LaHoste. "We challenged our funders to fund us off their regular cycle. The Rockefeller Foundation gave us $40,000 for development. Whether a play happened or not, we knew it would be an experiment in gathering material this way and building the company."

Equally important was the fact that *Gross Indecency* was the third-most-produced play in the American theatre last year. Its popularity gave Kaufman enough cachet to call out of the blue and introduce himself to Rebecca Hilliker, head of the theatre department at the University of Wyoming. When he told her the company wanted to interview people in Laramie about their response to Matthew Shepard's murder, she told him, "I feel like you just kicked me in the stomach. The students here need to talk, because the press coverage has cut off all dialogue on the subject." It was Hilliker's encouragement that emboldened Kaufman to proceed with the project and opened the first doors in Laramie.

The New Yorkers arrived in Laramie with a fair amount of trepidation, expecting to encounter a hotbed of Wild West homophobia. Kaufman decreed certain safety rules—no one works alone, and everyone carries a cell phone. Fondakowski and Pierotti, two gay members of the company who had a special interest in finding out about the gay community of Wyoming, prefaced their first trip to Laramie with a visit to Colorado Springs to interview John Paulk. A poster boy for the ex-gay movement that claims sexual orientation can be changed through the power of prayer, Paulk manages homosexuality and gender issues at the right-wing Christian organization Focus on the Family. Fondakowski and Pierotti were curious to explore why such groups had issued statements to the media distancing their work from the murder of Matthew Shepard. Although the Focus on the Family material never made it to the stage, it braced the company for the conservative sexual politics they would face outside of New York City.

"It's very scary how organized they are," says Fondakowski. "They get more mail than anyone in the country but the White House. After spending a couple of days with them, I was really frightened driving into Laramie at dusk. It took me four trips to feel safe jogging there."

Once they hit town and started meeting people, though, the theatre artists found they had to reconsider their stereotypes of small-town Westerners. Some churchgoers they interviewed held narrow-minded judgments about gay people; at the same time, one of the most heroically self-searching characters in the play is a Catholic priest. The artists met gay citizens who were political and outspoken, as well as many who were content to blend in with their surroundings rather than embrace public gay identities. They encountered not only female ranchers but also an Islamic feminist born in Bangladesh who'd lived in Laramie since the age of four. Nothing was as simple as it may have seemed.

The company members were clearly empowered by the experience of doing this kind of firsthand research. Back in New York, they transcribed tapes of their interviews and began developing performable impressions of the people they'd met. The first draft of the script was written in three weeks by 10 people. After viewing about 90 minutes of material in January, a team of four consolidated as the writers' group: actors Stephen Belber and Greg Pierotti, project advisor Stephen Wangh (who had served as dramaturg on *Gross Indecency*) and Fondakowski as head writer. (Fondakowski had been developing a similar kind of piece called *I Think I Like Girls*, based on interviews with lesbians from around the country, which is being co-produced by Tectonic and New Georges Theatre in New York.) Actors Amanda Gronich, John McAdams, Barbara Pitts and Kelli Simpkins each continued to feed material to Fondakowski and the writers' group. They are listed as contributing writers in the almost comically elaborate, but scrupulously respectful, program credits for the play.

Between November and April, company members returned to Laramie several times, to attend—among other things—the trial of Russell Henderson, one of Shepard's assailants. "In the course of six months, people changed," says Fondakowski. "For example, Romaine Patterson was incredibly young when we met her." Patterson, a 21-year-old lesbian who had been a friend of Shepard's, learned that his funeral would be picketed by Fred Phelps, the notorious Kansas-based homophobe, carrying signs saying "God Hates Fags." Patterson marshaled a group of people wearing gigantic white angels' wings to encircle the demonstrators and provide a buffer between their hateful chanting and Shepard's mourners. Patterson went on to form an activist group called Angel Action. "One of the great achievements of the piece was following the journey of various individuals and showing the magnitude of their change," Fondakowski says.

After a three-week workshop in May at New York's Classic Stage Company, the next stage of developing *The Laramie Project* took place at the Sundance Theatre Lab in Utah, whose artistic director, Robert Blacker, attended the first reading of the play. "Sundance usually brings in a writer and a director," says LaHoste, "but they actually paid to bring 12 of us out there for a three-and-a-half-week workshop in July." The first two acts were roughed out at Sundance and further developed at Dartmouth College in an August residency sponsored by New York Theatre Workshop. The third act, which depended on the outcome of Aaron McKinney's trial in October (he, like Henderson, was found guilty and sentenced to life imprisonment), was finished during the rehearsal period in Denver.

While the writers and actors were primarily responsible for boiling the research down to a text of suitable length, it was Kaufman's task to shape the piece theatrically. "Tectonic refers to the art and science of structure," he says. "We're interested in doing plays that explore language and form. As a gay man, I'm interested in revealing the structure: Who tells what story, and how, is important to me. How many stories of Oscar Wilde were told by gay writers? Most of the biographers I read referred to him as being 'diseased.' How do we tell stories? How do we construct our identity as a person? As a gay person, you're forced to define yourself—that's how we learn that identity is a construct." Kaufman's gift as a director lies in his ability to create a structure that allows multiple, potentially conflicting points of view to stay afloat at the same time. Rather than dictating a single truth or conclusion, he invites the audience to synthesize the material themselves—a classic Brechtian strategy.

Kaufman's key collaborator in shaping *The Laramie Project* theatrically was Steve Wangh, who had been a teacher of his at New York University. The oldest member of the company, Wangh kept a healthy distance from the interviewing process and every few weeks would meet with Kaufman for dramaturgical discussions on the level of theory and form rather than "carpentry conversations," as the director put it.

"We would talk about whether staging a particular moment would work better with a Brechtian approach or one from Meyerhold or Piscator," Kaufman recalls. "One of the big problems with this piece is how do you create a whole town on stage with only eight people? Meyerhold was a genius at doing that kind of thing." Asked to describe a Meyerholdian moment, he refers to the arraignment of the men arrested for beating Shepard: "All the chairs are facing sideways, and as the court officer reads aloud the details of the crime, you see the bodies of the people listening slowly implode as the horror of the scene sinks in. That's the kind of reaction that can only be done on stage."

There are, of course, many precedents for the kind of company-created, Living Newspaper–type work that *The Laramie Project* represents. In the 1970s and early '80s, Max Stafford-Clark's London-based Joint Stock Company unleashed actors to do the original research that culminated in such plays as David Hare's *Fanshen* and Caryl Churchill's *Cloud 9*. *The Laramie Project* calls to mind Emily Mann's "theatre of testimony," plays derived from verbatim transcripts of original interviews, especially *Execution of Justice*. And anyone familiar with Elizabeth LeCompte's work with the Wooster Group, especially *L.S.D. (. . . Just the High Points . . .)*, would surely recognize it as a model for Kaufman's split-level, highly presentational staging of *Gross Indecency*.

Kaufman acknowledges and admires these artists while carefully distinguishing his work from theirs. For instance, asked about another artist who has created powerful theatre from headline news, he says, "I love Anna Deavere Smith's work. She's interested in the intersection of language and character, though, while I'm interested in what happens on stage, the intersection of language and form." His biggest role model, he says, is Peter Brook's International Center for Theatre Research, especially the era in which Brook's company created *The Ik*, which Kaufman saw as a teenager.

"In Venezuela, because of the oil boom in the early '80s, they hosted an international theatre festival," he says. "When I was 14 or 15, I saw [Polish director Tadeusz] Kantor's Cricot 2, Pina Bausch, Peter Brook and Grotowski's *Akropolis*. That was the theatre I grew up with. So when I saw my first naturalistic play—it was Noël Coward's *Private Lives*—I thought: 'Wow, how avant-garde! Real props!'"

Born and raised in a Jewish family, Kaufman started college at a business school in Caracas, but his first accounting class was so boring that he sought refuge in the theatre department, where an experimental company called Thespis was in residence. He joined the company as an actor and spent five years performing Ionesco, Molière and new work staged by the artistic director, Fernando Ivosky, who was deeply immersed in the work of Brook and Grotowski.

In 1987, at the age of 23, he realized that he wanted to be a director. At the same time, he was coming to grips with his homosexuality. "At the time, I couldn't be gay in Venezuela," he says. "It was too much of a macho Catholic country." Moving to New York, he spent two years studying at NYU's Experimental Theatre Wing, where Brook and Grotowski were also major heroes. "I needed some theoretical basis, so I was able to study what I'd been doing for five years without knowing it," Kaufman says.

ETW turned out to be the launching pad for what would become the Tectonic Theater Project. "I told them all I need is space and actors to do what I want, and it was enough of a hippie atmosphere that they said, 'Great! Do it!'" *Women in Beckett*, an evening of short plays performed by actresses aged 65–80, led to incorporating Tectonic as a not-for-profit theatre, and Kaufman started building a reputation with striking productions of early plays by Naomi Iizuka (*Coxinga* and *Marlowe's Eye*) and Franz Xaver Kroetz's *The Nest*, which won an Obie Award in 1995.

David Rothenberg, a veteran producer and publicist of Off-Broadway theatre, recalls seeing Kaufman's production of *Marlowe's Eye* at St. Clement's Church in 1995. "It was very avant-garde," he says. "I couldn't tell if the play was any good. But I remember being constantly surprised by his creative staging, where people were coming from, how he used the set and the lighting. It was very innovative. It reminded me of certain landmarks in my own theatregoing, such as Ellis Rabb's production of *Pantagleize* with the APA or Peter Brook's staging of *Marat/Sade*. His direction was that extraordinary."

But it was *Gross Indecency* that really put Tectonic on the map. Kaufman gathered around him a company of actors and designers willing to devote two years to developing the piece from trial transcripts and other source material about Oscar Wilde. "Many actors just want to be given a script and five weeks' rehearsal," he notes. "This work attracts a very specific kind of artist. These are people who are thinking deeply about theatrical form."

Kaufman credits Brecht and Erwin Piscator as primary influences on his staging of *Gross Indecency*, in which eight performers played a variety of characters without ever "disappearing" into their roles. Literary sources, contemporary news reports and court documents were cited aloud in the text, and the characters who were speaking would be identified by other performers, the same way that TV sportscasters identify ball players for the viewing audience. As anyone who dares to follow Brecht's example all the way discovers, exposing the theatrical structure can create an almost paradoxically involving theatrical event. By admitting the truth that we are watching an artificially constructed event, rather than pretending otherwise, we are able to confront more directly and engage more fully with whatever moral or philosophical investigation the play is putting forward.

The Laramie Project goes even farther into Brechtian territory than *Gross Indecency*, which revolved around the central figure of Oscar Wilde. *The Laramie Project* ostentatiously declines to represent Matthew Shepard on stage. This choice ingeniously sidesteps sentimental images while at the same time giving the play a mysteriously satisfying spiritual dimension. The unseen presence is much more powerful than the overly familiar depiction of a crucified figure.

Kaufman's aesthetic is anything but dry and severe. The piece begins with actors, grouped around five tables and eight chairs, playing themselves—a theatre company sharing the results of their own investigation. However, as the play opens up and we meet the people of Laramie in various settings, the director and a skillful design team begin to fill the theatrical space with telling touches. A spotlit window box of cornstalks becomes the Wyoming prairie. As the media descend upon Laramie, TV monitors drop from the ceiling (a moment I couldn't help associating with the Wooster Group's *Route 1 & 9*, which displayed on similar TV monitors scenes from *Our Town*). In a scene at the Fireside Bar, the soundtrack features not country music but, more authentically, white-boy hip-hop. A video screen repeatedly shows footage of a two-lane highway late at night as seen in the headlights of a slightly wayward vehicle.

Still, the center of the performance is the actors. Donning a jacket or a pair of glasses, shifting a vocal inflection, the actors slide from one character to another, creating indelible impressions in as little as 15 seconds. For a play with no central character, it's almost miraculous how the actors sustain a compelling tension through a narrative whose outline is surely known to almost everyone in the audience. Two things help. One is the forthright way that the actors establish contact with the audience as themselves; we never lose sight of them even as they slip in and out of different roles. The other core element is the company's insistence on representing the people of Laramie in ways that allowed the residents to recognize themselves.

Easy as it would be to depict Shepard as a sentimental martyr, we hear friends of his describe him as "a blunt little shit" who lacked common sense. And rather than caricature the folksy humor and rural accents of Laramie residents, the performers mine those attributes for the savvy they mask. Commenting on the media's frenzied news coverage, Laramie's police chief drawls, "I didn't feel judged—I felt that they were stupid." A particularly haunting character is Reggie Fluty, the female deputy sheriff (played by Mercedes Herrero) who cut Matthew Shepard down from the fence where he was tied. Told by the hospital that Shepard was HIV-positive, she was treated with AZT, which made her lose 10 pounds and much of her hair. This information, not widely known, comes as a bit of a bombshell and raises numerous questions that the play provocatively chooses not to pursue. Instead, the anecdote resonates as part of Fluty's experience of the Matthew Shepard ordeal.

As *The Laramie Project* started coming together last summer, the Tectonic Theater Project began considering possibilities of where to perform the piece. They didn't want to open the piece in New York, as they'd done with *Gross Indecency*. "We needed some distance from New York," says Fondakowski. "This piece needs time to grow in front of an audience." A number of regional theatres, including the Seattle Repertory Theatre, Arena Stage in Washington, D.C., the Mark Taper Forum in Los Angeles and McCarter Theatre Center in Princeton, N.J., were interested in presenting the show. Kaufman was eager to mount it as soon as possible, and he wanted to do it somewhere close enough so that the people of Laramie could see it. Fortuitously, the Denver Center Theatre Company, whose production of *Gross Indecency* was so successful that they brought it back for a return engagement, had a sudden cancellation in the middle of its season. Since it is the closest regional theatre to Laramie, it seemed a perfect place to present the premiere.

On opening night in Denver, it was impossible not to be aware of the enormous responsibility that the actors felt to do justice to the people who had entrusted them with their stories and their innermost feelings. I found myself sitting next to Zackie Salmon, a 52-year-old lesbian university administrator, who was very attentive to how she came off in the play. Aside from some personal vanity about being seen as the "town nerd" in her oversized glasses, she generally approved, although she told *USA Today* that what didn't come through for her was "the depth of grief that was a communal grief. I don't know if it's possible in any way for anybody to capture that. I think they did the best they could." One of the central characters in the play is Matt Galloway, the bartender who served both Matthew Shepard and his assailants the night of the murder. As played by Stephen Belber, Galloway is effusive and somewhat comically self-possessed, yet highly articulate. Heart-breakingly, he questions whether he was to blame for not stepping in to intervene between Shepard and the men with whom he left the bar. After the show, a ripple of electricity ran through the lobby as we real-ized that the tall, handsome young man embracing Kaufman was Galloway himself, who was later heard saying to a friend, "I hope I'm not that bad . . . ."

Donovan Marley, artistic director of the Denver Center, told me how he felt about presenting *The Laramie Project* at his theatre. "Matthew Shepard's family and the people of Laramie have suffered way, way, way more than they should have to," he said. "Very frankly, I would not have taken on the project if I felt it was contributing to this suffering. But when I met Moisés, I was certain that it would be a pos-itive experience. It's not what he said, because I never listen to what people say. It was spending time with him and the people he had with him and coming to believe that they had been profoundly moved by going through the interviewing process. I just believed that their responses would have great generosity of spirit."

Journalist and critic Don Shewey lives in New York City. He has published three books about theatre. His articles and essays have appeared in publica-tions including the *New York Times*, the *Village Voice, Esquire* and *Rolling Stone*, as well as anthologies such as *The Politics of Manhood* and *Best Gay Erotica 2000*.

GONE WEST

By Jon Jory

July/August 2000

Okay, I'm outta here, 31 years is enough. I get the general idea. It's time to make way for a new generation, but I would be shirking my responsibility if I didn't pass on the 25 Sacred Laws that each retiring artistic director is supposed to leave, handwritten, in the center drawer of the office desk—only sometimes we forget. Nobody knows where they came from; a lot of people think they began with Bill Ball and Adrian Hall, whoever they were. Before I cut to the chase, a word of encouragement: Don't worry, young people, anybody can do this job. Only a genius could screw this up. Personally, I have only two regrets: Robert Brustein never gave me the secret handshake, and I'm still not sure how to pronounce Peer Gynt.

All right, here's the good stuff; don't tell it to anybody—I'm trying to give you a leg up.

1. The hard thing is to find enough rewarding and creative tasks to make everyone feel fully used but not murderously overworked.
2. Remember you're building the institution and not simply your own career.
3. Psychological realism may be dead, but the audience forgot to read the obituary.
4. Don't do a Boston season in Boise, or vice versa.
5. The profession loves novelty, and the audience loves the familiar. Now what?
6. What principle is at work when the carpenters make more than the stitchers? See, you already knew.
7. When everyone is underpaid and you buy a state-of-the-art lighting board, or renovate the executive offices, it's a political act.
8. Get as much mind as possible into the building.
9. Have passions and pay attention to what they cost.

10. You only get fired for losing money, but the board will say it's because "your work wasn't really exciting."
11. Only a few plays are guaranteed to make money: *The Wizard of Oz*, *A Christmas Carol* and *Dracula*.
12. If you produce any of those plays, it will be bruited about that you are not an artist.
13. If you don't produce them, you will be fired because your work "isn't really exciting."
14. A small-cast play is three. A large-cast play is eight. Once a year, you can have 12. If you do three two-character plays in a season, you can do Shakespeare. But you mustn't do plays anyone else does. Now plan a season that amazes everyone.
15. Since no theatre of any size ever played to more than two percent of its potential audience, you can stop worrying about being elitist.
16. To do new plays. To do classics. To do American plays. To do nonrealistic work. To do Shakespeare. To do seasons thematically. To have politics. To do musical theatre. To be an actors', directors' or playwrights' theatre. To do theatre that's sort of like dance. To be text-based. To do community-based work. To have puppets. To be a culturally exclusive theatre. To be a culturally inclusive theatre. Combine any two to have a fundable artistic policy. Combine any three to be profiled in *American Theatre*.
17. Process is the only reward. Concentrating is the only happiness. And hire people more talented than you are.
18. If you have a great success with a play in a rural setting, don't send it to New York. They can't follow the psychology of any character who wouldn't eat a bagel.
19. Don't forget to mention that you want to be "world class," and then—three years later—say you are.
20. It is important to remember that no artistic director notices when they are funded by corporations they ought to abhor. I mean, we've got casting to think about!
21. Directors who bar playwrights from rehearsal go to hell. Forever. Barefoot.
22. Have a life outside the theatre.
23. If the play isn't blocked after two-and-a-half weeks and the director tells you, "That's just the way I work," fire his ass.
24. After the third audition when you're sure she's the right actor, the agent will tell you she's unavailable, but she really wanted to meet you.
25. You'll know it's time to leave when there are more people in middle management than you ever have on stage, and you would rather kill someone than write another program note.

So, that's about it. I have to get going. I've had a really good time doing this stuff, and you will, too. Work from the heart, try to make sure everybody has a good time, respect your audience, take learning your craft seriously, trust your co-workers, and whenever they start talking about art, run like the devil was chasing you.

Bon voyage.

After 30 years as producing director at Kentucky's Actors Theatre of Louis-ville, where he founded the Humana Festival of New American Plays in 1979, Jon Jory left to become professor of acting and directing at the University of Washington in Seattle. He was also the founding artistic director of Long Wharf Theatre in New Haven, Conn., beginning in 1965. His books include *Tips: Ideas for Actors* (2000) and *Tips: Ideas for Directors* (2002).

A PLACE AT THE TABLE

By James Magruder

January 2001

The essay excerpted here was written in 1998 as an informal position paper to entice the Mellon Foundation into supporting dramaturgy at CENTERSTAGE of Baltimore, Md. The strategy worked; in the fall of 1999, the foundation awarded the theatre an unprecedented matching grant for dramaturgical activity. Former managing director Peter Culman raised $1 million before retiring in June '00; that was matched by a Mellon million, taking the total dramaturgical budget to $2 million.

Any dramaturg spends a significant portion of his or her time on the job responding to the question "What is a dramaturg?" Throughout my nine years in the business, I have explained and explained again—and again—to friends, actors, sixth graders, dates, dentists, donors and my uncomprehending family, that dramaturgy is a function more than a job description. To keep my answer fresh, I try to think up new images for myself every season. Sometimes they're lofty: The Keeper of the Flame of Thespis. The Conscience of the Theatre. The Bridge Between Page and Stage. Others are more pedestrian: The Artistic Enabler. The Resident Egghead and Cultural Flypaper. Always I try not to be defined by how others have historically viewed me. The Guy with the Library Card. The Useless Appendix of the American Theatre. Last-hired, First-fired. The Cheese Stands Alone.

We are a misunderstood lot, but not tragically so. Our (relative) enfranchisement as theatre professionals in America is recent; and if our progress as the closet idealists who attempt to forward the art form by our thoughts and deed has not been exactly swift, it's not surprising. We live in a young country whose biases are anti-intellectual, ahistorical, anti-art and utilitarian, and we work in a not-for-profit arts culture that is increasingly obsessed with the bottom line. Dramaturgy in America got started in the mid-'70s when regional theatres realized they needed "literary managers" to process all the new scripts for all the new-play programs generated by funding initiatives. Eventually, the more artistically minded theatres realized it wasn't a bad idea to have a smart person on staff to help select repertory, do research and educate the public as to the mission of the institution and the aims of the individual productions. As the money flowed through the go-go '80s, even the theatres that didn't know how to deploy dramaturgs hired them.

When I entered the dramaturgy program at the Yale School of Drama in 1985, I barely knew what a dramaturg was. I was just thrilled to have discovered a profession within the theatre that could make use of my writing skills, my critical eye and my brain *without* my having to be a director. I spent three years there explaining why I was not a threat to suspicious playwrights and insecure directors. My image for dramaturgy then was Chief Chair-Scoocher. At the first day of rehearsal, at the big table in the middle of the room, there were chairs for the director, the designers, the playwright, the actors and the stage manager. The dramaturg had to scooch his chair forward from the corner, making embarrassing noises and apologizing for being a bother as he hoped someone at the big table would make room for him to squeeze in. It was not a happy time. I was ready to leave the profession before I even started.

I came to CENTERSTAGE—a theatre with a long and abiding respect for the input of several eggheads—in 1991, during the season in which Irene Lewis began her tenure as artistic director. I expect that our collaboration will be the most fruitful of my dramaturgical life. Working against adverse circumstances for the arts, we have continued the mission of presenting challenging repertory, classics and new plays that lead, rather than follow, audience expectations with the finest theatre artists we can lure to Baltimore.

I read new plays; I cut Shakespeare; I agitate for Aeschylus and Marlowe in season planning; I take notes during run-throughs and previews, following the dramaturgical injunction to Make-It-Better; and I still get thrills in the rehearsal room and in the theatre when one of those indelible, alchemical, truly theatrical moments happens. There are, however, things I have done here no grad school could prepare me for: Writing an NEA grant proposal for Brendan Behan's *The Hostage* in three days. Speaking to the Rotary Club in Little Italy about the fate of theatre in the next millennium. Drafting an initial case study for an endowment campaign. Calling subscribers on the phone to ask them for money for the annual fund. Participating in a new-trustee orientation every fall, filling the freshmen in on critical concepts like "actor workweeks" and "artistically driven." Crafting copy for a television ad campaign. Whatever I do, whatever the season, the play, the audience, I am always making the case that theatre matters.

My latest image for the dramaturg is Practical Dreamer. Other theatres use terms like collaboration, diversity, artistic excellence, fiscal responsibility, new voices, educational outreach and a living wage. In my time here I have watched, and helped, Irene and managing director Peter Culman and board president Nancy Roche strive mightily to live by these terms. CENTERSTAGE doesn't need to have its dramaturgs be its conscience and its closet idealists. CENTERSTAGE itself is crawling with idealists of every stripe. CENTERSTAGE is also savvy enough to know how to perpetuate itself, how to preserve the continuation of its core values even as it prepares for inevitable transitions, whether they be internal changes in leadership or external changes in the business cycle. There is a very large place at the table for dramaturgs at CENTERSTAGE. Let it ever be so.

James Magruder was resident dramaturg at CENTERSTAGE from 1992 to 1999. His translations include Marivaux's *The Triumph of Love,* **as well as the book for its musical version, which ran on Broadway; Eugene Labiche's** *Eating Crow;* **Alain-René Lesage's** *Turcaret;* **Molière's** *The Imaginary Invalid, The Miser* **and** *Le Bourgeois Gentilhomme* **(as** *Bougie Man);* **and Carlo Gozzi's** *The Love of Three Oranges.* **He teaches translation and adaptation at Yale School of Drama.**

WHERE MYSTIQUE MEETS TECHNIQUE

By Randy Gener

January 2002

A mong the major figures of Japanese avant-garde theatre, Tadashi Suzuki—with his rigorous method of physical training that virtually remakes actors' bodies—has exerted the most powerful influence in this country over what an actor should be. Since his work came to the attention of American theatre practitioners in the early 1980s, the Suzuki method of actor training has swept through the acting community like foxfire. His training exercises re-ignited a landscape that, constrained by the boundaries of realism, was said in some quarters to be disintegrating into kitchen-sink clichés and self-indulgence.

Steeped in the austere performance styles of noh and kabuki, Suzuki seeks to create an actor who can "make the whole body speak, even when one is silent." This approach has been catnip to experimental seekers and utopian types who remain convinced that the key to the actor's craft lies in the nonverbal aspects of theatre—in physical actions and a heightened means of expression. Like Jerzy Grotowski's notion of "the holy actor," Suzuki's disciplined method fed the disillusionment that many actors and directors felt with the various Americanized variations of the Stanislavsky system.

Through an international exchange program that allowed young American actors to join Suzuki's Company of Toga in the mountains of Toga-mura (about 250 miles northwest of Tokyo), Suzuki quickly gained a worldwide following. None of his contemporaries in Japan's little-theatre movement (*shogekijo*) have inspired so many non-Japanese proselytes and disciples. Not Juro Kara, whose open-air Situation Theatre has only recently been called to New York's attention, thanks to the tireless efforts of the Japan Society. Not Shuji Terayama, whose meta-theatrical call for a "drama with no theatre" ended when he died in 1983. Not Satoh Makoto, whose anti-colonial politics have kept him rooted to the people's theatre in Asia, especially in the Philippines.

Other Japanese directors who have worked extensively in the international scene can't claim a comparable impact. Koichi Kimura's collaborations with Japanese playwright Hisashi Inoue and British playwright Arnold Wesker have largely been focused in Tokyo and London's West End. Yukio Ninagawa is internationally famous for his flamboyant productions of *Macbeth*, *Medea*, *The Tempest* and *King Lear*, but he has never theorized about acting or articulated his ideas about theatre in book form.

Suzuki, by contrast, has distinguished himself as a heady theorist of performance, thanks to the 1986 appearance of his first collection of theatre writings, *The Way of Acting* (TCG). In the United States he is a founder (with American experimental director Anne Bogart) of the international theatre institute and actor-training program in Saratoga, N.Y., known as SITI Company. Universities and institutions like American Conservatory Theater, Columbia University, University of Washington, University of Wisconsin–Milwaukee and Juilliard offer his regimen as part of their overall actor-training packages.

"I'm very interested in excesses of human energy that push our actions beyond the generally acceptable," said the 62-year-old director in a brightly lit conference room at the Japan Society in New York last November. After a 10-year absence, Suzuki was on the first leg of a month-long, four-city tour featuring members of the Shizouka Performing Arts Center, where he is currently artistic director. "I am not interested in naturalism. I am not interested in addressing plays that are realistic. All of the great plays by Shakespeare, the Greeks or Tennessee Williams feature protagonists who are criminals or are insane. They cheat, lie, kill. Beckett's plays are filled with weirdos listening to the sound of their own voices. The questions I am posing in my productions are: Who are these people? What are they about?"

Illness of the human psyche and mad power struggles in social institutions are recurring motifs for Suzuki. Fusing Western dramatic literature with the influence of traditional Asian styles, his austere productions ask us to identify with archetypal or trans-historical figures locked in the grip of insoluble conflicts (war, religious strife, sex, economic problems). In public appearances, essays, brochures and program notes, Suzuki reiterates and reaffirms his belief that "all the world is a hospital and all men and women are merely patients."

In fact, many of Suzuki's productions, past and present, literally situate classical figures in hospitals and insane asylums. In *The Tale of Lear*, Suzuki relocates Shakespeare's tragedy to a nursing home where an old man hallucinates that he is Shakespeare's mournful hero, betrayed and abandoned by his children, while a Nurse/Fool in a starched white uniform sits besides him reading the text of the play. The plight of *The Trojan Women* is seen through the eyes of a deranged Tokyo woman (played in the original production by Suzuki's one-time leading lady, the powerhouse actress Kayoko Shiraishi); a victim of the bombings of World War II, she relives the loss of her family in a cemetery and imagines herself as Hecuba and Cassandra.

Suzuki's potent 90-minute version of *Electra* is no different. (*Electra* is one of three Suzuki-helmed productions—none brand new—that recently completed touring the U.S. The others are *Oedipus Rex* and *Dionysus*.) Derived from an adaptation of the Greek myth by

Austrian dramatist and poet Hugo von Hofmannsthal, the play finds the main characters trapped in a mental asylum where a chorus of nurses and orderlies observes their every move and listens to their ghastly exhortations. Locked in solitary confinement, raging over the murder of her father Agamemnon, Electra plots and fantasizes the murder of his killer Clytemnestra, Electra's mother, at the hands of her brother Orestes. Pushed on stage and off in a wheelchair, Clytemnestra gutturally recounts her nightmare visions of the return of Orestes, whom she has exiled. A nubile, pretty Chrysothemis, whose dreams of getting hitched and bearing children have been stymied, wheels herself forward to rebuke her sister Electra's vengeful intransigence and murderous impulses.

Under the glare of the Sept. 11 tragedy, *Electra* plays like an ode to ruination, a hoarse symphony of scabrous eruptions and apoplectic fury. Moaning and groaning, virtually unable to speak, Electra embodies the disfigured shape of mourning and grief. Garrulous and bejeweled, Clytemnestra is the face of scathing guilt itself. "Greek plays overflow with characters driven to heinous deeds by excesses of energy," Suzuki said. "They depict how forces or systems beyond the control of the individual bring on misfortune. It is fair to say that Electra's abiding passion redirected is the passion of a terrorist. In my version, she is unable to execute her desire for revenge. She can only live it out in her imagination. She is relying on Orestes to do it, but then he turns out to be mad as well. The struggle between Orestes and Electra also reflects the battle between matriarchy and patriarchal lineage, which ultimately proved victorious in Europe. Because her abandon, energy and passion remain unexecuted, Electra is driven to madness."

Suzuki's personal vision throbs with the kinetic pulse of metaphor and mysticism. And it is never more bracing and visceral than when it is at a standstill: Suzuki's 70-minute adaptation of Sophocles' *Oedipus Rex*—unlike the eye-and-ear engaging *Electra*—dissolves into a formalistic series of tense moments and unwitting disclosures. In the simplest analysis, it is about the agonizing strain of unwitting discovery. With faces virtually still and impassive and movements sparse and formalistic, Oedipus and Jocasta look like totemic figures stuck in a crucible of indictment and prophecy. The pacing is deliberate, the action ritualized, the stage setting stark and shadowy. The production would have felt like a vacuum of tension and stasis had it not been leavened by rhythmic choral dancing, a lilting musical score and opulent costumes.

This is not an Oedipus who disgorges his eye sockets. "I actually had come to realize that Oedipus was sick," Suzuki said. "The play ends with the beginning of his illness. As long as he remains unconscious of what he did, the pollution that has struck Thebes was just weird or different. But once he comes into consciousness, he realizes that there is no way but to live with his disease. Only in the process of discovery does Oedipus become sick." So while achieving a healthy state of mind and body is a worthy aspiration, what's incredible about Oedipus is his will to action—his confident resolve to know what ails him.

"All of the characters in my plays are mentally unstable, and so am I," Suzuki declared during a post-performance discussion. "I'm drawn to the criminal within myself." His message, if you want to call it that, is that the root of our self-destruction lies in our own imagination. The virtue of the classical repertory is that it offers a profound and pitiless analysis of our spiritual crisis—if we are to survive, we must change in fundamental ways to be the kind of people that we are. Human perfection may be sheer impossibility, but Suzuki does hold out a glimmer of optimism. "Patients, at least, have a hope of getting better," he said. "Even prisoners are usually under a fixed sentence. I tend to portray humans as we must not be. Hope is all-important."

A distillation of techniques from noh and kabuki, Suzuki's training exercises build an actor's will, stamina and concentration. Somewhat akin to boot camp, they begin with the lower body, with an initial emphasis on the feet, and progress to an actor's breath, voice, energy and physicality. "It's really about maintaining a constant center of gravity," Suzuki explained. "When you see a ballerina turn or watch Michael Johnson on the track field, their heads never go up and down—there's a constant center of gravity. It's the same with actors."

Even those who know little about Suzuki's method know that it is "foot-oriented," but the director explains: "Instead of the emphasis being specifically on the feet, it's really about the lower body. You want actors to learn how to position their feet in relationship to the ground or the earth. What I am interested in is how the lower body is used in the service of supporting a performance, a swift movement or a large voice. You can't just have a smart brain or a beautiful physical body. The lower part of the body sustains the action and supports the voice over time. You can see this in flamenco dancers, noh as well as kabuki performers or in classical ballet."

The Suzuki method proposes a primal means of communication through bodies and actions rather than words. It was originally designed to accommodate his non-lingual, body-centered vision of how a play should be presented. This has led to the criticism that his method is applicable only to his own ascetic productions, an appraisal that is not without merit but which the director dismissed as a fallacy. Suzuki insists that his system does not conflict with the American acting tradition inspired by Stanislavsky and should pose no obstacle for actors working in realistic plays or even musicals. "If they find that there is friction, it's probably because the actor is not gifted," he said.

Suzuki cited the American actor Tom Hewitt as a model example. The Tony-nominated star of the Broadway revival of *The Rocky Horror Show* has previously tackled the role of Scar in Julie Taymor's *The Lion King*, and his work has ranged from classical Shakespeare to contemporary comedies by Wendy Wasserstein. After studying acting at the University of Wisconsin–Milwaukee, he commuted for six years to attend Suzuki's master classes in Toga-mura.

"When I did *Lear* with American actors, I cast Tom as the lead," Suzuki recalled. "Tom himself has told me how useful the Suzuki method has been. Even though *The Rocky Horror Show* bears no relationship whatsoever to the kind of *King Lear* he did in Toga, Tom asked me to come and see *Rocky Horror*, which I did. I can see how he's utilized aspects of the Suzuki method because he's a gifted, intelligent actor who can take what he's learned and alter it for the present circumstances. What this shows is that for all the years of commuting to Toga, he is able to be completely and totally adaptable, whether it's a musical on Broadway or a realistic drama at Arena Stage. What I don't want is a slavish mimicking of the exterior aspects of the training—robots of the Suzuki method—but an intelligent, gifted actor who can take the training and make it their own."

Although he understood English, Suzuki spoke through an interpreter, Linda Hoaglund. He confessed that he isn't aware of the extent to which his training method is being taught, used, exploited or put into practice in America. He has confidence in the quality of work being done by a select few former students with whom he has kept in close contact over the years, but he acknowledged there are potential problems in what he called "second- and third-generation teachings of the Suzuki method." There are about 15 Americans who have taken his master classes in Toga and are fully certified to teach the Suzuki technique. "The best way is to contact my office to find out who is or is not authentically trained," Suzuki added.

The Suzuki method requires a fairly long-term involvement. "I would say that three years would make sense," he said. "There are universities across the United States that have teachers who are certified instructors. So a person would have to start out there for a year or two. And then they may indicate an interest in coming to Japan. If they do well in their courses, they are eligible for master classes, which are about two months long."

But what ultimately matters to Suzuki is that an actor has prior experience, as opposed to someone who has no training or some training in a different system. "The reason I like working with experienced actors, even maybe actors who learned from other kinds of training methods (especially if they come from abroad), is that many people tend to feel confused about my training method," he said. "People tend to find what is exotic and different about my training methods. They think it's some Japanese cultural gobbledygook. It is nothing of the sort. It is not some strange Japanese cult or bizarre behavior. It's a very rigorous training method. I think the people who get the best results are those who are able to see for themselves that this method is a way of improving their range of technique."

He winced at the criticism that rasping, growling and throaty screams are a characteristic affectation of his method. "There is a theory that the Suzuki method is damaging to vocal chords, and that it's more akin to a calisthenics of the voice rather than actual acting training," Suzuki said. "I would like to know who are these teachers who are instituting it poorly. What's really important isn't just the rote transmission of the Suzuki training. It's really about understanding what the training is for and how a director will make it work on stage."

Despite the almost inhuman effort it takes to learn Suzuki's exercises for centering, breath-control, a powerful speaking voice, alignment and concentration, it is the mastery over stress and strain that makes it possible for a talented actor to play the heightened emotions that are laid bare in the great plays of dramatic literature. Its integrity lies precisely in the extremity of his technique. As Suzuki himself is quick to point out: "It's training, after all. It's not the act of creation. It helps as a *springboard* for the act of creation. The analogy I'd take is that for a plane to take off, you need a runway. In order for a car to drive fast, you need a highway. That's what the Suzuki training is. It's the runway. It's the highway. Whether or not the actor will really take off or not is up to the individual actor."

Amid the atmosphere of multiculturalism and the idealization of ritual forms that characterize so much of the postmodernist search for new acting techniques and directing styles, Suzuki's system calls into ideological question the weaknesses of so-called Method acting. During the 1980s and 1990s, the Suzuki system took stronger root in part because it had stimulating things to say about the nature of cross-cultural performance. Suzuki's innovative synthesis of traditional and avant-garde techniques, echoing back to Vsevolod Meyerhold's bio-mechanical ideas about gesture and Michael Chekhov's interest in the grammar of the feet, represents an advance in the evolution of inter-cultural theatre activity.

"When we in Japan want to learn, use or absorb something from out-side our culture, we do so with the expectation that it's going to be mod-ified when we use it in our system," Suzuki said. "No system can survive completely intact. I think the mark of a truly lasting art form, whether it's a cultural phenomenon or a training method such as the Suzuki method, is that it can survive in an altered form in another culture and still main-tain its integrity. In this day and age of international understanding and global communication, it would be strange if something survived exactly as it was in the original culture—rigidly in the secondary culture."

Since so much actor training depends so profoundly on gurus and their disciples, it remains an open question whether Suzuki's presentational approach will survive the ravages of time. Will it reign in the American acting community alongside Stanislavsky's representational system?

"I think what is upon us now is the necessary work of identifying indigenous practices and rituals," Suzuki said. "We really need to hold onto them and make them part of our world heritage. It's not just up to a particular region to try to protect its own culture. It's our collective responsibility. It's up to artists to devise a new strategy for unique and individual cultures to coexist in the future. We need begin to identify which cultural or artistic practices need to be preserved and should belong to the world—instead of just letting them fall under the sway of a particular language or be dominated by a particular culture that's becoming too powerful."

If nothing else, then, this disciplined training method offers a way out of what some have called the "Stanislavskian cul-de-sac." Breath-ing a new theatricality back into the actor's life, the Suzuki method fills a void in actor training in America.

Randy Gener is a senior editor of *American Theatre*.

INCIDENT AT AWASSA

By David Schein

May/June 2002

APRIL 2001, THE MARKET, AWASSA, ETHIOPIA: The audience closed in so tightly around the performers that there was hardly room to perform. *Too tight*, I thought, hugging the inside of the circle, one of two "forengis" in a crowd of over a thousand Ethiopians who were leaning in and starting to push, stumbling into the playing area. Someone could get hurt. The market police weren't helping matters. Every time they flicked their whips, the front row careened backwards onto the people behind them—who retaliated by pushing forward so that the crowd spilled back into the playing area, only to be whipped back again.

My cast of Ethiopian teenagers, performing the premiere of their *AIDS Education Circus* in the marketplace of Awassa, didn't miss a beat, adjusting their gymnastics to the ever-shrinking perimeter, fighting with cartwheels and flips to keep the death's-head AIDS-puppet monster in place, singing the audience back, performing on a dime. I roamed the inside of the circle, making pushing motions, using my full palm and spreading my fingers wide while I bowed, oh, so whitely, made eye contact, pushed softly, pleaded in my few words of Amharic, *"Amar say conalo"* ("Thank you"), *"Ishi"* ("Of course") and in English, idiotically, "Please, please, gentle, gentle, nice, nice," reaching down to pull squalling tots out from under the feet of the front line by their arms and handing them to the audience. If the crowd kept pushing forward, everyone would collapse in on each other.

This was at the point in the show when M'buye—my strongest teenage performer, so commanding in his half-mask, eye patch and big Batman voice—was supposed to call out in Amharic, "Only Condoms Will Kill the AIDS Monster," grab the garbage bag of condoms and throw handfuls of them into the audience. *No, M'buye*, I thought, *don't throw the condoms, please don't throw the condoms*. If he threw them, the young men might fight for them and the world's first Theatre Condom Riot would ensue. Many would die. I'd go to jail (they have great ones in Ethiopia, called "holes in the ground"), and in four years the American Embassy might get me a trial. All because of bad blocking. I'd figured on an audience of 200 and got 2,000. I thought the performers would be able to control the size of the circle. We'd worked so hard on expanding and contracting, but the lesson to be learned was: Once a circle is three deep, the perimeter can't respond.

I tried to get M'buye's attention with my eyes, but he was too busy fighting the crowd back. He threw a couple of condoms. *Oh, no.* There was a fight over the condoms in the back of the crowd. People were pushing in. *Oh, please, M'buye,* I prayed, hoping he'd see me shaking my head, *DON'T THROW THE CONDOMS.* I was scared to my bones, hyper-alert, ready to jump in and stop the crowd, ready to die *for the theatre.* But with the adrenaline of fear, there was a familiar companion—I have to admit it: that great big theatre glow, the one you get when your show is *really working.* Everyone wanted to see Mr. AIDS dance and blow kisses. The show was a killer.

Two weeks earlier I'd come to Awassa, capital of Sidama province in Southern Ethiopia, on the invitation of my German friend Dr. Hermann Hunzinger and his Awassan friend Aster Dabels, to make some theatre with teenagers, street kids. The kids had been initially collected by Aster's sister, Sunnait, who had started feeding them in her backyard and sending them to school. For four years now, Aster had been raising money to support the food and school fees, and Hunzinger had gotten involved. Meanwhile the kids, remarkably, without any formal coaching, had taught themselves tumbling, juggling and tightrope. An older boy, Berreket, who'd had some gymnastics training, had become their director, and they'd done well, placing in competitions with gymnastics troupes from other cities affiliated with the Circus Ethiopia movement. Hunzinger, knowing that I worked with kids in Chicago, had told me about these young folks and asked me, "Is there a way to do something with them—something special that could raise money for the project?" *Right, Hunzinger,* I'd thought, *it's hard enough to get money for teen theatre here in the States. In the second poorest country in the world—fat chance for slim pickings!* But somehow the phone conversation shifted to the subject of an NPR program I'd heard about how theatre and storytelling had been such an effective part of AIDS education in Uganda—perhaps we could form an *AIDS Education Circus* in Awassa? Hunzinger suggested that the Awassa market, one of the largest in Ethiopia, would be a perfect place for a show like that. Okay, I said, I could workshop the kids for an intensive two weeks. We'd build a show for the market and they'd perform it. "Okay, if you can get to Frankfurt and back," Hunzinger said, "I'll bankroll the rest. When are you available?"

It was a gig from Hunzinger heaven. I'd never been to Africa. I hit the library and the Internet and found that Ethiopia has the fourth highest rate of AIDS infection in Africa. Sixty million people and a 65-percent illiteracy rate. Little infrastructure. The one country in Africa that was never colonized. Three main roads in and out of a country the size of Spain and France combined. Landlocked. You can't get a boat up the Blue Nile to it. One railroad built in 1898. The Tibet of Africa, wedged in between the hornet's nests of war on either side in Sudan and Somalia; to the north, a recently subsided war with the present government's sworn enemy, Eritrea, had in three months taken 120,000 lives. What a place to do theatre: millions of people off the grid, way out in the highlands, no TV, no radio, no drama critics, no parking, a ready-made ensemble. The scheme could work. Maybe. Of course it would, I said to myself. Once you start folks singing and dancing, there's a common language. We'll develop a warm-up, the warm-up will become the show, and it'll be a piece of cake. Let them eat theatre.

When it came down to it, the project made as much sense to me as my latest piece, a choral work about my wife's underwear called *The Black Panty Suite*. I got my shots and then got more, packed malaria pills, did two months of fundraising in two weeks for my Chicago theatre company, Free Street Programs, and got on a plane for Frankfurt with a garbage bag of condoms and an alarmingly empty notebook.

Landing in Addis Ababa, my first images were of Hunzinger, my Swabian benefactor, and Aster, the Ethiopian princess-turned-German-housewife/social activist. True colonials can look at a place like Ethiopia and know that this world is their oyster and they can buy anything or anybody. But when I hit an underdeveloped country with my rucksack and my visa, I always feel fat, white and rich—that's who I am on the street: just look at my shoes, there's no denying it, the children know, they swarm around me begging, and I fill my pockets before I go out. Some days of silence are usually in order so that I can begin to understand, not what I see—that would take a lifetime—but at least my own reflection, who might I be to the people who see me.

First impressions of people: The women on the road crews swinging picks, lean sinew laying down cobbles. Solomon of the Van, our guide, a six-foot-two Oromo from Harrar (the town out toward the wilds of Somalia where Rimbaud died), always the watcher-outer for me with my eyes big and mouth shut, keeping track of my rucksack, my wallet. Light-skinned people with an African tinge, carrying the smell of coffee, roasting beans and eucalyptus. The "forengi" motel by the airport, a secluded outpost where various gringos on a mission could assemble forces before they took off for Ethiopia. The guy who was bicycling from Djibouti to South Africa. The Englishman from the British Museum with his safari vest of many pockets who had come to learn the Abore language before the tribe went extinct ("Only 25,000 left in Omo Valley, that's critical mass for a language"). The French travel agent who had come to investigate the possibility of producing tourist safaris in Ethiopia ("There is no infrastructure in this damned place," he said, as he headed home totally defeated). The pink-and-blue monoxide sunset on the airport road; the city sloping south to a darkening sky over the Rift Valley; the vans and taxis crammed, tens of thousands of people walking home; the begging children; the beautiful sign taking up a whole wall, blue and brown and yellow, a noble African couple with their well-dressed child, beaming with their creamy spoons in hand, the banner behind them proclaiming, "Yogurt, the

Wave of the Future." The leper clomping along on wooden hand-blocks, legs like brown rubber *sukinis*, face lit up in a huge smile by a small television on the counter of a tobacco shack on the airport road—and no, it couldn't be, the figure on the tube lighting that smile in the leper's face is "Judge Judy," piped in by satellite in English. The leper liked Judge Judy and basked in her glow, nodding approval to me at her verdict, which seemed to be going against the blonde with the beehive. We watched her together in the living room of the world.

We shopped for supplies before we left Addis, scoring a hundred pounds of rice for the kids, potatoes, and enough bottled water to last the forengis two weeks. We attended a meeting I'd prearranged by e-mail with the cultural aide at the concrete-barriered American Embassy, who told us that the ambassador's top priority was AIDS prevention, and set us up with contacts for meetings when we returned to Addis. Then we got in the vans bound for Awassa, 120 miles south past the lakes of the Rift Valley, Zway and Lengano, where we stopped to see the storks and the hippos. We drove past cattle herders and horse carts and charcoal stands by the side of the road, and everywhere, thatched huts and goats, cows, sheep, chickens, kids, camels, life, people, Africa.

We arrived in the dark at Sunnait's house in Awassa, a little bungalow in a walled compound, and suddenly I was the American, one of only a few who had visited since they'd all been thrown out in 1972. There was good Ethiopian beer and there were many people. I met Sensamo Mengistu, the sports minister of the province of Sidama; Dr. Million Tumato, who was in charge of HIV/AIDS education for the province; Girma Melesse, a round koala bear of a man who managed the project for Hunzinger and Aster; and young Berreket, the kids' director, who spoke just enough English to enable us to make a plan: a schedule and a pick-up time for me. I was taken out to meet the kids, in their eating tent, 40 of them. I said, "I'm David. I'm real excited about this," and they smiled, and one of them said, "We've been waiting for you," and I said, "See ya at nine," and another said, "At the soccer field," and I said, "I'm from Chicago," and in unison they said, "Michael Jordan," and then we were embarrassed and didn't know what more to say.

In the morning there were storks nesting in the trees by the hotel and big black-and-white monkeys clambering around. Berreket picked me up in a "cultural taxi" (a horse and buggy) and we clomped a couple of miles to the soccer field. At nine some of the kids were there, but by ten lots of people were there—the kids, various groups who had come to see the American forengi's first training, some men in suits (government?), some in traditional dress, and Hermann, Aster, Mengistu, Girma, Solomon and many additional teenagers. I shook hands with everyone and—feeling like a janitor posing as a surgeon before the first slice—I said, "Let's begin. Please, Berreket, show me what the circus can do."

Berreket clapped his hands and the kids lined up and began. *Thank God, a warm-up!* I could have kissed him. They were leading each other through moves, in rhythm, breaking sweat. What a relief. They spoke the language of theatre—it *was* an ensemble. I jumped in and warmed up with them. My audience laughed and pointed. I invited them to join in. Of course they didn't. But I got some kicks doing jumping jacks, push-ups, cartwheels and somersaults, and running a lap around the soccer field got rid of the fear.

They showed me what they knew: gymnastic moves, fast chains of front-flips, cartwheels, walkovers and half-gainers, and some circus stunts—juggling, slack rope, batons and chairs. They could build a pyramid. Sort of. What else? They did some "mime," which for them was acting scenes without words. I tried to guess the story of the scene and then somehow started directing. "Do it again. Use your hands. Try that. Use your eyes." We fell into the language of rehearsing. It was natural. One kid, Sentayo, spoke good English and that helped immensely. Soon I was teaching them Linklater breathing and sighing. And Lessac shapes, the inverted megaphone. Soon we were singing. And dancing in the circle, chorus and solo, the ritual of warm-up. Oh, could they sing. Oh, did we dance. When I looked up an hour later, the audience was gone. We had begun.

We put the *AIDS Education Circus* together in 10 days. We rehearsed in two shifts during the day, accommodating different school schedules, singing, dancing, drumming, trying gymnastic stunts and martial arts, laying down scenes. We wrote at night, after supper in the food tent. They wrote in Amharic with my facilitation, translating back and forth until I had an idea what was being said (at least I hoped I did). The kids wrote in their notebooks, choosing the best idea, translating it for me, arguing, finding consensus, sometimes getting pissed or tired, or just clowning around. It was just like making a show anywhere.

The show was simple. The troupe runs in with bodies held over their heads, throws them in the air. They flip down to the ground. *Bang*: We've got the audience. First song: Why did they die? Malaria, tsetse, pneumonia, TB, heart, stroke, alcohol, parasites, anything but . . . the relatives sing. Ghosts spring up: "You lie." Each Ghost tells its AIDS story: the truck driver and the prostitute, the wife and the husband, the kid who got it from her parents, the guy whose girlfriend lied.

Then in comes the big AIDS puppet, shaking and blowing kisses. They fight him with flips, kicks, cartwheels and somersaults. He always wins. Mr. AIDS blows kisses at the audience and shakes his ass. He drinks a beer. Sex is fun. Come on.

No, no, the children say, and keep trying to fight Mr. AIDS. But nothing works. How do you fight AIDS? Did someone say *condoms*? Yes! Be smart! An actor does a flip in place and when he lands he has a condom in his hand—and condoms work on Mr. AIDS like Kryptonite on Superman. The puppet fights for the condom, snatches it, tries to bite it, but too late—a little kid, the tiniest actor, flying through the air, gets the condom back. The puppet sags.

Someone calls out: "One to One" (monogamy). The girls stand on the boys' shoulders. Oh, poor Mr. AIDS, he doesn't like that. He's wavering and toppling, staggering now. The troupe dances to the hospital, the girls still on the boys' shoulders. They form a giant moving pyramid and unfurl a large banner that says, CONDOMS, MONOGAMY, TESTING, FIGHT AIDS TOGETHER. AIDS falls, AIDS dies, the puppet is carried off. The circle forms and a really simple rocking song ensues that says, again and again, CONDOMS, MONOGAMY, TESTING, TREATMENT, FIGHT AIDS TOGETHER. The children dance with the audience. Condoms are thrown to the audience, information about local services is distributed and broadcast by the AIDS truck, and condom demonstrations are given.

We cinched up the plan with the provincial HIV/AIDS education office (Dr. Million Tumato and his sound truck). The sports minister got the okay from the market authority and the city powers. Berreket took me to market day to scope out the scene. I'd never been anywhere like it. It was a huge place of 12,000 people, stuffed with hay and donkeys, piles of grain, beans, T-shirts, sneakers, firewood, camels, ghat, gange, baskets, kitchenware, heaps of coffee, bricks, cassettes, healers, peppers, potatoes, flip-flops, buffalos and lumber. It was like being inside a Jackson Pollock painting. We decided on three places to do the show. We'd perform, move through the market singing, perform, move, perform and move again. The AIDS truck would follow us.

Aster found a local artist to make a giant death's-head puppet: Mr. AIDS. The kids trucked out their old gymnastics costumes and on performance day we trooped, singing and dancing with our banners and Mr. AIDS, three miles through the town to the market. Little children followed us calling out "*Atto* AIDS" (Mr. AIDS). Hunzinger videoed. Aster and I had cameras. We set up. The crowd began to gather. I can't remember ever feeling happier than I did that morning. I was thinking, "I'm here in the market of Awassa doing a show. I've finally made it. This is my Broadway. This is my Hollywood."

In fact, it was nearly my Kent State. At the point when the market police were whipping the audience back as they surged forward, faces angry and fists clenched, I had to do something. I had to try to stop the show, somehow, before the audience fell in on the performers. I called upon Jesus, I called upon Ghandi, but it was Viola Spolin who saved me: Raising my hands, a lone forengi in an Ethiopian sea, I signaled the kids to stop. I placed myself between the police whips and the angry audience, stood high on my tiptoes and fell slowly onto the audience. They caught me. And held me. It was the "trust exercise." A strange stillness infected the market. And then, the group intelligence impelled the right movement: Slowly, everyone stepped back.

I nodded to M'buye. The company, undaunted, resumed, the audience again pressed in, but this time with care, and the kids, adapting our circle-your-wagons blocking to one-third the planned space, cartwheeled and tossed each other on a dime. At the end, they danced with the audience and handed out the condoms "*ant to ant*" (one to one). We made it through the show. I was shaking. Hunzinger was laughing with relief: "Oh, David, that was truly an unforgettable piece of theatre." And it was. We'd performed with conviction, we'd mesmerized the crowd, we'd shown enough love to miraculously get a thousand people in the heat of anger to take six steps back. No one died. Great show.

When we set up the second and third shows, I drew a line in the dirt, making a huge performance circle, put little kids in the front row and big guys behind them to protect them. The remaining shows were smooth, though the kids were hot and their voices were going. We handed out thousands of condoms and reams of information. Dr. Tumato and Mr. Sports Minister were happy. The market police calmed down. We marched home. I felt fabulous, and so did the kids. We'd won. Our Tony. Our Awassa Obie.

I bought three sheep and three cases of pop. We sang and danced goodbye that night, and the next day we drove north to Addis to do business. I had a show and I had to sell it, same in Addis as in Chicago, except in Addis UNICEF is Steppenwolf, and the regional reps are markets and refugee camps. I made the rounds: UNICEF, American Aid, Pathfinder and other international agencies with a focus on youth or HIV-ed. I returned to the U.S. and, lord help me, started raising money for the Awassa Children's Project. Last July, American Aid gave the circus a couple of thousand dollars. Folks from the embassy e-mailed me pictures of the show from the market of Shashemene. Now the kids are touring the southern towns on the road to Kenya, and I'm on my way back to tweak the show and to try to set up gigs in the refugee camps along the Sudanese border.

There's no end to this story, at least not at this juncture, but there is a point (and a glorious one) that that puts shivery hairs on end at the back of my neck whenever I think of it. The point is: There's a huge need for theatre in the real, vast "out there"—*way* out there beyond the loges and the balconies, beyond the struggling black boxes and the hot-tix booths and the developmental workshops, even beyond community theatre or street theatre as we know it. There is a need for theatre in the dusty markets of the globe . . . and with that need the possibility of making amazing artistic contact with fellow humans in the most faraway places, the possibility of doing exactly what we know how to do, what we've trained to do, what we are best at: warm-ups, rehearsals, writing shows, performing and producing in the world ensemble. Come join us.

David Schein is executive director of the Arts Council for Chautauqua County in New York and serves on the advisory board of the Awassa Children's Project. He led Free Street Programs in Chicago for more than a decade and has performed, directed and produced his own work across the U.S., Germany, France and England. He has created radio arts projects in Tijuana for NPR and taught theatre at the San Francisco County jail.

ART WILL OUT

By Jaan Whitehead

October 2002

The deepest essence of theatre is the connection of the actor to the audience. You do not need sets, lights, costumes or even a stage to create this connection or to create theatre; you just need an actor speaking to an audience. We tend to think of our theatre institutions as the means by which this connection takes place, the means by which we gather resources to produce the art and gather an audience to witness it. But we do not think very much about the fact that the theatre institutions we create are not a neutral means for doing this, that the institutions themselves affect not only what art is presented to what audience but which artists create the art and how it relates to the wider community. Because our institutions are so familiar to us—they seem so natural and inevitable—we do not ask the probing questions about how they affect and mediate the art. In fact, in seeming to be the obvious answer to the issue of how to produce theatre, the institutional model becomes a mask that obscures these deeper questions.

In recent years, there has been a growing chorus of voices expressing concern that, despite their many advantages, things are not well with our theatre institutions. The most commonly expressed concerns are that seasons are too bland, audiences too homogeneous and investment in new work inadequate to sustain a vital theatrical future. Usually, discussions of these problems tend to look outward at such things as the economy, the influence of television or conservative trends in the country. But I think we can see more clearly if we look inward, if we look inside our institutions and explore how they are, in fact, affecting the ways we develop and present our art. Rather than accepting institutions as inevitable, we can ask how their considerable resources are being used.

When you do ask this question, when you go behind the institutional mask, I believe you find that there is a dynamic in how our institutions developed that has undermined many of their original advantages. For, as theatres grow and become more institutionalized, they generate their own sets of needs that are separate from the art. With time, these institutional needs can become dominant, diverting resources from the art and altering sensibilities and values. Rather than being a means for producing art, institutions become ends in themselves, the art now serving the institution rather than the other way around. There is now an imbalance in how the art relates to the institution, a dissonance that pushes the art and the artists into a subservient role that is antithetical to the health of the theatre.

When this occurs, I think we honor our institutions best by challenging them, by asking how they actually are affecting the ways we practice our art on a daily basis. For instance, how does institutionalization affect the kind of work we do and the ways we develop our audiences? How does it affect the distribution of power in our theatres and how decisions are made? How does it affect our dreaming and how we plan for the future? And how does it affect the choices new artists have as they attempt to enter the field?

In this essay, I want to explore these questions, tracing first how this particular institutional model developed and why I think it causes distortions in how we practice our art. Then I want to look at what artistic alternatives already exist, alternatives that do put the art first and generate different kinds of institutional structures. Finally, I want to look at what might happen if we could break out of the framework of traditional institutional thinking and ask the fundamental question of whether we can use the advantages of an institution—its ability to gather resources and give visibility to the work—for the benefit of the art rather than the institution.

Institutional Art

Over 40 years ago, a group of pioneers founded the American regional theatre movement as a reaction against the growing restrictions of the commercial Broadway theatre. At that time, most professional theatre originated in New York and then spread out through the country in touring companies. The works of Arthur Miller, Eugene O'Neill and Tennessee Williams all were first seen in the New York commercial theatre. But as costs increased and popular culture changed, Broadway began to shy away from untested new work or serious classical work that might or might not draw an audience.

Frustrated with Broadway and wanting to step out from under its shadow, a small group of pioneers—Margo Jones, Nina Vance, Zelda Fichandler, Tyrone Guthrie—founded theatres outside New York where they could continue to develop new work and produce the classics. Supported by the newly established National Endowment for the Arts and innovative funding from the Ford Foundation, these theatres started a movement that grew and became part of the larger artistic renaissance of the 1960s and 1970s. Now, there are hundreds of large and small professional regional theatres spread out across the country.

In the early days of the movement, a particular model emerged as the institutional surround for these theatres—an artistic director and associates to produce the plays, a managing or executive director to lead the administrative side of the theatre, and a board of directors, who represented the public and carried the fiduciary role of seeing that the theatre's financial affairs were in order. It was a dichotomous structure—the artistic energy on one side and the administrative energy on the other.

As theatres grew, organizing themselves around longer seasons and larger audiences, a pattern emerged in which the administrative side became more and more prominent in how a theatre operated. With longer seasons, you needed development and marketing departments; with larger audiences, you needed box offices and outreach programs; with more complex budgets, you needed business offices and new administrative personnel. As institutions grew, boards also expanded, taking on more fundraising and community-liaison roles. And, as the field matured and theatres moved on to second- and third-generation leadership, the role of choosing the new leaders also fell to the board, which was drawn ever more deeply into the setting of artistic missions and institutional policies.

While the administrative side of the theatre expanded into a permanent institutional structure, the artistic side followed quite a different path. Although there was some expansion of the permanent staff, mainly artistic associates and dramaturgs, most of the growth took place through artists who were hired for the production of a particular play. Directors, actors and designers were all jobbed in, and, although theatres often developed longer-term relationships with particular artists, using them on a regular basis or bringing them in through residency programs, most artists really were pieceworkers who had little control over the evolution of a theatre's work. Larger theatres did create their own in-house production departments with set, costume and prop shops. And a few theatres had permanent acting companies. But both the shops and acting companies were quite removed from the institutional decision-making center of the theatre. Rather than becoming a fixed part of the institutional structure, many of the artists had little presence in the theatre on an ongoing basis—and little institutional power.

As theatres evolved along these separate paths, they became caught in a dynamic that reinforced the separation of the artist from the institution. For, when a theatre grows, the very elements that generate the growth—income from ticket sales and fundraising—need to be reproduced each year for the theatre to be sustained. Theatres become more and more dependent on the box office and on the marketing and fundraising departments that generate this income; maintaining the effectiveness of these departments becomes essential to the survival of the institution, and more and more resources go toward this effort. The institution now needs to feed itself as well as fund its art. I think you see this most clearly in times of financial stress, for when a budget needs to be cut, it is much easier to cut the artistic costs that vary with each production than administrative costs that are firmly lodged within the institution; it makes more sense to choose a play with a small cast and few production requirements—the proverbial

Love Letters—than to undermine the fundraising and box office that produce the theatre's income. The art becomes the flesh, while the economic imperatives become the bones of the institution. And, as the art becomes increasingly subject to the economic needs of the institution, the institution starts to drive the art rather than the other way around. The theatre now produces institutional art; the institution, not the artists, determines the ecology of artistic creation.

It is this imbalance between the art and the institution that I think causes many of the disturbing tendencies we see in our theatres today. Because we have such a wide variety of theatres, each with its own rich history, geography and values, these tendencies affect different theatres in different ways. Many theatres may not see themselves reflected in these tendencies at all, while others see themselves reflected very clearly. But I think the forces of institutionalization have affected enough theatres with enough force that the tendencies have become relevant to the field as a whole.

The most obvious, and the most often remarked on, tendency is for the process of institutionalization to insinuate itself into the very heart of the theatre, into the intimate connection between the art and the audience. Too often, the art is packaged into a season of plays with short rehearsal periods and prescheduled runs, while the audience is packaged into a group of season subscribers. Art and audience become two sides of a symbiotic process, each side dependent on the other and each a constraint on the other. The subscription audience is needed to finance the season, but the season has to be attractive enough to draw the subscription audience. It becomes a treadmill—find the plays to attract the audience and attract the audience to finance the plays. The box office now mediates the relationship between the art and the audience, too often becoming the definition of that relationship. What began as a success—the achievement of using subscriptions to build audiences and stabilize cash flow—often ends up reducing artistic options, rather than freeing them.

A less obvious tendency in institutionalized theatres is for power to shift away from artists toward administrators and board members. Power means *who* asks *what* questions of *whom*—who frames the questions and who answers them. A good way to see how this works is to look at a theatre's budget, the budget being an X-ray picture of a theatre's priorities—how choices are made among scarce resources. If you think about the budgeting process and who is most closely involved—who brings what priorities to the table—you see that the different constituents in the theatre have very different access to and power over the budget table. Think of how the different people in a theatre relate to each other, how well they know and understand each other and how they do, or do not, interact. What you see is that the people working in a traditional theatre tend to fall along a continuum, with the board at one end and the shops at the other. Where people fall on the line depends on whom they work most closely with and whose activities they best understand. So, next to the board, at one end of the line, is the administrative staff, particularly the executive, marketing and development directors, who work closely with the board on a regular basis. Moving along the line, the administrative staff, particularly the executive director, is most closely connected to the artistic director who in turn is most closely connected to the resident artists, then the production and technical staff, and finally the shops. So ranged along the line are the board, the administrative staff, the artistic director, the resident artists, the production and technical staff and the shops.

What is important is that, in most institutional theatres, the budgeting process takes place mainly at one end of this line, for it is usually the board that passes the budget and the administrative departments that prepare it with the artistic director. These are the people who sit at the budget table, and the further you are from this nexus of board, administrative leaders and artistic director, the less impact you have on the budget and, thus, the less power in your theatre. Because we tend to value the things we are most familiar with, it is not surprising that the urgency of your needs lessens the further down the line you are. And, of course, the actors, designers and directors who come in for each show are not on this line at all. To bring a better balance to the budget dialogue, the straight line would need to be curved into a circle, with greater connection and understanding among artists, administrators and board members and with more artists at the table.

Planning documents are also X-rays of a theatre's values and priorities, and a third troubling way I think institutionalization affects our theatres is that planning tends to replace dreaming—or at least constrain dreaming—in the life of the theatre. Planning for art is different than planning for an institution; to plan for art you would have to ask what is needed to make art flourish, to develop the art's potential, not just its survival. You would have to ask what is needed to support and nourish playwrights—and actors—and directors—and designers. And what is needed to support the development of new plays and to sustain vital productions of existing plays. In institutional planning, such wider questions about the potential of the art tend to be collapsed into questions about the survival or growth of the institution. The support of theatre buildings, administrative structures and education and audience-development programs all become fixed costs that take precedence over the art. In the end, planning often becomes a more sophisticated and long-term form of budgeting. But, because we really do believe in our mission statements and the value of our art, we tend not to see this, or, if we do see it, we justify it on the grounds that, without the institution, we would not be able to support the art. What this does to dreaming is to contain it within institutional planning; if the dreams cannot fit within the parameters of the institution, they become "impractical."

Finally, there is one last consequence that I find disturbing in how our institutions have developed: Because the funding infrastructure that has grown up around the field has come to expect theatres to take what is now the traditional institutional form, that form seems to be the only path new and emerging theatres can follow if they want to grow and gain financial stability. The regional theatre movement originally flourished with the support of the NEA and the Ford Foundation, because both of these funders were not only open to the ideas of the new theatres but actively sought their input on how to fashion programs to help them. The artists and funders built the theatres together. Forty years later, our funding community is not only much more entrenched; it is deeply invested in our traditional institutions, sharing many of their assumptions and values. Today, funders usually require new theatres to develop administrative structures along the lines of the traditional model before grants are forthcoming, inadvertently pushing them along the path to institutionalized art. It is very difficult for new theatres that do not have—or want—this institutional structure to break into the funding world, and traditional theatres do little to help them.

These are some of the problems that I think occur when theatres become dominated by institutional concerns. I am sure there are more. In many ways, the historical cycle is repeating itself; as our theatres have become more and more institutionalized, they are throwing the same kind of shadow over the art that Broadway did all those years ago. And, as before, a growing number of artists, particularly young artists coming of age in a new generation, are chafing to get out from under this shadow.

Artistic Alternatives

Alternative ways of creating theatre do exist, and have for a long time, but the importance and richness of these alternatives have been marginalized by the overwhelming dominance of institutionalized theatre. What identifies these theatres, what makes them alternative theatres, is that they have remained artist-based theatres, theatres created and run by artists who choose what work they want to do and what audiences they want to reach. Despite the constant battle for funding and recognition, they have chosen a path as independent as possible from institutionalization in order to preserve artistic control over their work and their lives.

Within the world of alternative theatre there are two distinguishable traditions, traditions that, although remarkably different, present revealing contrasts with institutional theatre. One is the tradition of experimental or avant-garde theatre, theatre that constantly pushes the art form in new directions, breaking boundaries and redefining ways of creating theatre. Provocative and challenging, this work is defined by its artistic aesthetic; it is art mediated almost entirely by the artists that create it. The other tradition is that of community-based theatre, theatre deeply rooted in a particular community, which itself is an essential partner and collaborator in the work. Not to be confused with the local amateur groups that are often called "community" theatres, the community-based theatres I am talking about are professional theatres, usually ensemble theatres, that choose to work and live in a particular community, articulating the voice of that community through their art. Going back to the central connection between the art and the audience, in both of these traditions, it is the artists who create and preserve this connection, experimental theatre devoting most of its creativity to the integrity of the art and community-based theatre to the integrity of the audience.

The first strong burst of American experimental or avant-garde energy occurred in the 1960s and 1970s in downtown New York. This was experimental theatre in its most radical form, challenging everything from the relevance of the written word to methods of acting, the role of audiences and the physical use of a theatre space itself. As part of the counterculture of the time, this theatre was political in its approach and communal in its creation, much of the work coming from ensemble groups of writers, directors and actors who wanted to create new forms of theatre as well as shocking audiences out of their complacency. Influenced by the powerful theories of Antonin Artaud, Jerzy Grotowski, Bertolt Brecht and Peter Brook, they wanted to break open the fourth wall and make theatre an authentic experience of transformation. Julian Beck and Judith Malina's Living Theatre, Joseph Chaikin's Open Theater and Richard Schechner's Performance Group were the most influential of these early groups. It was theatre that was both deeply intellectual and emotionally explosive.

Soon a second wave of experimental work emerged, partly in reaction to what was perceived to be a growing loss of rigor in the earlier work—a tendency toward emotional and physical excess—and partly due to changing times as the counterculture came to an end and a more individualistic and self-absorbed culture emerged. This new work tended to be visual and associative rather than linear and narrative, a reflection of the changing ways people were perceiving and absorbing information in the new age of technology. And, rather than being communally created, most of this work came from the vision of a single artist, an artist who often worked with a company of actors and ongoing collaborators but whose own vision dominated the process. Robert Wilson, Richard Foreman, the Wooster Group, and, more recently, Anne Bogart and her SITI Company are all examples of this wave of experimental energy. But, like earlier groups, these artists maintain a minimal institutional structure, create original pieces over long developmental periods and have an artistic aesthetic that is dynamic, not static, evolving with their work. And they continue to have close connections with international artists like Ariane Mnouchkine and Tadashi Suzuki who share their abiding interest in exploring the forms and meaning of theatre.

The other, so very different, tradition of alternative theatre is community-based theatre, which really had its origins in the Depression but has experienced its main growth in the past two decades. The Community Arts Network calls this "art made as a voice and a force within a specific community of place, spirit or tradition." The aim of community-based theatres is to become an indigenous part of the community, creating a theatrical voice for that community but also becoming one of its civic institutions, like schools and libraries. Many of these theatres reach audiences that have never experienced theatre before, and the relationship that develops between the artists and their audiences is very alive, a process of mutual creativity. And, although much of the work has intellectual roots in the ideas of the same thinkers who inspired the avant-garde such as Artaud and Grotowski, community-based theatres have added to their work other influences, such as commedia dell'arte, storytelling, folksongs and other more populist forms of expression.

These theatres have extended the geographical reach of the regional theatre movement, residing in many small towns and rural areas around the country and also in underserved neighborhoods of urban centers. Not unexpectedly, the tradition includes a rich variety of theatres—from the Roadside Theater of Whitesburg, Ky., which creates original work from the oral histories and songs of its Appalachian community; to the Cornerstone Theater Company, which originally created work in different rural communities and now works within and among the diverse communities of Los Angeles; to Traveling Jewish Theatre and the San Francisco Mime Troupe, which create specific kinds of theatre that tour here and abroad. Despite these differences, however, these theatres are unified in how they practice their art. Almost all are ensemble theatres whose artists collectively create the work; decision-making rests in the hands of the artists, and resources go toward supporting the artists and the artistic process—a very different model from the corporate one that dominates American theatre.

Both experimental and community-based theatres are important because they show clear alternatives to institutional theatre. But they also are important because both have experienced new bursts of energy in recent years and are claiming a stronger voice in the theatre community. Community-based theatres have begun to organize nationally, creating connections across geographical boundaries and establishing their work as an authentic movement that should be made known to young people coming into the field. And they have begun to create exciting collaborations.

For example, in the summer of 1999, the Touchstone Theatre of Bethlehem, Pa., created a play about the shutting of the steel mills in their town and the devastation this caused. Although conceived and produced by Touchstone, the play, *Steelbound*, was written by Cornerstone's Alison Carey and based on Aeschylus' *Prometheus Bound*. It was directed by Bill Rauch, also of Cornerstone; the costumes were designed by April Bevans of Pennsylvania's Bloomsburg Theatre Ensemble; and the lighting was done by Ken Rothchild of New York's Irondale Ensemble Project. Presented in the bold structural remains of an empty iron foundry, the play included three choruses of local people in the Greek tradition—one of steelworkers, one of women and one of youth—whose voices were central to the play. Expected to be a requiem for the losses to the community, the play turned out to be a healing experience, a beginning as much as an ending. This is just one example of the vitality that is energizing community-based theatres today.

Though the recent burst of activity in community-based theatres comes mainly from already-existing theatres, the new burst of energy in experimental theatre comes from the emergence of a whole new generation of artists who want to shake up the theatre world now, as their predecessors did before them. The range of the new experimental theatres is eclectic and, following the expansion of theatre to encompass the whole country, is spread out geographically rather than being concentrated in New York City. These small and energetic companies, created by artists in their twenties and thirties, place themselves in direct opposition to institutional theatre, deeply critical of the effects of institutionalization on the art and the life of the artist and shunning pressures to be pushed down similar paths.

Many of these theatres are close in spirit to the early wave of avant-garde art because they are deeply concerned with collapsing the distance between the artists and the audience and with issues of democratic community. They consider the idea of theatre space fluid, changing with the needs of a particular play, an environment for the actor and audience, not just a performing stage. And much of the work is multimedia, including film, music, dance and the visual arts, and, like other such original work, needs to tour to extend its life. These new artists want to reinvent a theatrical sensibility that is alive, not mediated by institutions as to form or content or place.

Of course, it is not possible to know how these experimental theatres will develop over time—where they will head artistically or institutionally—or how many will survive. Today they live with very few resources outside their own talent and energy. But they are the first real computer generation, collapsing geography with websites and e-mail and creating new ways of communicating and working. And they are consciously trying to develop a vocabulary that expresses who they are and how they work—a vocabulary that will better identify their differences with institutional theatre. But, perhaps most important, they are filled with the kind of anarchic energy that has always had the potential to create change.

Looking at how experimental and community-based theatres operate demonstrates that there are alternative ways for artists to be connected to their art besides the mediation of institutional structures. But, since it is still institutional theatres that dominate the field and absorb most of its resources, I think you need to circle back to the traditional institutions and ask what their potential is for change. And to ask how we can imagine such change taking place. We tend to think of our institutions as finished projects, but they are not; they are always in a state of becoming and can be sculpted with the same thoughtful creativity as our art.

Breaking It Open

Obviously many traditional institutions are what they want to be—happy in their mission and their audiences, while their audiences are happy with them. Many of these theatres, particularly the larger ones, are more than just theatres; they are cultural anchors that play important social and economic roles in their cities. In many cases, they are the main source of theatre education in school systems; they are

important and visible political advocates for the arts; and they contribute in significant ways to the economy of the community. As cultural leaders and prominent institutions in a community, their sense of
identity and worth has a broad base that goes beyond the theatre they
produce; they have genuine stakes that make them less likely to move
toward radical change.

There are also theatres that obviously sense problems with institutionalization and, consciously or unconsciously, are making efforts to
counter these problems. In a number of theatres, connections are
deliberately created between artists and boards, with artists giving presentations at board gatherings, artists actually serving on boards and,
in some cases, board members becoming interns for the production of
a play, following the play from the original design meetings to opening
night—all attempts to deepen board members' understanding of the
art and the artistic process. Many theatres have drawn more artists into
their permanent operational structure as dramaturgs, artists-in-residence
and education artists, adding more artistic voices to the institutional
mix. One theatre I know has a family dinner each spring, gathering
together everyone from stage managers to carpenters to box-office workers to board members, attempting to transform authority relationships
into human relationships. And some of our best institutional thinkers,
particularly Nello McDaniel and George Thorn, have worked with
theatres to develop alternate ways of organizing themselves—replacing hierarchical structures of authority with concentric circles of participation—and urging theatres to extend the collaborative artistic
process of the rehearsal hall to institutional decision-making.

Finally, there are theatres, particularly some younger theatres and
theatres with new artistic leaders, that are generating fresh energy in
the field by forging alliances either with other theatres in this country,
including some of the more experimental theatres, or with international artists who bring exciting new sensibilities to the work. And
some of these alliances are beginning to cross traditional cultural lines,
revitalizing audiences as well as the art. These theatres are finding
ways around their institutions to connect with their art.

These are just a few examples of the creative ways in which theatres are changing how their institutions operate. But, because these
strategies do not change the basic dynamic of the institution, they do
not reverse the tendencies they are trying to overcome. They are
working from the outside in, ameliorating many of the problems of
institutionalization but not reversing the institutional processes that
cause the problems. But what if you wanted to create more fundamental change—to work from the inside out, rather than the outside in?
What if you wanted to really break open institutions, creating new
ways of working and new relationships to the art? What would you do?
How would you begin?

If theatres really want to change, or even explore the idea of such
change, I think you need to start where all theatre starts, with the
artists. You need to bring the artists to the table, not in a token way but
as vital and respected members of the dialogue. The obvious reason for

doing this is so their needs and priorities are included in the theatre's decision-making. But, actually, I think there is a more compelling reason, which is that artists think differently from administrators; their imaginations, creativity and values come from a different internal place, making them more likely to bring whole new perspectives to the table. At a minimum, I think artists will identify many of the dissonances that exist between the art and the institution. But more significantly, I think they can open up a new dialogue, a dialogue of possibility in which alternative institutional realities can be explored. Not being so hampered by institutional baggage, artists are freer to turn the kaleidoscope, revealing alternative ways of defining and fulfilling a theatre's needs.

For example, maybe, if you look really hard, you would find that your mission statement has become empty as the real driving force of the theatre. If so, how would you change it or how would you change the institution to restore its vitality? Or maybe the box office has become too much of a stranglehold on the central relationship between the art and the audience. How could you redefine that art/audience relationship in ways that would, in turn, redefine the role of the box office? Or maybe you really are not sure what the term "governance" means. Who is governing whom about what? Is it enough for a board to hold the institution in trust—i.e., the financial integrity of the theatre—or should it also hold the art in trust? If so, what does that mean? Once you let the institutional imperatives be only one part of the dialogue, many new questions and possibilities emerge.

And there is one more reason I think artists belong at the table. In the press of institutional development, artists have inadvertently given over the guardianship of their art and lives to others. But it is *their* work and *their* lives that are at stake. One of the most important things alternative theatres show us is that there are artists who are willing to go to extreme lengths to maintain that guardianship. Artists should not be pieceworkers, occasional visitors to their theatres. They should have a dignified and integral role in those theatres and in the guardianship of their art.

Bringing artists to the table can change the scope and sensibility of the dialogue. But I think more is needed; I think you need to change the environment as well, to change the whole atmosphere in which the dialogue takes place. To do this I would move the table—figuratively and maybe even literally—out of the boardroom, the development office and the box office and onto the stage. It is on the stage—the very heart of the theatre, where the art and the audience live—that I believe a theatre can best find its bearings, where it can best see itself in terms of the art rather than the institution. I would put the planning table on the stage—and the budget table and the funding table and the board table. And sitting at each table would be artists and artisans, as well as administrators and board members.

If you are on the stage, the pressure is to look at the theatre through the eyes of the artists, for it is on the stage that artists have authority. This begins to put balance back into the power relationships at the table, the artists now having their own authority, not authority derived from others. So concerns about the art come to the fore. Planners have to ask what they really are planning for. Budgeters have to ask what they really are budgeting for. And board members have to ask what they are holding in trust for the community, what "fiduciary" means, beyond its narrow legal meaning. If it is the art that is being planned for, budgeted for and held in trust, then the knowledge and authority of the artists take on real meaning. Where before it was mainly administrators who defined the theatre's reality, now the question opens up: Whose reality is being created at the table and why? Whose views have authority and why? The conversation becomes a true dialogue.

And then there is one last step I would take in the effort to open up possibilities for change: to look outward to the larger environment in which the theatre operates, for change rarely happens in a vacuum. To imagine different kinds of theatre institutions, you also have to imagine a different kind of landscape for these institutions to live in, one that is more open, more multidimensional and has more points of entry for artists, audiences and new theatres.

Although there are many aspects to this wider landscape—cultural change, technological change, public policy, international influences— the most important has to be the funding community, for little significant change can happen without this community. So the real question is to what extent funders are willing to become partners for change. Obviously, the funding community is just as diverse as the theatre community, so there is a wide range of sensibilities and resources among the foundation, corporation, individual and government funders who make up this community. And, within this community, there already are a number of funders working creatively with theatres to support artistic and institutional change. But there are many more who remain tied to traditional approaches. To achieve the degree of change in the theatrical landscape I am suggesting, more significant breaks with traditional patterns, by a greater number of funders, will be needed. How might this happen?

The most obvious thing that comes to mind is that we invest so little in the development of our work and of our artists. In Moscow, a new theatre center is being founded just for the purpose of providing a nourishing and protective environment for creating theatre art. Named the Meyerhold Center after the legendary Russian director, the center will have no company or regular performances; it is a center that hopes to eventually enfold master classes, experimental productions, festivals, symposiums and a publishing program within its laboratory environment. It is a center for enriching art, not producing it. Can we imagine funding something like this? Or even providing more direct funding to artist groups such as playwright centers or acting companies so they could have autonomy as well as support in developing their talents. Or could we provide funding for artists, themselves, to create work that is then presented by traditional theatres, the model followed by successful experimental groups? Opening up funding to more ways of nourishing and producing theatre would certainly add vitality and depth to the theatrical landscape.

The second thing that comes to mind is to allow more people and more ways of working into the funding process, to open up funding to a wider range of theatres, particularly new and experimental ones. For instance, very small theatres could be helped if funders created pools of funds that could be distributed by local arts organizations or other neutral groups. This would save funders from having to invest in researching each theatre, an economy of scale of sorts, while providing an ongoing base for such theatres. Something like this occurred in New York City after the terrorist attacks when the Alliance of Resident Theatres/New York, the support group for New York theatres, was granted several pools of money to distribute to theatres, particularly small theatres, that had been badly hurt by the attacks. Or funders could provide more support for touring—one of the crucial needs of experimental and ensemble theatres that create unique work that cannot be easily duplicated. A good example of this is the National Performance Network, which was created to help such theatres form collaborations and tour as a way of expanding the reach of their work. More efforts like this could make a difference. Or perhaps funders could give traditional institutions incentives to include young artists and small theatres in their programming. They could be given grants to present this work during the summer, or at nontraditional times of the day, or in festivals drawing together a number of these groups. It would be exciting to walk into a theatre complex and be able to choose from a noon reading of a new play by a small theatre, a 6:00 multimedia performance by an experimental theatre, an 8:00 traditional performance by the host theatre and then, perhaps, a midnight jazz cabaret. What a diverse audience would be passing through the doors and what a wonderful mix of energies would be filling the spaces!

Finally, there is the question of the distribution of funds within the field. In a survey done for the year 2000 by TCG, 145 theatres of different sizes provided information on their total assets, including physical assets such as land and buildings and financial assets such as endowments, cash and securities. The results were that the 40 theatres in the survey with budgets over $5 million owned 79 percent of the assets; the 69 theatres with budgets between $1 million and $5 million owned 20 percent of the assets; and the 43 theatres with budgets under $1 million owned 1 percent of the assets. Put another way, the top 30 percent of the theatres held almost 80 percent of the assets, while the bottom 30 percent held only 1 percent. Obviously these numbers reflect the particular theatres in the survey, but, if anything, the skewed distribution is understated because there are hundreds of other small theatres and only a few other large ones that were not in the survey. Even acknowledging that the theatre field is deeply undercapitalized in the first place, it still seems clear that the scarce resources available to the field are concentrated in too few large theatres. So, a more even distribution of resources is certainly a further way funders could change the theatrical landscape.

Nourishing the art, inviting a wider range of artists and theatres into the funding process, allocating funds more evenly to theatres already there—these are just some of the ways the funding community could help open up the theatrical landscape, and many funders are already contributing to such change. But how do you accelerate the process? How do you think bigger? How do you show that the form or size of an institution does not determine the quality or value of its art?

Today we appear to be at another point of vital change in the American theatre, a time when the energies of new generations and changing times are again challenging how we create and present theatre. There are more questions and voices of dissent, more pressures from new artists coming into the field, and more consciousness of the need to move out from under institutional shadows. As our theatres settle into middle age, the time seems ripe for a new age of pioneers, pioneers who can put the art—and the artists—back into the heart of our theatres.

Jaan Whitehead has served on the boards of the Acting Company, Arena Stage, Living Stage, SITI Company, Whole Theatre, the National Cultural Alliance and TCG. She is a founding member of TCG's National Council for the American Theatre, and has been executive director of New York City's Theatre for a New Audience and development director for CENTERSTAGE in Baltimore, Md. A former teacher of political philosophy at Georgetown University, she is the co-editor, with Nancy Roche, of *The Art of Governance: Boards in the Performing Arts*, which was published by TCG in 2005.

THE SHAPE OF PLAYS TO COME

By Todd London

November 2002

> *It would take forever to recite / All that's not new in where we find
> ourselves.*
>
> —Robert Frost

How will the new come into our theatre? Will we recognize it? Will
we welcome it? Is it already here? If not, what's the best way to
make it happen?

There appears to be general agreement that the old ways aren't the
best. Rumors of the death of new-play development may have been
exaggerated, but the obituaries won't stop. Last spring, within a few
weeks of each other, three pronouncements signaled a new era for the
cultivation of work for the stage. First, Denver Center Theatre Company, one of America's wealthier nonprofits, and one with a long history
of support for new plays, announced that due to losses sustained in the
diving stock market, it would be suspending new-play development,
closing its literary offices, eliminating the position of associate artistic
director for new-play development and canceling its new-play festival
and the prestigious Francesca Primus Prize for women playwrights.
Within a few days, Lincoln Center Theater's Anne Cattaneo, one of
our most respected dramaturgs, was quoted in the *New York Times*, saying, "New-play development is dead. It just became too expensive to
do new work . . . . Today, instead of 50 regional theatres developing 50
new plays, what you have is one new play by an established writer that
gets done 50 times at 50 regional theatres."

Two months later, the *Times* ran another article announcing that
Jesse Ventura, pro-wrestler-turned-Minnesota governor (the muscular
butt of a nation's jokes) would help address his state's fiscal woes by
withholding money promised to major arts institutions, including that
flagship of flagships, the Guthrie Theater, which had counted on $24
million to construct a new $125-million facility. Joe Dowling, the
Guthrie's artistic director, responded to the governor's gambit with

one of his own: "In terms of encouraging new writers, staging new plays and co-productions, and sending our plays out to other places, we won't be able to do what we hoped."

Dowling's statement was revealing in a couple of ways. While the Guthrie has never been a hotbed of new-play development, by holding out its potential demise as a counterthreat, Dowling was making his priorities clear, despite a mission devoted to "classical repertoire" and "the exploration of new works." (Do theatres ever hold Shakespeare hostage in this way—no bucks, no Bard?) Second, as with the Denver amputation, it made palpable an attitude that many have noted over the years, a shared sense among institutions that work on new plays is dispensable, in a last-hired, first-fired sort of way.

Of course, no one asks playwrights if it's dispensable. Decisions about what appears on the nation's stages are mostly handed down without reference to the artists who write, perform, design and (with more exceptions) direct it. Like so many corporate actions threatened or undertaken in these hardish times—layoffs, division and regional office closings, corporate restructuring—they are top-down decisions. The workers (who, in the theatre, are precisely the "creators") are an afterthought, if that—pawns in negotiations with, say, Wrestler-Governors.

In the midst of the death knells, Theatre Communications Group, showing a will to positivism and a desire to spur radical rethinking, held a two-day "convening" in Portland, Ore., with an unlikely cast of characters. Joining a handful of playwrights and a slightly larger cadre of institutional theatre producers (managers and artistic directors, including a large children's theatre contingent) were an assortment of multi-arts presenters, ensemble-based theatre artists, directors, performance artists, literary managers and people who run small theatres and developmental labs. The gathering was a clear attempt to transcend the ingrown discourse of new-play development (the "developed to death" debate) that is nearly as old as the movement itself. With hope in their hearts, the folks at TCG skirted the debates (and once again showed their determination to break free of a past identification with the League of Resident Theatres) by bringing unusual suspects—people interested in the new anywhere, anyhow—and broadening the semantic umbrella. As if heralding an epoch in the making, they called it "New Works, New Ways." New-Play Development Is Dead! Long Live New Work Making!

> *The clashing point of two subjects, two disciplines, two cultures—of two galaxies, so far as that goes—ought to produce creative chances. In the history of mental activity that has been where some of the break-throughs came. The chances are there now. But they are, as it were, in a vacuum, because those in the two cultures can't talk to each other.*
> —C.P. Snow

In the '30s, Harold Clurman, that great inspirer and co-founder of the Group Theatre, was introduced to André Gide, novelist and Nobel laureate. "The problem with the theatre," Gide remarked, "is to find good plays." "The problem with the theatre," Clurman rejoined, "is to create a Theatre."

This exchange adumbrates a great divide in visions for the future: those who feel the American theatre suffers from lack of great, or even worthy, plays, and those who lay blame for a failing art at the feet of artistically deficient theatres. On one side sit, mostly, artistic directors and producers; on the other, writers, as well as a constellation of other independent artists.

Those who take the no-good-plays line often define quality by both artistic measures and those of the marketplace; a "viable" work is one that plays well and sells well. I've been talking with other artistic directors about this for nearly 20 years and have a sense that their complaints (which aren't always shared by their literary managers, whose tastes are often considerably more adventurous than their bosses') boil down to three: 1) American playwrights write too small; they aren't engaged enough with the wide world; 2) these playwrights don't understand structure; and 3) they aren't writing plays that will connect with "my audience."

The counterargument holds that we live amid a profusion of playwriting talent—that, as a profession, playwriting hasn't been this vital in decades—but that the theatres, long on business savvy and short on artistic vision, haven't kept up. Moreover, those theatres, having helped create a multigenerational playwriting community, have now abandoned it. Erik Ehn, playwright and co-founder of the itinerant, anarchic RAT conference—a shape-shifting network of small, experimental and alternative theatres—stood up for this view in a recent speech to the Literary Managers and Dramaturgs of the Americas. In "slightly doctored" notes from his talk, he contends, "There are plenty of plays out there, lots of excellence," adding, "To create a new theatre by developing plays first equals trying to build a new house by moving around the furniture." He compares mainstream new-play development, especially challenging or experimental texts, to Audubon twisting "the necks of exotic birds to help them fit the scale of his renderings." He calls for a change not only in theatre practice but also in theatre space and architecture, the expansion of time for creation and an emphasis on "hospitality over intellectualism." New, in other words, means creating a new theatre.

How will the new come into the theatre? How can we make it happen? Should our efforts be focused on the writing or the structures of production, the independent artists or the institutions? The answer, as well as the problem, lies in the relationship between the two.

Is it possible that at the heart of the creativity stoppage known as new-play development are not bad plays (I'm told they exist); bad working models (though these prevail everywhere, such as dead-end reading series and criticism from numerous people with no understanding of process and no interest in producing the play); or bad faith (which, god knows, pervades every theatre where programmers mentally doodle while the writers they've encouraged wait weeks or months or, yes, years before the inevitable rejection trickles down to them)? Maybe the fault lines are deeper, as deep as identity, the story we tell ourselves about who we in the theatre are.

I have a confession. For as long as I can remember, I have believed that theatre is singular—*the* theatre, or, just as grandly, the theatre *community*. I no longer do. I used to think the nonprofit theatre movement had given birth to a profession of shared values. I no longer do. Forty years after its seeding, this field (note the singular), which we've celebrated for its variety *and* its underlying unity of purpose, has become two, with a mostly unacknowledged rift running through them. Or, to borrow C.P. Snow's famous phrase, with which he dissected humanistic culture into natural scientists and literary intellectuals, it's become "two cultures." Two theatres, two cultures, two galaxies: that of the institution and that of the individual artist.

This dawning awareness has had, for me, the quality of slow-motion heartbreak. Like many theatre people born in the '50s, I was raised on the all-together-now harmonies of musical theatre and came of age under the sway of the utopian communality of '70s experimental theatre. As a young professional, I carried a torch for artistic homes, community regionalism and the company ethic implied by "resident." I've devoted much of my writing life since then to this magazine, in the belief that the "we" I used as the principal pronoun of address was actual, descriptive of a community in fact.

Now, as artistic director of a 53-year-old institution that serves playwrights—those most independent of theatre artists—I straddle two realities. One reality features a building, a board, a staff, a company of playwrights and a tight annual budget; it's driven by a clear mission and sense of institutional responsibility—for vitality, quality, stability and legacy. The second reality is that of the writers themselves. I'm fed by their inspired idiosyncrasy, dogged artistic ambition, bravery and skill. And I'm angry for them, because their stressful, unstructured, mood-swinging writing lives exist outside of the very world whose present and, even more, future depend on their articulated visions. Where are the theatres that are worthy of these artists? I don't see them. Not because there aren't theatres with the talent to stage their plays impressively, but because there are so few theatres willing to incorporate artistic lives and bodies of work into the institution's way of being. At best, playwrights (and, I suspect, all unaffiliated artists) are guests—sometimes welcome, sometimes tolerated, sometimes ignored—in the ongoing life of theatre buildings. It's worse, I'd venture, for playwrights of color, who bring even deeper cultural differences to bear on a divided situation—a double disenfranchisement. How will we welcome the new when we don't welcome the bringers of the new?

I don't mean to suggest that this disconnection is willful. The situation is no one's fault. It's an inevitable product of history, generational change and institutionalization. It's the American way: The innovative becomes the established. Yesterday's geek-renegades become today's corporate titans (All hail Misters Gates and Jobs!). The institutional theatre in America still sees itself as the alternative theatre, though the pioneers are gone, replaced by second- and third-generation artistic and management leaders without the pioneering spirit. It has become our Broadway, that which the new theatre must rebel against to get free.

Both sides of the theatrical divide contribute to the climate. Theatre leaders all too often fail to collaborate honestly or take responsibility for the huge imbalance in power that exists between those who hire and choose and those who audition and wait. The myth of community intensifies their astonishment at (or denial of) the depth of artists' alienation. You could read all about it in these pages last December, when Michael Maso, managing director of the Huntington Theatre Company and president of LORT, decried the use of anonymous sources in an article written by three designers about the difficult economics of freelance theatre design. Maso condemned the practice on journalistic grounds but missed the point. He assumed that freelance designers were part of his artistic village, where everyone should feel free to speak his or her mind. They aren't and they don't. Truthfulness endangered their livelihoods. They were whistle-blowers—nobody's idea of a pleasant hire—or, to steal a phrase from John Patrick Shanley, "beggars at the house of plenty."

Unaffiliated artists, by contrast, can be shockingly naïve about what's at stake when a theatre makes artistic decisions, about the complexities of running an arts organization, about its relationship with its audience/community, about the process by which it functions and the real human cost of programming risks. Moreover, unaffiliated artists in America (of whom playwrights are only one species) are too often mired in passivity, unable to imagine actions other than hitting their heads against the same closed doors. Where is a new generation of writer-founders, playwright-managers? Where are the manifestos?

At root, though, this division stems from the thousand particulars of daily life that create habits and systems of belief. What is a day like for the head of an institutional theatre? What's that same day for a writer or any freelance artist? The tendencies of those lives read like lists of bipolar opposites:

INSTITUTIONAL	INDIVIDUAL
Regularity of schedule and place	Uncertainty—every day is different
Public	Private
Top-down decisions	Solitary decisions
Selecting collaborators	Awaiting the invitation/knocking at the door
Planning/Knowing ahead	Flexibility/Finding out as you go
Problems of compromise	Problems of isolation
Tends toward the common denominator	Tends toward the esoteric
Attempts to unstructure the structured	Attempts to structure the unstructured
Organization	Improvisation
Calculating risk	At risk

INSTITUTIONAL	**INDIVIDUAL**
Programmed diversity	Sui generis of every possible kind
Serves many masters, and is served	One's own master, served by no one
Holds authority	Disempowered, except in the privacy of the work
Defense against people outside	Suspicion of people inside
Unnecessary busyness	Necessary idleness
The constancy of production	The inconstancy of productivity
Thinking outside the box	Living outside the box
Manic	Depressive

Add to the list or make up your own. Your story goes here.

One man cannot produce drama. True drama is born only of one feeling animating all the members of a clan—a spirit shared by all and expressed by the few for the all.
　　　　　　　　　　　　　　　　　—George (Jig) Cram Cook

As the multiculturation of the arts has shown, cultural differences make creative sparks fly. Moreover, there's a natural, generative tension between the solitary artist and the organization, between the private creator and the public producer. You can see this creative dissension up close and personal in that powerful first collaboration of the American art theatre—between Eugene O'Neill and the Provincetown Players.

In his lovingly detailed paean to Greenwich Village, *Republic of Dreams: Greenwich Village, The American Bohemia, 1910–1960*, the late Ross Wetzsteon retells the story of O'Neill's relationship with Province-town's founding spirit Jig Cook. O'Neill, young, tortured, almost fatally alcoholic, is introduced to the idealistic company by a fellow drunk who knows that Eugene keeps some plays in a trunk. These wildly uneven, blatantly experimental plays—and several subsequent ones—are just what the Players have been looking for. They thrill the neighbors on the Cape and stand out in the purposefully amateur evenings of one-acts mounted in several New York seasons. The newspapers discover O'Neill, Broadway beckons, a couple of Pulitzers follow and the playwright and soon-shuttered theatre part company. It's the Ur-story and the same old one: kindred spirits making dramatic whoopee, the lure of Broadway, loyalty betrayed, a playwright's posthumous profession of gratitude for the dead producer's grace. More important, it's a story of mutual dependence: a theatre helping the writer find a voice, a voice defining a theatre.

How would the emerging O'Neill have fared in today's theatre? Whose commitment would now buy that brilliant beginner the years of explosive experimentation he spent with Provincetown? Where would he go to find the heat to temper the talent expressed in his late, great works? And where would he find a statement like this one, taken from the Players's constitution:

> The president shall cooperate with the author in producing the play under the author's direction. The resources of the theatre . . . shall be placed at the disposal of the author . . . . The author shall produce the play without hindrance, according to his own ideas.

Is it the hothouse of Provincetown that grows an O'Neill, or the playwright's fervid imagination—Shakespeare's, Molière's, Sheridan's, Chekhov's, Churchill's—that dreams life into the Globe, Palais-Royal, Drury Lane, Moscow Art Theatre or Joint Stock? This year in New York, the Signature Theatre will dedicate its season to Lanford Wilson's work. What would the season look like if there'd never been a Circle Rep—an acting company, a director and a shared, evolving aesthetic to grow Wilson's corpus, play by play? Where are the new Circle Reps? It's hard enough to find an acting company of any size or consistency today, let alone one that includes a writer or writers in its ongoing artistic evolution.

The founding spirits of the American art theatre—Cook, Clurman, Hallie Flanagan, Zelda Fichandler, Herbert Blau, Malina and Beck, Douglas Turner Ward, Joseph Chaikin, Luis Valdez—knew at the start what we've forgotten. Unlike today, when the homogenous seasons of our national stages reveal a unanimity that feels like anonymity, these pragmatic inspirers shared a catalytic vision, one vision with a mess of names: company, collective, group, troupe, ensemble and clan. Every theatre must find its voice, and every writer must find her theatre.

> *People have asked me, "Why don't we have more good plays?" I said, "Why don't you ask why we don't have more bad plays, because if you have more bad plays you'll have more good plays, because that feeds the ground." That's the manure that makes things grow. It's very valuable manure, as manure is valuable to growth. We need activity, we need action, we need trial, we need error.*
>
> —Harold Clurman

Two things I know: 1) For writers to understand a theatre's community, they must be made part of it; and 2) the fusion of individual talent and collective energy fuels great theatre. Twenty-five hundred years of theatre history tells us this, but too few have been listening.

It's a sad irony that the very systems set up to nurture writers and involve them in the theatre have led to their disaffection. New-play development—reading series, literary offices, the emphasis on premieres—was conceived to foster both writers and work. Instead it demoted playwrights to overnight visitors—the artistic home as Motel 6—and created schism where there should be continuity—from development to production, page to stage.

These processes also disrupted what may well have been the most important theatrical relationship prior to the regional theatre movement: the tempestuous, vibrant, mutually self-interested partnership between the producer and the playwright. Certainly, the success of mid-20th-century plays and musicals brings to mind not only their creators but their producers, benevolent—Kermit Bloomgarden, Robert Whitehead, Alexander Cohen—and maniacal—Jed Harris, David Merrick. When writers and producers share a process, they can share a sense of direction as well; it's here, in relationship, that the scope of a play can be addressed, that the producer can cheer the writer's efforts to move away from the "small," to turn toward the wide world.

Before we knew it, artistic producers had literary managers/dramaturgs running blocking for them. Instead of being wooed, playwrights were customarily held at bay. The intimate producing partnership became a distant one, with the creator separated from the means of production. Moreover, the reading and discovery of plays has been delegated to such an extent that many artistic directors appear to have lost the patience, time and, consequently, the reading ability to wade through a play that may be different or difficult or in progress.

These systems and habits have altered the aesthetic landscape. The different, difficult and new are just what so many writers grope toward. I've come to believe that a most common feature of contemporary American playwriting is the search for form. The process of discovery and innovation is integral to the play, built in. Structure isn't imposed; it's immanent. Tony Kushner's *Angels in America* is a case in point. His "fantasia" structure is a kind of nonbinding structure, allowing Kushner's imagination to go where it wants, to digress, to elaborate, to move forward and back, like progress itself, one of the play's main themes. The play dreams itself into being. And then the second part, *Perestroika*, dreams itself another way. How many of the playwrights you admire possess this "setting out to parts unknown" energy? Think of Edward Albee, Maria Irene Fornes, Suzan-Lori Parks, Paula Vogel, Mac Wellman, August Wilson, John Guare, for example. Each of their plays is its own animal; each teaches us anew how to follow its tracks. American playwrights don't understand structure? They understand it well enough to know you have to discover it.

If these important writers—all important teachers as well—have made it up as they've gone along, pursuing those forms-in-formation, what undiscovered territory can we hope to stumble into as their students and less-established colleagues break ground? The solo mind will always be more nimble than an institution. So, playwrights, whether or not they write ahead of their times, will nearly always write forward of the theatres. But how will we welcome the new into the theatre if the theatres stand apart from it, if they no longer have the will or the skill to recognize it?

A second confession: I don't want to believe what I've written. My mind keeps doubling back, accusing itself of dramatizing—the institutional Pentheus on one side, the artistic Dionysus on the other. Pentheus, king of Thebes, up in a tree, decked out in the Maenad's drag—peeking down at the Dionysian revels (the drunken, theatrical revels), all the time thinking he's in control, in command. And I accuse myself of taking the analogy too far. Theatres are great ships turning in tidal waters; they resist change. Everybody in them, even the pilots, have their hearts in the right places.

Then I remember the hundreds of writers I've spoken to in the past few years, and how few theatres contradict the portrait of disengagement they've drawn. And I ask myself—and I ask you the same question—which theatres are truly important to me, which ones do I expect to lead, to draw us nearer to the future, to the new? And I know it won't be many of the ones our funding community has designated as "leading theatres," despite their impressive production values and eloquent leaders.

No wonder TCG invited all those ensemble folks to its Portland convening; it's natural to get excited about the work happening in companies. Who would not want what they have, those community-based and experimental troupes from Appalachia to Blue Lake, Calif., from Wooster Street to Cornerstone's corner of L.A.? You gotta love them. Collective models only apply so far, though; 999 times out of 1,000, someone will write the new thing alone in a room. But even the mammoth Oregon Shakespeare Festival, which boasts the largest acting company in the country, has been jazzing writers these days. And obviously, not all institutions are created alike: Some are born artist-centered (think Steppenwolf and South Coast Repertory) and remain so in their bones, even as they grow. And then there are the scrappy young theatres—gangs as much as theatres—with funny names, who are the real harbingers of the new, because they refuse to check their imaginings at the boardroom door.

Elsewhere, the century that invented directors also cursed the theatre with one dominant model, supported by theatre consultants and unwitting trustees: the director-led theatre. It's almost a given that the first choice to run most theatres is a director, and, having selected directors, most theatres define themselves as artist-centered. This unexamined practice, despite a few hundred years of counterexamples, has inflated the importance of the director and devalued the work of the writer and the centrality of the play. Director training, meanwhile, makes matters worse, by shortchanging new-play collaboration and overstressing classical interpretation. The coups of discovering the next fine writer or skillfully telling the new story have been supplanted by the interpretive thrill of tackling *The Winter's Tale* or *The Wild Duck* or mounting both parts of *Angels in America*. The system self-perpetuates, as board members (in the absence of ensembles and company playwrights) sustain contact with a single artist—a director. Real directors' theatres can be as compelling as any others—who can't wait to see what Robert Woodruff brews up at the American Repertory Theatre, in a season where he works side-by-side with Anne Bogart, Peter Sellars, János Szász and Andrei Serban? Not many directors, though, have developed a production "voice" rich and unique enough to compensate for the lack of other consistent, defining voices.

The gulf is real, and crossing it, bridging it, eliminating it is the primary work of this moment, more important than getting nonprofits and commercial producers together, more important even, I'd venture, than the financial health of institutions. What was envisioned as a community of artists has evolved into a community of institutions so cut off from its artists that it keeps looking outside for ways to save itself. The institutions envy performance ensembles, experimental troupes and community-based theatres for the vitality they know themselves to lack. They want the flexibility found only in playwright centers and labs. They look to corporate gurus from the business world to jar their thinking. Maybe it's time (to paraphrase the *New Yorker*'s Malcolm Gladwell) to stop trying to think outside the box and start trying, instead, to fix the box.

The archetype for creative progress in America pits the individual (often in concert with other individuals) against the institution. We're seeing the hypertext version this year, corridor after corridor: the abused take on the Catholic Church; middle managers and investors take on Enron, WorldCom and the FBI; Tony Soprano bada-bings the networks. House minority leader Richard Gephardt, citing a crisis of "faith in Institutions," suggests that our hope is in reform.

In the theatre—which, in spite of evidence to the contrary, sees itself as exempt from institutional abuse and corruption—the individual has remained mostly silent. Like an insular family—or people operating under a fragile myth of family—the unspoken agreement calls for silence. During 13 years of "culture wars," survival pragmatics demanded a unified front under attack. This summer, however, in the process of restoring a mere sliver of past cuts to the National Endowment for the Arts, some in Congress declared the "culture wars" over. Maybe we have a bit more freedom now, freedom to be divided, freedom for raucous in-fighting, freedom to fight for the future in loud, angry, impassioned voices.

My hope for the new rides in two directions at once—toward the playwrights who, on a daily basis, strike out into the unknown, and toward a new generation of theatres, a new generation of founders. And my wishes go to everyone who might want to pave the way for the new—individual artists, funders, trustees, future and present theatre leaders. The wish list includes the tentative, naïve, impractical and already-tried, but here goes.

I wish for a funding and support structure for nothing less than the total integration of companies of artists, including writers, in established theatres and new ones—not a place at the table but the table itself. I wish for funders who will reserve major backing for the theatres—most of them with budgets under $2 million—that are breaking ground for the future. Let young artists be the mentors, for a while, rather than senior administrators.

Any ideas that reverse the structure of power between institutions and independents make my list: Give artists money to choose which theatres they'll work with, rather than the other way around; let the writers of last season's hits—rampantly produced across the country—curate a second production by a contemporary playwright. (You do the 12th production of *Fuddy Meers* or *Dirty Blonde*? That's great. You should. Then David Lindsay-Abaire or Claudia Shear gets to choose another play for your season!) In fact, I can stand behind any idea that links the productions of premieres to those of second and third productions (all of which are necessary and lacking). How about making sure that every list of potential artistic directors contains a full complement of actors, playwrights, designers, nondirecting producers, literary managers and anybody else with a proven sense of service to artists other than themselves? And let's have a congress, not of commercial and nonprofit producers, but of institutional leaders and unaffiliated artists with full immunity for anything they might say.

I wish, too, that all director- and actor-training programs would devote at least half their production opportunities to the cultivation of new work—training for the real world and stimulus for the future, all rolled up. I wish we could find ways to add flexibility and time to development by partnering producing theatres with theatre laboratories, workshops, non-performance spaces and artist centers. I wish writers could drive and design their own process at theatres. And I wish producers would stop peeking at the schedules in this magazine to pick their seasons.

One final wish: more new plays in every season, more plays, more plays.

Todd London is the artistic director of New Dramatists in New York City, a former managing editor of *American Theatre* magazine and the author of several books, including *The Artistic Home* and the novel *The World's Room*.

36 ASSUMPTIONS ABOUT WRITING PLAYS

By José Rivera

February 2003

> *Art is the conversation between lovers.*
> *Art offers an opening for the heart.*
> *True art makes the divine silence in the soul*
> *Break into applause.*
>
> *Art is, at last, the knowledge of*
> *Where we are standing—*
> *Where we are standing*
> *In this Wonderland*
> *When we rip off all our clothes . . .*
> —Hafiz

Over the years I've had the good fortune to teach writing in a number of schools, from second grade to graduate school. I usually just wing it. But lately I've decided to think about the assumptions I was working under and to write them down. The following is an unscientific, gut-level survey of the assumptions I have about writing plays, in no particular order of importance.

1. Good playwriting is a collaboration between your many selves. The more multiple your personalities, the further, wider, deeper you might be able to go.
2. Theatre is closer to poetry and music than it is to the novel.
3. There's no time limit to writing plays. Think of playwriting as a lifelong apprenticeship. Imagine you may have your best ideas on your deathbed.
4. You write because you want to show something. For instance, you write "to show that the world is shit." "To show how fleeting love and happiness are." "To show the inner workings of your ego." "To show that democracy is in danger." "To show how interconnected we are." Each "to show" is active and must be personal, deeply held, true to you.

5. We write plays in order to organize despair and chaos. To live vicariously. To play God. To project an idealized version of the world. To destroy things we hate in the world and in ourselves. To remember and to forget. To lie to ourselves. To play. To dance with language. To beautify the landscape. To fight loneliness. To inspire others. To imitate our heroes. To bring back the past and raise the dead. To achieve transcendence over ourselves. To fight the powers that be. To sound alarms. To provoke conversation. To engage in the conversation started by great writers in the past. To further evolve the art form. To lose ourselves in our fictive worlds. To make money.

6. Each line of dialogue is like a piece of DNA: potentially containing the entire play and its thesis; potentially telling us the beginning, middle and end of the play.

7. If you're not prepared to risk your entire reputation every time you write, then it's not worth your audience's time.

8. Embrace your writer's block. It's nature's way of preserving trees and your reputation. Listen to it and try to understand its source. Often writer's block happens because somewhere in your work you've lied to yourself and your subconscious won't let you go any further until you've gone back, erased the lie, stated the truth and started over.

9. Language is a form of entertainment. Beautiful language can be like beautiful music. It can amuse, inspire, mystify, enlighten.

10. Rhythm is key. Use as many sounds and cadences as possible. Think of dialogue as a form of percussive music. You can vary the speed of language, the beats per line, volume, density. You can use silences, fragments, elongated sentences, interruptions, overlapping conversation, physical activity, monologues, nonsense, nonsequiturs, foreign languages.

11. Vary your tone as much as possible. Juxtapose high seriousness with raunchy language with lyrical beauty with violence with dark comedy with awe with eroticism.

12. Action doesn't have to be overt. It can be the steady deepening of the dramatic situation . . . or your characters' steady emotional movements from one emotional/psychological condition to another—ignorance to enlightenment, weakness to strength, illness to wholeness.

13. Invest something truly personal in each of your characters, even if it's something of your worst self.

14. If Realism is as artificial as any other genre, strive to create your own realism. If theatre is a handicraft in which you make one-of-a-kind pieces, then you're in complete control of your fictive universe. What are its physical laws? What's gravity like? What does time do? What are the rules of cause and effect? How do your characters behave in this altered universe?

15. You write from your organs. Write from your eyes, your heart, your liver, your ass—write from your brain last of all.

16. You should write from all your senses: Be prepared to design on the page, so it tells you exactly what you see, feel, hear, touch and

taste in this world: Never leave design to chance—that includes the design of the cast.

17. Find your tribe. Educate your collaborators. Stick to your people and be faithful to them for as long as possible. Seek aesthetic and emotional compatibility with those you work with. Understand your director's worldview, because it will color his or her approach to your work.

18. Strive to be your own genre. Great plays represent the genres created around the author's voice. A Chekhov genre. A Caryl Churchill genre.

19. Strive to create roles that actors you respect would kill to perform.

20. Form follows function. Strive to reflect the content of the play in the form of the play.

21. Use the literalization of metaphor to discuss the inner emotional state of your characters.

22. Don't be afraid to attempt the great themes: death, war, sexuality, identity, fate, God, existence, politics, love.

23. Theatre is the explanation of life to the living. We try to tease apart the conflicting noises of living and make some kind of pattern and order. It's not so much an explanation of life as it is a recipe for understanding, a blueprint for navigation, a confidante with some answers—enough to guide you and encourage you, but not to dictate to you.

24. You can push emotional extremes. Don't be a puritan. Be sexy. Be violent. Be irrational. Be sloppy. Be frightening. Be loud. Be stupid. Be colorful.

25. Ideas can be deeply embedded in the interactions and reactions of your character. They can be in the music and poetry of your form. You have thoughts and you generate ideas constantly. A play ought to embody that thought, and that thought can serve as a unifying energy in your play.

26. A play must be organized. This is another word for structure. You organize a meal, your closet, your time—why not your play?

27. Strive to be mysterious, not confusing.

28. Think of information in a play like an I.V. drip—dispensing just enough to keep the body alive, but not too much too soon.

29. Think of writing as a constant battle against the natural inertia of daily language.

30. Write in layers. Have as many things happening in a play in any one moment as possible.

31. Faulkner said the greatest drama is the heart in conflict with itself.

32. Keep your chops up with constant questioning of your own work. React against your work. Be hypercritical and do in the next work what you aimed for but failed to do in the last work.

33. Only listen to those people who have a vested interest in your future.

34. Character is the embodiment of obsession. A character must be stupendously hungry. There is no rest for those characters until they've satisfied their needs.

35. In all your plays, be sure to write at least one impossible thing. And don't let your director talk you out of it.

36. A writer cannot live without an authentic voice—the place where you are the most honest, most lyrical, most complete, most creative and new. That's what you're striving to find. But the authentic voice doesn't know how to write, any more than gasoline knows how to drive. But driving is impossible without fuel, and writing is impossible without the heat and strength of your authentic voice. Learning to write well is the stuff of workshops. Learning good habits and practicing hard. But finding your authentic voice as a writer is your business, your journey—a private, lonely, inexact, painful, slow and frustrating voyage. Teachers and mentors can only bring you closer to that voice. With luck and time you'll get there on your own.

Puerto Rican–born playwright José Rivera's plays have been produced all over the world, and his work has been translated into seven languages. His plays include *Marisol, Each Day Dies with Sleep, School of the Americas* and *Boleros for the Disenchanted*. He was nominated for an Academy Award for the adapted screenplay for *The Motorcycle Diaries* and has written the screenplay for a film of Jack Kerouac's *On the Road*, due in 2009. This article also appeared as an afterword in *References to Salvador Dalí Make Me Hot and Other Plays*, published by TCG Books in 2003.

WHITHER (OR WITHER) ART?

By Zelda Fichandler

May/June 2003

Not this or that, but this and that. Because one thing is true, it doesn't necessarily follow that the opposite is not also true. Up and down, back and forth, move ahead and drop back, no straight staircase to the sky but growth in a kind of spiral: success, success, success, then failure and disappointment, then the struggle to get unstuck and push ahead, to keep on keeping on, and the one who finishes last wins. Brecht has Galileo say, "As much of the truth gets through as we push through; we crawl by inches."

Over the holidays, I had the time to catch up with the October, November and December issues of *American Theatre* and was astounded by the thought-provoking riches I found in them. Every theatre worker in the land appreciates and needs Ben Cameron's recurring "Cheers!" Which is not to say that the TCG constituencies aren't always encouraged to think outside the box. But here is something else again, something new, I believe—challenges to and warnings about the box itself. Serious questions are posed about the very form and nature of what we know as the "institutional theatre"—a kind of theatre that in the past half-century has transformed the way we pro-duce (bring forth) our art. We are pushed to think about whether these institutions do or do not, did but now don't, nurture the art and the artists—measured against their founding mission. Since those who challenge and warn are our friends and colleagues and raise their voices not only out of anger, disappointment and frustration, but also out of love and a sense of responsibility, I take their queries very seriously. I hope we can avoid being defensive and can listen up. Here are some personal ruminations.

I left Arena Stage in 1991, and I know that much has changed since then. It has become increasingly difficult to keep a theatre pressing forward in a creative way. In my time with the Acting Company, Margot Harley's spirited young ensemble that tours the country with classics and new work, I continued to learn about the aspirations of young talent and about the amazing audience across America that is hungry for theatre. Leading an intense actor-training program within a large university has taught me how the weight of a highly structured, top-down institution actually feels; I have a deeper empathy with the artist's sense that the largest issues are decided above. I speak in this essay as a representative of what has come to be called the "institutional theatre," now under scrutiny, if not attack.

My six-year-old grandson is wont to ask me how things were in the olden days (starting with the Age of the Dinosaurs, followed by an unimaginably long historical period pre-TV and baseball computer games, followed thereupon by the more hospitable present, which he very much enjoys). My point being that I may be able to bring some information from my experience with the dinosaurs that others of you may not have.

What are the critics saying to us? What do they suggest as the next crusade? What have they misperceived, and what enlightens us? What is feasible and what is pie-in-the-sky? And the big issues: A new generation of founders? Challenge the power of our boards? No longer an alternative theatre as we were founded to be, pass the torch to the new alternatives? Fold up our expensive tents and silently steal away? Out with the old, on with the new and every dog has his day? These are provocative questions, indeed! How do we respond to them? Jaan Whitehead ("Art Will Out," October '02, included in this book on page 233.) acknowledges that not every theatre or board or mission statement is like every other, but feels that the pressure of institutional art (with the emphasis on "institution" rather than "art") is widespread enough to warrant sounding the alarm.

What does she mean by institutional art? The following, I think: Art that is made with the right eye on the dollar, the left eye on the stage, with the right eye dominant. Art that doesn't fly because it's tethered to the bottom line. Formulaic art—this was a hit in Cleveland (Boston, Milwaukee, on or Off Broadway), this could attract a star, this one got a Tony, this one would be great for group sales or students or at Christmas or for spring vacation or for St. Patrick's Day or around Rosh Hashanah, etc., etc.; too many lows and not enough highs—a sense of uniformity, predictability, a sense of low-grade depression. Where is astonishment, derring-do, originality, hoopla? Is it one from Column A and one from Column B, or does it all add up to something intentional and brave? Does what we think the subscribers want or what quickens the theatre's artistic heart come first?

Ah, what the subscribers want! The circle that Whitehead traces really exists—I've felt the clutch of it closing around me, and it's a circle from hell. To stave off death, the maw of the box office must be fed. We count on the subscribers who make up one-half (or one-third or two-thirds or 90 percent) of our audience to feed it. Indeed, if we appear plump and chipper, other sources of nourishment may open up; no foundation or corporation wants to feed a dying theatre. If things work well and we give our subscribers what they want (and, of course, what we can afford), they'll be back next year and we'll be set for another season on a full stomach. And while there's life, there's hope.

This looks like a fair exchange, almost too good to be true, but we become suspicious and look around. Aha! it's the audience who is running the theatre! No, the box office is running the theatre! No, the board and the executive director and his PR and marketing colleagues are running the theatre! No, the institution in general is running the theatre! That's it, we've abdicated our creative freedom—that which defines us and for which we struggled to be born—so as not to bite the hands that feed us. And where does that get us? What might be the unintended consequences? Whitehead has opened up some thoughts that we have probably thought before and pushed aside, for where do these thoughts lead?

A theatre gets the audience it signals to and deserves, and repertory is destiny. As in any real-life relationship, the response we get springs from what we send out, give off, invite. Are we underrating our subscribers? Why should their taste, curiosity and capacity to chew hard on some tough thoughts or forgive a well-intentioned miss be less than ours? Presumably, deep down they're very much like us despite differences in ethnicity, age, range of income. They come to the theatre to be awakened emotionally, psychologically, even intellectually and politically, and to have an adventure, to identify with a life that's similar enough to theirs so they can recognize it but that plays out in different circumstances. Maybe their numbers would increase if we shared our own personal tastes more fully, opened ourselves up through our work to our own deepest concerns. And how do we know what *they* want if we don't offer what we want? And how do they know what they want when they haven't seen it yet? This is a better line of speculation; we should think further.

And what if the real audience, the one we must have to complete our work, drifts away and another audience replaces it who is satisfied with less? Audiences are not interchangeable integers, after all. Do we think that when the world turns—which it will—and the economy recovers—which it will—and a new president stimulates a change in the Zeitgeist (maybe John Kerry?), do we think that *then* we can return to what we really want to do? And recover the audience we've lost? The future grows out of the present while the present seeps up out of the past. The choices we make today describe the theatre we'll have tomorrow. Process is everything, and the outcome can't be predicted. It's possible for a theatre to die of starvation, and that, of course, is very sad. It's also possible for it to wither away, and that is sadder.

Whitehead invites us to consider the relationship between institution and art. I think of an institution as a cradle and the thing we call art as the baby. There is reciprocal need: The baby needs the cradle, but the cradle is an empty, useless piece of wood without the baby. Baby Eugene O'Neill didn't have a cradle: He slept in a dresser drawer on the road with his actor-father and mother, but he created anyway, or perhaps because of. The institution can be as lean and simple as that dresser drawer or as elaborate and multileveled as money will buy; the sturdier-yet-flexible it can be, the more support it can offer. The cradle's/institution's function is to provide a continuity of comfort and stability, an opportunity for growth, an empathetic, responsive face, a respect for organic creative process, tolerance for behavioral slip-ups (like flops!) and pride in the baby's hijinks. The institution accepts that the baby will develop according to its own internal laws and dedicates itself to providing the environment to encourage that.

Or this metaphor: The main event is not the institution. The main event is under the Big Top where the performers with their feats of magic and daring and the audience with its imaginative belief and its empathy get together and all breathe the same air at the same moment. All of them are grateful to the management for seeing to it that everyone has been paid, the lights are on, the event has come in on budget, the seats are filled and that the tent doesn't leak. The president of the board and other board members have the best seats, as they deserve, and will later throw a party in appreciation of the extraordinarily audacious circus troupe. The clarity of this relationship is harder to maintain in threatening times because the board has the responsibility for the survival of the institution and can become excessively interested in what goes on in the tent as well as how much it cost to put it there. Tensions are to be expected and worked through, always remembering that while theatre is a business, its business is art, not business.

Because one thing is true it doesn't necessarily follow that the opposite is not also true. The artist must have freedom to be playful, to work from internal impulses. But he also shares responsibility for the fiscal health of the institution; it may surprise the board to hear that, but I've always found it to be so. The various production departments struggle to stay on budget and are proud when they do and actors extend themselves in many ways to build audiences. As an artistic director, I have always celebrated the box office. The dollar that came to us through it was twice-blessed: Once for what it could buy in goods and services and twice as a vote of confidence that bought us freedom. The first law of the theatre is success—without success there can be no theatre. That thought wraps around everything else one can say about what's right or wrong about our institutions. It's the iron-framework of fact. Since the norm of theatre is failure, not success, and since times are generally out of joint, the box office has come to be a place of special honor. Looked at in this way, the link between creativity and fiduciary responsibility is unbreakable.

Here's one from the Dinosaur Age that just surfaced in my memory, all of a piece down to what I was wearing and where I sat. President Eisenhower had moved into the White House and the Republicans moved into Washington with him, buying the houses from the Democrats who were moving out. Our audience at Arena dwindled, and it would take several years to cultivate another one. In that Republican year, we lost $10,000 at the box office—a large amount on such a small budget. My teacher and the co-founder of Arena Stage, Edward Mangum, had moved on, so that fingers pointed only at me at the final board meeting of the season where the loss was to be explained and justified. I did my best. The board members were my friends, hand-picked by Ed and me and Tom Fichandler for their love of theatre and their willingness to put in $1,000 each to get this idea off the ground. And they were pleased enough with the season. After I spoke, there was a fraught silence and then the chairman spoke up—heavily. This was the gist of it: "Of course we're committed here to a balanced budget and no red ink and so we regret the $10,000 that was lost in this year's operations. Zelda has explained to us how this happened. In the expectation that this was a one-time circumstance and that she will be able to guide us to a balanced budget next year and the years following, we accept the explanation and the loss." And then the chairman asked that the board give me a vote of confidence, which they did. This was very sweet of them, and I appreciated it. But I chiefly remember the gesture as a moment of profound and unexpected learning. For I had not for a minute anticipated that a vote of *no*-confidence was anywhere in the cards.

What I learned was that while I was entitled to enjoy the freedom to fail, it was anticipated that I would not indulge in it too frequently. Further, that it would be much more comfortable for me if the failure could be attributed to some outside power—the Republicans, the snow, a parade, a flood in the Potomac River—and not to my own bad judgment or creative misstep. The vision thing was mine to have as long as whatever that vision generated by way of art could pay for itself by way of money. When the Ford Foundation and W. McNeil Lowry entered the field toward the end of the '50s, Arena became not-for-profit in order to qualify for gifts and grants. But the same implicit understanding applied over the successive decades (and I never signed a contract; we would both know when it was time to part). Boards have become more sophisticated since the '50s—through experience, they've learned the ways of a creative enterprise (up and down, back and forth). But I lived through my long tenure at Arena Stage in a state of not this *or* that but this *and* that—Money *and* Art, Art *and* Money. In later days, the unresolved dialectic was not even imposed by the institution; it had become internalized because that's how things had to be. Since the late '80s, the balance has become even more difficult for the artistic leaders to maintain as financial support has dwindled.

Whitehead asks us to cease looking outside and turn our gaze inward, to the inside of our institutions for the source of our sense of oppression and ways we might free ourselves from it. And, indeed, we must do that. But the *outside* is the primary dimension within which our theatres live. A theatre is an organism, an artwork in and of itself, and the person who holds the vision is its primary artist. It's her angle-of-viewing that, like the super-objective of a play, animates all the rest. (Ralph Waldo Emerson was wise to note that "an institution is the lengthened shadow of a man." For *man*, read *person*.) It's as she confronts the sounds, sights, political conflicts, rhythms, scientific achievements, timbre of human relationships, status of minorities and women, contemporary forms of theatre and other art forms, and especially the economic support systems of her time that her vision for a theatre forms itself. An artistic director belongs to both worlds—one foot inside the institution, one outside. Consciously or unconsciously, a personal vision is born in reaction to a world.

Just imagine how the artistic director's vision would expand and her heart lighten if suddenly there were a generous infusion of funds and she could pay for everything that she and the artists gathered around her had ever dreamed of. Then the tension between art and money could resolve. Then the relationship between institution and art could become crystal clear, unclouded by the pressures of survival. To think this way is to play with fantasy of course, for the Great Benefactor has retired and departed on a long tour of the universe and we don't expect him back. But it's a good bit of fantasy for it helps us to perceive the difficulty of artistic freedom in a culture defined by success in the marketplace. "He who pays the piper calls the tune" may be an overstatement of our situation, but that notion does now thread through all aspects of our institutional life.

But let us imagine that the Great Benefactor does, indeed, return with a new perspective on the Good and the Beautiful and, particularly, on those needy arts institutions that are impeded in their flowering. Could he lull our anxieties (Am I talented enough? Was that the right decision? Is this play going to make it?) or endow us with the talent and wisdom that isn't already ours? Of course not. Take away our headaches, help us to sleep more soundly, provide more time with our families? Not a chance. Attract collaborators who will stake their creative fate with us? Show us how to build acting companies and use them well? Teach us how to be effective diplomats, fundraisers, problemsolvers, writers, speakers, psychiatrists, and still be prepared for rehearsals? No way. Reveal to us how to treat Molière and Chekhov as old friends we would never betray, yet move their texts into a contemporary world, or how to read a new script in an unfamiliar form and be able to imagine it living on the stage? Strengthen our will so that we can take the hills and valleys and not flee? Endow us with humor, tact, wisdom, patience and the capacity to affect others with our exhilaration in the work? Make clear to us the language of budgets and balance sheets so that we know how to match expenditures to a value system and spend money without wasting it? Sharpen our judgment and broaden our taste? Awaken our capacity for collegiality and our teacher's warmth so that we may give our personal attention and support to all the work, not just our own, and to all the people doing it? Keep us on the pulse of our community so we can fathom our neighbors' deepest thoughts maybe even before they themselves are aware of them? And keep us in touch with our world so its preoccupations can be reflected on our stages? No, he can't. Of course he can't.

I've just set down a job description for artistic leadership—the artistic director and his comrades who share the vision and contribute to it with their own skills. And that was the short form! So what *can* Mr. Great Benefactor do for us where Whitehead suggests we're remiss? First, he would allow us to use the planning process as a way to fulfill our artistic dreams. Planning for the future would cease to be merely a function of budgeting and become one of dreaming. We would be able to plan out of the images in our minds rather than within the vise of this year's (reduced?) budget and/or the nagging weight of accumulated debt. What else? He could lift from us the fears that repress the creative spirit. For it's fear, I suggest, rather than lack of talent or imagination or good will that leads to making what Whitehead calls institutional art. Which one of us wants to be the one to fold up the tent?

Fear encourages caution and conformity, and caution and conformity are antithetical to what we refer to as art, since art is always a personal and original way of knowing the world. Creativity is born out of the capacity to play, and it's the very capacity for meaningful play that defines us as human beings. We can play with political ideas, with scientific hypotheses, with new forms in literature, with bodies in space; we call a theatre production a play and we play the piano and the violin. The notion of play is indissolubly connected to the idea of freedom, and I left something out of the job description. It's the artistic leader's role to create a quiet and concentrated and non-judgmental environment so that the entire community can play within it without fear. Benefaction can help her with that. I emphasize the organic connection between funding and fear, for I'm not sure that it's fully understood by those pointing to our lapses, unfulfilled commitments, seeming inhospitality to artists, etc. (In addition to Whitehead, see Todd London, "The Shape of Plays to Come," November '02, included in this book on page 247, and Polly Carl, "Creating the Swell," same issue.)

London bravely opts for a new generation of artistic directors and a new generation of theatres and, for the companies and playwrights within them, not just a place at the table but the table itself. "Where is a new generation of writer-founders, of playwright-managers?" he asks. That's a rousing manifesto, and certainly anything conceived in the imagination has the potential to be born into reality. Let some talented, courageous new leaders come forward and hitch themselves to the wagon. They will be warmly welcomed into the field—and gently warned. For founding today is very different from founding yesterday.

News from the dinosaurs: Beginning in the '50s there was but a blank slate, and only a few of us were scratching on it. No models, just us, hanging onto skyhooks. An almost primitive instinct for improvisation and testing of reality was released. "What is to be done?" (by chance, the title of Lenin's revolutionary pamphlet!) and "*How* is it to be done?" were the subtexts of our daily lives. The sands take lines unknown, as the poet said, even as a painter lays down on his canvas a random sketch that will define the painting to follow. At Arena, we sketched as we went, rapidly producing one thing after the other (17 shows in the first year because the audience was very small and we had to turn productions over quickly). Poor, so poor! Tireless—no, tired!—we lived play to play, and all there was of the future was right now. Modestly, slowly, the audience grew. Unexpectedly, the foundations (circa 1957) and the NEA (1965) and, later, corporations and our own community found us. They gave us money, but better than that, they gave us respect. Respect: "to look more at, to give attention to, to regard." We felt important to more than this tiny unit on this tiny budget; we seemed to matter to the culture of our country. It was a heady ascent during those middle decades.

A kind of promise was made to us, not in so many words, but a promise: These agencies would continue to be there for us and would participate in our future, caring that we survive. The promise was kept over many years, deepening as time went on and as we evolved artistically. We enjoyed the sense that if we came up with an innovative idea—artistic or organizational (organization was also considered creation)—it stood a chance of being funded. Then, for reasons you know, the promise was broken; the official culture turned its back. The final signal for me, theatrical in its communicative power, was that during her term as chairman of the NEA, Jane Alexander was able to pin down only one private meeting with Bill Clinton, which lasted just 20 minutes and offered no assurances (as noted in her book, *Command Performance*). There was no longer any political capital to be gained for a sitting president to support the arts. And nothing has happened since then to suggest that the climate has changed.

Whitehead suggests the need to "move out from under institutional shadows" and the ripeness for "a new age of pioneers." Pioneers will come or not come without our intervention and will always be welcome, and our theatres cast far more light than shadows—just imagine the American theatre without them! I salute the work of avant-garde theatres, community-based theatres, ethnically diverse theatres, ensembles of form-seekers, playwriting collectives and all forms of socially based theatres. I admire their creativity and freedom. I've watched them proliferate since the '60s—often out of a singular aesthetic vision, the product of a single mind, or in response or antithesis to the institutional theatre. But while we come from the same line, the same root, these theatres are not "an alternative" but "a parallel" to the institutional theatre; they will neither replace nor inherit it, nor do we need to choose one form over the other. We are on different paths, with different tasks and structures that reflect them. Variants of the same species, each of us is a vital and essential part of the wonderful variety-within-unity that is the American Theatre. These parallel theatres are in great need of increased funding, which their flexibility and very variety make it hard for conservative funding agencies to categorize and, therefore, to support. That's a great injustice that won't be set right, I fear, until we have the seven years of plenty due us.

We should work together to discover and elect a president with an affinity for the arts. We should write and disseminate broadsides making the case for a New Deal for the arts in America. We should make immediate contact with Dana Gioia, the new chairman of the NEA, who promises to restore grants to individual artists and to find a way to increase federal funding. We should take inspiration from and look for another Helen Clark, elected prime minister of New Zealand in 1999, who promptly declared herself minister of arts, culture and heritage and within months injected tens of millions of dollars into a "cultural recovery package." Something like this grand boost could happen to us; hope is a thing with feathers.

This isn't the time, I suggest, to man the barricades and whip up an assault against a form of theatre that in the past half-century has become so imbedded in our theatrical way-of-life as to now be its dominant form, and which at the same time finds itself in the same position as many solo artists, locked outside and knocking at the gates. But is it not the time to listen hard with our inner ear and ask again as we asked before in that Age of the Dinosaur, "What is to be done?" And "How?"

There is an old Russian saying: "Circumstances alter cases," which I take to mean "depending on where you sit, is how you see it," or, "a thing changes depending on who's looking at it." It's about relativism and the subjective nature of truth. Institutions feel betrayed by this spate of critical articles in *American Theatre*, kicked when they're down—"After all we've done for you . . . !"—while the artists are frustrated and angry and prod the institutions to set new imaginative goals that will include them.

The feelings of the institutions are justified. Since mid-20th-century, they've been the primary developer of talent for the American theatre— for stage as well as film and TV. Go to a movie, turn on the tube, get tickets to a Broadway or Off-Broadway show, there our artists are. "We promised opportunity for artistic development, we delivered on that promise; there are more jobs for artists outside of New York than in it, the so-called center," the institutions say. Taken all together, our theatres constitute a kind of national bazaar where Broadway producers shop for next year's product and next year's Pulitzer playwright. Where else can our new playwrights and their plays be developed but with us?

And we've created the possibility of a new way-of-life for those who want it. Actors, directors, designers, playwrights can move from theatre to theatre, using themselves creatively in dialogue with intelligent audiences, often evolving a sense of belonging with one or several theatres where they can count on coming back. What with these "theatre gigs"—plus film, TV soaps and commercials, voice-overs, designing or directing for opera, teaching—an artist can have a respected, even fulfilling life while building funds for retirement. Besides, say the institutions, artists don't really want a home, they prefer moving along from choice to choice, it's hard to pin them down even for one project; their agents stand in the way of long commitments out-of-town.

So what's wrong with this picture? Nothing, if everybody's satisfied with it. Don't institutions tell it the way it is? Yes, but there are other voices, speaking up now loud and clear. They ask for involvement, a kind of permanence and continuity, the sort of emotional security and ebullience you feel in a personal relationship. They want their work to add to the overall work of the place, to build something with others and watch it grow. They want to belong to an idea they believe in and can serve with their creativity. They want to have a sense of self-determination and a role in defining the destiny of their institution.

Transient, temporary work sometimes feels as nothing but a high form of what the manufacturing industry calls "piece work"—you get paid for the number of "pieces of work" you turn out and how many you turn out is the measure of things, not you, yourself. On a rainy day, "jobbing-in"—our word for piece work—can make one feel devalued:

A "gig" can only be followed by another "gig." You may be moving along but only from here to there—moving, but not evolving.

If an actor is always cast because he's "right for the role" with no consideration for the development of his own range and versatility, if with each role he starts over again with a group of strangers who have no collective experience to draw upon, if he sometimes gets the sense of himself as a kind of commodity—paid to fill a need—and then "time's up and thanks," what is it we're saying to him? That "Theatre's a precarious profession, we always knew that, be glad you're working"? Is that okay? Is that enough?

Of all the artists, the playwright gets the most focused attention from the institution, and never more so than right now. That's been my experience and it's what I observe (see Lenora Inez Brown's article "The Real World," Nov. '02). But the number of productions the playwright receives may not be the main point to her. To have her voice mingle with the voices of others in a collective consciousness as the play is evolved from within itself into production; to know that even if this one fails, the next time she knocks with a telephone book of pages in her hands, they have to let her in—might weigh more than any number of exposures of her work produced out of any number of disparate motives in any number of theatres.

There's a tendency to romanticize our beginnings, as if we were an early Ideal Community. The beginnings weren't romantic—they were exhausting, impoverished and full of anxiety, but, yes, there was a specialness about that time because our intention was so clear and unconflicted. Each of the small band of beginners, flying blind in our separate air spaces, was struggling to create an artistic home: a company, an artistic collective, living and working in one place over a period of time, all of us with the same notion of why it was important to be doing that, having compatible skills and talents and a view of our world and the role of art within it, all of us together engaged in an ongoing dialogue with our audience via theatrical means. It didn't seem very complicated, it seemed entirely natural, inevitable, not even requiring elaboration in a manifesto or a mission statement. What else could a theatre be? How could you call it a theatre if it wasn't a *place*? Who else could define the culture of a theatre but its artists? Define its style? Didn't a collective art form require a collective? Weren't we here to protest and even replace the put-it-up, smash-it-down one-shot system of Broadway?

Our earliest banners were emblazoned with "Not a Hotel for Theatre, but a Home!" and a few of us held onto these (and still have them!), but not very many of us. As years went by, other slogans came into style. "Professionalism! You Can Count on Us!" or "Good Plays Well Done, That's the Ticket!" Or even "Eight-for-the-Price-of-Six!" And until I picked up my October, November and December issues of *American Theatre*, I had come to think that no one objected to the way things had become except some of my professional friends and my students, who want to be in companies, having been trained and proselytized for that kind of a life in art, but have not been able to find them.

The fact that artists are angry, frustrated and disappointed is not necessarily bad news. The other side of these feelings is that artists are insistent, energized, geared up to make larger commitments; they want in. Artists have become eager to become part of the warp and woof of institutional life and even take responsibility at its center (or as London puts it, *occupy* that center) but find institutions inhospitable or simply closed to them. Is this perception an illusion? How many artists have these thoughts and feelings? Six? Six hundred? Six thousand? If we were to throw a party, would they come? And is it true that the institutions are inhospitable or closed to artists? Is it too much of an ongoing responsibility to nurture a group of artists, drawing them into the center of the work? These questions are, of course, no use in a theoretical way, they need to be answered in practice. And the theatres would need to make the first move.

For starters, I suggest an effusive display of understanding that audiences come to the theatre to witness and partake of the work the artists have made—that it's art that makes the money and not the other way around. "Imagination is the nose of the public," wrote Edgar Allan Poe, "by this at any time it may be quietly led." What else? Pay those who are mature and committed artists the top salaries within the institution, at least equal to that of any (other) fundraiser or audience-builder. This gesture more than any other will signal where the artist stands as to recognition and power. In the deepest sense, artists are teachers—out of the darkness, they bring light—and their salary should be pegged to what a full professor makes at the university in the theatre's community. In some smaller communities, that may still not be enough, so that allowances should be made for commercial Time-Outs. (Time-Outs for creative refreshment need to be possible as well.)

Artists should be invited to become involved in the total life of the institution in order to provide it with their special knowledge and point of view and to have their say. I read that while Ingmar Bergman was heading the Swedish National Theatre, he established a five-member artists' council that he consulted about repertory, company membership, casting and the like. I don't know how this idea would play out in America, though I wish I'd tried it myself. And a proportion of board positions should be set aside in the theatre's bylaws or be established by common understanding for artists to occupy. This would be a very important change in the way we have operated, but it must be pressed for.

The presence of artists at board meetings would necessitate a transposition in vocabulary from a bottom-line, market-share, brand-conscious, focus-group lingo brought into the boardroom from a for-profit culture to a language of emotional meanings, thus bringing the board closer to the heartbeat of the theatre and unifying everyone around the real ideas that underlie the theatre. Significant issues do come up at board meetings, but are presented in such a way as to disconnect them from the life of the theatre as it's experienced by those living it. The artists' presence will focus these issue in a more appropriate way. Remember that artists are smart; planning is the strategy by which they bring art into the world; the artist's ability to juggle the animating idea along with time, money and materials is an aspect of her talent. Artists have much to contribute to the deliberations of a board.

To keep the artist outside the business of the institution (with which he's engaged, at any rate) is to romanticize him ("Artists are above business") at the same time that it miniaturizes him ("Artists just don't have the head for it, they're fanciful, unworldly creatures, we need to take care of them"). Why has it taken so long to see this?

The creative courage of the artistic director will inspire artists; they, in turn, will support the risks she takes on their behalf whether or not they succeed. The transparency she fosters so that information—whether good news or bad—is available to all, up and down and around the building, will deepen the sense of mutual respect and a communal destiny. And she will see to it that no one is made to feel intimidated to speak up; in story and myth, the figure of Death is always silent. The artistic director's acknowledgement of ambiguity, relativism, second thoughts and struggle that exist behind difficult decisions will draw the artists even closer to her, revealing her as worthy of having, using and sharing power. The blinding glare of certainty always reduces intimacy and trust.

And so on. There are myriad ways for the institution to build an interactive relationship with its artists that will create the sense of a home where each can be for himself and also for the other and where all are for the work. Both Whitehead and London suggest some of these. Eventually, all of us must come to a much deeper understanding of the nature of the organism that we call a theatre. I hold close Aristotle's statement: "What a thing can be, it must be, whether it be a horse or a man." Or a theatre, he might have added, had he thought of it. At some point in the future, we'll want to define ourselves by whether we insisted strongly enough on becoming what we can be, and therefore have become it. We will have come to consensus that artists *are* the theatre, not a separate tribe bussed in for the performances. The artists *are* the theatre, but administrators who protect and advance the artists' work are also the theatre. And the theatre is also its board, volunteers of time, money and caring on behalf of a profession that must sometimes seem to them a total mystery, operating as it does on hunches, gambles, the unknown. What else is the theatre? The repertory is the theatre, its very flesh and bones. Its ticket prices, its brochures and ads and newsletters, its spaces, even if they're humble, the intimacy of people pulling for the same thing, its respect for the intelligence of its audience, its restlessness and unceasing workload and so on and so on, and even the way the very air that hangs off the walls tells a stranger what kind of a place it is—all these are the theatre.

Everything both tangible and intangible is what a theatre is, and every thing is a part of everything else. A theatre is a refracted image of life itself and Life is All One, as Barbara exultantly discovers in the last act of Shaw's most revolutionary play. Being All One, a theatre must organize itself in circles—concentric circles, not vertically as in Enron, but rather like the rings of a tree trunk, with the artistic director and her artists in the center, yes, but what's a center without a circumference? It's the outer border of the cell that guarantees the integrity of the nucleus.

Since theatre is both art and money, money and art, how will we pay for our ultimate epiphany? "How?" The question hovers and Aristotle is silent. Margo Jones, who had the original idea of professional theatre outside of New York and with her small, 198-seat theatre in Dallas began the long revolution in which we are still engaged, would say, "If you have a million-dollar idea, you can raise a million dollars." She said this in the late '40s, however, and I don't know how many millions it would take to pay for that idea today. It might be that the roughly hundred million—plus or minus—that seems to be the price of a new theatre building could just as well be raised as endowment to support the idea of an artists' theatre. Or if the building is a must-have, then a half of what is raised, or if not a half, then a third or even a quarter, but no less, could be set aside for an artistic leap forward. What is a building but the enclosing of an Idea?

Here in the November '02 issue of *American Theatre* is a National Call for Manifestos concerning the American theatre. It's sponsored by the Playwrights' Center, Polly Carl, executive director, and the Guthrie Theater, Joe Dowling, artistic director, with other distinguished associates: Anna Deavere Smith's Institute on the Arts and Civic Dialogue, the Literary Managers and Dramaturgs of the Americas, Actors Theatre of Louisville and Vanderbilt University Theatre. The Call asks for manifestos "to imagine new possibilities for the future, engage in the idealism of the past, step forward and define our changing times, address the needs and necessity for the creation of new work of the theatre today." Among the judges of the winning manifesto are Morgan Jenness, Tony Kushner and Diana Son.

The engine of the Call seems to be "the need and necessity for the creation of new work" and the search for a contemporary American theatre that will define itself by responding to that thought. It's of note that the Guthrie, one of America's most esteemed theatres, whose artistic director is committed to developing new work, and Actors Theatre of Louisville, with its long history of important new plays and playwrights, will be involved in bringing the chosen manifesto to life. I hope that Carl will want to abandon her negative perception of what she calls "our behemoth institutions with their repressive powers," and that London will come to regard his rhetorical cry, "Where are the theatres worthy of these artists?" as somewhat hyperbolic, since the glass that is half full promises well-equipped stages, experienced staffs, practiced audiences, in-place administrative systems—the protection of an institution able and interested to embrace new thought.

While our institutions may not currently be satisfying all the needs and expectations of artists, it's only through and with them that there's any hope for growth. In both a Marxist sense and a practical, theatrical one, only the institutional theatres possess the "means of production" necessary to carry the work forward. Acquiring these took labor, love, grit and guts, as well as an act of large imagination sustained over a long period of time. There is accumulated wisdom within the institutional theatre. Suspecting or under-valuing these theatres as partners would be more than foolhardy and would demonstrate to the world an unfortunate lack of historical perspective. All of us have to listen up, not just the institutions.

Nothing is so irresistible as a good example. If the time is right, one or two examples can become two or four, can become eight or twelve, and so on. Transformation via contagion is the evolutionary pattern of the resident theatre movement.

The only way to begin something is to begin it. The only way to change something is to go yourself, not send someone else. You may not want to grab hold of your destiny; you may want someone to hand your destiny to you, while meanwhile you can keep on railing against your unjust fate. That would be too bad; there's so much future in the present moment.

I, too, send out a Call. It's not as resonant as the other Call and won't reach as far, but it could evoke an immediate response, and it's achievable within current circumstances. I call out to a leading American playwright whom the world admires and trusts to step up to the plate and to take on the responsibilities of artistic directorship of the next theatre that's looking for one and wants to devote three-quarters of its repertory to new work.

Our playwrights seem to be the most angry; the sense of exclusion, of disempowerment, seems strongest among them. Since their art is seminal to all the other arts, if it can be empowered to flourish, the other arts will bloom along with it. Beneath "the rage of powerlessness" noted in one of the articles can lie a deep and rich source of creative power, but it can be released only by opportunity. A director, designer or actor as artistic leader can surely provide this opportunity and each has done so. But a playwright-leader is one of their own and could serve them with a special understanding. The playwright whose authenticity is already established and whose empathy is assured carries a natural authority with other playwrights. Is it to be an impromptu table reading, a workshop, a lab production in an informal space, a full production—which is best for the playwright? The "workshopped-to-death" syndrome will be resolved by someone who has already been there, done that. The act of "auditioning" will have a different intention; from a test, a judgment, it will become an exploration, part of the overall process.

A number of our theatres focus very successfully on new work, but their relationship to the world's classics is casual, if they produce them at all. I would hope that a playwright's theatre would find the classics essential to its lab/teaching component: No playwright, no artist, was born yesterday; every artist stands on the shoulders of other artists working in other forms in other times. Classics in new adaptations and translations *are* new works and, representing profound excavations of the human spirit, belong in any theatre that claims to be contemporary.

In the work of a theatre, the playwright provides the scaffold of meaning and intention to which all the other arts attach. In performance, the actor is at the center; theatre as a performing art is an art of experience. Through the flesh and blood of the actor, the playwright comes alive, no matter when she lived. Playwrights and actors are natural companions, creating in a different way but always symbiotically. Anton Chekhov wrote to the company of the Moscow Art Theatre: "Never be afraid of an author. An actor is a free artist. You must create an image different from the author's. When the two images—the author's and the actor's—fuse into one, then an artistic work is created." There are soft rustles in the air; the idea of acting companies is blowing in again (and, of course, in a few theatres the idea has never left). Could it be that the playwright, actor, director could come together in a place in such a way as to form a dreamed-of golden triangle?

There will be a board who will understand the precarious nature of the undertaking and yet find it irresistible. The notion of research and development will be familiar to them; they will understand that it takes a lot of chaff to yield the wheat, that without bad plays there's no field from which the good ones can emerge. One doesn't know if the idea rates as a million-dollar idea that could raise a million (or whatever that is in current) dollars, but it's not beyond imagining that it could. The budget has to be large enough to support the goals, otherwise fear will take over from imagination yet another time. "Art requires luxury, even abundance," wrote Tolstoy. Indeed!

There is a level of fantasy to my line of thought, for is there an established playwright who would set aside his own writing for the arduous, time-consuming life of an artistic director? A playwright is the most solo of all theatre artists, while the artistic director belongs to the entire society of the theatre, last to herself. But there needs to be but one of you who hears the call. *Sui generis*, the example that occurs only once. And what follows is up to the others.

I was given for Christmas Mel Gussow's book *Conversations with Arthur Miller*. Here, from a conversation in 1986, is Miller's response to a question from Gussow about his use of time:

> If I had a theatre that I was connected to, a theatre of my peers, a working theatre with a good group of actors, I probably would have written a number of more plays. I had one experience like that and that was before Lincoln Center collapsed. I had done *After the Fall*, and Harold Clurman came to me and said, "Look, we've got to have another play. Do you have anything else? And I wrote *Incident at Vichy*. And it worked out magically; there was a part for every actor in the company. That never occurred to me. There was an excitement about it. You didn't have to run around finding producers . . . . It's very important. It's a defense against the outside. "We're all in this together."

Yes, we are.

Zelda Fichandler is the artistic director of the graduate acting program at New York University's Tisch School of the Arts, and served as its chair from 1984 to 2007. She is a co-founder of Arena Stage in Washington, D.C., where she was producing artistic director from 1950 to 1990.

GIRLS JUST WANT TO WRITE PLAYS

By Diana Son

May/June 2003

We were doing what playwrights always do during the rare times we're together as a group: playing Celebrity. It was winter in Montana and Doug Wright, Paula Vogel, Octavio Solis, Jerome Hairston and I—as well as composers Jeanine Tesori and Louie Perez—had flopped around in a nine-seater plane to get to the Sundance Playwrights Retreat at the Ucross Foundation in Wyoming, where we were spending three weeks together in February '00. This meant time for several rousing bouts of a game at which, I must demurely confess, I kick ass.

But my playwright colleagues offered mean competition. The names coming out of the Celebrity hat were challenging, but, like I said, I'm good at this. Tommy Smothers. Jello Biafra. Amy Fisher. I was reeling them off. But with 20 seconds left on Jerome's watch, I opened one tightly folded slip of paper—and was stumped. I had to sound it out:

"Okay, first name—sounds like a hairdo, uh, big, round, think '70s—"

"Afro!"

"Close enough. Second name—uh, Gentle, as in the bear. Or Big, like the clock in Lon—"

(*sound of a buzzer*)

"Afro Who?"

We all gaped at each other blankly. Then, accusingly. "Who the hell is Afro Ben?"

"You guys know Aphra Behn . . . don't you?" piped up Paula, revealing herself to be the trigger finger. "Aphra Behn." A charitable pause. Then, "She wrote *The Rover.*"

Doug Wright and Jeanine Tesori weakly mumbled, "Ohhhhh," without really opening their mouths. Paula continued in her ever-nurturing, forget-I-won-the-Pulitzer voice. "She's considered the first professional female playwright."

Never heard of her. None of us. The first professional female playwright? You mean, before Lillian Hellman?

Then, a couple of months ago, I got a call from Gwynn Mac-
Donald, artistic director of the Juggernaut Theatre Company here in
New York City, asking me to appear at a symposium she and Mallory
Catlett were organizing to celebrate the first 100-plus years of the pro-
fessional female playwright. "There were more than 60 professional
female playwrights writing between the years 1660–1800 with com-
mercial and critical success," she said, "but people only ever know
Aphra Behn." I clicked my tongue and sighed with empathic frustra-
tion. Meanwhile my mind hightailed it back to that Celebrity game,
scouring it for details. "Yes," I said haughtily, "because she wrote *The
Clover*." A kind pause. "Why don't we send you some materials," came
Gwynn's diplomatic reply.

Let me tell you—Gwynn MacDonald and Mallory Catlett had done
their homework. They did more than that. They did yours and mine.
The symposium—as well as the yearlong series of readings they curat-
ed with dramaturgs Andrea Watson-Canning, Branden Kornell, Toni
Moffett, Kimberly Megna and Maxine Kern—was called "The First 100
Years: The Professional Female Playwright." Focusing on five writers—
Aphra Behn (1640–1689), Susanna Centlivre (1669–1723), Hannah
Cowley (1743–1809), Elizabeth Inchbald (1753–1821) and Joanna Baillie
(1762–1851)—Gwynn and Mallory excavated a 130-year period in theatrical history when women playwrights triumphed. Rocked out. Not only
were their plays commercially and critically successful, but they artfully
folded barbed social criticisms—of subjects as wide-ranging as colonial-
ism, prison reform and a woman's role in marriage—into their comedic
plots. And these women accomplished this level of success in a male-
dominated society that was aggressively hostile toward them.

Gwynn and Mallory included three plays in my crash-course kit,
but there's this really cute little boy in my house who calls me Mommy,
and we do a lot of stuff together, so I only got to read one of the plays:
Susanna Centlivre's *The Basset Table*. It's a clever, twisty-turny play in
which the lead female character, Valeria, is an educated woman—a scientist—who aspires to marry her true love, a man who accepts her
intellectual ambitions, instead of the stiff her father has her arranged
with. Strong choices for someone writing in the early 1700s. I agreed
to appear at the symposium, held at the Roundabout Theatre's
American Airlines Nabisco Lounge (sadly, vanilla wafers were not
served) where Ellen McLaughlin and I were to be the "honored guests,"
which I hoped meant we wouldn't have to talk too much. What could
I say? "Wow, I never knew *any* of this."

As it turns out, that line was part of everyone's story at the symposium. "I didn't know about these women until . . . ," "I stumbled upon
this book in the library," "I was doing a web search on something else,"
"My friend took me to a production of . . . ."

The chilling and incomprehensible message being: These women
were at the top of their field, yet they've been pruned out of history.
I mean, we've all heard of Sheridan: Some actor friend's been in a production of *School for Scandal*, and we've trotted off to cheer him or her
on. Or Congreve. Every intro-to-theatre class makes you read *Way of*

the World. Why isn't Susanna Centlivre on the same syllabus? Or on the Roundabout Theatre Company's fall schedule? From the time she wrote her first play in 1700 to the end of the century, Centlivre had at least one play running at any given time. Elizabeth Inchbald had a similarly stunning record of productions. Joanna Baillie was considered the Shakespeare of her era.

How did their works get sucked into the vortex of obscurity? Imagine the futuristic equivalent. It's the year 3000 and, thanks to biotechnology, you're 130 years old but don't look a day over 85. Your great-granddaughter comes home from high school excited to tell you that they're starting to study the great playwrights of the 20th century. Ah, you say, ready to regale her with stories of how you rubbed against (or played Celebrity with) greatness, "Who are you reading? Caryl Churchill? Suzan-Lori Parks? Kia Corthron? Paula Vogel?" Your great-granddaughter screws up her face and says, "Never heard of *them*. But did you ever see a Neil Simon play?"

At the symposium, someone asked Ellen and me whether, if we had read these works as young writers, they would have had an influence on us. "Yes!" "Of course!"—we cried, with a tinge of anguish. Ellen answered most eloquently: "I can only imagine what would have happened to me in a parallel universe—if I had been growing up, falling in love with this medium, and had seen one of these plays . . . . If I had come into this world of playwriting thinking that I was standing on the shoulders of these women, and not always feeling like 'I will try to write a play and somebody will think: It's pretty good for a girl.'"

Pretty good for a girl is pretty good indeed. Consider that, in three of the past five years, the Pulitzer Prize in drama has gone to a woman playwright: Suzan-Lori Parks in 2002, Margaret Edson in 1999 and Paula Vogel in 1998. Theatre Communications Group reports that among the 10 most-produced plays nationally by its members in the most recent season, a solid half were written by women: Yasmina Reza's *Art*, Rebecca Gilman's *Spinning into Butter*, Becky Mode's *Fully Committed*, Margaret Edson's *Wit* and Claudia Shear's *Dirty Blonde*. Sounds like critical and commercial success to me. And yet, according to the Report on the Status of Women, authored by Susan Jonas and Suzanne Bennett, in the 2001–02 season, only 17 percent of all plays produced in the United States were written by women.

Huh?

How can it be that we're living in a time when women playwrights are among the most critically acclaimed and are writing plays that are making as much money as those written by men—and yet theatres are producing six times as many plays by men?

What can we do to ensure that history doesn't squeeze these contemporary women out of their rightful place in the canon?

First off—go to a reading of the plays featured in the First 100 Years series. In addition, most of these works are in the public domain, many downloadable off the web.

Secondly, go see plays and musicals by women. You might be as surprised as *Time Out New York*'s reviewer Sam Whitehead was when he went to see *Wit*: "That's what really knocked me out," he wrote in his positive review. "While it was about a woman, and a woman's problems, it was really about the human predicament." (See Jonas and Bennett, "Report on the Status of Women.")

Thirdly, buy published versions of contemporary plays by women. You have hundreds of excellent plays to choose from. Here are a few personal recommendations of plays recently produced and about to be published: *Breath, Boom* by Kia Corthron; *The Gimmick and Other Plays* by Dael Orlandersmith; *[sic]* by Melissa James Gibson; *Good Thing* by Jessica Goldberg; and *The Bubbly Black Girl Sheds Her Chameleon Skin* by Kirsten Childs. These writers deserve a more illustrious fate than to be stumper questions in a Celebrity hat.

Diana Son is the author of *Satellites, Stop Kiss, BOY, Fishes, R.A.W. ('Cause I'm a Woman)* **and other plays. She was most recently a writer and co-executive producer for "Law & Order: Criminal Intent." She is the mother of three boys.**

ON THE ROAD TO PALESTINE

By Kia Corthron, Tony Kushner, Robert O'Hara, Lisa Schlesinger, Betty Shamieh and Naomi Wallace

July/August 2003

In June '02, playwright Naomi Wallace traveled with British theatre director David Gothard to the Middle East. They met with Palestinian theatre artists in the Occupied Territories and set up meetings for a second trip that Wallace had, for years, been envisioning—one that would bring together a group of American playwrights and Palestinian theatre artists.

In August '02, that trip became a reality. Wallace, with the help of her friend Connie Julian, invited American playwrights Kia Corthron, Tony Kushner, Robert O'Hara, Betty Shamieh and Lisa Schlesinger to join her. The trip lasted seven days. It was financed by the playwrights themselves and by outside contributions from individuals.

This collectively written account of the trip is followed by six very personal essays in which each of the writers assesses and reflects on his or her experiences.

Our primary purpose was to meet with Palestinian theatre artists. We wanted to learn about the kinds of theatre being made under the harsh circumstances in Palestinian cities and in the camps: how playwrights, actors, designers and directors—our Palestinian colleagues—negotiated the checkpoints, curfews, occupations, gun and missile fire and catastrophic economy, as well as tensions and problems within Palestinian society. We wanted to see for ourselves, feeling as we did that the sporadic, lopsided glimpses into Palestinian life available in America were neither particularly trustworthy nor sufficient to the task of trying to comprehend the ongoing conflict and carnage, the appalling suffering endured on both sides—but especially, and for many long decades, by the Palestinians.

We wanted to make human contact with people we frequently hear dismissed or described as less than human. We hoped to break down some of the barriers dividing us from the Palestinian people. We went to gather ideas for projects we might undertake, together or individually, to facilitate an exchange between Palestinian and American theatre artists, to provide material and educational assistance to Palestinian theatre workers. We feel that personal contact, dialogue, lived experience, exploration and community-building are not ancillary to but rather the core—the life's blood—of our profession.

We stayed in a hotel in East Jerusalem, from whence we made day trips to Ramallah, Al Maghar, Hebron, Bethlehem, the Aida Refugee camp, Gaza City and the "beach camp" for refugees in Gaza. We toured various settlements as well, and one evening we drove to Tel Aviv, where we met with a large group of progressive Israeli theatre artists. Throughout our seven-day journey we met women and men who, against all odds, are creating theatre. Their immediate experience of theatre's power to make sense of misery and injustice and terror, of its power to organize and to heal, were incredibly inspiring, as were their courage, intelligence, decency and hospitality.

In Ramallah, the Ashtar Theatre, led by Iman Aoun and Edward Muallem, produces a show each year that, through the character of a cantankerous Palestinian patriarch named Ali Shakur, tackles issues of collaboration, corruption, even rape and incest, emphasizing Palestinian agency rather than Israeli brutality.

The Inad ("Stubborn") Theatre in Beit Jala is run primarily by women. Two of its members, producer Marina Barham and director Raeda Ghazaleh, told us hair-raising stories of the siege in Bethlehem, of their determination to rehearse their own work and hold workshops for traumatized children and adults, even in defiance of strictly imposed curfews. Our meeting took place in the theatre lobby, against a wall that still showed the traces of the enormous hole an Israeli missile had blasted away.

Adnan Tarabashi, who runs a puppet theatre in the Druze village of Al Maghar based in a center for the Palestinian deaf—a group for whom almost no services exist—is also a playwright and a filmmaker. Adnan, who is currently developing the first system of sign language based on Arabic, showed us a film of the trip he made with two deaf puppeteers from the village to an international puppetry festival in Cuba; and another film about two deaf sisters whose lives are tragically circumscribed by the lack of resources to adequately address the needs of deaf people.

Jackie Lubeck and Amer Khalil, the artistic and managing directors of Theater Day Productions in Hebron and Gaza City, create sophisticated children's theatre (50 percent of the Palestinian population is now under the age of 15) and run a school to train Palestinian actors and playwrights. At a meeting in Hebron with Theater Day's four actors, we saw an excerpt of their play, *The Walking Boy*, a fantastical dark comedy about a boy shot on his way to school. And we were regaled with another kind of fantastical dark comedy: the real-life kind, as the actors, who live in Hebron, told us of the six-day journey they had to make, through Jordan, Egypt, over the sea to Cypress and then by boat to Gaza, to get to Gaza City (less than a 40-minute drive from Hebron, usually at a cost of about $60) to perform the play before an audience of children. The return trip took another six days. Because of the way they had to go, the travel cost for the project, funded by an organization under the budget line for "international exchange," was $3,000.

Dr. AbdelFattah Abu-Srour, our companion for most of the trip and a playwright, painter and biochemist from the Aida Refugee camp, has created the Al-Rowwad ("The Return") Center in Aida, which provides local children with instruction in Palestinian dance, theatre and foreign languages and offers them a place to go when not in school, a service that is particularly crucial, since the checkpoints and curfews enforced in the past two years have affected almost every Palestinian child's ability to attend school.

Perhaps the most extraordinary encounter of our trip took place in Al-Rowwad, when we spent a couple of hours talking with the kids, mostly through interpreters (of our group only Betty Shamieh, who is Palestinian-American, speaks Arabic). They were remarkable children, beautiful, serious, curious about us, angry about what they see as worldwide neglect of their people, astonishingly aware of the injustice of their situation but lacking anything that sounded like self-pity. They were, rather, unbelievably ambitious. Even the very young kids seemed to have decided on a profession, doctor being the most popular choice. One boy, a 15-year-old named Abed, lectured us about the global situation, the history of the Palestinian people and his opinion about a peaceable solution, with a fluency and intelligence so unmistakable it transcended the language barrier. We spent the night at various homes in the camp, some of us with AbdelFattah's parents, who fled their home in a Palestinian village in 1948 and have been living in Aida, in a small United Nations–built cinderblock house, ever since.

In a rooftop restaurant in Jaffa we discussed theatre work and the political situation with about 50 Israeli theatre artists, including Igal Ezraty, artistic director of the Hebrew-Arab theatre of Jaffa; Sinai Peter, artistic director of the Haifa Municipal theatre; Jewish and Palestinian citizens of Israel who were actors and playwrights, and professors from Hebrew and Tel Aviv Universities. We learned that Palestinian theatre is a relatively new phenomenon. Nearly every artist we talked to traced her or his involvement in the theatre directly or indirectly to the work done, in the 1980s, after the Camp David accords, by the El Hakawati ("The Storyteller") theatre company in Ramallah and Jerusalem. Audiences must be developed; facilities must be developed; directors and actors (especially women) need to be trained and then paid for their work. Designers—especially trained lighting and sound designers—are as scarce as equipment. And everyone complained, worried, speculated about the lack of Palestinian playwrights, the lack of a body of dramatic literature in Arabic that addresses Palestinian life—though it must also be said that nearly everyone we met was writing or had written plays, and we returned to the U.S. with a number of scripts, in Arabic.

Non-theatrical sights and encounters also moved us, angered us, gave us material to discuss, to ponder. We spent hours getting through the checkpoint to Ramallah, getting into Hebron and Gaza; and we watched lines of Palestinians who were clearly going to spend many more hours than we had. These checkpoints frequently cut off Palestinian cities from towns in the West Bank, making it difficult for family members to see one another, for children to attend school or for anyone to be employed outside their immediate area. At one juncture, Robert O'Hara was held at gunpoint by border guards at an Israeli checkpoint. The guards turned their Uzis on him and started shouting at him in Hebrew, a language he does not speak. After some more shouting, Robert showed the guards that he was not carrying anything dangerous in his backpack, and they eventually let him pass.

We spent an afternoon visiting settlements in the Territories, Gaza and Hebron. We met with Dr. Mahdi F. Abdul Hadi at the Palestinian Academic Society for the Study of International Affairs, a Palestinian think tank in East Jerusalem, who talked about suicide bombers, the future of peace negotiations and the prospect of a solution, and the effects of Sept. 11 on the situation in the Middle East. And in Gaza we visited the vast pile of rubble created when the Israeli Defense Forces fired a missile into an apartment complex to kill a Hamas lieutenant, killing 14 civilians in the process. Children were playing near the site when we visited; someone had spray-painted on each of the three standing walls surrounding what had been the apartment building "This is the American Missile."

With our Palestinian colleagues, we are working on establishing the American & Palestinian Playwrights Exchange, designed to send American theatre artists to the Palestinian Territories and to bring Palestinian actors, playwrights, designers and directors to the U.S. At present we are working to bring a Palestinian writer to the International Writing Program in the University of Iowa. We have also delivered a computer to the Al-Rowwad Center and are raising funds to buy another one.

Our Palestinian associates are creating theatre under extraordinarily difficult conditions. The spaces where they work are continually threatened by missiles and bullets. Their artists face harassment, arrest and violence. They must negotiate curfews, checkpoints, uncrossable borders and bureaucratic quagmires in order for their work to continue. Their audiences, which now largely consist of young children, are also under siege.

Despite these almost unimaginable obstacles and dangers, Palestinian theatre artists and workers refuse to give up their goal of making vital theatre for their communities. We hope that by forging links between Palestinians and Americans we can work toward building a global community in which all artists can work in safety and freedom.

M-60 SHELLS BY THE SEASHORE
By Kia Corthron

There are plenty of things I'm scared of—heights and the dark—but when I was invited on the trip to Palestine my answer without pause was a resolute "YES!" And since we never climbed mountains or traipsed through the night woods, I was rarely afraid—but there were a few exceptions. Like walking by the Israeli settlements in Hebron, thump thump my heart, these people seem hostile, hateful, and I am even more fearful for Lisa and Tony: traitors.

Friday, our last day, we are in a Gaza community center, one of two spaces utilized by Theater Day Productions. While we wait for logistical arrangements to be made, Betty finds a little boy in the corridor. He looks five or six, grinning ear to ear. She asks him his name: "Mohamed"—the only word he will speak. She asks how old he is. He stares at her, grinning. She holds up two fingers. He nods. Betty: "No!" She holds up four fingers. He nods. Eventually she walks him over to Tony, who tells him what a beautiful smile he has. He keeps grinning. Tony brings him to me. I talk to him, let him touch my dreadlocked hair. His hand slides down lazily, lifelessly. Grin grin. I play "patty-cake," having to move his limp hands. "Put it in the oven for Mohamed and me!" I notice he has stopped grinning. Staring at my lips, seeming to have forgotten there is a face attached. "Patty-cake! Patty-cake!" I laugh. He doesn't hear. I am still laughing, still talking, but now feeling nervous, distressed, I've heard of shell shock, but the horrible words won't come to my mind, and mercifully Betty brings Mohamed's little sister in, walks him over to her. She bawls uncontrollably. He stares at her, blank.

We stand before rubble. Sixty people died here, a residential building, babies and five-year-olds and elderly and one suspected Hamas. The graffiti in English: "This is the Israeli peace," "This is the American missile." Children come to peek and giggle and pose for our cameras.

There's a parade to the Mediterranean! The children in front of us and behind, hordes of them from all over this desert slum, and for fun one adolescent boy tosses a stone and it harmlessly hits my foot. For a moment I am cautious, then the moment passes. Party again! I am stunned at the openness of the Palestinian people, beyond all logic their welcoming us, Americans. If the worst we got is a pebble to my shoe, we got off damned easy.

IN SEARCH OF THE UNBEARABLE
By Tony Kushner

I went to visit the Occupied Territories, the West Bank, East Jerusalem, the refugee camps and Gaza; I went because I am an American and a Jew and a playwright. I carried with me as reading material the recently published volume of Gershom Scholem's letters. This seemed, among other things, an economical choice: In one volume I carried a glorious example of what I loved and valued about Judaism and Jewish thought, and also an example of those aspects of my tradition from which I dissent, with which I profoundly disagree, or into which I simply cannot find an opening, an entrance; in this book I carried as well stunning, devastating evidence of the agony of Jewish history and of the fate of the Jews in world history; and in Scholem's letters, if read carefully, there is a history of Zionism, its complexity and contradictions preserved, scrutinized, brooded over by a great intellect, an ethical, poetic, rigorous, honest intellect, an intellect writing from a point in time when one could be ethical, poetic, rigorous, honest and still be a Zionist.

I've never been so glad at having made a trip, and I urge anyone with the time and the money to go and see for yourself. It will change you. Of course, during the trip I felt, at times, disloyal to my Jewishness, to the Jewish people, but that's why I went, in part: to examine these feelings of loyalty, and also feelings of danger and distrust and anger and grief, in the context of an encounter with living human beings on the actual ground from whence my immaterial (but no less living or actual) feelings sprang. I returned more certain than I was before I left that the Sharon government, supported by the Bush government, is criminal in its brutal policies toward the Palestinians and a catastrophe for Israelis as well; that the occupation is unjust and inhuman; that the settlements are the principal barrier to negotiating peace; that only a two-state solution policed by an international force can save both the Palestinian people and the people of Israel.

I knew before I left that Palestinians are decent, generous, smart, caring people, just like Jews, just like Americans, just like people I know intimately and love. I knew before going to East Jerusalem or Hebron or the Aida Refugee camp that Palestinian kids are spectacular and heart-stirring, just like any kids are. I knew before I left that these people, for all their differences of history and culture, are also utterly recognizable; and I already knew before I went that these people have been made to suffer unimaginably for an unimaginably long time.

But I've returned with specific memories, faces, sights, sounds, tastes, all attached to what I knew before, increasing my urgency, my unhappiness and my certainty that this situation must be addressed, redressed—that peace negotiations must commence again, no matter who tries to stop it, and that American aid should not go to anyone who refuses to come to the negotiating table. Now when I read that a town is under siege, there's a good chance I know what that town looks like, what the children look like who play in its streets, what food is being served in its restaurants. This makes everything harder to bear, and, in a situation like this, unbearable is good.

Because I went with a diverse group of people, I saw things I might have missed, and because I am a Jew I think I saw things others didn't see, and I learned a lot about how ideology and history both open your eyes and blind you. I long to return to this great and terrible place.

I AM A WITNESS
By Robert O'Hara

I am a Witness. I was born in 1970, not 1960. I have a grandmother who grew up in a Segregated American South with a sixth-grade education. I have never seen the words "Whites Only" over a Bathroom Door or a Water Fountain. I have never had to eat at the back of a restaurant. I have never had to sit in the back of a Bus. I have never seen a lynching. I have never marched through the streets of a city for Civil Rights. I have never been in fear of being Drafted. I was on a Cruise Ship in the Caribbean with my family on Sept. 11. I have never witnessed my Mother being publicly humiliated by a Policeman. I have never been barred from moving freely around my country. I have never been searched because of the ethnicity of my traveling companion. I have never run for my life. I have never been more afraid for the destruction of our society than I am right now. I have never seen ordinary citizens carrying Guns. I am the descendant of Slaves, and I have traveled through the landscapes that hold their blood in its soil. I am a Homosexual. I am a Wimp. I am an Artist. I am a Witness. I am Crazy. I love Life. I love Love. I had never met one Palestinian. I do not believe in One God. I do not know Arabic. I have a lot of Jewish Friends. I don't know what it is like to awake and sleep in hunger. I love my Country. I did not vote for Bush or his Father. I do not believe Hatred is Easy. I am a Writer. I have only been abroad to Europe. I am 32. I want the world to get smarter. I am a Witness. I had never stood in the middle of Horror. I believe in the power of Theatre. I am a Storyteller. I am a Myth Creator. I am a Liar. I am a Witness. I want to give to this earth more than was here when I arrived. That is why I went on this Trip. That is what I got from the Trip. I carry the Scars of those that came before me. I am a Witness.

A DREAM OF BECOMING
By Lisa Schlesinger

In August, my aunt gives me a key chain with a prayer for travelers on it. The prayer beckons peace, safe return—simple things anyone would want when leaving home on a journey. At the time, I don't know I am going anywhere. A couple of weeks later I am packing for Jerusalem.

My 16-year-old son says, *Mom, are you nuts? You're going to a war zone.* I pack a photo of him. He looks like the perfect soldier—strong, robust, young. I think airport security might notice that. I pack the photo for that reason, though my primary reason for going to the Promised Land is to find avenues for peace.

Don't go, my younger son says.

Let's say we are living in a refugee camp and we are waiting to go home, I say. *Wouldn't you want someone to come see us? To say I haven't forgotten you?*

How long have we been waiting?

Thirty-five years.

He thinks about that. Thirty-five years is beyond his imagination.

Usually the day I travel I have a stomachache. On this trip it never goes away. The reasons are all about guts. I have none.

The destruction in the Territories is pervasive: the bulldozed orchards and villages; the tanks charging through tiny streets; the innards of houses hanging out of walls blasted through in the middle of the night; blockades made from the rubble of these houses; the Israeli snipers on the top floors of the remains; the U.S.-made M-16s the IDF carry. The real violence is the invisible one underneath it all.

At every checkpoint, the greatest hope is that the soldiers will let one pass with relative ease. The greatest fear is death. In between hope and fear is the daily humiliation that Palestinians experience at these checkpoints. The steady, torturous breaking of the spirit.

At the Al-Rowwad Cultural Center in Aida camp, the children offer to dance for us. They squeeze into the other room to make a dramatic entrance. First the girls dance and then the boys. As often happens, art renews my resolve, intention, hope.

Afterwards, a boy, Anas, asks, *What do you know about us?*

Robert [O'Hara] says, *We've seen you on TV. Throwing stones at the tanks.*

Someone says, *We saw you dancing when the planes hit the towers on Sept. 11.*

That wasn't us, Anas answers. *We don't hate the Israelis or the Americans. Why do they hate us? We only want what all children want. To be safe, to learn, to go to school, to play . . . .*

I can't paraphrase the hope of a child—the only way to imagine it is backwards: *What if this were my child? What prayer would be on a key chain for these children?*

God grant me a dream of becoming.

At night I lie down on Anas's sister's bed and dream of my grandfather. He sailed to the U.S. as an orphan, with a head full of lice and the ghosts of his mother and brother in the wake of the ship. He fought in World War II fortified by his experience of being hated because he was a Jew. He told me his dream of the Promised Land. But not the cost.

Some months later Anas is shot when a tank enters Aida Camp. He is dancing in its path.

LIVES I COULD NOT HAVE LED
By Betty Shamieh

When Naomi Wallace asked me to go with a delegation of American playwrights to meet with Palestinian theatre artists living and working under Israeli occupation—the longest military occupation of one people by another in modern history—my first reaction was "Hell, no!"

I did not want to confront what my life could have been like if my parents had not immigrated to America in the 1960s. It's the luck of the draw that I was born in San Francisco rather than Ramallah, where my ancestors founded a small Christian village over 400 years ago. I was born after Israel captured the West Bank and Gaza in the 1967 war, so, if I lived in Ramallah, I would never have known a life in which I did not live under military occupation. Access to water for my family would be limited. But from places in Ramallah, I would have clear views of swimming pools and sprinkler systems fanning lawns of Israeli settlements upon the land they acquired by war—an acquisition that almost every country in the world has acknowledged as illegal and a roadblock to peace. Yet, every year, I would watch those settlements grow.

Instead of Harvard and Yale, I would have likely attended Bir Zeit University, also known as the Harvard of Palestine. I was a student during the first intifada, so I would be behind in school, because the

educational institutions that I would have access to would have sometimes been shut down for as long as a year.

As I do in New York, I'd probably teach at a small college to support my playwriting habit. If I taught at a place like Bethlehem University, I would live under the threat of curfew and be confined to my
home 24 hours a day for weeks at a time. For the past two years, I'd have
waked every day and waited to see if the tanks and snipers—who shoot
anything that moves—had retreated, meaning that was a day I could
teach, walk outside, get fresh food, visit a friend or, if need be, a doctor.

I know myself, and I am not a brave person. If I were an Israeli,
I would probably not have the courage to be a refusenik, like the Israeli
director who helped organize a meeting between the Arabic-Hebrew
Theatre and our delegation—who faced possible jail time for signing a
document that says, "We shall not continue to fight beyond the 1967
borders in order to dominate, expel, starve and humiliate an entire
people." Perhaps, unlike the Israeli refuseniks whose numbers are 500
strong (and growing), I would have followed orders. But I know for
certain that I would not attend a demonstration where I knew I could
be killed—attend it in hopes that someone, somewhere, might catch a
glimpse of me and actually think about what has happened and is happening to my people. Not me. I'd be at home, perhaps writing a play,
but I'd be at home. I know myself. If someone threatened to harm or
torture me, I'd turn on everything I hold dear. In a heartbeat. That is
not something one likes to see in one's self, and I see it clear as day
every time I go back there.

So I wanted to tell Naomi, "No! I don't want to see what my life
would and would not have been like, thank you very much! Then, I'd
have to return to New York and try to talk about what I saw and who
I met in the Palestinian Territories, using every forum available to me,
no matter what the cost to myself personally and professionally."

And yet I went. The cost of ignoring what is happening there—
and ignoring how those happenings affect the stability of the entire
world—is unbearable.

WE ARE ALSO EACH OTHER
By Naomi Wallace

"Politics is not separate from lived experience or the imaginary world
of what is possible," writes historian Robin D. G. Kelley in his book
Race Rebels. And it was this very idea of interconnectedness and imagination that led me to envision making a trip to visit the Occupied
Territories, the West Bank and Gaza.

A few months since our return, two things especially have stayed
hard in my mind. One of these is our trip to the Aida Refugee camp
outside Bethlehem, where our visit interrupted a dancing lesson in
progress. The children, aged eight to fourteen, were training in traditional Palestinian dance, the *debka*.

I had never before encountered such an informed and politically
mature group of young folks, children who could make the distinction

between the actions of a government and its people. The miracle was that these children did not spit at us for the three billion dollars a year in U.S. military aid that supports their occupation. They did not shout at us for the American-made Black Hawk helicopters, F-16s and Cobras that terrify them, even in their sleep, day in and day out. They did not say, "Yankee, go home." They did not hold us accountable, as citizens, for the deaths of their friends at the hands of Israeli soldiers firing American bullets. One could not have blamed them if they had.

Instead, for half an hour in the tiny, hot room of their refugee camp, these children danced for us. Afterward, a boy of 10 said to us, "Yes, I throw stones at tanks. But I would rather play." A 12-year-old girl with her arm in a cast said, "When I grow up, I want to be a doctor." I pray that she will. On both accounts.

Another piece that stays with me is also a memory of children: the almost-still-children of the Israeli army, the shock-troops for a colonial settler state. Along the roads and at each town, we were stopped, our identification was checked and we were questioned. When approached by an armed soldier, one looks first at the gun and only afterward at the face. From the face, one's focus goes quickly back to the gun, then to the hand that holds it and the finger, almost always on the trigger. I was disturbed and moved by the beauty of these young soldiers' hands, the fine hair on their forearms, and simultaneously appalled by the monstrous obscenity of these almost-still-children of Israel sent out for decades to brutalize and subdue an entire people. These young men should have been out kicking a soccer ball, shouting with the excitement of play, not war.

To visit the Occupied Territories, the West Bank and Gaza as theatre writers is not simply an exercise in forging links between ourselves and the Palestinians. Rather, it is to realize that we, as Americans, are, on an intensely intimate level, already fused, through the overt involvement of our government, with the history of these people. The challenge, then, is to recognize this, and ultimately to do something about it that makes a motion in the direction of that long, hard struggle for peace. As Mahmoud Darwish says in his poem "Psalm 11," "Nothing remains for me / but to inhabit your voice that is my voice." We are not, I thank the gods, only ourselves and our own personal experience. We are also what happens to one another.

And so? In a way, it's a simple aspiration: So we can all meet in the morning on the soccer field, our weapons stacked to make the goal posts, our children dancing with their wild feet, the ball going up, up, somewhere in the big sky, then coming slowly down; and then that enormous, ecstatic, thrilling cheer, because all of us at the end of the day are safe, and we will eat together at dusk, after the sweat and play of the game; and we will sit at the same gigantic table, cooling our hot arms in the bowls of fruit.

And look! Those who want to, even with their shoes still on and muddy, even in the midst of the meal—they can get up on the table, among the vegetables and water, and begin to shout and cry and argue and laugh and forge an uncontrollable, dream-worthy theatre that inscribes every one of our names in the footlights, that changes us all in mid-sentence, exactly in mid-flight.

Kia Corthron's plays include *Breath, Boom, Light Raise the Roof, Snapshot Silhouette, The Venus de Milo Is Armed, Force Continuum* and *Slide Glide the Slippery Slope.* She has written for television's "The Wire" and "The Jury." In 2004, on a travel grant from Minneapolis's Guthrie Theater, she traveled to Liberia and is developing *Tap the Leopard* with the theatre.

Tony Kushner is best known for his two-part *Angels in America,* also a six-hour television event produced by HBO. His other plays include *Homebody/Kabul, A Bright Room Called Day* and *Slavs!*; as well as adaptations of Corneille's *The Illusion,* Ansky's *The Dybbuk* and Brecht's *The Good Person of Setzuan* and *Mother Courage and Her Children.* He wrote the book for the musical *Caroline, or Change* and the screenplay for Steven Spielberg's film *Munich.* The Guthrie Theater of Minneapolis will premiere *The Intelligent Homosexual's Guide to Capitalism and Socialism with a Key to the Scriptures* in May '09.

Robert O'Hara wrote and directed his groundbreaking play *Insurrection: Holding History* in 1996. He is also the author of *Antebellum, Good Breeding, American Ma(u)l, The Spot, Down Low* and *B.Candy.* He received a 2006 Obie Award for his direction of *In the Continuum* and has directed across the U.S., in South Africa and at the Edinburgh Fringe Festival. His feature film directing debut, *My Place in the Horror,* is forthcoming from Duty Noted Inc.

Lisa Schlesinger's stage and radio plays include *Wal-martyrs, Celestial Bodies, Same Egg, Manny and Chicken, Rock Ends Ahead* and *The Bones of Danny Winston.* She is the co-author, with Naomi Wallace and AbdelFattah Abu-Srour, of *Twenty-One Positions.* She is currently working on an opera, *Harmonicus Mundi.* Her essay "Postcards from Gaza and Other Unspeakable Geographies" is forthcoming in *Out of Silence,* edited by Caridad Svich. She is a professor at Columbia College in Chicago.

Betty Shamieh is a playwright, author, screenwriter and actor. Among her 15 plays are *The Black-Eyed, Territories, The Machine, Chocolate in Heat* and *Roar.* In 2008 she was playwright-in-residence at San Francisco's Magic Theatre.

Naomi Wallace's plays *In the Heart of America, One Flea Spare, Slaughter City, The Trestle at Pope Lick Creek* and *The War Boys* are collected in one volume, *In the Heart of America and Other Plays,* published by TCG Books. Her most recent works are *Things of Dry Hours* and *The Fever Chart: Three Visions of the Middle East.* She is a recipient of the MacArthur "genius" grant, among other awards, and divides her time between Kentucky and Yorkshire Dales, U.K.

FOUND IN TRANSLATION

By Eisa Davis

July/August 2004

I said it before, and I'm-a say it again. I belong to the church of hip-hop. Cain't help it. If your after-school program is dancing to a boom box made out of two speakers, a suitcase and a skateboard spray-painted gold, if you remember when the *Source* magazine was just a double-sided Xerox copy, if you've got Queen Latifah's autograph from back when she used to be a dope MC, you are a hip-hop head, without a doubt. And that I am.

I also belong to the cult of theatre. My other after-school program was playing Bilbo Baggins in *The Hobbit*, Teeta in Alice Childress's *Wedding Band*, crying through the monologues from Ntozake Shange's *for colored girls who have considered suicide / when the rainbow is enuf* over and over to the bunks on my bunk bed. When I saw Anna Deavere Smith's *Fires in the Mirror* at the Public Theater in New York City and then Tony Kushner's *Angels in America* at the Mark Taper Forum just a few months later in Los Angeles, I knew that theatre was a place I could make my home.

One MFA and several jobs later, I heard about something called hip-hop theatre and lost my natural born mind. I was already doing this—writing plays with hip-hop in them—but had no idea that this sort of work was being created by artists all over the country, all over the world. In New York, Cincinnati, D.C., London, San Fran and L.A., a new movement was being born, a syncretic art form that, in combining two genres, was actually revitalizing the aesthetics of each.

Having a name for what we did suddenly meant we had a community. We were not alone, we had crew, comrades, an umbrella 501(c)(3). Having a name meant we were consciously developing artistic voices unique to what had come before us. Today, the name hip-hop theatre still brings people together, recognizing that the separation of hip-hop from theatre to begin with was an unnecessary, artificial split. Hip-hop theatre is a family reunion, says Javier Reyes, artistic director of Colored Ink of Oakland, Calif. It's a clarion call to artists who want to resurrect American hip-hop by siphoning the formaldehyde out of its commodified veins, and to infuse theatre with our bright, fresh blood. It's the child of hip-hop and theatre. Perhaps it has another name, which it has yet to find. For now, it carries the name of its parents—and is more than the sum of its parts.

What is hip-hop theatre? When did it start? Lot of heat around this form, not enough light. Here are a few samples. Some take it all the way back to Amiri Baraka's *Dutchman*, the Last Poets and Ntozake Shange— works from the '60s and '70s that exemplify what Paul Carter Harrison calls the "African continuum." Then came the Santa Claus skit by the Treacherous Three in the movie *Beat Street* and the interludes on De La Soul's debut album *Three Feet High and Rising*. All of the B'boying and breakdance from *Flashdance* and *Breakin'* to GhettOriginal and *Noise/Funk*. The graffiti writing in *Wild Style*. Might have been recorded on film or on tape but was theatre just the same. Some pioneers of the recent wave working explicitly in traditional theatre venues include Will Power, Universes, Danny Hoch, Hip Hop Theatre Junction, Sarah Jones, Jonzi D and Full Circle. There's no way to essentialize their work. Each artist re-creates the genre as s/he creates individual pieces. Some artists are more interested in innovative theatrical form, utilizing one or more of the four elements of hip-hop (rapping/MC'ing, DJ'ing, B'boying/breakdancing, writing grafitti) for storytelling, and others are more interested in innovative narrative, making use of the sensibility, language and stories of the hip-hop generation for content. You could break down the difference between these creative styles like this: Whether it's Jay-Z rhyming (hip-hop form) or Latrell Sprewell playing basketball (hip-hop content), both are hip-hop through and through. Like Anna Deavere Smith and Tony Kushner, hip-hop theatre artists are pushing the envelope and creating culture instead of just riding it. With hip-hop theatre, we have what rapper KRS-One calls "edutainment." There is ritual, call and response, and an amped, young audience of color that actually wants to be in their seats.

But hip-hop theatre is a name, and names hold water, weight, sway. Names can be outgrown. Names can be used to pigeonhole, denigrate, exclude. "You mean you're 'doing' poetry instead of writing it? Slam poems instead of page poems?" "How can you be a hip-hop theatre artist and write a traditional play set in 1955 in the California redwoods! That's not street; write something uglier." "If you don't use the four elements, you are not hip-hop." "You're Asian, you're white, you're Pacific Islander, so you are not hip-hop." "You're black, so why are you so smart and articulate?" These attempts to limit expression don't just come from outside the community, they come from inside. Even when comments don't intend to be exclusionary, there is no agreement on what hip-hop theatre is, whatsoever. It's like that, and that's the way it is. It's the internal dialogue that keeps the form vital, relevant, and enhances the ability to be participants and observers simultaneously. Which is what artists must always be.

I like the name "hip-hop theatre," because when it's ascriptive, voluntary and utilized by a self-described hip-hop generation that speaks through theatre, we are found in translation. Finally, a form that describes and comprises our multi-ness. When U.K.–based artist Benji Reid dances his monologues, it's new, and it's the best kind of new—the kind that plays with conventions and serves up their permutations. And we've got all kinds of historical precedents. Art forms progress when they mimic other art forms, whether it's Langston Hughes writing the blues on the page or Aaron Copland building symphonies from folk tunes or Lee Strasberg bringing the therapist's couch into acting. The purists shriek, the open-minded are jazzed, and the culture follows.

There's an intergenerational dialogue that's going on with hip-hop theatre, too. Sometimes it's a screaming match, sometimes it's a passing of the torch, sometimes it's an active collaboration. But it's a dialogue that is entirely welcome, and it has to do with the conscious relationship that hip-hop has always had to the past. When you sample old records and quote lyrics, you're not just stealing, you're showing respect. A DJ is doing her job when she generates nostalgia for music itself. When we convened a presentation and discussion of hip-hop theatre at New Dramatists in February, I was heartened to hear from Baraka Sele, curator of New Jersey Performing Arts Center's World Festival, and Gwendolen Hardwick, program director of Creative Arts Team, that we are doing exactly what they were doing in the Black Arts movement of the '70s. Trying to make theatre that was for us, by us, about us; being ignored by the mainstream; funneling the same raw energy into work that takes a stance in the endless struggle for socioeconomic, racial, gender and sexual equality.

And hip-hop theatre is already happening to older, primarily white subscription audiences in mainstream theatres, even on Broadway. A recent example is Regina Taylor's *Drowning Crow*. An adaptation of Chekhov's *The Seagull*, the play dramatizes the conflict between mother and son as an aesthetic war between traditional and hip-hop theatre, between Arkadina's fading glory as a Negro Ensemble Company actress and Constantine's youthful search for "new forms." Of course, Chekhov wrote himself in as Konstantin—with *The Seagull*, he was attempting to create a new form himself. In Marion McClinton's Manhattan Theatre Club production, Constantine, or C-Trip, as Taylor renames him, was played by Anthony Mackie. As an actor, his hip-hop cred is high after playing Tupac in Michael Winn's *Up Against the Wind* at the New York Theatre Workshop, and for penning his own rhymes as Papa Doc, Eminem's archrival in the film *8 Mile*. So when Mackie as C-Trip presents his play within a play on the lake in the first act, guess what it is? Hip-hop theatre. He recites blank verse and rhyme to a beat, dancing expressively as he speaks. Before presenting the play, C-Trip even speaks to other characters with rhyme and rhythm, revealing that his artistic experimentation with new forms is taking place in every facet of his life. And because the play unfurls from his perspective, the entire production employs the projections and dance and sampling that hip-hop theatre is known for.

But back to C-Trip's play. What does Arkadina (played by Alfre Woodard) think of it? She thinks it stinks. Why couldn't he do an excerpt from August Wilson's *Seven Guitars*, she asks. Eventually, C-Trip kills himself, because he can't get any love, can't get any understanding. And even if Regina Taylor had changed the ending to spare his life, Ben Brantley slayed the whole show in the *New York Times*, and no one could be caught dead appreciating the bold stylistic leap that Taylor had taken.

I appreciated it. Playwright and poet Cornelius Eady, author of *Running Man* and *Brutal Imagination*, always insists to his students that the instructions for hearing the play must be written into the play. We must always be sure that every audience member has a way into our work. In *Drowning Crow*, the instructions were there. But in our world of de facto cultural segregation, some audience members may not know the language in which those instructions are written. So we keep trying to be found in translation.

When I was in grad school, the director/actor Stuart Vaughan once came and spoke in our Shakespeare class. He talked about two major epochs in drama: the theatre of the articulate and the theatre of the inarticulate. Vaughan used Shakespeare as his prime example of the articulate, where each character eventually says exactly what s/he feels. Sam Shepard was his example of the inarticulate, where much of the play's meaning takes place in the subtext, in what is not being said or is unable to be said. Articulate theatre recognizes a one-to-one correlation between thought and word, whereas inarticulate theatre does not trust words to say it all, recognizes that expression, let alone communication, is often impossible. Hip-hop joins the articulate with the inarticulate. The lyrics provide the articulation of intellect, the need to speak plainly or with complexity, with irony, local and personal specificity, satire, longing—and the beat brings the inarticulate release of pure music, of the drum, of our primal rhythm. And we can flip it. The lyrics can be inarticulate, the pure feeling evoked by a curse word, a nonsense rhyme—and the beat can be intellectual, not danceable, just something to contemplate, to analyze. When hip-hop moves from the corner and into a theatre, you get the one-two punch. Articulate inarticulateness. Restoring theatre to its full power.

In just 25 years, we've already got a classical hip-hop aesthetic. Just as ballet technique became codified over the years—first through fifth position for legs and arms, arabesque, tendu—so have hip-hop music, lyrics, dance and visual art developed a stable vocabulary—battle rhymes, freestyle, uprock, poplock—that can be taught and used to tell anybody's story. Philly collective olive Dance Theatre (Jamie Merwin and Raphael Xavier, artistic directors) demonstrated this loud and clear in its recent piece *tOy bOx*, which imagined a set of mechanized children's toys dressed in green and red coming to life through breakdancing moves. Harlem Renaissance writer James Weldon Johnson once said that history judges a race by the quality of its literature and art. If jazz and modernism are the formal legacies of his generation, hip-hop and postmodernism may well be the formal legacies of ours. Content may never change, stories always stay the same, but new forms alter consciousness, actually change the way we imagine ourselves.

So if hip-hop is now at the center of global culture, how long will it take our theatres to catch up? We're on the bound. Four years ago, I wrote an article in the grownup, glossy version of the *Source* magazine about hip-hop theatre. I didn't coin the term: It actually had appeared some months before in an *American Theatre* article by Holly Bass, who would go on to curate for the Hip-Hop Theater Festival. But she didn't coin the term either. I think that just like calculus being invented simultaneously by Leibniz and Newton, hip-hop theatre simply arrived because of evolutionary necessity. Because my article was in the March '00 issue of the *Source*, a hip-hop magazine, the term "hip-hop theatre" was able to galvanize a community of artists already developing the form, some of whom had never met before. Danny Hoch and Kamilah Forbes and Clyde Valentin started the New York Hip-Hop Theater Festival that year. In the *Source* article, *Noise/Funk* co-creator Reg E. Gaines said that "hip-hop theatre becomes valid if Puffy [Sean Combs] or Russell or Master P reads this, invests and puts hip-hop theatre on Broadway . . . until they invest, nothing matters." Since then, Russell Simmons has won a Tony for producing *Def Poetry Jam* and MC/actor Mos Def has starred in Suzan-Lori Parks's Pulitzer-winning *Topdog/Underdog*. And regardless of your opinion of Sean "P. Diddy" Combs playing Walter Lee Younger in *A Raisin in the Sun*, by simply being on stage, he is creating an excitement around live theatre that many young people have never felt before. Will Power and Universes and Danny Hoch work at New York Theatre Workshop and the Mark Taper Forum. We've had a Future Aesthetics retreat for artists spearheaded by Roberta Uno at the Ford Foundation, and plays by Ben Snyder, Indio Melendez, Gamal Chasten, myself and others are being developed by theatres nationwide. Through such grassroots initiatives like the International Hip-Hop Exchange, the roots of hip-hop are being nurtured by MCs in Colombia, Brazil, Mexico and Cuba, and hip-hop theatre's got a multi-part series in *American Theatre*.

And we don't stop. We're in both worlds, and we want you to be, too. Keep learning about us, and we'll keep learning about you.

Eisa Davis's plays include *Bulrusher*, a finalist for the Pulitzer Prize in 2007, *Angela's Mixtape*, *Warriors Don't Cry*, *Hip Hop Anansi* and *Umkovu*. As an actor, she has appeared in the rock musical *Passing Strange* at Berkeley Repertory Theatre, the Public Theater and on Broadway; the films *Robot Stories*, *Pretty Bird* and *The Architect*; and the TV series "The Wire" and "Law and Order." She also performs original songs and released her first full-length album, *Something Else*, in May '08.

THE FOLLIES OF CHINESE DISSIDENT POLITICS

By Zhang Xian
Translated by Tang Ying

November 2004

One of the basic contradictions of my life is that as my theatre struggles with the fast, changing realities of China, my plays have to be produced in an environment that is closely guarded by my government. That is the source of my life's frustrations. I am considered a political playwright because so many of my works have been turned down for production or performance. Because I never cared whether or not my plays would see the light of production, I call them "closet plays," and I am, to some extent, an underground writer.

Because of the theatre's power and appeal, traditional Chinese audiences have a tendency to blur the distinctions between what is staged and what is real. Audiences often think that the stage—which is tightly and severely controlled by the Communist Party—exists in the same continuum as reality, and that a play that has been given the green light must also have been true to life. Indeed, the lives of the *laobaixing* (common people) have changed drastically in the past 20 years. (Today, with the popularity of illegal DVD copies of American television dramas like "Sex and the City," Chinese audiences like to say, "These kinds of stories are also taking place in our own lives.") But the magnitude of those transformations has not been fully and accurately reflected on stage—except on occasion, when, for brief spurts of time, the Chinese authorities relax their repressive hold and the theatre's post-revolutionary avant-garde seems to display greater degrees of boldness, unconventionality and sexual frankness.

The avant-garde's reaction against the institutional role of Chinese theatre, however, is frequently less daring and less frankly sexual than contemporary Chinese literature, and it takes place in an environment of confusion, quick changes, subterfuge and illusory surfaces. Such was the case last January when an alumna of Shanghai Theatre Academy returned from the U.S. to visit her parents in China and called me up to ask in amazement, "What is happening in Shanghai?" Her voice a mixture of excitement and bewilderment, my friend declared, "Shanghai stages seem so open now—much more so than American stages."

Her shock was understandable. At the time, several Chinese plays that were given the green light teemed with graphic details and sexual indulgences—stories that in an earlier time would have been deemed polluted and corrupt. In October '03, for example, Li Rong's *Please Forget Me Immediately at Night* told the story of a wife who discovers her husband has had an affair, and in retaliation finds herself looking for affairs of her own. (Her husband eventually has a nervous breakdown.) That November, *Let Us Live a Night Life* by Zhou Xiaoli concerned a woman novelist who, following the instructions of her publisher, fakes experience as a prostitute in her résumé to sell her books. After landing on the best-seller lists, she actually becomes a hooker. Xiu Guochun's *Break Up When It Is Dawn*, in December '03, offered a comic moral lesson about sex: If you think one-night stands are foolish, *not* breaking up after a one-night stand is even more foolish. January '04 saw the debut of *Life Should Be in Bed* by Yu Rongjun, in which a woman throws herself into serial sex after the breakdown of her marriage.

My alumna-friend was most surprised to find out that several Chinese female actors actually were rehearsing *The Vagina Monologues* for a Shanghai-style performance. A huge rose opened up on stage; a giant uterus was revealed in the center of the petals; and three actresses voiced the Eve Ensler play, which incorporated the stories and thoughts of several Shanghai women about their own vaginas.

In disbelief she asked, "Has *wenyi* finally thawed out in China?"

"Yes—and no," I replied. *Wenyi* is the Chinese word for "arts and literature." The early 1980s were hailed by the Chinese as "the spring of art and literature," meaning a cultural awakening after the death of Mao Zedong in 1976, or a thawing-out from the freeze of Maoism. But in China, *wenyi*'s true meaning encompasses not just the arts (theatre, movies, fine arts, literature) but also the entire media culture—all publications, newspapers, television stations, entertainment places, propaganda agencies and cultural administrative departments. *Wenyi*, moreover, is supposed to bear a direct relationship to our social culture, morals and customs: Real cultural workers must shoulder a social responsibility. Addressing a Beijing gathering of 2,000 artists and writers in December '01, President Jiang Zemin stated: "Literary and art workers should adhere to the truth, oppose falsehood, glorify beauty and goodness, advocate science and combat foolishness."

A spring of *wenyi* suggests, in other words, that the Chinese people are experiencing greater freedoms in our social life. But since the theatre challenges reality and often dares to go against official rules and controls, how could it be possible for the party cadres and Chinese authorities to now suddenly tolerate free expression in the theatre?

Looks can be deceiving. The Chinese dramas mentioned above—commercial vehicles with hackneyed plots—do challenge the severe moral limits of society far more openly than before, but they do not sharply criticize the system itself. Unlike my plays, they do not reject the authoritarianism of cultural institutions, and they have not infuriated government officials. On the plus side, these popular plays do reflect something of the real lives of Chinese citizens, daily existences that were once held in a kind of semi-secrecy, witnessed by Chinese writers but never actually told on Chinese stages. In China, where theatre is a state institution, like the church or the court systems, theatrical affairs are always carefully reviewed and inspected. [*Editor's note:* Most dramas in Shanghai are produced by two state-owned theatres, the Shanghai Drama Arts Center and the Shanghai Theatre Academy. Since independent theatre, where it does exist, falls way below the radar, many directors have to turn to these institutions for cooperation to get their productions off the ground.]

In the 1980s, after Mao, reforms, economic liberalization and personal freedoms emerged, and those exciting years broke down the limits of fundamentalist Confucian morality, leading to a situation where legal penalties, like re-education, didn't befall a majority of the people. However, alternative lifestyles and illegal existences continued to raise political flak if realistically shown or depicted on stage.

The battle for the hearts and minds of the Chinese people is not over. It has intensified in other, often covert, ways, since all public-security bureaus have never truly given up the privilege of keeping a close watch on people's affairs. At any time, according to certain needlessly high moral positions or ambiguous criminal codes, Chinese women who, in real life, might behave like Carrie, Samantha, Charlotte and Miranda in "Sex and the City" can be arrested and labeled "criminals" and "gangsters."

Beyond reflecting high rules of conduct, artists are supposed to act as agents who contribute to expanding China's advanced productive forces and raising the people's ideological and moral standards. Moral lessons, the Chinese government believes, should be contained in any theatrical production: If something is deemed illegal in social life, it is frequently deemed illegal on stage. Chinese officials constantly worry that a subculture of disaffected communists might arise from the underground and enter the mainstream, so the Communist Party's exertions of its political power and control always reflect its fear that any audacious production or any freedom shown on stage might bear some political risk.

You might even say that during the past 20 years of "reform and openness" since the death of Mao Zedong, China has undergone several springs of *wenyi*, each one having briefly come and gone, always discontinued by orders "from the top." Sometimes the government's Ministry of Culture issues these orders; most of the time "from the top" refers to the party's Department of Propaganda. You are not allowed, for example, to mention the Cultural Revolution, or talk about layoffs, relocations and Chinese migrations. Punishment for violation of any ban ranges from writing self-critiques, receiving wage deductions or being demoted or discharged to being charged with a crime. Instead of nakedly forcing policies upon the masses, the party has taken closer cover; in recent years, bans have become more obscure and less unbridled.

In 1993, Deng Xiaoping urged the whole nation to concentrate on making money in earnest under a socialist-capitalist economic structure. But the nature of totalitarianism in China today is such that even if a degree of economic liberalization is allowed, such liberalization is certainly not allowed in the realm of *wenyi*. And it is certainly not allowed in the realm of politics.

The results are entirely predictable: Performances of the Shanghai-style *Vagina Monologues* that was rehearsed last February were ultimately prohibited. A few days later, a musical version of Ensler's script that had just completed rehearsals was also prohibited from being performed. Rehearsals for two of the more salacious plays mentioned above—Xiu Guochun's *Break Up When It Is Dawn* and Yu Rongjun's *Life Should Be in Bed*—were promptly shut down. A ban against one play gives a strong hint, for institutions like the Shanghai Dramatic Arts Center, to steer clear of similar plays that might also be deemed unsuitable.

I began my struggle as an individual playwright upon learning the tragedy of my situation some 20 years ago: Politically, I was being buried alive. To be told to say nothing, I felt, was the same as dying. [*Editor's note:* At the onset of the Cultural Revolution in 1966, Zhang's family became a Red Guard target and was ostracized. Zhang was exiled to remote Yun'an in southwest China until 1978, when college entrance exams were reinstated and he entered Shanghai's drama academy. After a couple of years, he was sent back to Yun'an where he was assigned to work in a sweater factory. He continued to write stories, poetry and plays, until he drifted back to Shanghai in 1986.]

In the 1980s a lot of theatrical productions went on to condemn, rather than extol, the Cultural Revolution that had just ended. Musical revues that sang the praises of the Communist Party claimed that the Party is always right, that the Revolution was caused by a few bad eggs, and that the Chinese people will love the Party forever. When these criticisms reached their limit, soon plays about the Cultural Revolutions became prohibited.

Retreating to a distant and lonely place, I began creating several fable plays. *A House-bound Owl*, written in 1986 and produced in Shanghai in 1989, is about a woman living in the seclusion of her apartment who becomes so immersed in her dreams and recollections that she loses all sense of reality. Her husband, whom she discovers is impotent, uses hypnosis to give her an orgasm. A 1987 play, *Fashion Street*, produced two years later, centers on the exploits of a fashion designer aspiring to be on the cutting edge and to become a darling of the elite. Ironically his unconventional concepts are quickly picked up and copied among the masses. Later he ceases designing trendy outfits altogether and decides to show only his naked body. But then the fashion district becomes ridden with naked people. Furious and unable to set himself apart, he tears away his skin.

Just three years prior to the recent "spring of *wenyi*," I wrote *Calling Life*, which depicts the inconstancies of life through the story of a Chinese man who orders all his services by phone, everything from laundry and cooking to a weekend-wife. A disguised form of prostitute, weekend-wives offer their special services for some male customers who are tired of ordinary prostitutes. My protagonist finds a qualified "wife" who doesn't offer him sex at first and simply keeps him company. He falls in love, and they sign a one-year contract agreeing to make love every weekend. Eventually the man discovers that it is he that is being used by the uncaring woman as her sex partner—and he feels as though he has become her prostitute.

Calling Life, which takes the form of a "daily drama," is representative of a number of my new plays, including *Backroom*, in which a middle-aged single man taken by a friend to an illegal nightclub in search of sex suddenly suspects he has fallen into a trap set up by the secret police; and *Join the Party*, about a philosophy student who informs his professor of his interest in joining "the Party," but whose motivation is finally revealed as increasing his chances of being hired as a university professor after graduation.

Unsatisfied in the 1990s with writing table plays, I wrote new works that run the gamut of styles: verse plays like *Insomnia Makes Me So Happy* and *Remember the Woman Who Fell*; installation and game plays, like *Chinese Dog, Salty Fish*; parade plays like *Long Live the People*; musical plays like *What We Like Eating* and *The Cover on the Sewer*; and so forth. None of them have ever been produced in China.

Are these political plays? They are, in the special environment of Chinese culture. Because my plays often show lives that exist outside the accepted moral limits, they look like political provocations in the eyes of the Chinese government. I think of them as consciousness-raising plays, reflecting a social ideology. If they were to be actually mounted, managers of the state-owned theatres or the producers themselves would be in greater trouble than I would as the author. Some of my friends in the theatre have suggested that these plays should remain hidden in the closet until the policy of *wenyi* is looser. Because I have been considered a "dangerous figure" by the government, everything I write is thought to challenge the political system, even though sometimes the plays themselves don't involve political matters.

The Communist Party's control of Chinese culture began in 1949, after the People's Liberation Army (made up mostly of poor young peasants) came to Shanghai and quickly established the committees on military and cultural control. The latter committee's job was to root out the urban culture of Shanghai and assist the government in completely transforming a very modern and cosmopolitan place (the fourth largest city in the world) into a huge collective. All entertainment places, including ballrooms and skating-rinks, were shut down. All theatrical troupes were folded into the system of state ownership and were turned into propaganda entities. Appointed by the party, their leaders selected the playwrights and directors, who were required to report their subject matter and stories before they created plays and productions. No work was to begin without the leaders' approval. The average personnel of each troupe participated in the dissection of plays under review. Plays were checked again and again until they were confirmed to have no political problem—only then could rehearsals begin. Officials of the Culture Ministry and Propaganda Department attended dress rehearsals.

Worried that they would lose their political power after the Tiananmen Square massacre of 1989, Communist Party officials have since adjusted their tactics and started to carry out a policy of internal control. On the outside they seem lax, but on the inside they have remained rigid, underhanded and austere. Outside China, authorities foster an image that favors an open-door policy for the purpose of attracting international investment. Behind the scenes, meanwhile, these same officials have strengthened their ideological control and concealed their methods.

Chinese officials today still issue documents about their new policy to manage *wenyi*, but more often orders are given through a simple phone call, asking for changes in everything down to the smallest details, like the title of an article or some questionable word.

In the summer of 1994, an officer of the Shanghai Propaganda Department found many political problems in my play *Margin Calls* when she attended the dress rehearsals. At midnight the Propaganda Department held an urgent meeting and decided to send orders by calling different media outlets before 5 a.m. the next morning: All reports, articles and production photos of *Margin Calls* were to be prohibited. My name was disallowed to see print in the next two years, although, as a matter of fact, no media reported on any theatrical activity of mine even after the two years expired. "The ban was never withdrawn," one reporter told me.

The following morning, radio and television stations and newspapers withdrew their articles and reviews about *Margin Calls*; that afternoon my producer called different media representatives and got the same reply: "We got a call from the Propaganda Department. We have been notified to stop reporting on *Margin Calls*. You should know, it came 'from the top.'"

As he put down the receiver, my producer remarked, "The Communist Party is the party in power, but its style looks more like an underground mafia."

In China, all political persecutions are justified for reasons of national security. Apparently, China is always at risk, and a theatrical production or a movie may subvert government policies. Individual rights have to be sacrificed. We must keep our silence.

When I was arrested 20 years ago in the library of Shanghai Theatre Academy, I suddenly understood that everyone in China is living a "National Drama." While in jail I realized that, ever since we were children, we have been actors playing our parts in this super-theatre; we have all been cast in faceless roles, the action has to follow the director, and everyone speaks and moves in accord. I didn't understand at first the reasons for my arrest, although I did know that I had written some articles for an underground publication and made contact with several foreign students. I was sentenced, in the end, to one year in jail on a charge of malfeasance, which meant that I leaked out state secrets by giving a foreign student a factory newspaper published during the Cultural Revolution. But the truth is that I was punished for not playing my role well in China's National Drama.

This National Drama is directed by a powerful and mysterious will. We follow it blindly, although we don't truly understand what it wants. But we know it requires us to attend the same national ceremonies and say the unified actors' lines. All of our expressions look alike; we wear face masks. Our bodies operate like wooden figures.

At first I thought of this National Drama as a tragedy, but then later I came to understand that it was a comedy, a kind of farce, and I pledged that I should start writing my own drama when I got out of jail. It was a drama that would belong only to myself. It would be an individual theatre that exists inside and yet is in opposition to the National Drama. Because I want my theatre to be a weapon against the autocracy and injustices of my society, it would be a kind of anti-drama under the National Drama.

The subject matter of China's endless and everlasting National Drama shifts and changes according to the winds of political movements, ranging from Communism and Cultural Revolutions to economic reforms.

Today the subject is money. Because productions of plays are viewed as commercial gambits, some degree of boldness and sexual frankness are allowed—every once in a while—to be shown on stage. State-owned theatres mimic shows that are initiated and produced by small independent groups, belonging to what I call a "civilian theatre," a notion that is deliberately alternative and counterpoised to "the people's theatre." For in China, companies that are routinely described as "the people's" are not truly "the people's" at all, and those who are conscious of their "civil rights," "individuality" and "civil society" are derided as *xiao shi min*, or "little citizens."

Under the auspices of this "civilian theatre," two of my plays have been produced in the tighter post-1989 climate: *Margin Calls*, about a Chinese overseas broker who tries unsuccessfully to become involved with two women in the futures market of Shanghai in 1990, and *His Wife Back from America*, about an ambitious Chinese woman who returns to Shanghai from the U.S. to file divorce proceedings against a husband who never left China. Though financed by several business investors, both shows used the production licenses of state theatres, which require that any show be subject to propaganda-department checkups. Performed in Shanghai's "little theatres," both deliver their social messages with greater complexity than the ringing party/state discourse favored on Chinese television and other propagandistic *wenyi*.

I was very surprised to find that both productions had box-office appeal. It felt strange to suddenly realize that I had become a force in China's new mainstream theatre, so I withdrew immediately and had two other plays produced with a radical posture. *Crowd*, about the abuse of power by an aggressive man who attacks other people in a congested bus, had strong runs in Guangzhou and Shanghai. However, *Tales of a Vat Player*, which ridicules Chinese intellectuals who play games with influential government officials, was shut down after the Propaganda Department realized that it was an allegory of the regimes of Mao Zedong, Deng Xiaoping and Jiang Zeming.

My theatre today, it seems, has become a new barometer of the *wenyi* policy in Shanghai. Some people say I am a loser. Others consider me a success. But for me, success and failure are no different from each other. I would rather spend all my life as a kind of "special society performer"—a dissident actor playing his unofficial part in China's National Drama. I write plays with the knowledge that they will be forbidden. I am like a social performer always acting on society's stage and always clinging to my theatrical role in the individual struggle against the National Drama.

At the beginning of 2004, the news from Beijing is that newer reforms will be instituted, and all Chinese theatres, which have been owned by the state for 50 years, will return to private ownership. This year, the central government has cut off all subsidized funding for state-owned troupes. Theatrical workers will be thrown to the mercy of market forces. They are to become self-supporting.

Will the theatres still play their part in the National Drama or become independent players? Who knows what will transpire in the next act? Thousands of Chinese theatre workers, of course, will do anything for their art and their own survival. As they explore the borders of the commercial market, and advance to the last realm—politics—they will come to understand that the political realm is full of commercial potential.

Zhang Xian, a freelance playwright and theatremaker in Shanghai, has written 40 plays, 9 of which have been produced in China.

Tang Ying, the translator, is a freelance writer and filmmaker who has written seven works of fiction.

IS YOUR PLAY A VIRGIN?

By Theresa Rebeck

January 2005

Sheri Wilner has written a play. Apparently it's a pretty good play—when her agent sent it out she got three offers for productions, in addition to strong interest from other theatres which weren't yet quite ready to bite. Unfortunately, when they found out there was already a production slated for spring of 2005, all the other theatres withdrew their interest. "If they couldn't be first, the play was dead to them," Wilner says.

Ronan Noone has written a play. It received a workshop production at the Boston Playwrights' Theatre, got raves from the critics and won all of the Boston area's major theatre awards. It has never had another production. "The thing won a ton of awards, and I've only ever seen 12 performances of it, with student actors," Noone admits. "Who were great. It was a terrific production. I'd just like to see it again."

Suzanne Bradbeer has written a play. Her work has been seen in many theatres regionally and Off-Off Broadway, where she has a growing reputation. A New York theatre actually commissioned this play and paid her $1,000 to write it. Then, a larger theatre in Connecticut read it, and now they want to produce it as well—but may back out, because they want the premiere, which has been promised, even though the commissioning theatre is only slated to present an Equity waiver production not open to critics. "It took me two years to write this thing," Bradbeer says. "Am I being told that a thousand dollars is all I'm ever going to make? Is one Equity waiver production all I'm ever going to see?"

For those of you who don't know about this dandy system, here is how it works: The vast majority of American theatres are obsessed with producing World Premieres. Some theatre people call this phenomenon "premiere-itis," identifying it, appropriately enough, as a disease. Premiere-itis demands that if 12 theatres like that play and want to produce it, then the playwright has to pick only one of those productions and dismiss the other 11—even if they are all in different cities where there will be no possible overlap of audiences whatsoever. Of course, if after that one production, the play gets picked up by a New York theatre, and if the New York production goes well, and if the reviews are good, and if the play gets an extended run, then other theatres around the country can, again, do it. So, if what happened to *Proof*, or to *Wit*, or to *Art*—or to my play *Bad Dates*—happens to you, eureka, good for you. But if you don't have all of those nearly impossible things happen to your play, then the likelihood is that one three-week production somewhere will constitute its life. This is the rule of premiere-itis.

Sometimes more established writers can put together co-productions or juggle the system better than less established writers can. Some plays and playwrights just get a pass on premiere-itis altogether, for reasons which are desperately mysterious to everyone else. But exceptions are just that, and the unfortunate rule is: Once your play has lost its virginity, it's ruined. And virginity is easy to lose. A non-Equity waiver showcase might be enough to pop the cherry. And then your play is ruined.

As one might imagine, this is not a formula that actually works for, or even makes a shred of sense to, most playwrights. When it happens that you write a play which excites people to the point that it attracts several offers of production, only to find you have to pick one—and only one—you really just want to blow your brains out. "If you ask me, the theatre that gets the so-called 'sloppy seconds'—the already premiered play—is probably getting a better play than the first theatre," notes Wilner. "So many kinks are worked out during that first production. Unanticipated problems discovered and solved; audience reactions gauged and changes made accordingly—how many times do we walk out of the final performance saying, 'Okay, now we know how to do this play?'"

So why do so many theatres seem to like the one-production arrangement? When you check in with theatre management, their answer is pretty simple: grants. According to Karen Chilcote, associate director for corporate and foundation relations at Seattle Repertory Theatre—which supports new plays with admirable consistency—the number of grant-writing opportunities for a world-premiere run is in the double digits. She knew of no grant-writing opportunities that would provide funding for plays that were not world premieres.

Janice Paran, dramaturg at the McCarter Theatre Center in Princeton, N.J., sees a second factor playing into the obsession with premieres. "Marketing departments further hope to generate enthusiasm by broadcasting a play's status as a 'world premiere,' an 'American premiere,' or even a 'regional premiere,'" she states. "I'm not sure those marketing tags make a lick of difference, but everyone uses them."

In a completely unscientific poll conducted to find out whether or not those tags make a lick of difference or not, I asked random theatregoers what they looked for in a new play. These were their responses:

"I usually look for an actor I like or playwright or topic. I'm looking to be challenged by plays and to have a different type of thinking in the theatre than I do at the movies or watching TV, where I usually do three things at once."

"Usually I go because Rusty (my stepson, an actor) or one of his actor/director/writer friends is involved and has said this is something they are excited about. I guess that would fall into the broad category of 'word of mouth.'"

"Sometimes we're looking for a different viewpoint. Sometimes a validation of our views. Sometimes just for fun. There's nothing wrong with enjoying yourself."

I also asked if anyone was more interested in world premieres than in any random new play that was out there. These were their responses:

"No."

"No."

"No. Whether a play has been done before is never an issue—the point is, it's new to me. Theatres that want to do only world premieres seem to be practicing a bizarre type of fetishism."

Out of 30 answers to this question, I got not one "yes." Okay, so obviously someone needs to explain to marketing personnel that this whole "world premiere" thing is a boneheaded maneuver, if you're trying to attract people to come see your play. Someone also needs to explain to funding organizations that obsessing on world premieres is completely counterproductive in terms of the health of the art form, not to mention the mental health of the playwright. Can't somebody tell these people that second and third productions are just as important as the first? I contacted TCG and several research foundations that track grant-writing policies, and none of them knew of grants for second or third productions. Nor did they seem terribly interested in the question. Too many people in management seem to accept that new-play grants are necessarily going to support world premieres. But why?

At this moment in time, the choice to be a playwright is absurdly optimistic in its embrace of the belief that stories told outside the crushing demands of corporate capitalism will have significance and weight for a community. Playwrights are, in fact, optimists, once you get past all the depression and anxiety. And our playwrights are asking a serious question here for all of us in the American theatre: What kind of theatre survives, much less thrives, without a commitment to the overall life of the play?

Theresa Rebeck's plays include *Our House, Mauritius, The Scene, Bad Dates, The Family of Mann, Spike Heels* and *View of the Dome. Omnium Gatherum* (co-written with Alexandra Gersten-Vassilaros) was a finalist for the 2003 Pulitzer Prize. She is also the author of *Free Fire Zone*, a book of comedic essays about writing and show business, and the novel *Three Girls and Their Brother*. In television, she has written for "Law and Order: Criminal Intent," "Third Watch" and "NYPD Blue," among other shows. Her produced feature films include *Harriet the Spy, Gossip* and the independent feature *Sunday on the Rocks*.

THE LYING GAME

By Zelda Fichandler

January 2005

Stella Adler once quoted her father Jacob, patriarch of the Yiddish theatre, on the reasons why someone wants to become an actor: "You don't want to get up early, you don't want to work and you're afraid to steal."

But seriously, why does someone want to become an actor? To enter that arena with the lions and subject oneself to rejection on a regular basis? To chance the masochism of love for a profession that makes no promise to love you back? To risk a life of temping and maybe even poverty? To postpone having a committed relationship or raising a family? Why in the world would you even dream of becoming an actor, let alone audition for a graduate acting program—running up a debt that not only means you'll go without steak dinners and dental work, but that could define your choices until you're almost middle-aged?

If you're in such a program, I'm sure your mother asked you these very same questions. I hope you didn't get angry when she did. And I hope you didn't respond, "I wouldn't even consider, simply can't imagine, would rather die than be a lawyer or a doctor or anything but an actor! Why, ever since I was in the third grade, remember when we went to see *The Sound of Music,* how excited I was . . . ."

That's not enough; that won't see you through. You have to really understand the nature of your commitment, the depth of it and its sustainability under pressure.

Let's say you've chosen—you insist on it—to defy the odds and become an artist at all costs, financial as well as psychic. In an act of strong will, and after a period of ambivalence, I'm sure, you've decided to make your way in a crowded, competitive, inhospitable profession. I congratulate you for that leap and offer some words of advice.

At Tisch School of the Arts, where I teach, we ask our students to hang on stubbornly to the "why" of their presence there. There are periods of not knowing how one thing relates to another. An actor in training must live in that state. In moments of doubt or fatigue or tedium, when you are doing repetitions for a voice class or memorizing lines or rehearsing a scene at a God-awful time of night, when you think that you'll never live up to expectations, repeat the mantra of your commitment and stay the course.

Since you know why you are on this path and how urgent it is for you, please give your teachers your trust; the longer you withhold it, the longer will the changes within you be delayed. Do your best to be open and vulnerable. Surrender cynicism. If you experience fear or shame, thrust through it. If you enjoy the work, that's a real bonus. You should *expect* to feel joy.

Adopt an attitude of curiosity that will lead you into the work rather than away from it. In your training, you will be bombarded with many new things to do and new ways to do the things you've always done. There's juggling and the trapeze, simulating punches and slaps and fighting with daggers and swords. There's researching the world that gave birth to a particular play. There's breathing in a new way and learning muscular relaxation. (A word of caution: Never confuse relaxation with nap time—in class, rehearsal or, Thespis forbid, on the stage!—or with being anything other than alert, poised to act, to do, even if you're sitting quietly in a chair. The basic law of our technique is that something inside of us is always in motion.)

The hardest thing may turn out to be not what we traditionally think of as "working"—not physical or even intellectual effort—but rather, the act of surrendering; allowing things to happen to you rather than lunging after them. This may be the most revolutionary notion to master after a lifetime of slogans like "Good, better, best / Never let it rest / Till the good is better / And the better best." Numberless demands are made on us even before we're old enough to internalize them. Clean your plate or you can't go out to play. You have seven minutes to finish the test. Big boys don't cry . . . . It takes time to dissolve the restrictions of an educational system where answers are either right or wrong and where uniqueness can be perceived as disruptive. Be patient as you discover the ways in which you are not replaceable by anyone else.

In thinking about my own life, I've decided my greatest talent has been in receiving criticism, incorporating it into my "attend-to" list and moving on. I learned somehow that criticism is a gift, or at least a commodity that can be very useful (and, after all, comes free). If you are defensive or too frightened to listen, or if you mistakenly think it is easy for others to find the precise way to move your work forward without demolishing your sense of self, you are holding back your own progress. If you see how everything contributes to your becoming an artist—from fixing your slouch, to ridding yourself of speech regionalisms, to gaining flexibility and daring within your very psyche—perhaps you will come to welcome critical evaluations as a demonstration of interest in you and of a desire to help you to claim and evolve your talent.

I return to my first question: Why would someone want to be an actor? The response to this is crucial and is the reason I've been besotted with the theatre for most of my life.

If I had the gift of being an actor, I would have bent my will, energy, time and money to become the very best one I could be. I chose instead to produce, direct, teach, and especially to create structures that would make it possible for others to live their lives as actors. Actors are the very center of the theatrical experience, for only a human being can embody another human being. It's to see what can happen to a human in this time between two darknesses—and imaginatively what, then, could happen to one's own self—that audiences need the living experience of theatre.

Each of us is given but one life: the life of a fly measured against eternity. That life might seem to us to be a free one in terms of choice and possibility. In limited ways it is, but in major ways it is quite determined. Chromosomes decide our sex, the color of our skin and eyes, our bone structure, our predisposition to certain talents and tastes and even to the illnesses that ultimately will whisk us away. The one life we have is determined, too, by how the knobs of inherited characteristics are turned by the culture into which we happen to be born.

Do we want to be hemmed in by one fate? Especially for a creature with high imagination, who is naturally empathetic, curious and daring, is one life enough? I think the sense of the possibilities of other lives within us propels some of us to want be part of the maddening, glorious world of theatre.

The ultimate companion of mankind should be *com-passion*, "feeling with." That message threads through the body of Shakespeare's work. Perhaps even if you were a Jew, you could find a way to play a Palestinian suicide bomber, depending on how far you could stretch that ability to *feel with*. Would you choose to play him—or her—as a crazy? An uncultured bandit? You could, surely. Or you could play him as someone who has not received from life what he has expected, has seen atrocity, who looks at this singular act of terror as an "instant of courage," as it is propagandized by his society. If you choose to play him this way, you would find support in Mahmoud Darwish's "Psalm 11": "Nothing remains for me / but to inhabit your voice that is my voice."

I don't know if you would want to undertake this role. But if you did, and chose to play the character from his own point of view, you would have the opportunity to open the mind of the audience to a different, and perhaps to them dangerous, way of looking at a reality they thought they already knew. You would give them sight into an alien soul. *Tikkun olam*: in Hebrew, "to repair the world." We are the only animal who strives to do that. In my view, that is the specific creative mission of the actor.

Another "why": The actor is allowed the ultimate reward—the enduring thrill of human encounter. There is ebullient joy in performing as an acting company, as an individual part of an organic whole that would not be the same without you, nor you the same without it. The company is the natural habitat of the actor; alternate systems fall short. It's possible that an acting company can be assembled for a single production and work out quite well, or a company could be brought together for administrative and economic reasons. But neither of these systems provides the creative advantages of a company that has evolved from the same aesthetic root, in which you're all playing the game by the same rules. Without its members having a basis in common training, the words "acting company" are misapplied.

If professional actors are members of a company, they've learned to live within the same world in any given production. They've mastered the technique of give-and-take. They are comfortable with the notion of spontaneity within form (or form to support spontaneity; it can be stated either way). It feels natural to vary their performances slightly now and again, as they suddenly understand a line in a new way, while still maintaining the overall pattern laid down in rehearsals—with confidence that no one will report them to the stage manager. The sense of competition—"this is my performance, don't get in the way of it"—gives way to the collective will.

Let's say you're on stage in the Ides of March scene from *Julius Caesar*. Here comes Caesar himself, Cassius and Brutus, Metellus Cimber, Cinna the Poet. You know what your relationship to them will be for the next 12 minutes, what will transpire. But what is most important, you know who's inside the togas and under the helmets: It's Sanjit and Bill and Harry and Peter and Mano and so on. They're the ones you've eaten lunch with, criticized in class, took to the emergency room, begged to clear their rotting fruit from the dressing table. Now you're playing a game together—the great, profound, physical, fun game of acting. Afterwards maybe you'll go out for a beer. You're from the same tribe; you have elders to learn from and youngsters to initiate. An acting company both avoids and civilizes what is truly barbaric about the one-shot production method of the Broadway theatre, which sees the actor as another commodity from which to grow rich and is oblivious to him as an ever-evolving artist equally as important to society as a teacher, doctor or spiritual leader.

I think the following is *my* "why" for sustaining a life in the theatre for over half a century. It's about the audience: my friends and neighbors; the visitors of different colors; the despairing who lead tight, circumscribed lives; the rich and comfortable who in the dark may experience guilt and the rich and comfortable whose hunger can never be assuaged; the wide-eyed children in their one good dress; the lonely one in a single seat; the Masons in their funny hats; the cognizant and the non-knowing; the old who can forget about dying for a few hours; the egoists; the damned; the teenagers who under their bravado and with rings in every part of their anatomy yearn to be useful. The Audience, the terminus of all our work. God bless them all.

They enter into a conspiracy of belief with us, and it would not be moral to betray them. I called what we do a game, and I don't take it back. But it's a game with stakes higher than any other game I know. It's not about getting the shuttlecock over the net or about having your foot on the plate, more important even than flirting to snag that handsome guy at the buffet table. This quirky game is also an elaborate deception, prepared over months and years. We must admit theatre is a lying game, and actors lie to play it. But they are lies designed to trap the truth, and the more convincing they are, the deeper the truth that is exposed.

The audience eggs us on: "Just lie like mad, and give us your golden truth. The Prologue asks us, 'Think when we talk of horses that you see them / Printing their proud hoofs i' the receiving earth / For 'tis your thoughts that now must deck our kings.' Yes, of course we'll imagine right along with you. Give it to us, we'll give it back; play with us, we'll play along."

A conspiracy of belief, I said, and we mustn't disappoint. We have to believe in the imaginative world with everything we've got. But, I remind you, that belief has to stop just short of falling into the orchestra pit, or, as Medea, howling in anguish on the street outside the theatre after you've killed your children, drawing the police with your cries and jeopardizing tomorrow's sold-out matinee. Just short of this formless excess must we play out our "as ifs." If the actor can contain herself just below the level of the truth, she has an opportunity to reach a *supra-truth* and move us to understand the un-understandable—that a woman's feelings of rage and abandonment could be so ravenous as to lead her to destroy what she loves. Theatre does indeed fabricate everything from the storm's roar to the lark's song, from the actor's laughter to her nightly flood of tears. That actor may nevertheless construct a vision of the human condition that opens us to a new understanding of ourselves. What could be more important than that?

How actually one does this is, of course, the subject matter of actors' training. All technique is in the service of spontaneous life. A famous Hungarian bassist said the same thing: "One must work one's fingers again and again so that one is able to say the things of one's heart."

Or, to take the stunning statement that concludes Arthur Miller's essay "On Politics and the Art of Acting": "However dull or morally delinquent an artist may be, in his moment of creation, when his work pierces to the truth, he cannot dissimulate, he cannot fake it. Tolstoy once remarked that what we work for in a work of art is the revelation of the artist's soul, a glimpse of God. You can't fake that."

Zelda Fichandler is the artistic director of the graduate acting program at New York University's Tisch School of the Arts, and served as its chair from 1984 to 2007. She is a co-founder of Arena Stage in Washington, D.C., where she was producing artistic director from 1950 to 1990. This essay is drawn from remarks she delivered to 2003–04 students and faculty of the Tisch graduate acting program.

CHEKHOV: SHORTER, FASTER, FUNNIER AND UNCUT

By Tom Donaghy

May/June 2005

In the Novodevichy Cemetery, on the outskirts of Moscow, the legendary director Konstantin Stanislavsky lies entombed under an enormous marble gravestone. The marker is etched with the slightly abstracted image of a seagull, the icon of the Moscow Art Theatre, where Anton Chekhov's play *The Seagull* premiered, and where, not so arguably, modern drama was refined in the wake of Ibsen and launched into the world.

A few yards away, the gravestone of Chekhov himself can be found. It is, compared to Stanislavsky's, demure. Perhaps four feet tall, it is a white obelisk, hewn from unpolished marble and capped with a bronze gable. On it, the playwright's name is spelled out in Cyrillic lettering, slanting in the triangled cursive that was the style of the then flourishing Art Nouveau movement. Chekhov's wife—Olga Knipper, who would perform in his masterwork, *The Cherry Orchard*, for some 40 years (photo records show her becoming stout and severe as the decades pass)—is buried at his side.

On July 15, Chekhov will have been dead for a century and a year. He breathed his last in a ritzy spa in Badenweiler, Germany, 1,500 or so miles from his grocery-store beginnings, after drinking a glass of champagne and sighing, "It's a long time since I drank champagne." His body was returned to Moscow, and since then his legend has grown there and everywhere. A portraitist by nature, originally writing humorous sketches and stories for newspapers in St. Petersburg, Chekhov was revered in his lifetime for four complex and cherished plays before tuberculosis and its ravages exiled him to the seaside resort of Yalta. It was a Chekhovian end to 44 years of labor, love, ennui and empathy.

His legacy is certain. His plays, however, remain open to interpretation. He himself notoriously insisted that *The Seagull* and *The Cherry Orchard* were "gay, lighthearted, comedies," but this was ignored by Stanislavsky, who directed the plays, according to Chekhov, as "weepy."

The two men were often at loggerheads as a result. The premiere production of *The Cherry Orchard*, rehearsing in Moscow while the playwright withered in Yalta, gave Chekhov his final chance to decry what he saw as Stanislavsky's enduring misinterpretation of his work. As his strength evanesced, he roused himself, fired up his pen and dashed off acid-tinged missives that warned Stanislavsky against employing his familiar, cloying theatrical tricks. These usually involved the offstage sounds of dogs barking, birds singing and frogs croaking. Early in their collaboration, an exasperated Chekhov even exclaimed, "I shall write a new play and the first words will be, 'It's wonderful, this calm! No birds, no dogs, no cuckoos, no owls, no nightingales, no clocks, no sleigh bells, no crickets.'"

But Stanislavsky ignored the directives, and Chekhov, when finally taken to Moscow to attend opening night, was more or less disgusted by what he saw on stage. "Stanislavsky has ruined my play," he wrote Olga. "Oh well, I don't suppose anything can be done about it."

He supposed right. And in the 100 years that followed, something intractable began to take hold. By ignoring the playwright's intentions, Stanislavsky seems to have established a tradition for how Chekhov's plays would be directed—and often misdirected—to this day. They have been remade and deconstructed. They have been springboards for directorial theories, from Eva Le Gallienne's to Joshua Logan's to Andrei Serban's to Peter Brook's. A recent production of *The Cherry Orchard*, directed by Eimuntas Nekrosius of Lithuania, clocked in at six hours. New York City's Wooster Group refracted *Three Sisters* through live video feed. The plays have been set in decrepit theatres, Northern Ireland, the Gullah Islands—you name it. They have often bored audiences to tears, and sometimes they have been as full of bells and whistles as a Ringling Brothers dressing room. They have played like Strindberg at his gloomiest and Neil Simon at his schtickiest. No doubt somewhere on this earth the curtain is about to rise on a shadow puppet version of *Uncle Vanya*.

What of the text, though, untethered to directorial interpretation? What does it say to us on its own? Even more important, how does it say it?

Lately, I've been reading a literal translation of *The Cherry Orchard* for an adaptation I'm creating for Atlantic Theater Company's current season. The work is by Ronald Meyer, director of the M.A. program in Russian literary translation at Columbia University. It is a verbatim translation from the original Russian text to American English—as close to reading Chekhov's original script as any non-Russian-reading reader can get. What's more, it is eye-poppingly different from any "Chekhov" I've ever read in the 20 years that I've been familiar with his plays.

What is striking at first about the translation is the text's sui generis nature. It is its own thing—exotic and resistant to seeming like anything else, adaptable to no other settings. Its integrity is utterly sound; to transpose its characters to a different time or place seems unnecessary and slightly cuckoo. And yet, of course, Chekhov's plays—more than any other playwright's save for Shakespeare's—seem to suffer a kind of mania for interpretation.

The other striking thing about the translation, which is apparent from the first page, is its twin strains of brutality and hilarity. The play possesses both, with very little transition between the two. The characters and their emotions, are, as Australians say, "all over the shop." At a moment in time when drama seems to need to explain, spell out, comfort and offer lessons, Chekhov's final play stands in gorgeous resistance to these tasks. It jerks you through the air; yet there is no net below. It does not comfort; on the contrary, it agitates—but at the most fundamental and emotional level. This is upsetting, but also exhilarating and, yes, very funny. You are unprepared as a reader—and even though you think you might be familiar with the play, you have no idea where you are being taken.

And you are, no question, being taken. For something that seems on the face of it plotless, nonlinear and willfully static, there courses underneath this play a vitality that is antic and not entirely kind. The play wants to toss you about. Similar to the vertiginous feeling you get as you try to grab hold of Virginia Woolf's sentences, with their incautious swoops, Chekhov's play can fling you somewhere, and you arrive before you even realize you've been flung. And then you are off again. At the end of the play, when axes are heard taking great chunks out of the cherry trees, the reader is breathless, shaken and suspicious of the ground beneath. But giggly—giddy even. People behave ridiculously; this is life.

Then why is it we don't always feel this when seeing a production of these plays? I have a hunch the problem begins with adaptations. Adaptations happen. But how? One of two ways, really. They can be generated from a literal translation of the original text (what I'm doing): the translator one person, the adaptor another. Or, in rare cases, such as when a playwright speaks Russian, the translator and adaptor can be one and the same. This is the case with the elegant adaptations of the scholar and theatre artist Paul Schmidt.

There are, however, a whole lot of dunderheaded adaptations of Chekhov's plays, such as the one I—and many others—first read in college by the artistically named Constance Garnett. The fault with these adaptations seems to be embellishment: straightening out the kinked way Chekhov's scenes proceed; having the characters make more "sense" by smoothing over what seem to be their abrupt reversals of mood; theatricalizing the plays, akin to what Stanislavsky did in his productions, in order to foster a kind of naturalism that the plays do not really possess on the page. Often adaptations want to make the characters merely tragic, or worse, loveable.

In Janet Malcolm's *Reading Chekhov*, she observes that when you utter the name "Chekhov" in Russia, no less than in our own country, people "arrange their features as if a baby deer had come into the room." This fawning reference surrounding Chekhov's reputation has transferred itself to the adaptations and productions of his plays, resulting in a kind of pretty veneer that has built up over them in the

course of the last century. But this gauzy, huggable overlay is not war-
ranted. It would have outraged the famously unsentimental playwright, who spent many years hacking due to the blood in his lungs.

There are also adaptations that politicize the plays, by tilting them
toward a prescient and specific awareness of the Russian revolution to
come. But Chekhov was not concerned with politics. On the subject of
political action his plays are, if anything, about people's inability to
actually engage in it. Chekhov is not like his friend, the revolutionary
Maxim Gorky. Chekhov wrote about people and their inability to
organize their own world, not about people who were able to reorga-
nize—or even truly interested in reorganizing—the larger one.

All of these interpretations have the ability to distort adaptations
and wrench Chekhov's plays from their very simple conveyance of life
as it is actually lived—even today. People go about talking and making
love and hoping and having tea, and all the while things are being simply, effortlessly lost.

The most striking thing about the literal translation I am basing
my adaptation on, however, is its remarkable brevity. It is 73 pages. As
many of us know, a playscript is usually nearer 120 pages, signaling—
the rule is a minute a page—a two-hour play. A 73-page play starting at
8 p.m. would then come down about 9:13 p.m. This begs an important
question: Who among us has ever seen a Chekhov play and made it to
dinner by 9:45?

When I asked Meyer what he may have cut to make the play so
short, he said, "Nothing. You're getting it word-for-word from the
original Chekhov text." Why then have we endured three-to-four-
hour versions of *The Cherry Orchard*? Chekhov himself said the last act
should run 12 minutes—he even wrote it this way because the characters are running for the train.

And as I read the translation for the first time, I saw exactly why
the play shouldn't be long: Its brevity is precisely what creates the 3-D
nature of its power. It is fast because it is dire. One wants it to slow
down for the sad parts, and it does, but then it lifts again with velocity
because it is inexorably moving toward its end—an end, by the way,
that has shades of both light and dark. Before seeing the literal translation, I only ever remembered the tragedy of the characters losing their
cherry orchard, but Meyer's translation suggests there is, for the characters, just as much relief as grief.

Indeed, one gets the feeling that Lyubov Ranevskaya, the owner of
the orchard, will be able to finally axe this Russian part of her life, lived
near the river where her only son drowned, to return to Paris where
she can continue to cheerfully—as they say today—reinvent herself.
When she's asked when she'll return to visit, she evades the question.
Leonid Gaev, her brother, remarks that everyone seems much more
content now that the orchard is sold. Her daughter, Anya, is made positively buoyant by what we have come to think of as a crippling loss. A
new life without the worries of a big estate sounds just peachy to her.
There are only three characters who seem to be truly put out: Varya,
but she is heading to a new job in town; Charlotta, the governess, who

as a former circus performer has been itinerant her whole life anyway; and the ancient servant and former serf, Firs, who wants nothing more than to die, and then promptly does—it seems so anyway—as the lights come down. What is so "weepy" about this?

In the end, perhaps, any adaptation should adhere to the only dictum I was able to glean from Anatoly Smeliansky, an associate director at the Moscow Art Theatre and head of the Moscow Art Theatre School. I met Smeliansky, an elfin man full of charm and seriousness—considered by many to be the world's foremost authority on Chekhov—in his offices on Kamergersky Lane, several floors above the stage on which Chekhov's plays were first presented. When I asked him how long my adaptation should be—or how many minutes he thought the play should run—he gave me a level look. "The play works long, and it works short," he said in his thick Muscovite accent. "Yes, but—" I said. "Listen to me," he said, cutting me off. "If it takes four hours, fine. If it takes 90 minutes, that's fine too. The important thing is that your audience understand the story you think Chekhov wanted to tell."

"Aha," I thought—and set about my work.

Tom Donaghy's plays include *Down the Shore, Northeast Local, Minutes from the Blue Route, From Above, The Beginning of August, Boys and Girls* and *Eden Lane.* Produced by some of the most prestigious theatres in the country—including Atlantic Theater Company, the Goodman Theatre, La Jolla Playhouse, Lincoln Center Theater, Playwrights Horizons, Seattle Repertory and South Coast Repertory—the plays are published in a collection by Grove Press.

THINKING ABOUT WRITING ABOUT THINKING ABOUT NEW PLAYS

By Jeffrey M. Jones

October 2005

> *He's the kind of character who really deserves to be in his own play,*
> *but we've denied him one.*
> —actor James Urbaniak, on the character of Thom Pain

It's easy to get discouraged about the theatre. What I find most discouraging (you may disagree) is the prospect of nothing ever changing about the way plays are imagined or written or written about or understood. How off-putting it would be if the theatre just kept presenting the same kind of plays based on the same small set of templates—year in, year out, same as it ever was—while I grew older and older and finally . . . stopped going, I suppose.

But another part of me says that's nonsense. Theatrical experiment is thriving as never before: Why, in the past year alone in one little enclave by the Hudson River, we've had wildly unorthodox new plays (in the sense that everyone understands the term "play") from Banana Bag and Bodice, Sheila Callaghan, Erin Courtney, Will Eno, Madeleine George, Rinne Groff, Rob Handel, Ann Marie Healy, Julia Jarcho, Len Jenkin (a known offender against the cult of orthodoxy), John Jesurun, Karinne Keithley, Kristen Kosmas, Paul Lazar and Annie-B Parson, Young Jean Lee, Ethan Lipton, Kirk Lynn, Richard Maxwell, Charlotte Meehan, Sally Oswald, Kate Ryan, Kelly Stuart, Alice Tuan, Anne Washburn, Mac Wellman (another known offender), Gary Winter—and who knows what-all elsewhere (for theatre is always local) across the land. Playwriting, it turns out, is in fine shape. The problem I'm really having is with the state of theatre criticism, which is largely unequipped to deal with this phalanx of new writers.

And no—I'm not going to say terrible things about critics. But consider the case of Will Eno, who earlier this year received a truly jaw-dropping rave in the paper of record, the clear and stated purpose of which was to make everyone want to rush out and see *Thom Pain (based on nothing)*, which they did. And why would this be a bad thing? Well, the night I went, the audience was pretty much the sort of folks you'd expect to be shelling out 60 bucks for an Off-Broadway show—theatre veterans, happy to have a hot ticket—and no sooner had the play begun than a miasmic pall fell over them, and there they sat glumly for another 70 minutes, resisting the show with a dull ferocity until they were released. And as they trooped out, what they said to each other was some variation of: "I don't know what that thing was supposed to be, but it sure as hell wasn't a play."

An off-night, I am told. But even so, isn't this the Artistic Director's Nightmare? You do a risky play (and Eno's play is, *inter alia*, weird, unpleasant, irritating, aggressive, manipulative and, like his *Tragedy: a tragedy*, a theatre of absence and withholding rather than presentation and presence); you have a critic who understands and loves the play for what it is; and then your audience comes and hates it for the very thing it is. If this is what necessarily happens—and I believe most theatre practitioners in our country have this expectation, born, alas, of painful experience—then why bother?

Does this mean, then, that the great bold dream of the not-for-profit movement—of revitalizing an art form by expanding the definition of what's possible—stands now revealed, some 40 years on, as a snare and a delusion? Is it in fact the case that theatre is so locked into a set of expectations—about what a play is, about what audiences want—that it is effectively paralyzed?

Of course, at any point in time, any art form consists of expectations with established thresholds beyond which most people cannot readily be led—"The Shock of the New," etc.—and, by the same token, there will always be a handful of people poking around beyond those very thresholds, making unorthodox work, which at the time will appeal to only a few. The problem is not that there are limits. The problem arises when, over time, those limits never change. In other words, the problem of theatre isn't that audiences will only go so far, but that over time, and despite 40 years of effort, they still seem unwilling to go anywhere except where they have gone before. And this, rightly, is recognized by theatres and artists as a paralyzing condition which is bad for all concerned (especially theatres and artists, even if a preponderance of those theatres and artists are—at any given time—quite happy in the mainstream).

If the field as a whole cannot include the new—or can only include it so incrementally as to make it imperceptible and marginal and irrelevant—then the field as a whole is profoundly and inherently conservative. I believe even artists with little personal appetite for radical work find this prospect troubling. Which may be why any discussion of The Problem of New Work so often takes the form of bafflement yielding to truculence: "So, is this how it is? Well, okay, then—get used to it. Unless you've got a *better idea* . . . ?"

The fact is that as long as the question is "How can anyone ever get an audience to accept and enjoy new and difficult work?" the cycle of frustration will be perpetuated, because the premise is based on the assumption that no one knows the solution. But once the question is reframed, and one inquires whether any other art form has faced a similar problem, the experience of 20th-century American painting surely becomes relevant.

I'm old enough to remember when educated Americans could claim, in print and for attribution, that Modernism (by which they actually meant an undifferentiated grab-bag of styles from Picasso to Pollock) was a "fraud," something "a six-year-old child could do better." Today nobody would dare make that claim. Nobody, that is, who isn't prepared to be dismissed as an ignoramus or cultural provocateur (with Tom Wolfe's 1975 *The Painted Word* leading that particular Pickett's Charge). Nor is the reason mysterious. Wander into any blockbuster Modernist exhibit, and you will find little old gray-haired ladies going through the galleries, nattering on about "the flatness of the picture-plane." Once little old gray-haired ladies feel comfortable discussing the flatness of the picture-plane, you can't write off Henri Matisse as no better than a six-year-old.

Now I had to go to college and take an art history class to learn about the flatness of the picture-plane; where on earth do the little old gray-haired ladies come by it? No mystery there, either: They can simply rent a headset and let Philippe de Montebello tell them what it is, and where to look for it, and why it matters so. They have, in other words, been taught to use a few terms and concepts—just as I was, just as Philippe de Montebello was, via the very process Robert Hughes describes in *The Shock of the New* (1981)—and, having acquired a handful of terms and concepts with which to discuss the work, they are suddenly and magically able to discuss and understand it—and, lo, the scales fall from their eyes and they see . . . .

Starting shortly after the Second World War, advocates of the visual arts in this country put an enormous amount of effort and energy into disseminating a core set of terms and concepts by which the "difficult" stuff could be discussed and understood. By the mid-1980s, their battle was essentially won, and the halls of the Guggenheims, Dias and MOMAs still swarm with gray-haired ladies and their descendants. Theatre, unless I have been missing something, has spent almost no effort or energy in defining, let alone disseminating, a core set of terms and concepts by which new plays might be discussed and understood. And I believe even the gray-haired ladies aren't subscribing the way they used to.

No museum of any size, no gallery of any importance, for heaven's sake, would mount a show without a catalog. And while a pricey museum catalog may sell on the basis of the souvenir value of the reproductions or its coffee-table cachet, the actual purpose of the catalog is to provide an essay that places the work-at-hand in the context of that shared set of core terms and concepts. In so doing, the catalog directly rebuts objections of fraud or technical incompetence. One need not read the catalog (I suspect hardly anyone does); the catalog does its essential work merely by existing. The catalog stands as a sentinel; its mere existence demonstrates that the work-at-hand cannot simply be dismissed. The catalog raises the bar of the discourse; it sets the tone and chooses the weaponry. One cannot impugn (let alone dismiss) the art on the walls without going through the catalog, and the catalog gives no quarter. The catalog does not even pretend to be easy or simple. The catalog merely insists that you must respond, if you dare, on its own terms.

Not that the art world is incapable of hubris or folly: You can't plop Richard Serra's aggressive whorl of Cor-Ten steel down into a corporate plaza without a reaction from the lunchtime crowds. You cannot really (and why was this ever a surprise?) expect the average sensual museumgoer to contemplate Robert Mapplethorpe's hardcore candids of sex on the pier without flinching. But these are tiny setbacks in an otherwise triumphal campaign for mass acceptance—a campaign echoed if not quite matched by similar efforts on behalf of dance, symphonic music, the novel and poetry. Which is why I humbly suggest that if little old gray-haired ladies can be taught to "read" Pollock and de Kooning and Anselm Kiefer and Gerhard Richter and Dan Flavin and Donald Judd and John Currin (because even figurative art dare not venture forth without a bodyguard today), they can surely be taught to "read" Mac Wellman, Melissa James Gibson, Will Eno and stranger, wilder creatures.

A true story: Some years ago, the Wooster Group was invited to remount *Rumstick Road* at New York City's American Place Theatre after its original run downtown. Artistic director Wynn Handman thought he could serve it up to his subscription audience, and I'd heard nothing but horror stories from my buddies in the Group—how almost as soon as the lights went down the audience started to get up and leave, continuing out in a steady stream until by the end there was hardly anyone left.

Imagine, then, my surprise upon attending a Wednesday matinee (!!) to find a crowd of fashionable middle-aged ladies not only sitting through the thing but paying attention and obviously having a grand time. This was so against expectation that I had to seek an answer, and it turned out they were a theatre group from Westchester whose leader had given them a little orientation on the bus ride down. Nothing, mind you, on the order of the "flatness of the picture-plane." The palpable pleasure these women derived from watching and "getting" the show—a pleasure indeed compounded both of enjoying the show on its own terms and feeling the self-congratulation which comes of "getting" something you've been told is "hard" and "difficult"—sprang entirely from this "explanation": that *Rumstick Road* a) was a piece about a mother's suicide, which b) was made by a younger generation of artists who c) had a lot of technology and media in their lives (hence all the tape recordings and slide projections and aggressive scoring) and d) watched a lot of television and liked to switch channels all the time (hence the disjunctive and associative structure of the piece).

That's all. Yet that simple and reductive explanation was enough to give the matinee ladies enough confidence to face *Rumstick Road* with the expectation that they would understand and recognize what the artists were doing. And sure enough—the lights went down and there were all the tape recorders and the slide projections and the loud blaring music and the mention of the mother's suicide and the jump-cuts between the scenes—and the women were so happy they practically cut each other off in mid-sentence trying to tell me that they enjoyed the show so much because *it happened just the way they'd been told it would.* This fulfillment of an expectation—their recognition of what they had been told to look for—was what made the show enjoyable. Whereas with *Thom Pain (based on nothing)* it was just the reverse. There was an audience that showed up to see a play (in the sense that everyone understands that term) and found something different—something that in fact was clearly not a play (though it stands in a clear and complex relationship to the sense in which everyone understands the term)—and for want of a context—the shared terms and concepts— found themselves baffled and alienated, hating the experience of being there and thus hating the "play."

So, is it realistic to expect art theory in a daily newspaper? I will let you compare the level of art and theatre criticism in your local paper (I'd say the answer is a qualified "yes"), but the dissemination of shared terms and concepts doesn't depend on a newspaper. And am I seriously suggesting that difficult, strange new plays—plays that are not plays in the sense that everyone understands that term—can be presented to a mainstream theatre audience? I am, indeed—presumptuously and in defiance of everything everyone "knows" about theatre—as long as one adopts the tools and techniques of the visual arts:

1. Theatres must accept that the presentation of new plays is Smart Fun, and be prepared to promote it accordingly. Theatre is so afraid of seeming "elitist" that it often pretends to be dumber than it really is, then tries to mend the damage by claiming that somehow, within its precincts, the "challenging" will be made "accessible." Which is nothing but a fiddle, which an audience will recognize as a fiddle, thereby leaving all parties to the transaction feeling sheepish.

   Is there really any reason not to appeal to intelligence— or at least, to the level of intelligence which is assumed, say, by the *New Yorker* or the *New York Times Book Review*? Is anyone likely to be put off by a presumption of intelligence? Is it possible that major American cities do not host even a few thousand people who would want to see new, strange, unusual plays—people who might find the very invitation bracing—as long as it came with the assurance that they would also be provided with the terms and concepts that would allow them to follow such current explorations at the forefront of theatre?

2. (And this follows from the previous.) The enterprise is not the work itself; the enterprise is creating a context for the work. In fact, the context is even more important than the work, and this is true especially at places like the Perform-

ing Garage and the Ontological-Hysteric Theater. *Those venues are the context.* Your experience of a production by Richard Foreman or Elizabeth LeCompte stands or falls by what you make of Foreman or LeCompte themselves (which is to say, the context). The piece itself—the actual lines spoken and actions performed on stage, the "content," if you will, or even, God help us, the "meaning" of the actual work-at-hand—is understood to be secondary if not irrelevant to the ongoing fact of the theatre and the artists whose work is shown there. The piece itself is just another instance of that true and ongoing work. So at any theatre presenting new plays, it must be the context that the audience is asked to attend more than any particular play. It is that context that the theatre, by its existence, proposes to establish—a context of explication—which must prove itself reliable and dependable and constant. Within that abiding context, the plays themselves will come and go.

3. Therefore (and this too follows from the previous), the context specifically must be, and be known to be, about providing ways to read and understand and discuss the work. Before spending money on production—even before spending money on development—a theatre devoted to new work should spend enough to commission serious and substantive critical essays by smart, literate thinkers, and these essays should all be published in a big fat catalog called the Program, and every effort should be made to get this 50-page booklet into the hands of anyone who buys a ticket—if they don't, in fact, get the thing in the mail beforehand. And these essays need to be top-drawer, high-powered, literate criticism—which doesn't mean they can't be fun and snarky and even perhaps a little heavy-going from time to time. Because, like the museum catalog, they are setting the terms of the discourse. I'm not suggesting anything approaching the current excesses of the MLA; plain English, finely wrought, will suffice. But the writing must show evidence of original thought, and it cannot, ever, excuse or plead or truckle.

When the New York City group Clubbed Thumb mounted its Wellman Festival in 1998, its program was a 50-page brochure that included essays by the likes of Marjorie Perloff. Is there any reason why major regional theatres can't engage leading critics, essayists, novelists, poets and playwrights for such a project? Can you imagine a season of new plays culminating in a combined catalog, now of book-length form, with essays by the likes of Camille Paglia and Luc Sante and Don DeLillo and Marjorie Garber and Tony Kushner and Joyce Carol Oates and Michael Chabon and Paula Vogel and Daniel Mendelsohn and . . . ?

Wouldn't that change forever the way new plays are presented?

And wouldn't that be pretty darn cool?

Jeffrey M. Jones's plays include *70 Scenes of Halloween, Nightcoil, A Man's Best Friend, Der Inka Von Peru, Tomorrowland, Wipeout, Stone Monkey Banished* and *12 Brothers* (with Camila Jones). He is also the author of two musicals: *Write If You Get Work* (with a score by Dan Moses Schreier) and *J.P. Morgan Saves the Nation* (with a score by Jonathan Larson).

ON DIRECTING: A MODEST PROPOSAL

By Steven Dietz

March 2007

The roughly 120-year experiment in placing the stage director at the center of theatrical creation has run its course. While the previous century of primarily director-based theatre was one of notable achievements, and while its momentum will no doubt carry forward for many years to come, a new century requires a new approach.

To be clear: What must be achieved is not the abolition of the director's role, but its continued evolution. As with any ongoing experiment, the director's role must be candidly and regularly interrogated—with the goal of having it grow and change at the pace of the art form, embracing the changing dynamics and collaborative challenges of this burgeoning theatrical age.

The role of the director in America grew through implication—an often unspoken covenant which over time served to transfer creative power away from the "generative" artist and toward the "interpretive" artist. And while the history and status of this approach must be respectfully noted, I believe our work must now be grounded in a differing philosophy. We must acknowledge the centrality of the explicit elements which comprise the theatrical event: text, performance and design. In an effort to embrace the primacy of these central elements, the director—the implicit element in this process—must be trained to be a unifying, rather than stratifying, presence in the "artistic workplace" we call the theatre.

A key component of this evolution is the growth and preponderance of interdisciplinary work being created for the stage. Actors, musicians, dancers and designers are increasingly joining playwrights as generative theatre artists. It follows then that many of these artists wish to both create and conduct the events which comprise their performance, and thus are challenging the prevailing hierarchies which evolved over the previous century. Furthermore, as "psychological realism"—which helped cement the director's position in the American theatre—is joined by new forms and paradigms of narrative, the training of directors must expand to keep pace with this new artistic landscape.

As theatrical craft begins to be viewed as inherently interpretive, the traditional model of the director as the singular person who interprets the script and determines how the play is presented to the audience is rendered obsolete. The new director must be trained to be a crucial bonding agent among the participating artists—rather than a necessary filter between them. The director of the next century shall, therefore, often be an artist who embraces the role as an organic extension of his or her creative contribution (as writer, actor, dancer, designer, etc.) to the event at hand.

While I am not calling for the extinction of hierarchical systems in the collaborative process, I am strongly advocating for an aesthetic hierarchy—one based on need rather than formula, as practical as it is fluid, and determined by the specific artistic needs of the given project and the artistic tools of its participants. Let us not seek a diminishment of the director's contribution, but rather let us bring the explicit creators (the writer, the actor, the designer) forward in the process—empowering and emboldening them to be accountable for their creation. Let's put an end to the blaming of directors for "failing to realize the artistic vision" of the project's central creator(s). It is time for generative artists to stand up, step to the fore and take full responsibility for the fate of their work.

Let us seek to eliminate the hyphenization of artists ("playwright/director," "actor/director," "choreographer/director") and instead actively foster the integration of these disciplines. Let us recognize that the essence of the director's craft must be inculcated in not only our directors, but in each generative artist—be they writer, performer or designer—who seeks training in the theatre.

I am not advocating that "all writers should direct their own work" (though, historically, they often have)—but I am saying that writers who emerge from training programs should be expected to attain a strong, practical working knowledge of the craft of directing: exploration of text, communication with performers, the realization and unification of all aspects of design. In this way, these students will begin to bridge the considerable distance between the private act of writing, the collaborative act of rehearsal and the public act of presentation.

I am not advocating that "actors don't need a director" (though, historically, of course, they have not)—again, I am simply saying that young actors should have sufficient knowledge and mastery of the theatrical event as to enable them to be not only in the service of their directors—but, first and foremost, in the service of their plays.

Nearly every theatrical director of note in recent history has claimed her/his position not by fiat, but rather by emerging from a creative melting pot of writers/actors/designers—the exact paradigm, in fact, which first produced what came to be known as "the director" over a century ago. To this end, I believe we must widen the pool of talent from which young directors emerge. We must target not only student directors in the traditional sense, but also recognize, nurture and support the directors of tomorrow from among our many generative disciplines—be they writers, actors, designers, etc. Whereas the traditional model has been to bring in aspiring directors and have them leave as collaborators, let us instead bring in aspiring collaborators— and have them leave as trained directors.

The training of directors warrants vigorous experimentation and a visionary spirit. The emerging director must become as fearless and facile as the art form itself, wrestling with the demands of many texts— classical and new, realistic and experimental—as well as the challenges of many collaborators: writers, performers and designers with a variety of interests, styles and passions.

Finally, we must remember this: Directors do not make the art form—but, rather, the art form makes directors. To this goal—and to this grand, maddening and ever-evolving craft which we have been fortunate enough to inherit—let us continue to dedicate our time, our passion and our resolve.

Steven Dietz is a director, playwright and visiting professor at the University of Texas–Austin. He is a longtime member of both the Society of Stage Directors and Choreographers and the Dramatists Guild of America. Among his many plays are *Fiction, Still Life with Iris, Lonely Planet* and *Sherlock Holmes: The Final Adventure*. He has directed at many of America's leading regional theatres and was a resident director for 10 years at the Playwrights' Center in Minneapolis.

GETTING STANISLAVSKY WRONG

By Charles Marowitz

March 2007

In 1923, all of New York was bowled over by the first visit of the Moscow Art Theatre to America. No one in this country had seen such synchronized ensemble-playing or a troupe of individual actors of such power and persuasiveness. When the company returned to Russia after a triumphant national tour, actors such as Maria Ouspenskaya stayed behind and, along with Richard Boleslavsky, an earlier drop-out, began instructing American actors in that strange doctrine known as the Stanislavsky System. One of Boleslavsky's most attentive students was Lee Strasberg. Both Strasberg and his close friend Harold Clurman were early converts to Stanislavsky as handed down by Boleslavsky.

The fact is many of the tenets of the system passed on by Boleslavsky had already been surpassed by Stanislavsky even as the System was being absorbed by the Group Theatre under Strasberg's aegis. After a visit from Stella Adler to Paris, where she received private instruction from Stanslavsky, it became clear that elements such as "emotional memory" had been virtually abandoned by Stanislavsky and a new and stronger emphasis placed on "playing actions." These unexpected developments caused severe upheavals within the Group, and there were some, like Robert Lewis, who believed it was this schism which eventually triggered Strasberg's resignation from the company and brought about the disintegration of the Group Theatre itself.

During the next six decades, the precepts derived from the Stanislavsky System became the prevailing mode of tuition for professional actors both in America and Europe and, in many countries, is still the official doctrine for people pursuing theatre studies.

However, no dogma is so persuasive that it does not eventually create skeptics, apostates and even iconoclasts, and, in recent years, aspects of the Stanislavsky System have been seriously questioned and, in some instances, abandoned. Theorists like Michael Chekhov (who broke with Stanislavsky in the 1920s) and Bertolt Brecht (who found the System abhorrent) have fostered a whole series of alternative approaches inspired largely by a body of plays less naturalistic than those that stemmed from the repertoire of the Moscow Art Theatre. In some quarters, the very ethos of the Stanislavsky System has been attacked and its efficacy put into question.

The Stanislavskian practice most adhered to among students and professional actors is the formulation of "actions"—that is, a choice made about the central drive of a particular scene, what a character is going after. It is often the case that an actor in conjunction with a director can come up with three, four or even a half-dozen actions for a particular scene, the justification being that a character's action is never static but always changing. This approach often produces a series of impulses, each duly labeled in advance; these impulses are then assembled as if they were playing-cards, and then tossed out one after the other until the hand is played and the next round of the game begun.

What this tends to do is to divide a scene into a series of finite units with prescriptive action-titles, with actors proceeding on the assumption that these units cover all the minute changes that take place between characters in some dramatic interaction. What it actually does is over-systematize the actor's work and lead him or her into believing every moment of the scene should be strictly accounted for. What it does not do is allow the actor to organically adjust to the variation of circumstances as they unfold in what is supposed to be a spontaneous volley of behavior. In other words, it substitutes cognition for instinct.

In real life, we often go into a situation with a clear-cut objective in mind. Almost always, that objective encounters unexpected resistance or diversions from the people with whom it collides. Our "action" (i.e., fundamental "want") in the situation does not change, but it does alter according to unexpected pressures brought to bear upon it. In adjusting to these unexpected changes we, in a sense, improvise our way around obstacles as dictated by the overall objective that first placed us into those social circumstances. But if an actor has worked out every aspect of what is to come, every buffet, challenge or untoward development, he knows more than he should about his character's activity. He is robbed of the spontaneity that comes—as in life—from instinctively adjusting to whatever obstacles he may encounter in the pursuit of his objective.

Recently, in Copenhagen, I was assisting a young director with what she referred to as her "game-plan." We had spoken loosely about the character's "want," but what she had formulated was an action for every vicissitude in the scene—a scene of about seven minutes' duration to which she had attached over a dozen banner headlines. "Why be so fastidious about every single nuance?" I asked. Reply: "Because I want the actor to understand all the minute adaptations he has to make in pursuing his objective, and therefore every moment has to be accounted for." But if the actor has a handle on what he fundamentally wants, won't he steer a course based on that original desire? That is, won't he logically equivocate or elude, camouflage or conceal, become wary, suspicious, insistent or frightened? Perhaps, said the young director, but this way he knows every twist and turn the scene will take and can prepare for it beforehand.

That may be true, but such an approach siphons off much of the spontaneity that would occur if the actor was not so totally conscious of every emotional change he was expected to make. What the actor gains in certainty, he loses in spontaneity. Having already decided precisely what his reactions are supposed to be, he merely posits them—rather than allowing them to evolve organically from the stimuli of the given circumstances.

It may seem like splitting hairs, but the underlying object of all acting is to create and sustain a spontaneity which, we all know, is rooted in a priori choices. But if the central thrust of a scene is clearly understood, and its overriding action correctly selected, all of those meticulously prescribed reactions take care of themselves—and in so doing, retain some of the surprise that life is always handing us just when we are expecting something different.

Overloading the actor with minute actions rather than permitting him to fend for himself in the hurly-burly of changing circumstances is only one of the many Stanislavsky postulates that need overhauling. The notion that all an actor needs do is determine his "action" in a particular scene or formulate a super-objective for the entire play is based on the fallacy that all one ever wants in life is the fulfillment of one overriding conscious desire. Hamlet wants to revenge the death of his father, we are told; Katherine wants to assert her independence from male domination; Macbeth plots and plans to acquire the crown which he believes has been supernaturally promised him. These are time-honored generalizations and, like all generalizations, may be either confirmed or contradicted. Hamlet can just as readily want to do everything he can to avoid revenging his father a) because he is never entirely sure that the "ghost" he saw was a benevolent or malignant spirit; b) because he has scruples about regicide or endangering his mother's status after her hasty remarriage; c) because he recognizes that he will never be the man his father was and therefore could never possibly rule the Kingdom of Denmark, a position he would be obliged to undertake as the natural heir to the throne. Conceivably, Katherine, rather than confirming her desire for independence, may secretly be longing to relinquish it because she has met her match in Petruchio but is now stuck with a fiery and belligerent persona which she cannot shake off. Macbeth, conscious of his indecisive nature, may be terrified by a prophecy which is beyond his true station, and he may sense that the Witches' prediction may be a snare to bring him down rather than raise him up.

Stanislavsky-based actors frequently base their choices on textual considerations rather than subtextual ones. What is apparent in the words a character speaks in a play often has no bearing on what is essentially motivating him—which is why we can and do have innumerable interpretations of what, at the outset, appears to be self-evident material. Actions based on professed sentiments almost always produce stale and repetitive theatre. It's only when an actor comes up with a new and previously unconsidered objective—one that had never occurred to us before—that we experience the frisson of a fresh interpretation.

The other and more perilous Stanislavsky fallacy is the assumption that a character can only want one thing at a time—the carefully analyzed "action" that he gleans from a reading of the text or is dogmatically handed him by a director.

But as we know from our own psychological experience, one can simultaneously have multiple goals and mixed feelings. In the first court scene under the aegis of the newly anointed King Claudius, Hamlet may want to show his contempt toward the ruler because of the incestuous union with Gertrude; he may be squirmingly aware of the fact that there are people at court who recognize that his position as the heir-apparent has been usurped and he has to brazen out his humiliation in public. He may be yearning for a show of solidarity from his mother, whom he may believe was coerced into marrying Claudius; he may be scotching down his contempt for Laertes, who is being given leave to go to France, whereas he is not being allowed to go back to Wittenberg; he may be feeling utterly helpless in a court where there is not one person he can call friend. The list of possible moods and mood-changes is endless, and each one of them dictates a different "action," and each action, a different mode of behavior. How can one, in light of all those possibilities, single out a single "action" and say resolutely, this is how Hamlet "feels" and this is precisely what he "wants"?

In the 20th century we learned a lot about the psychology of acting from Stanislavsky, and much of it still applies, but not all of it. In the decades that followed his earliest work, the theories of Michael Chekhov have provided a useful corrective to many of the tenets of the System that had previously gone unchallenged. Acting theory has been evolving since Quintilian (and probably before), and the drama has gone from artifice to naturalism to psychological realism, expressionism, magic realism and the discontinuous demands of performance art. Acting technique has gone from "rules" to assumptions about behavior and widely differing notions of interior reality; from clashes between Diderot and Strasberg to theoretical differences stemming from Jung and Freud. If we revise or even discard certain basic Stanislavsky precepts, we are not dishonoring the Father of Psychological Realism but acknowledging his own belief that in art, the only constant is change.

Critic, playwright and director Charles Marowitz was a close collaborator with Peter Brook at the Royal Shakespeare Company and the founder and director of the Open Space Theatre in London. His most recent works for the stage are *Silent Partners*, a dramatization of Eric Bentley's *A Brecht Memoir*, and *Murdering Marlowe*. His free adaptations of Shakespeare are collected in *The Marowitz Shakespeare*. Among his more than two dozen books are *The Other Way: An Alternative Approach to Acting and Directing* (2006), *How to Stage a Play, Make a Fortune, Win a Tony and Become a Theatrical Icon* (2005) and *The Other Chekhov: A Biography of Michael Chekhov, the Legendary Actor, Director and Theorist* (2004).

AWAKEN AND SING

By Steven Sater

July/August 2007

> *When we were young Frank Wedekind was the Masked Man of our
> Spring Awakening . . . . This was the turn of the century. Bourgeois
> ideas lay in their agony.*
> —Berthold Viertel (1885–1953), *Writings on Theatre*

Suffice it to say, by the time I thought of introducing Wedekind's
Masked Man to the American musical theatre, those same "bourgeois ideas" had more than managed to rise again.

It was indeed the turn of a new century when I first gave Duncan
Sheik a copy of the play. Some months later, in the wake of the shootings at Columbine, its subject felt all the more urgent; I approached
director Michael Mayer about working on it with us. These days, a
short eight years later, in the shadow of the shootings at Virginia Tech,
I am often asked why I ever thought *Spring Awakening* could work as a
musical. And my only real answer is that I knew and loved the play, that
I had long felt it was a sort of opera-in-waiting, and that somehow
I could already "hear" Duncan's music in it.

Subtitled "A Children's Tragedy," Wedekind's play is full of the
unheard, anguished cries of young people. It struck me that pop
music—rock music—is the exact place that adolescents for the last few
generations have found release from, and expression of, that same
mute pain.

"The flesh has its own spirit," Wedekind once wrote. And surely
his gorgeous threnody already has the soul of song within it. But
I never dreamed that, by letting his characters actually sing, we would
end up so profoundly transforming his work.

Then, perhaps there is something in the nature of song itself that
opens the door to story—that admits us to the heart of the singer—as
if every song tells of a sort of unacknowledged "I want." For what we
sing is what is unspoken, what is hidden. The "real story."

As we began work, I vowed to remain true to Wedekind's fierce original intent. But I soon found that once we had access, through song, to the inner workings of our characters' hearts and minds, we engaged with them differently—we embarked on journeys with them. Before long, we found ourselves altering the structure, even the substance, of our source material, to account for the places those songs had taken us.

From the start, my thought was that the songs in our show would function as interior monologues. Characters would not serenade one another in the middle of scenes. Rather, each student would give voice to his or her inner landscape.

Surely, the original play is full of exquisite monologues—a dramatic technique Wedekind inherited from his countrymen Goethe and Schiller. But our monologues were meant to be truly interior—a technique more familiar in 20th-century fiction.

Instinctively, I felt I did not want to write lyrics that would forward the plot, and so chose not to follow that golden rule of musicals. I wanted a sharp and clear distinction between the world of the spoken and the world of the sung. And yet, I also wanted to create a seamless and ongoing musical counterpoint between the languages of those distinct worlds.

Ludwig Wittgenstein famously wrote: "What we cannot speak about, we must pass over in silence." And, yet, song seems to let us pause within that silence, to find ourselves articulate within it.

Within our show, the songs soon came to function as subtext. The boy and girl fumble to make polite conversation; but underneath, each of them already senses the enormous story about to unfold between them: "O, I'm gonna be wounded . . . ."

We wrote songs as confession ("There is a part I can't tell, about the dark I know well"). Songs as denial ("Uh-huh, uh-huh, uh-huh . . . well, fine") or admission ("It's the bitch of living as someone you can't stand"). Songs as cri de coeur ("But there's nowhere to hide from the ghost in my mind . . ."). Somehow, I felt, we still remained true to that inchoate yearning of Wedekind's youths.

But of course we were also up to something else: In our show, the scenes set out the world of 19th-century repression, while the songs afford our young characters a momentary release into contemporary pop idiom. (Caught in the relentless dramas of our adolescent lives, we are all still rock stars in the privacy of our own bedrooms.) The time-jumping structure of our show is meant, thus, to underscore the sadly enduring relevance of our theme.

Some of my earliest efforts to transpose 19th-century yearnings into contemporary attitudes and idiom were fairly straightforward. A failure at school, a virtual pariah at home, stymied in his efforts to flee provincial Bavaria, Wedekind's Moritz wanders to the river at dusk and declares: "But then, it's better this way . . . . I don't want to cry again— not today . . . ." Our Moritz wanders into the same dusk, but soon ignites into neon—a post-punk kid at a mike who sings: "Awful sweet to be a little butterfly . . . . 'Cause, you know, I don't do sadness . . . ."

Certainly, my original vow was to remain true to Wedekind's text. Still, I have been alternately touched and bemused that so many critics have spoken so highly about how faithful we have been to the original, how admirably we have distilled it. Maybe. But, at the same time, we have fundamentally altered it. (I remember when Stephen Spinella, who joined our show just before our Broadway transfer, asked to see my uncut translation from Wedekind of several of his scenes. I had nothing to show him. He continued to press his suit: He really wanted to see Moritz's scene with his father in its longer form—a scene in which the man humiliates, strikes and effectively renounces his son. Alas, I had to report that we never see Moritz with his father in the original play.)

Still, it has been more than merely adding new scenes, or thoroughly rewriting those already extant. We have created journeys for our three lead characters which do not exist in the original dark, fractious fable.

As others have noted, the two biggest shifts we made to the tale occur at the ends of Act 1 and Act 2—in the hayloft and then in the graveyard. In Wedekind's script, Melchior "date-rapes" Wendla. We wanted to see him make love to her. More: We wanted to show how this young man (who jests at his friend's puberty wounds) first uncovers ineluctable sexual feelings; how he begins to own his sexual identity; how he helps Wendla awaken to hers. The truth is, we had already, irrevocably, set Melchior on this path when we gave him the song "Touch Me." There, he articulates his sense of "the female" yearning for pleasure, singing as if in some hypothetical woman's voice: "Touch me, just like that. Now, there, that's it—God, that's heaven . . . ." Sheltered in a hayloft in a rainstorm with an actual young woman—Wendla—and confronted with the possibility of giving her that pleasure, Melchior cannot restrain himself.

As for the graveyard . . . suffice it to say, after seven years' labor, we finally dispensed with the notorious Masked Man. This Symbolist figure appears—literally out of nowhere—in the last scene of Wedekind's text. He confronts the despairing Melchior and assures him that with a warm meal in his belly, he will no longer chafe to join his friend Moritz in the grave.

Without a doubt, this character is a sort of throwback, a deus ex machina, like those in Ancient Greek tragedies who appear in the final scene to resolve the issues of the play. And yet, his appearance, along with the ghost of Moritz, who rises from his grave to tempt Melchior to suicide, effectively marks the birth of the Expressionist Theatre (a world where iconic figures body forth the emotions of the central characters).

Since high school—when I first read the play—I have been haunted by the Masked Man. I struggled so long to incorporate him into our show, offering him up in one incarnation after another: as a sort of somber emcee, as an ever-present silent specter, as an actor who (living or dead) somehow survived the Allied bombing of a German theatre. But we finally realized that within our piece the music already performs the role of the Masked Man, for it gives our adolescent characters a voice to celebrate, to decry, to embrace the darker longings within them as *part of them*, rather than as something to run from or repress.

As for Moritz arising from his grave to tell Melchior how good the dead have it, hovering high above joy and despair . . . it just seemed wrong to us—a cop-out, for dramaturgic effect, on a character we cared about and had worked so hard to illuminate. In our show, we witness Moritz's struggles at school and home firsthand; his devotion to Melchior is his sole anchor. In song after song, he utters heartfelt, would-be defiant cries of anguish at the world grown dark around him. In the Expressionist original, the Moritz we meet in the graveyard is largely an aspect of Melchior's feeling—a projection. But for us, he was still our gangly Eraserhead. We didn't want to see him extend a rotting hand in an effort to betray his friend.

And yet, it felt appropriate to hear from him again, and also from Wendla. The question was: What did we want to say? If the answer wasn't a "warm meal" in a young Bavarian belly, then how was Melchior to find the strength to go on? Ultimately, the lyrics—the message—of Melchior's final song, "Those You've Known," came to me while writing it. I found the lyrics telling me: It was the love still felt for those we have known that enables us to continue in the face of losing them.

Now we had the end of our tale: a boy left thoroughly distraught, his rebellious spirit broken by The System, somehow finds sustenance at the source of his sufferings. He has learned to learn from his heart.

If the lesson to be learned was of the heart, then it made sense that we would introduce Melchior as a guy with a naïve rebellious pride in the power of his own mind. And so (working backward from that lesson learned by show's end), we wrote his opening number, "All That's Known":

All they say
Is "Trust in What Is Written."
Wars are made,
And somehow that is wisdom.

Thought is suspect,
And money is their idol,
And nothing is okay unless it's scripted in their Bible.

But I know
There's so much more to find—
Just in looking through myself, and not at them.

Still, I know
To trust my own true mind,
And to say: "There's a way through this . . . ."

The realization of how our story should begin led us to construct an entirely new opening scene for our young rebel—the Latin Class—

which does not exist in the original. This scene allowed us to see the boys in school. It allowed us to introduce a world of repression, where students are struck for giving the wrong answers. It let us see Moritz floundering. Most important, it showed us Melchior standing up for his friend and defending him.

In contrast, we were clear from the beginning about how to launch Wendla's story, and "Mama Who Bore Me" was one of the first songs Duncan and I wrote. I always felt our show should begin with this determined young woman asking her mother how babies are born, only to be rebuffed, coddled with bourgeois evasion.

In the original, this classic scene falls in Act 2. Wendla has already met Melchior, has indeed already been beaten by him. Moving the scene to the top of the show allowed us to make a political point right from the start: The seeds of the entire "children's tragedy" are sown by this one willful act of silence—a parent failing to talk honestly to her child about sex.

I saw Wendla as a girl with a mission—a 19th-century teen with a quest that could also feel contemporary. Thwarted by her mother, she keeps looking for answers: She wants to know the world of her strange new body. Disturbed but also darkly intrigued to learn Martha's father beats her, Wendla turns, searchingly, to Melchior. In the original script, when she asks him to beat her, he is dumbstruck; all she can offer is that she has never been beaten, her entire life. When our Wendla asks Melchior to beat her, he demands: "How can you even want such a thing?" And she responds: "I've never felt . . . anything."

As Wedekind scripted it, the hayloft scene is brief—startlingly brief. With next to no acknowledgment of the horrific beating Melchior has inflicted on her, Wendla kneels beside him in the hay, and he begins kissing her. A moment later, he forces himself on her. We worked hard to flesh out a fuller scene between them, to let our would-be lovers struggle to make sense of what they have so brutally done—to offer one another forgiveness, before they fall into each other's arms.

From the top of Act 2, we wanted to see Wendla confusedly awakening to her own womanhood, owning her lovemaking, claiming her part of the pleasure. Where Wedekind gives her an Ophelia-like morning after, our young heroine celebrates in song the sweet unknown world she's just discovered. The final arc of her journey, however, came late in the process. Our producer Tom Hulce felt, and repeatedly warned, that we were letting our sometime-fearless young woman conclude her story as a "victim," lamenting the incomprehensible news that she was with child. The problem was, we all loved her sad song, "Whispering." One day, Michael proposed we try intercutting that song with the scene between Melchior's parents that follows it. As Wendla discovers the consequences of her night with Melchior, the more progressive Gabors, hearing the same news, give up on their son and send him to a reformatory.

It was an inspired idea. Somehow, in cutting those scenes together, it became plain that, over the course of her song, Wendla could undergo a transformation. Her song would then play in counterpoint with their scene: as Frau Gabor bows to her sense of duty and condemns Melchior, Wendla sets aside her grief and trusts what her heart found with him. And so I rewrote the words of "Whispering"—what had been, from near the beginning, my favorite lyric:

> See the sweetheart on his knees,
> So faithful and adoring.
> Says he loves her,
> So she lets him have her—
> Another summer's story . . . .

As the story of the song changed, this chorus became:

> Had a sweetheart on his knees,
> So faithful and adoring.
> And he touched me,
> And I let him love me.
> So, let that be my story . . . .

While Moritz finally succumbs to the humiliations of society (he can no longer face the prospect of a world that brooks no failure), our Wendla chooses to remember the love she has felt, to ignore the ghostly whispers of society, and embrace the new life already whispering within her.

And with that move, our play made its pro-choice stance explicit. Wendla's abortion was, in a sense, transported into our own century: a century in which a "bourgeois idea" such as abstinence is still widely preached as the only form of safe sex; where the widespread dissemination of contraceptive devices is described by some within our Department of Health and Human Services as demeaning to women. One can only hope that a century from now the world will finally hear, and honestly answer, the cries of its Wendlas.

And so I am left pondering how and why all this ever came to be. I remember the first time I walked by our marquee, feeling almost baffled: "*Spring Awakening*—A Musical? Wait, no, isn't that just the name of a book in my room?"

I can honestly say that my earliest sense of why this *kindertragödie* could work as a piece of musical theatre was instinctual. Even so, the entire eight-year siege of developing it entailed nothing harder than learning to trust our instincts. As Michael has recently said, we didn't set out to "revolutionize the musical theatre," nor with the express intention of doing something different. Rather, we had a story we wanted to tell, and a way we all felt we wanted to tell it.

Through all those years, through the darkest hours when our project fell off almost everyone's radar, Michael never lost heart, never lost faith in our ability to pull the thing together. For all the endless nights he spent going through line after line, every syllable of this text with me . . . well, this text—the show itself—are all I have to repay that.

As for the debt to Duncan . . . who can explain the mystic thing that happens when I hand him a lyric and he somehow hears a song in it. When (in a moment indelibly etched in my memory) he first looks through those words, picks up his guitar and strums: "There's a moment you know . . . ." And then he pauses, looks up with a grin, and sings: "You're fucked."

Steven Sater won two 2007 Tony Awards for *Spring Awakening*, for best book and best score. In addition to *Spring Awakening*, he has collaborated with Duncan Sheik on the plays *Umbrage, Nero (Another Golden Rome)* and *The Nightingale*; the album *Phantom Moon*; and songs for the films *A Home at the End of the World* and *Brother's Shadow*. His other plays include *Carbondale Dreams; Perfect for You, Doll; A Footnote to the Iliad; Asylum*; and a reconceived version of *The Tempest* with music by Laurie Anderson. This article is reprinted from the preface to *Spring Awakening*, published in 2007 by TCG Books.

THANKS, BUT NO THANKS

By Richard Nelson

September 2007

I think this will be the first "speech" I have ever given; 56 years old, and I've managed to escape giving a speech until now. I suppose I never thought it was my "thing." I love hearing what I write spoken by others, not myself. But things change; we change. I remember when I became a father for the first time. Suddenly I found within me an ability to fight for my child in ways that I could never have fought for myself. A year and a half ago I began teaching young emerging talented playwrights at the Yale School of Drama. Tonight I want to talk about issues that are important to them—and to me and, I believe, to all American playwrights—but mostly to them. I suppose it is because of them, and because of the hundreds of playwrights whose work I now read each year, that I feel the need, the passion, but more importantly the responsibility to discuss the state of our profession with you tonight.

So much has happened to the profession of playwriting since I had my first professional production in 1975. And so much of what has happened has not been good for playwrights.

The profession of playwright, the role of the playwright in today's American theatre, I believe, is under serious attack. Some who attack are simply greedy; some are ignorant; some can't understand why theatre isn't TV or film. But perhaps the greatest threat to the playwright in today's theatre comes not from the greedy and ignorant, but rather from those who want to "help."

"Playwrights are in need of help." This is now almost a maxim in our theatre today. Unquestioned. A given. But where does this mind-set—for that is what it is, a mindset—come from? Of course playwrights need things: money, productions, support, encouragement. So do actors, directors, designers, artistic directors. But this mindset is different, because what is meant here is: Playwrights are in need of help—to write their plays. They are in need of help—to do their work. They can't do their work themselves.

How strange. What other profession is viewed in this way? What other person in the theatre is viewed this way? Imagine hiring, say, a director, with the assumption that he couldn't do his work himself. Now, I am not saying that a director shouldn't listen to others, receive notes, be open to discussions and so forth. Quite the opposite, for this is all part of what a director does. And I am not saying a playwright shouldn't listen to notes, be open to discussions and so forth—because this is what a playwright does. What I am saying is that the given mindset should not be that the playwright cannot be trusted to lead this process, cannot be trusted to know how to work within the collaboration of theatre.

Nor am I talking about mentoring or educating young playwrights. I'm talking about how our professional theatre looks at playwrights and the playwright's play—about assumptions made, and about the various specific solutions theatres make based on these false assumptions.

What is really being said to the playwright by all the help? From the playwright's perspective it is this: that what a playwright writes, no matter how much he or she works on it, rewrites it at his or her desk, the play will always not be right—will always need "help." In other words, writing a play is too big of a job for just the playwright to achieve. This, I believe, is now a prevalent attitude in the American theatre. And this mindset is devastating.

[Playwright and artistic director] Emily Mann told me the other day that in her 17 years running the McCarter Theatre Center, the greatest change has been that now more and more plays are submitted that are obviously unfinished. Writers today recognize that if they wish to participate in a process that perhaps will lead to the production of their work, this will require rewriting and revision, guided and cajoled by others. So why finish anything?

I sit with young writers and hear how they now leave chunks of their plays purposely written badly—hoping that the "help" they receive will concentrate on these areas and not on others that they care about. These are tricks, games that many a screenwriter has learned over time, now finding their way into the writing of plays.

No doubt many of you are thinking: But the plays *aren't* finished; they need help; and they *do* get better.

Again, I'm not saying that a playwright should ignore comments about and reactions to his work—quite the opposite. But I am saying that our mindset toward playwrights should be this: that the playwright knows what he is doing; and that perhaps the play, as presented, is as it should be—so that the onus for change is not on the playwright but on others, on the theatre. And the theatre is there with a full array of tools to support the playwright as he or she attempts to improve upon his or her play. How to improve a play should be the domain of the writer, with the theatre supplying potential tools—a reading, say, or a workshop with clearly delineated goals. These are tools that should evolve out of a need, as opposed to being a given.

A culture of "help" breeds a culture of dependence, and this is what I believe we now have in the American theatre: the culture of readings and workshops, which would have been unimaginable when I was a young playwright 30 years ago. A culture of "development." And this culture—more than being an activity, a process—is a mindset. Having spent a great deal of time in classical theatre, I have watched actors and directors approach classical plays that have massive contradictions, and address those plays not as works to be fixed, but rather to be solved. So I am arguing for a theatre where the mindset is not to fix new plays, but to solve them.

If it is assumed that all plays need to be helped along, then no playwright actually has it in his or her power to complete his or her play. Therefore, can it really be called his or her play? Ah—now we come to the other, trickier sides of the equation, where the "help" given writers also has strings. I'd like to look at just a few—there are many—examples of how this mindset has infiltrated our theatre and what it is doing to my profession.

Let's get specific. Let's look at the actors, directors, even audiences who have been taught, or re-educated, by this culture to feel a responsibility to "help" the playwright write his or her play—producers, literary managers and dramaturgs who "help" with rules about what makes a good play; who "help" by mandating readings because they must be "helpful." Let's look at managers who "helpfully" organize commissions so that the theatre can encourage (or is the word "enforce"?) changes that are "helpful" to the play. There are contracts that demand remuneration for this "help." There are foundations that allow their monies to be used in a developmental hell that breeds the loss of confidence and control that every playwright needs—must have—to succeed.

Readings. Mandatory readings of plays for judgment or to "give help." Be careful. This is dangerous, and has already caused great harm. A play with two people at a table having a conversation—this works in a reading, we get a good sense of what the writer is after. But what about seven people in a room, moving about, talking to two, then three, unheard by a fourth, and so on? This makes no sense in a reading. And so playwrights, practical people that we are—slowly, like a bad evolution—stop writing in forms that don't work in readings. Again, slowly, our plays begin to look dramaturgically similar. Of course a playwright can benefit from a reading, but one needs to be so very careful about why the play is being read, what one hopes is being gained, and what is being lost. All those reading series out there—careful—in the long run are they doing much more harm than good?

Workshops: What are they? What is the role of an actor or a director in a workshop? To direct or act in a play requires, I believe, a strong element of confidence in the play; a belief that the answer to one's questions or confusions can be found in the play. This is what a director or actor does; this is their talent and how they explore. But if the playwright is encouraged—no, celebrated—for rewriting during this process, then where does that put the actor, the director? Not acting or directing, but there "to help." Isn't this the wrong mindset for a director or actor to have? Couldn't their talents be put to better service trying to solve what the writer has written, as opposed to trying to help him fix it?

Audiences: By involving them in readings and discussions and, god forbid, workshops, we are apparently asking for their "help" with the play. But doesn't this confuse, even warp, the role of the audience? In terms of new work, doesn't this put an audience's focus overwhelmingly on "does it work?" as opposed to "what is it about?" or "why was it written?" or "does it matter?" Aren't these the questions we want discussed? Aren't these the questions that help generate the sort of substantive discussions we in the theatre wish to have with an audience?

Rules for writing plays: My god! One hears young playwrights being told what a play "must do," or "how a play works." One hears writers being told that a character's "journey" isn't clear enough, or that the writer needs to determine a character's "motivation." One hears how a play has to "build" in a certain way, or how "the conflict" isn't strong enough. These are terms that seem to suggest a deep understanding of what a play is and how it is put together, but in fact they tell us very little. Perhaps a particular play might be helped by one of these suggestions, but they (and other "rules") are too generally prescribed. To see how silly this prescription is, one has only to ask: What is the clear motivation of Lear? The playwright doesn't write out of "motivations" but rather out of truth and reality, out of people and story and worlds he or she wishes or needs to create for us. These terms are perhaps useful to the critic or the dramaturg in finding a way in for themselves to these plays, but such considerations are not how plays—good plays, great plays—are made.

The word "text": I may be crazy, but I think I woke up one day and suddenly people were talking about "the text" instead of "the play." How did this come about? Since when does a playwright only write words? Isn't that the hidden meaning of this—to make the playwright the "word guy" and leave the theatremaking to others? As if the writer were only a source from which words flowed that others made into plays. As I tell my students endlessly, theatre is the only artistic form that uses the entire live human being as its expression. Playwrights write people, not words. We write words to convey the people. To push us aside, to make us the "text guys" rather than the "play guys," is a subtle but dangerous change in thinking and betrays a new mindset about the place of the playwright in the making of theatre.

Step commissions: These are fairly prevalent commissions by which the playwright is usually paid in three stages. First, when he agrees to the commission and signs the contract; the second when he submits the play; and the third when he submits the rewrite. Now, what is wrong with this picture? What is the underlying assumption here? That the play the playwright submits will need to be rewritten and that the playwright will only do this rewrite if he or she is paid for it.

Now, as we all know, the playwright still is the owner of the play; he or she owns the copyright. So—say you build a house. You own this house. Suppose a guy comes along and suggests you add a window. Now, if you agree this would improve your house a great deal, you'll add the window. However, suppose the guy says he thinks you should add a window and you need to be paid to do so. To your own house! How bizarre. This guy must be thinking maybe you don't want to add a window and you need to be paid to do it. Well, that is very much what these step deals suggest—once again, insidiously, the role of the playwright, or at least the playwright's judgment and understanding of his own play and what it needs, is being doubted, questioned. In his mind he's thinking he's being paid to do what he doesn't necessarily want to do.

Here's one that will upset some of you and the one that will take the longest to explain and discuss: the idea of "participation." You should see my first-year students' faces when I explain what participation is.

"You mean," they say, "that I give up a percentage of my play forever? Why?" "Because," I say, "the theatre has done your play."

"Why?" they ask again.

I tell them theatres will give two reasons: They have enhanced the play's value by producing it in an important "market," and because the theatres have helped the writer with the writing of the play. Ah, there's this help again, which may have been unwanted, and now we have to pay for it! How did this happen?

A little background that most of you know, I'm sure. Participation has been around a long time in the commercial theatre, but it is a fairly recent development in the nonprofit theatre as a pervasive practice. And it just sort of happened—there was no real debate that I know of. Now, who is to blame for this? Of course, playwrights themselves need to accept a good bit of that blame for not fighting this harder when it began to occur in nonprofit contracts. But—and I would guess that those who now run the Dramatists Guild might even agree—until very recently, our Guild was pretty myopic, and saw theatre only through the lens of Broadway, where participation was a given. So there was no understanding of why it should be stopped in the nonprofit theatre. And so there was little, if any, serious debate or opposition. Only when Gregory Mosher and Bernie Gersten took over Lincoln Center Theater and refused to take any participation from new work was there even the glimmer of discussion—and certainly nothing involving the praise that those two gentlemen deserved.

So, it happened because no one fought it. The playwrights were too weak and disorganized to fight back and understand what was being done to them. So, I suppose it's our fault. However, as we all know, that's not how the serious theatre works.

I remember an executive committee meeting many years ago at the Guthrie Theater, where I was working, when we were going over salary increases for the next season. When it came to the proposed raise for actors, one new board member said, "But I understand that there are always lots of actors who want to play each part. So why are we now going to pay actors more? We should pay them less and save money." A few minutes later a couple of more experienced members of the board took this gentleman aside and explained. And what they explained is obvious to all of us in this room: We in the theatre have a responsibility not just to our immediate bottom line, but to the future of our art and profession. You apply principles of hardnosed business to every element of the theatre and you will destroy the theatre. So, yes, we playwrights did not protect or fight for ourselves. Yes, we should have. But that failure does not make us fair game. We write our play, we own our play, and we should continue to own our play—all of it, at least as long as we stay in the nonprofit theatre, which is a theatre that raises its money often on claims of producing new writing.

Only one argument about this has ever made sense to me: If a playwright has a huge hit, shouldn't that money come back to the theatre and support other writers and other productions? I have signed many contracts in England stating just that: that should I make a very large amount of money from the play during a given year, then a percentage is owed to the theatre. That makes sense. That is responsible. But I have never seen an American theatre contract with anything like that language. If theatres won't take it upon themselves to rectify this situation, if playwrights prove as a group too weak and unfocused, then I say let's turn to the funders themselves, the foundations and donors, and ask: Does this make sense to you? That healthy percentages of future incomes from plays presented in smallish theatres with small royalties, requiring months and months of work and involvement by the playwright—should these theatres now have a right to own part of these plays? What signal does this send to the writers, especially the young ones?

These are a few—there are many more—specific examples of how this mindset toward the playwright has found its way into all reaches of the theatre and therefore how difficult it will be to change.

Empowerment, I suppose, is what this is all about—allowing the playwright to feel that he or she owns the play, in all meanings of that word, to have pride in that ownership. Prescribed "rules"—this does the opposite. A culture with a mindset of "help" does the same. The loss of a percentage of one's play—the same again. And so it is my hope—and, I believe, my profession's best hope—to change this mindset and the culture based upon it.

When I was asked to give this speech, I was told to speak about anything I wanted. I knew right away that this is what I wished to talk about with all of you. Because it is my great belief and hope that it will be from gatherings like these, gatherings of caring, dedicated theatre professionals, lovers of theatre, that we can change how we think, change the broken ways, and reinvigorate, even reimagine, our theatre.

Playwright Richard Nelson won Britain's Olivier Award for *Goodnight Children Everywhere* **and the Tony Award for best book for** *James Joyce's The Dead.* **From 2005–08 he was the chair of the playwriting program at the Yale School of Drama. This article is reprinted from Nelson's Laura Pels Keynote Address to the Alliance of Resident Theatres/New York in April '07.**

WRITING ABOUT SEX

By Wallace Shawn

April 2008

For whatever reason, and I don't remember how it happened, I am now what people call "64 years old," and I have to admit that I started writing about sex almost as soon as I realized it was possible to do so—say, at the age of 14—and I still do it, even though I was in a way the wrong age then, and in a different way I guess I'm the wrong age now. Various people who have liked me or cared about me—people who believed in my promise as a writer—have hinted to me at different times in my life that an excessive preoccupation with the subject of sex has harmed or even ruined my writing. They've implied that it was sad, almost pitiful, that an adolescent obsession—or maybe it was in fact a psychological compulsion—should have been allowed to marginalize what they optimistically had hoped might have been a serious body of work.

Meanwhile, people I don't know very well have tended over all those decades to break into a very particular smile, one I recognize now, when they've learned that I've written something that deals with sex—a winking smile which seems to suggest that a trivial, silly, but rather amusing topic has been mentioned. It's a smile not unlike the smile that would appear on the faces of some of our more conservative teachers in the 1950s when the topic of "jazz" was raised—a smile sometimes accompanied back in those days by a mocking, suggestive swaying of the hips.

I suppose it goes without saying that James Joyce, D.H. Lawrence and others were expanding the scope of literature and redrawing humanity's picture of itself when they approached this subject in the earlier part of the 20th century. But by the time I came along, many of my friends were embarrassed on my behalf precisely because the topic I was writing about seemed so closely associated with an earlier era.

So why *have* I stuck with it? I suppose it has to do with the point I've heard boringly expressed by writers in one way or another all of my life—the thing they always say, while in a way always hoping that no one will believe them, though what they're saying is true—some variation or another of "*I don't do my own writing.*" I personally sometimes express the point, when pressed, by saying that I see my writing as a sort of collaboration between my rational self ("me") and the voice that comes from outside the window, the voice that comes in through the window, whose words I write down in a state of weirded-out puzzlement, thinking, "Jesus Christ, what the fuck is he saying?"

The collaboration is really quite an unequal partnership, I'd have to admit. The voice contributes everything, and I contribute nothing, frankly, except some modest organizing abilities and (if I may say so) a certain skill in finding, among the voice's many utterances, those that are most successful. (I suppose I'm quite a bit like one of those young college graduates in jacket and tie who help some unruly but for some reason celebrated man to write his autobiography.) But when I try to define the voice, I say, weakly, "Oh, that's the unconscious." And eventually, if I brood about it, I'm forced to conclude that, if the unconscious has thoughts, it has to have heard these thoughts, or at least their constituent fragments, from human beings of some description— from the people I've met, the people I've read about, the people I've happened to overhear on the street. So it's not just a theory that society is speaking to itself through me. If it were not so, all I would be able to hear, and all I would be trying to transcribe, would be the sound of my own heart sending blood through my veins.

Obviously society has asked writers, as a group, to take time out from normal labor to do this special listening and transcribing, and each individual writer has been assigned a certain part of the spectrum. No writer knows—or can know—whether the section that's been assigned to him contains the valuable code that will ultimately benefit the human species or whether his section consists merely of the more common noise or chatter. But obviously the system can only work if everyone dutifully struggles to do his best with the material that's been given to him, rather than trying to do what has already been assigned to somebody else.

The voice outside my own particular window has repeatedly come back to the subject of sex. And sure, I regret it in a way, or it sometimes upsets me. But if I were to conclude that the voice is fundamentally not to be trusted, where would I be then? The enterprise of writing would have to come to an end for me, because on what basis could I possibly decide to reject what the voice was saying so insistently? The truth is that, even if I wanted to reject my voice and try to listen to somebody else's, I wouldn't be able to hear it. And without an outside voice, what would I write down? Who would I listen to? "Me?" It doesn't work that way. So at a certain point—and with a certain sadness, because of how I knew I would be seen by other people—I decided I was going to trust the voice I was hearing. And of course, like every writer, I hope I'll be one of the ones who will be led to do something truly worthwhile. But in another way, it actually doesn't matter whether it's me or not. That's just a game—who did the best? The actually important question is not whether "I" am one of the better cogs in the machine—

the important question is whether the whole mechanism of which I'm a part is or is not one of evolution's cleverer species-survival devices, one that might be very helpful—even at the last minute.

Why is sex interesting to write about? To some, that might seem like a rather dumb question. Obviously when someone interested in geology is alone in a room, he or she tends to think a lot about rocks. And I imagine that when many geologists were children, they put pictures having to do with rocks on their bedroom walls. And I would have to guess that geologists find it fun to sit at a desk and write about rocks. So, yes, I find it enjoyable. But apart from that, I still find myself wondering, "Why is it interesting to write about sex?"

One reason is that sex is shocking. Yes, it's still shocking, after all these years—isn't that incredible? At least it's shocking to me. And I suppose I think it's shocking because, even after all these years, most bourgeois people, including me, still walk around with an image of themselves in their heads that doesn't include—well—*that*. I'm vaguely aware that while going about my daily round of behavior I'm making use of various mammalian processes, such as breathing, digesting, and getting from place to place by hobbling about on those odd legs we have. But the fact is that when I form a picture of myself, I see myself doing the sorts of things that humans do and *only* humans do—things like hailing a taxi, going to a restaurant, voting for a candidate in an election, or placing receipts in various piles and adding them up. But if I'm unexpectedly reminded that my soul and body are capable of being totally swept up in a pursuit and an activity that pigs, flies, wolves, lions and tigers also engage in, my normal picture of myself is violently disrupted.

Writing about sex is really a variant of what Wordsworth did, that is, it's a variant of writing about nature, or as we call it now, "the environment." Sex is "the environment" coming inside, coming into our home or apartment and taking root inside our own minds. It comes out of the mud where the earliest creatures swam; it comes up and appears in our brains in the form of feelings and thoughts. It sometimes appears with such great force that it sweeps other feelings and other thoughts completely out of the way. And on a daily basis it quietly and patiently approaches the self and winds itself around it and through it until no part of the self is unconnected to it.

Sex is really an extraordinary meeting of the meaningful and the meaningless. The big toe, for example, is one part of the human body, human flesh shaped and constructed in a particular way. The penis is another part of the body, located not too far away from the big toe and built out of fundamentally the same materials. The act of sex, the particular shapes of the penis and the vagina, are the way they are because natural selection has made them that way. There may be an adaptive value to each particular choice that evolution made, but from our point of view as human beings living our lives, the evolutionary explanations are unknown, and the various details present themselves to us as completely arbitrary. It can only be seen as funny that men buy magazines containing pictures of breasts, but not magazines with pictures of knees or elbows. It can only be seen as funny that demagogues give speeches denouncing men who insert their penises into other men's anuses—and then go home to insert their own penises into their wives' vaginas! (One might have thought it obvious that either both of these acts are completely outrageous, or neither of them is.) And yet the interplay and permutations of the apparently meaningless, the desire to penetrate anus or vagina, the glimpse of the naked breast, the hope of sexual intercourse or the failure of it, lead to joy, grief, happiness or desperation for the human creature.

Perhaps it is the power of sex that has taught us to love the meaningless and thereby turn it into the meaningful. Apparently, amazingly, the love of what is arbitrary (which one could alternately describe as the love of reality) is something we human beings are capable of feeling (and perhaps even what we call the love of the beautiful is simply a particular way of exercising this remarkable ability). So it might not be absurd to say that if you love the body of another person, if you love another person, if you love a meadow, if you love a horse, if you love a painting or a piece of music or the sky at night, then the power of sex is flowing through you.

It is often noted that writers like to write about conflict, and of course conflict is built into the theme of sex. A story about a person who wants to have a plate of spaghetti might be interesting, but a story about a person who wants to have another person—now, that is potentially even more interesting, because the person who is desired may not want to participate. But even leaving aside the conflict involved in the fact that people's desires are often at cross purposes, sex has always been known to be such a powerful force that fragile humanity can't help but be terribly nervous in front of it, so powerful barriers have been devised to control it—taboos of all varieties, first of all, and then all the emotions subsumed under the concepts of jealousy and possessiveness, possessiveness being a sort of anticipatory form of jealousy. (I noticed recently that a sociological survey of married people in the United States found that when asked the question: "What is very important for a successful marriage?" the quality mentioned most frequently—by 93 percent of the respondents—was "faithfulness," while "happy sexual relationship" came in with only 70 percent. In other words, to 23 percent of the respondents, it seemed more important that they and their partner should *not* have sex with others than that they themselves should enjoy sex.) Sex seems capable of creating anarchy, and those who are committed to predictability and order find themselves inevitably either standing in opposition to it, or occasionally trying to pretend to themselves that it doesn't even exist.

My local newspaper, the *New York Times*, for example, does not include images of naked people. Many of its readers might enjoy it much, much more if it did, but those same people still might not buy it if those images were in it, because if it contained such images it couldn't be the *New York Times*, it couldn't present the portrait of a normal, stable, adequate world—a world not ideal, but still good enough—which it's the function of the *New York Times* to present every day. Nudity somehow seems to imply that anything could happen, but the *New York*

Times is committed to telling its readers that many things will *not* happen, because the world is under control, benevolent people are looking out for us, the situation is not as bad as we tend to think, and while problems do exist, they can be solved by wise rulers. The contemplation of nudity or sex could tend to bring up the alarming idea that at any moment human passions might rise up and topple the world we know.

But perhaps it would be a good thing if people saw themselves as a part of nature, connected to the environment in which they live. Sex can be a very humbling, equalizing force. It's often been noted that naked people do not wear medals, and weapons are forbidden inside the pleasure garden. When the sexuality of the terrifying people we call "our leaders" is for some reason revealed, they lose some of their power—sometimes all of it—because we're reminded (and strangely, we need reminding) that they are merely creatures like the ordinary worm or beetle that creeps along at the edge of the pond. Sex really is a nation of its own. Those whose allegiance is given to sex at a certain moment withdraw their loyalty temporarily from other powers. It's a symbol of the possibility that we might all defect for one reason or another from the obedient columns in which we march.

Wallace Shawn is the author of *The Fever, Aunt Dan and Lemon, Our Late Night, Marie and Bruce, The Designated Mourner, Grasses of a Thousand Colors* **and other plays. With André Gregory, he co-wrote and starred in** *My Dinner with André.* **In addition to his work for the theatre, he is known for his television and film roles. This article is reprinted from Shawn's introduction to** *Our Late Night and A Thought in Three Parts,* **published by TCG Books.**

AN EYE ON THE FUTURE

By Joseph Haj

April 2009

Borrowing from Facebook's ubiquitous "25 Random Things," here are 25 thoughts about the next 25 years in the American theatre:

1. We will recognize that we are the servants in this game, not the masters, and that our theatres belong to the communities that they serve.
2. The sector will realize that all theatre is local.
3. There will be fewer LORT theatres.
4. We'll finally be able to offer a more articulate defense of the value of our work than "we think you should fund it because we like making it."
5. We will make the argument so beautifully that asking why theatre is important will be like asking for a flashlight to find the sun.
6. The next 25 years will include the passing of some of the giants in the field; we will find ways to put young people at their feet to learn everything before they go.
7. There will be many more women and people of color as leaders of our major institutions . . .
8. . . . and so we will see still better guidance of our institutions than we have seen in the past 25 years.
9. There will be increased intolerance of arbitrary, capricious and mean-spirited leadership.
10. There will be more resident acting companies.
11. There will be more artists in leadership positions.
12. It will all be about the Vision Thing.
13. The days of "come admire our work and get the hell out of the building" are over.
14. Fiscal responsibility will be a value held as closely as artistic excellence in all surviving institutions, and not just by the managing director.

15. Deliberate artistic and administrative opacity will make way to transparency and invitation into process.
16. The field will learn how to take care of its artists, particularly actors, more responsibly.
17. Social networking is not the future (not even sure it's the present).
18. Stewardship will not be enough. Leadership is required, and the field will find a comprehensive way to identify and develop it.
19. An end to constructing buildings bigger than the ideas that they hold.
20. An end to vilifying mature audiences.
21. An end to infighting about who is making more meaningful theatre.
22. Finally figuring out how to engage young people meaningfully in our work.
23. There will be no such thing as a newspaper critic.
24. Future leaders will need to do two things: First, learn everything from those who have come before . . . and second:
25. Take the old way outside and shoot it.

Joseph Haj is the producing artistic director of PlayMakers Repertory Company in Chapel Hill, N.C. He has directed and performed at major theatres across the country and abroad, including leading workshops with Palestinian and Israeli actors in the West Bank and Gaza.

THE CONVERSATIONS

RHYTHM AND TRUTHS

An interview with Sam Shepard by Amy Lippman

April 1984

As you are writing a play, do you have a certain idea of what the play's ending will be?

No. I think for me, every play has its own force, its own momentum, its own rhythm and tempo. That's the fascination of it. It's like people who hear music in their heads, or in the air, or wherever. They attract it in a certain way and it begins to speak to them. It has its own peculiar set of rules and circumstances, and complicated structures that you can't necessarily dictate. I think a play is like that. What you're trying to do, in a way, is have a meeting. You're trying to have a meeting with this thing that's already taking place. So, I can't really say that I have a beginning, middle and end every time I sit down to write a play. Every moment of the play is a beginning, a middle and an end.

So, it's a very ephemeral process?

Yeah, it is. A play's like music—ephemeral, elusive, appearing and disappearing all the time. You never reach a final point with it.

Do you see productions of your own work?

No. For the most part, it doesn't interest me, no. The initial production is very exciting because you're involved, you're engaged in it. After that point, though, I'd just as soon let it go and go on to the next play, because the next one's going to be even that much more exciting than the one before it. Once that first production happens, then I don't care what happens to it really. I'm not concerned in tracking it down, in following it around like an ex-lover or something.

Critics of your plays such as *Curse of the Starving Class*, *Buried Child* and *True West* have often referred to them as chronicling the break-up of the American family. To what extent is that a legitimate reading of those plays?

I'm not interested in the American social scene at all. It totally bores me. I'm not interested in the social predicament. It's stupid. And the thing you bring up about the break-up of the family isn't particularly American; it's all over the world. Because I was born in America, it comes out as the American family. But I'm not interested in writing a treatise on the American family. That's ridiculous. I mean, that's not fair or unfair to read that into my plays. It just seems an incomplete, a partial way of looking at the play. People get off on tripping out on these social implications of the play and how that matches up to contemporary America. And that's okay. But that's not why I'm writing plays.

So, why are you writing plays?
I have to. I have a mission. (*Laughs.*) No, I don't know why I do it. Why not?

You collaborated on the writing of two of your collected plays, *Tongues* and *Savage/Love*.
Yeah, the ones with Joe [Joseph Chaikin]. Well, that was a very unique circumstance, working with someone that I'd known as a friend for a long time and never really had a chance to work intimately with, one on one. I was hanging around the Open Theater and I knew Joe. We had a lot of things in common. So we just sat down and collaborated on this thing, just cooked it up. The thing that was unique about them, I think, is that they were designed for one performer, for him in particular. That was the impulse behind the whole thing. It's very different from writing by yourself.

Do you consider your work to revolve around myths?
Well, so many people have different ideas—of what the word means.

What does it mean to you?
It means a lot of things to me. One thing it means is a lie. Another thing it means is an ancient formula that is expressed as a means of handing down a very specific knowledge. That's a true myth—an ancient myth like Osiris, an old Egyptian myth that comes down from antiquity. The thing that's powerful about a myth is that it's the communication of emotions, at the same time ancient and for all time. If, for instance, you look at *Romeo and Juliet* as a myth, the feelings that you are confronted with in a play like that are true for all time. They'll always be true.

What relationship does that have to your plays?
Well, hopefully in writing a play, you can snare emotions that aren't just personal emotions, not just catharsis, not just psychological emotions that you're getting off your chest, but emotions and feelings that are connected with everybody. Hopefully. It's not true all the time; sometimes it's nothing but self-indulgence. But if you work hard enough toward being true to what you intuitively feel is going down in the play, you might be able to catch that kind of thing. So that you suddenly hook up with feelings that are on a very broad scale. But you start

with something personal and see how it follows out and opens to something that's much bigger. That's what I'm interested in.

Should one then be able to project his own experience onto what has occurred on stage?
Yeah, you can do that if you want to. But it doesn't have any real value. The only time it has value is when you hook up with something that you don't know. Something that you can't pin down. Something where you say, "I feel something here that's going on that's deeply mysterious. I know that it's true, but I can't put my finger on it." I'm not interested if it reminds you of your mother, or your sister, or your cousin, or anything like that. So what? Everybody has something like that. That's what I mean about this social thing, that similarities between social neuroses in American society really don't mean much in the long run because they're always going to change. But if emotions that come up during a play call up questions, or seem to remind you of something that you can't quite put your finger on, then it starts to get interesting. Then it starts to move in a direction we all know, regardless of where we come from or who we are. It starts to hook up in a certain way. Those, to me, are mythic emotions.

What ties do you feel to the American West?
Well, it's all subjective. I just feel like the West is much more ancient than the East. Much more. It is. I don't know if you've traveled out here at all but there are areas like Wyoming, Texas, Montana and places like that, where you really feel this ancient thing about the land. Ancient. That it's primordial. Of course, you can say that about New England. But it doesn't have the same power to me, because it's this thing about space. No wonder these mysterious cults in Indian religions sprang up, you know? It wasn't as though these people were just . . . just fell down from the sky. It has to do with the relationship between the land and the people—between the human being and the ground. I think that's typically Western and much more attractive than this tight little forest civilization that happened back East. It's much more physical and emotional to me. New England and the East Coast have always been an intellectual community. Also, I was raised out here, so I guess it's just an outcome of my background. I just feel like I'll never get over the fact of being from here.

There's a very disorienting element in some of your plays. In certain places the dialogue is very realistic but the situation seems very surrealistic, and this dichotomy is never resolved.
I think it's a cheap trick to resolve things. It's totally a complete lie to make resolutions. I've always felt that, particularly in theatre when everything's tied up at the end with a neat little ribbon and you're delivered this package. You walk out of the theatre feeling that everything's resolved and you know what the play's about. So what? It's almost as though why go through all that if you're just going to tie it all up at the end? It seems like a lie to me—the resolutions, the denoue-

ment and all the rest of it. And it's been handed down as if that is the way to write plays.

What's the alternative?
Well, there are many, many alternatives. But I think it's all dependent again on the elements that you start with and what your interest is in those elements. If you're only interested in taking a couple of characters, however many, and having them clash for a while, and then resolve their problems, then why not go to group therapy, or something?

What do *you* do?
I think of it more like music. If you play an instrument and you meet somebody else who plays an instrument, and the two of you sit down and start to play music, it's really interesting to see where that music goes between two musicians. It might not go anywhere you thought it would go; it might go in directions that you never even thought of before. You see what I mean? So you take two characters and you set them in motion. It's very interesting to follow this thing that they're on. It's a great adventure—it's like getting on a wild horse.

But aren't you, the playwright, controlling everything? You're *creating* it, aren't you?
I'm not creating that.

It doesn't happen by itself, does it?
No, but in a way, it's already in the air. I really believe that's true. These things are in the air, all around us. And all I'm trying to do is latch onto them. I don't feel like it's a big creative act, like I'm inventing all of this. I mean, I'm not putting myself in the same category as Mozart at all, don't get me wrong, but the story with him was that he heard this music. It was going on, and he was just open to it somehow, latched onto it, and wrote it down. *True West* is like that. *True West* is following these two guys, blow by blow, just following them, trying to stick with them and stick with the actual moment by moment thing of it. I mean, I wrote that thing . . . it took me a long time to write that play.

Why?
Because I went down a lot of blind alleys. I tried to make them go in one direction, and they didn't want to go that way.

How did you know when it was right, then?
I just know. Just like you know it's right when you're with somebody. You don't know it through the head—you have a feeling.

How did you know when to end it?
Well, I've always had a problem with endings. I never know when to end a play. I'd just as soon not end anything. But you have to stop at some point, just to let people out of the theatre. I don't like endings and I have a hard time with them. So *True West* doesn't really have an ending; it has a confrontation. A resolution isn't an ending; it's a strangulation.

Is the point then to leave the audience hanging?
No, no. I'm not intentionally trying to leave people up in the air. But I also don't want to give people the impression that it's over. (*Laughs.*)

Do you write for an audience?
Well, you know, that's an interesting question because, here again, the question comes up, what is the audience? Who is the audience? In a way, you must write for yourself as a certain kind of audience. In the midst of writing, it always feels as though I'm writing for the thing itself. I'm writing to have the thing itself be true. And then I feel like an audience would be able to relate to it. The theatre's about a relationship.

Between the actors and the audience?
If there's no relationship on stage, there's not going to be any in the theatre. But that has to be answered first in the writing. If you and I sit down on stage as two actors, and we don't have a relationship, what's the point? A relationship's both invisible and tangible at the same time, and you can see it between actors. You can also see the absence of it. If it's there, the audience is related immediately.

How are you affected by criticism, both favorable and unfavorable, of your work?
Well, I'm not immune to it. But you've got to follow this thing that keeps telling you blow by blow what to do, no matter what. It's very apparent [to you] what the next thing is. But critics can't tell you that. How could a critic know what your inner condition is as a writer? I'm not saying [criticism] doesn't have a pull on me. It has a definite pull on me. But whether you believe it or not is what counts. I've been in a few rodeos, and the first team roping that I won gave me more of a feeling of accomplishment and pride of achievement than I ever got winning the Pulitzer Prize. At the same time, I'm glad that the plays are successful and that they do something to people. But I'm not trying to win another Pulitzer Prize or anything.

Do you feel as if the media has certain expectations of you?
Sure. It's hard to know what they're expecting. If they're expecting me to be myself, I can guarantee that will happen all the way down the line. If they're expecting me to be Eugene O'Neill, they may be disappointed. (*Laughs.*)

What writers have influenced you? What playwrights?
I don't know. What's the point?

Do you go to see plays?
I don't go to the theatre at all. I hate the theatre. I really do, I can't stand it. I think it's totally disappointing for the most part. It's just always embarrassing, I find. But every once in a while, something real is taking place.

So, as for contemporary influences on your work—
Have you ever been to a rodeo?

No.

Well, there's more drama that goes down in a rodeo than 100 plays you can go to see. It's a real confrontation, a real thing going on. With a real audience, an actively involved audience. You should go to a couple of rodeos after you go to the theatre.

Do you consider your plays "experimental"?

I guess they are. I mean, it's all experimental. Experiment, by its very nature, has to do with risk. If there's no risk, there's no experiment. And every play's a risk. You take a huge risk with something like that.

In its appeal? Its success?

No, a big risk in going into unknown territory. You don't know where you're going.

Are the risks in creating unusual situations, or a totally new way of presenting something? What risks do you mean?

Well, I don't know if you feel this or not, but I feel like there are territories within us that are totally unknown. Huge, mysterious and dangerous territories. We think we know ourselves, when we really know only this little bitty part. We have this social person that we present to each other. We have all these galaxies inside of us. And if we don't enter those in art of one kind or another, whether it's playwriting, or painting, or music, or whatever, then I don't understand the point in doing anything.

How does that relate to your own work?

It's the reason I write. I try to go into parts of myself that are unknown. And I think that those parts are related to everybody. They're not unique to me. They're not my personal domain.

Is there then something cathartic about the whole process of writing?

No. Catharsis is getting rid of something. I'm not looking to get rid of it; I'm looking to find it. I'm not doing this in order to vent demons. I want to shake hands with them.

How long have you been writing plays?

Seventeen, eighteen years.

How have your plays changed?

Well, actually, they're the same. They're just closer to a verification of what these emotions are. In a way, that old cliché about somebody doing the same thing over and over and over again his whole life is true. I'm doing the same thing over each time. I'm trying to get closer to the source.

Are you more adept at doing that now than you were 18 years ago?

I'm more . . . not adept, I'm more *determined* to do it. I'm less afraid. Because there's something absolutely terrifying about going into yourself. . . . It's something that I don't understand. If I understood it,

I probably wouldn't write. That's why it's very difficult to talk about, and why a lot of this sounds like it's evasive.

Do you feel that you have discovered certain things, dealt with them in your plays, and then moved on to something else?
Well, I haven't left anything behind . . . . That's not true. I've gotten rid of a lot of useless stuff. A lot of tricks.

Dramatic tricks?
Yeah. Like allowing things to unravel in a direction that you know they're not going to go by themselves. Like this play [*Fool for Love*], for instance. I wrote about 16 versions of it, and every time I came back to the first five pages. I'd write like 70, 80 pages and then bring it all the way back to the first five pages and start again—throw out 60, 70 pages. So, I've got literally at least a dozen different versions of the play, but the first five pages are the same in every one.

Is that because what you felt initially about it was the truest?
Yes. The very first meeting there was something there. I knew there was something there, and I just had to keep trying. They weren't just drafts. Every time I think *this is the play*. I'm not writing a draft—I wrote 12 *plays*.

As an actor, how do you approach a role?
I don't really consider myself an actor. In film you can get away with a whole lot that you can't on stage. I think almost anyone can get away with being in a film.

Is that just the nature of the medium?
Yeah. Because if you're in a tight close-up, you don't have to do much: You don't have to do anything; you just say the lines. You don't have to act. So, I mean, with film acting, for me, it's just a matter of corresponding certain parts of myself to the character, finding corresponding parts and just becoming those parts all the time. I'm not a method actor or anything. I don't have any complicated scheme behind it.

Could you act in your own plays?
I could, but I don't want to.

Why?
Well, because part of the reason for writing them is to see them. You can't see them if you're in them at the same time. I like having that distance.

Music plays a more significant role in some of your plays than in others.
I think they're all musical. I like to look at the language and the inner rhythms of the play, and all that to me is related to music directly. In *True West* there are coyote sounds and crickets and things like that. And the dialogue is musical. It's a musical, *True West*. I think it's very related to music, the whole rhythmic structure of it. Rhythm is the

delineation of time in space, but it only makes sense with silences on either side of it. You can't have a rhythm that doesn't have silence in it. I studied for a long time with a drummer from Ghana. He was totally amazing. And I found out that, particularly in African music, every rhythm is related. You can play 4/4, 5/8 and 6/8 all together at the same time and at some point there's a convergence. Even though it sounds like all these things are going off in totally crazy directions that are beating up against each other, they'll always come back. That was a big revelation to me, that rhythm on top of rhythm on top of rhythm always has a meaning. So the same is true on the stage. There are many possible rhythmic structures that an actor can hit, but there's only one true one. There's one moment that he has to meet.

How do you find that moment?
Well, that's very complex. It has to do with an emotional relaxation, where suddenly the tension goes and it's just *there*. I was a drummer for a long time and I realized that a lot of the time you're straining to keep the time. And then there are times when all that drops away and everything just . . . it all just rides together. And those are the times it became simple. Absolutely simple.

Do you feel closer to certain plays because they contain more of a sense of that?
Oh, yeah. Some of them have real dumb rhythms. It depends on each piece, though. There's only one little part of *Buried Child* that I like, that I could watch over and over and over again. One little tiny section. It's at the beginning of Act 2, I think. Just the little dialogue between the children and the old man on the couch by the television. That's the only part that interests me anymore.

Why?
Because the rest of it just seems verbose and overblown. It seems unnecessarily complicated. But that little simple scene at the beginning of that act, it's great. It's perfect. I could watch that all day. It's just got a musical thing to it, you know? That kind of thing happened.

It's been said that nothing can shock anymore. Still, there's an element in some of your plays that seems determined to shock us.
Yeah?

In *Curse of the Starving Class*, for example, you have a character pee on stage.
Well, I wouldn't do that again if I had to do it over again. I was looking for a gesture, for something without words. It's funny how you look, you know? You look at all parts of yourself for it. Sometimes it comes out when someone pisses on stage. It's a little flashy, you know, and overblown, and maybe embarrassing, but that's the way it came out. It's just a gesture. Like the toasters in *True West*. There's an intention there that's intrinsic to itself. It only makes sense to itself. It doesn't *mean* anything. You can call it absurdist or whatever you want to; I don't care what you call it, but it's true to itself. It takes the impulse that was

behind it to its absolute extreme, further than you would expect. And that's what I wanted. Trying to figure it out is not the point. I think explanation destroys it and makes it less than it is.

How do you write?

You mean the technical thing? I write by hand first, I write everything in notebooks. Then, after I get everything where I want it pretty much, I start typing it. And as I'm typing it, I'm rewriting it. I'm copying from the notebook and I'm rewriting on the typewriter.

Do you consider yourself a poet?

That's a very high thing to be, a poet. César Vallejo is a poet. I'm not a poet yet; I'm working on it. I think a poet is a musician. Poetry is music. So it doesn't matter what form it's in, whether a line extends across the page or goes vertically. That has nothing to do with it. It's the musical nature of the language and everything that's going on in it. Vallejo, Neruda, Hank Williams. He was one of the original country-western singers. Have you ever heard any of his stuff? Great American poet. "I'm So Lonesome I Could Cry"? You never heard this? Jimmie Rodgers? You've got to look into this.

Do you see your work as evolving to a certain point?

No, I don't see it like that at all. Maybe it's just going in a circle. I don't know; I really can't tell you whether it's evolving or not. I mean, it's definitely different. There's more at stake now; there's a bigger risk.

Amy Lippman is a television producer and screenwriter. She was the co-creator of Fox's "Party of Five" and is currently a writer for HBO's "In Treatment." This interview was first published in the March '83 issue of the *Harvard Advocate*, while Lippman was a junior there.

ARTICLES OF FAITH

An interview with Lillian Hellman by Marsha Norman

May 1984

L illian Hellman's house is hidden from the road, but everyone knows where it is. Knowing where it is, however, is not knowing what it is, or who it is that lives there. The house has thick white walls that face the world, and clear glass panes that face the water. It is a writer's house.

Inside her house, Miss Hellman is quite thin and very sick. There are nurses round the clock, but there is also a boat on call, for the fishing that is as good for her as the medicine, her friends say. Readers will, perhaps, expect me to describe her more fully, as she is rarely seen in public anymore. But my desire is to protect her. Quite simply, I owe her a great debt. And if leaving her privacy undisturbed is what I can do for her now, then that is what I will do.

Robert Brustein made the arrangements for this interview. He joined Miss Hellman and me as we talked in the house on Martha's Vineyard during the summer of 1983.

LILLIAN HELLMAN: I hear your play is very good, Miss Norman.

I am so surprised by the reaction to *'night, Mother*. When I wrote it, I was so angry, I didn't care if anybody ever saw it. And I was convinced nobody would want to.

HELLMAN: Well, that's the way to write. The idiot Pulitzer Prize people picked right for once.

It's so good to have an opportunity to say what you did for me. But I don't know if you want to hear that.

HELLMAN: Oh, I'd love to hear it.

I was a kid who didn't really know it was possible to write for a living. I grew up in a religious fundamentalist family in Kentucky, and Mother hoped I would work

for the airlines for a few years and then marry a doctor. But all through high school, there were teachers who put your plays in my hands. And finally there was a moment during my first marriage, when I had begun to refer to my first husband as "the keeper," when Martha Ellison, a dear friend and former teacher, gave me *An Unfinished Woman* and said, "Lillian Hellman said this better than anybody has ever said it," and she was referring to your line about the driving desire to be alone when you want to be and not alone when you don't want to be.

HELLMAN: It's still true for me, isn't it for you?

I don't even like to think about how true it is.

HELLMAN: That one gets more and more true. And I am less and less alone. It's not possible for me to be alone any more. I have three rounds of nurses. And I have so much more desire to be alone, and I'll never be alone again.

Why is it people are afraid when you tell them you want to be alone? Why does that scare people?

HELLMAN: I don't think it scares them; I think it offends them. Also I think it attacks them in some way. They don't want to be alone. It's very hard to explain to somebody who always wants to be with somebody. It must sound awful. Hammett used to say that you could watch me plan to be alone. You could watch me sit on the couch and say, "Now how can I get out of this room in 10 minutes?" I once had a beau who went to Hammett for advice. This particular beau wanted to marry me for money, of course, but can you imagine going to Dash for advice? Isn't that wonderful?

ROBERT BRUSTEIN: You were living with Dash then.

HELLMAN: Yes, I was living with Dash. And he went to Dash for advice. And this man said, "You know, Dash, I don't know what to do, I love Lillian very much." (Probably what he loved was what he thought was money.) "But," he said, "she seems to leave the room every now and then. I know what she's doing, she must be having these wonderful deep, profound thoughts, but what should I do?" And Hammett said, "If I were you I would do nothing. If she's thinking anything at all, it's not very profound. Maybe she's thinking how to move the sofa up against the chair. The only other thing it could be is she's trying hard to find out how to leave you." And so this man asked me if that were true, and I said it was, and I never saw him again. I literally never saw him again.

I'd like to keep asking you about these lines of yours that have meant something to me. Right at the beginning of *An Unfinished Woman*, you say that your mother fell in love and stayed in love with Max for her whole life. Is that possible, or how was that possible with your mother?

HELLMAN: To answer that, we'd have to discuss the nature of in-love-ness, which I think we'd better not do. What I meant was her passion was as great, wherever passion comes from. She was on her deathbed and accusing him of infidelity, which was probably 25 years after the original marriage. I don't know whether it means in-loveness or not, but she was still fascinated by him, or interested in him. After all that time, she still wanted him.

You don't hear about that kind of love anymore.

HELLMAN: Women like my mother—whether they knew what they were doing or not—they sort of invented it, perhaps. I think it would be wise to go back to inventing it.

I'm very concerned, right now, about those articles of faith that we have left behind.

HELLMAN: I am too.

I hated that old religion. I fought it, I rebelled, but now I find myself coming back and wanting there to be things to believe in.

HELLMAN: I find myself in exactly the same stage. I don't know whether I want that religion to believe in, but I want other things to believe in. I don't look on the past with the glamour that most people do. It's too bad that certain moralities have been lost. I think that's one of the reasons I like John Hersey. Because there's an uprightness to him I miss. He's very pleasant. He's reassuring to me. Someone who will not be evil, who will not betray, some elegance of spirit is what I really think it is. There's an enormous amount of betrayal along with the violence now, isn't there? That makes me almost sicker than the violence.

There's a line of yours about fear, about "showing off against it." I see an awful lot of that.

HELLMAN: I think we all do.

What do you know about fear now that you didn't know when you wrote that line?

HELLMAN: A lot. I have a lot of physical fears now that I never knew anything about. This illness has taught me a bit. How physically frightened I am. I am a total coward. Hammett guessed it once. He said I acted bravely so I wouldn't show the fear, and he was absolutely right.

BRUSTEIN: Lillian, you forget how you behaved before your operation last fall. You were out having a dinner party at the Parker House and then you cooked a goose the next night.

HELLMAN: Did I?

BRUSTEIN: You were showing no fear whatsoever.

HELLMAN: I didn't know what the operation meant. I blocked out the whole thing, all of last summer. I can't remember anybody who was here. Thank you for telling me, Bob, that's wonderful. Where did I do this?

BRUSTEIN: In Boston. You came out of the hospital and took us all to the Parker House for dinner and the next night you cooked two geese.

HELLMAN: Oh, that's right.

BRUSTEIN: And the next day you went in and had those operations.

HELLMAN: That's just my way of forgetting things. That ain't brave. Oh, how nice of you to tell me. What a pleasant memory that is.

If that isn't brave, what is?

HELLMAN: Well, you see, I don't know. Maybe it is brave, I don't know. I think of myself now as a mass of fears. I had totally forgotten about the geese.

Then there is a discussion of the Styrons' anniversary party the previous night, to which Miss Hellman had sent a case of beer with a card saying, "This will be clearer and better than I am." One of the housekeepers lights a cigarette for her.

There's another one of your lines I want to ask you about. You said the theatre had been your life but not your world. I have the feeling that you were never comfortable in the theatre.

HELLMAN: No, I wasn't. Not with the people. I feel comfortable in a theatre, I feel comfortable in a rehearsal, for example, but I don't like theatre people very much. Never have. A few isolated instances, maybe.

What was it, exactly, you didn't like about theatre people?

HELLMAN: They're silly people, most of them. They're very vain. Vanity is a disease in theatre, it's actors, it's directors, it's everybody. God knows I have it, but I've tried very hard not to let it control me. It's a very dangerous streak in all of us.

Do you think there's a way to make theatre without vanity?

HELLMAN: No, no. You have to have some, but you don't have to let it run away with you. You don't have to be that interested in yourself. You don't have to get up every morning and stand in front of the mirror and then spend the day there.

What advice do you have for dealing with success in the theatre?

HELLMAN: Just forget it. Just earn the money and forget it. Don't let all those silly people tell you how wonderful you are. It's very nice to listen, just don't pay any attention to it.

You just see so many people who have been destroyed by their success in the theatre.

HELLMAN: Yes, but we destroy everything else by success in America. We want it so terribly and we don't handle it very well. We feel we have to top ourselves every time around. We can do anything—sexually—we want, but we cannot have an artistic failure.

I think the truth is, nobody really knows whether they can survive an artistic failure. I worry about that. But people keep saying, "But Marsha, you're so strong . . . ."

HELLMAN: Oh, they always will, darling. Any successful woman they'll always talk about this way. It's partly to put you down, I must warn you. It's not always entirely admiration. It's probably to make you feel that they're tiny and attractive, and you're the strongest, most miserable piece of fascist violence ever put on earth.

Is there a good way to deal with that?

HELLMAN: I don't listen to it anymore. When men do it, it's for another reason. But when women do it, it's exactly what I describe, to say, "I'm pretty and so darling and look at you, over there earning a living. And you're powerful and ugly and miserable."

BRUSTEIN: Who was your favorite director, Lillian? Who were you satisfied with?

HELLMAN: Herman Shumlin was. We had terrible fights, every other day, but we did fine together. We used to actually throw things at each other.

Do you find that a lot of your fights are about the same things, even though they're with different people?

HELLMAN: Well, I made the unfortunate mistake of having an affair with this man. And he made the even more unfortunate mistake of falling in love, or whatever you call it, with me.

Who have you really liked working with?

HELLMAN: I liked Maureen [Stapleton], I still like her. But one night . . . .

There ensues a largely unprintable discussion of a dinner which ended with the restaurant staff escorting them both to the door. Hellman calls a nurse to come and stand her up and massage her back.

Are there things you would like to have done more of? More war reporting, for example?

HELLMAN: I would like to have had the courage to *do* what I wrote about. You remember I once had an offer to go with the Russian army to Berlin? I wish I'd had guts enough to do that. I wish I'd been there for that.

That's exactly what I was wondering about. If you were writing today and able to move around, would you be in El Salvador?

HELLMAN: I hope so. I've been thinking about it anyway, to tell you the truth, and I realize I couldn't take a nurse to El Salvador, but I've been in constant communication. I fortunately have an ex-student who is among the rebel leaders, who gets in touch with me all the time.

Then she tells how this man gets in touch with her and where they meet and what he brings her from El Salvador, and she asks me not to print the details because it could be dangerous for him.

What is it about those people that excites you?

HELLMAN: Oh, I like the idea of people revolting against what they have, what they haven't got. It's a wonderful human quality. In the end, you can't fool people. You can't keep them down. I come from a banana republic family, and my Sundays were spent with my Uncle Willie getting up, pushing the table aside and saying, "Well, we'll send Johnny Christmas down with some guns."

So your family would have been on the establishment side.

HELLMAN: Oh yes.

How did Vietnam seem to you?

HELLMAN: Absolute crap. Some series of dopes, here, thought it would work. Disgusting. The most disgusting event of my whole life. We don't know anything about the rest of the world and we don't care about ourselves. Imagine sending Americans to die in that place. Most Americans couldn't even place it on the map. And we don't give a damn about the people who came back from it either.

Another piece of yours that I love is the introduction to the Chekhov letters. And in it, you say that all great art requires a kind of spiritual violence.

HELLMAN: Did I say that?

You sure did.

HELLMAN: Thank you very much. That's very nice. That translation has been under attack.

There's another place in it where you talk about the "need that shallow people have for emotional fancy dress. Their desire to deck out ordinary trouble in gaudy colors, and to teeter around life like children in their mother's high-heeled shoes."

HELLMAN: Did I write that? That's good.

Well, there's so much more. All you have to do is ask me and I'll come read you the whole thing.

HELLMAN: That would be wonderful. Do you live in New York?

Yes.

HELLMAN: Well, maybe you'd come down and see me. Would you?

I sure would.

HELLMAN: I'll fix you and your husband a goose.

And the nurses take her upstairs and Bob and I walk out of the house. He says she liked me. And I wonder why the National Endowment for the Arts doesn't have a program that sends unemployed actors over to old writers' houses to read their work to them.

Marsha Norman was awarded the 1983 Pulitzer Prize, Susan Smith Blackburn Prize, Hull-Warriner and Drama Desk Awards for *'night Mother*. She won the 1992 Tony Award for her book for *The Secret Garden*. Her other plays include *Traveler in the Dark*, *Getting Out*, *Third and Oak: The Laundromat*, *The Poolhall*, *The Holdup*, *Sarah and Abraham*, *Loving Daniel Boone* and *Trudy Blue*. She has served on the faculty of the Juilliard School since 1994.

MAKE NEW SOUNDS

An interview with Lorraine Hansberry by Studs Terkel

November 1984

When *A Raisin in the Sun* opened at the Barrymore Theatre on March 11, 1959, the late Lorraine Hansberry became Broadway's first black woman play-wright—and, in short order, the chronicler of the black experience and strug-gle for a generation of Americans. Two months after the opening—after Hansberry had upstaged Tennessee Williams, Eugene O'Neill and Archibald MacLeish by winning the New York Drama Critics' Circle Award—she was interviewed by Studs Terkel for his "Almanac" radio show in her home town, Chicago. On the occasion of the 25th anniversary of *Raisin*'s opening, excerpts from the interview are printed here for the first time.

CHICAGO—MAY 12, 1959

Someone comes up to you and says, "*A Raisin in the Sun* is not really a Negro play. Why, this could be about anybody!" What is your reaction? What do you say?
What people are trying to say is that this is not what they consider the traditional treatment of the Negro in the theatre. They're trying to say that it isn't a propaganda play, that it isn't a protest play. They're trying to say that the characters in our play transcend category. However, it is an unfortunate way to try to say it, because I believe that one of the soundest ideas in dramatic writing is that in order to create the univer-sal, you must pay very great attention to the specific. Universality, I think, emerges from truthful identity of what is.

In other words, I have told people that not only is this a Negro family, specifically and culturally, but it's not even a New York family or a southern Negro family—it is specifically Southside Chicago. To the extent we accept them and believe them as who they're supposed to be, to that extent they can become everybody. So I would say it is def-initely a Negro play before it is anything else.

You've spoken of Walter Lee Younger, the focal character of the play, as an affir-mative hero in contrast to many of the heroes of theatre such as we see today.

Walter is affirmative because he refuses to give up. There are moments when he doubts himself and even retreats. But I supposed thematically what he represents is my own feeling that sooner or later we are going to have to make principled decisions in America about a lot of things. We have set up some very materialistic and overtly limited concepts of how the world should go. I think it's conceivable to create a character today who decides that maybe his whole life is wrong, so that he ought to go do something else altogether and really make a complete reversal of things that we think are very acceptable. This is to me a certain kind of affirmation. It isn't just rebellion, because rebellion rarely knows what it wants to do when it gets through rebelling.

There was another affirmative character to emerge in the theatre in the last few years, who interestingly enough chooses death, when he stands up against the Salem witch hunts in the 17th century—John Proctor in *The Crucible*. This is choosing death for a reason that's going to substantiate life.

For life as a man rather than as a cipher.
Exactly.

Walter Lee's mother is a remarkably strong character. In Negro families, the mother has always been a sort of pillar of strength, hasn't she?
Yes. Historically this has something to do with the slave society, and was sustained by the sharecropper system in the South and on up into even urban Negro life in the North. There's a relationship between Mother Younger in this play and Juno, the protagonist in Sean O'Casey's *Juno and the Paycock*. No doubt there was a necessity among oppressed peoples, black or Irish or otherwise, for the mother to assume a certain kind of role. Obviously the most oppressed group of any oppressed group will be its women, who are twice oppressed. So I should imagine that they react accordingly: As oppression makes people more militant, women become *twice* as militant, because they are twice oppressed. So that there is an assumption of leadership historically.

You have often mentioned your feelings for O'Casey.
Yes, I love O'Casey. He is the playwright of the 20th century who accepts and uses the instruments of Shakespeare, that is, the human personality in its totality. I've always thought this should be a profoundly significant model, or point of departure, for Negro writers. O'Casey never fools you about the Irish, you see: He shows the Irish drunkard, the Irish braggart, the Irish liar, who is always talking about how he is going to fight the Revolution, but when the English show up he runs and hides under the bed and the young girl goes out to fight the Tommies. There is a genuine heroism which must naturally emerge when you tell the truth about people. This to me is the height of artistic perception and the most rewarding kind of thing that can happen in drama. If we believe people completely, as drunkards or braggarts or cowards, then we also believe them in their moments of heroic assertion.

In your work, you showed Walter Lee's frailties throughout, and when he did emerge in the heroic moment, we believed.

That was the hope. That was the intent. What I do *not* believe in, to turn for a moment to technical dramaturgy, is naturalism. I think naturalism should die a quiet death. I *do* believe in realism.

What's the difference?

There's an enormous difference. Naturalism is its own limitation—it simply repeats what *is*. But realism demands the imposition of a point of view. The artist creating a realistic work shows not only what *is* but what is *possible*—which is part of reality too. The point in O'Casey is the wonder of the nobility of people. It is this dimension of people's humanity that he imposes on us. And he uses something which I can't imitate because I'm not equipped to—poetic dialogue, which moves it into the sphere of great art.

But there is a great deal of poetry in *Raisin in the Sun*. A feeling that is larger than life. Isn't that what theatre should be?

Always. Always. There used to be a ballet in this play. (*Laughing.*)

There was a ballet?

That's right. The motifs of the characters were to have been done in modern dance. It didn't work! But I think that imagination has no bounds in realism—you can do anything which is permissible in terms of the truth of the characters. That's all you have to care about.

Is the play autobiographical?

No, it isn't. I've tried to explain this to people. I come from an extremely comfortable background, materially speaking. And yet we live in a ghetto, you know, which automatically means intimacy with all classes and all kinds of experiences. It's not any more difficult for me to know the people that I wrote about than it is for me to know members of my family. This is one of the things that the American experience has meant to Negroes. We are *one* people.

I guess at this moment the Negro middle class—the comfortable middle class—may be from 5 to 6 percent of our people, and they are atypical of the representative experience of Negroes in this country. Therefore, I have to believe that whatever we ultimately achieve, however we ultimately transform our lives, the changes will come from the kind of people that I chose to portray. They are more pertinent, more relevant, more significant—most important, more *decisive*—in our political history and our political future.

The very charming and lively little sister—is she slightly autobiographical?

Oh, she's *very* autobiographical! (*Laughing.*) My sister, my brother would tell you that! The truth of the matter is that I enjoyed making fun of this girl who is myself eight years ago. I have great confidence about what she represents. She doesn't have a word in the play that I don't agree with still, today. I would say it differently today.

I've been interested in some of the criticisms of the play—there was one letter in the *New York Times* from a very sophisticated young man who said he regarded it as a soap opera. Which amused me. Soap opera implies melodrama, of course, and melodrama has a classical definition. If you can prove that there are no motivated crises in this play, I would be astonished. Or a "happy ending"! If he thinks *that's* a happy ending, I invite him to come live in one of the communities where the Youngers are going! So I don't think the play qualifies as melodrama; it is legitimate drama.

It's very interesting to me that no one has picked out something that is a very genuine criticism of the play—that is, that it lacks a central character in the true classical sense. There is a *pivotal* character . . . .

In Walter Lee.
Yes.

But some will tell you Mrs. Younger.
That's right. And some people are so enamored of the daughter that they're not sure that *she* isn't the most relevant in some way. This to me is a weakness of the play.

Is this really a weakness? I'm thinking of Clifford Odets's *Awake and Sing!* There was no central character in this excellent play of Jewish lower-middle-class family.
Well, obviously, when you start breaking rules you may be doing it for a good reason. But in my view of drama, the great plays have always had a central character with whom we rise or fall no matter what, from the Greeks through Shakespeare through Ibsen.

May I ask you about Asagai, the African suitor?
My favorite character.

He's a remarkable figure. Who is he? What is his meaning in the play?
He represents two things. The first is the true intellectual. This is a young man who is so absolutely confident in his understanding and his perception of the world that he has no need for any of the façade of pseudo-intellectuality, for any of the pretense and the nonsense. He doesn't have the time or interest—except for amusement—in *useless* passion, in useless promenading of ideas.

The other thing he represents is much more overt. I was aware that on the Broadway stage they had never seen an African who didn't have his shoes hanging around his neck and a bone through his nose, or his ears, or something. (*Laughing.*) And I thought that just theatrically speaking, he would be a most refreshing character. In fact, this boy is a composite of many African students in the United States whom I have known. They have represented to me in life what this fellow represents in the play: the emergence of an articulate and deeply conscious colonial intelligentsia in the world. He also signifies a hangover of something that began in the '30s, when the Negro intellectuals first discovered the African past and became very aware of it.

Garveyism.

Yes, that was part of it in a different sense. But I mean particularly in poetry and the creative arts. I want to reclaim it. Not physically—I don't mean I want to move there—but this great culture that has been lost may very well make decisive contributions to the developments of the world in the next few years.

The New York Times recently quoted you, speaking of a certain irritation you felt in seeing plays about blacks written by people wholly removed from the situation. You said something about Carmen Jones ....

I probably alluded to the whole concept of the Exotic. In Europe, you know, they think that the Gypsy is just about the most *exotic* creature to have walked across the earth—that's because he's isolated from the mainstream of European life. So, obviously, the natural parallel in American life is the *Negro*. (*Laughing*.) Very exotic. So whenever it's time to do something like a Bizet opera which involves the Gypsies of Spain, it's translated, they think, very neatly, into a Negro piece. I just think this is sort of a bore by now.

The clichés are there.

I'm bored with clichés. I don't think very many people realize how *boring*—aside from being nauseating—those stereotyped notions are. This is not said often enough. It's not only a matter of works like *Porgy and Bess*—I'm talking about the DuBose Heyward book now, not the music, which is great American music in which the roots of our native opera are to be found someday. But the book is not only offensive, not only insulting because it's a degrading way of looking at people, but it's *bad art* because it doesn't tell the truth! And fiction demands the truth. In other words, there is no excuse for a stereotype. I'm not talking socially or politically. I'm talking as an artist now.

Aesthetically, it's bad.

Exactly. If a work of art is a lie because it just tells *half* a truth, then the artist should shudder for reasons other than the disapproval of the NAACP. And the responsible artist will.

Art must tell the truth.

I think so. It's almost the only place where you can tell it.

Now that A Raisin in the Sun has been so well received, what about this little goddess, Success? What does it do to you?

It's wonderful, and I'm enjoying it! I don't have the right to be very personal about the reception to this play, though, because I think it transcends what I did, or what Sidney Poitier or Lloyd Richards or any of us connected with it did. I think it reflects at this particular moment in our country—as troubled and as depressed as I, for one, am about so much of it—it reflects a new mood. We went through 8 to 10 years of misery under [Joseph] McCarthy and all that nonsense, and to the great credit of the American people they got rid of it. And they're feeling like: *Make new sounds!* I'm glad I was here to make one.

Make new sounds! The best of jazzmen say that, too.
It's a close relationship. I've often said that the glory of Langston Hughes was that he took the quality of the blues and put it into our poetry. And I think when the Negro dramatist can begin to approach that quality, he might almost get close to what O'Casey does in putting the Irish folksong into a play.

I think Lorraine Hansberry is on the road, certainly.
I spoke of how there's a new affirmative political and social mood in our country having to do with the fact that people are finally aware that Negroes are tired, and it's time to do something about it. But beyond that, in terms of the total picture, I'd like to see a parallel movement, I'd like to see a parallel movement in the culture of our country. I see no reason in the world why the American theatre should be lined up on about six blocks on Broadway in New York City. I'd like to see a little agitation to get a national theatre and other art programs in this country so that kids all over the United States can go see Shakespeare without thinking it's a bore. Or Eugene O'Neill. Or Lorraine Hansberry!

Studs Terkel was a prize-winning author and radio broadcast personality. His first book of oral history interviews, *Division Street: America*, was published in 1967. It was followed by a succession of oral history books on the 1930s Depression, World War II, race relations, working, the American dream and aging. He was the first Distinguished Scholar-in-Residence at the Chicago Historical Society. His last book, *P.S.: Further Thoughts from a Lifetime of Listening*, was released in November '08. He died on Oct. 31, 2008, at the age of 96.

AN AFTERNOON WITH ARTHUR MILLER

An interview by Mark Lamos

May 1986

I'm standing on the porch of Arthur Miller's house in Roxbury, Conn., and two German shepherds are barking like crazy but looking pretty harmless. A bustling, friendly old German woman lets me in, asking if I'm there to see Arthur. "Yes," I tell her, and then I see him. He's silhouetted tall and lean against a bright autumn sky, smiling broadly. We shake hands.

"You look great."

He asks, "You want a pear or an apple?"

"An apple," I decide.

"Oh." He looks at the woman, who is briskly polishing pears on a picnic table. "Here," he says, and leads me off the porch and into the late afternoon light.

We step out onto a hill of grass and walk toward a large, gnarled apple tree. The grass around it is dotted with mottled fruit. He picks up an apple and turns to me. His rag-knit beige sweater has holes in the elbows, the jeans on his stork-like long legs are worn. Despite (or perhaps because of) his glasses, his eyes are the same as I remember them—like bird's eyes, hawk's eyes: skillful, watchful, aware.

Time stops. My mind flashes back to 1972, when I was acting in his play *The Creation of the World and Other Business*. It lasted some 20 performances on Broadway, and its birthing was the beginning of my theatrical loss of innocence. Harold Clurman had been the director, but he was fired during previews at Boston's Colonial Theatre. Hal Holbrook and Barbara Harris were the original stars, but we opened in New York with George Grizzard and Zoe Caldwell. Miller rewrote the third act 14 times. I played Abel. I spent the first two acts in the dressing room at the Shubert Theatre and then got bonked on the head by Cain in Act Three. At that time in my life, it was just about the most glorious opportunity a fledgling New York actor could hope for. I was in a play by Arthur Miller. Ironically, by the time it opened in New York, I had worked with more stars and directors than if I'd done three Arthur Miller plays in a row.

Looking at Miller now, 14 years later, I find myself remembering the way he used to stand in the auditorium at the edge of the stage, slapping the floor of Boris Aronson's fiberglass set with a rolled-up script, barking up at the actors with a smile, "This is the best god-damned play I've ever written. It's better than *Salesman*!" I believed it.

I still believe in Arthur. He hands me an apple covered with yellowish lumps and splattered with as many colors as an oak leaf in October. "You can eat all that," he assures me. "It looks that way because I don't spray."

He picks up an apple from the grass and bites into it. We begin walking up the hill towards a weathered cabin, chomping on our apples.

"How much land you got here?" I ask.

"Two hundred acres. That apple tree was here before I came."

Idly discussing Connecticut real estate, we arrive on the cabin's rickety deck, he pulls aside the sliding glass doors and we enter what seems to be an abandoned study. Cobwebs tie the typewriter to a mug full of pencils. Card tables sag with the weight of notebooks and piles of dusty papers. The room is very spare, even haphazard. There are old chairs, a fireplace, a few shelves of books with water-warped covers. A perfect place, it strikes me, to get some writing done when the time is right.

We settle into chairs and I set up a tape recorder. Since I'm hoping to direct a revival of *The Crucible* at Hartford Stage Company in the coming season, we decide to start the interview on that subject.

I read somewhere that you enjoyed the writing of *The Crucible* more than any other play because you didn't have to worry about the plot.

Yeah. You could write all day and when you got to a standstill, you'd think, oh shit, what do I do now? But then all you really had to do was open the history books.

Is everyone in *The Crucible* a real person?

Oh, yeah. They all really lived. Most of that really happened. I made Abigail a little older. You know, in those days, a girl could get married very young.

You wrote *The Crucible* in response to McCarthyism, a movement many people said couldn't happen here. Could what happened in Puritan Salem happen again in the 20th or 21st century? Did Americans learn anything from Salem?

There was a lesson learned, both by intellectuals and people in general, and I don't see the possibility of a hysterical reaction on that level. On the other hand, look what we did in World War II with the Japanese on the West Coast. This internment of people was done not by some arch-revolutionary racists, but by Franklin Roosevelt with the consent of a lot of us who got stampeded into it. It was born, as such things always are, of some concrete circumstances.

You see, in Salem a new governor had come in—the king's representative passed an edict that all land titles were up for grabs. There was a disputation about who owned what. If you're dealing with thousands of acres in a community that couldn't rely on a proper survey, and then suddenly the government says, "Well, you may not own what you think you own," a roiling uneasiness begins to develop, and a lot of people begin to talk about some kind of spirit abroad—of the Antichrist moving in to disturb the good sheep.

This had been going on for years in Salem before the outbreak of witchcraft. And Salem was a very isolated community—there wasn't any traffic going through Salem to Boston, a town that was, relatively speaking, far more sophisticated. Nevertheless, all the great preachers in Boston at the time were preaching witchcraft—they thought it was a great idea to "go hunting." So I guess they weren't that sophisticated! (*Miller laughs heartily.*)

I'll tell you a quick story about the son of the governor. He and his buddies from Harvard thought that all these local yokels in Salem who were carrying on about witches were touchingly stupid. These boys had read about it, and they thought it might be fun to horseback down to Salem early one morning and watch a witchcraft trial in one of the churches . . . which they did. At one point something so absurd was said by one of the witnesses or the preacher or somebody that the Harvard boys burst out laughing. They were promptly put in jail, and they were going to be condemned to hang. But by passing some money to the guards, they got out of there—and they didn't come back to Salem very soon! (*More laughter.*)

Can you talk a little bit about the Wooster Group's production of L.S.D., which used parts of The Crucible and reorganized it, deconstructed it? Your lawyers used an injunction, right? You closed the production.
There was no permission asked to do anything, although the Wooster Group later asserted that they had asked. The other thing was, I didn't agree aesthetically with it—it was a simplified cartoon of a much more interesting and complicated phenomenon. Had I thought it was wonderful, I wouldn't have objected—they owed me the right to agree with their production concept. I resented the arrogance in relation to me, which I didn't think the play deserved.

My impression of L.S.D. was that they used The Crucible as a theme for a set of variations. Did you see it?
Yeah, I saw it. What they did was abstract a whole play into one brief act. The rationale was that since everybody knew the play, the actors could verbally maul it. It was a demonstration of their boredom rather than their getting to the center of everything in it. Well . . . it's a boring time in the arts. I told them when I'm dead and gone they could do what they liked with it. But for now I'm still around. See, they were treating the play like a "found object." And I said, "But it's a found object that nobody lost." (*Much laughter.*)

You mentioned the Japanese situation on the West Coast during World War II. That reminds me that you once said, in response to some criticism of After the

Fall, that concentration camps seemed to you to be the logical conclusion of 20th-century life. Do you still feel that?

Oh, yeah. Such camps occurred not just in Germany, you know, but also in Russia as a tremendous reaction to what you could call the Liberal Idea. They were the statement of people who were against the idea of a mixed society, where people have the opportunity to do anything they choose to do. The idea of a mixed society disturbs a lot of people, and the 20th century has by now so demoralized people as far as their individual existence is concerned that people are tempted—in every direction, from the point of view of dishonesty in business, even sexually—to be essentially out for themselves. I think the purging of the Jews was a logical consequence of the desire to make all people part of a single larger organism.

A phrase you have used to describe your work as a playwright is "unearthing an inner coherency." Often in my own work I find people saying to me, "Gee, it's amazing what you evoke by creating this or that stage picture." It seems to mean something to them outside of the theatrical moment itself. Now, of course, sometimes you strive for an effect; but at other times, people see things in your work that you didn't even know were there. A subconscious coherency. Do you feel that most of your work comes from a desire to make something knowable out of our chaotic responses . . . ?

Yes. That's why I write, I think. I've often wondered why I went through all this, and I suppose it's the need to *make form*—and form is simply consistency. You find relationships between otherwise disparate things. Suddenly you see that there's a common thread running through everything, and when you locate that thread, you've got an organism. Incidentally, the actor and the director finally have to do the same thing: They have to find it for themselves—and that may be a different thread from the writer's, but it's a thread, nonetheless. Otherwise, there's no forward motion—you're not discovering anything.

The horrible thing is, though, when the thread that you're discovering isn't the thread that the auditor is discovering—which is maybe what happened with *After the Fall* when audiences first saw it and perceived it as simply a play about Marilyn Monroe.

Yeah. But maybe we shouldn't think of that as a defeat in any way. After all, look at Shakespeare, at how many ways you can do a Shakespearean play, because each one is so rich. You can endlessly interpret them, just as you can, say, the Bible. And why should there be one meaning? When six people look at the same inkblot in a Rorschach test, they come up with six different images. And I'm afraid that's the way it's gonna be with art as well. However, if there is some rudimentary consistency, some form, some thread in the first place . . . .

I see a play now and then in New York that seems to have no reason for existing at all. It just seems to be an effusion of some kind, under the license of I don't know what—free association or something. Which is very boring: It's too much like life. You don't want life in the theatre, you want art.

Do you find that the way your plays are directed, designed or acted may give them differing focuses?
Oh, yes. For example, this last production of *Salesman* [on Broadway and for television], I realized at a certain point, was far more the story of Biff, the son, than it was of Willy Loman, the salesman of the title.

Because of John [Malkovich]?
Because of John. But I also think it was because of what's happened in the past 30 years—that is, the coming into consciousness of a youth culture, and the demands of youth. When I wrote *Salesman* there was no such thing—I didn't regard Biff as the leader of some movement.

Incidentally, when I directed *Salesman* in China, the guy playing Biff asked me, "Now is he speaking for the movement?" And I said, "Well, the movement was as yet 20 years off in the future; that rebellion of youth against the parent and society." That baffled the Chinese actor, because the idea of one man making a decision like Biff makes—to disregard his father's tradition and go off on his own—seemed very strange to him, unless it was couched in a political rebellion. The Chinese found it very crazy that Biff might be doing that just for himself.

And many Chinese people also regarded the play as very much a story of the mother. In China it would often be the woman, the mother, who would be worrying that way about the careers of her children. China is a hidden matriarchy. As in a lot of these macho-suppressed societies, it's the women who make the important decisions.

You've just had your 70th birthday, and I wonder what you want to accomplish next?
Well, I've got a big play that is lying right over there in those notebooks, and I'd like to do that. I get very discouraged about *how* to do it, how I'm going to finish it. I need one scene, the last scene. I've been mulling that over for a couple of years. But when that's done, it'll be my big play. And I'm writing a book here about my life—I'm about half finished on it.

Is it more difficult to get things on stage now than it was when you started writing?
Oh, yeah. As bad as it was back in the '40s and even the '50s, it's harder to do now because of today's costs—it's as simple as that. I've just recently written two one-act plays involving four actors, but I'm sure that if you tried to do them in the conventional way on Broadway today, it would cost you a quarter of a million dollars.

The cost factor is ridiculously prohibitive today, even in the so-called nonprofit theatre. And with ticket prices so high, it no longer seems to be a theatre for the people.
What are your prices now?

Twenty-one bucks is our top at Hartford Stage.
You see, this is a bitch, this is a terrible problem.

I see a different audience in our theatre during the previews when they can come for eight bucks, and at the matinees which combine student groups with senior citizens. But the rest of the time, the level of excitement and of interaction between audience and actor often seems less variegated, certainly less vigorous, less invested.

I kept saying this for years; I gave up saying it: There's a deal going on between a play and an audience, an unspoken social arrangement in which they're agreed to come and you've agreed to talk with them. Now if, for one reason or another, certain people are strained out of the audience, the nature of the event changes, it's weakened. You see, I go by two theatres of the past—the Elizabethan and the classical Greek. In both cases you had more or less the whole society in those theatres. In America this happened during a short period in the '20s, when there were touring companies going around the country to places without a big middle class. These touring companies were drawing people out of the factories and the lower income groups in order to survive. They were competing with vaudeville, which certainly had a universal, working-class appeal.

But I think we have a theatre now which loses its political quality. By "political" I don't mean Republican, Democrat, Socialist or Communist—I mean it was theatre addressed to the *polis*, the Greek idea of community. And even though they don't realize it, the playwrights themselves are sensitive to that little segment of the community, and they begin writing plays for this narrow audience. When I began writing, when Tennessee Williams began writing, we shared the illusion that we were talking to *everybody*. Both of us wrote for the man on the street. So consequently the architecture of our plays, the embrace of our plays, their breadth, was in accordance with that conception. It was the very opposite of an elitist theatre, the very opposite of an intellectual theatre.

And by the way, *Hamlet* is that kind of a play . . . .

Exactly! *Hamlet* **was written for beggars as well as kings.**

You see, if you had the whole society in the theatre, it would temper the elitism—because those people of narrow mentality would hear laughter at moments in which they couldn't see the humor, or they would hear people gasping with feeling at something which they may have resolved to remain remote from. So a new aspect of social behavior and human interaction would begin to open up—the members of each part of society would become affected by their fellows in the audience. The less culturally hip would benefit as well and pick up some cues from those who were more hip.

So our earlier playwrights assumed everyone would share the theatre experience and benefit from that sharing?

Absolutely. In America during the '20s and '30s, the person who went to see the *Ziegfeld Follies* would also be interested in seeing O'Neill. Nobody thought that was particularly amazing or even contradictory. What we've gotten in the last 15 years, as the theatre became more constricted, is a critical apparatus that reinforced the division. We got fewer and fewer plain, educated reporters writing reviews, and more "trained critics" who were bringing academic standards to bear on the theatre and looked down on stuff that had more feeling in it. I think there is a failure of many critics to allow themselves to react to feeling. It's an awful situation. In New York, it's catastrophic because there's only one newspaper—and even if you had the greatest critic in the world on that newspaper, it would only make it *worse*, because it would reinforce a single authority.

I want to ask you about TV and film acting. Somebody said that it's not really a performance controlled by the actor, it's just behavior that the camera picks up. Do you agree with that?
Yeah, maybe it is true. In the theatre, "as if" is very important. It's got to be "as if" you're doing it because you can't literally be doing it. But the "as if" is *gone* in film. That element has been eliminated. When we started shooting *Salesman* for TV, we had to throw out the first two days of film because all the actors were doing it the way they'd done it on stage. And the director said, "This is intolerable. You can't watch this for two-and-a-half hours. It's too big, it's too loud. It's too demonstrated." Well, Dustin [Hoffman], being a film actor, understood that. But everybody starting talking (*softly*) like that, and I said, "There goes the whole play, there's nothing gonna happen!" But finally it did happen. We found a completely different level.

Somewhere you talk about how listening to Beethoven and reading Dostoevsky had an effect on climax and structure in your work. You said, for example, that listening to Beethoven you realized how the climax was withheld and withheld, and this musical idea influenced your work.
When I started thinking about writing for the theatre, I thought of the play as a symphonic organization. The whole convention, the way of thinking about life in drama, was that stage action was a culmination of the past—through development, characterization, complication and so on—and through the whole first act you would tell about matters of the past that led to a specific dilemma. And the dilemma in the second act came to a crisis, and that crisis came to a climax in the third act. Well, this meant that you drew strands of meaning from all over the place to gradually show the wonder, the wondrousness of the event—how seeming accident, seemingly disconnected events, were really connected by one fatal element—be it the fatal flaw in the character who drew it all together, or in society itself. Everything was drawn together. Well, that's very symphonic. It's also very Greek.

And, with variations, that was the basic method of playwriting I employed. What happened was that sometime in the '50s, all that really broke loose. The new dramatic writing that came from the sense of disconnection in that time seemed to contradict the idea of the well-made play. Impressionistic writing emerged, the kind of thing Beckett was doing. His characters lived not in a specific place . . . but rather "on the earth." Ionesco's characters were . . . angles of irony. Characters like that had no personalities beyond the most blatant qualities—one was a rhinoceros and the other was a firebug or whatever—so that the whole idea of bringing the past to bear on the present, as such, was gone.

We don't have any past anymore. And we've got little plays as a result. They're little in the sense that they're about one small segment of an event. They don't need a past. Movies, incidentally, don't really have any past either.

In the case of the Greek plays, how much did the audience's knowledge of the plot help to create theatrical excitement? How much do you think the excitement and power of Greek plays depended on the audience in Athens knowing the plot, those old stories—as we know Bible stories or, say, *A Christmas Carol*?
I think a lot; it gave the writers and presumably the actors as well the license to create their variations. The audience could relax. The story was familiar. It's a little bit, I suppose, like going to church and hearing a sermon on a Bible story. There's no question about how it's going to come out. But there's the atmosphere and the beauty of the actual telling, the minister's voice and his wearing of various sacred garments . . . . After all, what is a minister doing with most of these sermons? He's taking a well-known theme and making variations.

Like a Greek *stasimon*. An ode. But then Ibsen really changed all that because he deliberately didn't want you to know the story.
That's right. *That* is melodrama. The evolution of the tale then becomes at once extremely important. You know, when we revived *Salesman* last year, 90 percent of that New York audience knew the play or at least they knew the story. But they wanted to see how we did it this time. We could have run it five years.

Do you think a playwright has a moral obligation as a writer?
I don't like to call it a moral obligation. It's really . . . well, take Chekhov. When we read Chekhov now, we see his time through his plays. They get more journalistic to me as I read them—I notice the speeches where people are saying, "Why don't we do something?" You get the sense of a whole society that's stalled, mired, doesn't know how to work anymore. Chekhov proved to be politically prophetic. And I'm sure he was eager to say, "This is what's happening NOW." Otherwise, why would he have written those speeches? It's a long and honorable tradition, this business of telling the news. That's all the obligation I'm interested in. Certainly Ibsen was up to his neck in the news of the day. But I think it's harder to do now as brilliantly as it once was, because this society is so *various*. Everything is disconnected somehow, and nothing coheres. Look at President Reagan—his supporters chucklingly acknowledge that you can't quite believe anything he's telling you. He's a nice guy—he just says things that have no basis in fact. And he says them very often and about very important things, like Star Wars. Even his advisors admit that it's a fantasy, not to mention the whole scientific community! But Reagan's gonna appropriate some trillions of dollars to this thing, and there's no *connection* made. The

wires are being pulled out. That has to be said, you see? What I just said is a *statement*. It's a critical stance.

What other writers have been influences on you?

I think probably the single greatest discovery I made was the structure of the Greek plays. That really blinded me. It seemed to fit everything that I felt. And then there was Ibsen, who was dealing with the same kind of structural pattern—that is, the past meeting the present dilemma. I loved the spirit of Chekhov more than anybody, but I could never think of writing that way—when you sit down to write, it's hard to be that wise and tolerant and loving.

What about Clifford Odets?

He had a remarkably short career—less than five years. After he went out to Hollywood he ceased wanting to be a playwright. He wrote two more plays, one of which I thought was half a terrific play—*The Flowering Peach*—together with *The Big Knife*, which has some wonderful stuff, too. But even at that time he was disintegrating.

You see, to be alive in those days was to feel certain communal passions which everybody on the Left and all the artists felt—namely that the country had come to a moral halt, so to speak. The powers-that-be were morally bankrupt. The only alternative was the explosion of authority in the outside classes, the lower middle class and the working class. They were going to restore honor to the human race. Odets's career starts fundamentally in 1935 and it's over by 1940—the years of the Depression outcry. As soon as life got more ambiguous, which soon happened, his style seemed to be inappropriate. But while it was going, it was powerful—not just what he had accomplished but the idea of a playwright being a spokesman for something. After all, there *was* no politics in the American theatre until Odets. It was pure entertainment.

Watching Larry Kramer's play about AIDS, *The Normal Heart*, at the New York Shakespeare Festival, I got so riled up, so disturbed. I felt I had to walk out of the theatre and do something—begin organizing and demonstrating and raising money. I wondered if I was feeling something akin to what audiences felt in the '30s when they saw Odets's *Waiting for Lefty*. Didn't they used to leave the theatre yelling, "Strike! Strike! Strike!"?

When I saw *Waiting for Lefty*, I really believed that some of those people on stage were taxi drivers. What was happening on stage was part of what was happening on the *street*. Mostly you got the sense that Odets was reporting some inner life about which you knew very little. You felt too that he was making a statement: "IT'S ALL WRONG!" The statement was all the stronger because everything else that was going on in the theatre at the time was just entertainment, pure entertainment.

It's interesting to look at writers as part of their times. Odets happened at a particular moment in American time; if he had come along a decade later, perhaps he wouldn't have written plays. Looking at Shakespeare, you think he could only have

let that extraordinary mind loose in the Elizabethan Age, that age that had just discovered that the world was round, not flat, that there were stars, planets . . . .
Everything was possible.

Shakespeare is really the playwright of the possible.
I think that's true. But Shakespeare also had a mythology to draw on. I learned how important that is in writing *The Crucible*, where I had the history there, the myth to go back to. It's funny—Shakespeare didn't really invent his stories . . . well, maybe *The Tempest*.

What I love about *The Tempest* is that it's based on a news event.
A shipwreck.

Absolutely. You know, Shakespeare was a member of the Virginia Company. He may even have been an investor in that ship. The play couldn't have been written if America hadn't been discovered. The storm that begins the play was talked about all over England. So *The Tempest* really was "news of the day."
No kidding.

The afternoon sun is setting. We continue talking as I pack up the tape deck and we make our way back to the house at the bottom of the hill. There we meet Miller's wife, photographer Inge Morath. She's as handsome and energetic as I remember her being 14 years ago.

As we pass into the kitchen, Miller points to a framed poster of the French premiere of *The Crucible*, which starred the late Simone Signoret. Looking at that, I think of all the questions I didn't ask. But then the dogs begin to bark again, the old German lady (who turns out to be Inge's mother) shakes my hand, and Miller and I go out to the car. He remarks on its newness, we trade quips about foreign cars, and in a moment I'm wheeling down the drive under the rain of yellow leaves and onto a winding country road past leaning mailboxes, stone walls, barns.

Actor and director Mark Lamos took on the artistic directorship of Connecticut's Westport Country Playhouse in early 2009. He led the Regional Tony Award–winning Hartford Stage from 1980 to 1997 before leaving to pursue a freelance career. He has directed around the country and on Broadway and Off Broadway. He received a Tony Award nomination for directing when the Hartford Stage production of *Our Country's Good* transferred to Broadway in 1991.

JOSEPH PAPP GETS BIG IDEAS

An interview by Ross Wetzsteon

September 1986

To understand Joseph Papp, perhaps the most powerful figure in the American theatre for the past three decades, it's helpful to paraphrase a line from one of his greatest hits, *The Pirates of Penzance*—a Pappadox, a Pappadox, a most ingenious Pappadox. He's a financial genius—yet his greatest achievement has been free summer theatre in New York's Central Park. He has, his critics contend, lowbrow taste and little aesthetic vision—yet he's famous for reviving interest in Shakespeare and for nurturing new playwrights. He relies on gut instincts, liberal politics and personal loyalties—yet, those critics argue, his career has been built on shrewd calculation, imperialist exploitation and cold-blooded betrayal. And finally, he has fought the establishment all his life—yet now he is the mainstream, in the very center of both commercial and experimental theatre.

In the late '50s, Joe Papp was working out of an office in a cloakroom at a children's theatre on 103rd Street, but he also had a truck stage in Central Park. He didn't have a permit—he just moved in, and when the Parks Department asked what was up, he mumbled something about "a mechanical breakdown." Almost before Parks Commissioner Robert Moses realized what was happening, Papp had presented a couple of summers of free Shakespeare—and when Goliath finally got around to confronting David it was too late. Papp had only one strength going for him—his weakness. But he played the cocky underdog to the hilt, and after the battle was waged in the courts—and in the papers—Moses had to back down. Thirty years later, Shakespeare in Central Park is one of New York City's major cultural attractions, and has played to three million people.

In 1966, taking advantage of a new landmarks law, Papp raised $575,000 to buy the old Astor Library building and turn it into the Public Theater and headquarters for the New York Shakespeare Festival. Within a year, he renovated the building into six theatres, rehearsal space and office quarters, and opened with a hippie musical called *Hair*. But Papp was soon running up a million-dollar-a-year deficit. So he leaned on the city, which, in 1971, bought back the building for $2.6 million and leased it back to Papp—for a dollar a year. In those five years, he'd parlayed half a million dollars into a million-dollar debt, and gone on to parlay that debt into a $2.6 million sale and six theatres for 16 cents a year each. Joe Papp was giving chutzpah back its good name.

In 1973, Papp was called in to save Lincoln Center's Vivian Beaumont Theater. The saga of a bisexual go-go dancer, a comedy about mastectomy, Puerto Rican child molesters in prison—the establishment wasn't ready for his kind of fare, and he left in 1977 "to concentrate all my energies at the Public Theater." But, "defeated" by the establishment, he *became* the establishment, and when his theatre recently celebrated its 30th year he could point to three Pulitzers, more than 30 Tony Awards and almost as many Obies as the rest of Off Broadway combined.

"Robert Moses's power made him arrogant," Papp told me a few years ago. "You know what Lord Acton said: 'Power corrupts.' That's what power does to people." But when I pointed out to him that he himself probably had more power than anyone in the American theatre, he covered himself magnificently. "I don't feel the power myself," he said quickly, "but it's marvelous for the people who work for me. I have the power to keep them functioning because I'm fighting the powers that are trying to destroy them." A man who can turn Lord Acton's aphorism about power into altruism—now there's a man who understands power.

But like all powerful personages, Papp has made his share of enemies. He has no guiding aesthetic vision, they say—he merely has an uncanny sense of the next bandwagon and skillfully positions himself as its driver. He may say he uses his power to protect the people who work for him—but, ask his critics, who protects those people from him? He announces ambitious new schemes with a fanfare (a four-year contract with CBS television, plans to create an American National Theater Service Agency), then quietly walks away when they fail to get off the ground. He poaches productions from smaller theatres and turns them into hits. He pays lip service to artistic merit while lusting after blockbusters. The litany goes on and on—but then so does Joe Papp. And for every theatre artist who's vowed never to work for that son-of-a-bitch again, a dozen will tell you he's the single person most responsible for their success.

Nor is Papp the kind of person who keeps clear of controversy. He led the futile battle to save the Morosco and Helen Hayes Theatres, his ardent testimony helped pass New York City's gay rights legislation, and he stepped into the middle of the fight at this year's Festival of Nations in Baltimore, arguing on behalf of the exclusion of the National Theatre of Great Britain's production of *Animal Farm* from the program when he could easily have avoided taking what he surely must have known would be a highly unpopular stand.

Finding out where Joe Papp stands is never difficult—what's hard is getting a word in edgewise. Try to ask him a question and he's off on a half-dozen topics at once. This trait was even more evident than usual when I visited him early this summer at his office on Lafayette Street, since he'd just embarked on yet another major new project.

This seems to be particularly felicitous time for you. The New York Shakespeare Festival recently celebrated its 30th anniversary, *A Chorus Line* is in its 11th year, *The Mystery of Edwin Drood* has just won a Tony as . . . .

That's all in the past. I'm not interested in any of that. This is what interests me now. (*He holds up an advance copy of a full page ad in the Sunday* New York Times.) A new play by a new writer, *Cuba and His Teddy Bear* by Ray Povod—I'm moving it to Broadway. I'm experimenting, taking the first step toward a low-priced theatre on Broadway. Not musicals, dramatic works. We have 250 seats at $10 a seat, with the rest of the house at regular Broadway prices. That's not my desired price structure down the line—I'd like to average $15 or $20.

You mean this isn't just a one-time . . . .

People are saying, "Oh, now he's going to charge less and people will start running." Getting a new audience into the theatre—that's what I want. The Broadway houses will really be Off Broadway on Broadway. We're starting with a top name, Robert De Niro, one of the best actors in America. Even though he hasn't done much on the stage, he's turning in a brilliant performance—just brilliant. But I want to introduce the notion—as I was negotiating with the unions regarding our schools program—the notion that theatre people have to step back, for dramas in particular. The unions have to step back to make it possible to have a grace period of about 10 weeks where union conditions are very loosely applied in terms of salary, in terms of work, so that it'll be possible to charge very little money to be able to break even, to be able to perpetuate productions of plays. Maybe even doing two plays in repertory with two stars. I want a few hundred thousand people who will come to see four plays a season at one or two theatres. Why stop at one or two? Why not three or four? If there are four theatres, there are going to be 16 productions. Think of that—16 new productions a year.

Hold it. I haven't even asked a question yet, and already you've mentioned a schools program, union negotiations and an experimental program for new plays on Broadway—you've gone from one trial run to 16 plays a season—you've intimated both a revolution in the economic structure of the commercial theatre and in the make-up of its audience. Let's take it one step at a time. What about *Cuba and His Teddy Bear?*

This is a 10-week dry run. I want to produce low-priced plays with big stars every season in Broadway houses at low rent, or rent-free. My goal is to create a theatre constituency in New York for plays that have something to say, at affordable prices, and in Broadway houses that are empty or threatened with demolition. The reason, the necessity to do this is for a decent living for people in the theatre. In the noncommercial system, without government support, people cannot make a living. Under our program, during the 10-week grace period, the writer, for example, will get the highest salary, probably $1,000 a week, no royalties, no nothing. All the rest will get less. The stars, the unions, everybody. If you charge low prices, you may break even or you may lose money, so you need a fund to compensate. If you have three or four theatres, some plays will do very well and some may not, so if this play does very well, we'll have this other play that's not doing too well—it's a consortium of theatres.

There seems to be some sort of threefold paradox at work here. For one thing, you're aiming at a more populist theatre. For another, you're stressing quality dramas. And for another, you're heading toward a star-oriented theatre.
The idea is to get people of some reputation to appear in these plays, so that people who ordinarily don't go to the theatre—even those who do go to the theatre—have a reason to go aside from the play itself. Because dramas are dead now, they virtually disappear as soon as they arrive. Even Sam Shepard's *A Lie of the Mind* couldn't run, and he's one of the most important writers we have.

But to gain this new constituency I'm after, this new audience, you have to create a different kind of theatrical culture. The old theatrical culture had great stars, stage stars—Katherine Cornell, Helen Hayes, all those great names, going way back—and it was those people who attracted audiences. People never went just to see a play. Oh, they'd go to see an O'Neill play, but O'Neill usually had major actors in his plays. But because of what has happened over the years, Broadway has diminished. Top actors, even top press agents, are few and far between. We're seeing the diminution of everything, even top *tailors*—because the whole industry has shrunk and its economic base is very small. All you get are a few shows that try to become blockbusters, that try to attract audiences who don't have a stake in the theatre itself. So what you get is a constituency of people who are essentially credit-card people, who do not establish a standard. In fact, by the high prices they're willing to pay, they encourage a certain kind of pure entertainment, and generally not very good entertainment at that—just a kind of theatrical product. And what we miss most from this constituency is the New York input. We don't have a real New York audience of any size that can establish standards and create the kind of energy that we need in the American theatre.

By New York audience, do you mean an ethnically diverse . . . .
I'm not finished with Broadway yet. Now, I'm not foolish enough to think that we're going to bring back the 19th century. Times have changed, there's new technology—you can't beat it, you join it in the proper way. But we have Broadway theatres that are in danger and will continue to be in danger in the immediate future—theatres that have no economic viability, no reason for existence. And you know how it is in our society, if things have no reason for their existence, we wipe them out. This brings back this craw in my side, this rat in my throat—which is the tearing down, the demolition of two marvelous theatres, the Morosco and the Helen Hayes. That was the beginning. But it

could get worse. To quote Gerry Schoenfeld, he's with the Shubert people—and I don't have to hear it from him—I asked him, "How many theatres do we actually need on Broadway, based on the present economy?" And he said, "We could certainly get rid of a third and feel no pain." I think it's even more than that. So consequently, by beginning to make those theatres function—not as landmarks with plaques on them but as working theatres—by beginning to draw a new audience, by beginning to get new writers from that audience—because audiences create writers—we can begin to turn things around.

This new audience, these new writers—that's what every producer dreams about. But where are they going to come from?
They're going to have to be more representative of what constitutes the New York population. That includes our own black communities, our own Hispanic communities—which are very large—our own Asian community—which is growing—and other communities of different nationalities. We have very rich, fertile ground for a different kind of theatre to supplement the middle-class theatre. We're still going to depend on the middle-class audience, and we don't want to preclude people who are 70 or 80 or 90—but there's a core audience out there somewhere between 17 and 27 years of age, active, animated groups who have shown an interest in or who could become interested in the theatre, particularly my theatre. I want to get a survey and try to find out how many people would become constituents, members of this theatre. I'm thinking about 50,000. And there's no shortage of plays if you open up the possibility that plays can be produced and playwrights can make a living. You'll get more people writing, you'll get new people—like we got Ray Povod, who came with very little education, a product of the Lower East Side, and who turned out a marvelous play. This city is alive with talent. This country is alive with talent. We have a tremendous amount of culture—we just have to focus it and put it someplace.

Speaking of focus—it all sounds very noble and ambitious, but are nobility and ambition going to impress the unions?
I'm asking the unions for this grace period of 10 weeks for new productions, during which time pay would be lowered to let the play get off the ground. Then, if that creates an audience, we'd revert to regular union scales. Of course it still has to be negotiated, though it's already been negotiated for the schools program—but you pay actors somewhere around $400 a week for this 10-week period. Right now, with *Cuba* moving into the Longacre, we haven't done that well. But all the actors will be working for the Broadway minimum, $700 a week. That includes all the stars—Robert De Niro, Ralph Macchio, Burt Young—everybody is working for $700 a week to make that production possible. Even the lighting designers and costume designers are getting only a fraction of what they would ordinarily get. Because everybody says, "We want to keep making those theatres come to life." Sure, the unions hate to step back after they've won certain minimums.

But there are so many theatre people unemployed that it's just academic to discuss those things. Create employment! Create the possibility of something succeeding! That's what I'm talking about, and that's why they'll listen to me. And I'm not talking only new plays. I'm talking classics as well. We put on *Hamlet* at the Public last year with a company of 35 people. On Broadway that would have cost a couple of million dollars, but we did it for under $400,000. And nobody is being exploited because nobody is making any money.

You've mentioned your schools program several times. Tell us a bit about that.
I'm doing both these projects at once because obviously the two are connected. We have a company, led by Estelle Parsons, made up of black, Hispanic and Asian actors, doing *As You Like It* and *Romeo and Juliet*—we'll be adding other plays as we go along. We bussed in more than 500 students a day for two performances daily at the Anspacher Theater this spring. Then this fall we'll move into the Belasco Theatre on Broadway for 10 performances a week, a thousand students per performance, two a day. There'll also be preparation for their classes, analysis and backup after their classes, meetings with their teachers, teaching the teachers how to teach Shakespeare. Then on weekends, which are very important for us, we're going to try to re-create some semblance of what once existed in middle-class life—parents bringing their children to the theatre; only now the children will be bringing their parents to the theatre. It's not just work in the educational system—once you work in the educational system you're doing social work, too, and you're dealing with all the problems of poverty. I'm interested in organizing New York City for the theatre. In each of the boroughs, through the borough president, I'll have a representative who will be a kind of coordinator who will make contact with existing institutions and help create an audience so that we can begin to unleash what I consider the New York energy. And if it functions here, it'll go out to the rest of the country.

So the main purpose of the schools program is to create that new audience for serious drama?
I want these kids to have an interest in the theatre. And I want them to be *able* to go to the theatre—the two programs are interrelated. I want them to know that there are going to be dramas on Broadway of a serious nature, that they would be interested in them, that they could affect their lives. And at the same time I don't want them to find that tickets are $75 by the time they get out of school. There's an audience, and I think it numbers in the hundreds of thousands, that has been disenfranchised or alienated from the theatre, either because it's too expensive or because it has no intellectual base. Most of the stuff today is junk. You find more interest going to a good movie, or reading a book, or even going to a restaurant. So we have to begin to deal with these two problems. What we're setting up are two systems—the noncommercial system adjacent to the commercial system, which will feed the commercial system.

How do you plan to finance this program?

Other governments, like Britain, can give $65 million to the Royal Shakespeare Company, but in this country we have to struggle. I put up all the money up front before I get a penny from anybody else because if I wait until people give me money I'll never get it. We've even taken money out of our endowment, which hurts us because we need that money to survive. We have almost a $3 million deficit, but we're still moving ahead with the schools program—we've spent over $600,000 on it already. We're waiting now to see how much the city will come through with as its contribution. The program is budgeted at $2.5 million—we're putting up a million-and-a-half and we expect a million from the city. If that money doesn't come through, I don't know what I'm going to do—but I'll do something. But it's interesting that the Board of Education, which has extraordinary needs right now for all kinds of programs, has taken the position, having seen the work, that this is very important to the school system.

Getting back to your program for drama on Broadway, you say you're basing this effort on using major stars—do you have any in particular in mind?

Yes. But I wouldn't tell you. Not yet. I can tell you, though, that people didn't come to see *Hamlet*, they came to see Kevin Kline. The way to attract new audiences is to get actors who are already well known to them—from television or film in particular. There just aren't any great stage actors anymore who people instantly recognize. I'm very conscious, for example, that if I do a black play, I want to make sure I have a major black actor in that play. The same if I do an Hispanic play. Because there's not an immediate audience that's just going to come running if I put up a sign, or an ad in the *Times* or the *Village Voice*. Ninety percent of this is organization. You have to organize it. Like being a union organizer. You have to get out there and get people, and I'm working at it. Above all I want to create the attraction of major actors. I can get any major actor I want. A major actor on the stage is someone who can make the walls rattle without shouting, someone who can rivet your attention. The very being of that actor is a magnet.

But isn't one of the very things wrong with the theatre today that it depends too much on the star system?

When I say star, I'm not talking about a star *system*. A star system is when you get one major star and then you get a second rate company together because the star wants to look good and the producer doesn't want to pay people. What I'm looking at is different—a major actor like De Niro or Meryl Streep can attract other actors who want to work with that person; they get together for artistic reasons. England has been the best example—you have the finest actors working in all the media. I think we have to begin to make that happen here. I'll get them. And I'll get them to do classics as well as contemporary plays— and at low prices too. Don't worry, I'll get them.

Some of your critics find it hard to see a consistent guiding artistic vision in your career. They say you chase after fashions—that you go for political plays one year, for ethnic plays the next year, for British plays the year after that— whatever happens to be "in" that year.

But I've had a very consistent vision! Never changed! It's been addressed primarily to reaching audiences, new audiences, people who can't afford to go to the theatre. This new Broadway program—didn't I start out with the same idea 31 years ago, bringing audiences to free Shakespeare? And I've always had a strong social base, always. You'll find that 80 percent of my plays deal with problems that are issues of today. Is that chasing after fashions?

Let's take the last two years. Start with Larry Kramer's play, *The Normal Heart*, a hot political play dealing with a major issue, AIDS. Look at *Map of the World*, David Hare's play. *Aunt Dan and Lemon*, Wally Shawn's play, was highly controversial—I was even accused of being anti-Semitic in doing that play—where's the fashion for a play like that? Keith Reddin's *Rum and Coke*. Ray Povod's *Cuba and His Teddy Bear*—a crucial play about a poor family. I do a lot more black and Hispanic works than anybody. Is that chasing after fashions? That's part of my artistic vision. These critics, they want an artistic vision where an individual is the director of a theatre that turns out only one kind of art, but I'm not that kind of person. I've always been rooted in the city; I want my theatre to reflect what exists in the city of New York, in terms of population, the nature of its different cultures. Sure, I'm interested in music, I love music, but you'll find that all my musicals have had a high standard—you can't say that's not consistent. Take an old chestnut like *The Pirates of Penzance*, an operetta, a gorgeous piece of work, get Linda Ronstadt to attract people to the theatre, and make it a popular piece. I've tried to do that with Shakespeare, same thing. If that's not an artistically consistent line, I don't know what is.

I think some of those critics are still living in the '60s, when there were individuals who had a particular kind of artistic bent, like Grotowski. I'm not a Grotowski. Grotowski didn't care if he played for 45 people. I do care. I want lots of people to see my plays. I believe in a popular, democratic theatre. I want the theatre to reach great numbers. Sure, I enjoy it when Robert Wilson does his thing because he's been very consistent with his art and I love it. But I don't have just one single artistic thought or style. I want to do a great variety of plays to satisfy all kinds of audiences, not just some coterie. I am interested in the avant-garde. I love the work of Mabou Mines—they were here for years. I encouraged that work. And Richard Foreman. And Joe Chaikin. They both worked here. And finding young writers, giving them a chance. That's my policy.

What fashion do I follow? When I introduced *A Chorus Line*, there was no fashion for *A Chorus Line*. There was no fashion for *The Pirates of Penzance*. There was no fashion for *Two Gentlemen of Verona*. There was no fashion for bringing a play like *Sticks and Bones* to Broadway, a play which I knew would lose money. Those critics, they weren't doing plays about Vietnam; I was doing plays about Vietnam. They weren't doing plays with blacks; I was doing plays with blacks. Who was doing the first plays about women? I was doing them. That's not fashion, that's tied in to what's going on with the world, so that the theatre has some life. There is very clearly a social consciousness in all the work I'm doing.

Okay, let's move . . . .

No consistent artistic vision? In fact, I've made a complete circle. More so than ever I'm doing what I originally started out doing. I haven't changed a bit. The only difference now is that I have more power, more clout, more prestige, more possibility of having an impact on the American theatre. Just changing the economics, to make it possible to do dramas on Broadway and open up four or five of those dark theatres and have lights in those streets—if I can do that, that would be amazing, because we're going against history. History is going to tear all those theatres down, history is going to build more of those goddamn hotels—that's what history is doing.

Speaking of what history is doing, and your hopes of turning the tide—the critic Robert Brustein says that we're entering a new Golden Age in the American theatre, while other people argue that the American theatre is in the greatest crisis in its history. What do you think?

They're both wrong. First of all, theatre isn't going into a Golden Age. There are a lot of talented people around, but I don't see where this Golden Age is. On the other hand, sure, the American theatre is in a state of crisis; but theatre writers and theatre artists are not. The institutions may be in a crisis, but institutions alone don't make up the theatre. The theatre will survive because there's a lot of unselfishness and people need to do theatre. Writers, despite the fact that they know there are very few outlets for them, despite the fact that it looks like they have one chance in a million of even getting a play put on—they still write, they still keep going. It's that kind of drive which seems to be organic. That sense of survival will keep theatre artists alive.

How do you feel about the decentralization of the American theatre—the fact that New York isn't the center of the country anymore?

It's still the central theatre, but we're just holding on by our teeth. New York doesn't have the kind of impact it used to have. Still, that doesn't say very much for the rest of the country. There are, here and there, some companies that are interesting, that are doing exciting work, but not on any extraordinary scale. I haven't seen any place in the country where there's any kind of really powerful manifestation of a Golden Age, not at all. Bob Brustein could mention a Golden Age from his point of view—he's had some very interesting people working there [at American Repertory Theatre in Cambridge, Mass.], but that's hardly an example of the rest of the country.

Who are some of those companies whose work you admire—anybody you'd like to single out?

A guy like what's-his-name, Peter Sellars. He's a talented guy. I like Des McAnuff's work in San Diego. And there are small groups here and there that are doing interesting work. But of the major groups around the country I don't see anything that I can say is outstanding or changing anything.

Where do you see yourself in relationship to the American theatre? Do you consider the Shakespeare Festival a kind of regional theatre that just happens to be in New York? Do you consider yourself part of the nonprofit theatre community? Or do you see yourself as entirely independent, almost sui generis?

I have a certain amount of independence because I don't depend entirely on support from charitable or eleemosynary groups. I have to make it on my own. But I'm essentially a not-for-profit organization. Now a not-for-profit organization is actually the most expensive in some ways, because you have to maintain it year-round. It's easier on Broadway—if the show is running, fine; if it isn't, you close up, you don't have to carry the institution all the time. But I don't consider myself a Broadway producer. Essentially, I identify myself with Off Broadway.

What do you think of the current state of theatre criticism?

What's that?

Is it good, bad, useful, stimulating, irrelevant, what?

I didn't know it existed.

Well, that's an answer, I guess. But do you think the fact that it's generally so unintelligent is harmful to the theatre? You're well known for not having official opening nights, for inviting the critics only in the middle of or near the end of a run. Do you think more intelligent discussion in the dailies and weeklies would help the theatre, or would you like to be independent of criticism altogether?

I'm not interested in intelligent discussion, except among the people who actually create the work—the writer, the director, the actors, the people in the play development department, that kind of discussion. I really do not need, personally, to have someone who happens to write for a newspaper give me his opinion. His opinion is like anybody else's opinion—except that it's based on power. On the other hand, people respond to reviews. So I'm very much for reviews, but I don't consider that criticism. I like the reviewer when he gives me a good review; I dislike him when he gives me a bad review. As far as the opinions expressed in that review—other than generally favorable or unfavorable—I don't pay much attention to them.

Well, there are two ways of looking at it—one, that reviews help sell tickets, and the other, that informed criticism helps writers and directors and actors develop their craft, that perceptive discussion helps generate and stimulate a vital theatre community.

I have no time for that. Most of these things quickly deteriorate into very unintelligent discussion. We've lost an intellectual base for the theatre, so consequently most of the discussions in print are vapid—people don't know anything, and yet they go on to talk about it. John Simon of *New York Magazine* is always tearing individuals apart, which I despise. When he praises something I've done, I always think I must have done something wrong. As far as Frank Rich is concerned, I don't agree with a lot of his positions but he has the *New York Times*, so I want a good review from him. But as far as their value in any kind of intelligent, lively discussion, I don't think they have any at all. Too much discussion about the theatre, theoretical discussion, I find extremely boring. I don't even like to read books about theatre—who cares? I used to read them when I first became interested in theatre. I read all of Stanislavsky. That was a good education. But I'm growing up—at my age, I'm not interested in theory anymore.

Now I have to just work. The actual work sparks my creativity. My theory comes out of my practice. I do things and I understand. I analyze plays constantly, for instance. I analyze the weakness or the strength of the play. I'm very good at structure. I can tell you exactly what's wrong with a play in a few minutes—exactly. It's like being a diagnostician, who can look at you and immediately know what your general health is. I can do that with a play. I have a discussion with a writer about his play—you need to do this, this is missing, this doesn't pay off because you don't have it set up beforehand. Sheer nuts and bolts. Of course you have to be extremely careful how you handle that because you don't want to impose anything on the writer. It's an extremely delicate matter, it's surgical.

You say that you "don't want to impose anything," but there are dozens of people who've worked with you who feel that you've often imposed your own judgment, as a producer, on writers and directors. You're not exactly a passive person. Do you feel that sometimes you've stepped in too actively as a producer?
Sure, but I only do that when it's necessary. I only intervene when I feel the work is going poorly. My whole desire is to stay away as best I can. I try to avoid work, that's my main goal. Sometimes I do get involved too much, but when I do that means something is wrong with the product—there's something wrong, there's a crisis. Ask the writers I've worked with—except Sam Shepard, because he was never here—ask them how I work, how much I interfere. I would never touch them. First-class writers I will never touch. But if someone needs help, the writer is grateful that I came into it. Ask Albert Innaurato, he's a perfect case. He's the touchiest man in the world, but I worked beautifully with him. The one play of his we did [*Coming of Age in Soho*] I turned completely around through my idea. Ask him what he thought of the way I criticized his play. Ask Wilford Leach [principal director of the Shakespeare Festival] if I interfere with his productions. I respect his work. He's a first-class artist. Why am I going to interfere and screw it up, unless I'm a destructive person? I can't build an organization by interfering with people's work. They wouldn't work here!

You're a highly visible producer. Was it a conscious decision to make yourself into a kind of celebrity by participating so actively in advertising campaigns?
In the first years I didn't want my name mentioned at all. I just buried myself. What happened was that as a result of our successes, my name became important to a certain kind of identification with this particular theatre. So actually I didn't sell myself, they were selling me. It doesn't mean very much to me, personally, but it brings attention to the theatre. I don't have any ego about that. But if my name helps, use it.

I was also thinking of your *USA Today* and American Airlines ads—you were used as a celebrity; the ads didn't have anything to do with the theatre.
Oh, yes they did! That American Airlines thing—we shot the marquee so I'd be seen coming out of my theatre. Also, all the money I make from ads goes to the Public Theater. I don't keep any money I make from anything. I just have my salary. Any money I make—like when I went to teach at Florida State University, I got $60,000—it all went to the Public. Any advertising I do also provides revenue for us. We're still collecting on American Airlines.

Would you care to share with the readers of *American Theatre* just what your salary is?
No, I don't think so. Let's just say it's consistent with the job I do. I have a board of trustees, and my salary is evaluated with comparable jobs in other institutions, based on a $12 million annual budget. I don't make more or less money if a show is a hit or if it fails.

Your connection with England is fairly well established, with the continuing exchange program with the Royal Court, but now you seem to be looking more and more to Latin America. I understand you're even learning Spanish.
Yes, I'm studying Spanish. I knew Spanish before, but not so well—I need it now that I'm speaking and traveling in Latin America so much. But it's hard to learn a language when you're older.

How old are you?
I'll be 65 next week. I've lived awhile, see.

Do you see yourself retiring at any time in the near future?
I have no idea of age at all. I don't know what the hell it is. I'm in very good shape. I started working out four or five years ago, I have a very tough regimen. I work out like someone who is 35. As far as my health is concerned, I'm okay. I don't see any reason to even think of retiring. You think of retiring when you're tired and bored. Right now I feel that I know more than I've ever known. And I'm doing the most important thing I've ever done right now. These programs—the Broadway dramas and Shakespeare in schools—they're the quintessential programs.

Most institutions make plans for a succession, for continuity, if a strong leader were to suddenly die. But if you were to get run over by a bus, is the Public set

up in such a way that it could continue to function? Or would it slowly die, lacking its central focus, its aggressive guiding personality?

I've already made arrangements. There are two or three people, one in particular, who would step in immediately.

Could you tell us who they are?

No, I don't want to embarrass them. But the Public will go on. I've added people to the board who will follow the basic precepts of the organization. I have also made provisions—well, let's say my recommendation—for the next president. So the institution will go on, but what will happen next is questionable. It'll change. It has to change. But the institution itself is well grounded. The tradition will always be there, one way or another, but it will be something different. What would I do if I were the next person to sit here? (*He gestures dismissively at the framed posters of dozens of famous Papp productions covering the walls of his office.*) I would immediately take all these off the wall. They'd have to come down immediately.

People don't realize what a short lifespan theatres usually have—even the most important theatres in our history. The Group Theatre, for all its influence, actually lasted for only a few years, and the Provincetown Players were a vital force for only four or five years. Yet the Public is now over 30 years old.

Theatres have a limited life. They don't go on forever. And if they do go on, generally they become very institutionalized. I think 10 years would be considered a long time. The creative life of a theatre is almost like that of an individual—it hits a height at a certain time and then it starts to decline. It's very strange. Yet this theatre breaks all the rules. I think we're in a very high position right now. The work still has a cutting edge. So that defies tradition.

When I talked to you a couple of years ago, you seemed to have a very despondent view of American culture and of theatre's role in society. In fact, you seemed to feel that theatre couldn't really lead but was merely a prisoner of the social context in which it existed. Now it would seem that we're living in a time when theatre is an even more marginal part of American culture, when American culture itself is very much in a down cycle. Yet you seem far more optimistic, far more adventurous then you were just three or four years ago.

You're right. A few years ago I felt despondent because we weren't doing anything, but now I feel more on the upside. Not like Brustein, not like the Golden Age. I think we're in the Copper Age right now, but at least we have some mettle! (*He smiles broadly at his pun.*) So I feel positive about that. We're engaged in something. And I feel that there will always be a theatrical energy that will emerge. New forms have to come, new structures. But if theatre is marginal now, as compared to television and movies—and even baseball and restaurants—remember that even at its best, in the '20s, when theatre was doing very well, it was still relatively marginal compared to the other arts.

It's amazing—theatre is so small, yet so *powerful*. You can feel its power over time. It's hard to describe: It has to do with human resources, because living actors on stage do something that is not provided in any of the other media. No matter how good a film is, the impact of the thing in the theatre is different—it's live, people are sitting there and going through an experience. You've heard this over and over again, but it has that *liveliness* to it, it's the closest thing to a human experience. People want to go to a live show. It has to do with ritual. I'm not saying that can't be wiped out, it can be—Broadway can be destroyed. But you notice that there's still theatre in all the Western countries—theatre still plays a role. Not a dominant one, but a role. So to answer your question—no, I'm not despondent these days.

As a matter of fact, you seem more ebullient than ever. Learning a new language at 65, that's . . . .
That's nothing. I'm learning new things all the time. Still, these projects I'm working on now—they're important because I feel I have to do something that's going to impact on the entire theatre, to find myself useful in the world. Let me put it this way: To be in the theatre is such a privilege that I feel I must do something important.

Ross Wetzsteon was a longtime editor at the *Village Voice* who helped build the Obie Awards into major theatrical accolades for Off and Off-Off Broadway. He is the author of *Republic of Dreams: An Intellectual History of Greenwich Village*. He died in 1998.

BORDER TACTICS

An interview with Luis Valdez by David Savran

January 1988

One month into the 1965 Delano grape strike, which solidified the power of the United Farm Workers, 23-year-old Luis Valdez met with a group of union volunteers and devised a short comic skit to help persuade reluctant workers to join the strike. He hung signs reading "*huelgista*" (striker) on two men and "*esquirol*" (scab) on a third. The two *huelgistas* started yelling at the *esquirol* and the audience laughed. Thus began Valdez's career as founder and director of El Teatro Campesino—a career that in the more than two decades since has thrust him to the forefront of the complex and politically charged Hispanic search for identity in the Anglo culture of the United States.

Riding the wave of growing Hispanic numbers and influence, Valdez has come into his own in no less than three media: His latest play, the comedy *I Don't Have to Show You No Stinking Badges*, drew cheers in recent seasons at the Los Angeles Theater Center and San Diego Repertory Company; *Corridos*, a series of staged Mexican folk ballads, was videotaped and aired as a PBS-TV special in October; and *La Bamba*, a movie about '50s rock-and-roller Ritchie Valens that Valdez wrote and directed was released over the summer (in English and Spanish versions) to critical accolades and box-office success. "There was a time when I spoke only to Chicanos—now I want a national audience," Valdez admits. But the recent mainstreaming of his work has not obscured the continuity or clarity of Valdez's intention: to communicate the Chicano experience in all of its political, cultural and religious complexity.

That intention was shaped in El Teatro Campesino's early history and fired by its struggles. During the company's first years it was a union tool, performing in meeting halls, fields and strike camps. Drawing on commedia dell'arte and elements of Mexican folk culture, Valdez created *actos*, short comic sketches designed to raise political awareness and inspire action. *Los Vendidos* (*The Sellouts*, 1967), for example, attacks the stereotyping of Chicanos and government-sanctioned tokenism. A Chicano secretary from Governor Reagan's office goes to

Honest Sancho's Used Mexican Lot to buy "a Mexican type" for the front office. She examines several models—a farm worker, a young *pachuco* (a swaggering street kid), a *revolucionario* and finally a Mexican-American in a business suit who sings "God Bless America" and drinks dry martinis. As soon as she buys the last, he malfunctions and begins shouting "*Viva la huelga*," while the others chase her away and divide the money.

At the same time that he was writing and performing agitprop for the Farm Workers, Valdez turned to examine his pre-Columbian heritage, the sophisticated religion and culture of the ancient Mayans. The Teatro settled in two houses in San Juan Bautista in 1971, where they farmed according to Mayan practices and Valdez developed the second of his dramatic forms, the *mito* (myth), which characteristically takes the form of a parable based on Indian ritual. For Valdez the *mito* is an attempt to integrate political activism and religious ritual—to tie "the cause of social justice" to "the cause of everything else in our universe." *Bernabe* (1970) is a parable about the prostitution of the land. It opposes the pure, mystical love for La Tierra (the earth) by the mentally retarded *campesino* of the title against its simple possession by landowners and banks. At the play's end Bernabe is visited by La Luna (the moon, dressed as a 1942 *pachuca*), La Tierra and El Sol (the sun) in the guise of Tonatiuh, the Aztec sun god. In a final apotheosis, the "cosmic idiot" is made whole and united with La Tierra, at last revealed to be Coatlicue, the Aztec goddess of life, death and rebirth.

In the 1970s Valdez developed a third dramatic form, the *corrido* (ballad), which, like the *mito*, is intended to claim a cultural heritage, rather than inspire political revolution. The *corrido* is Valdez's reinvention of the musical, based on Mexican-American folk ballads telling tales of love, death and heroism. *Zoot Suit* (1978) is perhaps his best known *corrido* and was the first Hispanic play to reach Broadway, after a long and successful run in Los Angeles. Mixing narrative, action, song and dance, it is the story of members of a zoot suit–clad *pachuco* gang of the '40s, their wrongful conviction for murder and the "Zoot Suit Riots" that followed.

I Don't Have to Show You No Stinking Badges takes on the political and existential implications of acting, both in theatre and society. It takes place in a television studio in which is set the suburban southern California home of Buddy and Connie Villa, two assimilated, middle-class Chicanos, "the silent bit king and queen of Hollywood." Their son, Sonny, who has just dropped out of Harvard Law School and has returned home with his Asian-American girlfriend, tries to find work in Hollywood, but despairs at having to become one of the many "actors faking our roles to fit into the great American success story." With Pirandellian sleight of hand, Valdez uses a director to interrupt the scene (which it turns out is an episode of a new sitcom, "Badges"!) in order to debate the social function of art. "This isn't reality," Sonny protests. But the director assures him, "Frankly, reality's a big boring pain in the ass. We're in the entertainment business. Laughs, Sonny, that's more important than reality."

Although closer to mainstream comedy than mystery play, Valdez's exploration of role-playing represents more a development of than a break with the technique of his early *mitos*. Both *Bernabe* and *Badges* eschew naturalism in favor of a more theatrically bold style, the earlier play drawing upon a naïve former model and the later a sophisticated one. *Bernabe*, in keeping with the conventions of religious drama, opts for a simple, mystical ending, while *Badges* refuses the pat resolution of television sitcom by offering several alternative endings. Both examine the spiritual implications of material choices; both are celebratory despite their socially critical vision.

Deep connections are evident in Valdez's uniquely diverse collection of plays. As he shapes the experience of Chicanos into drama that speaks to all Americans, he is also examining the interrelationship between the political and the metaphysical, between historically determined oppressive structures and man's transhistorical desire for faith and freedom.

I spoke with Valdez in May 1987, in his El Teatro Campesino office in San Juan Bautista.

How did you get interested in theatre?

There's a story that's almost apocryphal, I've repeated it so many times now. It's nevertheless true. I got hooked on the theatre when I was six. I was born into a family of migrant farm workers and shortly after World War II we were in a cotton camp in the San Joaquin valley. The season was over, it was starting to rain, but we were still there because my dad's little Ford pickup truck had broken down and was up on blocks and there was no way for us to get out. Life was pretty meager then and we survived by fishing in a river and sharing staples like beans, rice and flour. And the bus from the local school used to come in from a place called Stratford—irony of ironies, except it was on the San Joaquin River. (*Laughs.*)

I took my lunch to school in a little brown paper bag—which was a valuable commodity because there were still paper shortages in 1946. One day as school let out and the kids were rushing toward the bus, I found my bag missing and I went around in a panic looking for it. The teacher saw me and said, "Are you looking for your bag?" and I said, "Yes." She said, "Come here," and she took me in the little back room and there, on a table, were some things laid out that completely changed my perception of the universe. She'd torn the bag up and placed it in water. I was horrified. But then she showed me the next bowl. It was a paste. She was making papier-mâché. A little farther down the line, she'd taken the paper and put it on a clay mold of a face of a monkey, and finally there was a finished product, unpainted but nevertheless definitely a monkey. And she said, "I'm making masks."

I was amazed, shocked in an exhilarating way, that she could do this with paper and paste. As it turned out, she was making masks for the school play. I didn't know what a play was, but she explained and said, "We're having tryouts." I came back the next week all enthused and auditioned for a part and got a leading role as a monkey. The play was about Christmas in the jungle. I was measured for a costume that was better than the clothes I was wearing at the time, certainly more colorful. The next few weeks were some of the most exciting in my short life. After seeing the stage transformed into a jungle and after all the excitement of the preparations—I doubt that it was as elaborate as my mind remembers it now—my dad got the truck fixed and a week before the show was to go on, we moved away. So I never got to be in the Christmas play.

That left an unfillable gap, a vacuum that I've been pouring myself into for the last 41 years. From then on, it was just a question of evolution. Later I got into puppets. I was a ventriloquist, believe it or not. In 1956 when I was in high school, I became a regular on a local television program. I was still living in a *barrio* with my family, a place in San José called Sal Si Puedes—Get Out if You Can. It was one of those places with dirt streets and potholes, a terrible place. But I was on television, right? (*Laughs.*) And I wrote my own stuff and it established me in high school.

By the time I graduated, I had pretty well decided that writing was my consuming passion. Coming from my background, I didn't feel right about going to my parents and saying, "I want to be a playwright." So I started college majoring in math and physics. Then one day late in my freshman year I walked to the drama department and decided, "To hell with it, I'm going to go with this." I changed majors to English, with an emphasis on playwriting, and that's what I did for the rest of my college days.

In 1964 I wrote and directed my first full-length play, *The Shrunken Head of Pancho Villa*. People saw it and gave me a lot of encouragement. I joined the San Francisco Mime Troupe the following year, and then in '65 joined the Farm Workers Union and essentially started El Teatro Campesino. The evolution has been continuous since then, both of the company and of my styles of playwriting.

During that period, what was your most important theatre training—college, the Mime Troupe?

It's all important. It's a question of layering. I love to layer things. I think they achieve a certain richness—I'm speaking now about "the work." But life essentially evolves that way, too. Those years of studying theatre history were extremely important. I connected with a number of ancient playwrights in a very direct way. Plautus was a revelation, he spoke directly to me. I took four years of Latin so I was able to read him in Latin. There are clever turns of phrases that I grew to appreciate and, in my own way, was able almost to reproduce in Spanish. The central figure of the wily servant in classical Roman drama—Greek also—became a standard feature of my work with El Teatro Campesino. The striker was basically a wily servant. I'd also been exposed to commedia dell'arte through the Brighellas, Arlecchinos and Pantalones. I saw a direct link between these commedia types and the types I had to work with in order to put together a Farm Workers' theatre. I chose to do an outdoor, robust theatre of types. I figured it hit the reality.

My second phase was the raw, elemental education I got, performing under the most primitive conditions in the farm labor camps and on flatbed trucks. In doing so, I dealt with the basic elements of drama: structure, language, music, movement. The first education was literary, the second practical. We used to put on stuff every week, under all kinds of circumstances: outdoors, indoors, under the threat of violence.

There was a period during the grape strike in '67 when we had become an effective weapon within the Farm Workers and were considered enough of a threat that a rumor flashed across the strike camp that somebody was after me with a high-powered rifle. We went out to the labor camp anyway, but I was really sweating it. I don't think I've sweated any performance since then. It changed my perspective on what I was doing. Was this really worth it? Was it a life-and-death issue? Of course it was for me at the time, and still is. I learned that in a very direct and practical way. I was beaten and kicked and jailed, also in the '60s, essentially for doing theatre. I knew the kind of theatre we were doing was a political act, it was art and politics. At least I hope I wasn't being kicked for the art. (*Laughs.*)

What other playwrights had a major impact on you in those days?
Brecht looms huge in my orientation. I discovered Brecht in college, from an intellectual perspective. That was really the only way—no one was doing Brecht back in 1961. When Esslin's book, *Brecht: The Man and His Work*, came out in 1960, I was working in the library, so I had first dibs on all the new books. Brecht to me had been only a name. But this book opened up Brecht and I started reading all his plays and his theories, which I subscribed to immediately. I continue to use his alienation effect to this day. I don't think audiences like it too much, but I like it because it seems to me an essential feature of the experience of theatre.

Theatre should reflect an audience back on itself: You should think as well as feel. Still, there's no underestimating the power of emotional impact—I understand better now how ideas are conveyed and exchanged on a beam of emotion. I think Brecht began to discover that in his later works and integrated it. I've integrated a lot of feeling into my works, but I still love ideas. I still love communicating a concept, an abstraction. That's the mathematician in me.

How has your way of writing changed over the years?
What has changed over the years is an approach and a technique. The first few years with the Teatro Campesino were largely improvisational. I wrote outlines. I sketched out a dramatic structure, sometimes on a single page, and used that as my guide to direct the actors. Later on, I began to write very simple scripts that were sometimes born out of improvisations. During the first 10 years, from '65 to '75, the collective process became more complicated and more sophisticated within the company—we were creating longer pieces, full-length pieces, but they'd take forever to complete using the collective process.

By 1975 I'd taken the collective process as far as I could. I enjoyed working with people. I didn't have to deal with the loneliness of writing. My problem was that I was so much part of the collective that I couldn't leave for even a month without the group having serious problems. By 1975 we were stable enough as a company for me to begin to take a month, two months, six months, eventually a year. I turned a corner and was ready to start writing plays again.

In 1975 I took a month off and wrote a play called *El Fin del Mundo* (*The End of the World*). We began to create it the year before and did it through 1980, a different version every year. The characters were people born of my experience, and they are still alive for me. Someday I'll finish all of that as a play or else it will be poured into a screenplay for a "major motion picture." (*Laughs.*) Shortly after that, in 1977, I was invited by the Mark Taper Forum to write a play for their New Theatre for Now series. We agreed on the Zoot Suit Riots as a subject. *Zoot Suit* firmly reestablished my self-identity as a playwright. Essentially I've been writing nonstop since '75. That's not to say I didn't write anything between '65 and '75. *Soldado Razo*, which is probably my most performed play around the world, was written in 1970, as was *Bernabe*. *The Dark Root of a Scream* was written in 1967. These are all one-acts. But I used to work on them with a sense of longing, wanting more time to be able to sit down and write.

Now I'm firmly back in touch with myself as a playwright. When I begin, I allow myself at least a month of free association with notes. I can start anywhere. I can start with an abstract notion, a character . . . it's rarely dialogue or anything specific like that. More often than not, it's just an amorphous bunch of ideas, impressions and feelings. I allow myself to tumble in this ball of thoughts and impressions, knowing that I'm heading toward a play and that eventually I've got to begin dealing with character and then structure.

Because of the dearth of Hispanic playwrights—or even American playwrights, for that matter—I felt it necessary to explore the territory, to cover the range of theatre as widely as I could. Political theatre with the Farm Workers was sometimes minimal scale, a small group of workers gathered in some dusty little corner in a labor camp, and sometimes immense—huge crowds, 10,000, 15,000, with banners flying. But the political theatre extends beyond the farm worker into the whole Chicano experience. We've dealt with a lot of issues—racism, education, immigration—and that took us, again, through many circles.

We evolved three separate forms: The *acto* was the political act, the short form, 15 minutes; the *mito* was the mythic, religious play; and the *corrido* was the ballad. I just finished a full-length video program called *Corridos*. So the form has evolved into another medium. I do political plays, musicals, historical dramas, religious dramas. We still do our religious plays at the Mission here every year. They're nurturing, they feed the spirit. Peter Brook's response when he saw our Virgin play, years ago, was that it was like something out of the Middle Ages. It's religion for many of the people who come see it, not just entertainment. And of course we've gone on to do serious plays and comedies like *I Don't Have to Show You No Stinking Badges*.

It seems that a play like *Bernabe* aligns the *mito* and the *acto*, the politics and the myth. It uses religious mysticism to point out the difference between simply owning the land and loving it. The political point is made by appeal to mystical process.

The spiritual aspect of the political struggle has been part of the work from the beginning. Some of that is through César Chávez, who is a spiritual-political leader. Some people—say, the political types—have had trouble dealing with the spiritual. They say, "It's a distortion. Religion is the opium of the masses." But it seems to me that the spiritual is very much part of everyday life. There's no way to exclude it . . . we are spirit. We're a manifestation of something, of an energy.

The whole fusion between the spiritual and the material is for me the paradox of human existence. That's why I connected with Peter Brook when he was here in '73—his question was, "How do you make the invisible visible?" To me myth is not something that's fake or not real. On the contrary, it's so real that it's just below the surface—it's the supporting structure of our everyday reality. That makes me a lot more Jungian than Freudian. And it distinguishes me, I think, from a lot of other playwrights. A lot of modern playwrights go to psychoanalysis to work out their problems. I can't stop there, that's just the beginning for me. I've had to go to the root of my own existence in order to effect my own salvation, if you will. The search for meaning took me into religion and science, and into mythology.

I had to sound out these things in myself. Someone pointed out to me the evolution a couple of years ago. *The Shrunken Head of Pancho Villa* is theatre of the absurd. One of the characters, the oldest brother, is a disembodied head, huge, oversized. And he eats all of the food that the family can produce. So they stay poor. He has lice that turn out to be tiny little cockroaches that grow and cover the walls. He sings "La Cucaracha" but cannot talk. And he can't move. He's just kind of there. In a metaphorical sense, that was me back in the early '60s. That's the way I felt—that I had no legs, no arms. By 1970, when I got to *Bernabe*, I was the idiot, but I'd gotten in contact with the sun and the moon and earth. Fortunately, out of these grotesque self-portraits, my characters have attained a greater and greater degree of humanity.

I've always had difficulty with naturalism in the theatre. Consequently, a lot of people have looked at my work and said, "Maybe he just can't write naturalism. His is the theatre of types, of simplistic little stick figures." What I needed was a medium in which to be able to do that, so I came to film. *La Bamba* is naturalism, as well as of the spirit. There I wanted the dirt, so I got the dirt. I wanted intimate realistic scenes between two real people. I can write that stuff for the stage too, but it just doesn't interest me. The stage for me—that box, that flat floor—holds other potentials; it's a means to explore other things.

As much a ritual space as anything else.

Most definitely. It seems to me that the essence of the human being is to act, to move through space in patterns that gives his life meaning.

We adorn ourselves with symbolic objects that give that movement even more meaning. Then we come out with sounds. And then somewhere along the line we begin to call that reality—but it's a self-created reality. The whole of civilization is a dance. I think the theatre celebrates that.

So religion functions in your work as a connection with the past, with one's heritage and one's bond to all men.

Sounding out those elemental drums, going back into the basics. I was doing this as a Chicano but I was also doing it as someone who inhabits the 20th century. I think we need to reconnect. The word religion means "a tying back." The vacuum I thought I was born into turned out to be full of all kinds of mystery and power. The strange things that were going on in the *barrio*—the Mexican things, the ethnic things—seemed like superstition, but on another level there was a lot of psychic activity. There's a lot of psychic activity in Mexican culture that is actually political at times.

Zoot Suit is another extremely spiritual, political play. And it was never understood. People thought it was about juvenile delinquents and that I was putting the Pachuco on the stage just to be snide. But the young man, Henry Reyna, achieves his own liberation by coming into contact with this internal authority. The Pachuco is the Jungian self-image, the superego if you will, the power inside every individual that's greater than any human institution. The Pachuco says, "It'll take more than the U.S. Navy to beat me down," referring to the Navy and Marines stripping zoot suiters in the 1940s. "I don't give a fuck what you do to me, you can't take this from me. And I reassert myself, in this guise." The fact that critics couldn't accept that guise was too bad, but it doesn't change the nature of what the play's about. It deals with self-salvation. And you can follow the playwright through the story—I was also those two dudes. With *Zoot Suit* I was finally able to transcend social conditions, and the way I did it on stage was to give the Pachuco absolute power, as the master of ceremonies. He could snap his fingers and stop the action. It was a Brechtian device that allowed the plot to move forward, but psychically and symbolically, in the right way.

And Chicanos got off on it. That's why a half-million people came to see it in L.A. Because I had given a disenfranchised people their religion back. I dressed the Pachuco in the colors of Testatipoka, the Aztec god of education, the dean of the school of hard knocks. There's another god of culture, Quetzalcoatl, the feathered serpent, who's much kinder. He surfaces in *La Bamba* as the figure of Ritchie Valens. He's an artist and poet and is gentle and not at all fearful. When my audiences see *La Bamba*, they like that positive spirit. The Pachuco's a little harder to take.

But these are evolutions. I use the metaphor of the serpent crawling out of its skin. There's that symbolism in *La Bamba*—it's pre-Columbian, but it's also very accurate in terms of the way that I view my own life. I've crawled through many of my own dead skins.

Although *Badges* and *Bernabe* are very different, in both of them the meta-physical is given a political dimension.

I like to think there's a core that's constant. In one way, what I have to say is quite basic, quite human. In another way, it's specifically American, in a continental sense. I'm reaching back to pre-Columbian America and trying to share that. I feel and sense those rhythms within me. I'm not just a Mexican farm worker. I'm an American with roots in Mayan culture. I can resonate and unlock some of the mysteries of this land which reside in all of us. I've just been in the neighborhood a little bit longer.

What about the endings of your plays? *Zoot Suit's* seems very Brechtian, a happy ending immediately called into question. Then you present three different possible futures for the characters. And *Badges* is similar. You present what could happen, depending on the choices the characters make.

Multiple endings—multiple beginnings, too—have started to evolve in my work. I don't think there's any single end. I firmly believe that, we exist simultaneously on seven levels—you can call them *chakras* if you're so inclined, or you can call them something else. In the Mayan sculptures, there's a vision of the universe in those ancient headdresses, in which you see the open mouths of birds with human heads coming through them, and then something else going in through the eyes and coming out again. That's a pulsating vision of the universe. It might have been born from the jungle but is, nevertheless, an accurate description of what is going on below the surface, at the nuclear level, in the way atomic particles are interacting. To me the universe is a huge, pulsating, enormously vital and *conscious* phenomenon. There is no end. There is no beginning. There's only an apparent end and an apparent beginning.

We had an ending and beginning to *La Bamba*, which I had scripted and seemed right on paper. But our first preview audiences rejected them. So eventually we snipped them. What we had was not exactly a Brechtian turn, but it was a stepping back and looking at the '50s from the perspective of the '80s. They wanted to stay in the '50s. I had been trying, on some level, to alleviate the pain of Ritchie Valens's death, but audiences told us, "Leave us with the pain." So that's where we left it.

Can you describe how you work as a director with your own material?

As a director I switch gears. Writing is a solitary process—you're in there with the words, and I love that. But I also love directing, getting out of myself and into other people. As a director—and this again comes from my experiences in the Farm Worker days—I have to know who I'm working with. And what they are like. If I have four actors, or a dozen actors, plus crew, my first job as a director is to get them to become one, to get them hot enough about doing the project so that there's a lot of enthusiasm.

More and more the first thing I want to establish in character development is movement. You can't have a feeling, an emotion, without motion. You can pick up a lot from the associative school, referring back to your own experiences, but I think it's also possible to get people to laugh and cry through what they do to their bodies.

Very often that's the difference between acting for film and acting for the stage. You can't get away with "acting" on film. You have to cut it so close to the bone, you have to *be*, to get down-and-dirty. It's "the Method," to be sure. So you have to make it small, intense and real. On the stage, because you have to project, things sometimes get out of whack. And you have to switch to a new mentality. This is where ritual comes in. Performance on the stage is much more like dance than anything else. Dance is real. You can't fake dance. But somehow a lot of people start acting as if they're "acting," and think they're doing it right. In fact, acting is something totally different: It's a *real act*. Which gets back to politics, in that our first theatrical acts were real political acts. That's why that dude was out there with a high-powered rifle—he wasn't seeing theatre, but a threatening political act.

Now it seems that the political dimension has become sublimated, less explicit. You're no longer writing agitprop.

There is a time and place for all forms. It's 20 years down the road. But the political impact is still there. The only difference is that I'm being asked to run for governor now, which I'm not interested in doing. My purpose is still to impact socially, culturally and politically. I'm reaffirming some things that are very important to all of us as Americans, those things that we all believe to be essential to our society. What I hope is changing is a perception about the country as a whole. And the continent as well.

I'm just trying to kick my two cents into the pot. I still want El Teatro Campesino to perform on Broadway, because I think that's a political act. El Teatro Campesino is in Hollywood, and I don't think we've compromised any social statements. We started out in '65 doing these *actos* within the context of the United Farm Workers. Twenty-two years later, my next movie may be about the grape strike. My Vietnam was at home. I refused to go to Vietnam, but I encountered all the violence I needed on the home front: People were killed by the Farm Workers' strike.

Some critics have accused you of selling out.

I used to joke, "It's impossible for us to sell out because nobody wants to buy us." That doesn't bother me in the least. There's too much to do, to be socially conscious about. In some ways, it's just people sounding me out. I don't mind people referring back to what I have been. We're all like mirrors to each other. People help to keep you on course. I've strayed very little from my pronounced intentions.

In '67 when we left United Farm Workers and started our own cultural center in Del Rey, we came out with a manifesto, essentially stating that we were trying to put the tools of the artist in the hands of the humblest, the working people. But not just 19th-century tools, not clay and straw or spit and masking tape or felt pens. We were talking about video, film, recording studios. Now we're beginning to work in the best facilities that the industry has to offer. What we do with them from here is something else.

Do you read the critics?

Sure. I love listening to the public. They're the audience, who am I to argue with them? They either got it or they didn't. The critics are part of the process. I do have some strong feelings about the nature of American criticism—I don't think that it's deeply rooted enough in a knowledge of theatre history. Very often newspapers just assign reporters, Joe Blow off the street. Perhaps it would be too much for the public to have somebody that's overly informed—is that possible?— about the theatre.

How do you see the American theatre today?

The overwhelming impression for me is that theatre's not nearly as interesting as it could be, that it's been stuck in its traces for many, many years. Broadway has not moved out of the '20s, from what I can see. It might be due to the fact that so many of the houses on Broadway are 19th-century playhouses. But much of the material that I see—and I don't see nearly enough—is too anemic for my tastes. I have trouble staying awake in the theatre, believe it or not. I can barely stay awake at my own plays.

I feel that the whole question of the human enterprise is up for grabs. I don't think this country has come to terms with its racial questions, obviously. And because of that, it has not really come to terms with the cultural question of what America is. There are two vast melting pots that must eventually come together. The Hispanic, after all, is really the product of a melting pot—there's no such thing as a Latin-American race. The Hispanic melting pot melds all the races of the world, like the Anglo melting pot does; so one of these days, and probably in the United States, those two are going to be poured together— probably in a play, and it could be one of my own. (*Laughs.*)

There's a connection with the Indian cultures that has to be established in American life. Before we can do that, however, we have to get beyond the national guilt over the genocide of the Indian. What's needed is expiation and forgiveness, and the only ones that are in a position to forgive are the Indian peoples. I'm a Yaqui Indian—Spanish blood, yes, but largely Yaqui. I'm in a position to be able to forgive white people. And why not? I think that's what we're here for, to forgive each other. Martin Luther King speaking in 1963 at the Lincoln Memorial was a beginning. It didn't reach nearly far enough. We're still wrestling with it. Deep fears, about miscegenation and the despoliation of the race, have to be dealt with. I'm here, through my work, to show that short, brown people are okay, you know what I mean? We've got ideas, too, and we've got a song and a dance or two. And we know something about the world that we can share. I'm here to show that to other brown people who don't think very much of themselves, and there are a lot of those.

I wish there were more plays that dealt with the reality of this country. The racial issue is always just swept aside. It deserves to be swept aside—once it's been dealt with. We cannot begin to approach a real solution to our social ills—a solution like integration, for instance, or assimilation—without dealing with all our underlying feelings about each other. I'm trying to deal with my past, not just with respect to Anglos, but to blacks and Asians. I draw on the symbolism of the four roads: the black road, the white road, the red road and the yellow road. They all meet in the navel of the universe, the place where the upper road leads into the underworld—read consciousness and sub-consciousness. I think that where they come home is in America.

What are your plans for the future? And goals?
I'm into a very active phase right now, as writer and director, but with writing as the base. I have a number of very central stories I want to tell—on film, on television and on the stage. I want to be working in the three media, on simultaneous projects that feed each other. I like the separation between film, television and theatre. It makes each a lot clearer for me. In theatre, there are a number of ritualistic pieces I want to do that explore the movement of bodies in space and the relation between movement and language. That sphere I can explore on film, too, or television. What film gives me is movement around the actor—I can explore from any viewpoint, any distance. But theatre's the only medium that gives me the sheer beauty, power and presence of bodies. Ritual, literally.

I've got a piece that I've been working on for many, many years, called *The Earthquake Sun*, about our time. All I can tell you is that it will be on the road one of these days. I have another play called *The Mummified Fetus*. It takes off from a real incident that happened a couple years ago: an 85-year-old woman was discovered with a mummified fetus in her womb. I have a couple of plays that the world has not seen, that we've only done here with the company.

In television I have a number of projects. *Corridos* has begun to open up other possibilities. I talk about video as electronic theatre. I'm getting into the idea of doing theatre before cameras, but going for specifically theatrical moments as opposed to real cinematic moments. *Corridos* is an example of this.

I hope a more workable touring network will develop in this country. The links between East and West must be solidified. I think it's great for companies to tour. We're very excited about the possibility of our company plugging into the resources of the regional theatres, as we've done with *Badges* in San Diego and at the Los Angeles Theater Center, even with the Burt Reynolds Playhouse in Jupiter, Fla. We hope to be able to go from regional theatre to regional theatre all the way across the country, including New York. In that way, we'll be able to reach a national audience.

I still want to experience the dust and sweat occasionally. I'm trying to leave time open for that. This month we're going to celebrate the 25th anniversary of the United Farm Workers, and we'll be back on a flatbed truck, doing some of the old *actos*. I don't want to lose any of our audience. I want worldwide audience. We had that—up until 1980 we were touring Europe and Latin America. We want to tour Asia with the Teatro Campesino. Essentially, I would like to see theatre develop the kind of mass audience—it's impossible of course—that the movies have. I wish we could generate that enthusiasm in young people and in audiences in general, get them out of their homes, away from their VCRs, to experience the theatre as the life-affirming, life-giving experience that it is.

David Savran is a specialist in American theatre, popular culture and social theory. Among his books are two volumes of interviews with playwrights, *In Their Own Words* and *The Playwright's Voice*, both published by TCG, and the forthcoming *Highbrow/Lowdown: Theater, Jazz, and the Making of the New Middle Class* from University of Michigan Press. He is professor of theatre at the Graduate Center of the City University of New York and editor of the *Journal of American Drama and Theatre*.

CONTROVERSY AND GORDON DAVIDSON

An interview by Arthur Bartow

May 1988

Gordon Davidson has a nose for the kind of theatre that attracts heated debate. For more than 20 years, as artistic director of the Mark Taper Forum in Los Angeles, controversy has followed him like a friendly pet that can't be shooed away. Davidson has time and again presented plays for his community that raise deep social and political questions. And when audiences have reacted with shock and indignation, no one has been more surprised than Davidson himself. How could his earnest vision of a theatre whose mission it is to embrace and enlighten the community earn the enmity of some of its most respected and powerful citizens?

It was in 1964 that the 32-year-old, Brooklyn-born Davidson became the producing head of the Theatre Group, sheltered on the L.A. campus of the University of California. The group had been formed in 1959 in response to an emerging hunger for culture in southern California, spurred on by the growing pool of actors, directors and technicians who had been displaced to Hollywood from New York when films began to open their doors to theatre-trained artists.

Davidson sees the UCLA company's founders—John Houseman, Robert Ryan, Abbott Kaplan, Jeff Hayden and Lamont Johnson—as initiators of "a lineage, a heritage. And I don't want to break that. It's very important to me, especially in an age in which everything is used up and nobody is aware of anything that happened before." A brief two years after he assumed the group's directorship, the Los Angeles Music Center sent out the word that it was seeking a resident company for its new 750-seat thrust-stage space, the Mark Taper Forum. Davidson's nationally visible success with such productions as Rolf Hochhuth's Holocaust drama *The Deputy*, which had toured the U.S. for 26 weeks, made the UCLA company seem an obvious choice. The invitation was issued and the company, rechristened Center Theatre Group, moved in.

The Mark Taper Forum opened in 1967 with Davidson's production of *The Devils*, based on Aldous Huxley's novel *The Devils of*

Loudun, and the Center's wealthiest conservative Catholic contributors immediately called for the new director's ouster. They wanted the play stopped and the theatre closed; their attacks were leveled not only at Davidson but at the Music Center itself, and at philanthropist Dorothy Chandler, who financed it. Newspapers headlined the controversy and the county board of supervisors considered establishing a local censorship committee. But Chandler became Davidson's strongest supporter and a new group of underwriters stepped in to fund the Center. The conflict ultimately opened the way for the Mark Taper Forum to continue to tackle controversial subjects.

And tackle them it did. Although Davidson went forward with a well-rounded repertoire of modern and classic plays, he tended to prefer directing contemporary works, some of which raised eyebrows and ruffled feathers—and in short order earned for him and the theatre an international reputation.

The Taper's 1967 premiere of Heinar Kipphardt's *In the Matter of J. Robert Oppenheimer* drew fire from participants in the Atomic Energy Commission hearings on which the play was based, and Davidson and his translator Ruth Speirs were forced to change certain names and portions of dialogue. Davidson's much-admired production of Daniel Berrigan and Saul Levitt's *The Trial of the Catonsville Nine* in 1969 again stirred great opposition from some factions in Los Angeles; the play had premiered at the Taper, opened for a subsequent run in New York, and was being remounted in Los Angeles when legal action was instituted by a right-wing group calling itself the Citizens Legal Defense Alliance. Their suit, brought against the Music Center and Center Theatre Group, termed *Catonsville* "vulgar, obscene, licentious, indecent, immoral, illegal, scandalous and objectionable."

Davidson weathered these and other attacks, going on to direct the premieres of such works as Mark Medoff's *Children of a Lesser God*, Christopher Hampton's *Savages* and *Tales from Hollywood*, and Conor Cruise O'Brien's *Murderous Angels*, and to produce such works as the premieres of Luis Valdez's *Zoot Suit* and JoAnne Akalaitis's *Green Card*. After introducing Michael Cristofer's *The Shadow Box* at the Taper in 1975, he subsequently directed it at New Haven's Long Wharf Theatre and then on Broadway, receiving a Tony Award for best direction in 1977 while the play received a best-play Tony and the Pulitzer Prize. All in all, the Taper has collected 11 Tonys, 58 L.A. Drama Critics Circle Awards and some 200 other prizes for outstanding theatre; today it has a budget of $8.3 million and more than 30,000 subscribers. Davidson can rattle off the numbers, but he is more likely to wax enthusiastic about his "New Theatre for Now" series, one of the nation's earliest developmental programs for playwrights and directors, or the ongoing accomplishments of the theatre's weekly literary cabaret at the Itchey Foot, its television and film productions overseen by Taper Media, or the traveling theatre for young people known as ITP.

Controversy, international attention and the wear and tear of 20 years of building the Taper have not diminished Davidson's concern for the health of his profession, his audiences and society. He still believes in introducing new experiences to theatregoers and is still puzzled and frustrated when they resist. He doesn't believe in patronizing his audiences, whether or not they share his vision of what theatre should encompass.

Your first production at the Mark Taper Forum, *The Devils*, was highly controversial.

I didn't do it to be controversial, nor did I know it was going to be. I didn't think that as a company we were equipped to do Shakespeare, but I wanted to open with an experience that dealt with large, humanistic issues. *The Devils* is Shakespearean in scope. I did not detect one ounce of controversy in it—it was a little risqué, maybe, but cloaked in respectability, and in theatrical and historical authenticity. I didn't really know the community power structure of Los Angeles, even though I was living there. Some of the conservative Catholic community leaders were on the county board of supervisors, and the Music Center is on county land. All of these forces—mostly people who had not seen or read the play—came together to attack it. They had "heard" that it was terrible. The great thing was that it unified support behind the theatre in a way that I don't think could have been created had I started less dramatically. It brought people to the defense of freedom of expression in a much better way than any manifesto or proclamation that might have said: "Theatre is potentially controversial, full of ideas and images and material that may not please everybody." It rallied people, although there are wounds to this day, despite the fact that times have changed.

Over the years, controversy at the Taper has centered on politics and sexually explicit language. Although I've been criticized, I've never veered from my path. I don't do anything for the sake of shock—that alone is not a valid intention—although there are always people who are convinced otherwise.

The truth is that the controversy actually started before I opened the theatre. *The Deputy* was potentially a very controversial play. It criticized Pope Pius's actions during World War II. But I was protected because it was done in a university setting. Chancellor Franklin Murphy buffered any criticism.

Why was the American premiere of Kipphardt's *In the Matter of J. Robert Oppenheimer* delayed until 1967?

I had a chance to do it a bit earlier, but Oppenheimer was still alive and it was made known to me that he would be very unhappy if the play were done, because he didn't want that whole period of his life dished up. After he passed away, I felt that it was necessary to do it.

I've only directed plays that I've wanted to do. Each one has had its own particular challenge and meaning for me. Plays like *Hamlet, Henry IV, Part I* open up worlds of study; like the world of Africa in Conor Cruise O'Brien's *Murderous Angels* or the radical Catholic community in *The Trial of the Catonsville Nine*. I do these plays at the Taper in a controlled, protective, supportive, embracing atmosphere. When I've directed elsewhere, especially on Broadway, it's usually a fight just to get it on. It's hard enough to do what we do without that.

Children of a Lesser God was developed at the Taper. How long did you work on that play?
It all came about rather quickly. That was an occasion when a change made in an emergency—a slot became available in the season—and the acceleration and intensity of that paid off. In general, I prefer to develop a play with a long gestation time. Mark Medoff, the playwright, thrives on pressure and likes to work fast.

His script had been workshopped at New Mexico State University, but I didn't see it. I read it later. The interesting thing about that play was that my readers, who screen our plays at the Forum, rejected it. That's one of the constant fears that anyone running an organization lives with—that something good will be passed over. You have to allow the people who read new plays their independent judgment and strong opinions—but they must also have that particular insight that permits them to say, "Gordon, you have to pay attention to this play."

How did you overcome the difficulty of communicating with Phyllis Frelich, who could not hear you?
You mean my not being able to speak her language. It is a two-way street. The interpreter was actually the lesser way of bridging the gulf, while being the most practical. The real gulf was bridged by time, by gaining confidence, by the fact that we are both very expressive people. We understood each other best by way of our passion and the expression of our faces. What we constantly had to improve and deepen was the actual language communication, the use of sign and the sensitive use of the interpreter. When we rehearsed the play for the first time in L.A., the interpreter was a young man. When we rehearsed for Broadway, Phyllis requested that the interpreter be a woman because she felt that a woman could better convey what she wanted to say. And I liked the idea that when she was interpreted, I heard a female voice. The third time we worked together was in Mark Medoff's *The Hands of Its Enemy*. By that time, she didn't care whether the interpreter was a man or a woman.

The Taper production of *Children* was enormously successful. Then we had a three- or four-month hiatus between the Taper production and re-rehearsing it for Broadway. In that time period, we created a new second act.

What was the process that went into that rewriting?
My way of working, to the distraction of some writers, is to ask questions. I try to provoke and prod and get the writer to respond to the questions that I have about the material, or that I think the writer should be asking himself or herself about the material.

What if you don't get the answers that you think you ought?
We live in an imperfect world. And, as I get older, I'm realizing more and more that you're not always going to get it right in your lifetime and, to a certain extent, the work itself has some right to be imperfect.

The final judgment is how the work connects to an audience—
whether it's tapping some of those mysteries that make it work for
them. We premiered Lanford Wilson's *Burn This* at the Forum in 1986,
which is dramaturgically not a perfect play, but which speaks with a
voice that quite mysteriously makes an audience feel wonderful about
being in the theatre. Because it is a play in Lanford's style of lyric realism, it defies a certain kind of analysis. *Burn This* touches a chord of
modern emotional sensibility about the complexity of relationships in
the 1980s. But it does it in a more abstract, poetic way than, for instance,
The Catonsville Nine, which was about the Vietnam War, dealing with
conscience and what it takes finally to stand up and be counted.

**That play came along in 1970 just as there began to be a perception of what our
nation had gotten itself into.**
It was slightly ahead of its time. I've been lucky over the years in that
respect, because you can't necessarily predict when a work will be on
the leading edge. At that time, there hadn't been a hundred plays written about Vietnam. *Catonsville* came to my attention during a trip to
New York, when I was given a set of galleys to a book called *The Trial
of the Catonsville Nine* by Father Daniel Berrigan, S.J. I didn't know
Daniel Berrigan and only vaguely remembered reading about the
Catonsville raid in Maryland in 1964 when the Berrigan brothers
protested by burning draft documents. I read Berrigan's organization
of the trial transcript on the airplane. It was very poetic and formal.
Each person spoke his testimony; then there was a kind of summary.
And I started to cry on the airplane. As soon as the plane landed, before
I got my luggage, I called Flora Roberts, the agent, and said, "I don't
know what this is, Flora, but I have to find a way to do it." She was very
excited, and that started the whole journey.

I met with Father Dan Berrigan and started to study what actually
happened. I decided to do it in the Taper's New Theatre for Now
series, essentially with the script that he wrote. When we did it the first
time, there was great power, but I could feel the audience begin to wear
out—they heard the first testimony, the second, the third. Each one
was very moving, but I could see people thinking, "We're up to four—
there are five more to go." Based on that experience, I realized that to
make that play work the material would have to be reorganized. Saul
Levitt, who had written *The Andersonville Trial*, turned out to be a perfect person to do this. Without writing a single new word, he organized it into a more successful dramatic structure. I remember sitting
in his studio down in the Village with pieces of the script all over the
floor. We essentially reassembled what Dan had written.

Catonsville turned out to be one of the most exciting presentations
of a play I've ever experienced, because between the time that I first
met Dan and the time we went into rehearsal, he went underground.
Dan had been out on bail awaiting appeal, which was turned down. He
was going to have to serve his sentence and he decided that not to serve
would be a further escalation of his protest. So he went underground,
as did a number of other Catonsville people. Philip, his brother, was

captured first, and finally Dan. During the time he was underground, I made contact with him and said, "You know, Dan, usually an author is present for a rehearsal, and I wonder if there's a way for you to say something to the company?" A few days later, a tape arrived—a wonderful tape with his statement for the actors. Dan talked about darkness and light, about the actors' moral force pushing against the darkness. When I played that for the actors, it was an extraordinary experience.

There must also have been a certain element of danger at that point with Berrigan a fugitive.
Here's what happened. My phone was tapped. There was a nondescript repair truck curiously parked in front of my house for the entire duration of rehearsals and the run of the play. It disappeared once the play closed. A number of the actors were hassled by the FBI, especially one who had some previous liberal and possibly communist relationships. On the opening night, the FBI was an obvious presence in and around the theatre. I had decided to edit a portion of the tape that Dan had sent and to make it the beginning of the play, so that when the house lights went out the first words one heard in the darkness were, "Hello, this is Father Dan Berrigan speaking to you from the underground." The FBI agents in the audience leapt out of their seats because they couldn't take the chance that he wasn't there hiding in the rafters.

There have been many special plays like that—*Murderous Angels* about Dag Hammarskjold, *Oppenheimer, Savages, Ghetto, Children of a Lesser God*. Those are the ones where the rehearsal process becomes part of a bigger experience, the creating of a community of actors who are being put in touch with another community, the community of the world of the play; this in turn makes a larger connection to the community of people who come to see it. This creating of a family and a commonality of experience has involved research, field trips, resource people, things that extend the rehearsal process over and above and beyond the simple reading of the text. Some plays don't require any more than bringing your psyche to bear upon a particular character involved in particular events—a play about a family, a mother, a father, whatever. In those cases, it may be better for the actors not to go outside the world of the play, just to find it totally within themselves. The plays that I have always been attracted to require a larger investigation.

At one time you felt uneasy because you did not have a trained actor's background. What is the method you use with actors?
I'm not an actor, but I love and respect actors. I don't think it's necessary for a director to have acted, but you have to know something about the psychology of human beings and the techniques with which actors work. One of the most difficult things about directing a play is working with actors from a great variety of backgrounds, trying to create a single production style out of this incredible variety. I am not schooled in Stanislavsky, the Method, or any one particular viewpoint, but I have an interest in them all. I try to use those things that pertain to the play to weld together something that represents a single point of view.

Clearly, I feel more comfortable with plays that come essentially out of reality behavior, have some sense of immediacy and make a connection between the human scene and the material. From the earliest days, I always tried to stretch myself by inviting people like Joe Chaikin, Peter Brook, Lee Breuer and JoAnne Akalaitis to come to the Taper to do workshops. All of these artists have experimented with forms that are now very much part of our theatre. But my métier is related more to taking simple human truths that are inherent in an individual, marrying them with the style of material and letting the actor speak through that.

My way of working with actors is to build trust. I really do believe that the work is a collaboration, that the actors have an absolute right to experiment and fail. There's as much chance that they're going to teach me something about the event or the character as that I'm going to be able to teach them.

What do you seek or admire in an actor?

I like actors who try to develop and explore the play rather than trying to please me; actors who do homework, who don't wait to be told everything, who are flexible, willing to make changes. I don't direct every pinky move, every turn of the head. My agenda is the totality of the piece, and I bring a strong sense of timing, of how to get where we're going. I have a clock ticking in me that says, by now we should be here, and by now we should be at another place. It's my responsibility to get the production and the actors up to a certain point for the first run-through, the first tech, the first audience, opening night. One of the happiest rehearsal times is the previews. Most theatres have two or three and then they open, but we always have ten. It's during previews that I shape the show.

Do you come back to a production after it has opened?

Absolutely—although because I run an institution, and have put everything else on hold during rehearsals, what often happens is once we open I have to plunge into other things and don't get back as much as I want.

A play goes through a gestation cycle. I always feel that a show, once it opens, should play for a week or so without the director around, and then, in the ideal world, go back into rehearsal again. I don't often get to do that. There's a time about the second week of the run when growth has taken place and you can do a certain kind of work. At about six weeks, which is usually when you are coming to the end of a run, there's another good period for work. I've been fortunate in having had experience with some long runs like *Children* and *The Shadow Box*. I've noticed that at the three-month period, the growth and solidity start to deteriorate a bit and you have to find a new way of getting it back on track.

How have you learned to communicate, to collaborate with designers?

When I was a young stage manager, I worked for Martha Graham, and I think that I learned more about the theatre from being in her presence than I could from any directing teacher. I will never forget going to a preliminary design meeting about a new ballet that she was going to choreograph based on the Phaedra legend. She summoned Isamu Noguchi, who was going to do the set, Jean Rosenthal, the lighting designer, and me. Having attended a number of design meetings like that in the past, I expected a certain procedure to be followed. I had my pad ready, expecting to learn where the platform had to be, or the doors, or what have you. To my surprise, delight, puzzlement and amazement, they never talked about the ballet. We sat down in Martha's apartment on the East Side. She said, "I'm thinking of doing a new ballet based on the Phaedra legend." She reached over to the table and picked up a rock. She handed it to Noguchi. It was an interesting shape and he felt it. He gave it to Jean Rosenthal. She felt it. I looked at it and gave it back to Martha. And that was the end of the meeting. Noguchi went off and designed an extraordinary set. Jeannie lit it. It was a wonderful ballet. To this day, I still don't know how that happened, although sometimes I've experienced the kind of communication that happens among artists who have worked together over a long period of time.

Over the years, I've had some very important relationships with designers—Peter Wexler, Sally Jacobs, Ralph Funicello, Ming Cho Lee and Doug Stein, particularly. The best work gets at the essence of something and defines it. Out of that emerges a design and, therefore, a concept. Of course, you can't make anything like that work every time. When creative people get together they don't always make it happen. The longer the gestation time, discussion time, the longer you have to live with it the better. Sometimes you can press the right buttons and release the right ideas, and other times you don't.

When Doug and I did the Benjamin Britten opera *A Midsummer Night's Dream* for the Los Angeles Opera in 1988, we needed to find the right visual language for the piece, and we did that by looking at a lot of paintings. Lewis Brown joined us for costumes, and we all agreed that it was necessary to get the right visual metaphors. The mechanical detail would follow. We settled on a common visual stimulus, a Victorian pre-Raphaelite painter. Once we hit on that, ideas started to flow. But the production didn't really fall into place until Doug constructed the model, because it lived in three dimensions and not in the sketches. In contemporary design, more often than not, models have become the key method of expression. In an earlier time, sketching, painting renditions were principally used, partly because it was the period of proscenium and drops.

One of my great dreams is to be able to evolve the design from the work rather than conceptualizing it in advance and pouring the actors into it like so much liquid into a vessel. Actors have a way of creating a shape within that, if you allow enough freedom for them to do it, but it would be more interesting the other way.

Over the years, you've directed a fair amount of musical theatre and opera. Is there a basic difference in the way you approach directing a musical piece as opposed to a play?

Music can be extremely stimulating and rewarding because it often transcends the problems of dramatic structure and illuminates in a more abstract, and therefore more profound, way. I have tried to bring my knowledge of the theatre to opera in order to make the work have a greater dramatic sense. That's really common these days with young directors—they want to strengthen the libretto and its marriage to the music through better staging and interpretation, as opposed to just presenting the voice.

My first professional job directing an opera was in the 1950s with a little-known work called *The Barrier*, with text by Langston Hughes and a score by Jan Meyerowitz. It was based on Hughes's 1935 play *Mulatto*. The opera was short-lived, but the original play had been a scandalous success because it was about miscegenation. Hughes was alive when we did the opera at Columbia University with Lawrence Tibbett in the role of the Southern Colonel. In the first rehearsal, the musical director, Maurice Peress, went over the score with the singers and I realized that the singers had been working only on their vocal parts and didn't have a clue as to what the opera was about. So I stopped the rehearsal and said, "Before we get into the staging, I think we ought to read the libretto." They had never heard of such a thing. And it isn't easy to read a libretto. But I said, "Let's try it even though a lot of it may not make sense or will sound like doggerel." I wanted everyone to have some common experience with the piece—not only with the storyline and what was being stated in the arias, but what was being said in the duets, trios and quartets. It was an extraordinary revelation.

I direct a musical or an opera every couple of years and then I vow never to do it again, primarily because the system for doing opera is very frustrating, partly because of the lack of training of the singers and partly because of the lack of rehearsal time. One of the great tyrannies of opera is that the technical and preparation time is very truncated. In the theatre, the dress rehearsal marks the beginning of a whole new phase of work; but in opera, the dress rehearsal is really the first performance. You can't even give notes because there is a day off and then the show opens. Technically, you may be able to make some adjustments. It's a ludicrous system. You get it on by sheer dint of effort and the knowledge that somehow people will find their way. But you never get to refine anything, let alone make radical changes. Fundamentally, you have to wait until the next time you do the opera to cash in on how much you've learned. It's very, very frustrating.

Have you had experiences with opera where your input was closer to what you do in theatre?
Thea Musgrave composed and wrote the libretto for a new opera about Harriet Tubman and the Underground Railroad, a wonderful piece called *Harriet* that I staged in Virginia in 1985. She came to me very early in its development, so there was always a gap between seeing the work on the libretto and finally hearing the music. The process went on for a couple of years during which there were some radical changes in thinking—we went into rehearsal just as Thea completed

the music. That meant we had to design it before the score was finished and I didn't really hear the full score until the first rehearsal. And no amount of study of the libretto can reveal an opera. You have to know it through the music.

Harriet wasn't in repertory so we rehearsed it more or less like a play. However, we still had to get it on the stage quickly; then, at the dress rehearsal, the leading singer broke her ankle and we had to make amazing compromises in the first performance. We did the usual handful of performances, and I wanted to go back to work on it. But there's been no opportunity.

Is the purpose of the opera director to focus the audience on the story or the music?
I saw a dress rehearsal of Giorgio Strehler's *The Abduction from the Seraglio* at La Scala. He used a lot of side and back lighting, so that you often didn't see the faces. Every time he came to an aria, as opposed to the recitative, he would take the front light off the singers. I realized that what he was doing was forcing one to listen to the music in a different way. The arias are definitely about the music and not about interacting—the force of the aria is communicated through the music and through the interpretation of the musical line. So the idea of lowering the lights during an aria is an interesting idea. Again, like most interesting ideas, if everyone starts doing it then it's no longer interesting.

Do you think that technique could work with the texts of the classic plays?
It's conceivable that if you wanted the audience to listen to "To be or not to be" in a new way, rather than contemplating the Dane, one might indeed use that technique. In Strehler's production of *The Tempest* for the Olympic Arts Festival, one critic missed the point when he wrote that it was "dim." There may not have been enough light to suit the critic, but it wasn't dim; it was carefully controlled. The difficulty with removing lighting with the spoken drama is that the way we understand the words is often through seeing. I encounter that problem constantly on the thrust stage with full lighting because there are moments when an actor's back is to a portion of the audience. That sometimes impedes comprehension, because lack of hearing in older people often has just as much to do with failing eyesight.

It's been said that you can't have great theatre without a great audience. Do you think it's possible to develop a great audience?
I have changing views on that. Over the years I've committed myself to the building of an audience and I like our audience; we don't talk down to them. I worry that they are growing older with me. I do have a sense of family. And then I get letters that depress me when they say how much they hated a particular play. It disturbs me that they don't seem to have built a vocabulary that helps them to grow. It shows that there isn't a real consistency of taste or values.

Are you referring to objections raised about plays that are presented in a non-realistic style, that affect audiences on another level and sometimes make them uneasy?

On a certain level, it's no different from a person who stands in front of a photo-realistic painting, as opposed to an expressionistic painting, and says, "This is what I like because I understand it." There is an audience for abstract work. You see it at dance and New Wave concerts. In theatre it has been harder to develop that audience because our approach has not been consistent. A company like Mabou Mines will find its audience. What's hard to do is to take an audience like the Taper's—or that of any institution that produces a wide variety of work—and build a consistent level of catholicity of taste. I understand that. If I'm dealing with 30,000 subscribers, I can't get every one of them to grow in the same way. But I am puzzled and worried about people who are consistently unable to build on their experience. I have discovered that the possibility of such growth is more theoretical than actual.

Do you think such reactions from audiences will tempt you to choose less dangerous work in the future?

I've always felt that the theatre has a function in society which goes beyond entertainment. Theatre includes entertainment—but should we settle for fun when we could be pushing the boundaries of man's psyche? The arts are perhaps the best medium for expanding those boundaries. They're about finding a way to tell some truths. In the theatre, I can express something to satisfy my own soul and share it with my fellow citizens. That demands being more creative, going deeper and taking more chances!

Arthur Bartow joined the undergraduate drama department at New York University's Tisch School of the Arts as chair in 1990, and from 1995 to 2006 was the department's first artistic director. He was formerly associate director of Theatre Communications Group and artistic director of New Playwrights' Theatre in Washington, D.C., and the Theatre of the Riverside Church in New York. This article is adapted from Bartow's *The Director's Voice*, published by TCG Books in 1988. His most recent book is *Training of the American Actor*, published by TCG Books in 2007.

A CONVERSATION WITH PETER ZEISLER

An interview by Anna Deavere Smith

July/August 1995

Peter Zeisler has been a leading player in events that have transformed the face of American theatre since the 1950s. He co-founded the Guthrie Theater in Minneapolis with Sir Tyrone Guthrie and Oliver Rea in 1963. He became the executive director of Theatre Communications Group in 1972. On the occasion of his retirement, he talked with actor, educator and playwright Anna Deavere Smith at the TCG offices in Manhattan.

I want to start by asking you some things about your youth. I heard through the grapevine that your grandmother was a pianist and you traveled with her when you were, I suppose, a young boy.
An infant, really; she died when I was four. Her name was Fanny Bloomfield Zeisler, and she was a concert pianist. She was the Myra Hess of her day, the first acknowledged woman concert pianist.

How long has your family been in the United States?
Her parents came from either Czechoslovakia or Austria, depending on where you drew the border. It would have been in the early 1900s.

Was she the only entertainer in your family?
Yes.

So how did you come to theatre?
I don't really know. I started going to plays very early in life. I grew up on Riverside Drive where, every Saturday, my mother would give me two dollars and I would go off for the day. My lunch would be at Nedick's—an orange juice, hot dog and sugared donut for a quarter— and I would go to Gray's Drugstore at 43rd and Broadway, on the west side of the street, and get whatever 55-cent tickets they had. I would see two plays for $1.10, a matinee and an evening play on Saturday.

And your mother, did she like to go to the theatre?

Yes. Both my parents did. The marvelous thing was that they didn't try to dissuade my passion. My father didn't want to be a lawyer, but his father sort of forced him into it. The only advice my father ever gave me was, "The one thing I'm not going to do is tell you what to do, because my father told me what to do." He hoped I would not be a lawyer.

And then did you go to college?

I went for one year to Oberlin College, which was the blandest, most uptight, boring school in North America. All the boys ate in the girls' dormitories. And at each table, there was a house mother who sat there to make sure that nothing was going on under the table.

The first morning, I went to have breakfast, and I took a taste of Midwestern coffee. Do you know Midwestern coffee? It's just colored water. I took a sip of it, and said, "Jesus Christ, what is this?" I was invited by the matron to go into her parlor and talk to her, and I was invited not to eat in the dormitory anymore. Obviously, my language was too disrespectful. So I stayed one year and that was enough. I transferred to Columbia.

Did you know at that point that you were going to try to make a career in theatre? That would have been your late teens, early twenties.

Yes, I knew, but I had no idea what I was going to do.

Did you want to act?

I guess so, because everyone wants to act. I had a marvelous teacher named Paul Morrison, who had been a scenic designer for the Group Theatre. I went up to his apartment one morning and talked to him, asking him what the hell I was going to do. As he was shaving, he looked at me in the mirror and said, "You know, you're never going to be Cary Grant." Which was his way of telling me, don't be an actor.

But you ultimately became a stage manager.

I wanted to direct at that point, and the way to get into directing was stage managing.

It must have been much simpler then to get an assignment as a stage manager.

No. I was lucky. Just by a fluke, after I got out of school, New Stages— the first sort of "Off-Broadway" theatre since the days of O'Neill and the Provincetown Playhouse—was being started by a group of professional actors. They had turned to radio to make a living, but they wanted to get back to doing theatre. We renovated a theatre, which is now Circle in the Square Downtown. I built that theatre with my own hands. 159 Bleecker Street.

And the first play, Jean-Paul Sartre's *The Respectful Prostitute*, was an extraordinary hit. It transferred to Broadway and I transferred with it. So here's this little putz who's a stage manager on Broadway, working with stagehands five times his age. I started out that way. I was unbelievably lucky.

How many years were you in the commercial theatre?
From 1948 or '49 to 1963.

Can you talk to me a little bit about the difference between the commercial theatre then and now?
I very seldom go to Broadway now because there's seldom anything I really want to see. The thing I remember fondly about Broadway was the extraordinary level of craft you found at all levels. You found it in the technical theatre, you found it in the acting and the directing. Superb technical control of the material. But remember, it was all really kitchen drama—four-wall realistic drama.

One of the most amazing things about the nonprofit theatre is how it has changed the concept of training in this country. For years, you were only training for the commercial theatre, which was light comedies and naturalistic acting. Then the nonprofit theatre came along and made demands on actors they simply couldn't deal with because they had no voice or movement training.

So was Shakespeare first done in the nonprofit theatre?
Well, no . . . there were a couple of rudimentary attempts at doing classical theatre on Broadway, one by Eva Le Gallienne and her company, another by Orson Welles. Maurice Evans did a series of plays, but that was not a company, really.

The classics were done in the nonprofit theatre primarily because it was an alternative to the work being done in the commercial theatre, but also because we couldn't get access to new plays—agents simply wouldn't give them to us. The first one, I guess, was Arthur Kopit's *Indians* at Arena Stage, which was too big to do on Broadway. But we did the classics primarily because that was all we really *could* do.

So how do you think the classics became what, in training, we all aspired to?
We had no role model of American classical theatre, so we had to accept the model of the British. Unfortunately, for many years, we imitated British Shakespeare rather than trying to reassess it. We then went to the other extreme, where we were doing Shakespeare in name only, making it so "relevant" it had nothing to do with the text. We're beginning now to really find our voice, but it's taken a long time.

Do you think it makes a difference whether people are trained in schools?
You've got to have technique in your background, in your consciousness, whether or not you use it again in your professional life. There are exceptions, of course. One of the best American actors I ever worked with (and I did three shows with him) was Robert Preston—a terribly underestimated actor in this country because he never got to play the parts he should have played.

Bob had no training, but he had an absolutely ironclad technique. He could do anything. And he could do it over and over and over again and make it fresh each time. Where he got that from, I don't know. He didn't get it from training, but he had it. Let's face it. Great actors don't need to go to school. Olivier didn't go to school. Gielgud didn't go to school. The geniuses don't need schools. The ones who aren't geniuses need school.

Three sentences and you can tell if there's training. Any pianist is expected to play Mozart, yet in many cases actors are not expected to be able to play the equivalent of Mozart—Shakespeare. In the absence of that elusive quality of genius, craft is the key to being a serious artist.

Unfortunately, we've grown up in a society that picked up the Betty Grable mythology that you could be a star by being discovered on a stool in Schwab's drugstore in Hollywood—that craft had nothing to do with acting, that acting had to do with personality. It took us a long time to learn differently.

We also suffered for many years with an extraordinary "quirk of fate." Stella Adler went to Moscow to meet Stanislavsky and brought back the "Torah," *An Actor Prepares*, but didn't bring back the second book, *Building a Character*, that's primarily about the physical demands of acting. But nobody learned that. So even in the heyday of what I think was probably the best training program in New York in the '50s, the Neighborhood Playhouse—Sandy Meisner was a stunning, brilliant teacher—and although Martha Graham taught movement at the Playhouse, there was no voice work, really, and there was no work done on classic text.

I want to ask you about being blacklisted during this period.
This is my favorite story of the blacklist. I was a young apprentice director at the Actors Studio (which is where I first worked with Alan Schneider). Elia Kazan did his great apologia and took a full page ad in the *New York Times* to explain why he ratted on his friends. (The Saturday paper, of course, because nobody read it.) I took a Saturday night class at the Studio with Gadge [Kazan's nickname]. We all got to class that night and, of course, we had all read the paper. And everybody is clucking—oh, my god, how could he do this, blah, blah, blah.

I stood up and made a very simple suggestion: that we write to Cheryl Crawford, who was then the administrator of the Studio, saying that we loved the Studio, we loved working at the Studio, but we did not want to work with Gadge anymore. We would like to work with Bobby Lewis or somebody else who was teaching. At which point two enormously successful New York actors stood up and said, "Oh, my god, how can we do this? He hires us." I said, "You can't have it both ways." Out of that entire class, two of us left. It was a terrible time in New York, people turning other people in. I was caught up in the hysteria, and I didn't work for over two years as a result. A very strange feeling, because in offices that I could walk into at will before, suddenly the doors were just slammed shut.

I'm not clear how you actually found out you were blacklisted.
Well, it was a very simple exercise. I was stage managing a play at the Royale Theatre, *Affairs of State*, in 1950. The Royale shares a common alleyway with the Majestic, where *South Pacific* was playing. Four theatres all have a common alleyway there.

The stage managers would always stand outside before a Wednesday matinee and talk about whatever came up. One Wednesday, telegrams were delivered to the four stage managers asking that we post on the callboard the fact that the Hollywood Ten were going to appear at the old Capital Hotel at 50th Street and Eighth Avenue to explain why they had taken the Fifth Amendment.

The stage manager of *South Pacific* put it on the callboard. We all did. My company manager at that time was late getting to the matinee because he was out picketing on behalf of the Catholic War Veterans in front of Loew's State, where Judy Holliday's movie *Born Yesterday* had just opened.

He got back from the theatre in hysteria, tore the telegram off the callboard and came backstage demanding to know why it had gone up. I said, it's a point of information for the company. Whether they go or not is up to them. But this is a callboard and I put that notice on, and it's going to stay there.

Well, it didn't stay there, and that night, I was given two weeks' notice. I was fired because I was a "Commie."

Did somebody actually say that to you?
The company manager said that to me. I did appeal it to Equity Council. A very distinguished character actress on the Council turned to me and said, "Why is it all you young Jewish boys are making 'trouble'?"

How long were you blacklisted?
Between two and three years.

What did you do?
I worked as a soda jerk at Schraft's drugstore.

Do you think anything like that can happen again, or that it does happen?
Well, as the result of the last few weeks with the Michigan Militia, I think it probably is happening right now. There's a growing timidity out there. I think people are increasingly afraid of taking a stand. It horrifies me. I don't understand what is happening in this country, and I don't understand what has happened to our moral values, and it scares me.

Can you talk to me more about that?
What I'm seeing is much worse than McCarthy, because it's more central now to the system. It's not just one bigot. I see a terrifying recurrence of anti-Semitism, homophobia, every kind of multicultural discrimination. I find it being heightened daily.

How do you see that scenario turning into someone deciding who can or cannot work? Could there be a McCarthy? Is there a McCarthy?
Of course. Jesse Helms is a McCarthy. There are five or six of them in the Senate.

My formative years were the '40s and '50s. I lived in New York; I was a West Side New York boy. I grew up on 114th Street and Riverside Drive, and my two bibles then were the *Partisan Review* and the *New Yorker*, and maybe *Harper's*. They really formed my ethical education. I still cannot understand what happened to that generation of liberal New York Jews, many of whom came here as a result of Hitler—that marvelous, tough, liberal point of view. There was a marvelous left-wing—not radical, just left-wing—stance on the part of the *Partisan Review* about ethics and morals in the country all through the '40s and '50s—Mary McCarthy, Phil Roth. We don't have those voices anymore.

What about in the theatre? I don't suppose the theatre was a part of that, at any rate, when you were younger.
Well, yes, the Group Theatre was making those kinds of statements when I was a child.

What about during the McCarthy era? What theatre group was holding to a moral core?
There wasn't any theatre group. We didn't have groups. By then, the Group Theatre had disbanded. But that's when Arthur Miller wrote *The Crucible*. We did have some extraordinary producers. Cheryl Crawford, who later became the administrator of the Actors Studio, and Kermit Bloomgarden—the two of them were the liberal producers and they were doing avowedly political work, Kermit more than anybody else. Kermit was Arthur Miller's producer.

When we think about the current drama at the NEA, for example, and think about Jesse Helms, what pleases you and what disappoints you about how we in the theatre have positioned ourselves?
I don't think we should have a purely political theatre, but we have an apolitical theatre now, largely because we've given it over to either documentary film or television. We're not making those kinds of political statements now. I think it started going downhill during the Vietnam War when, suddenly, every day on television you got images that the theatre couldn't provide. That was the first time television became testimony to our time, much more than theatre. The theatre has never found out how to react to the television documentary.

What's keeping us from being more responsible?
I think there are a number of things that have happened. The first is that we don't have the role of "producer" in the nonprofit theatre. It started really with Mac Lowry at the Ford Foundation, who thought the title producer connoted "sleazy" Broadway practices, and that theatres should be run by artists. Well, actually, many of the best theatres in this country are run by artistic directors who are not necessarily good directors but are marvelous producers. We have to get over this mythology that a producer is bad.

We invented the title of artistic director at the Guthrie. We didn't want to do it, and it was a terrible mistake. But people kept saying: What does Tyrone Guthrie do? What do you do? What does Oliver Rea do?

We sort of had to give ourselves titles, but Tony and I both objected to the title of artistic director as terribly pompous and pretentious.

Another problem is that the nonprofit theatre started in a much different age, the Kennedy age. It started in an age when there was a spirit of *don't ask what your country can do for you, ask what you can do for your country.* There was a great feeling of being of service, almost a missionary feeling—how could we serve? That's not true anymore. Twelve years of Reagan and the me-too generation pretty well knocked the idealism out of young people in this country. We've never regained that sense of commitment.

I think the thing that I'm most disappointed in is the fact that I always thought a theatre should lead the community. Not reflect it, but lead it, the way Arthur Miller led it when he wrote *The Crucible* and really made a very strong statement about blacklisting. In 1995, I think the ability of the theatre to reflect its society is virtually nonexistent. I don't see enough people of color in determining positions in the theatre. I think if we don't start moving, the theatre is just going to be irrelevant in the society.

But it's going to be irrelevant for other reasons besides race, don't you think?
Yes, yes. But we still have this glorious opportunity that no other art form has. It's the only place you meet person-to-person. It really goes back to primitive man and the campfire. It goes back to the need to go to the church, to be with other people to discuss issues.

Do you think there's a possibility that we'll be in a dry spell for a while, until people realize they need us?
We have a bankrupt educational system in this country. Unless we fix that, we're not going to have any arts.

And television just exacerbates the problem. People don't read. It's frightening. There was a period in the '50s in England with all the "Peter" directors—Peter Brook, Peter Wood, Peter Hall, everybody was Peter. And, interestingly, most of them went to Oxford, where they all "read" the same thing—they all read Greats, which is the toughest philosophy course in the Western world, except for the Sorbonne. They didn't learn craft, they didn't learn that upstage left is the weak entrance. They learned how to think and they learned how to synthesize, and that's what made them brilliant directors. But we've lost the intellectual fiber in the theatre.

As well as the moral fiber?
In my first Broadway show, *The Respectful Prostitute*, the second lead was played by John Marriott, who was considered by many the leading black actor in New York commercial theatre. John showed up for rehearsal late the first day, and he was late the second day and he was late the third day. John was then a man of about 50; I was 27 years old.

After the third day of rehearsal, I got him in a corner and I gave him stage manager's lecture 132/5 about respect for his fellow actors and respect for the director and said, goddammit, be on time. And the more I talked, the more he sort of giggled; the angrier I got, the more he laughed.

Finally, I said to John, "What is so funny?" He said, "Well, Peter, this is my 40th Broadway show. This is the first time anybody has talked to me as an actor and not as a black man." It just broke my heart. We then became the best of friends.

The fact is, we won a partial victory over segregation, right? So we have similar frames of reference now. And that's the plus of television. It's not like it was. So why is it, given the fact that we all have had similar experiences, why can't we desegregate our theatre?

I can't answer you. We're going through a period now where there is rightful indignation on the part of small, culturally specific theatres against the large theatres that are getting money for doing multicultural work, and this has, unfortunately, exacerbated the either/or situation.

As the money crunch gets worse and worse and worse—and it's at really epidemic stages right now—I don't know how most of the theatres are going to do next season. There's so little money out there.

The only reason theatres have tax exemption is because they are considered to be providing educational and social services in their communities. It's the thing that separates them from commercial theatre. But increasingly, I find the choices theatres must make are based on how many tickets are going to be sold rather than, is this a play that has to be done?

You didn't ask me about the Army. You know, I was court-martialed for saluting a black officer.

Tell me about that.

It's one of my favorite stories. I was in North Camp Hood, Tex., because it was the nearest thing General Patton could find to the desert in the United States. Only white troops. I was a sergeant, and the sergeant acts on behalf of the platoon. I was leading a platoon down the street with my buddies and facing me was a black major. I hadn't even seen a black private first class and here was a major. Well, he turned out to be a doctor. So I gave the snappiest salute I had ever given in the Army. That night, the company commander called me in and wanted to know why I had saluted a nigger. I said, "I didn't salute a nigger, I saluted a uniform."

"Well, soldier, we don't salute niggers in Texas." I said, "I do." I was cited under the 96th article of war, "conduct unbecoming to a soldier." I was a sergeant and got broken to private. Thirty days in the guard house.

What did you think about when you were in the guard house?

Not much. It was awful.

Yet you still turned around years later and put that telegram up on the board. What gave you moral values? What makes you stand up for things that you believe in?

The interesting thing is that I am a born-and-bred agnostic. I've never had religious instruction or any religious desires or any religious interest all my life, which is strange.

Do you have any spirituality at all?
I don't think so. You know, there was that old adage during the war, "There are no atheists in foxholes." Well, this one was. I was in prison camp for over a year.

Where were you in prison camp?
A little country club the Germans had, called Dachau. I never felt that religious need. I'm not proud of it. It's just a fact.

How did you end up in Dachau?
I was inducted in the Army when I was a student at Columbia. Despite the fact that I knew my entire Army career would be based on the intelligence test you take, I was given a sendoff by all my friends, a very alcoholic sendoff. I had to report at 0600 hours and we sat outside the gate till 0559 drinking, and I could hardly walk through the gate. I remember being given a uniform and I sort of remember having powdered eggs given to me for breakfast. I don't remember anything else.

About three days later, in formation, a bunch of names were called out. I was one of them. We walked down this long alleyway into a classroom and a very smug sergeant said, "I'm here to teach you how to read and write." I had signed my name on the intelligence test and passed out!

So I raised my hand in righteous indignation. He started to explain the alphabet. I went back to the barracks after class was over, and the bright guys—they had been on the infiltration course and had marched about 10 miles. They were exhausted. I felt fine. I decided to cool it.

So about three weeks later, we were up to two-syllable words like "rifle" and "soldier." Suddenly, I was called before the company commander, and he wanted to know what kind of school Columbia was. The game was up. I said, 'Well, it's got a lousy football team . . . ." He made me take the test again, and somehow I passed this time.

Two weeks later, I was called in again, and was transferred from Army illiteracy school—the "dummy platoon," as we were called—to Army intelligence school. So my service record reads, Army illiteracy school *and* Army intelligence school.

I ended up as Patton's intelligence noncom—noncommissioned officer. I was on an intelligence mission in civilian clothes with a Dutch passport, and I was captured. They never knew I was American; they sure as hell never knew I was Jewish. I wouldn't be alive if they had.

Did you speak Dutch?
I spoke German. The northern Dutch speak uninflected German.

What did you have to do for a year? Did you have any relationships there?
No, you try to live. You weigh 85 pounds when you come out. You're a vegetable.

Did you see Jewish people there?
We were segregated by degrees of calumny. The American Jews had the worst treatment, the German Jews had the next worst treatment, and I was a "Dutch gentile," so I was relatively well off.

How did you ultimately get out?
At the end of the war, Dachau was liberated by American troops.

Peter, when you look back over your career, what is the most satisfying thing to you?
The beginning of the acceptance of the theatre as an art form in this country, which it never was before. It was always considered "entertainment." Forty years ago, whatever anybody in the country knew about American drama originated in New York. Now, theatre starts allover the country. The fact that we have reversed the methodology is, I think, the most exciting thing.

What would you like to have had the opportunity to do that you didn't get to do?
I think the fact that we did not stay the course and form true acting companies in this country is my biggest disappointment. Everybody thought that all the theatres were going to be resident companies back in the early '60s. When the money started getting tight, that's when people gave up on companies. But it entails so much more, because it really was the end of an apprenticeship into the companies by young actors. It removed the relationship of training to theatre companies. It became a less organic business.

I also regret that we were never able to get artist salaries to a satisfactory level. When an actor gets to be 40 years old and has to start thinking about putting his kids in college, he can't afford to live on what he makes in the theatre.

I think we made too many compromises. I don't think we dug our heels in enough. We're the most accommodating profession in the world. We all want to work and we'll do anything in order to be able to work. I can't have an English army if I'm going to do *Henry V*—all right, so I'll do it with two soldiers. Nobody is going to do *Swan Lake* without swans. We should have dug in our heels and said, it's the cost of doing business, and we didn't do that. Because of the love of the work and the need to work, we always "make do."

We can't really end on this note. Even for a man who is a proclaimed agnostic, do you really not have a source of faith?
I guess I must. But I can't verbalize it. I have, unfortunately, a rigid sort of moral code for myself.

What are some of the rules in that code?
It has to do with fairness and it has to do with thinking in terms of individuals.

What are you going to do now?

I have no idea. I want to travel. I just got back from two weeks in Japan. The Japanese are interested in nonprofit theatre—it's a totally alien concept to them. I did a series of seminars with them and I would love to do more travel, and I'd like to do some teaching. I have no other plans yet.

Actor and playwright Anna Deavere Smith is known for her interview-based solo theatre pieces, such as *Twilight: Los Angeles, Fires in the Mirror* and *Let Me Down Easy*. She founded and directed the Institute on the Arts and Civic Dialogue from 1998–2000 at Harvard University, and became the Ford Foundation's first artist-in-residence in 1997.

EARTH MOM

An interview with Olympia Dukakis by Timothy Near and Krissy Keefer

September 1995

In 1994 the entire city of San Francisco was seduced by a minute-long commercial for *Tales of the City*, a controversial ratings blockbuster for PES-TV. The commercial, a short scene on a park bench between a mature man (Donald Moffat) and a sympathetic stranger (Olympia Dukakis), was intoxicating for the honesty, warmth and sensuousness that emanated from the couple's simple conversation. Portraying Anna Madrigal, an unconventional landlady in her late fifties, in the mini-series based on Armistead Maupin's seriocomic novels, Dukakis created a wacky-wise, fully sexual woman so against the tide of mainstream female characters on television that critics and viewers alike were startled by the uniqueness and genuine humanity she exuded.

Tales of the City, of course, was no debut for Olympia Dukakis, on screen or off. As an actress, teacher, activist, producer and director, she has a career that spans 30 years. For the past 10 of those years, she has been the unlikely star of films such as *Steel Magnolias*, *The Cemetery Club*, *Dad* and *Moonstruck* (for which she won a best-supporting-actress Oscar, one of numerous acting awards she has garnered during her career). But perhaps Dukakis's most valuable contribution has been her giant compassion for the women she has played—her ability to convey an intensity, wisdom and intelligence that comes through rarely in American theatre and even more rarely in American film.

This season, Dukakis has come to San Francisco's American Conservatory Theater to work with artistic director Carey Perloff on a new adaptation by Timberlake Wertenbaker of the ancient Greek tragedy *Hecuba*. During the production's run in June and July at the Yerba Buena Theatre, one cannot help but notice that there are women over 50 everywhere—walking in groups, in pairs, alone. They have come in droves—many without their husbands—to see this play about revenge and betrayal, about the consuming love of children, about the men who control women's lives but aren't integrated into their lives. On the

ACT stage, they discover a play written centuries ago that somehow parallels and illuminates their contemporary experiences.

Dukakis's Hecuba seems to be grounded deep in her body. Carey Perloff and designer Kate Edmunds have given her a set where the character, daughter of a river god and a nymph, can fulfill her relationship with the elements. The Greeks believed that Heaven and Earth were the first parents, the Titans their children and the gods their grandchildren. Dukakis, herself the daughter of Greek immigrants, works on this tragedy as if her ancestors were indeed Heaven and Earth: At times she moves with the grace and power of the ravaged Queen of Troy, but more often she lashes out with the focus and darkness of an impending hurricane, speaking with a voice that seems to come from somewhere deep underground.

Hecuba is a war widow and now slave to Odysseus. Eighteen of her nineteen sons have been killed; only two daughters survive. When the play starts, this mother of dead children digs in the earth like a dog until she uncovers a light which reveals a dream. When the dream is over, she pushes the earth back over the light as if to bury the unbearable truth that she has learned.

When she discovers that her daughter Polyxena is to be sacrificed by the Greeks, she rises up out of the dirt and reaches for the child, slamming her body to her own; they appear glued together, almost as if Hecuba is trying literally to absorb Polyxena's body into her own pores. Her physical expressions of Mother as Protector take on animal form: a lion, a bear, a dog. When her reasoned appeals for mercy and justice seem to have no effect on Odysseus, she becomes a strutting, screeching bird ("*I* am the one who gave birth to Paris and it was the arrow from Paris's bow that killed Achilles. Take *me* to his mound and stab me there"), attempting with great intensity to distract the enemy away from her child.

When Polyxena is taken away, the Chorus sings a song familiar to women taken in war: "Who will buy me? Whose slave will I be?" During this song of sorrow, Hecuba walks slowly down the hill holding her daughter's dress, and it is clear that she is reliving the moment Polyxena learned to walk. Her child has gone to her death. She flails her thin arms, claws at her own face. She curls up in the dirt and becomes very small, very frail—an image of aching loss.

Later, when she finds that her one remaining son has been murdered for greed, we understand that Hecuba has united with an underworld darkness inside herself. Her voice lowers to an animal growl. Her body crouches more toward the earth—like a woman giving birth standing up; at one point she almost seems to be attempting to suck her dead son back up into her womb so that time can be reversed, and he can be safe. When she sees no one will help her find justice, she becomes vengeance itself, killing her enemy's children.

The play is over. In the aisles, in the lobby and out on the street women cry and argue, struggle to absorb the impact of what they have just seen. Backstage, Dukakis is gracious and charming to her fans, joking with and complimenting the stage crew. I find her instantly likeable. As we go to find a place to eat and talk, her hair is wet and San Francisco is windy, but she's not worried. Although the performance exhausts her, her voice is strong, and she's not worried about losing it. We find a quiet soup, salad and pizza place. We talk, we eat, we eat and talk. She's half my size and eats twice as much. And why not? She needs to be strong as an ox to be doing what she's doing on stage.

Dukakis has a face and body that can be surprisingly young one moment—innocent eyes, *open, open* smile that is irresistible—but in the next moment you glimpse great age, sorrow and wisdom that feels ancient. Wizened weltschmerz. Global sadness. She takes in *everything*.

I am still thinking about the last moment of the play where you carry your son to the ship's prow. You stand there as Polymestor makes his prophecy that you will leap to your death on your way to Greece and your watery grave will be named the Bitch with Burning Eyes. Holding your dead son, you crouch like a dog rising on its back legs, protecting its pup.
The fierce protectress mother, that's right. I really love doing that. *Hecuba* is about taking care of the children. That, to me, is what it is at the end. Because of greed and of revenge, children die. It's about these children and what we're doing to them.

What does that last line mean: "History has no compassion"?
Actually, I think the winners write history, so history is often distorted. But in this case I think the author doesn't want the audience to start getting personal and say, "Oh, too bad for that woman, oh, too bad for that man, or too bad for those kids." There *should* be no compassion. Compassion doesn't get us far. You have to take a look at the lesson to be learned. It's a little Brechtian, as a matter of fact.

You know, I saw this play in Greece with my husband [actor Louis Zorich] 34 years ago. Katina Paxinou was playing Hecuba. The women next to us in the theatre were crying and pulling their clothes away from their body, as if even the very cloth of their clothing was painful to them—they felt such sympathy for Hecuba's *lament*. Lamentation in Greece doesn't just mean to cry and carry on—it is a political act and anti-military. In fact, the Greeks eventually outlawed lamenting. But these Greek women felt sympathy for Hecuba. And today it was the women who stood up—they stood up! You know, women so seldom see images and scenes in plays that contain the complexity and depth of who we are.

You seem to use every nerve ending, every fiber in your body to express Hecuba. Did you train for this over the years?
I love these kinds of parts where I feel my body can get embroiled; whether it's a character, like Soot in *The Marriage of Bette and Boo*, or more subtle work like in *Rose Tattoo*. I have a great time with those roles. Peter Cass was my teacher. A great teacher! He taught the physical, the vocal, the whole thing. Over the years I have moved toward this physical expression on my own, and I'm always pushing for more flexibility and more articulation. It's harder now that I've gotten older.

In the mornings I have to do yoga. When I was younger I used to hurl my body through time and space. Sometimes with *Hecuba* I've had to get up in the morning and take two Advil. Rehearsal was . . . I was on my knees for days! I thought, Christ, if this doesn't get me, nothing else will. (*Laughs.*) I seem to have survived it.

Your political views about the world seem always to inform your art. Where does this connection of art and politics come from?
Our families—all the Dukakises—would get together and have discussions about social issues, and it was always expected that you would be engaged. It was just assumed that of course you would be informed about the issues of the day and have opinions. My father used to engage me in discussion and take the opposite side because he wanted me to become combative and a strong debater. That's very Greek. It's not necessarily something that Greek women at my time were doing, but my father was a kind of unusual man. He started off as a socialist and ended his life as a Republican. But my mother remained a Democrat all her life. She maintained that she was at the heart of the matter. My mother and I would be talking about *why* somebody did such and such, and my father would say, "Why are you talking about this? It doesn't matter. *Character is destiny*." Actually, Aristotle said that, too.

Your parents were Greek immigrants?
My mother came to the U.S. from mainland Greece when she was six, and my father came from Asia Minor when he was sixteen. They met here in America. I grew up during World War II. My parents were involved with the Red Cross and Greek war relief. Hitler starved the Greeks. [Director] Nikos Psacharopoulos grew up at that time, and he told the story that he picked through the garbage to stay alive. It helps you understand Nikos a little better.

You did a lot of work with Nikos.
I did Chekhov over and over with him until we finally began to learn something about it. But I learned just as much from my husband, who seems to have a real affinity for the material. With Nikos [at Williamstown Theatre Festival in Massachusetts] I played Carlotta, Luba, Paulina and Arkadina, and some of the roles in *Three Sisters*. So Nikos was important for me. You know when you work with people over and over again, they hold in their memory your work. They tend to tell you the truth quicker.

Yes, to be a part of a company seems very important to you. You and your husband, your brother Apollo, and several other actors, directors and designers founded the Whole Theatre Company in Montclair, N.J., in 1973.
Yes, and what's interesting is that most of those people had already started theatres before that. I'm a founding member of the Actors Company and Charles Playhouse in Boston, and we had people who had started the New York Free Theatre and the Performance Group with Richard Schechner.

What was the impulse that started the Whole Theatre?

To create a place where you could do work that was important and timely in your life—to do work that mattered to the world around you.

And you were artistic director?

No, as a matter of fact. We didn't organize ourselves that way at all. We organized ourselves by committee. You had to be the chair of one committee and sit on another one. We had co-chairs, so I was always one of the co-chairs of the artistic committee, and got rotated to the other committees, like development, marketing. It was amazing. My experience with the Whole Theatre really forced me to learn a lot about everything. It was like playing different parts.

One day you're playing the role of a fundraiser . . . .

Right, then you're the person who keeps the staff together, and then you're the person who figures out how to deal with the latest changes in the fire laws. The Whole Theatre also sponsored an outreach group for children called Thunder in the Light. We modeled it after Bob Alexander's Living Stage [in Washington, D.C.].

Did you change as an artist during the Whole Theatre era?

Yes. As it evolved, what I wanted as an actress evolved as well. At first acting was a way of defining myself. My first impulse was to be a very good craftswoman. I was told in my first acting class that it takes 20 years to make an actor. I believed that. Then competition became very important—to be better than the others. But when you compete you are alone on stage, and at some point my desire *not* to be alone became very real. The original impulse for me to be in theatre was to play *with* people. Not everyone plays the way you want to play, so then you find your tribe—the people you want to work with. And of course, a company allows you to have that honesty and familiarity with other artists.

The next phase of the evolution was to realize what my place was in a play in relation to the experience the audience was having. I'm not there to teach them; we are all there together, the actors and the audience. The actors are there as a catalyst to help us *all* remember something that we *all* know. When I was in the Whole Theatre I had this Lorca poem hanging on my office wall. Do you know it?

> *The poem, the song, the picture,*
> *Is water drawn from the well of the people*
> *And should be given back to them in a cup of beauty*
> *So that in drinking they may know themselves.*

At the Whole Theatre, you did a lot of early work on multicultural and political themes, didn't you?

I tried to do plays that were very much of our time, and that's how we got into trouble. When the Mapplethorpe thing happened, everybody decided it was better to fund education and health, not a theatre that the season before did a comedy about two lesbians having a baby!

You were in existence for 19 years. Why did you close?

Many complicated reasons. Not just one thing. We were carrying a debt, but not a huge one. We had raised $7.25 million toward a new building. The audiences were good, responsive. Then the political climate changed. Governor Florio cut the state arts budget by 46 percent. We had struggles with the city arts council. The board wanted cuts that I couldn't support, like the salaries of the staff. And one of our key fundraisers had a heart attack. So funding, space, politics . . . . We decided to close while we were still feeling good about the work. The last play I did was Beckett's *Happy Days*. The audience was incredibly reactive to that play. People would come expecting to see the me in *Steel Magnolias*, and instead there I was in a mound of dirt. They loved it.

You seem to get these roles where you're in the dirt a lot.

Winnie in *Happy Days* says, "Everybody eats a peck of dirt before they die." My husband says, "Everybody eats a bushel of shit before they die." (*Laughs*.)

Talk to me about yourself as a teacher.

I taught beginning classes for Peter Cass, and then I taught for 15 years at New York University. Peter was a great teacher—he helped me learn how to teach. Every time I would get to the point where I would say, "I just don't want to teach anymore. I'm not doing anything any good anyhow. I'm not really helping anybody," Peter would come to watch me teach. Then once he said, "Don't get up from your chair, stay in your chair." That's because when I first started teaching I was always up on my feet walking behind students, moving and talking, blah blah, you know. "Sit in your chair," and he was right. I began to create ways of working with students to help them become willful and make their own choices instead of me doing it for them. It was very difficult. He asked me, "What's the most important thing to you?" I said, "The most important thing for me is that they become independent." That is the most difficult thing for actors. To claim their own work, claim their own process without being defensive.

How did your teaching affect your directing?

Initially, when I started to direct I would get too embroiled in the actors and their problems. By the time I finished with the Whole Theatre, I couldn't wait for techs to come, because I wouldn't have to talk with the actors. You'd sit out there and talk about other things.

Your brother Apollo is also a director and an actor.

Apollo is a wonderful actor of tremendous range. He's also a great director. Once he directed me in *Long Day's Journey into Night*. Louis, my husband, and I were doing the opening scene (I'd already done this play with Louis twice before). Finally I stop and say, "I don't know what to do in this scene—I can't even see your eyes, Louis. They're totally closed, and you won't look at me." And Apollo says, "What's the problem?" I say, "I can't play the scene, he won't look at me, I can't see his eyes. I don't know what's going on. Do you know what's going on?" Apollo says, "No, I don't know what's going on, any more than I know why you have to control the stage all the time." (*Laughs.*) It was awful, and there ensued screaming and yelling and much carrying on. Of course, Louis, who's from Connecticut, is not saying anything, while these two crazy Greeks are screaming and yelling at each other.

Then Apollo said something to me that was so great. He said, "You're not vulnerable to other actors unless they're playing what you want them to play. When you approve of it, then you're vulnerable. That's no way to play with people." Well, that piece of criticism was quite a revelation. I mean, it was a case of somebody who loves you telling you those things—most people just go off and talk about you behind your back, but he actually said that to me. I had to totally accept in that moment that this was not Louis the actor who wouldn't look at me but Louis the character in *Long Day's Journey*. The moment I realized that, the scene was right.

What do you look for in a director?
Somebody who can tell me what they see. I mean, who can really tell you what they see, instead of manipulating you. I frequently ask directors, "So, well, what do you see? Do you see the story? What's coming across?" In other words, what's the *audience* gonna see? Initially you can do that for yourself. But for me, as I get into something, I become less and less able to do that.

Are you a different person when you direct? Do you draw on a part of your talent different from the actor part? Can you act and direct at the same time?
That's too hard. I could produce, I could be an artistic director and act. But directing is so consuming. I feel more comfortable acting. When you're directing you've gotta be everybody's babysitter, and you've gotta be the crossing guard, and you've gotta be the mother, and then you've gotta be the lover and you've gotta be everything. Of course there are directors who don't do that.

Do you feel fame has changed your life?
Yeah. Absolutely. I used to worry a great deal about money. Now I'm still a worrier, you know—I guess I'm a Depression baby—but I now feel that there are possibilities for me to remain financially secure, whereas until 1988, the year *Moonstruck* came out, we were sending our daughter to college on credit cards.

How about privacy?
Oh, that is important. I'm not, you know, like a star. People know me and they come up and say things, and then it's always nice. Most of the time it's very quick and sweet and people go on their way. In New York people are very respectful of your privacy.

How does fame affect the work. Is there more pressure?
No, not in the work itself. I think I was fortunate that my film work happened so late. (*Laughs.*) But the pressure I do feel is to try to take

advantage of it. There are certain things that I care about—issues about women and children, violence, abuse of the planet. I try to help raise money for those organizations.

How does your activism and art overlap?
To try to bring your work and your life together is really the trick. You do things because they want to pay you, and you do the best damn job you can. And that's nothing to be ashamed of. And then there are other things that you feel you're in sync with. I felt that with *Tales of the City*.

Is it hard to go back to theatre after having walked through the Hollywood door?
It was hard in the beginning. I would say, oh well, I can only do theatre work in December or January, which is a kind of down time for Hollywood. With *Hecuba*, I said to my agent, "I don't care when it is. If I don't do this, I won't know who I am."

Anyhow, there have been very few parts for women my age on television and in the movies. Movies, it's a business, right? And who are you selling to? Primarily you're selling to 24-to-27-year-old white males. That's the predominant audience out there. And what do you think they want? You think they want middle-aged women? They want action and testosterone. They're not necessarily interested in middle-aged estrogen problems. They want action, whether it's sexual, or physical, or fear.

Your daughter Christina is an actress. Do you see yourself in her work?
Yeah, every problem she has spills out. I was and still am like that. Everything comes out. Which is good, because then it gets dealt with—it's not hidden or perverted. But she has a more interesting range than I do. It was hard for me to learn to do light comedy. I was too worried about people laughing at me. Christina is very good at comedy. She makes me laugh—I say this and now I start to cry! But she really makes me laugh. Her timing, her physicality, her little body things are very funny.

You told me that your study of Greek mythology started with your family, that you read Greek myths as a child. These childhood stories continue to influence your work. Especially with your present theatre company, Voices of the Earth. How did that company get started?
It's a not-for-profit company that started about three years ago in New Jersey, consisting of four actresses—me, Joan MacIntosh, Leslie Ayvazian and Remi Barclay Bosseau [who also appeared in *Hecuba*]. It started with a grant I got from the Geraldine Dodge Foundation to work on goddess-related questions. In Voices of the Earth we work with a pre-patriarchal Sumerian myth called "Descent of Innana." In this myth there are two sisters, Erishigal and Innana. Erishigal is confined to the dark underworld, and Innana lives in the world above where she has learned to manipulate, survive and be really good. Erishigal feels betrayed by her sister because Innana has been complicit in the effort to get rid of her. Innana seeks to know about the mys-

teries that her sister knows. Erishigal seeks to revenge herself and to name her betrayers. An unexpected transformation takes place and makes possible a uniting of these two aspects which have been separated for so long.

We are guided by the dynamic of the myth—we don't perform the myth literally. We create performance pieces where we try to discover those events in our own experience that have created a similar separation and unification and find a form for them. It is difficult to give voice or expression to these things. So we have found clarity in metaphor. For example, nobody in the world above is interested in what Erishigal has to say. So to explore who Erishigal is, we wrap each other up in a chair with cloth, head to toe, like in mummification. The voice has to come from very deep within because of this total confinement.

The performances are, at times, very funny, very fierce, very moving, and, I hate to admit it, but at times very confusing to our audience. Actually, we recently had a lot of men in our audience, and they were very responsive. We were playing our fathers. The audience was pleasantly surprised at the humor and the passion, and the fact that we receive and express information from both sexes. They were relieved we weren't bashing men. I'm not in the business of bashing men. God, I have a husband and two sons. I'm in the business of exploring what has happened between men and women over the centuries.

So it is Innana's voice that Hecuba uses when she speaks with Polymestor— soft, flirtatious, supplicant? And when your voice gets very low?
That is Erishigal. I worked a whole year to lower my voice—I wanted to go down, down. It's a voice that doesn't want to conform. No compromises. No capitulation. It refuses to betray women. It is a voice of the avenging spirits. It's sexual and it's fierce and it says the truth.

Timothy Near spent two decades as artistic director of San Jose Repertory Theatre in California. She is an award-winning director who has worked at numerous theatres around the U.S., including Minneapolis's Guthrie Theater, Berkeley Repertory Theatre, Atlanta's Alliance Theatre and Washington, D.C.'s Ford's Theatre.

Krissy Keefer is artistic director of the Dance Brigade in Oakland, Calif.

I HAVE SOMETHING TO SAY

An interview with Jonathan Larson by John Istel

July/August 1996

ON POP MUSIC IN THE THEATRE

Do you see your music as part of the American musical theatre tradition?

My whole thing is that American popular music used to come from theatre and Tin Pan Alley, and there's no reason why contemporary theatre can't reflect real contemporary music, and why music that's recorded or that's made into a video cannot be from a show. Popular music being a part of theatre ended with *Jesus Christ Superstar* and *Hair* and rock musicals in the late 1960s. A number of things happened. One was that there had been singers in the '40s, '50s, even early '60s, who would sing anybody's material—Frank Sinatra, what have you. Then, beginning with the Beatles, you had songwriters and bands who were singing only their own material. So you didn't have that venue for theatre music to be popular.

What do you think about Randy Newman's latest musical project [*Faust*] and other pop stars working in the theatre?

New York Magazine ran this article [about what was killing Broadway]. The last part had a 12-step program—12 ways to renovate Broadway. Number 12 was bringing new music to Broadway. They were getting all excited about Randy Newman, and Prince evidently is thinking about it, and Paul Simon is working on a new musical. That's exciting if they're successful and if they bring younger people to the theatre who wouldn't normally go. But it's almost going backwards to have a musical that is songwriter-generated because of the traps they can fall into.

They're used to a number of things: not collaborating, not making changes and writing in their own voice. There's so much that Rodgers and Hammerstein and Sondheim have taught us about how to advance plot and character and theme in a song. Often, you get contemporary pop writers who know how to write a verse and a chorus, but they don't necessarily know how to write an inner monologue where a character goes through a change by the end of the song so the plot and story continue.

On those messy concept albums like *The Who's Tommy* or the Kinks's *Soap Opera* there's so much left to the imagination or that isn't spelled out because you don't have to physicalize it.

Right. And that was the problem with *Tommy*. At least Pete Townshend knew he had to work with a book writer, Des McAnuff, who was a theatre person. Even if I don't agree with the story they chose to tell in *Tommy*, which was this sort of return-to-family-values thing at the end, at least he understood the concept of collaborating. It's easy to write 18 songs, but it's not easy to write a two-and-a-half-hour piece that has an arc.

ON THE MATURATION OF A MUSICAL WRITER

What's Jonathan Larson's style?

I'm a rock-and-roller at heart and I'm influenced by contemporary music. There is a Jonathan Larson style, but I can't totally describe it.

Who were your favorite composers?

Well, I loved Pete Townshend growing up, and I loved the old Police and Prince—or whatever his name is—he's brilliant. I love Kurt Cobain and Liz Phair. Beatles. And in the theatre—Leonard Bernstein, Sondheim. I absolutely love them.

Were you a theatre major in college?

Yeah. I was an actor, too. I had a four-year acting scholarship to Adelphi [on Long Island, N.Y.]. Adelphi was a lousy place to go to school in the sense that it's in suburbia and that's where I grew up. But it was run by a disciple of Robert Brustein's named Jacques Burdick, who basically made an undergraduate version of Yale School of Drama. And I was mature enough coming out of high school to appreciate it. I got to do everything from Ionesco to Shakespeare to original plays or musicals.

The best thing, though, was that, like Yale, they had four original cabarets a year, and they were always looking for people to write them. So by the end of my time there I had written eight or ten shows. And I found that I liked it as much as performing. I had a skill doing it. When I came to New York, I had gotten my Equity card because I had done summer stock. I started going to cattle calls, but at the same time I had my first musical, which was a really bad rock version of *1984*, based on Orwell. It was getting a lot of attention and serious consideration—basically because the year was 1982. We came close to getting the rights, but it was a good thing we didn't because it was not a very good show. But it was my first real attempt to write a big show.

At Adelphi we wrote the original Nick and Nora Charles musical—it was called *The Steak Tartare Caper*—10 years before they did it on Broadway. We did *ShoGun Cabaret*—we were way ahead of our time.

Then, when I came to New York, Sondheim was always a big mentor. He encouraged me to be a writer as opposed to being an actor, and suggested that I join ASCAP and do the musical theatre workshop. ASCAP was sort of a 12-step meeting for people who write musicals, but you get to show your work to top-notch professionals in the field.

Two things amazed me at ASCAP: One was that I had written 100 songs by then, had seen them in productions, and had seen them work or not work with audiences. If Peter Stone, head of the Dramatists Guild, or Sondheim, said something that I disagreed with, I said, "I disagree and I'll tell you why." Some of my peers, and those even older, had never had their work performed. And they would be like, "Okay, I'll just throw out my project. You're right—it sucks."

ON THE GENESIS OF *RENT*

Ira Weitzman put me in touch with Billy Aronson, who had an idea— years ago—to do a modern-day *La Bohème*. Billy's done stuff at Ensemble Studio Theatre and with Showtime and TV, and he's a sort of Woody Allen type and he wanted to do a modern-day *La Bohème*, set it on the Upper West Side, and make it about Yuppies and funny. I said, "That doesn't interest me, but if you want to set it in Tompkins Square Park and do it seriously, I like that idea a lot." He had never spent any time in the East Village, but he wrote a libretto. He wanted to write the book and lyrics, and I was to set a few of the songs to music and see what everyone's response was. I also came up with the title of *Rent*. So I wrote "Rent," "Santa Fe" and "I Should Tell You."

I found different types of contemporary music for each character, so the hero [Roger] in *Rent* sings in a Kurt Cobain–esque style and the street transvestite sings like De La Soul. And there's a Tom Waits–esque character. The American musical has always been taking contemporary music and using it to tell a story. So I'm just trying to do that.

We made a demo tape and everyone loved the concepts, loved the music—but when they read the accompanying libretto, they weren't too strong on it. So we just put it on hold. I loved the concept, but I didn't have a burning reason to go back to it. And then I did.

Two years later a number of my friends, men and women, were finding out they were HIV-positive. I was devastated, and needed to do something. I decided to ask Billy if he would let me continue by myself, and he was very cool about it.

I am the kind of person that when I write my own work, I have something I need to say. It surprises me that in musicals, even plays today, sometimes I don't see what the impetus was, other than thinking it was a good smart idea or it could make them some money or something.

ON COMPOSING IN THE AMERICAN MUSICAL THEATRE

What's it like making a living as a composer in the theatre these days?

Well, the old thing about how you can make a killing but you can't make a living is absolutely true. I'm proof of that. Now, I have the ability to compete trying to write jingles, trying to do other kinds of music that makes money, and I haven't put myself out there. My feeling is that it's not what I want to do, and I would be competing with guys who do want to. So I'm just working on musicals—it's like this huge wall, and I'm chipping away at it with a screwdriver. I just keep making a little more headway. I've had a lot of very generous grants, but they all go to the play. I get a little stipend, but I can't live off the commissions.

I work two days a week waiting tables at Moondance in Soho. I've been there for eight-and-a-half years but I don't mind it. In fact, I love the customers—the regulars are fantastic. The management and the owner totally support me. I can take a couple of months off when I need to do a show, come back, and I've actually gotten work there twice. There was a little piece on me in *New York Magazine* a few years ago, and one of the regular customers who I'd known for years, Bob Golden, brought it up and said, "I saw that you were in *New York Magazine* and that you wrote for 'Sesame Street.'" I said, "Yeah, it was mostly freelance." He said, "Have you ever considered making a children's video yourself? You can make a lot of money." I said, "I'd love to but I don't have the capital to put up." He said, "Well, I do."

And the next week I brought in a five-page budget and concept, and handed it to him with his eggs, and he totally went for it. It's a half-hour video called *Away We Go!*. [Golden co-wrote and composed the video with Larson.] It stars a puppet called Newt the Newt. (Unfortunately, we came up with that name before it took on other connotations.) It's for very young kids—"Sesame Street" age. The great thing about that—besides that someone was trusting me and putting up the money—was I had something tangible that no one could take away from me. Theatre is so ethereal. You have programs, and you have maybe a recording of the show, but that's it. It's such a weird medium.

John Istel is a freelance editor and arts writer based in New York City. He was the editor in chief of *Stagebill* from 1996 to 2001.

ART, EXILE AND RESISTANCE

An interview with Wole Soyinka by Dale Byam

January 1997

Even the briefest of encounters with Wole Soyinka—celebrated playwright, essayist, activist and winner of the 1986 Nobel Prize for Literature—is enough to make evident the qualities that are at the crux of his accomplishments. A formidable and centered man, he speaks with a quiet and utter confidence—a confidence that belies his personal fury for the events of June 12, 1993, which rendered him into exile from his native Nigeria.

It was on that day that a military coup prevented a newly elected civilian government from assuming power. Large numbers of Nigerians had voted across ethnic and regional lines in what was widely seen as the country's most democratic election ever—an event that, in Soyinka's eyes, was his homeland's last best hope of becoming a free and viable nation. But the military strongman General Ibrahim Babangida, who had ruled Nigeria for eight years (in the process building one of Africa's largest private fortunes), forbade publication of the voting results and, in place of the election's ostensible winner, installed his own deputy, the brutal General Sani Abacha, as head of state. Soyinka celebrated his 60th birthday with a protest march against Abacha's takeover, an action that led to threats of house arrest and the writer's movement into exile.

From this vantage, stateless but hardly alienated, Soyinka has continued to bring the issues of Africa to the table, so to speak. His most recent play, *The Beatification of Area Boy*, arrived in America in October at Brooklyn Academy of Music, following its debut in Leeds, England, last year; his impassioned philosophical essay *The Open Sore of a Continent: A Personal Narrative of the Nigerian Crisis* was published last August by Oxford. The two works illuminate distinctly different but complementary sides of Soyinka: the anecdotal, celebratory playwright with a penchant for portraiture and whimsy, and the fiercely angry polemicist, producing what he once called "monster prodigies of spleen."

A full measure of the writer's righteous anger cannot be taken without considering a second incident of outrage: On Nov. 10, 1995,

Ken Saro-Wiwa, Soyinka's friend and fellow dissident writer, was executed by the military government, along with eight other members of the Ogoni ethnic minority. Soyinka, himself a member of the Yoruba majority, had arduously campaigned throughout the world community for their release, and for the cause of the Ogoni, who have waged a desperate battle for survival against overdevelopment and international oil interests.

Soyinka's plays—the best known of which is the Yoruban epic *Death and the King's Horseman*, which was directed by the author in an acclaimed 1987 production starring Earle Hyman at Lincoln Center Theater— keep such practical political matters at arm's length, or at a poetic remove. *The Beatification of Area Boy* takes the form of a lively slice of life as it explores the condition of Nigeria's urban poor, young boys who survive in the environs of a shopping complex in Lagos through a savvy that almost always involves hoodwinking the unwitting, innocent shopper or tourist. Sanda, a failed revolutionary, surreptitiously manages the "boys" while serving as the complex's chief security guard. Street vendors and madmen are the play's other principal characters. The plot thickens when Sanda encounters Miseyi, a former lover and college student, on the eve of her wedding to a key military officer. But flowing like a stream beneath the play's buoyant surface is an underlying awareness of the offstage exodus of a million people, forcibly resettled at the whim of the military government.

Soyinka the dramatist clearly shies away from prescribing solutions to the wretched conditions in the play, reserving his ideas about correctives for *Open Sore of a Continent*. There Soyinka summons the international community to discuss the urgent problems of African nationhood, fashioning a philosophic imperative to do the right thing in Africa. The Nigerian people, he points out, did not repudiate nationhood—they voted their hunger for it, only to see their will criminally denied. "A nation is a collective enterprise," he writes; "outside of that, it is mostly a gambling space for the opportunism and adventurism of power."

As one talks with Soyinka about his art—an art indelibly linked to his ideas of nationhood in this age of Nigerian uncertainty, and to the rich and complex mythology of Yoruba culture—his countenance betrays neither lament nor brooding. Rather his indomitable spirit is a nourishing symbol of African perseverance.

Do you write in response to something, or can it simply be a mood?
A mood, or just an idea in my head. I know there are writers who get up every morning and sit by their typewriter or word processor or pad of paper and wait to write. I don't function that way. I go through a long period of gestation before I'm even ready to write. Take *Death and the King's Horseman*. The story of that play [based on a true incident in 1946, in which the horseman of the title was prevented by resident colonial authorities from following his deceased king to the grave by committing ritual suicide] is something I had known for about 10 years before I got down to writing it. One day it was just ready to be written. The muse had mounted my head, shall we say, and I sat down and wrote the play, and that was that.

When you write a play, is there a particular audience that you have in mind?
It would be more accurate to say I have a company in mind to perform the play. I used to work very closely with two different companies in Nigeria, and while I'm not writing the plays as vehicles for them, in certain cases I do have certain actors in mind for certain roles. One of the companies I used to run did what I call guerrilla theatre—we made instant improvisations on themes of the day and gave performances in marketplaces, outside civil service offices, outside the houses of assembly members. Obviously the plays were targeted not merely at the specific audience, which is Nigerian, but also created for a specific time when certain events are fresh in the mind.

There are other plays like *Opera Wonyusi*, my adaptation of Brecht's *Threepenny Opera*, which are particularly targeted at Nigerian audiences. Even though this play was written before the hanging of Ken Saro-Wiwa and the eight Ogoni people, there's no way anybody would see this play—which involved the military, and takes place in Nigeria—without immediately thinking of this universally traumatizing event. I know that for me, who went to speak to heads of state after the sentences were confirmed, it was so disquieting that I couldn't function for about three days.

It is pleasant to find that even though *Opera Wonyusi* was produced outside Nigeria, it is receiving a tremendous response. I saw it in Zurich with mixed audiences, and it's amazing how people responded to it.

Do political events direct your work, or are they a distraction from work that you ideally want to do?
My creative temperament is rather eclectic. I find I'm in the mood some days to write a densely mythological play like *Death and the King's Horseman*; at other times, I write lighthearted "scoops" like the Jero plays [such as *The Trials of Brother Jero*, about the power trips of a prophet who feeds on his followers' dissatisfaction]; then there are ritualistic plays like *Strong Breed*. Anything which agitates me sufficiently to start conceiving of an event to strike a feeling of revenge, a projection in creative terms—that's what gets onto the paper.

Are there any plays that have worked better on paper than on stage?
For me a play can never work better on paper than in performance. You can say, perhaps, that the performance has not quite fulfilled the expectations of the play; the performance may understate the playwright's intentions, or distort them completely. But the play on paper isn't working yet. You can enjoy reading it like a piece of literature, yes, that's true. Some read better than others, but they don't come to life until they're on stage.

I understand the director of *Area Boy*, Jude Kelly, actually visited Nigeria to find actors. Is it necessary to have Nigerians in the play?
Well, yes, even when I direct my plays outside Nigeria I always do everything possible to bring a core of my company—four, five or six actors—to participate in the production. It makes a difference with

certain plays. You try to create a certain atmosphere in the kind of plays which involve community. To create the atmosphere, the color, the tone, to infect the others who are alienated from that environment, you cannot guess the difference it makes to have a community of actors. Also, in this kind of play I use a lot of local music.

Because you are of the Yoruba culture but very representative of the whole of Nigeria, have you managed to straddle the ethnic contradictions?
First of all, I don't believe in ethnic contradictions. (There are, however, collisions of ethnic interests which the government orchestrates.) Take *Strong Breed*, for instance—the ritual of the carrier I used in that play is not a Yoruba ritual at all. It is a ritual from the Ibo, in the eastern part of Nigeria. Others of my plays incorporate many things which most Nigerian ethnic groups will recognize. But essentially, my culture dominates my plays, and naturally it is the Yoruba culture.

No one considers it a transgression when you incorporate ethnic rituals in your work?
They have no right. Culture is not their property. Culture is universal.

Even when it is attached to a religious framework?
Oh, some people find, for instance, my spoof *Brother Jero* offensive—it's offensive to the Christian religion, although others of my plays have spoofed religious extremism all over the place. But there has been no price on my head yet.

Sitting in a New York cab driven by a Nigerian, I mentioned your *Beatification of Area Boy*. This taxi driver became so excited by the mere mention of your name. He had read your work during his school years in Nigeria. How do you reconcile your celebration in that society with the present reality that you are in virtual alienation . . . exile?
My condition is not one of permanent exile. There's no question at all, though, that my condition is one of partial alienation. That alienation, of course, triggers off the need to respond in some fashion—in some creative way. If you're a painter, you respond as a painter; if you're a musician, you respond as a musician. It's no surprise that some musicians have been jailed by this dictatorship for their music. [The Nigerian pop idol] Fela has been persecuted by a number of regimes—that's become his way of life. It's not just writers who are in exile.

But there is no conflict: If you live in a state of social disjunction, on certain levels that becomes your reality. You operate within it, you critique it. From time to time, you act as a citizen and join others in resisting it. You become part of an oppositional movement which cuts across your profession. During the protestations to remove Babangida, you would see all sorts of people there—civil servants, union members, policemen, market women. There were the "touts," the area boys, as well, some of whom were totally committed, others who took the opportunity to pick a few pockets. The whole society is involved, and the question is which is the real society at that moment? Is it the preda-tors who are sitting on top, immune in their fortifications? Or is it those masses on the street?

Which is the reality?
Oh, the people on the streets . . . with whom I find myself.

Even though a culture of silence prevails amongst these oppressed people?
No, it is not a culture of silence. Sometimes, yes, there is stasis, a seeming acquiescence. But, believe me, there is simmering ferment going on all the time. People may be hobbled by the superior power, the ruthlessness, of a regime like Abacha's. But talk to those taxi drivers—even those who are here in the U.S.; talk to people who come out from time to time; look at the vibrant underground press in Nigeria, the risks that they take. They are jailed, they are brutalized by the police, their families are sometimes taken hostage. For me, this is the reality, this underground reality. The culture of resistance begins gathering force, sometimes slowly, sometimes suddenly. You never can tell which way it will go.

As a Yoruba, how do you see yourself in relation to Nigeria?
I am undeniably a Yoruba because I was born into Yoruba; I am a Nigerian because I born into a certain definable entity called Nigeria. What I am saying is that when you compare that entity called Yoruba—or Ogun, or Hausa, or Ibo—when you compare it to the entity called Nigeria, you see that one is not the result of any artificial creation or agreement. It happens to be. It's like your blood. The other, however, something called Nigeria, was not there 50 years ago. It was invented. What was the purpose of that invention? Was it simply to supply raw material to Great Britain and to the international and commercial world? Or was Nigeria invented in order to cohere all the disparate elements into a single entity, where all have the right to life, liberty, means of education, health, etc., etc.? You must decide, what should be my definition of a nation?

Are both *Open Sore of a Continent* and *Area Boy* responding to the military rule in Nigeria?
Open Sore of a Continent is a large discourse. *The Beatification of Area Boy* is a vignette, a microcosm of society. The characters in the play are not concerned with issues of nationhood—they're concerned with issues of community and how best to survive; they are responding to the cruelty of a singularly insensitive regime. I wouldn't say the two works cover the same ground.

The military expulsion, the removal of a million people, which actually happened there, horrified me—it made me feel ashamed to be a Nigerian in a time when such things could happen. One wonders how there can be a nation where people could wake up and be rendered homeless in peacetime, for no reason other than greed. But I'm not asking that question in the play.

Having now traveled so extensively, do you see parallels between the Nigerian condition and elsewhere?

Oh, yes, no question at all there are many such spots on the African continent, and look at what's happening in some of the Latin American countries—look at "class sanitation," which takes place in Brazil, when the police go and round up all these area boys, little ones, not even the grown-up ones, and shoot them because they think they will grow up into thugs and thieves. Repression is not peculiar to Nigeria.

So what can the performing artist do?
The performing artist is at a disadvantage, as his resources are limited. All an actor can do is join forces. He or she may also decide, "I will not do this kind of play, it's reactionary or corrupt." Remember, a writer, a musician, a painter, a sculptor, an architect—these are first of all citizens. Their responsibility is no different from any other citizen. There should be no unfair burden being placed on the artists in society—each artist must choose the degree and capability of his or her commitment to certain issues. You cannot say that an artist 24 hours a day, 7 days a week, must be politically engaged. That's madness. You cannot make that imposition on a bricklayer or a craftsman; you cannot make it on the artist.

But you find yourself in that position?
It doesn't mean that I believe that this is the best life. I do what I do because I'm temperamentally inclined to do it. All writers are not the same, just like all preachers are not the same. Some preachers believe that religion should be an instrument of social change, and thank God for that; but there are others who believe that their function is simply to minister to the spirit. Similarly, you have artists who believe that their function is to be revelatory, to open up certain horizons for human striving. I'm an artist and a producer, a creative person, but I'm also a consumer—I like to go into galleries, to listen to music, to read books—and I don't recall screaming in outrage if a work is not politically engaged, because what I'm consuming at that moment fulfills a certain part of me. The kind of spiritual elevation that is also a part of the function of the artist should never, never be underestimated.

Does your condition overwhelm you?
Oh, yes, sometimes.

How do you temper that?
I go for a drink. At home I'll pick up my gun and go hunting. The thing I miss here is getting lost in the bush. I just go. I call it sometimes "just taking my gun for a walk." I can get lost in the bush for hours. I come back very much refreshed, feeling more benevolent towards life in general, because I've seen animals who act better than human beings.

Dale Byam teaches in the Africana Studies department at Brooklyn College and previously taught theatre for the Tisch School of the Arts at New York University. She is the author of the book *Community in Motion: Theatre for Development in Africa*.

THE GESTURE OF ILLOGIC

An interview with Kate Valk by Bevya Rosten

February 1998

For more than two decades, New York's Wooster Group has sliced, diced and rearranged pre-existent texts, film, video and original material in a never-ending attempt to face off against conventional narrative. *House/Lights*, a new work currently being performed at the company's Manhattan home base, the Performing Garage, is no exception. The piece is the company's take on *maman terrible* Gertrude Stein's opera text, *Dr. Faustus Lights the Lights*, combined with an obscure 1964 exploitation film, *Olga's House of Shame*. Infused with frenzied energy, *House/Lights* unearths the satiric and erotic aspects of Stein's text while exploring the nature of female power struggles.

The Wooster Group's interest in Stein's fractured use of language continues a long tradition of avant-garde luminaries who have been attracted to *Dr. Faustus Lights the Lights*. Judith Malina directed a production in 1951, as did Lawrence Kornfield in 1979, Richard Foreman in 1981 and Robert Wilson in 1993. However, what's fascinating about the group's approach is its interest in process as product, collage rather than narrative. The integration of disparate materials in *House/Lights* is nothing new for the group. *Route 1 & 9* (1981) combined Thornton Wilder's *Our Town* with a homemade sex film; Frank Dell's *The Temptation of Saint Anthony* (1987) spliced the words of Flaubert and Lenny Bruce with those of the Irish spiritualist Geraldine Cummins; *Brace Up!* (1991), the company's deconstructive rumination on Chekhov's *Three Sisters*, made ingenious use of TV monitors and popular Japanese entertainment forms. The Wooster Group is not interested in interpretation (neither was Gertrude Stein, for that matter) and its end products are not necessarily linked by thematic similarities.

Since 1979, actor Kate Valk has been a driving force with the Wooster Group, whose other veterans include Peyton Smith, Willem Dafoe and the late Ron Vawter. In *House/Lights*, Valk embodies the heroines of both *Dr. Faustus Lights the Lights* and *Olga's House of Shame* as well as the character of Faustus. Much like her role in *Brace Up!*, she also serves as a self-described "onstage dramaturg"—fulfilling a dramaturgical function, but from the inside of the piece rather than as an outside observer.

Valk joined the ensemble when she was a student at New York University, assisting with costumes for the final Elizabeth LeCompte/Spalding Gray collaboration, *Point Judith*. Since then, she has become a company mainstay, appearing in all its pieces, from Tituba in its adaptation of Arthur Miller's *The Crucible* [*L.S.D.* (. . . *Just the High Points* . . .)] in 1985; to Brutus Jones, Eugene O'Neill's doomed Caribbean monarch, in *The Emperor Jones*; to, most recently, a cartoon-voiced debutante in giant toe-shoes in *The Hairy Ape*. According to Valk, *Dr. Faustus* and *Olga's House of Shame* metamorphosed into *House/Lights* because the two "happened to walk into the space at the same time and there was a vibration between them." Stein's piece is a send-up of Faust plays, damsel-in-distress conventions and the Romantic tradition; *Olga's House of Shame*, with its scenes of torture and homoeroticism, unconsciously addresses themes of female domination and submission. Valk reveals that the Wooster Group was interested in, among other elements, investigating relationships between women: older/younger, dominant/submissive, good looking/better looking. In one of the work's racier sections (re-creating a scene from the film), two women lead another two around on leashes. "We're playing with what this kind of image evokes and what it says about power," Valk explains.

In a series of conversations last fall, while *House/Lights* was still in development, Valk helped to demystify the group's process, as well as its approach to Stein. (During the interviews, Valk sometimes used the term "mask" to describe a "secret technological construct that helps to structure a performance"; at other times, she used the same word as someone else might use "character" or "style.")

How did *House/Lights* evolve?

It's hard to figure out where one idea emanates from because the Wooster Group's been together for a couple of decades. But we were working on a film [*Wrong Guys*] and we needed some torture footage for a fever sequence. We asked a friend of ours, Dennis Dermody, who's kind of a living, walking film archive, if he could think of anything—and he showed us *Olga's House of Shame*. We used a small snippet of it at that time. Liz [LeCompte, the company's director] became interested in using the *Olga* movie as a pattern and translating it to theatrical space. At the same time, she was considering doing a Stein piece. We started working with the film and reading Stein's works concurrently.

We have quite a long and developed relationship with television—we use the monitors as mirrors, or as sources of information that either illustrate what we're doing or disrupt what we're doing. But in this instance, we were using the monitors very directly as a way of channeling something: We had the performers watching the *Olga* film on TV and mimicking exactly what they saw gesturally and translating the logic of the camera—close-up, medium shot, long shot—into the theatrical space. It was making for a very quirky physical vocabulary. Then we did readings of Stein's works. When we read *Dr. Faustus Lights the Lights* aloud, we said, "Ah, this is it! This is what we want to do." It struck an emotional chord. That began our journey into merging those two worlds.

Did you discover that working on a Stein text was significantly different from other material you've dealt with?
We're used to working on American classics. Because Stein is abstract, we found *Dr. Faustus* a real beast to wrangle with. But as with our other pieces, we let the style arise from the material. Our idea is not to put a certain spin on something. We are always facing off with the text and finding a way to hear it in the space.

The Stein, we knew, was a comedy. Someone told us that when Stein read it to Picasso she was hysterical with laughter. It didn't have to be heavy, formal, highfalutin art, where the language is precious. We were also very interested in this piece having a heavy technological mask that might be invisible to the audience. In all our pieces we find a lot of constructs that might confine the performer, but through that comes the liberation.

How did you go about exploring the constructs for this production?
We'd been interested in the Yiddish Art Theatre, so we listened to, say, the performances of Maurice Schwartz and fitted the memorized Stein text into the cadence of those performances. We eventually let that go, since we felt like we'd done it before. Another influence was the Marx Brothers—the kind of physicality that was developing in one sequence was highly stylized movement not unlike that of the Marx Brothers films. We also listened to Cantonese opera and did Stein texts along with that. Usually a woman is at the center of the Cantonese opera, and that high voice led us to the little cartoon voice I use.

We also started working with battery-operated wireless receivers so that we could tune into different soundtracks in the space. We tune into the Olga film and into Hans Peter Kuhn [composer for Robert Wilson's production of *Dr. Faustus Lights the Lights*, who is also creating music for *House/Lights*] reading the entire text of *Dr. Faustus* on tape. I don't say anything unless I hear Kuhn say it. I channel the text. It's liberating. I don't have to search for a psychological thrust.

Stein's text leaves a lot of room for "intervention," something which seems to be of great interest to the Wooster Group.
When we pick a text, we want to do the text; we don't go about saying we're going to deconstruct it. We're doing the best we can to get the text on its feet, but what we deal with is the reality of the time and space and the people performing—if we don't have anyone to play a particular role, we ask, What will be fun? Maybe to make that character an intrusion on the television? It's a lot of problem-solving and creative solutions to not being able to do the entire text that prompts us to make a condensed version—or what some people might call a deconstruction and others call cannibalization. Call it what you will, we're not semioticians and we're not ideologues, we're thespians (*laughs*) with a wry sense of our own lim-

itations, and a place, the Garage, with technology available. So when we go to problem-solve, we think of the most fun way to get around not being able to present the text in its entirety.

How did you combine the characters from the two works?
In the *Olga* film the narrator says, "To incur Olga's wrath is to invite the Devil from Hell," and that, for us, was connection enough. Peyton [Smith], who plays Olga, is also Mephisto. So it's between the low and the high and the merging of these texts.

Could you give me a blow-by-blow breakdown of the evolution of the piece in rehearsal?
Initially, we worked with the televisions to mimic the film and translate the logic of the camera and the edit into the theatrical space. Then we watched Marx Brothers films—maybe they'd inform us, maybe they wouldn't. Then we did some work using the *Olga* film as a pattern and developing the physical language at the same time the space was developing—that was crucial. First, there were just railings and ramps; then the ramps got put on a teeter-totter; then the ramps were altered not only to teeter-totter, but to move forward; then stools went in front of the ramps. All of this was developing when we were working on the Stein text. The space was getting more specific and we were making rough sketch after rough sketch, while we also were finding the mask for the Stein through the use of the Yiddish Art Theatre and the Cantonese opera.

Then we let the heavy Yiddish theatrical mask go, although we had gotten pretty far along in developing it. What's really great about the way we work is that even when we let something go, it'll come back. What we didn't let go was the Cantonese opera, which led us to the high little cartoon voice. Then we played around a lot with starting both texts at the same time, meaning the film and the Stein, and running them simultaneously to see how they overlapped and what came forward and what receded. Then we got more into really defining the physical movement in the space.

There was a point where we threw out the Stein text—it was so huge we didn't know how to hear it. Then we started working purely physically from the *Olga* film and defining the space as two filmic frames that were either scanning or mirroring. For a while we decided to do the Stein only as a small talking-head monologue—that was one way of hearing the text in the space. Kuhn came much later. We originally had this idea that we would bury the Stein in a melodrama, knowing that somewhere it had already gotten its "highbrow" treatment, and we wanted to find the "lowbrow" humor.

Director and writer Bevya Rosten, who died in 2003, was the author of many articles and reviews. Her Ph.D. dissertation at the City University of New York, written in 1998, was titled "The Fractured Stage: Gertrude Stein's Influence on American Avant-Garde Directing as Seen in Four Productions of *Dr. Faustus Lights the Lights.*" She was on the faculty of New York University's Tisch School of the Arts and of the Mason Gross School of the Arts, Rutgers University, and in 2001–02 was visiting faculty at the Yale School of Drama.

DRIVING MS. VOGEL

An interview by David Savran

October 1998

In her playwriting classes at Brown University, Paula Vogel asks her students to write the impossible—a play with a dog as protagonist, a play that cannot be staged, a play that dramatizes the end of the world in five pages. While these provocative exercises stretch students' imaginations in remarkable ways, they also inadvertently reveal much about Vogel's own playwriting: All of her plays endeavor to stage the impossible. They defy traditional theatre logic, subtly calling conventions into question or, in some cases, pushing them well past their limits. What other playwright would dare memorialize her brother who died of AIDS in a play filled with fart jokes and riotous sex? What other feminist would dare write so many jokes about tits?

Vogel's complex relationship to feminism is in part the result of contradictions that molded her when she was growing up. The daughter of a Jewish father from New York and a Catholic mother from New Orleans (her father left home when she was 11), Vogel has always been just a little schizoid. A lesbian who loves men and John Waters movies, she came out when she was 17. Brought up in a working-class family, she nevertheless entered academia, graduating from Catholic University and spending three years in the doctoral program in theatre at Cornell. A devotee of Büchner and Sigmund Romberg, Maria Irene Fornes and Judy Garland, *In the Summer House* and *The Bad Seed*, she is a fierce defender of the theatre in an era when it is under fire from all quarters. Since 1985, she has been director of the graduate playwriting program at Brown University in Rhode Island and has fashioned it into one of the country's best. As she explains it, she longs, both in her own writing and that of her students, to unleash confusion, to make sense out of a world—and a society—gone terribly awry.

A Paula Vogel play is never simply a politely dramatized fiction. It is always a meditation on the theatre itself—on role-playing, on the socially sanctioned scripts from which characters diverge at their peril and on a theatrical tradition that has punished women who don't remain quiet, passive and demure. Take, for example, *The Mineola Twins* (1996), which chillingly manipulates the age-old farcical convention of using one actor (and a battery of wigs) to play two startlingly dissimilar identical twins. Or *Hot 'n' Throbbing* (1994), which transforms a theatre into a living room and a living room into a theatre in order to dramatize the fatal consequences of stage directions gone out of control. Or her Pulitzer-winning memory play, *How I Learned to Drive* (1997), which accomplishes far more than explaining the effects sexual predation can have on a young girl; it literally splits the lead character (L'il Bit) into two—a body and a voice—in order to represent the radical alienation from self that results from having been molested by her Uncle Peck.

If L'il Bit is haunted by Peck's unquiet spirit, then so is Anna in *The Baltimore Waltz* (1992)—a character who, like the playwright herself, is haunted by the spirit of her dead brother, Carl. In attempting to remember, Vogel's theatre calls up ghosts, figures lighter than air yet heavy with the past. It is obsessed with commemorating what has been lost, while understanding that loss always pays a kind of dividend that is experienced both on a personal and cultural level. Vogel's ghosts always materialize at the place where history intersects with memory, the universal with the particular. Thus, *Baltimore Waltz* becomes an exhilarating tribute and love letter not only to Carl, but to everyone who has died of AIDS.

For all their precision in documenting the act of remembering, Vogel's plays are perhaps unique in the way that they locate memory in the body. It is far more than her punning sensibility that inspires her to title her most recent collection *The Mammary Plays* (recently published by TCG). Summoning up big-breasted women, both *Drive* and *The Mineola Twins* play off and critique the 1950s cliché of the "stacked" femme fatale. Both tacitly acknowledge that female bodies are steeped in history, that "sometimes the body," as Peck puts it, "knows things that the mind isn't listening to."

As a feminist writer, Vogel attends to the deeply contradictory representations of women in our culture. From the sprightly geriatric prostitutes of *The Oldest Profession* (1988) who have seized the means of production, to the lesbian parents of three imaginary little boys in *And Baby Makes Seven* (1984), Vogel's women are themselves playwrights who attempt to write their way out of difficult situations and script more creative, bountiful lives. Like Vogel herself, they are committed to redressing a history of oppression by rewriting the scenes they have been handed. By turning her female characters—and her students—into playwrights of no mean achievement, she suggests that although a triumphal feminist theatre seems an impossibility in our time, one can attempt to stage that impossibility, along with the glittering promises it holds.

I spoke to Vogel in New York City last summer.

What drew you to theatre?

I got interested in theatre growing up in Washington, D.C., as a way of staying out of the house. My first experience was some god-awful opera at the National Theatre. It was a school trip, and they put us in the very upper gallery, which is way up there, and what I most remember is that the boys were leaning over the balcony because from that point of view they could see the soprano's cleavage. We didn't hear a note of the opera, I just remember their entranced gazes, and I think I knew even then that theatre had to be seductive in order to work.

Then I stumbled into a drama class and high school productions, when I was a sophomore. I walked into the room and I felt, "This is home." I also pretty much knew my own sexuality, and in this high school drama class there were very few boys because to take drama in those days meant you were admitting you were homosexual. So I was chosen to play all the male leads, and I did them very well. I thought I made a superb John Proctor.

But I pretty much knew I couldn't be an actress. I was petrified of exposing my own body. I had enormous problems with it in that I didn't want to act the role. It seemed to me that acting was great for young gay men because they had to act heterosexual in order to pass in a straight, pre-Stonewall world. Directing seemed to be the province of straight men—prescribing the roles that everybody else played. And because figuring out where I fit was a real problem, theatre became a home that included a spectrum of possibilities in terms of gender. For gay women, tech theatre was perfect—you were out of sight, you could watch everything.

So I spent three wonderful years being a stage manager. One of the things I loved about stage managing was that you got to see backstage as well as on stage—that you were immersed in the culture of making theatre seemed as important and vital as the actual theatre itself.

By the end of my senior year, when I had already had my first affair, it was pretty clear to me that I would have to make a choice in my life, and that included my sexuality. At that point I was a good public speaker—I was class president—but I suddenly became aware that if I went in the track of law school and politics, my sexuality could not be hidden, which was unthinkable during the '60s. I realized immediately in my first moment in bed with another young girl, I can never stop doing this. I can never not have this be a part of my life. And I immediately said, goodbye politics, goodbye being a public servant. And what else is there to fill the gap? I think I chose the theatre because it was a home that could include my sexuality.

So by the end of my senior year I was starting to write. I thought I'd actually write for the Broadway stage. I loved musicals. I was writing lyrics, writing little books and revues and that sort of thing.

More and more I thought maybe I could write but I didn't know of any women writers. By the time I got out of Catholic University, the only place I knew to apply to was Yale School of Drama. It was the only program in the country I was aware of where one could study to be a playwright, and I was turned down. I didn't know what else to do with my life. I put my head on the table and wept. I was turned down in the class of Christopher Durang and Wendy Wasserstein. I've charted the impact that being admitted to Yale has had in people's lives, and it seemed in one more way I was outside the club when Yale turned me down.

Because of public speaking and my personality skills, I figured I'd probably enjoy teaching—it was just a hunch. I then decided to apply for a Ph.D. program, got into Cornell, and pretty much used Cornell as a backdrop to continue the playwriting and try to figure out how to do it my own way and teach myself a method.

What's your process of writing? How do you usually start a play?
Time and again I've said this: If I had sat down and said, "I'm going to write a play about my brother's death from AIDS," I never would have written a play, I would simply have curled up in a little ball and wept. But if I say I'm going to write a play on language lessons, knowing full well it's about my brother's death, I allow myself to forget. The only way you can do that is by playing games with yourself. It's a very conscious craft.

I usually start by trying to escape, closing myself away from people, going and finding a place that's remote, where I can't be reached. I start writing by spending a week doing nothing but staring at the ceiling and getting bored out of my mind. It's almost a retreat.

I do a lot of reading and research. For example, I read a lot about the '50s, '60s and '80s when writing *The Mineola Twins*. I did a lot of reading about automobiles for *How I Learned to Drive*, which I really enjoyed. There are thousands of books on automobiles—such a fetish—and I plunged into that. I construct a lot of tape loops. I spend a huge amount of money on music. Interestingly enough, I don't have any good music. I have only schlock for a particular play that creates a distinctive sound world. I create a sound loop that I play over and over again. It may be Strauss waltzes, as for *Baltimore Waltz*. It was the Mamas and the Papas, "Dedicated to the One I Love," and Roy Orbison for *How I Learned to Drive*, with a little bit of Melissa Etheridge thrown in so that I could craft the end of that particular voyage.

Then I do a general plot outline. I try to figure out where I'm going. But I'm not figuring out the absolute ends of my plays anymore. I'm figuring out the peripeties and the beginning points. Then I usually surprise myself in the last moment. Not always, but often. Or the sequence surprises me. You let the plot take over. Take notes, and then let it rip. I usually try to get a draft out in two to four weeks. It depends on the material. Sometimes I'm lucky. *Baltimore Waltz* came out in three. And then I changed maybe 10 percent. *How I Learned to Drive* came out in two weeks. I changed even less. But *Mineola Twins* is a year-and-a-half-long baby. *And Baby Makes Seven*—we're talking about plays for which I wrote 15 to 20 drafts. I also believe—and this has to do with the unconscious versus the conscious—that on plays like *Hot 'n' Throbbing* or *The Mineola Twins* the best thing to do is to start a new play at some point before I return to rewrites. So I keep an ongoing cycle in which the new play tells me how to rewrite the older play.

What do you think makes for a really good production of your work? I know you've had some wonderful experiences, particularly working with Molly Smith.
What makes a really good production is letting a play be mysterious and fragile, and having a director come in and not try to figure out

what my intentions are or what will please me. Rather, a director has to figure out her or his relationship to the material in the way that I did when I started to write the play. So the director says, "This is the tale I want to tell with this script. Not the relationship of Paula Vogel to her dead brother, but here's the person I'm grieving, or the person I want to celebrate, or here's my homage to my first love affair, or my homage to my brother or sister." That's a director that's going to come in with a resistance to my play.

I'm now thinking that what makes a good production is avoiding the kind of marriage model that we use in directing and playwriting collaborations. I think marriage is a terrible idea in the theatre—you get a compromise and a collaborative vision. It just creates mush. Much better is a kind of resistance, and a vibrancy, in which at times the playwright is speaking and at times the director responds—at times the designer is speaking and the actors respond. So it's more a response to the text than trying to let the text be the guiding principle. Now that may sound kind of fluid, but I'm really thinking synthesis is wrong. More interesting to see *that's* Anne Bogart, *that's* Vogel, *that's* Mark Brokaw, *that's* Vogel, *that's* Molly Smith. Or to say, "Oh my god, *that's* Cherry Jones, *that's* Joe Mantello." So I'm now using the "call and response" mode of gospel singing. The leader stands up and then the chorus responds. At times the text is the chorus, and the director is the leader, at times the actor, at times the playwright, the designer, the audience. That creates more of a collective response.

When you're writing do you have an imaginary audience in mind? Do you write for a friend, for a family member, for your lover?
It depends on the play. I don't think of an anonymous mass audience. I don't think of the theatre company, "Oh, I'm gonna pitch this to so-and-so." I don't think of the market—in other words, the way that one might think if one were sitting down to write a screenplay for hire. I don't think playwrights usually think that way. I do think occasionally, for example, "I want to write a play for Anne Bogart to direct," or "I want to write a play for Cherry Jones," or "I'm writing this for my brother." But usually, I'm the only audience in the room and I try to write just for me. As a result of some 19 years of teaching, of seeing a lot of plays in development, of being ill myself, and of witnessing death, I have far less patience. What I say has to be said—I call it the "now we're two hours closer to death" principle. The last thing I want to do when I go out of the theatre is think, "I'm two hours closer to death and I could have been spending that time . . . ." There's got to be something so compelling that I'm glad I spent those two hours in that theatre. So I'm a little more aware of sort of cutting to the chase at the top of the play. Each time I sit down to write now, I feel a greater urgency.

I do discern a change in your writing since about 1985 when you started teaching at Brown.
I think teaching has had a huge impact on me. Coming face-to-face with the younger generation and seeing how they don't ask permission

to break the fourth wall has been very liberating. Reading a lot more contemporary dramatists has been really helpful. I also think it's probably a process of aging, which may sound strange. Aging does not necessarily mean solidifying or becoming more rigid. Aging could also mean, "Well, what the fuck. I don't give a damn anymore." Letting go, not being embarrassed, and in a strange way for me, aging is a process of just giving over.

So I think a number of things are happening. One is that I think my plays are reflecting at a deeper level a sense of loss. There's a sense of yearning and mourning. Mourning for a protagonist, yearning for a well-made play structure or plot. There's a sense of what is lost, a 19th-century theatrical tradition as much as my youth or even people who are alive. You can see aging as a kind of coming apart in a good and liberating way. So I think my plays are coming apart. I think at some point I decided, "I'm never going to get done. I'm never going to break through, let's just give it up." The second I stopped trying to please the dramaturgs of this country, the second I accepted that I wasn't going to get through the door—and I still haven't gotten through the door of a lot of places—the more I started writing for myself. So I also think that's in there: a kind of giving up on American theatre, on commercial theatre, on pleasing people, or on what people are going to think. I really don't care what people think anymore.

The difficulty is that it's easier to find proponents of *How I Learned to Drive* and *Baltimore Waltz*, and much harder to find supporters of *Desdemona*, *And Baby Makes Seven* and *The Mineola Twins*. I'm not really sure why that is. I'm feeling that my actual physical shape on the world, being a "lesbian, female playwright," interferes with the reception of the play. I think we do this game. We look at a play and receive the play according to what we think a woman playwright or a lesbian playwright should write. There's a decorum here, and when you go against that decorum of what we should be writing, there's a real resistance.

Although that policing is, of course, primarily directed at persons of color, at sexual minorities and at women because it's assumed that white men can write anything.

Tom Stoppard can do *Rosencrantz and Guildenstern*, but Paula Vogel can't do *Desdemona*. There's a latitude given those in the majority that just does not exist for the others. There should be a word—it's beyond homophobia and misogyny—for a bias against lesbians that's very particular.

There are, I think, two things going on. One is that language that is particular to the male gender is now starting to attach itself to the female gender. For example, I have long felt and thought that women are virile, that there's a sense of female virility. Thanks in large part to women songwriters and singers, we're starting to see desire expressed by women in a profound way. The second has to do with our arts—we've castrated our arts. To isolate, to put on a pedestal, to make special is to take away power, to make impotent. We are so petrified of genius. Instead of saying that genius is just what happens when you work in a community for a long, long time, it's quarantined. We see art as something God-given and one-of-a-kind, and not as a way of working, as labor, something that is attached to so many other disciplines that give it meaning.

Since the 1960s, the American theatre has in a large part been defined in opposition to mass culture, especially to television, but also, to some extent, to film. I think that's been changing in the past 10 years or so with the explosion of independent film, but is there something that makes theatre distinctive?
Being with so many wonderful younger writers, I see there's no problem with theatre as an art form speaking to a younger generation. But you have to get the structure and the production out of the hands of older generations that don't want to give it over. Independent films have shown there's a way for a 25-year-old to make something with $200,000 and go to Sundance. So you suddenly have an art form that's addressing the current moment, and that's different from someone who's got access to studio financing. And similarly in New York right now we're seeing a proliferation of places like the Drama Dept. or the New Group or Tiny Mythic Theatre. If you turn over the theatrical apparatus to artists that have been dispossessed by the not-for-profit LORT structure, and by the Broadway and Off-Broadway structure, you're going to get theatre that's vibrant and speaking to audiences that traditionally haven't gone to the theatre.

It's almost like you're talking about the development of a new Off-Off Broadway.
We have to have a new Off-Off Broadway. No one's going to pay you to do Genet, you're going to have to do it on top of your day job. Is there something that's unique about theatre? Yes, there is, and I think it is making a comeback in the same way that, for example, poetry slams are suddenly being discovered by a younger generation. There is a live connection between the audience and the stage. That's the most terrific asset.

Unfortunately, there's also been a connection between theatre and film at a studio level—people trying to figure out, "What market are we talking about? How do we do this commercially?" when they're not directly connected. But if you get any poet up on stage live, with an audience, there is going to be a vibrant connection. It's just that it's not worth anything in a capitalist country. It's art, it's not a money-maker, and we've developed a notion of entertainment that has confused the two. That's not to say you can't have theatre that makes money and isn't also art. But the means of production in this country have been in the hands of people who feel that theatre should be a money-making proposition or now must be a money-making proposition since foundations and the NEA have turned their back—since we've forsaken the great experiment of the '60s. I do think theatre is going to specialize. Small theatres, doing what only theatre can—forget the helicopters—that's what's going to flourish. I'm not worried about theatre dying. I think to some extent, we have to die off. By that I mean our generation and those older have to give up the reins to let younger people in.

I'm feeling very, very good about recognizing that generational gap. Aging allows you to come apart and deconstruct your own generational art. You're unknitting and unraveling the commercial theatre of your time and actually speaking to audience members a generation younger than you. Your own generation wants to see everything comfortably put together in the status quo, they don't want to see it taken apart. You've got to reach the age and have the experience with the theatrical apparatus to be able to take it apart.

So you think it's essential that theatre artists start addressing younger audiences?
We talk to ourselves, and the people who pick up on us are younger. Suzan-Lori Parks and Mac Wellman are understood with perfect ease by 20-year-olds in our classes at Brown. We have to explain Mac and Suzan-Lori to our own peers in their mid-forties because they're saying, "I want a tune that goes bum-bum-bum-de-dum." It's like Sondheim dismantling the Broadway musical, speaking to people 20 or 30 years younger than he is. It's not intentional, but as we dismantle the apparatus of our time we are speaking to a younger generation. That then becomes their legacy and they will dismantle it further.

What playwrights do you think are doing the most important work now?
That's two questions. First are my gods, who've already had a major impact on me. Second are my peer group and younger writers who are doing what I think is really interesting, major work. I have three gods. One is John Guare, the second is Maria Irene Fornes and the third is Caryl Churchill. They've transformed the possibilities, the vocabulary. I wouldn't be able to exist without them. In terms of who's doing fascinating, fabulous contemporary work out there, I would say Suzan-Lori Parks, Mac Wellman, Chuck Mee, Elizabeth Egloff, Connie Congdon, Naomi Wallace . . . . I'm very excited to see what Tony Kushner writes in the next few years. It's actually a vibrant time for contemporary writers. And Philip Kan Gotanda's *The Ballad of Yachiyo* is a remarkable work.

There's a rising generation that I've encountered that excites me a great deal, like Stephanie Page Miskowski from Seattle. She wrote a play called *Feasting* that I read 10 years ago, and boy, it still haunts me. It's a *Peer Gynt* of the '90s. Nilo Cruz is somebody I just adore on the page. Madeline Olnek is producing incredible contemporary masterpieces. Donna DiNovelli's work remains with me. I often think of starting a theatre just to see her work get done.

It's not that theatre is unvital or on the decline. But the only theatre being produced is in such an ensconced, safe system that people aren't seeing what's out there.

What are your writing plans for the future?
I'm hoping I can finally do this full time. That's my goal. And I've been thinking a lot more about film. I'm taking myself back to school in a way, reading as many screenplays as I can to try and figure out what my voice is cinematically. I'm starting an adaptation of *How I Learned to Drive*, which I originally saw as a movie and not a play, and I'm getting

very excited by the movie in my head. So I want to continue screen-writing. I want to start to write for musical theatre. I don't think I'll be writing for straight theatre as much. I'm feeling the restrictions of the space, of the apparatus.

What is it about the musical stage now that excites you?

I think it's an emotionally overpowering form. And because it's so over-powering, it's political dynamite. When you can play with emotions like that, you can get all kinds of nifty things in politically. My father said something when I was a child that he repeated when I met him again 25 years later. He asked me if I liked musical theatre, and I said, "Yes," and he said, "Well that's good, because only through the Amer-ican musical theatre can this country ever approach what Bertolt Brecht did in Germany." And I remember staring at him and saying, "Dad, did you tell me that when I was a child?" And he said, "Yes." I said, "I teach that now"—for precisely that reason.

I'm not opposed to mass culture at all. I think amazing things can be and are done on TV and in film. You just have to realize that you're not going to get certain things done on a big budget. If your budget's big, you can forget your voice. Know where your voice is. My voice is not going to be in a high-concept film—although ask me again in two years. If I can't pay the rent, it may be very appealing. I've enjoyed the collaboration of the stage. I think I know how to collaborate now. Which means I think I'm ready for musical theatre and for film, where, as David Mamet once said, when they say collaborate they mean bend over. I think I'm less attached to my writing than I was as a younger woman.

There are no longer any straight plays that I'm burning up to write. I'm mostly burning up to write musicals and movies. It's an interesting thing. A lot of people stay away from those forms because they see them as selling out. There's a defensiveness about the forms in which we write and I'm not feeling defensive anymore. I feel like I'm ready to work with more people in the room, and I'm ready to learn new forms.

David Savran is a specialist in American theatre, popular culture and social theory. Among his books are two volumes of interviews with playwrights, *In Their Own Words* and *The Playwright's Voice*, both published by TCG, and the forthcoming *Highbrow/Lowdown: Theater, Jazz, and the Making of the New Middle Class* from University of Michigan Press. He is professor of theatre at the Graduate Center of the City University of New York and editor of the *Journal of American Drama and Theatre*. This interview is excerpted from *The Playwright's Voice*.

A CRITICS' SUMMIT

An interview with Robert Brustein and Frank Rich
by Robert Marx

May/June 1999

Back when new Broadway plays and musicals were rushed into print, collected drama criticism also took up prime space on bookstore shelves—until the business changed two decades ago. Major companies like Random House stopped publishing drama, the work of older critics like George Jean Nathan and Stark Young disappeared from the catalogs, and most contemporary critics were relegated to academic or alternative presses, if their work was anthologized at all.

The simultaneous publication last winter of collected theatre writings by both Robert Brustein and Frank Rich helped restore theatre criticism to the prestige of hardcover sales and front-line history. Brustein's *Cultural Calisthenics: Writings on Race, Politics and Theatre* (Ivan R. Dee, Chicago), like so many of his earlier books, consists largely of vital material that appeared originally in the *New Republic*. Leaving aside Brustein's volumes of literary criticism and autobiography, this new book is his ninth rigorous collection of theatre reviews and related essays—an extraordinary sequence that began with *Seasons of Discontent* in the early 1960s. With the possible exception of Walter Kerr, no American critic of Brustein's time has had the persistence and good fortune to see so many articles from a prolific career republished in such controversial volumes that chronicle a theatregoing lifetime.

Frank Rich's *Hot Seat: Theatre Criticism for the* New York Times, *1980–1993* is, astonishingly, the first-ever collection of reviews by the critic who loomed over American theatre for 13-plus seasons. This weighty and generous 1,000-page enterprise has been published by Random House as if the firm had never left the theatre business. It is an essential book, documenting not only the major and minor New York plays of a generation, but the arc of a preeminent theatre critic's influential taste, leadership and commitment.

In *Hot Seat*'s final pages, we learn that after years of mutual antagonism Brustein recently offered to "bury the hatchet," and that Rich gladly agreed. Taking advantage of the truce, *American Theatre* invited both writers to meet in New York to discuss their careers, drama criticism and current issues in the theatre. An edited transcript of their wide-ranging conversation follows.

Bob, when you started writing criticism in the 1960s, you were part of a prominent community—Eric Bentley, Harold Clurman, Kenneth Tynan, Walter Kerr, Richard Gilman, Stanley Kauffmann. It was an amazing group.

ROBERT BRUSTEIN: And Susan Sontag. Everybody wanted to write theatre criticism in those days. Eric Bentley had a profound influence on me when I was a young, evolving intellectual. He was one of the few in our time who took theatre seriously as a genuine art form and not simply entertainment (although it must be that, too, of course). I read his books religiously and scoured the *New Republic* for his reviews. He was my idol, as it were, and he stimulated me through his work to go into theatre criticism.

When I eventually became drama critic for the *New Republic*, it was his example that led me to make really stringent demands on the editorial staff there before I took the job. He claimed that he'd been treated very badly by the *New Republic*—that they dropped a lot of his articles and edited others. So I demanded that every word be published as written, and any changes had to be checked with me. As a result, my editor would call me every week and read to me from Washington my copy over the phone. It was a great time for criticism, for me personally, anyway.

FRANK RICH: Fascinating generational changes. When I was at Harvard as an undergraduate in 1970 and '71 and working for the *Crimson*, I wanted to write drama criticism, and people thought it was a joke. I was told, "You're going to have to talk about movies, because there's so little interest in the theatre at this moment that you're not going to get a job writing about your first love." And indeed it was years before I got a job as a drama critic; it was regarded as an eccentric interest in my generation. When I began my career in New York, the community of critics I admired and learned from were all older than me and they were all film critics, such as Pauline Kael and Andrew Sarris and John Simon (who also wrote about theatre, but I met him as a film critic). I was part of the young generation of film critics that was coming along, like Janet Maslin and David Denby. Later, when I became a drama critic, there really was no community like the one Bob describes. To me, that's a fantasy—Paris in the '20s, or New York in the '50s or Hollywood in the '30s. It just didn't exist.

BRUSTEIN: I want to add a few more names to the list of people who were writing in those days: Wilfred Sheed was writing criticism at the time, as was Albert Bermel, and so was Richard Hayes, who was doing extraordinary work for *Commonweal*. I had taken my doctoral work under Lionel Trilling, who was my real god as a critic. But he had nothing but scorn for the drama—he didn't think it was worthy of a man of intellect. I was determined to demonstrate, if I could, that the same values could be brought to bear on the theatre that were being used by him and others like him on literature and poetry.

RICH: I became a drama critic in 1980, and the changes, just since 1980, are extraordinary. When I was writing about film at *Time* magazine in the late '70s, there was a full-time drama critic, Ted Kalem. He died in the early '80s and was succeeded by Bill Henry. When Henry died, that was the end of it. Similarly, at *Newsweek*, theatre coverage must be a quarter of what it was. Even in the 1980s at *Newsweek*, Jack Kroll reviewed pretty much what a first-string critic of the *Times* would review. That's gone.

The editors don't consider theatre a national art?

RICH: Not unless it's produced by a national corporation like Disney. Then it's a national art. That's the problem.

BRUSTEIN: In fact, it's become a different kind of national art. The theatre has decentralized itself, even though obviously there's still an enormous amount of activity in New York. But the reasoning of editors is, if you go to Boston, Louisville or Chicago, you're not talking about something that the readers of the *New York Times*, for example, can connect with, because they can't get to it.

There are terrific critics these days in dance and in music—such as Tim Page at the *Washington Post*, Mark Swed at the *L.A. Times* and Joan Acocella at the *New Yorker*—but I can't think of a young critic in the theatre today who can analyze an actor's technique with the same skill that Acocella has brought to analyzing a dancer's technique. Why have wonderfully agile, committed critics emerged in those disciplines but not in the theatre?

BRUSTEIN: I think one reason is the theatre is still considered to be an entertainment for tired businessmen. It's been very hard to persuade people that the theatre is an art form on a par with dance, symphony and other classical music, opera and literature, even though Frank and I, along with other critics, have been working very hard to persuade people that this is true. But our editors—not my editor, but I think a lot of editors, particularly on newspapers—don't think it's true. What they prefer is someone to arbitrate the consumption of entertainment—a consumer guide—and tell people where to go, as they would recommend restaurants. It's what I call Himalaya criticism—loved him, hated her.

There's also a Puritan aspect to this, which I never tire of mentioning. Remember that this country was founded by Puritans who were fleeing England, where the first thing they did in power was to close down the theatres. Plays could be performed if there was musical accompaniment, if they were called operas. In short, music was sacred, the theatre profane. In my neck of the woods, in New England, there's lip service for support of theatre but very little money for it. The money goes to music. It goes to the symphony. It doesn't go to the theatre.

RICH: I think what Bob says is entirely right. There's still that cultural bias. I don't think, however, that explains entirely why there are so few young writers who match Joan Acocella. I have a child who is a freshman in college, and for his generation, theatre is hardly on the map culturally. It's not hip. No one is trying to indoctrinate children in the theatre more than I have with my kids, who love culture and are big culture buffs. They'll go to the Pollock show at the Museum of Modern Art, or they'll go to see the newest film at the Angelika theatre, or they'll go see Philip Glass in Brooklyn before they will go to a Broadway house, or an Off-Broadway house, or to the New York Shakespeare Festival. I can't quite explain why this is so, but it's not that there hasn't been good theatre—there has been. Still, surveys actually show that virtually no young people are going to theatre. And if they are going, they're going to big commercial crap.

BRUSTEIN: The median age of our audience at the American Repertory Theatre is 41. It's a very young audience, which is why we don't have a large subscription base, because they don't buy subscriptions. But they're a passionate audience, deeply involved in theatre.

RICH: But you're in a college town.

BRUSTEIN: I don't think it's college kids that are going—I think it's young professionals.

The habit of theatregoing is lost in a lot of ways, and that's where price enters the picture. I'm of the last generation of New York outer-borough kids for whom it was not unusual to get on the subway from the Bronx or Brooklyn to come downtown and pay $3 to sit in the balcony of a Broadway theatre—even less Off Broadway. It was as easy as going to a movie. Now those same seats are $55, apart from formal discount programs.

BRUSTEIN: Price is important. In the case of New York audiences, I think it has something to do with all those standing ovations and endless bravos—people seem to be not applauding the show, but their own expenditure. You don't see that in any other city in the country, really—people don't go that ape shit when a play is over. They respond with affection and with enjoyment, but this is an unnatural condition.

What is the best training today for theatre critics?

BRUSTEIN: At the Yale School of Drama, we thought we were giving excellent training to drama critics. Looking over the field, we saw most drama critics didn't know anything about dramatic literature—or *any* literature. They could not put the play in its time—its social, political or metaphysical contexts. They didn't know anything about production, or about theatrical process. So we thought it was our obligation to train people in those areas. And we turned out some really first-rate people, none of whom could get jobs in the major media because they didn't appeal to the average theatregoer. They were not going to connect with a reader who would trust them regarding whether to see *Chicago* or *Fosse* or whatever the latest musical hit was. We lost heart about training such critics, because there's no sense training people for nonexistent jobs. Now we train them to be dramaturgs.

We're having this discussion a week after the end of the impeachment trial. Where does theatre fit into the culture wars now?

RICH: I haven't seen any intersection. You see, I feel that theatre is a minor player in the culture wars. The only example of recent vintage is *Corpus Christi*, and that was a political football created by a group that was just scouring to find something. If it hadn't been *Corpus Christi*, it would have been the Paul Rudnick play, *The Most Fabulous Story Ever Told*. It's simply happenstance.

Is the NEA still an issue now?

BRUSTEIN: It's always relevant.

RICH: It's relevant, but it's arguing about a symbol rather than a thriving, monied enterprise. I don't think the theatre is on the front lines of the culture wars. Gangsta rap is.

BRUSTEIN: I don't agree. But I think there's a sufficient number of really important and powerful playwrights around who aren't simply writing editorials—they're not journalists in that sense. What may be making people lose interest in the theatre is that so many playwrights in so many theatres are telling us over and over what we already know: that it's important for all the races to be equal; that it's important for women to share power with men; that it's important for gay people to be respected and not abused. These things are all true and important, but they're not interesting as art because there's no surprise in it. And art has to be surprising. The truth is surprising. Life is surprising and unpredictable, and not a sufficient number of playwrights are being unpredictable.

RICH: I agree with you, and I feel that makes my point. That's why the theatre is not at the center of the cultural debate. Even *Corpus Christi* said nothing shocking. It was manufactured as shocking by its political opponents.

I have a friend whom I never reviewed, Jonathan Reynolds, who wrote a play, *Stonewall Jackson's House*, that was, I would say, the kind of iconoclastic play that you're talking about. It was saying everyone isn't created equal. It was talking about race in a way that you never hear in the theatre. In spite of good reviews, not a single nonprofit theatre in the country would produce that play except the one in New York that originated it, the American Place Theatre.

BRUSTEIN: I was desperate to do that play. The reason I didn't was because it wasn't a good enough play, despite its reviews. It did everything I thought a play should do, except it simply wasn't written well enough.

RICH: Let's say that for the sake of argument you're right—it's a flawed play. But I think if it had been more on the side of the angels on the issues you mentioned, people would have worked it through another draft. No one wanted to touch it. There are plays of far less quality that get a million productions. What it didn't have was all the truisms that congratulate an audience on their moral superiority instead of challenging them.

BRUSTEIN: I think it's crucial that artistic directors be willing to put on plays that they disagree with ideologically but that have quality as plays.

RICH: But who's writing them?

BRUSTEIN: David Mamet is writing them. Paula Vogel's writing them. Paula Vogel has written very unpredictable, idiosyncratic, kinky plays, like *Hot 'n' Throbbing*, for example, or *How I Learned to Drive*. Those are very subversive plays. *How I Learned to Drive*, to me, is almost as subversive as *Lolita*, because she doesn't take the approved, politically correct position on sexual harassment.

Bob, looking back on your debate [at Town Hall in New York City in January '97] with August Wilson, what was learned from that experience?

BRUSTEIN: One thing I learned was the inability of journalists to get their facts right. I think there was only one accurate report in the *Times* out of the four or five that appeared that really reflected what happened that night. I've forgotten who did it, but it didn't take sides.

RICH: Probably William Grimes, our new food critic. Shows you all talents are transferable.

BRUSTEIN: Yes, that's right. I think that it was a very healthy and salutary debate, frankly. It didn't seem so at the time because it was so divisive and such fault lines were drawn between members of the audience. But it was very important that we finally began to talk about some of these things that we only mumble about in secret. And the fact is, Wilson had said some really quite outrageous things regarding the capacity of black artists to work only in black plays. It seems to me that was a very restricting and segregating thing to do, and I thought it had to be challenged. Every time I talk to a group of black people, once they hear what the issues are, they respond positively to the fact of the debate. They don't see it as in any way a racist assault on themselves.

RICH: Without rehashing the whole thing, I certainly agree with Bob that Wilson's position that black artists should be segregated and can only do each other's work is totally untenable. To me, what's interesting about the debate is that it was a dead end. I saw people, some public intellectuals in New York City, at that debate that I've never seen in the theatre. People were eager for that conversation. But how is it being played out in terms of the theatre and its art? There's been no significant play that I've seen from August Wilson or anyone else—I may have missed it—that deals with the issue of race in America. I haven't seen those intellectuals who turned out to take one side or the other turn out again for a play. So to me, it's kind of another version of the *Corpus Christi* debate. The issues are very interesting, but where are they being played out in the actual life of the theatre, as opposed to being played out in journalism, and pieces by me or Bob, or in *American Theatre* magazine?

Is our theatre immobile right now? Is it the opposite of the theatre of the '60s?

RICH: I agree with Bob that plays don't deserve brownie points because they deal with political issues. I'm not saying that we should now have a Group Theatre about race, or we should have *Viet Rock*, or that all plays have to be David Rabe plays, or whatever. But I do feel that, even in terms of metaphor and of a real pursuit of cultural issues that are not journalistic, it's not happening. I really admire Paula Vogel—she's a superb writer. But I would be hard-pressed to argue that her plays are on the cutting edge of cultural debate. And race. Where's race? August Wilson has fallen silent since then.

BRUSTEIN: Suzan-Lori Parks is for me the most exciting African-American voice today, the most original and most innovative. She's got two new plays coming out. If I had thought of it, I believe I would have said at the debate with Wilson that the major issue that we're wrestling with today is not just racism. Clearly there's a lot of racism in this country, and it must be confronted. But I think there's another issue and another danger, which is a suppression of thought and language considered by some to be racist. If people become so sensitive that words like "niggardly" are taken to be racial insults, all you will do is drive feelings underground where they fester and become very ugly. I believe in more speech rather than less speech. I'm very fearful about "freedom from speech," the suppression and control of speech being demanded by otherwise worthy groups. Minorities are better off when they know who their enemies are, rather than muzzling them through guilt or fear.

And is that suppression and self-censorship evident in the theatre?

BRUSTEIN: Very much so.

RICH: *Stonewall Jackson's House* is a perfect example. This is a play that most readers of *American Theatre* aren't going to see, because they can't see it. What you're saying about the suppression of conversation about race—I don't think that's really happening so much in the public sphere. Whether it be conflicts over words like "niggardly" or "Ebonics" or whatever, there's a tremendous amount of debate in the public sphere. But in the case of the theatre: Why would, for lack of a better term, politically incorrect debate about race be less welcome than in all the other arts? This is not a problem in television. It's not a problem in movies. It's not a problem, certainly, in contemporary fiction, where politically incorrect stuff happens all the time. And kids, my kids, talk about it. "The Simpsons" and "South Park" deal with more subversive, challenging, politically incorrect notions about race than the American theatre does.

BRUSTEIN: Absolutely. I think it's possibly because the theatre community is made up of what Howard Rosenberg once called "a herd of independent minds." They herd together and communicate the same ideas to each other. And it may be—we can only speculate psychologically as to why it's so—because people in the theatre are among the very few people in this country who really love what they do, and who are being paid for something they love. Most people in this culture are doing things they hate and are being paid a lot of money for it. For the most part, theatre people have a lot of guilt about that, which transmits itself into this kind of obligatory social conscience on the part of some who really don't have that much social conscience. That's where we get into trouble.

Has the resident theatre movement that began in the '60s achieved what it set out to build?

BRUSTEIN: The resident-theatre movement is not in a very healthy or buoyant state at this particular moment. It had its great days. I think its great days will come again. It's going to need another Sputnik—by that I mean it's going to need some external impetus that will get everyone so scared that they say, "We have to support the arts," and "We have to support education in order to keep up with international competition," which we're not doing now. It's in the schools that the audiences are developed for the theatre and for all the arts, and frankly, they're not being developed now. Kids are growing up thinking that graffiti is great art and that gangsta rap is great music. They're helped in this by *Time* magazine, which runs a cover telling you that these are the great art forms of our time. Multiculturalism—which has been so effective in giving a voice to people who have not had a voice in the past—is now becoming a kind of *uni*culturalism, in the sense that it creates hostility about so-called Eurocentric culture, which is a crucial part of American culture.

RICH: The fact remains that if you're not seeing plays, and therefore all you're getting is the pop culture that is sent on the pipeline of cable TV into your house, there's no alternative. One of the horrible things that has happened over the course of the culture wars has been that the demonization of the NEA has been used to demonize spending on culture, period, by every segment of government—federal, state and local—in many parts of the country. The bashing of the NEA had the effect of making the arts in general subversive, and making culture the first thing that can be slashed out of a school budget. That, by the way, was the intent of a lot of people on the Right. They've done as much damage as multicultural madness has from the Left, I would argue.

BRUSTEIN: I think that's an extension of the Puritanism we were talking about, and it's also a demonstration of hypocrisy, which we haven't talked about, but which is rampant in our government. I mean, *Tartuffe* is being enacted every day by the religious Right and the freshmen Republicans.

But as far as objections to the NEA are concerned, they essentially come out of deep homophobia, deep sexual nausea and a deep hatred of the "dirty little secret," as D.H. Lawrence called it, that the theatre seems to be identified with. The notion that the theatre should be funded according to so-called community standards is the death of the theatre, the death of the arts. When in history have community standards told us what quality is, or excellence, or value? Great thinkers throughout history, starting with Shakespeare, have scorned the whole notion of community standards.

RICH: Including the thinkers who created the country. Once again, the Right doesn't say, "All right, if you want to do your salacious, anti-God, anti-patriotic play, no one's saying you can't do it with private money. But why should we federal taxpayers have to pay for it?" The fallout politically goes beyond NEA money—community standards are being used to beat up people who are using private philanthropy and not public funds. *Corpus Christi* had no public money in it.

BRUSTEIN: I want to quote Shaw on community standards: "Forty-million Frenchmen can't be right." (*Laughter.*) And the other thing I want to emphasize is this horrible, nauseating content-restriction clause that, for some reason, the Clinton Administration pushed to the Supreme Court after it had been struck down by a federal court in California. Now we have the Supreme Court on record as validating a violation of the First Amendment.

RICH: What I find equally appalling are these enhancement deals— you've written very well about this, Bob—in which the nonprofit theatre is playing footsy with commercial theatre. In my view, the Alliance Theatre of Atlanta serving as a tryout for Disney is simply whoredom. And it blew up in their face, because it bombed.

I feel that this development—this so-called merging of the non-profit and the commercial—is culturally significant for two reasons. First, that's one less original American play or musical on the schedule for a theatre that supposedly exists to do the kind of plays that Bob does or that any self-respecting nonprofit theatrical institution would do. Also, it contributes to the coarsening of theatre, which should be providing alternatives to *Beauty and the Beast* and *Riverdance*.

Then we have the Lincoln Center Theater situation. With *Parade*, they got involved with another Disney wannabe company that has now gone belly-up, stuck them with bills and given them a show that's going to have lost perhaps five or six million dollars—in a not-for-profit institution? I think there's something seriously off. There was a Faustian bargain there, and it should be a wake-up call that Livent turned out to be engulfed in fraud. How is the American theatre served by that arrangement?

BRUSTEIN: Everyone involved with the commercial theatre is under the obligation to make money for his or her investors and for himself or herself. When that is your animating motive, then all decisions are made accordingly: the choice of the play, the choice of the director, the choice of the theatre, the choice of the star, how and when you get the critics in. The alternative—in which your animating motive is to create a work of art, a collective work of art—is a socialist idea, not a capitalist idea. And it's very hard for a socialist idea to survive in an essentially ravenous, capitalist society. That's why the nonprofit theatre is now fighting for its life and its virtue, because it is so easy to succumb to the various temptations that are out there just to stay alive.

As the two of you look back at your critical writing, are there opinions that you've changed or topics you would approach differently?

RICH: Well, of course. In fact, in my book it's one of the issues I try to address. By and large, my opinions have not changed. But in terms of what I stressed, the things I emphasized, the harshness of tone, the over-generosity at times? Sure, there are things I'd change. I think any writer of any kind, including a critic, who remains completely frozen in sensibility and whose writing style doesn't mature and improve over a 20-year period is dead. That's just not the way writing works.

BRUSTEIN: I had occasion to look over *Seasons of Discontent*, my first book of collected criticism, recently. I didn't read the whole thing. But I read a few essays and I was appalled at how harsh I was, and how judgmental and stupid I was about the process of theatre. It just didn't occur to me that I was talking about human beings. I was talking about an art form all the time. I think John Simon admired me in those days and copied that style. The more I got involved in theatre and making theatre, the more I saw the incredible difficulty that goes into getting something on stage.

One of the reasons I gave for not taking the *Times* job in the early '60s—and it was the major reason, I think—was that I was privileged to be as tough as I was as long as I wasn't affecting anybody's livelihood. If I'd gone on the *Times*, obviously, I would have affected people's livelihood. Whereas today, my concern is that I may be affecting people's sense of themselves. The actor has nothing but himself or herself to offer—that's the instrument. It's not a flute or a fiddle or a cello. That's why I do deplore some of the crueler opinions being voiced by a few of our professional colleagues. I'm looking for other ways to go about criticism.

RICH: My experience, obviously, is different from Bob's in that I did not enter the theatre. But life experience changes you, too, and over the course of this job I came to have a different sense of the people who were involved in the theatre and what they were up against. I have also looked at some of my earlier stuff and said, "I can't believe how harsh this was, and how unforgiving it was, and how I was so concerned with artistic principles that I forgot that there was any kind of humanity involved." Ideally, you grow up—and it's shocking when you have colleagues who actually don't grow up. One place where we may differ is that I still feel very conscious of a certain kind of reader—the angriest, most intelligent mail I got as a drama critic was from people who didn't like things that I had sent them to. It was not from people saying, "Oh, why didn't you like *Starlight Express*?" It was from people saying, "Why did you send me to *Glengarry Glen Ross*, with all that dirty language, and what was it about? It had no story." At the *Times*, you're writing for a million people. That can mellow you a bit in terms of trying to be clearer in your arguments, clearer in what you're saying so that people, whatever your opinion is, can better understand where you're coming from and what they're in for.

BRUSTEIN: The great value of my writing for the *New Republic* is I'm writing for a readership that probably doesn't go to the theatre and, therefore, doesn't need guidance from me. However, I do get a lot of mail about the things we produce at ART from people who say, "How can you do this to the classics? Why did you think this was a good play?" I respond to all of them personally. And we try to talk to our audience a lot though symposia and pre-production discussions to explain why we go about doing the things we do and to make it clear that there's a purpose behind them. We don't try to insult audiences. I think the ultimate corruptibility of criticism is its lack of accountability. As critics, we're not accountable to anybody, except maybe our editors or our readership.

RICH: You are accountable. The readership can turn on a critic. I've always been struck by the example of the film critic Bosley Crowther, who had dismissed *Bonnie and Clyde* as just a routine gangster film. I was going through *Times* microfilm and I found two full pages in Arts and Leisure of letters attacking his review of *Bonnie and Clyde*—people were outraged that he had missed what was then and probably still is a turning point in American cinema. The audience really got him. I think that led directly to his being replaced by Renata Adler, who could not have been more different.

More proof to your point that the pendulum does swing back and forth. That brings to mind a topic I want to address—the whole question of experimental theatre in America. Is that extraordinary movement past?

BRUSTEIN: No, there's the Wooster Group, and Richard Foreman, and people like Bob McGrath with the Ridge Theater. You know, whenever we tend to generalize about the death of the theatre, someone comes along and revives it. All it takes is one artist. It took Chekhov to revive the moribund Russian theatre. It took Brecht to revive the moribund German theatre. They're out there, and they'll reappear. Whenever anyone asks me, "What's the future of the theatre?" I always have to say, "The future of the theatre is whatever artists are coming along to revolutionize it."

RICH: I totally agree with that. We have to have an infrastructure, for lack of a better term, that supports that artist when he or she does come along. We have to make sure that that artist gets an audience. And that's why I'm worried about things such as the commercial theatre so boldly annexing nonprofit theatres on Broadway. It wasn't that long ago that you could do *Glengarry Glen Ross* on Broadway, you could do *Angels in America* on Broadway. You wouldn't get rich doing it, but Broadway would give plays like that cultural prominence that would help speed up productions at nonprofit theatres and help disseminate them the way that Broadway once helped disseminate *A Streetcar Named Desire*. Now, it's almost impossible to do that unless it's a British import or there's a star. And it's going to become less and less possible as these corporations gain more and more power. *How I Learned to Drive* could've been done on Broadway 15 years ago. It wouldn't have been a better or worse play for having been, but it would have meant that "Theatre X" in Omaha might have found it a little earlier and would've taken more of a shine to it.

I agree with Bob that artists always come along, and people who love the theatre want to work in the theatre and can't be talked out of it no matter what new media there are. But there has to be a theatre there to receive them.

Robert Marx is a foundation director, producer and arts essayist. He has been executive director of the New York Public Library for the Performing Arts and has led the theatre programs of the National Endowment for the Arts and the New York State Council on the Arts. He has developed projects for the Salzburg Festival, Lincoln Center, Brooklyn Academy of Music, Carnegie Hall, the Julliard School, the Mark Taper Forum and the Los Angeles Olympic Festival. For many years he served as commentator and intermission host of the Metropolitan Opera's live Saturday radio broadcasts.

BALANCING ACTS

An interview with Anne Bogart and Kristin Linklater
by David J. Diamond

January 2001

A year ago in the pages of *American Theatre*, Kristin Linklater, chair of the theatre division of Columbia University, spoke out against student actors' diluting their training by taking bits and pieces of craft from other cultures. "Actors-in-training are often submitted to a kind of transcultural grafting that dilutes their art," she opined in "Far Horizons," an article that outlined eight theatre practitioners' views on training, "instead of getting deep nourishment from the meat and potatoes of our own European-based, verbal traditions."

The iconoclastic teacher of voice, text and Shakespeare went on to say that, while good actors can pick up ideas from many sources, "they should be wary of becoming whores with low self-esteem. They and their teachers sell themselves short when they bow down to foreign gods."

Linklater's colleague Anne Bogart, who heads the directing program at Columbia's theatre division and is also the renowned artistic director of Saratoga International Theatre Institute Company, took exception to Linklater's remarks. In a letter to the editor that ran in the April '00 issue of *American Theatre*, Bogart and SITI Company wrote that Linklater's suggestions "are as uninformed as they are destructive." Stressing the fact that the work of SITI "is enriched by contact with other cultures," the letter went on to say that Linklater's remarks "demonize the possibility of cross-cultural exchange. This creates a reactionary conservatism that does not belong in the arts."

In that same issue of the magazine, Linklater responded to the Bogart/SITI letter by saying, "I certainly don't have the power (or the inclination) to demonize cross-cultural exchange." She also objected to Bogart's characterization of her as "xenophobic, exclusionary and borderline racist."

With the aim of allowing Linklater and Bogart the opportunity to explain their positions more fully, we invited them to a face-to-face debate at the *American Theatre* offices. We also asked a dozen directors to listen to the exchange and join in the discussion. During the course of the afternoon, we discovered that, while Linklater and Bogart may radically disagree on methodology, their opinions about the discipline and goals of training are much closer than their original statements might have led one to expect.

KRISTIN LINKLATER: On many occasions, I've heard the suggestion that the American theatre and American-theatre training were inferior to those of other cultures. Now I have taught in many parts of the world, and I'm always struck by the fact that wherever I am, there are workshops in American actor-training going on—the basic stuff, the Americanized version of Stanislavsky, what came out of the Actors' Studio and dominated the actor-training studio scene in New York for many, many years. Now, the fact that our actor-training is so sought after, all over the world, it seems to me, is something we should be proud of. American artists don't have to look elsewhere for their roots. We have very deep roots.

ANNE BOGART: I actually don't care for most American actor-training. I think that Stanislavsky was strangled, mostly by Lee Strasberg. I'm very frustrated with what a rehearsal is for most American actors. It seems a little bit small. As a director, when I hear an actor say, "Is that what you want?" I think, "Is a rehearsal about doing what the director wants?" And that worries me. So, my entire life I've gone elsewhere for inspiration. I went to Germany to work as a young director, and I suddenly had an epiphany: that I'm an American artist. My roots are back in vaudeville. I have an American sense of rhythm, an American sense of humor, an American sense of structure. Oddly enough, the way I get closest to my American roots—and most of the work I've done in the past 15 years is about American culture or American artists—is by going away. When I go to Japan and work with Tadashi Suzuki, for example, I'm thrown against a wall of my own assumptions. I have to choose what I want to own.

I formed a company based on a celebration of this issue. We meet people of different cultures who do things differently, and that act challenges us to grow—to become, oddly enough, more American. So, as the years go by I feel more and more militantly against the Americanized, misunderstood version of Stanislavsky we seem to suffer under. The biggest issue I have is with the actor's thinking, "If I feel it, the audience feels it."

Kristin, what is wrong with different cultural influences bearing on American actor training?

LINKLATER: There is nothing wrong with it, once students have acquired roots in the Western theatre tradition. Those roots are deep; they go back to the Greeks, grow through Shakespeare and on to the 20th-century American classics. The tradition is densely verbal. It's based in the revelation of the human being through the human psyche, the human emotions, the intellect, the imagination—as shaped by a particular culture.

I think if you get your roots deep enough into this tradition you have earned the right to meet other, international ones. The depth and discipline of those traditions are extraordinary. If we come to them as if we're going to the street fair—to see what we can pick up to decorate our living rooms—then we're in trouble.

Anne, don't you think that there's a wildness and an excitement— an extension of the human expression—that comes from very deep inside the good American actors? The good American actors can blow the English actors off the stage, for a start. And there's also an excite- ment here, which has to be admired and respected. The frightening alternative to, "If I feel it, the audience is going to feel it," often seems to be, "I'll just tell the audience about it." And that's where a lot of theatre training and directing is going—"Don't be emotional, whatever you do. Just say the words."

I just love the fact that the Actors' Studio happened, and that it totally bastardized Stanislavsky, and Strasberg took people down into those depths of the neurotic self, to the point where nobody could hear a word for 25 years afterwards. The fact that he went so far in that direction and that we then started coming back, I think, is enormously valuable.

BOGART: This business of contacting an emotional memory and using that in relationship to a text causes a sort of narcissism that I find unbearable. I think that emotional recall is particularly dangerous because it works beautifully on film and television, where you want to be photogenic and spontaneous. After the moment happens, you never create it again. The technique doesn't work in the theatre, where it's not about being photogenic. Of course, the theatre is about being spontaneous, but in a way you can repeat. So the search in a rehearsal is to find a vehicle in which the emotions can change all the time.

My problem is this: The emotions are such powerful tools that a lot of rehearsals become about generating an emotion and then the director saying, "Keep that." Now, for me the emotions are the most precious things we experience—I don't even want to use the word "have," because they're not a commodity. Therefore, I believe that the emotions should be left alone in a rehearsal. What you're looking for in rehearsal is an action or a shape or a form in which the emotions can always be different. Because the minute you pin down an emotion, you cheapen it.

So I prefer to look at the body, at placement, at arrangement. I'm interested in the emotions, but I don't want to strangle them. I think that the work of the Actors' Studio, especially, while fantastic on film or television, is deadly in the way it separates actors from each other. That's because the emphasis is, to a large extent, on trying to generate feeling, instead of on being present in the room.

The type of work that you do in rehearsal—what tradition does that come from, if it doesn't come from a Western tradition?

BOGART: Oh, I think it comes from a very Western tradition—it comes from vaudeville, from postmodern dance, especially of the Judson Church era. My influences are both international and American, and my company does two separate kinds of training—Suzuki training and Viewpoints. The Suzuki is like a barre class for a dancer, and the Viewpoints is a way to practice creating fiction using time and space. One is vertical; the other is horizontal. One is you and God; the other is you and the people around you.

How does that jibe with the training in deep traditions that you were talking about?

LINKLATER: I have benefited both from the British version and the American version of those deep traditions. In London I was trained by people from the Old Vic Theatre School created by Michel St. Denis, who had come out of Jacques Copeau's Company. Jacques Copeau did in France what Stanislavsky did in Russia—he looked at conventional acting and said, "Where is the humanity?"

Then when I came to New York and started teaching at NYU, I encountered a holy madman of the theatre: Peter Kass, whose whole point was that there is no limit to what the actor can do, what the actor knows—the actor is always bigger than the character. I found that my voice work fitted extraordinarily well with that approach because my voice work involves freeing the human being from the constraints that our culture puts on us as we grow up. The actor's duty, as far as I'm concerned, is to have a free and open body without tensions and a voice that can express the full gamut of human emotions and an intellect that will channel those emotions. And the balance between voice, body, emotions and intellect has to be exact; otherwise, you're going to get a skewed communication. The training I'm talking about, which is aimed toward that balance, comes out of everything I've learned since coming to this country about psychology and the self and the deep value of the imagination and individual creative spirit—and that's not the same as narcissism.

This training, for me, is the equivalent of your "barre class." When I worked with Shakespeare & Company [of Lenox, Mass.] and then with my own company, the Company of Women, our barre was a 45-minute or hour-long warm-up before every single rehearsal and performance—an inventory of our bodies and our voices, but also our emotional selves that day. And sometimes it was a mess. Everybody would have to cry for 20 minutes before they could get on with anything. To treat one's own emotions as part of one's technique, I think, is really important. And it's very different, by the way, from the emotional memory stuff that leads you down memory lane into some dark place. That has to do with neurosis, not free emotion.

So I believe basic training frees an actor from the constraints of habit, which is always a diminishing, reductive force. I could not train young actors in voice work if they were doing equal amounts of time in Suzuki. Suzuki involves building muscular control, and the work I do involves giving up external muscular controls. Lots of other kinds of training are incompatible with my kind of voice work, too—modern dance is hopeless; ballet absolutely undermines every inch of the training. If an actor's psycho-physical system is constantly being thrown in one direction and then another, it won't learn as fast.

BOGART: For me, interesting acting training is just the opposite. I think that actors are not asked to do difficult enough things. I think on a daily basis actors need to do something that's almost impossible. I think they should study opera and ballet—three or four techniques that are next to impossible—and then try to do them as a professional. Try to walk into the room as ballet dancers, even though they're actors. Of course, I'm not an actor, but I actually think it opens them up.

LINKLATER: Do something that's nearly impossible . . . . I spent an hour and a half this morning with my first-year students at Columbia, and they were convinced that I was asking for the impossible—that was to open up their throats and stretch their tongues out of their throats while their throats remained open. This was as hard as doing three pliés and a pas de deux.

I think actors come up against things that are impossible all the time. An actor might say, "You want me to speak while I remember the dreadful thing that my father did to me when I was six?" The answer is: Yes! Otherwise, how will you learn to open your throat while you're playing Iphigenia? Often in my classes a memory of something horrific comes up, and a student just wants to leave the room. I say, "You've got to stay in the room. Now is when you have to talk. Because that's when you're going to restore the relationship between your brain and your feelings so that you can be eloquent with your emotion."

BOGART: When I do actor-training, I do a lot of physically exhausting things—running and jumping and stuff. At a certain point people get really exhausted. And what I say is, "You're in the fifth act of *Hamlet.* You can't say, 'I'm tired,' and shut down!"

Is there any danger of dilution when an actor tries to get a little bit of Suzuki here, a little bit of Grotowski there . . . .

BOGART: This is where I really agree with Kristin—"boutiquing" is dangerous. In a way, I think, it doesn't really matter what you choose to study, but you have to stick with it. The word I look for in actor training is rigor.

LINKLATER: Absolutely. Any art that's achieved a high level has gone very, very deep into its disciplines. I think there are parts of the brain that get engaged when you go long and slow and demandingly. When I do my Shakespeare training, we spend five weeks leading up to one sonnet, first trying to get the voice to move the body from inside-out, then going to the color work, and then vowels and consonants, and so on.

I want to go back, Anne, to something you talked about earlier—the relationship of emotion to physical movement, especially as rehearsal moves into performance. How do you get the actor to the right emotional place?

BOGART: I don't get actors to emotional places. I try to create an environment in which many-colored emotions might occur. I find that if I try to make emotions happen, the environment is cheapened. So I try to create the circumstances in which emotions can be free.

Now what I find is, in rehearsal, if you concentrate on detail, things start happening. The trick is to keep working on something. And eventually the emotions that need to happen—the arc of the scene—emerges, not because you're trying to make it happen, but because you're taking care of things around it.

MARCY ARLIN of Immigrants' Theatre Project and Lincoln Center Theater Directors Lab: How do you keep a wonderful, spontaneous, magic moment that happens in rehearsal and translate it into the performance?

BOGART: When I was a young director and had no pay and no theatres to work in, and did work on street corners and rooftops, and worked with young inexperienced actors who didn't mind not being paid, I choreographed everything. I set moments of imbalance—sometimes it was just something that was really hard to do, like, "Can you get your elbow over here on this word and make sure you're looking behind you?" So that the actor then was actually straining *against* something and that made the juices go. When you watch artists work, you watch them throw themselves off balance and then fight for balance. And that is a heroic act. After all, great plays start when something goes wrong, so that the characters have to scramble to re-create harmony inside an imbalanced state.

The most important thing to do as a director is to *see* the person you're in the room with—what their hair's like, how tall they are, how heavy their body is. *That's* what you're working with and not something in your head.

LINKLATER: I'd like to pitch in on that one, too, because I think that's really at the heart of good acting. It sounds terribly simple, and it's very hard: to be really in the moment. To be here *now*. My job as the actor is to be open to the play, to let the play *play* me from beginning to end.

I think it boils down to the rhythm of your breathing. After the outgoing breath, there's a moment of nothing, and that's the moment of imbalance, as far as I can tell. And then breath comes back in again. You can train yourself to consciously say, "What a surprise! The breath came back in." I think training involves training oneself to be surprised.

NATALIA DE CAMPOS of LCT Directors Lab: Kristin, you mentioned the balance of the four aspects of actor's training—voice, body, emotions and intellect. Do you really think American training can fulfill those four aspects?

LINKLATER: I think American training is getting better and better. For a long time, stage movement for actors was not very well looked after here, but now we're into the second generation of Lecoq-trained teachers, and I think that's fantastic training for actors. And—god, it sounds a little immodest to say so—but in the 30-odd years that I've been here, voice training. Before, it was not an essential part of actor-training programs in all these universities. Now it is. And then there's the discipline of scene-study work, which has always been part of American training but was not part of British training until very recently. I think there's some very good training happening in this country. To the young American actor, I always say, "Don't go to London for your basic training. Stay here!"

FROM THE AUDIENCE: I'm wondering if the differences in your approaches might have something to do with a difference in the way you relate to your audiences.

BOGART: I'm interested in the creative role of the audience. My frustration with a lot of theatre is that all the answers are given and there's no room for the audience—and I think that comes, again, from film and television. There are two ways of thinking about the audience. The first is to want everybody in the room to feel the same thing. I tend to think of that as what Spielberg did in *E.T.* You cry at all the right places, but everybody is crying at those places too, and at the end you feel like a manipulated rag. It's actually easy to make a whole audience feel one thing. It's also called fascism.

The second way is to create a moment on stage that triggers *different* associations in everybody in the audience. It's much harder to do that. I try to set up contradictions on the stage. In between those contradictions lives something very bright. I try to think of the audience as detectives; I'm leaving clues for them. The older I get, the more I try to do the least I possibly can on stage, so that the most happens in the audience's head.

LINKLATER: I would say I'm really old-fashioned, and I still believe in catharsis. If there is an emotional moment on the stage that triggers an emotion in an individual in the audience, then that emotion sheds light on the condition of that individual. And it's highly unlikely that you'll get everyone crying at the same moment. Of course, the kind of plays that I'm working on are mostly very verbal. The voice can, and should, have a powerful emotive effect on the audience. It actually moves sound waves physically through the air and hits bodies.

Two things that I see coming onto the live stage from film upset me very much. One is that actors are being trained in what I call the Mametian style, in which the voice is purely outward signage and is not meant to carry the story or carry the imaginative transformation from within the actor to the audience member. The age of irony has undermined the emotive power of the voice on the stage.

The second thing is this idea of soundscapes on stage. I have heard music on stage that *tells* the audience what it's meant to feel. That happens instead of the actor's voice, with its own intrinsic musicality and power, arousing an emotional response from the audience. Now, that is a serious evisceration of the art.

MONIKA GROSS of LCT Directors Lab and the Women's Project Directors Forum: I'm an Alexander instructor. I wanted to go back to something that Kristin touched on earlier about modern dance. If we're looking for American psycho-physical traditions, early development of modern dance in America seems to be somewhat of a model for training.

LINKLATER: Martha Graham was one of the great, great American artists of the last century, there's no question about that. But Graham's technique is deadly for actors. Because if you contract in there (*indicating the diaphragm*) you can't breathe.

GROSS: With Graham, the emphasis is a lot on contraction, yes, but it's also on release.

LINKLATER: But it's for a different art.

BOGART: It's not a different art! I think Martha Graham is the most important theatre person of the century. I think she really got it in terms of character. I play a game in my head sometimes: "What would have happened if the Moscow Art Theatre never came to the U.S. in 1922 and '23?" I think, "Maybe Graham would have been our entire theatre!"

DIAMOND: Anne, actors in your company spend a lot of time working around Suzuki. What does Suzuki training give an actor?

BOGART: The results I see are incredible concentration, focus, strength and the ability to change quickly. And I've found that when actors do Suzuki in conjunction with the Viewpoints—which deals with spontaneity and flexibility and being in the moment—it's a magic, chemical combination.

AINNA MANAPAT, *American Theatre* intern: You were saying that you don't think American actors should go to England for their training, and I know that, among a lot of young actors right now, the buzz is that American schools are just not as good as RADA or BADA or whatever . . . .

LINKLATER: It's very colonial thinking. The BADA program I think is terrific for young folk who have not been exposed to any serious training at all. But the dreadful, awful thing is that in this country there are so many undergraduate actor-training programs turning out people who think they are actors—it's drowning the profession in mediocrity. Some of them will get jobs anyway because those programs also train people how to sell themselves. And if they're aiming for the American professional theatre, these actors have to have an ear cocked to the marketplace. And if they go over to England, they will tend to come back with an English accent. English people coming here tend not to pick up the American accent in the same way—I don't know why that is. There are also certain emphases in the English training which may not be all that helpful for the serious, professionally directed young American actor.

SHEELA KANGAL, TCG staff: I feel that the goal of so many training programs is to strip the student, leave him or her naked and exhausted, saying, "I don't know what I'm doing"—and then somehow, at that point, then they can start again. I just don't see the justification in that. If I go into a kind of training, I don't want to be called to a place that's unsafe.

LINKLATER: An actor who wants to stay safe is a boring actor. One of the things you have to learn as an actor is how to go into dangerous places. And you don't do that by being confirmed in what you already know. If somebody comes to me for training, I'm assuming they want to change, dig deeper or go further, get more dangerous, tap into their own individual creativity. Creativity is not a comfortable land to live in.

BOGART: All the really great actors I work with are willing to throw away everything they've done a night before opening and change it. And I think that's a quality of a great artist, and it takes a lot of bravery. Training should develop that bravery.

LINKLATER: Some thinking has said that the greatest spiritual level is insecurity.

BOGART: Heisenberg proved that. Mathematically.

LINKLATER: There you are.

David J. Diamond is a theatre consultant, producer and career coach for artists. He organizes and coordinates, along with Ellen Stewart and Mia B. Yoo, the La MaMa International Symposium for Directors in Spoleto, Italy, each summer. He previously spent nearly a decade as executive director of the Stage Directors and Choreographers Foundation and was general manager of United States Institute for Theatre Technology and managing director of the Barrow Group Theatre Company.

SIDE BY SIDE BY SIDE

An interview with Stephen Sondheim by Frank Rich

July/August 2002

This is America's Sondheim summer.

Through the final days of August, the nation's capital will remain a destination point for musical-theatre aficionados from around the world, as the Kennedy Center throws its considerable resources behind an unprecedented tribute to composer and lyricist Stephen Sondheim. Six Sondheim musicals, mounted in overlapping repertory with the participation of some of the brightest talents in contemporary musical theatre, along with two concert programs of his songs (by Barbara Cook and Mandy Patinkin), are on the Sondheim Celebration program, described by Kennedy Center president Michael M. Kaiser as "a theatrical version of a museum retrospective."

The first three productions—*Sweeney Todd*, directed by Christopher Ashley; *Company*, supervised by Sean Mathias; and *Sunday in the Park with George*, mounted by the event's overall artistic director, Eric Schaeffer—were scheduled to run through the end of June. Still to come are *Merrily We Roll Along*, opening July 13 under Ashley's direction; *Passion*, beginning July 19 with Schaeffer at the helm; and Mark Brokaw's staging of *A Little Night Music*, due Aug. 2.

The affair kicked off on April 28 with "Sondheim on Sondheim," a public conversation between the composer and former *New York Times* chief theatre critic Frank Rich, during whose tenure on the theatre beat many of Sondheim's greatest works appeared—and who was once facetiously dubbed by industry insiders as "the demon barber of Broadway" for his harsh reviews (not usually of Sondheim shows, which he, for the most part, championed). Here are excerpts from their wide-ranging conversation.

The first time I was in the same theatre with Stephen Sondheim was, indeed, here in Washington—at the National Theatre—and I looked up my old playbill and it was literally 40 years ago today: a Saturday matinee on April 28, 1962,

when John Kennedy was in the White House and had not yet lent his name to a cultural center. Tell us what went on that day.

Well, it was a matinee of *A Funny Thing Happened on the Way to the Forum*, and there were almost fewer people in the audience than there were on the stage. In fact, I said to Hal Prince, the producer, "Let's invite them all back to the hotel for a drink after."

That would have changed my life.

The show was a disaster in Washington—it was very badly received. I remember that [critic] Richard Coe said in the *Post*, "*A Funny Thing Happened on the Way to the Forum* gives it the old college try, but the colleges do it so much better." Those things stick in your mind. However, we put in a new opening number, took it to New York, and everything was fine.

The new opening number was "Comedy Tonight." Where and when did you write it?

I think I was staying at the Jefferson Hotel, and Jerry Robbins came in at my suggestion and worked with us for the last week when we were in Washington. He said that what the show needed was a number at the beginning that told the audience what kind of an evening they were in for—a "baggy pants" number, meaning low comedy. Then he said something that rather put me off. He said, "Now, I don't want you to tell any jokes; let me do the jokes." That's why the lyric of "Comedy Tonight" is just a list of things. And for those of you who have had the pleasure of seeing that number, it's one of the two or three best opening numbers ever. It would be very hard to have a flop show after that number, because Robbins did all these physical jokes on the stage. It was a dazzler.

What is it like when you have to produce a song like that on demand out of town?

It's always easier. Historically, some of the best songs get written out of town because you know whom you're writing for. At that point, I knew exactly Zero Mostel's strengths and weaknesses. I've often said as a joke that I really don't want to write the score until the show is cast and in rehearsal—then I wouldn't make any mistakes. Silly as it sounds, it's true, because by then you know the qualities of the people that you're writing for. For example, I wrote "Send in the Clowns" during rehearsals of *A Little Night Music* for Glynis Johns—not just for Glynis Johns, but for Glynis Johns playing the part of Desiree in a specific situation, and as staged by Hal Prince. And when you have all those . . . parameters, if that's the right word—when you have those, it's so much easier to write. I wrote that song in two or three days, and it was a cinch because I knew all the materials. Writing *Gypsy* for Ethel Merman took about four months, which is a very short time to write a show. And it was because we knew the performer, as well as the character, so well.

You wanted to write the music and lyrics for Broadway shows, but the first two shows you actually got on, *West Side Story* and *Gypsy*, you could only write the lyrics. Was that frustrating? And did you learn the things from Leonard Bernstein and Jule Styne that you expected to?

The answer to both questions is yes. I got the job doing *West Side Story* by accident, by running into Arthur Laurents at a party. I didn't know him at all, but I had auditioned for him for another show. I asked him what he was doing, and he told me he was about to start on this musical of *Romeo and Juliet* and they were looking for a lyric writer. He said, "Well, I never thought of you. I didn't much like your music but I thought your lyrics were terrific. Why don't you come in and play for Leonard Bernstein?" Well, I wasn't the least bit interested in writing just lyrics, but I sure wanted to meet Leonard Bernstein. I went up the next day and played for Lenny and he said, "Actually, Comden and Green are supposed to do the lyrics but they may be stuck in Hollywood. We'll find out within a week and I'll let you know then." I was thinking to myself, "It doesn't matter anyway, because I don't want to do just lyrics." But Oscar Hammerstein, who was, as most of you know, my mentor, said to me, "I think it would be very smart of you to take this job. You would be working with men of high quality in the theatre: Robbins, Laurents and Bernstein. You'll learn something from them." And, boy, was he right.

It was very frustrating not writing the music, but, because I was a composer, Lenny listened to me when I talked music, so we had a collaboration that was closer than it might have been if I weren't a musician. I was able to learn a great deal from him, musically. What I learned from him most, though, is that Lenny was never ashamed to fall off the high rung of the ladder—whenever he failed, it was always because his reach was greater than his grasp. He never had a piddling little failure. They were big failures and I like to think that my failures are big failures, too. (*Laughter.*)

As for *Gypsy*, I was supposed to do music and lyrics for it, but Ethel Merman didn't want an unknown composer. She had just done a show called *Happy Hunting* that was not a success, and she was feeling very skittish and defensive. But she had seen *West Side Story*, so she was perfectly willing to have me aboard as lyric writer. And, again, I balked, and, again, Oscar told me to do it. He said, "You'll have a different experience this time. You'll be writing for a star. It's a quite different process." So I figured there was something to be learned there, and, indeed, there was.

About Oscar Hammerstein: Sometimes people have trouble making the connection between the man who wrote *Oklahoma!* and *The Sound of Music* and the man who wrote *Sweeney Todd* and *Pacific Overtures*. Explain what you learned from him.

Well, I learned a lot about technique from him, and, up until the day he died, I always showed him everything I wrote. But the major thing I learned from him came about when I was 16 or 17 and starting to write under his guidance. He taught me a very simple and very profound lesson. As you know, he used a lot of nature images in his work, lots of larks learning to pray, cattle standing like statues and that sort of thing. (*Laughter.*) And though he lived on a farm much of the time, he was a city boy, absolutely urban. People think of him as a sort of simple kind of fellow with hay in his mouth. In fact, he had a very sharp tongue and was a very good and articulate critic. But that was not how he wrote. So the first songs I started to write were full of clouds and, you know, not necessarily cattle but a tree here and a tree there . . . and a bird, maybe. And he said, "You're writing like me. You're trying to imitate me. Write what you feel. Write for the character and for the way you feel the character feels." That seems like a very simple lesson but, you know, it takes a lot of guts to share your own emotions and observations publicly—you're naked when you write something and it's out there in public. Oscar told me not only to be not ashamed but not to imitate—and to try to find, in myself, a way of relating to the characters so that it would be unique to me. Again, I'm sure that sounds simplistic, not just simple, but, boy, it has stood me in good stead for a long time. Anyway, that's why what I write is so different from what he wrote.

It's amazing to me that you can get into the head of everyone from a flight attendant in *Company*, to a 19th-century Japanese peasant in *Pacific Overtures*, to the demon barber of Fleet Street. Where did you get that kind of chameleon-like quality?
Well, it may sound ridiculously modest, but it's because of the librettists I work with. These are good writers who imagine vivid characters. The characters—I've said it before and I'll say it many times—are their inventions. What I am good at is imitating. I have the approach of an actor. I get inside the character the way an actor gets inside a character. I never write a song—a lyric, anyway—until there are at least one or two scenes written by the librettist so that I can get into the diction. That's the talent I have, for mimicking. In fact, when I was in college, I was a pretty good actor. I'm terrible now. I got much more inhibited as I got older, although I act pretty well when I sing. But, where I really act well is when I'm writing for characters that somebody else has created.

Of all of those diverse characters you've written, are there some that you particularly liked inhabiting more than others, or vice versa?
No, I enjoy all the characters I've ever written for. I think they're all terrific. You have to like your villains as well as your sympathetic characters. And you get to know them so well. They do become—this all sounds so corny—they become family. While you're writing something, you're really living with those people. The most interesting one was Georges Seurat in *Sunday in the Park*, because he was so secretive. Very few people knew anything about his life. They referred to him as "the notary" because he was always formally dressed and very reserved. The only things he ever spoke with passion about were color and his experiments with color. He did not consider himself a painter, he considered himself a scientist about color. He lived a few blocks away from his mother and would see her once a week for dinner. His life was very, very organized that way. And only after his death did she learn that he had a child by his mistress—that's how secretive he was; he kept his life compartmentalized. Well, when you have a character like that, you can fill him out in any way you want.

You were talking before about how you sometimes write your characters with specific performers in mind. Is it weird to then see them, as you are about to see them here, in other productions with actors that you never knew existed when you were writing?

No, it's not weird; it's what makes theatre so much more satisfying for a writer than the movies. I mean, performances in movies don't get any better. When you see *Gone with the Wind* again, they're still giving the same performances—they're very good, but they don't get any better. (*Laughter.*) It's really wonderful to see different actors do the same piece. Actors are so different from each other. For example, in the new production of *Into the Woods*, when the Witch, who was originally played by Bernadette Peters, is played by Vanessa Williams, all the values start to change. The other two leading characters—the Baker and the Wife—are played by actors with entirely different weight and sensibility than the first cast, which is very deliberate on the part of the director James Lapine. The idea is not so much to reconceive the show as to give it a different tone, both in its visual approach and in the choice of actors. And the result is that it's alive.

What about the way the shows change? I saw *Into the Woods* last week in New York and there was a palpable feeling in the second act of something that was obviously not your intention when you wrote it—of Sept. 11. It was upsetting. The show played somewhat differently because of things falling down, massive destruction from an evil outside force. A show like *Company*, to take another example, was written about New York and a sort of social milieu of 1970. Is it applicable now?

No, *Company* is topical in the same way that, let's say, Gilbert and Sullivan is. It's very much of its time. I mean, if it's still fresh, it's fresh because of the writing itself, but it is very much of its time. When, however, you deal with shows like *Sweeney* or *Sunday in the Park with George* or even *A Little Night Music*, all of which take place in an era that's so long ago, it's much easier to absorb them into whatever is going on today. Similarly, *Into the Woods* takes place in fairy-tale time— let's call it medieval times. Therefore, any of the actions and overtones in the play may become relevant (that awful word, "relevant") to what's going on, may take on colors the way any so-called classic work does (classic meaning something that takes place in a different time).

You know, there's a scene in *Company* where a couple is being turned on to marijuana for the first time, and all the humor in the scene comes from that. I happen to think that scene is still as fresh as it was back then, because it's not about marijuana, it's about something else— a relationship in which the marijuana cigarettes become the . . . the means by which we discover who these people are. And they, too, discover something about themselves. But you think, gosh, what year are we in? People who try to update *Company* make a mistake, I think. It should either be performed as a '70s piece or with no date, but not with an attempt to make it '90s or contemporary.

As a child, which came first for you in terms of passion—music or the theatre?

Oh, I guess the theatre, but it wasn't a passion, it was just fun. I was a movie buff; movies were my passion. And I took piano lessons like nice Jewish boys on the Upper West Side did, when I was six and seven years old; but, you know, it was so that my parents had something they could show off at cocktail time. I would play "The Flight of the Bumblebee" and everybody would say, "Oh, he's so gifted!" (*Laughter.*) I had a very good right hand. I still have a very good right hand, very fleet. But I stopped. Then, when I was in military school at the age of 10, they had this huge pipe organ there. That was the next time I encountered music. I wanted to press all the pink and yellow buttons and use the four manuals—it was just great. Then I lost interest in music again until I met Oscar and got interested in writing music for the theatre.

If you hadn't hooked up with Oscar Hammerstein might have you gravitated toward Hollywood or . . . ?
I don't know. What I really loved was mathematics, and I think I might have become a mathematician. In fact, I deliberately didn't take any math courses in college because it was like candy to me. I thought, if I get into math I'm going to distract myself.

You could've written *Copenhagen*.
Copenhagen!, the Musical. (*Laughter.*)

A couple of years ago, we did an interview together for the *Times* in which you were very, very gloomy about the state of the theatre and what's happened since your career began. Do you still feel as gloomy?
Well, I feel pretty gloomy about the commercial theatre, yeah. Young writers aren't getting a chance, that's all. It's simple, it's the old cry. Nobody does plays anymore, everybody does musicals and musicals and musicals and musicals; they're the badge of contemporary theatre. I'm not biting the hand that feeds me—I love musicals, but I also love plays. And plays are mostly done Off Broadway, and therefore playwrights can't, even when they're successful, make enough money to write another play. The young people who write musicals may get their work done, but they don't earn enough to support a family—so most of them end up writing for television and movies. The theatre, as you know, is a profession you learn by doing. It's a performing art. It has to be on a stage with performers, professional performers; and, in the case of musicals, not with a string trio but with an orchestra.

You've played an Oscar Hammerstein sort of role with some very talented young songwriters, the late Jonathan Larson, the author of *Rent*, and Adam Guettel, of *Floyd Collins*. I know you've been involved with the Young Playwrights Festival. You must hear from a lot of young people who want to do what you did. What do you tell them?
I tell them to just put it on anyplace. That's the only way I can think of to be encouraging to people. One good thing about the current situation is that you can get your work heard. When I grew up, there was no

such thing as Off Broadway—it was invented, I believe, in 1954. Now with Off Broadway and regional theatre, you can get your work heard a great deal. And once the work is heard, then sometimes a commercial producer will take a chance and put your work on in a commercial theatre. That has happened a number of times and continues to. I wish it happened more.

What do you think about the role of the theatre in American culture as a whole? Is it destined to be smaller in the age of television?
Yeah, I think so. The word "theatre" causes people's spines to curl—it's elitist. I'm talking, again, about the kind of theatre that is in the big cities, that affects the public in a big way. I think there will always be live theatre: people wanting to put on plays, whether they're in communities or in schools or in other places. But the business of a healthy commercial theatre, a supermarket where there you can find everything from, you know, sex farces to classic tragedies—yes, that's all over.

Two developments that began in the '80s were the growth of musicals that are sung through—rock operas, pop operas, whatever you call them—and the growth of musicals as spectacle. Sometimes they're one and the same. What did you think of those two developments?
Well, you'll notice they've disappeared. They have now been replaced by self-referential musicals in which you make fun of all other shows: *Urinetown*, *The Producers*, that's the trend now. But rock opera and spectacles? What did I think of them? I suppose there may be elements of them that will find their way back in and help inform things. But they tend to be ponderous, and I don't think they'll have any particular lasting effect by themselves. I think that one of the reasons we're getting so many of these self-referential shows now is that humor has been missing so long from the musical theatre—anything that's fun and funny is very welcome now.

Of the seven shows that are going to be part of this Washington festival, five of them you did with Hal Prince, two of them you did with James Lapine. To what extent did they influence you and how is it different to work with the two of them?
Well, first of all, Lapine is a writer as well as a director, so he and Hal are different in that way. Hal's not a writer, but he is a creator, and his vision of what a show should be extends far beyond just the visuals—although he always starts by thinking visually. He's primarily a visual man, but he's also very literate. He has opinions on storytelling that are quite often different than mine. We're working together now, with John Weidman, and together we cause the best kind of abrasive creation. That's what I think a good collaboration is; it's not two or three people thinking exactly alike but two or three people who want the same thing, yet go at it from different angles.

Hal and I grew up in the commercial theatre—we're Broadway babies. One of the joys of creating with Jim Lapine is that he comes from a different generation—he grew up in Off Broadway. Off Broadway has a different sensibility; it's a much looser way of putting on a show—although James is a meticulous writer and plots very carefully. But his approach to a show, even his approach to writing, is not necessarily traditional—for example, the notion of starting at the beginning. Sometimes he starts in the middle. Working with Lapine was startling to me because of the different approach not only to the actual writing but to the producing. James said, "Come on, I have friends at Playwrights Horizons, we'll put it on there." With Hal it was, "Okay, I think we can get the Majestic Theatre next fall, so we'll do it then." It gears your mind differently. Hal makes me bubble with vitality. The minute a meeting or a phone call or a conversation with Hal is over, I can't wait to get back to the yellow pad and the piano. Once I'm there, however . . . ? (*Laughter.*)

Correct me if I'm wrong, but it seems to me that of the great songwriters in the theatre that came before you, the two composers you seem to most admire are George Gershwin and Harold Arlen. Why?
Oh, boy, it's hard to talk about music and say specifically what you like about it. I can tell you that in both cases it's about harmonic richness. Harmony is, of the three elements of music, the one that gets me—it's not melody or rhythm, it's harmony. The way one recognizes composers—not just Gershwin, Arlen, Kern, Rodgers, Porter, but Beethoven, Brahms and Stravinsky—is by their harmonic language. And the richest and most inventive harmonies in show music, I think, are those of Gershwin and Arlen. I could wallow in *Porgy and Bess*, the chords alone. And any song by Arlen is just, you know . . . .

You once said that when you found your voice as a musical-theatre writer in *Company* in 1970, you were shocked by the hostility that it provoked.
Still am.

I know this experience. (*Laughter.*) People have said that your work is too intellectual, it's not melodic enough, it's too angry—whatever. What's that about? And what do you think are the biggest misperceptions about your work, positive as well as negative?
I think, like a good play, a good musical should be worth more than one visit. I like to write with writers who have the same interest in—I don't want to say complexity—complications, with layers still to be discovered, discovered on a second view. Most people go to musicals for the one-time experience. Generally, I find that people who have seen a show of mine that they disliked the first time may not like it any better the second time around, but they don't dislike it the same way. (*Laughter.*) I didn't mean that humorously, unfortunately. (*Laughter.*) Then of course there's the matter of "unhummability." There are two kinds of songs that are hummable: one, the song that you've heard before you go into the theatre and you're just hearing another version of; and two, a song that is reprised 64 times during the course of the evening and you can't help going out humming it. At the end of the

first act of *Night Music*, people in the lobby were humming "Weekend in the Country." Why? Because they had heard nine choruses of it in the space of six minutes (*Laughter*.)

Until about 30 years ago, people went to musicals not wanting to be anything but entertained on a very easy level. But starting in the late '60s and early '70s, we began experimenting with form, with content. Musicals were trying to encroach on territory that previously had belonged solely to plays. They started to become plays with songs, plays told through songs. That's pretty well accepted now. Audiences have come to realize that when they go to a musical, sometimes they'll get just a finger-snapping, easy kind of experience, but sometimes not. The easy ones will always be the bigger hits, but that's been true for 2,000 years. I suspect Aristophanes would have outsold Euripides, but I may be wrong.

The beginning of that, at least in my time frame, was *West Side Story*, which did try out in Washington in 1957 and was considered sufficiently shocking that I know my parents wouldn't take me to see it. I was eight, so they may have had a point. What was it like to play that in Washington in 1957?

Well, it was a shocker, but it got audiences. I mean, it sold well. It was kind of chic in Washington, but it didn't sell very well in Philadelphia, which is where we went next. People think of *West Side Story* as being this smash hit. It wasn't. When it opened on Broadway it got a very mixed reception from both the critics and the audience. On the second night—remember, this was my first Broadway show and, boy, was I pleased and proud—I thought I'd go in and stand in the back. Well, the curtain went up and there were the six Jets on stage, gang members in color-coordinated sneakers, going (*snapping fingers*) like that. (*Humming*) Da-da-da-da-dum, da-da-da-da . . . and then one of them went like that (*gestures flamboyantly*) and another went like that (*gestures again*), and this guy in the second row from the back got up, put his coat over his arm and made his way through the row, saying "Excuse me, excuse me, excuse me, excuse me, excuse me." When he saw me standing in the back looking kind of gob-smacked, he just fixed me with a baleful stare and muttered, "Don't ask." (*Laughter*.) That's when I knew we were not going to have a smash hit.

West Side Story ran less than two years, with the last six months on "twofers" in New York. Then it went on the road and came back for another six months. I think the total number of performances was something like 719. It made its money back, but that's partly because the cast were all under 25 and they didn't get very big salaries. (*Laughter*.) The only Tony Award it got was for choreography. It lost everything to *The Music Man*—and there's a perfect example. *The Music Man* has a lot of original stuff in it, but it doesn't exactly threaten an audience. I'm not putting it down—the opening number of *Music Man* is about as original a song as I've ever heard in the theatre.

Speaking of *The Music Man*, it had a great star performance in it. *West Side Story* was an ensemble piece. Is the day of the big star in the Broadway musical over?

Yes, because stars are not created any more. They don't stand a chance. There are lots of talented performers around, but not enough musicals are being done for them to get a chance to be seen. Some of those talented people are going to be down here over the next few months—people like Raúl Esparza and Melissa Errico and John Barrowman, not to mention established people like Christine Baranski and Brian Stokes Mitchell and Lynn Redgrave, just to name the ones who'll appear first. How many chances do they get to do musicals? The Mary Martins, the Ethel Mermans, were created by doing dozens of shows. I don't know who the last star created on Broadway is—maybe Bernadette [Peters]. I mean, a star in the sense of someone who sells tickets.

What is your role in these productions that are coming to the festival in Washington?
Oh, what I'm doing in each case is primarily making the cast feel good. (*Laughter.*) Somebody's got to tell them they're good before the audience does. And general checking-up. I'll come down for run-throughs and check things like tempo and interpretation, and help any of the performers who are having difficulty—not necessarily with the singing but, say, blending the song in with the scene. Or telling them what I intended. It's important to tell performers what you intend and let them take off from there. In short, I'll come down when I can be useful and when the director tells me that I can be useful.

We'll take a few pre-written questions from the audience. Prepare yourself for a little shift in tone. (*Reads question.*) If you could have someone's head on a platter, who would it be?
The temptation is to say, 20 years ago it was . . . (*gestures to Frank Rich; laughter*). But I won't—it wouldn't have been true, anyway. Actually, in my old age I've mellowed. I'm afraid the answer is: Nobody at the moment.

Many new musicals are based on movies these days—even your *Passion* had a movie as a source of inspiration. If you were to create a new musical based on a film, which film would you choose?
I think *Groundhog Day* would make a really good musical. Now somebody will do it and I'll be sorry I said it, although I suspect I'm not the first person to have thought of it. It's a wonderful movie, and it's a wonderful idea for theme and variations, which is a kind of musical I want to do. That's a theme-and-variations story.

Leonard Bernstein said that every composer steals from others. Are there any lifts that you would like to cop to?
Well, not specific lifts. I don't know of any conscious melodic lifts, but there are harmonic lifts all the time. I constantly use chord progressions from Ravel and Rachmaninoff, although I can only think of one specific one: The opening chord of "Liaisons" in *A Little Night Music* is the opening chord of "Valses Nobles et Sentimentales," which is one of my favorite pieces. I remember thinking, "Oh god, I've got to use

that chord, nobody has ever used that chord except Ravel, I've got to do it." (*Laughter.*)

Can you comment on the decision to postpone the New York revival of *Assassins* after Sept. 11?
The day after, John Weidman and I spoke and agreed that this is not the time now. We were about to go into rehearsal one week later, but we felt this was just not a time when an audience could hear what we have to say—not just because of the wave of patriotism, but because of the fact that *Assassins* raises some questions about the purpose of this country and what people expect from it. A number of the characters—a number of the assassins—anticipate something that the country seems to promise them, etc., etc. Well, that just wasn't a time to bring such things up. I don't think an audience would hear it. I wouldn't want to hear it. Six months later, the situation had changed. And if all goes well, we'll be doing *Assassins* next year at the Roundabout Theatre.

Here is a really terrific final question from a member of the audience: What do you still want to accomplish?
Gee, I wish I had a dramatic answer. The fact is, I really like writing shows. It gets harder as time goes on. I thought I'd get more confident. And you'd think something like this Washington celebration would make me more confident—but it doesn't. I think the more you write, the more you realize how much you don't know. You get a view of yourself and your weaknesses, the dangers of things like repetition, the feeling that you've written it all before. Those things make it harder to write. But, in a way, that also makes me want to write more, because I want to overcome it. And, to put it sentimentally, there are just so many wonderful stories to tell, and I really would like to find some that would lend themselves to music that I haven't heard before.

Frank Rich has been an op-ed columnist for the *New York Times* since 1994; before that, he spent 13 years as the *Times*'s chief drama critic. His criticism has been published in a volume titled *Hot Seat*. He is also the author of *Ghost Light: A Memoir* and *The Greatest Story Ever Sold: The Decline and Fall of Truth in Bush's America*, and the co-author (with Lisa Aronson) of *The Theatre Art of Boris Aronson*.

ADAM GUETTEL FACES THE MUSIC

An interview by David Savran

January 2004

An innocent young American woman and her wealthy, protective mother spend a glorious summer in Florence, seduced by Renaissance art, the Tuscan sun and the *ragazzi*. A handsome stranger sweeps the daughter off her feet and she savors her first, sweet taste of love. Her mother's fears, meanwhile, about calculating, manipulative Italian men—it is 1958, after all—prove unfounded. Despite an unlucky misunderstanding (followed by a timely reconciliation), daughter and boyfriend at long last tie the knot in a *matrimonio splendido*.

Although this sketch makes it sound like little more than a fairy tale, the new musical *The Light in the Piazza* is in fact the product of two of the most uncompromising talents in the American theatre today, composer/lyricist Adam Guettel and playwright Craig Lucas. While the pair describe the piece as an old-fashioned musical, it is old-fashioned with a difference—neither writer is noted for romantic clichés, uncomplicated characters or cockeyed optimism. Their musical adaptation of Elizabeth Spencer's celebrated short novel (also the basis for a forgettable 1962 Hollywood film featuring Olivia de Havilland as the mother) uses the fairy-tale plot to focus on the deeply ambivalent emotions aroused in Margaret when her daughter, Clara, falls rapturously in love with the dashing Fabrizio. For the secret that Margaret keeps inside is the knowledge that her vivacious, 26-year-old daughter's mental development was in fact halted by an accident at age 12. So in dealing with Clara's all-consuming passion, Margaret must also confront her own personal disappointments, anxieties and guilt. Because Guettel and Lucas dramatize the emotional and moral complexities of this story with startling richness and subtlety, even the happy ending remains slightly off-kilter, posing as many questions as it answers.

After a critically acclaimed run last summer at the Intiman Theatre in Seattle, this groundbreaking musical opens at the Goodman Theatre in Chicago this month, directed by Bartlett Sher.

Guettel and Lucas have been working on *The Light in the Piazza* for more than three years, and their perfectionism shows. As a play-wright, Lucas is known as a restless experimenter whose richly tex-tured and evocative plays range from the mysteriously ironic comedy of *Reckless* to the wrenching tragedy of *The Dying Gaul*. But this is his first book musical. He notes that one of the main challenges for him has been to take "what is essentially an interior monologue" and find the dramatic means to convey both the story's psychological intricacies and its large-scale, almost cinematic scenes of Florentine life. He has solved these problems by "consciously seizing and capitalizing on the dramatic action," both of the piece itself and of each character, and "condensing them to their essential gestures." This economical and precise mode of storytelling dovetails with Guettel's radiant, chamber music–like score that combines the lush harmonic world of Fauré, Debussy and Ravel with an Italianate lyricism.

Although Craig Lucas used to perform in musicals (including *Sweeney Todd* on Broadway), Adam Guettel has a longer and more com-plicated involvement with musical theatre. From the time he was a toddler, he was lucky enough to be taken to see the musicals of his mother, Mary Rodgers, and his grandfather, Richard Rodgers, begin-ning with a revival of *Oklahoma! The Light in the Piazza* represents only his fourth professionally produced, full-length work, after three col-laborations with director Tina Landau, including *Floyd Collins* and *Saturn Returns*. A trained musician (like his grandfather) with an inspired musical and theatrical imagination, Guettel represents per-haps the most accomplished of a new generation of musical theatre writers who are building on the innovations of Stephen Sondheim and bringing the sophistication of opera to the most distinctive, misunder-stood and maligned of American theatre forms.

While it is always risky to generalize about the work of a develop-ing artist, Adam Guettel's musicals are distinguished in part by his sub-tle and knowing manipulation of the conventions of musical theatre. This is coupled with an almost uncanny ability to penetrate characters psychologically and dramatize both their intensely personal struggles and the social circumstances swirling about them. *Floyd Collins*, for example, based on a true story from 1925, focuses both on the plight of the title character, a "caver" trapped in a cave that 15 days later becomes his grave, and on the media circus that his confinement unleashes. But even more important is Guettel's ability to turn a form that has always depended on wish fulfillment into an examination of what happens when you are granted what you wish for. *Floyd Collins* is, above all, a tragedy of American entrepreneurship. Floyd finds what he's looking for—the perfect cave, media attention, fame and fortune—yet he is destroyed by it. The very myth of success, which the musical theatre has so often extolled, is revealed to be a hollow, self-defeating promise. Moving back and forth between the cave and the world beyond, between fantasy and reality, between hope and despair, Guettel's music and lyrics render Floyd's aspirations and dreams—as well as his terrify-ing predicament—with a hushed yet exhilarating intensity.

I talked with Adam Guettel in his New York City loft on Oct. 21, 2003.

What got you interested in theatre?

I saw *Oklahoma!* when I was two and I still remember some glints of light from that production. I think it was a Lincoln Center revival. It was incredible—I kept asking my mother, "When is it going to be over?" And finally she hauled me off and said, "You don't like this?" "No," I said, "I love it, I don't want it to be over." I had a visceral reaction to the experience of live musical theatre.

But my household growing up was not by any means alive with music—unless my mother was writing, in which case there was not to be any noise except her piano. We didn't listen to my grandfather's music or to Steve [Sondheim]'s music. We didn't listen to music because it was too distracting for Mom. But we went to see a lot of theatre, and I remember going to the first productions of *Follies*, *Company* and *A Little Night Music* and really loving them, even when I was five, six, seven years old. I think you know what good music is when you're really young.

But then as I entered my teen years I really didn't want to have anything to do with this field, for obvious reasons. The last thing I wanted was, a) to try to follow my grandfather's footsteps or, b) to be a part of what was—as was increasingly apparent—marginalized culturally. The more theatre I saw, the less "good" theatre was becoming. And so my ego kind of took over and I thought, "Well, I'm going to make my own world here, and I'm not going to have anything to do with that lame, fairy-tale, unsophisticated, boring, clunky old art form." And that's how I felt for a long time—pretty much until my late twenties.

What theatre did you see—so-called straight theatre?

Not much, actually. Read a bunch of plays in high school. But I didn't see many. So that wasn't a big part of my education. I came to straight theatre through the written word, really.

What about at Yale?

Then I started to read more and see more—Caryl Churchill's work, for instance. But I was also new to Miller and Albee and Ionesco and all that stuff. I don't know—I don't feel my dramatic impulses come from that world but from a more compressed, less prosaic form: musical theatre.

Compressed?

A song usually occurs at the dramatic apex of a scene. Or the song takes care of that which is most dramatically compressible and most readily made into metaphor. That discipline seems to be more a part of the practical implementation of musical theatre. When you're dealing with songs, which are by nature compressed, you have to find lyrics that are equally compressed and carry metaphor and have—as Johnny Mercer used to say—a bicycle. That is, you have an idea that generates the song, usually a metaphor, something that has compressed energy that can spring outwards. That's something I want to continue to learn how to do. In a way, it's unnatural—and, in a way, it's part of everyday living. We extrapolate from mundane details outwards to the metaphoric and the universal.

How did you get back into musical theatre?
At Yale I wrote some songs and I did a one-act opera based on a Dr. Seuss book, called *The Butter Battle Book*, which I never got the rights to, so it sits over there in a drawer. Orchestrated. But I still wasn't sure. I was playing upright bass a lot. I was singing.

What's your primary instrument?
I suppose my voice. I'm not really much of an instrumentalist, but I play a lot of things not very well—guitar and piano.

I read that you played rock-and-roll for a while.
I was in a bunch of bands throughout my teens and early twenties. I went through a phase of thinking I could somehow cross from the life with which I am blessed into an art form based on defiance. But those were not the cards I was dealt. I was dealt lovely, luxurious, moneyed, educated, elitist cards and I felt insincere in trying to put on airs. I'd rather fantasize and make things up from my experience. Which is not to say I plan to write *Brideshead Revisited: The Musical* or anything. Also, I didn't pursue rock because I felt I wanted to say more than, "I wanna get laid," "I get laid a lot," "I'm not getting laid right now," "I wanna get laid with you."

Although there are other conventions in rock.
Absolutely. But the form itself didn't feel right for me. Theatre songs, for the most part, need to go from one emotional state to another. And pop songs need to be a really engaging, catchy examination of one state. But I'm wired to want to morph within the form.

This brings up something I find distinctive about your song structures. They are always focused on what's called the release. As you know, this contrasting section is sometimes labeled the bridge. But to describe your work, the word release seems particularly apt. Virtually all of your songs are structured around a release, sometimes several releases. Many do not use traditional A-A-B-A form. The release makes the song into a dramatic structure.
Tension and release—that's the basic dynamic of listening to music. I suppose the core guide for me in writing is to make sure I pay people back for all the loans they've made me over the course of the song. They say that you get 10 minutes for free at the top of a show in terms of audience engagement. I think that's true of a song. They're willing to listen as you start to establish your vocabulary. But if you don't begin to use those words syntactically to make sentences they can identify, you're asking too much.

You're taking them on a journey. That's what song structure does.

And A-A-B-A is just a slight twist on sonata form, and we all have these basic physical needs as listeners. If you don't establish your enharmonic home—this is how I put things together—then you don't create a value system and the subliminal emotional communication between you and your audience. How can you establish tension if there is no return to comfort and consonance? As you work with an "A" section and you screw down all the bolts and make sure it hangs together right, there's internal pressure that builds and you really do need out of there. That's a musical experience. I'm not sure what a lyricist goes through when he or she puts pen to paper, because I always write lyrics second. But it seems that there isn't the same build of visceral pressure. There's a necessity to create a different feeling in this "B" section. I'm not sure. I know that my worst lyrics have been written first.

I hear both your individual songs and your plays as being more harmonically driven than melodically or rhythmically. Or lyrically, for that matter.

I think that's fair.

You write great tunes—any good songwriter has to. But you have a very distinctive harmonic signature. And your vocabulary is simply more chromatic than those of your contemporaries—or Sondheim's, for that matter.

I start to find the language for a song, the harmonic ambience, the words that are going to become sentences—because chords feel like words to me, like parts of a thesis statement. And chords have syntax, and there's a developing process wherein (to mix metaphors) chromaticism is the ligament. It ensures that things stay cohesive. If you use harmonies that are heard a lot, you're not making your own emotional/harmonic syntax or stirring emotional heat—you're provoking associations and recollections and nostalgia. And because people tend not to know chromatic harmonies, I end up heading in that direction.

What's your process of writing?

I usually start with music, a few notes of a melody or a vamp. For instance, in the song "Fable" [in *Piazza*] there's a kind of 6/8 vamp that establishes the emotional context, the ambience of the song. And the melody came out of that ambience. It wasn't that the harmony dictated the melody. It said: This is the world this song is going to live in. And then you apply simple music-writing principles, like contrary motion. I was a terrible student in music theory, but I adhere pretty closely to those principles because I think there are certain physical needs to keep things together and strong.

What you're describing I hear as a productive, live tension in your work between melody and harmony, which, I think, makes for unusually complex and contrapuntal theatre, both musically and dramatically.

I think that's one of the reasons why my stuff tends to be difficult on first hearing. But it's the kind of thing you go back to because you know that the counterpoint and the melody are referencing each other.

I think it's also something that increases the velocity of the experience, even though the tempo may be slow. There's a kind of accrued momentum that you get from the material, elegantly dovetailing and proceeding forward in a contrapuntal way. It's about deepening the engagement of the listener. That's what momentum is. It's not about increasing the tempo. It's about going further in.

At what point do the words come?

When my collaborator says, "If you don't finish that fucking lyric, I'm never going to talk to you again." That's when they come in. Lyric writing is really rewarding and really, really grueling to do. There are a few exceptions. A couple of songs in each score just kind of come to you, and you feel like you were just given a pass. The language of music is infinite, and you can say, "I love you" or "I want you" in music in a zillion ways. But in any spoken language, most of the really good ways have already been done. So it's about finding a broader language in which you place a phrase like "I love you" that inflects it in a way that makes it feel fresh. Avoiding saying "I love you" can be very time-consuming and sometimes impossible.

What classical music has been important to you?

Do you see that multicolored record set? That's the complete Stravinsky. That was my high school graduation present. It's absolutely worn out. I adore him. I think *Rake's Progress* is one of the three best operas of the past century. He redefined recitative and orchestration for opera. And Britten. Those are my contemporary faves. And Barber would probably come in there somewhere. Then we're getting into a kind of mushy Elgar, Korngold territory. I'm a sucker for that, for sure. Ravel was a steady diet for a couple of years. Then I got into a really intense early music period: Gesualdo and Josquin Des Pres and Adam de la Halle. I listened mostly for monody and a sense of line and the exquisite message coded in a single line.

In preparing *Floyd Collins*, some of the greatest material I listened to were Folkways recordings of toothless old ladies from the Civil War. You know, (*sings:*) "Came to this country in 1864 . . . ." It's like you can tell they have exactly one tooth. And in that one line is this beautiful melody—such a world. Just to go to the fourth degree, by harmonic implication, is to have a sea-change emotionally. And all that is encoded in the single line. The more notes you put on the keyboard, the more you tend to water that stuff down. I think counterpoint helps one move away from vertical construction toward horizontal construction. Because vertical tends to make us think, "It has to be more moving, so I'll just add more notes to this big pile I have on the first beat of the measure." But it's getting to that note that makes the note valuable, not just plunking it down.

What about Aaron Copland? That classic American sound?

He was one of the best theatre writers in the classical music business. Even in his non-dance scores, he—like John Adams—understands dramatic frames. He's so lucid and transparent dramatically. And he doesn't feed you too much at once. I haven't listened to nearly as much Copland as Stravinsky because I realized that every movie score I'd heard in 30 years had been copying his thing, even though his was the best version. And I wanted to be around stuff I hadn't heard. Not that Stravinsky hasn't had an incredible influence. But in terms of pop culture—Copland you can get in a Wal-Mart commercial. Yet he's very painterly and powerful.

Unlike earlier generations of musical theatre composers—and I include Sondheim among them—your generation of writers is choosing to work with innovative and risk-taking collaborators like Tina Landau and Craig Lucas. Colleagues of yours are working with George Wolfe, Tony Kushner and other major playwrights. Have you thought about this change?
I would not want to be in this field if I had to do it all myself. I would love to open my life up even more to collaborators. It seemed that in the so-called Golden Age of the theatre, everybody collaborated and there was a healthy, self-perpetuating group of people working in the theatre because it was the dominant popular art form. Now they all go to Hollywood, because that's the dominant thing, and I don't blame them. So there are not too many people to work with. If I was thriving in pop culture, I don't know that I would want to devote myself to writing for the theatre. There is a real dearth of book writers, lyricists especially, and a lamentable surplus of composers. (*Laughs.*)

My boyfriend described the work you and your contemporaries make as boutique musicals, for a very different kind of audience.
That is at once the most lethal and accurate criticism that gets leveled at me. And I have no rebuttal. I think it's true that there is not currently a nexus between a mass audience and the way I approach what I think to be universal ideas and experiences. But I don't think that's likely always to be the case. It just may be a question of having missed the bus and needing to wait for the next one. You know, it would be really great if I was able to do something that was both new and appealing on a massive scale.

To some extent, isn't that what you're trying to do with *Piazza*?
That's not the goal. I would say it's more appealing to a broader audience. But you heard the score. There's plenty in there that people will say is, well, elitist. For classical music nerds. Solipsistic. Not easily metabolized.

But these are the same charges that have been leveled against Sondheim and virtually all of your contemporaries.
Right. And one of the great sources of inspiration for me in Steve's work is that it continues to be done all over, all the time, people going back to it, plumbing it for more, and getting more, and seeing more, and hearing more in it—because there is so much in it. That's why you don't get it right away. I don't want to bore your readers, but I want to

make the point that I do not ever—and never would—assign blame or responsibility for the cultural obscurity of what I do to anyone but myself.

For the past few decades, most theatre in America has been marginalized to the extreme.
I hope I can figure out how to do something really original and genuine and legitimate that's also wildly successful. I haven't done that yet. I wouldn't ask any close friends to put money on that happening with *Piazza*, although I'm very proud of it.

Although until the 1960s musicals were a part of popular culture.
If you do some quick math and you add the movie of *Chicago* to *Moulin Rouge* and you add in Rufus Wainwright—whose work has a certain theatrical quality—and you subtract *Umbrellas of Cherbourg* from the equation because most people have forgotten about that, and you put it over the quadratic formula, which is *The Sound of Music*, *The King and I* and all those movie musicals, and then you divide the whole thing by *Rent*—you might get a quantity that is workable.

How did you work with Craig on *Piazza*?
When I got together with Craig the first time, I played him six or seven songs from the score. At the time I think there were only lyrics for one. Then I explained where I thought the songs would belong—or for what situation those songs had been written—and for the most part that stayed the case, although some of the songs have moved around. Beyond that, we would sit in a room and figure out what each song needed to say, and who was likely to be involved, and how long it should be, and what the feeling might be, and all that normal stuff. And then I would take 19 years to write it. When you're in this field and you want to work with collaborators, finding one who's really good is the equivalent of getting a kidney transplant. If you don't have working kidneys, it makes life very, very difficult. And if you don't have a good collaborator, it's just impossible to imagine life—if this is what you want to do. So I just feel that Craig is that much of a treasure to me.

So the two of you finish the architectural work before you compose a new song.
Yes, and I do a lot of that anyway in terms of tone and feeling. Just as a song has its own emotional ambience, established by harmony, the score has its own broader harmonic palette. That gets established usually in the first three or four songs. And then I'm able sometimes to stray as a way of foiling expectations. As long as I have that beachhead.

I want to get back to the question of song form, because I've noticed that your work is so consistently about release, transcendence. In *Myths and Hymns*, "Saturn Returns" is all about flight. In one of the pivotal moments in *Floyd Collins*, "The Riddle Song" that ends the first act, Floyd and Homer sing about their swing tree—all that upward movement. Then there's the obverse fantasy of falling into the pit, the grave. Your work is so much about vertical movement.

Of course there are many different ways of thinking about that. One word you use is spirituality. I prefer to think of those moments as utopian figurations.

On a practical musical level, some of this may come from the fact that I always have had a high voice. So before I knew more complicated ways, more sophisticated ways, I knew I could achieve certain musical or dramatic goals simply by having a singer sing higher. So that aspiration has been a constant and a source of problems, because not all singers have the range I have. It makes it very difficult to transpose a song when the range is greater than an octave and a third or an octave and a fifth. And I regularly did that. But on *Piazza*, some of the songs are only an octave in range, and that's been a kind of personal goal for me. My first attempts at creating drama in music were just to go up.

Also, on a personal level, there's just this thing for me of not being particularly comfortable here on earth—and I don't say that ruefully. I think it's given me the energy to do the work that I've needed to do. But this is not, like, home for me. I love my life, I really like it here. I don't think that my work will always go in that escapist direction. Then again, how much art is about scrubbing potatoes? I don't feel particularly original or unique in this. It just happens to be true of me.

It's like one time I was outside late at night with my brother, out in the countryside. And I saw colored lights getting larger and coming toward us. I started jumping up and down, saying, "We're here, come get us! Take us away!" I've always had this great desire to be abducted. I'd be abducted right now if I could be. "Take us away! We're here!" There was a long pause and then my brother said, "Leave me." Because he likes it here. He's cool with that. I feel very comfortable with the idea of somewhere else. That's why I like drugs and alcohol, which is a kind of weakness. The reality is that I'm here. I do the best I can with this. I'm not particularly proud of this.

This figuration—which I read as utopian—is one reason why I respond so to your work. But I was also thinking about the fact that historically, musical theatre has functioned to provide a way of imagining the unimaginable. It goes all the way back to *Show Boat*, and before.

And that's where effective harmony is essential. If you can't create the musical and emotional legitimacy of that other place that you go to when you're watching a show—if that landscape is not actually created, so that you can really live there for two hours—then there is no escape. There might be an escape through a satire of musical theatre itself, or through ego-bolstering, in the sense of, "Oh, I'm not like that." And that's perfectly okay—it's just a different kind of escape. But making another world where you can live for two hours is what I aspire to do with my life.

How does that work with *Piazza*?

The world of *Piazza* is that real—but totally invented—world that is summoned by true romantic love. That first bloom of romantic love is a kind of overwhelmingly real reality that's unlike anything you get when you're actually living. And I'm trying to invoke, if not evoke, that with the sound of the score. The other point I try to make with the score is that the sound of having that and the sound of losing that are the same. The feeling within one's stomach and heart of having it and the feeling—the actual physical feeling of losing it—are the same. It's just contextualized differently.

So the moment of discovery is always shadowed by loss, or the fear of loss. I hate to get Freudian about it, but Freud writes that finding something means in fact re-finding it.
It's the sweetness of remembering something that you've always known, and that's what it is to meet someone you've always hoped to meet. And to lose them, as you always knew you would, somehow. That's the sound I'm going for in the score.

What draws you to a story? What attracted you to *Light in the Piazza*?
I think it's that I suspect, or I know, there's a chance that I'll never find romantic love in the way that I hope to, and I knew that I had the sounds available to represent that desire. And that equals a tremendous amount of energy, which is necessary for me because I'm a lazy, trust-fund dilettante and unless I feel that level of personal energy, unless I have that investment . . . it's usually rooted in a kind of sadness.

In *Myths and Hymns*, "Icarus" is about the anxiety of influence, the challenge of having to answer to celebrated forebears. The path you've made for yourself is very different from that of your grandfather or your mother.
This may sound cavalier, but the easy part has been being my own person musically. To carve out, to etch one's own profile, musically, lyrically, dramatically is the only way to go, and if you can't do that, just give it up. That's the easy part. I think I do know who I am in these respects, but it is difficult to feel legitimate in society when you're not actually creating jobs and generating lots and lots of dough. It's hard not to feel those pressures and not to feel sort of pathetic. It's bad for the work to have these pressures if you happen to have carved out a profile that is not particularly commercial.

The other anguishing thing is to know—to feel and know—how much is inside, and how much you could be putting into the world that would give people some small amount of happiness, but that you can't let out for spiritual arrogance, for fear, and the worry of not meeting expectations. I'm over-porous to all that stuff. . . . Three or four times, after a period of high exposure and accolade, I have had a period of anguishing paralysis and fear. And only by feeling forgotten do I find myself again and start to really focus and work. I have to feel the underdog to get anything done. It's that coming through the back door.

It needs to be a struggle.
Yes. And one doesn't think of art as something produced by the House of Windsor, which is what, in the musical theatre, this family is thought of as being. I think it's lessening as Rodgers and Hammerstein

recede into history and kind of start to get the status of Gilbert and Sullivan. The fact is, I struggle with that every day.

Dare I ask, what are your favorite Richard Rodgers songs? Could you answer?
I don't think I can. I often say "Glad to Be Unhappy," and that's become kind of a pat answer for me. But I do love that song. It's difficult, because I appreciate Richard Rodgers's work in its totality rather than for its individual parts.

What about other composers and lyricists of the Golden Age?
In terms of encoding a certain line of music, making highly sophisticated melody, a very condensed message: Jule Styne and Frank Loesser. Bernstein, not a tunesmith, for my money, but a fabulous theatre composer. You said the Golden Age?

For me the Golden Age begins in the '20s.
Right. Kern. And Gershwin. Arlen was like a lush decorator. His music makes you want to have a drink and hors d'oeuvres. It's a lifestyle. But silver in your pocket? I'll go with Gershwin any day. "Don't be a naughty baby / Come to papa—come to papa—do!" The world is inside that. Yeah, the harmonies are implied, but that guy really knew how to parse it out slow and lead you through it. He was heartbreakingly good.

What about Porter?
I think his songs are like wonderful machines, with an emotional wetness I don't really get too well. But they're so beautifully constructed. They're like Longines watches. Repeater mechanisms. Chimes and cuckoos. I love Porter, and one of the reasons Porter sometimes replaces my grandfather on the shortlist is because he so much more fully embodies that time and that place, politically, socially. He's like a Carr's water cracker, whereas I think my grandfather's social aspirations were greater, and the music reflects that. Gershwin was, by the way, the only person my grandfather was ever really jealous of. My mother has spoken about that.

You're co-orchestrating *Piazza*, using a small ensemble?
Yeah. That's been fun. Piano, cello, violin, harp and upright bass. We were thinking about adding percussion for Chicago, but we decided to keep it the way it is, and if we are lucky enough to take it somewhere else, we might expand it. We'll see. There should be one version of the score that's producible cheaply. Eight people on stage, five people in the pit, no conductor, thank you very much. Because of the material, it's probably not going to be some type of mainstream thing. Who knows? So we better make damn sure it's producible in small places.

As has been the case with *Floyd Collins*.
Right. And that taught me the lesson. Your work can have a life. It doesn't need to be at the Winter Garden. When I go see shows by my

contemporaries like *Urinetown* or *Avenue Q*—and they're not even my contemporaries, they're younger—I just pray that I can have a show in a Broadway house someday.

David Savran is a specialist in American theatre, popular culture and social theory. Among his books are two volumes of interviews with playwrights, *In Their Own Words* and *The Playwright's Voice*, both published by TCG, and the forthcoming *Highbrow/Lowdown: Theater, Jazz, and the Making of the New Middle Class* from University of Michigan Press. He is professor of theatre at the Graduate Center of the City University of New York and editor of the *Journal of American Drama and Theatre*.

THE EVOLUTION OF JOHN PATRICK SHANLEY

An interview by Robert Coe

November 2004

John Patrick Shanley's Bronx characters don't sidle up and ask—they demand to be seen and heard. Saying exactly what they feel, almost without appearing to think about it, they're posturing and naked at once, far-fetched, mercurial and profane, and they effortlessly own the stage. This fall theatre season in New York is offering a major revival of Shanley's electrifying first drama, *Danny and the Deep Blue Sea*, a 1984 two-hander "dedicated to everyone in the Bronx who punched me or kissed me, and to everyone whom I punched or kissed"—by a man inducted this past summer into the Bronx Walk of Fame. The play opened at Second Stage on Oct. 21. Five days later, New York audiences began catching up to Shanley's present work at the Public Theater's Shiva Theater, where the LAByrinth Theater Company is presenting the world-premiere production of one of the playwright's most radical stylistic experiments to date: *Sailor's Song*, a love story with dancing (to waltzes by Johann Strauss), set in an imagined seaside town, about a cynical man and a true believer battling over two beautiful women and the nature of love.

A second new play will open on Nov. 22 at Manhattan Theatre Club's New York City Center Stage I, and will play this spring at California's Pasadena Playhouse: *Doubt*, a drama set in the 1960s at a Bronx Catholic School—the story of a stern principal, Sister Aloysius (Cherry Jones), who grows suspicious of a priest who seems to be taking too much interest in a young male student. Night and day from the animal vitality of *Danny*, *Doubt* unfolds in a spirit of poetic restraint and deep seriousness, and it reads as Shanley's most powerful play in years.

This would seem an ideal moment to reconsider the career of an off-center playwright frequently viewed as an eccentric, vulgar provisioner for scenery-chewing actors, but who is in fact a deeply ambitious artist working through primal themes, in a language that people actually use and a voice as recognizable as David Mamet's (although less easily caricatured). An overview of his work reveals a more substantial, shapelier body than this reader had previously imagined, as well as an integrity and steadily deepening gravitas suited to a writer now nearing 54 and living comfortably in Brooklyn Heights, with a leafy school ground for a backyard, since 2000.

Formerly married, now divorced and co-parenting 12-year-olds Nick and Frank, and after two decades toiling with mixed success and failure in the killing fields of Hollywood, Shanley has settled into a solid maturity that, as he once told a journalist, leaves behind the "electric leaps" of youth in favor of "a more considered attempt to converse and discover connection."

It was slightly over 20 years ago that *Danny* burst onto the American theatre scene with two vivid characters, described by the author as "violent and battered, inarticulate and yearning to speak, dangerous and vulnerable," locked in mortal combat, longing and, eventually, a kind of love. From the beginning Shanley exhibited a seemingly effortless mastery of the rhythms of hostility and longing, along with a natural gift for instilling tremendous spiritual ambition in his characters— a willingness to leap, to let go, far more often than to hesitate and cling. Whether in doubt or rapture, Shanley's characters are unafraid of speaking in banalities or in wild poetic flight—or, when they *are* afraid of something, then the playwright confronts those fears head-on. (Courage and determination are subjects that Shanley has revisited throughout his career.)

Each of the Bronx plays that followed *Danny* would be about people wanting either IN or OUT—another way of saying that these plays are about dramatic change and a challenge to imposed definitions and boundaries, especially the ones between the Bronx/Manhattan and victimhood/liberation. Shanley's characters seek transcendence, connection and new identities, via more than words alone: They touch, sweat, spit and spray every available bodily fluid in that alternately claustrophobic and explosive atmosphere that has characterized most of the canonical mainstream of 20th-century American drama.

Shanley worked outside this atmosphere as well. *Welcome to the Moon . . . and Other Plays*, which ran in the fall of 1982 at New York's Ensemble Studio Theatre, introduced a strain of surrealistic experimentation that established Shanley's parallel career as a radical stage formalist, not unlike that of another hard-living, essentially naturalistic Irish-American writer, Eugene O'Neill.

Shanley remained in his imagined Bronx and delivered further on his promise with *Savage in Limbo* (1985), "dedicated to all those good assassins who contributed to the death of my former self." Working with multiple characters this time, Shanley stood closest to his eponymous heroine, the pained and caustic Denise Savage: "We're on the cliff. We were born here. Well, do you wanna die on the cliff?" *Savage* was in part about the animals lurking inside human beings, just as *Danny* was, but with a caveat offered by Denise's friend in boyfriend trouble, Linda Rotunda: "It ain't the new clothes that make the man. It's what he does with his dirty things." The project of self-discovery becomes one of finding determination within the grope and flailing of tongues. As the aptly named bartender Murk opines: "The problem with people is they think they're alone. They think what they say don't do nothing. So they say every stupid thing that goes through their gourd, and they do shit they don't even know why. Which leads to what? The world looks like homemade refried shit."

Shanley could not keep working forever in this tortured Italian-American ghetto. *Women of Manhattan* (1986)—this time the inevitable and telling dedication was "to women, women, women . . . [written 23 more times] and a guy named Larry Sigman [a dying friend, now deceased]"—headed down to a lower borough, away from working-class, ethnic concerns, to address the issue and substance of self-esteem, a screaming lack in all Shanley's earlier characters. *Women of Manhattan* moved through the animal appetites to search for grown-up identities. I have probably undervalued the verbal intelligence and wit on display in these early writings, but this play, while beautifully written and complete, feels a little weightless.

Shanley wasn't through with the Bronx: His 1985 fantasia, *the dreamer examines his pillow*, dedicated, simply enough, "to my family," introduced family members for the first time—a daughter, Donna, who is unable to live with her lover, Tommy, or without him (especially after she discovers he's sleeping with her 16-year-old sister). Like *Women of Manhattan*, *the dreamer* pursues questions of identity, as opposed to merely coping or desperately surviving: "You are somebody, " Donna tells Tommy. "Tell me who . . . . You know what it is down there inside the last Chinese box?" Dealing with their pie-in-the-sky romantic dreams, she realizes they will always find themselves "back down in this shithole room or some other shithole room, and I can't feature that no more." *The dreamer* is a dark attempt to chart the intellectual/emotional terrain of Shanley's imagination, leading to an ambiguous recognition that in sex we can discover identity, and escape it.

Shanley's best work simultaneously imagines and exposes the failure of "the key that lets me outta my life," as Donna puts it. Self-knowledge is far more difficult to obtain than simply escaping the past or some shithole room. In the end, *the dreamer* reaches for a deeper question: Why live at all? A didactic element entered Shanley's work for the first time: "You gotta make the big mistakes," says Donna's dad. "Remember that. It makes it easier to bear. But remember, too, that Sex does resurrect. Flyin in the face of the truly great mistakes, there is that consolation."

Shanley's constant implicit theme—the marriage of two people—became comically overt in his popular *Italian American Reconciliation* (1988), the first of his plays the author directed, with a cast including John Turturro (the original Danny), John Pankow, Laura San Giacomo and Shanley's then wife, Jayne Haynes, at Manhattan Theatre Club. *Reconciliation* had a simple, outrageous plot involving an inappropriate seduction (the commedia aspect of which was inescapable), a hilarious momentum, and an almost maudlin denouement reached when Aldo (Turturro) announces: "And this is the lesson I have to teach: The greatest, the only success, is to be able to love."

The years 1982 to 1988 were ones of extraordinary creativity for the former juvenile delinquent and NYU grad. By the time of *The Big Funk* (1990), he was arguing for the interconnectedness of everything. But an undercurrent had entered his work that was not so empathic. Shanley prefaced the published version: "And so I ask the question: Why is theatre so ineffectual, un-new, not exciting, fussy, not connected to the thrilling recognition possible in dreams? It's a question of spirit. My ungainly spirit thrashes around inside me, making me feel lumpy and sick."

The Big Funk was formally adventurous, employing nudity and direct address of the audience, while also reminding us of the Greeks by essentially being about a dinner party—a Symposium. But it also removed all recognizable contexts of time and place—as if the playwright wanted to address the interconnectedness of everything at the expense of its specificity. From this turning point, Shanley wheeled back to a theatrical beginning he never actually had and wrote a nakedly autobiographical family play: *Beggars in the House of Plenty* (1991), about how some siblings make it and others don't. *Beggars* is arguably his most successful work employing surrealistic elements, while also breaking from his usual intense dramatic focus to explore a more studied irony. Out of the cauldron into what fire? (The old Shanley did periodically surface, as his stand-in "Johnny" intoned: "I look like the Bronx inside. I could vomit up a burning car.")

Inevitably, Shanley stepped back from his investigation of an increasingly distant past: *Four Dogs and a Bone* (1993) was his first play not driven by insatiable personal demons. Instead, it used bitter, excoriating comedy to limn a social world in which two actresses battle to have their parts beefed up during an indie film production. By the end of the play it's the screenwriter who grows some balls, or is corrupted (it's hard to tell which, but he does take over the show). Shanley knew something about Hollywood wish-fulfillment: Back in the early '80s, watching funds from a large NEA grant dwindling, he had decided that instead of returning to painting apartments, moving furniture or tending bar, he would write a screenplay. *Five Corners* (1987) ended up being produced by Beatle George Harrison, and was followed shortly by Shanley's signature achievement, *Moonstruck*, the Norman Jewison film and Cher vehicle that won Shanley a well-deserved Oscar for best screenplay.

Moonstruck brought together all his insights into Italian-American culture with a brilliantly funny, wise and balanced screenplay that holds up, to this day, as a masterful comedic melodrama. This was followed by *The January Man* (1989), a botched thriller; *Joe Versus the Volcano* (1990), which Shanley also directed, starring Tom Hanks and Meg Ryan, in an odd turn that died at the box office; *Alive* (1993), about a plane crash and cannibalism in the Andes; and *Congo* (1995) a jungle-based techno-thriller about mutant apes—none of which came close to matching his early success.

Shanley returned to the stage with new aspirations: *Psychopathia Sexualis* (1996) was a clever, entertaining boulevard comedy about sexual fetishism and a loony shrink. *Cellini* (1998), his first-ever stage adaptation, drew on the notorious Renaissance autobiography; *Missing/Kissing* (1996) proved a not-particularly-engaging romantic study; *Where's My Money?* (2001), his first experience with the LAByrinth Theater Company, was a wholly satisfying dark comedic drama about a kinky affair, a cynical marriage and the loss of romantic sentiment—for my money, Shanley's best play since the '80s, although more West Side comedy of manners than raw exposé.

Then came 9/11, which inspired Shanley's topical *Dirty Story* (2003), featuring characters intended to represent the U.S., Israel and Palestine—a comedic parable so cartoonish that some critics had a hard time taking it seriously, even while the *New York Times* called it "appallingly entertaining." [Denver Center Theatre Company's production runs through Nov. 13.] Shanley was staying on a Mideast beat: *Live from Baghdad*, a 2002 film written for HBO, about CNN at the start of the Gulf War, earned an Emmy nomination for him and other co-screenwriters. (My favorite line: "If we can keep talking, then maybe we won't kill each other.") Shanley also recently completed a new script for *Moonstruck* director Norman Jewison, *The Waltz of the Tulips*. Apparently the moonstruck writer is thinking in 3/4 time these days.

Which brings us up to *Doubt* and *Sailor's Song*—two new plays, each a major return to form, both resounding evidence of a new confidence, maturity and economy from an artist who has always maintained that "writing is acting is directing is living your life."

We meet at his request at the Soho Grand Hotel for tea and cookies. Shanley is grayer than the last time I saw him, back in the early '90s, strolling in a black leather jacket down Lafayette Street in Manhattan with the actress Julia Roberts. His explosive, raucous laugh and the classic Irish twinkle in his eye haven't changed; he seems eminently sane, focused, amiable and self-examined. He tells me that today is his son Frankie's birthday, and that after our interview he will be picking him up to celebrate. Both sons were adopted at birth, four-and-a-half months apart, so for the next seven-and-one-half months, Shanley laughs, "both my sons are 12." Speaking with the rhythms of his native Bronx, he is still asking ambitious questions and giving big answers, but with a new subtlety, new tools and a steady, jovial demeanor.

When was the last time you actually saw *Danny and the Deep Blue Sea*?
It's been a few years. Some of my plays I've never seen done by anybody since the original productions. *Danny* I've seen done maybe three times in amateur productions that somebody got me to go to. Actually, the last time I saw it was in Paris, in French.

Did you think you were watching *No Exit*?
(*Laughs.*) No! Because *Danny* has a catharsis. Catharses build up a lot of energy, and when the energy is metabolized, it is released, and the audience is released. That can be really important! You have to legitimately achieve it. It's one of the big reasons that I would go to the theatre—in the hopes of experiencing that.

Who will be playing Danny and Roberta this year?

I don't know. Second Stage suggested Leigh Silverman for director—she had done well at the Public [with Lisa Kron's acclaimed play *Well*], and I met with her and thought she was smart and driven and completely unlike me. I can't explain that any more than to say she's made of different stuff. So I said, "All right, let's see what you'll do. You're free. I want the Leigh Silverman production."

You really don't want to haunt the rehearsal hall?

Nah. I'm not much for going back. You can either have a career or chase it, and I don't particularly want to chase my own shadow back through time. With the number of workshops of my plays in New York alone, it could have been my career, just going to my own shows—and how sad would that have been!

"Is Shanley here again?"

(*Raucous laughter.*) That's right. "Poor guy."

So let's jump forward 20-plus years to your new play *Sailor's Song*. The publicity makes it sound as if you were inspired by the two Genes: Kelly and O'Neill.

Sailor's Song is about—just to pull a figure out of the air—35 percent dance. But it's not performed by dancers, it's very much a play. A very, very romantic play—almost a tragic-romance. I'll be very involved in this one. *Sailor's Song* and *Doubt* are only four days apart in rehearsal schedule, so I couldn't direct either one of them. Doug Hughes is directing *Doubt*, and he's great; the other show's got a much greener director, Chris McGarry, who's been an actor mostly, and who I did *Dirty Story* with. He's very intelligent and I wanted to give him a shot. The music is extant—it's waltzes, used in a very unusual way. It's almost all three-four time—"Tales of Vienna Woods," "Blue Danube," all that stuff. Johann Strauss mostly, right down the line! And it works! I did a workshop of it last fall to make sure, and it's really fun to listen to that music. All the music that's ever been written is still around, but it's amazing how pop music has pushed out everything else, for the most part, except for in formal dance. And it doesn't have to be so.

You've written so much about the nature of love and romance. I sense in *Sailor's Song* a new wisdom and maturity—almost a mellowness that does not suggest complacency, just a longer overview and a deeper perspective.

Yes. I'm savoring life now, whereas I used to just wolf it down. This play is all about savoring the moonlit moment of romantic choice—that place on the dance floor of the heart when two people could kiss but they haven't yet. You are a dancer and the music is playing like a blue river around you. Everything is on the move and yet, paradoxically, time has ceased its forward motion. And this liquid pulsing photograph of possibilities is placed side by side in this play with mortality, with the certainty of death, with the brevity of youth, and with the importance of *now*. So *Sailor's Song* is about the almost unbearable beauty of choosing to love in the face of death. Love is the most essential act of courage, isn't it? Will you choose to love before you are swept away by oblivion? I hope so.

Now tell me about *Doubt*.
I went to a Catholic Church school in the Bronx and was educated by the Sisters of Charity in the '60s. That's a world that's gone now, but it was a very defined place that I was in for eight years. I realized later on when the Church scandals were breaking that the way a lot of these priests were getting busted had to be by nuns. Because nuns were the ones who were noticing the children with aberrant behavior, distressed children, falling grades, and in some cases they had to be the ones who discovered what was happening. But the chain of command in the Catholic Church was such that they had to report it not to the police but to their superior within the Church, who then covered up for the guy. This had to create very powerful frustrations and moral dilemmas for these women. It was very shortly after that that they started to leave the Church in droves.

I was not aware of that. Has this been noted elsewhere?
As far as I can make out, never. So showing this experience was one of the motivations behind *Doubt*. Another was that I saw a dark side to the Second Vatican Council's message of "go out into the community." When I was a kid, priests were not going to take boys out of church [to outside activities]. They were priests, they were in the rectory. And so I think this explosive combination of celibacy and "go out and make believe you're just one of the other folks" had a lot to do with the problems that followed.

But over and above that, the more interesting thing to me doesn't have anything to do with the scandals, and that is the cathartic, philosophical power of embracing doubt—of embracing not knowing, embracing that you may never know the truth or falsity of a story, of a scenario, and that you cannot morally stand in judgment from any place that is utterly firm in relation to another person's life. And yet actions must be taken if you feel the imperative, if you feel that you have the clarity of thought and know what should be done. And that powerful, explosive dilemma for an individual is really fraught for me. Here are these women who stumble on what may be something—and the choice is to go through the normal chain of command, which will lead to the complete exoneration and literally the *safety* of an abusive priest.

You know a member of my own family was molested by [Father John] Geoghan, the guy who was strangled in prison. And my family members went to Cardinal O'Connor, after they'd gone to everybody locally and gotten no satisfaction, and Cardinal O'Connor took them by the hands and said, "I am so sorry this happened. I will take care of it." And then he *promoted* him. Unbelievable. So they left the Church, but after 10 years they went back, and that Sunday the Monsignor got up and gave a sermon saying that these children who were abused, it was the parents' fault. That's when they left the Church again.

So this material is very close to home.

It is, but I think when you see the play you'll see that my relationship to it is very complicated. There's an even weirder level: Is what some of these guys do totally bad? That I also have doubts about. When I was growing up, at certain points I was championed by homosexual teachers who were the only people watching out for me. And why were they doing it? They were really into boys. They were really into my problems. Did they do anything *to* me? No. Did they want to? I don't know. Did they make a pass? No. Was that in the air? Somewhere, yes, it was in the air. Did I take advantage of the good things they were offering me? Yes, because I needed to, because I was isolated and there was no one else. Did that make them bad people? Not to me. Not to me at all.

It's only acting out that compromises a child.
That is correct. And, even then, if it's like some guy putting his hand on my leg and me saying, "Get your hand off my leg," and that's it—frankly, I wouldn't have been traumatized. But, of course, what happens is that a lot of kids who are more confused than that about their sexuality, which is perfectly natural at that age—and also out of tremendous need—can become *very* confused. So there are a lot of levels to it. I'm not interested in issue plays per se, although I'm more interested in them now than I used to be. What I'm *not* interested in is writing polemics on one side of an issue or another. Doubt does not have to dismantle passion. It can be a passionate exercise.

When you look back, do you see any arc or evolution in your career?
One of the ongoing concerns that I have is how to be intimate with another human being. Another is how to invite everybody to the party. We have to be able to find a way to communicate so that we can talk about anything. That's the one thing we should be able to do—to talk about *anything*.

We don't necessarily have to be able to do everything.
That is correct. Right now, the Democrats and the Republicans, for instance, are never able to cede anything to the other side. Everything has to be crossfire! Which can be a fun part of a play, but that's a play that never goes to catharsis. It ends up forever stuck in some kind of French existential hell! And that's not what's interesting to me. I want to find the dynamic door that leads out of the dilemma and on into the future.

I grew up in a violent place where people did not communicate well, but where there were big feelings and big longings, and I remember that some of the most interesting people were also the most doomed, because they had no tools to save themselves. In some weird way, the Palestinian character in *Dirty Story* is a descendent of those people: "If you won't solve my problem, if no one will listen to me, then I'm going to blow you and me up." I certainly knew that guy, I certainly grew up with that guy—and I've got a little bit of that guy in me. I always said that if things went well I would spend the first half of my life writing about my problems, and the second half I would write about other people's problems, and that's sort of what happened—I'm able now to start turning *out*. Maybe that's why I was able to write *Doubt*, and why I was able to write *Dirty Story*. Of course they're personal plays, but they are about larger social concerns.

Your own ethnic background provides a great example of communicating across boundaries and bridging differences.
Yes. I'm very Irish, from an Irish-Italian neighborhood in the Bronx. I grew up in a household where talk was important, music was important, clothing was not important, food was not important. Then I went over to my Italian friends' houses, where the guys were combing their hair with "Hidden Magic" which they'd stolen from their mothers, and spending an hour getting dressed, and talking openly about sexuality, which was *bad* in my household! It was just a much more sensual, ebullient world, I went to their houses to soak up the sheer pleasure of it, the stimulation—and I was like, "I want what they got, *plus* what I got!"

My father came from Ireland when he was 24, had a brogue and was raised on a farm, basically in the 19th century. And my mother was first-generation—her parents were from Ireland as well. And when I went back to the farm where my father was born—he died two years ago at 96—the people on that farm spoke in poetry, and we really got along. And I thought, "This is much closer to my true family than the particular culture I grew up in!"

Most of your plays are language-driven, and yet we know movies generally aren't—the engine of a film is imagery. How do you think writing screenplays has affected your playwriting?
Actually, the influence is very much the other way around. Playwriting has continued to make my screenwriting possible. Without that constant feedback from the audience, writing can become ungrounded. Audiences show up too late in cinema; you don't get a chance to fix it after they get there. So you better have a very strong sense of what you've got, of what the music is between you and the audience. The theatre gives so much back in that way. I feel genetically born to be a playwright. When I started writing in the dialogue form, I had a complete moment of recognition, like, "Oh! This is what I do!" I'd written in many other forms before that—I started writing when I was 11 and I was a poet, exclusively, for several years. But it wasn't until I was 23, 24, that I tried the dialogue form, and it was instantaneous. I wrote a full-length play the first time I ever wrote in dialogue, and it was produced a few weeks later.

When you reflect back on your personal journey, are you ever amazed that here you are, this troublemaker from the Bronx, who ended up a playwright with something to say that lots of people want to hear?
Yes. My life is both inevitable and surprising to me. But I've never had the slightest sense of future. I did not envision a fate. So I don't know why I should have any feeling of surprise.

Robert Coe is a screenwriter, playwright and journalist living in New Jersey.

HOW DOES YOUR GARDEN GROW?

Conversations with F. Murray Abraham, Olympia Dukakis, Floyd King, Marian Seldes, Fiona Shaw and Gary Sinise

By David Byron

January 2005

> *The most plausible Objection to our Administration seem'd to be that we took no Care to breed up young Actors to succeed us, and this was imputed as the greatest Fault, because it was taken for granted that it was a Matter as easy as planting so many Cabbages. Let it be our Excuse then that since there was no Garden where accomplish'd Actors grew, we could only pick them up, as we do Pebbles of Value, by chance.*
> *—An Apology for the Life of Colley Cibber* (1740)
> by Colley Cibber

> *Everybody in the world thinks they know two things—what they do and acting.*
> —Floyd King

Poor Colley Cibber, the most popular comedic actor of his time, he's mostly remembered today as the hapless sod who was overshadowed by the Colossus-like imprint of David Garrick and ridiculed and dismissed by the likes of Johnson, Fielding and Pope for being a hack. But if he was behind even the times he lived in, he did put his finger on two significant truths that continue to resonate today: The world seems to need actors. And good ones aren't easy to come by.

Laurence Olivier, addressing a commencement class of acting students at the Central School of Speech and Drama in London in the 1950s, said, "Above all, the actor must be the great understander—and that puts him in a category with the philosopher, the poet and the priest,"

It's a lovely sentiment, but how much have attitudes changed toward actors and actor training since the time of Colley Cibber? Anyone familiar with the drama departments of most universities across America will tell you that those beleaguered bastions are routinely less funded than other departments and staffed with fewer tenured professors.

The situation mirrors the way we view actors overall. We deify them (endless awards programs) or we dismiss them (especially when they speak up during an election season), but we haven't yet seemed to find a niche for them outside the pages of *Entertainment Weekly*. Fiona Shaw believes that the situation is especially problematic in America. But even Richard Eyre, former artistic director of England's Royal National Theatre, lets down the cause in his otherwise all-encompassing survey of contemporary theatre history, *Changing Stages*, in which he and his co-writer Nicholas Wright only tangentially mention actors at all. In the process they not only marginalize actors' role in the social order, but erase them even from theatre history,

It's in this dispiriting context that the efforts of six actors who teach, profiled here, are especially gratifying. They know that the best way to elevate the position of the actor in America is to elevate the quality of work being done. They teach, as often as not, with little or no pay and because they believe that the training of actors is not just important, it's relevant—both within a proscenium and on the world stage—now more than ever.

F. Murray Abraham, Olympia Dukakis, Floyd King, Marian Seldes, Fiona Shaw and Gary Sinise interviewed separately, but united by a vision, tend the "cabbages" that Colley Cibber neglected—root by root, plant by plant, one class at a time. In the process, they cultivate respect for the actor, respect for acting. Uta Hagen, herself a teacher of three of these teachers, would be proud.

DAVID BYRON: How were you first exposed to acting and how did it change you?

F. MURRAY ABRAHAM: An acting teacher saved my life: Lucia P. Hutchens, El Paso, Tex., right on the border of Mexico. I was scattered and a little crazy, and in some trouble. It was the beginnings of the gangs then, the *pachucos*. I was just a fuck-up. I'd been in jail a couple of times and was barely making it through school. I was taking the easiest classes I could. One of them was speech and drama—it sounded like a simple thing, and I always liked to tell jokes and there couldn't be much homework, I supposed. I got in that class and she saw something. She said, "Read this out to the class." My first brush with Shakespeare, at 17 years old.

Literature wasn't a big part of my family's life. But she praised me and talked about the school play. That was it, as soon as I stepped on stage. It's as simple as that. But the fact that she took the time, to me that's a real gift. Amazing. It was great, great good fortune. How else would I have become associated with the theatre? It was not part of my blue-collar family at all. My father was a mechanic. We were steelworkers, coal miners and farmers. I feel that it saved my life.

GARY SINISE: Disney honors a teacher every year with the American Teacher Award, and they asked me to present it. They said, "Do you have a teacher in mind?" And I said, "Oh, yeah. You called the right guy." Barbara Patterson—she was it. She got me into the theatre at Highland Park High School in Illinois, and once I was in, I was hooked. That's where I met Jeff Perry, and we became best buddies and eventually started Steppenwolf. Barbara was really a sort of you-gotta-make-theatre-wherever-you-can kind of person. "Don't wait around," she said. So we ended up starting our own theatre, and it's 30 years old now.

FIONA SHAW: I was trained at the Royal Academy of Dramatic Art, and it was really the best training in the world—it was revelatory. Not least because of the totality of it. I do think that the immersion in a total acting-training is the key. You have to sort of leave the world and join the world of the harnessing of the multiple skills of your body and your mind. So, really, I found that very, very good. There was a man there called Hugh Cruttwell. He was able to hone in on everybody's individual skill, everybody's individual development and everybody's individual weakness.

OLYMPIA DUKAKIS: My mother was my first acting teacher. She would periodically decide we were going to do little skits and musical revues in the kitchen and we'd jump up and sing songs to each other. She and my father started the Dionysus Club in Lowell, Mass., in the '20s, and did *Oedipus* and other classical Greek plays, and the two of them put on musical-revue-type things for the Red Cross and the Greek war relief. The first time I was on stage I was the Spirit of Young Greece. I'll tell you how sweet it was. I had two doves, and they were supposed to fly out into the audience and they crapped all over me. I should have known then what show business was like.

FLOYD KING: Michael Kahn was a huge, huge influence on me. I wasn't a formal student of his, but he taught me everything I know, sometimes the hard way. Before I met him I was a performer. After I met him I began to become an actor. Before it was all instinct, but he kept me at the Shakespeare Theatre Company in Washington, D.C., for 20 years and I've slowly learned to act. That kind of chance is so rare these days. It's like England in the old days.

MARIAN SELDES: I had great teachers, and I remember everything. Certainly Sanford Meisner and the Neighborhood Playhouse. And Martha Graham and the marvelous discipline of the dance world thrilled me. Shortly after I graduated from the Playhouse and was on tour with Judith Anderson in *Medea*, Uta Hagen was teaching in Chicago and playing Blanche DuBois at the same time. She let me audit her classes, and she had an enormous influence on me—I mean as a teacher. One of the first scenes I ever saw in her class was the scene between Ophelia and Hamlet, and the Hamlet had a southern accent and the Ophelia was a larger person than the Hamlet, someone you would think of maybe working on Gertrude, and I saw right away that it was not the result that Uta was interested in, it was the process.

What makes a good acting teacher?

SELDES: I think it's all a question of giving the young actor confidence and the place in which he or she can develop without humiliation, without terror, without any of those things people warn you about. After I've been teaching a class for a certain amount of time, I feel my students become so welcoming of the talent of the others that it really does happen. It's a utopia.

SINISE: There are probably a lot of teachers who shouldn't be teaching, you know? It's all about being a drill sergeant—they want to break you down and get you to the point where, "If you can't survive in my class, you'll never survive in this business"—all that kind of stuff. But they're doing it because they're bitter and don't have anything else to do. If you have the wrong teacher, it can really mess up your life.

ABRAHAM: I would prefer a teacher who has considerable experience on the stage. But as with Uta Hagen, the danger is that a good teacher, a great teacher, carries a real charisma, and a charismatic teacher is a dangerous teacher. The longer I was with Uta Hagen, the worse I became, because I was falling under her spell. What I began to do incrementally with every class was to erase what I brought, who I was, in order to do precisely everything that she was recommending. I wanted to please her. By the end she threw me out of her class, and I think she did me a favor by getting rid of me.

How do you teach?

KING: I only teach Shakespeare, classical comedy. I call it "the brain surgery" of acting. Sometimes I get a whiff from the other teachers of, "Thank God it's not me." But I don't think teaching comedy is a special art, it's a matter of releasing. I think the word "comedy" scares everybody to death. So I never talk about being funny. There are lots of people who aren't funny people who do comedy brilliantly. That's another thing I teach them. It encourages them if I can get them to believe it. You don't have to be funny to do comedy. And vice versa: You can be a funny person and not be funny on stage.

SELDES: The kind of work I do is based on script. That's what all my work is about: for actors to find themselves in the material and to get them to read plays. When actors say they're between jobs or something, I say, "What's the last play you read?" Because you would never think of a doctor not reading what's new about medicine. I think my strong point is the connection between the actor and the playwright.

KING: One of the assignments I give is to take a piece, from either a Shakespeare tragedy or history, and do a scene from it as if it were a comedy. They can't pull their pants down, they can't make fun of the material. It's not about satire. It's about playing the objective so strongly that it's funny. The more tragic it is, the funnier it can be. *Romeo and Juliet* is hilarious. Look at the balcony scene. Lots of laughs, because it's not a tragedy *yet!*

SHAW: What I don't deal with particularly is character. Situations are character, rather than character "not being you." I don't know how one could "not be you." I think the literal transformation that American acting has been so brilliant at is often a way of . . . I don't know, there is something about the desire by Americans to use theatre or acting as an escape from life rather than an investigation of life. People often feel very released when they become bag ladies or kings, but I think what's interesting is not the bag lady or the king or even the transformation, but what is the situation the bag lady or the king finds her or himself in.

Why teach if you don't need to?

KING: I don't think it's altruistic; it helps me as much as it helps them. I like the energy of the youngsters and seeing all that raw talent, but also what it does for me. It constantly is a refresher course in process. Sometimes, in your own work, you have a tendency, maybe, to skip over things. And when you're teaching them you're seeing your own particular problems as an actor.

ABRAHAM: I think that people who are successful in this business, those who have lots of experience, should give themselves to teaching, a bit anyway. For one thing, it clarifies your own ideas. It insists that you codify your knowledge. I wanted to start finding out what I didn't know. I began teaching because my dear departed friend, Geraldine Page—a terrific, gifted teacher—called me in one day and asked me to take over her class because she was busy. So I had to examine what I knew to be able to verbalize it. And you begin to understand that perhaps you have been coasting in this area. And if you have really good students, they won't let you get away with that.

SHAW: I teach because I live in the middle of this stuff all the time. It's like saying your prayers; you get a chance to revisit scenes from plays that you do or don't know. I mean, I'm often doing something from *King Lear* in class. I didn't know *King Lear* at all, but I know lots of bits of it now. It's a great way of doing the unknown. Once you discover the center of the play, then you're not trapped by the historical moment of it, because the play could be written now or anytime. You're just interested in the scene and what the scene reveals. So the exercise is a mantra and entirely new each time. Maybe the story has been held tight for 2,000 years. It's been reworked and reworked and refound, so it's polished to a kind of nugget—it's there for the releasing. I would say that acting is the creativity of one generation over another, the reexplosion of the same thing again and again.

DUKAKIS: It's a great adventure. You know the thing Tennessee Williams says: "Make voyages, there's nothing else."

Is the actor a proactive, creative force, not only on the stage but in society as a whole?

SELDES: I don't see the actor as a person who can influence and make a change. We are absolutely the servants of the writer. That's a tremendous conviction I have.

KING: It's the playwright who's the proactive one. We're the interpreters; It's not our words, it's not our thoughts, it's not our principles that we put up there on stage. It's the playwright's. If we're doing our job right, that's what we're serving. If anyone's going to change the world, it's going to be a playwright.

SINISE: In the scheme of things, you know, there are more important things than acting.

ABRAHAM: It's the most important thing in the world!

SHAW: Apart from everything else, the actor's a brilliant unifying force for seeing that all of us live just now, and we all will die. The life of the actor is that you actually have the opportunity to labor over what it might be like to stand in a different corner of the world—and that has to be a good thing, doesn't it? I think it's a marvelous thing. Reading a novel is a marvelous thing, but acting is almost better, because if you read a novel you sit and you experience it in your mind; but if you act something, you actually take responsibility for it.

SINISE: Do I look for things I can make my political statement in? No, I never have. You know, I played Harry Truman, and I played George Wallace, too. If you're going to take them on, you've got to play them both with conviction and commitment and with no holds barred. It doesn't have to have anything to do with your political point of view.

ABRAHAM: I think acting is definitely subversive. There's an anarchic quality to acting that people envy and lash out at. Actors represent a danger to society. It's that discovery of a thing in each of us that we'd rather not examine, we'd rather not touch on. And the better the actor, the closer they are to that truth, and that makes them dangerous, because it wakes ourselves up to who and what we are.

Take *Medea* for example. To do a really satisfying Medea, truly, you have to find in yourself that part of you that would kill your own children. If you have a child who has colic, who screams for six months (because that's how long colic lasts), you will think about killing that child if you allow yourself to. Now what actress is willing to examine that? A great actress. But once she does, she communicates that to the house. She discovers what that awakens, on stage, in front of you, live, there. When she does, you do. And that is scary.

SHAW: I don't think that good acting is polemical, but I do think that the choices the actor makes are, of course, political. The explosive poetical concentration of your revelation of a character in a situation results in a moral universe: You're being offered to an audience, who then have to make their choice.

DUKAKIS: We don't have political theatre anymore, the way we did in the '60s and the early '70s—at least not here in America. Europeans have it much more. People here try to stay away from politics and religion because they're controversial, and controversy makes it very hard, especially, say, in the regional theatres, to raise money.

SHAW: America is obsessed with money; the value of a person is connected to their power, which equals their money. It is the only value, the only standard, whereas in Europe, in Spain and Italy, still, the intellectual power or the imaginative power somebody has gives them a certain status in the community. Long may it last, I say, but America is unique in that. This is a very anti-intellectual moment in American life.

ABRAHAM: The people that we call leaders these days, at least in America, seem to have almost no leadership stature. One of the reasons I love *Oedipus* is the fact that this political leader, a king, Oedipus Rex, says, "There's a cancer on society. We must find out what the cause is and then we must, whomever, whatever, wherever falls the blame, get him out." And then we find out that it's him, though in fact he really is innocent. He did not know, but that's not the point, is it? As the leader, it's his responsibility, and he does this thing he does. It's not enough to say, just, "I'm leaving." He punishes himself, and in that way he purges his guilt, he purifies the country that he says he loves.

Now, in contradiction to that noble example of leadership, we have so many leaders who refuse to take responsibility. Kenneth Lay: "I didn't know." Nixon: Practically everybody in his cabinet went to jail. Bush today: He's propagating this mantle of irresponsibility, of non-responsibility. It's the sign of our times. What's going to happen to our country? Now is the time to do *Oedipus Rex*!

SHAW: I think it's fascinating that 10 years ago in drama classes we used to be reaching for ways of conjuring up extreme situations, and now they're all too immediate.

You have to believe that human nature remains the same. If anything, the terror today brings up the same questions it always has, which are: Who are the baddies? Are we them? These are good questions for young people to have to answer because they always assume they're in the moral right. It's absolutely marvelous if you're not—and much more interesting, if you ask me.

Will acting and the teaching of acting continue to be relevant in years to come?

KING: Acting certainly will, because people want to hear stories and see them acted out. And the teaching of acting is really the teaching of process and helping someone to find and bring out what's inside them. There'll always be a need for that.

SELDES: Aristotle said that theatre is a healing art. It's a medicine. It teaches us that we are more alike than different. It brings us together. It's being there at the moment it happens. Television and films and the Internet can never replace that immediacy.

SHAW: I think studying acting is a beautiful way of investigating the unacceptable, and it produces compassion, it produces understanding. It celebrates human nature even at its worst, and I think that that's of brilliant value—that humans don't have to die in the darkness of ignorance. That's not going to change.

DUKAKIS: I think it has a lot to do with the way we dream. These dreams are revelatory and informing and empowering, and I think that's what the arts do: Whether you're looking at a single image, like a painting, or watching a dance or listening to music, it's all about being involved in a collaborative way in the storytelling. That really does it. That's where you really get off.

KING: Not all these students are going to be actors, but they're going to be audiences—and they're going to be educated audiences. They'll see the magic, but they'll also be able to see the craft.

ABRAHAM: But these kids, you're really giving them something that is so hard for them to find outside of our little protected enclave, because their parents and grandparents and friends think they are damn fools. This is not so much an encouragement as an affirmation: "It's okay, you can have your dream for as long as it lasts, as long as you understand that if you leave the business or the process of studying, when you leave—and this is very important—it's not been wasted time. None of it is wasted."

SHAW: I'm concerned that there are so many institutions teaching acting, and you wonder: Do we need to be producing these hundreds of actors every year, when we only need 10 new ones who are good? But I do actually think that for them, to study acting and then to go and become lawyers or housewives—I think it affects those other roles. I think it makes them better housewives and better lawyers. I think it's a wonderful thing to have studied, and the really great thing is that if they learn anything in their classes, they can use it in their kitchens.

David Byron has taught theatre history at Yale and at the British American Drama Academy (BADA) in London and Oxford.

THE REAL THING

An interview with William S. Yellow Robe Jr. by David Rooks

July/August 2005

> *This whole thing of who is more Indin, what we do to be Indin, or don't do because it might make us look less Indin, is a sickness beyond any thinking.*
> *—Grandchildren of the Buffalo Soldiers*, Act 2, Scene 1

I was a Lakota man/child in my twenties, hungry for work. A job search took me in the late 1970s from my home on the Pine Ridge Indian Reservation in South Dakota to a solitary junction in northwestern Montana called Wolf Point. Located on the Fort Peck Indian Reservation, home of the Assiniboine *oyate* (people), Wolf Point lives in my memory as an old service station/convenience store, where a framed but faded photograph hung prominently on a wall near the store's entrance. The yellowed black-and-white print held a scene of frigid winter. Centered in the photograph, over deep snow, a stack of wolf carcasses rose about 15 to 20 feet high: if not a thousand, at least hundreds of wolves slaughtered in a single season. Beside the stack of wolves stood the proud bounty hunters: a few white men. I wondered how the local Assiniboine had fared in such a climate.

What I didn't know was I had sojourned in the homeland of a then budding Assiniboine playwright named William S. Yellow Robe Jr. Today, when I read Yellow Robe's plays, the sagebrush and coyote vistas of western Montana return. So, too, do the problematic shift and chant of Native culture in flux, whether it be Assiniboine, Lakota, Pequot or Mohawk. William S. Yellow Robe's plays cast a sharp and unsentimental eye on modern Native life: all its broken-mirror reflections on identity, social and familial ties, the destructive fallout of chemical addictions, and, yes, the compassionate acceptance that we are what is left, and that that must be good, and must endure.

At the behest of *American Theatre*, I caught up with Mr. Yellow Robe in a coffee shop in Providence, R.I., this past midwinter. He was serving as a guest faculty member at nearby Brown University and also as playwright-in-residence at the estimable Trinity Repertory Company. With the support and cast of a local avant-garde troupe called the Perishable Theatre Company, his sharp-witted play *Better-n-Indins* had just opened in downtown Providence. Concurrently, plans were underway for a national tour of another new play, *Grandchildren of the Buffalo Soldiers*, staged as a co-production of Trinity Rep and Penumbra Theatre Company of St. Paul, Minn.

Grandchildren will premiere in St. Paul Sept. 15–Oct. 15 and will continue to tour widely through February '06. According to Emily Atkinson, communications director at Trinity Rep, the production is noteworthy as "the country's first fully mounted professional touring production by a regional theatre of a Native American play by a Native playwright." The production is supported by grants from the Ford Foundation and the National Endowment for the Arts Regional Touring Program.

Former Trinity Rep artistic director Oskar Eustis, who has just assumed the helm of New York City's Public Theater, speaks glowingly of Yellow Robe's work. "I think William is really one of the great American playwrights—he has an extraordinary body of work created over the past 20 years." Eustis first met the writer in Los Angeles about 15 years ago on the occasion of a production of Yellow Robe's *The Independence of Eddie Rose*, a coming-of-age drama about a Native family torn apart by alcoholism and abuse. "I've taught that incredible play over the years to groups of non-Native students, and it's interesting how powerful and revelatory—and upsetting as well—it is for those students," avows Eustis. "It's very exciting being able to introduce people to Bill's work that way."

"My sneaking hope is that after Trinity Rep is through with *Grandchildren of the Buffalo Soldiers*, they'll do *Eddie Rose*," Eustis goes on. "It is hard to write a play that is so honest about such brutal things, but, nonetheless, hopeful at the end. It really has positive energy in it. This is the thing I love about Bill: There is a real sense of spirituality, and it feels like it's hard-earned, in his work. It doesn't make it seem as if things are easy or somehow automatic, like a formula. He has struggled to find what his connection to a higher power is, and what room there is for redemption.

"My hope is that the way we're producing this touring production of *Grandchildren* will set a pattern for other Native American plays that could be produced that way, too. We are hoping to build an audience and employment opportunities, not only for Bill but other Native American theatre folk."

Artistic director Lou Bellamy says he founded the African-American company Penumbra as part of the Black Arts Movement, and though *Grandchildren* deals with the black community only tangentially, Bellamy believes the tenor and content of Yellow Robe's writing is essentially in sync with the company's mandate. "*Grandchildren of the Buffalo Soldiers* is significant for all kinds of reasons," says Bellamy. "There aren't many Native American writers who have dealt with the history of the Buffalo Soldiers. What Bill has done is what artists do:

He has personalized a very large issue and brought it down to one family. He knows what he's writing about from a very intimate point of view, and it's because of that that we can use this play to do further education and healing. That is why I think people like Bill and myself are in theatre—not for the bows and the curtain calls but because this is the way we exercise our citizenship, our humanness."

From Wolf Point, Mont., to the footlights of theatres from Los Angeles to Providence, Yellow Robe's journey has been a remarkable one. My interview with him is wide-ranging, but that is perhaps simply a reflection of the playwright's work. Mr. Yellow Robe was gracious, generous with his time and patient—a true *ikce wicasa*, to employ a Lakota phrase. Which is to say: He remains a common Native man, with humility and humor still intact.

Your play *Better-n-Indins* just opened. How was it received by the critics and audiences in general?
The first perception has been that the stories—the issues and themes—were coming from the Native community. The play is about issues that are present in various Native communities. The point is not that it is a quintessential spokes-vehicle for all Native groups—different Native people from different tribes could sit in the audience and say, "I can't really identify with this," or, "This doesn't speak for me." And they're absolutely right in saying that. At the same time, there are other communities that would go, "This is what I've always wanted to say," or, "This supplies me support, so I can say these things myself." The Perishable Theatre itself is a realm that was formerly foreign to Native American audiences, so that made it especially interesting.

The critics that came were used to seeing plays that talked to them, tickled their fancies, dealt with issues they could comprehend and situations they have a shared experience with. In some ways, I think it was sad that many non-Natives in the audience for *Better-n-Indins* were uncomfortable, because they did not know whether or not to laugh. For them, it was seeing a part of America that was just up the street but that they were not even aware of. At one point, near the end of the show's run, I was actually requested by Mark Lerman, then artistic director of Perishable, to add into the opening monologue of the play that while there is a difference between Indian humor and non-Indian humor, they both require laughter—so please don't be afraid to laugh.

How would you define Native theatre?
If you look at it historically, there is no architecture for Native American theatre. In other words, it doesn't have a home yet. Native theatre, for me, comes from one specific tribal community: It incorporates that tribe's language, their history, their culture, everything. In another sense, there are experiences in Native theatre that everybody has shared; for instance, in *Better-n-Indins*, there's a scene called "Hold Me Closer Tiny Fancy Shawl Dancer." The young girl in the scene has been rejected by her peers and by her family. Coming home after years of being absent, she has to be reintroduced to the community and to

her extended family. A lot of tribes have individuals who have gone through that very difficult experience.

So it's not monolithic?

No. I would call what I do intertribal theatre, and I should explain that, too. I work with different tribal groups, making theatre that allows this exchange of tribal culture—it's not based on race, it's based on how well you know yourself. How well do you know your people, your community, your family and so on.

There are threads in much of your writing of longstanding feuds, cross-generational wounds and anger in Indian country. Could you speak to that?

When I wrote *Sneaky* at the University of Montana, I was trying to explain this concept—that sometimes generational anger can be held onto for a long time. Growing up on the reservation, you could be at a pow-wow [a formal social gathering of Native peoples for thanksgiving] and all of sudden you would get jumped. Then you'd realize you got jumped because you beat up so-and-so's cousin when you were 10 years old, and this was payback. It might not be right now, it might not be tomorrow, but it's gonna happen. That's why in *Better-n-Indins* I wrote a scene called "Casino," with, basically, a mocking mentality. I took it a step further by adding the language of a Martin Scorsese movie, with its Italians. I've got these Native guys talking like big-time gangsters in their casinos.

It's such a rage—that whole thing of honor, keeping it within the family. You know, we might be able to sit down and bad-mouth so-and-so, but he's *our* cousin. Nobody else can do that but us. You don't talk bad about so-and-so to anybody else but a family member. That's how it's always been.

But what about rage at the white man—how is that depicted in your plays?

Part of that anger is an ongoing process, because a lot of things have not been taken care of. We're all [in this country] supposedly on a level playing field, and that's perhaps the biggest misconception. Sure, we're all on a playing field, but it's never been level. I'd like to say everything's fine and dandy. But, no, we still have high unemployment in our Native communities; we still have problems with basic physical needs such as housing. Environmental conditions? Rivers are polluted. We have need for medical assistance, because we have such high rates of diabetes and heart and liver ailments. Now cancer is growing. In three generations, it hasn't changed.

But I take the opportunity as a playwright to show that you can put the anger to the side rather than use it as a destructive force. It will still be there on a day-to-day basis. You know, I go into Providence and people come up to me and say, "Hey, you're a real Indian." I don't get mad. It just amazes me that in this day and age, it still goes on. You don't see someone go up to a black man and say, "Hey, you're a real black man."

Is there a casino on your reservation?
No. We have a small bingo palace called the Silver Wolf. They have video slots, but nothing in comparison with the Mohegan Sun or Foxwoods Casino.

When you write about casinos, how cynical can you be, especially when it's how many tribes support themselves?
They're economic band-aids. They're not going to solve the problems, they're a service industry. I don't know how long they're going to last, but people should try to make as much money as they can because you never know when they'll go belly-up.

Part of what I feel about casinos is this: First, Native communities can't exploit their resources, because they've already been exploited. A lot of tribes can't nurture their timber industry, especially when their timber has been almost wiped out. A lot of the natural resources that traditionally gave sustenance to the tribes are gone. We have a situation where there is really no economic development happening. There are now places where tribes are harnessing wind for energy, but the days for exploiting coal or oil are almost over. On my reservation, we have a large deposit of lignite coal, but, culturally speaking, you just can't tear up the land. Training and education are so desperately needed on the reservations right now. A lot of these kids don't see a future from where they're standing. And what they're being taught in school has no relevance to their community.

Do Native American youth assimilate popular culture like most other kids?
Oh, yeah. But because the traditional culture has always been attacked from the outside, a lot of kids haven't been raised with any knowledge of their own culture. Their culture is not being validated in the school process. I mean, you turn on the radio and you don't hear the Badlands Singers, you don't hear the Black Lodge Singers, you don't hear a traditional drum group. On almost every FM station you hear U2, you hear rap songs, you hear 50 Cent.

It's interesting, though, how we can take on stereotypes, too. You know, we've appropriated other cultures. For a while, there was such negativity against African-American culture—but then you had fry bread being presented as Indian soul food. You had the Temptations being blared out by these Native fancy dancers, who began adding R&B and hip-hop to their tape collections.

From my perspective, there seemed to be an excessive amount of self-congratulation among non-Indians for their "wonderful" treatment of Native peoples in movies like *Dances with Wolves*. Will there be anything like that attached to *Buffalo Soldiers*?
No, there's absolutely nothing like that going on. With this play we're trying to develop a strong educational component, so you'll have a reference list of materials where you can go to learn more. We're establishing a website where you can download information written by

Native people concerning the topic of the Buffalo Soldiers. We're going way deeper.

We did a panel discussion following a reading of *Buffalo Soldiers* at Brown, and one student asked: "What are Buffalo Soldiers?" And this African-American woman stood up and said, "Well, the Buffalo Soldiers were honorable, trustworthy, loyal"—she noted all of the good things from the African-American perspective. And so I said: "That's one definition. From a Native/Indigenous perspective, they were brutal, violent, vicious men who did not respect surrender. They fought you till the enemy was wiped out."

Do you sense doors are opening for Native Americans in theatre?
Yes, and this has to be mentioned. The thing about Oskar [Eustis] is that he took a big risk by actually allowing me to be a playwright-in-residence at Trinity Rep, beginning with the Four Directions playwrights festival in 2002. Oskar has opened a door for Native people on the East Coast that hasn't been open for a long time. I think the last guy that did it on the East Coast was Joseph Papp. He worked with Hanay Geiogamah and the Spiderwoman troupe. The big fear I have is: Will other doors open? And is this door going to close? That's what scares me the most—you realize you're the first one here, but at the same time you want to make sure the door always stays open for others to come through.

***Buffalo Soldiers* opens with a silhouette of a cowboy and a Native woman. Then it moves to the same view 100 years later, but with a contemporary couple replacing the originals. How much has rapid change affected Native societies?**
Oh, it's central. Things have changed so drastically. I remember the day when my dad was first trying to start a new record machine we just bought. Dad had gone to JC Penney because my mother had all these old Canyon Records, with recordings of all the local drum groups. He tried to put on the album, but he didn't know how to do it. I can see that image of my dad, with his T-shirt and his jeans, trying to turn that thing on. There are moments like that where you're happy that he's doing it, but it's so sad that you want to cry. It hurts you in different ways. My father spoke fluent Assiniboine when he was young, and when he died I looked at his birth certificate and until the age of seven he was known as Old Rock. No Christian name, nothing. That was it. The other thing is that he was not an immigrant—he didn't come from Italy, he didn't come from Russia. This was his homeland; and he became a stranger in it.

A friend of mine, a Native colleague, used to say: "Bill, do you know how to start a fire? If 10 of your relatives came over, would you know how to feed them?" It's a good question. You see, this is information that's not being shared nowadays. Do you know how to drink from a stream? Do you know the way the ancestors used to test water to see if it was drinkable?

All ethnic groups have had to absorb technology into their ways of life. Has this been particularly troublesome for Native Americans?

Yes, because we're not an ethnic minority. We're indigenous people. This is our homeland. You can't lump Native people as ethnics, we're not ethnic, we're indigenous, we're aboriginal.

I kind of feel guilty sometimes because I'm not a full practitioner of many of my tribe's cultural aspects. And I feel angry about that, because when my mother and father died, that was a link to the culture that is no longer here in this world. I feel regret that they're not here. But that's me—it's not a general statement about how others feel.

Do you feel our young people are often angrier than other kids?

Once a woman who was Southern Cheyenne and Arapaho came to me and said: "Mr. Yellow Robe, can you talk to my son? He's so angry and it scares me." That kind of anger turns into self-hatred. It also turns into the need to escape into something else other than one's self. We've allowed that to happen. It could be alcohol, it could be drugs, it could be a whole disassociation with Native culture. But for me, there was writing and theatre. Theatre was a way of dealing with the anger, and a way of presenting these problems. One of the things about this Euro/colonial art form known as theatre is that if Native people can form a relationship with it, it is a way for communities to develop their own Native language, to practice it, to teach it, and to share their culture within their communities—to basically, share their history. Theatre is a way for a community to empower itself.

How much were you a part of what went on in the '60s and '70s, that whole restoration of Native culture thing?

Because I was pretty young, I was mostly an observer. I remember when I was in high school I was elected president of our American government class, and there was a bill introduced by a Native woman to terminate the reservations, and we had to debate it. Some people I grew up with refused to partake, because the debates got really emotional and heated. They were raised with the idea that Native people aren't worth anything. But I was up there debating this—even then, I was politically and socially active within the community at Wolf Point.

I had always asked the question: What is the catalyst for change? I read a lot of essays by Martin Luther King Jr., and after college I read Malcolm X's autobiography. At the end, he said: "You know, when I actually went to Mecca, I realized that I can't make generalizations any more. I can't condemn anybody with a broad stroke." And I really believe that, because you have to go beyond color. Judging people based on color is a luxury I have never had. With Martin Luther King it was civil rights; with Malcolm X it was human rights—the right to be ourselves. I don't want to be your equal, I want to be myself. The recent generations have concentrated on making us equal. In the old tribes, they were themselves. We had Iktomi (Spider) stories, Coyote stories—Coyote turned himself into a mouse, a rabbit, a duck. The moral was: Be yourself!

You have spoken eloquently about the need to just be yourself among Native peoples.
How soon we forget that. That's the reason why, when I first came to the East Coast and lectured at colleges or universities or social gatherings, I would say: I am honored to be in the home of the Narragansett, or, I am honored to be in the home of the Wampanoag, but I am Assiniboine from Montana. I don't want to be a Narragansett or a Wampanoag or a Navajo. I want you to know that. I am honored to be with you, but I am not trying to be one of you. I'm Assiniboine, and I'm proud of it.

The reason I say that is to show these people I respect them. I respect you, I think you people are strong, I think you people are good, but I'm not trying to be like you. You see a gopher come across a deer, the gopher doesn't all of a sudden try to grow antlers, the deer doesn't all of a sudden try to go in a hole.

I am an Assiniboine playwright, not a Native American playwright. I can speak on some level to Native Americans in general, but when I write a play I'm talking from my heart, and that heart is Assiniboine. And sometimes there are good things and sometimes there are bad things, but I can't really control that.

There seems to be a fierce need by certain non-Native people to embrace Native culture. Why is that, do you suppose?
My feeling is there is really a lack of fulfillment in their own humanity, in their own spirituality, in their own culture. They're just looking to fill the void. It goes back, I suppose, to the question: Why did non-Natives feel the need to come to the so-called New World? You didn't hear about a bunch of Sioux getting together to build a monster canoe and paddling to France. I go back to what Chief Red Stone said when he signed the Fort Peck Treaty: "Just listen, we don't want you to get mad, we don't want you to feel this way or that. Just listen. That's all we want."

On our homelands, you don't have the grandchildren-come-latelies that you have here on the East Coast. The grandchildren-come-latelies exist in the more urban areas, but they hide; they don't show up at the pow-wows because they know if they do they'll get called out on that. This means they'll be asked to stop simulating ceremonies because they're not Native, or they don't know what they are doing, and that it's basically insulting. Instead of bringing honor and respect to yourself, you're bringing disrespect.

Here, they show up at pow-wows in some of the strangest outfits, some of them pretty suggestive. I had a lot of East Coast people ask me: Does that happen out west? And I said: No! At our pow-wows, we have the whip man—you start going around bare-ass-naked dancing, he'll throw you out. If you don't have an outfit, they'll suit you with an outfit so you can go out and dance. You see people trying to adorn themselves with all these respectful entities and eagle feathers, eagle claws, and they're trying to appropriate a look without knowing anything of the culture. Ultimately, you know, you can't get mad, you can't laugh at them, because in the end they're pitiful. They just don't know any better.

When I came out here, I made the mistake of all western people coming out to the east. I made fun of some of the dance outfits. They were pretty funky. I went to a pow-wow here and I was watching a girl dance, and I was saying: Wow, that's really a clingy buckskin outfit—she must have thrown that deer hide in the wash a couple of times to get it to shrink and shine like that. When I got up close, I realized her deer hide was made out of vinyl. There was another woman I used to call Dances with Pelts. She had all these damn pelts—when she'd get going in pow-wow, all the kids would come up and pet her pelts.

I felt bad for making fun of that, so for all this I had to apologize. That's the reason I wrote, in their honor, the "Hold Me Closer Tiny Fancy Shawl Dancer" scene in *Better-n-Indins*. In it I show that some of them are just really trying, in a good way, to respect Native culture. I mean, who the hell am I to disrespect them? I'm not even from here. I can't judge them.

How do you see this bleaching of tradition affecting Native spirituality?
Around here, everything is sacred. I used to do this routine during rehearsals of *Better-n-Indins*: "Now I'm going to sit down and drink from my sacred cup, and drink my sacred coffee, and if I get really gassy, I'll go and release to the god what is there in a sacred way." You know, when everything is sacred, *nothing* is sacred—it loses its meaning. We had this kid reading poetry one time: "*Aho* for the bears, *Aho* for the water, *Aho* for the bleachers, *Aho* for my car . . . ." I thought: Gee, "*Aho* for this verb, *Aho* for this conjunction, *Aho* for this adjective, *Aho* for this pronoun . . . *Aho* for my dentures that came early from the Indian Health Service this week, *AHO!*" (*Laughs.*) "*Aho* for the fact the dentist had the Novocain on a swab and not on a needle."

They say everything is so sacred around here. I say if you're going to do it, use the real thing. Don't try to pass off these painted feathers as eagle feathers.

What could be an example of how to understand if something spiritual is the real thing?
The real thing is when you have an awareness and a clarity of what you're doing. You're doing it not because it will make you look good or make you feel good, but because you're willing to sacrifice something of yourself. That's the big difference. You're not always thinking of yourself, you're thinking of those around you—your family, your loved ones. That's the reason I do what I do. When I do a play, it's not really about me. For some reason, that can be hard to grasp for non-Natives. But we must be able to do our work without having to explain everything. Neil Simon doesn't have to write a glossary in his plays to explain everything that might have something to do with Yiddish. O'Neill didn't need a glossary to explain something that might be peculiarly Irish.

From Victor Mature to Kevin Costner, the popularity of Native people seems to wax and wane in the public imagination. Unfortunately, what seems to happen is new stereotypes get grafted over the old. Do you see that in theatre?

Yes, in theatre we have the same situation. I always tell people: If you've come [to one of my plays] expecting the magical mystery tour, you've come to the wrong play. If you're expecting to see friendly, happy brown-skinned people, you've come to the wrong play. But if you want to see people celebrating life—this is it.

Are your characters celebrating life? A lot of them seem to be trapped in really traumatic situations.
Well, yes. But for a lot of the characters, they stop just trying to survive and they actually begin to live. They're no longer just trying to get through, they're actually living. People have always asked me: "How did you get out of this stuff?" I say: "I never left." I never got out. It's still with me. It will always be with me. But you can't explain that concept—you can't explain it to the people who don't know. You can't expect them to understand.

Could you define "this stuff"?
I grew up with so many different misconceptions of my people and myself. There was always that big myth that, you know, the only thing Native people can do is beadwork, the only thing they can do is drink. To be Indian you were required to accept this list. I remember one time my late wife, Diane, lost two hundred dollars. She felt so bad she cried. I told her not to panic, and I went downstairs to look for it in the car. After I was gone, the landlord came up to my wife and asked her outright: "Did he beat you?" And she said: "No, I lost this money and he went down to look for it." But, see, the landlord had already decided because she was crying that I beat her. Part of it is gaining the acceptance of oneself—just being able to recognize the truth from lies.

As a staff writer at *Indian Country Today*, I had a non-Indian editor who told me Native/Indigenous people could not be racists. As an Oglala Lakota, my experience told me different. *Buffalo Soldiers* treats a very sticky issue in Indian country—Native on Native racism.
I always talk about this in my classes when they ask me about me being part black, because I'm five-eighths Assiniboine, three-eighths black—I was called "nigger" for the very first time when I was in the third grade by a very good friend of mine. So I went home and asked my mother: "Am I part nigger?" She looked at me, shook her head and said: "You know, Billy, you're part colored, but I didn't raise you to be part colored, I raised you to be Assiniboine." And that's the way I conduct my life. My late wife, who was the catalyst for *Grandchildren of the Buffalo Soldiers*, wanted me to write about this experience growing up on the reservation. I was sort of isolated—I couldn't run to the white community like some of the other breeds. Those who were part white, if they got the Native community mad, they would run to the white community, and if they got the white community mad, they could run to the Native community—they would hide in both places. I couldn't. There was no African-American community to hide with. But within that process, I had a chance to see both sides, and I've never hated

either. I know a person who actually hated that he was part black. He launched himself totally into the Native culture. When he was a freshman he dropped out of high school, yet he could speak five different Native languages, including our own. He could look at a piece of beadwork and say, "That's Crow, that's Northern Cheyenne, that's Blackfeet, that's Cree." That's how good he was. But he hated the fact that he was part black. In fact, at one point he wanted to change his name. I would never do that, because I was proud of who and what I am.

If you were to prescribe a good way for Native peoples to accept modern life, what would that way be?
There are two misconceptions. The first is that we Native people have to reach out to the world. No. The world has to come to us. The world must continue to come to our nations. Columbus came here, the British Empire came here, the German Empire and the French Empire—they all came here and they stayed. Show me in any world history book where a boatload of Sioux went to China, or a boatload of Blackfeet went and set up a colony in India.

The second misconception is that being a "breed" is just an issue of being white and Indian. There are black Indians, Asian Indians, Chicano Indians—we're related to the world now. We have relations with the world. We are traditional people, but whoever honors Indian people has to recognize that being Indian has to include being able to absorb change. Change doesn't necessarily mess you up. It's the hardest thing for a lot of people: to receive change. But that's what we need to do to survive. Craig Robe in *Buffalo Soldiers* has changed when he comes back to the reservation. He realizes after he meets his family that he still has a lot more changing to do. The question is: Can he deal with it? If he's going to get on with life, he's going to have to.

In the final analysis, why do you write plays, and could you comment on other Native American performers or writers that you admire?
I do plays to show the Assiniboine are still alive, and that we are a part of the great Lakota Nation [according to oral tradition, the Plains Assiniboine separated from the Lakota Nation some time before 1640], and that I honor and celebrate the fact that my people are still alive today. The other reason is I try to create opportunities for younger people. The ultimate thing is to make it easier for the younger ones who are up and coming. The main responsibility I have is to make it easier for the next generation so they can step up and do it. In order for indigenous theatre to survive, it has to be generated by indigenous people. It has to be developed with tribal people; it can't be from the outside.

There are a lot of Native American theatre artists I admire. I really enjoy Hanay Geiogamah and his work as a playwright. There's Phyllis Bryson—she's a Fort Peck Sioux who's a director and actress. She's from my reservation, though she's originally from Poplar, Mont. There was John Kauffman, a Nez Perce, who passed away in 1990.

One of the main things hindering the movement for Native Americans getting into theatre is the lack of financial resources. One reason for that is that we get homogenized with "ethnic theatre," and we're not. Even the term "Native American theatre" lumps all these nations together, and that's kind of dangerous, too. The cultural differences can be incredibly distinct. But there are some Native groups that are doing really good stuff: There's the Tulsa Indian Actors Workshop in Oklahoma; Red Eagle Soaring, out of Seattle; there's the Project HOOP at UCLA that's providing a lot of good information for Native communities. Thunderbird Theatre at Haskell Indian Nations University in Lawrence, Kans., is still going strong; and there's a host of other community groups doing their best on pretty much nonexistent budgets.

What do you hope your plays accomplish for non-Native audiences? And what do your people think of you back in Wolf Point?
To answer the first part: That they'll listen. And that, listening, maybe they'll realize they don't know all the answers. Because we don't know them, either.

As for the second part of your question: It's mixed. Some people remember my family, and my father, and they don't like me—you know, old tribal politics. Sometimes, the biggest fear I have when I do a play is: What if back in Fort Peck they don't like it? You know, for Native people you can go home again, but the biggest question is: Will they want you? In the end, if you were raised within the circle of your people, you are never out of the circle, no matter where you are.

David Rooks, a tribal member of the Oglala Lakota Nation, is a journalist living in southwestern South Dakota who reports regularly on issues affecting indigenous tribes of the Western Plains.

THE LIGHT IN AUGUST

An interview with August Wilson by Suzan-Lori Parks

November 2005

In the middle of the summer, *American Theatre* magazine asked me if I would interview August Wilson for an article that would accompany the publication of *Radio Golf*, the last play in his unparalleled epic 10-play cycle. I'm a fan of Mr. Wilson's and was grateful I'd been asked. I began to prepare: rereading his plays and taking deep breaths. Although I'd met him several times, now I was actually going to have an *in-depth conversation* with one of my literary heroes. On the day of the interview, just an hour before I was scheduled to talk to him, I got a call from a friend telling me that Mr. Wilson had just announced to the press that he was ill and had been given only a few months to live. An hour later, when we spoke, my heart and mind were clouded with sadness. I could hardly keep from crying, but Mr. Wilson was clear, focused, funny and, as always, brilliant as hell.

I just want to say for the record: You are our king. And your work is so thrilling and delicious and dazzling and funny.
Well, thank you.

I loved *Radio Golf*. I saw it at the Taper; it's a great, great, great production.
I wasn't able to see it, but I'm pleased with the work that's gone on with it. We have a great cast there.

You always get great actors. Everybody is jonesing to work with you.
I've been fortunate in that regard. Absolutely.

Seeing *Radio Golf* was such a pleasure because we were seeing the end of your great 10-play cycle, but also a whole new beginning. It's like a brand-new day at the end of the play.
Hey, you have to go forward into the 21st century. I figure we could go forward united.

You say "we." Who's "we"?

I'm talking about the black Americans who share that 400-year history of being here in America. One of the things with *Radio Golf* is that I realized I had to in some way deal with the black middle class, which for the most part is not in the other nine plays. My idea was that the black middle class seems to be divorcing themselves from that community, making their fortune on their own without recognizing or acknowledging their connection to the larger community. And I thought: We have gained a lot of sophistication and expertise and resources, and we should be helping that community, which is completely devastated by drugs and crime and the social practices of the past hundred years of the country. I thought: How do I show that you can go back and that you can't—nobody wants to be poor, nobody wants to live in substandard housing. No one is asking them to do that. But I think that here again we have resources.

For instance, the NAACP is concerned with middle-class issues. I thought if you rename yourselves the National Association of Black People, you get in that community, you can solve some of those problems, provide some of those people with free legal services, lobby the government, the school boards, the communities. Put that expertise that we've gained to some use. But you can still be middle class; you can still live the life you want to; you can still be contributing to where you came from. If you don't recognize that you have a duty and a responsibility, then obviously you won't do that. Some people don't feel that responsibility, but I do, so I thought I would express that in the work. In the 21st century we can go forward together. That was my idea behind the play.

Is there resistance to going forward together because some black middle-class people define themselves as "successful" by the distance between where they are and where their not-so-fortunate brothers and sisters are?

Yeah. Because that's the way society defines success now. In other words, they have adopted the values of the dominant society and have in the process given up some of their cultural values, so in essence they have different cultural clothing. Some people make that choice; it's certainly not only black people—a lot of ethnic Europeans have made that choice completely. They have been so anxious to become Americans that they've changed their names, forgotten the old ways and don't want to be reminded of them. Other people go, "No, I want to go live in Little Italy. I'm Italian and I'm an American too." You can be both. It's as simple as that.

Why do you think that in our society success is defined by how much you can leave behind while you climb the ladder?

I think we're all trying to imitate the British to become lords and aristocrats, have a bunch of servants and a gardener, all that kind of stuff. We were founded as a British colony—that's a large part of it. We've managed to be immensely successful in pulling the energy and the brilliance of all those European immigrants that came here and worked hard. Their imagination—Carnegie coming up with the new way to make steel, all that stuff—and we've become the most powerful and the richest country in the world. So we've adopted those materialistic values at the expense of some more human values. There are ways to live life on this planet without being a consumer, without being concerned with acquiring hundreds of millions of dollars. I think, God, you have $100 million; don't you think that's enough? But a guy that has $100 million is trying to get $200 million.

(*Laughing*.) You're right, you're right.
I just find that mind-boggling, personally. These people that stack it up, man.

What's he going to do with it?
He's going to die! And what always amazed me is your children have to wait till you die before they get hold of it. Why don't you give it to them while you're living? It's a crazy society. In many ways, again, it's immensely successful, it has some wonderful values, it's able to create some great works of art. And we're moving toward this art being American art—that means being influenced by all of the different ethnic groups that make up America—and further and further away from the old, old Western conventions of Europe. We're turning out novelists whom you can only describe as American novelists. They're not building on Western convention anymore, but on this amalgam of ideas and thoughts and necessity and struggle of all the various ethnic groups in America. Eventually we are going to become an American culture, an American society unlike any other.

Yeah, hopefully a little more Left, you know?
We have to find our way and we're still in the process, I believe, of defining what "American" is. It's not all bad and it's not all good, either.

When you wrote *Jitney* in 1979, did you see the whole plan of the 10-year cycle from the jump?
No, I did not. I was taking one decade at a time, and looking where that decade left us, and then I would look at the whole thing and see what was missing. So, for instance, in *King Hedley*, I had to deal with the '80s, and I realized that I had written these plays, but hadn't really dealt with what I call a "male play," even though I have a bunch of male characters. So I needed to have King and Mister and Elmore at the center of that, and to deal with the absurd conditions of the '80s—kids out there murdering each other over $15 worth of narcotics or a pair of tennis shoes. That became the male play—the aspect I think was missing from the cycle.

But what's amazing is that, in the middle of what you're calling a "male play," you have Tonya, who gives that beautiful, excellent, perfect, perfect speech about why she doesn't want to have another child. In the middle of this "male play" you have this bloom of a beautiful woman who totally expresses the hope

and the despair at the same time, which is so mind-blowing. You sure you weren't writing a female play too?

When you have the males, you have to have the females. What happens is the male goes off to the battle, if you will, and when he comes home, the woman nurses his wounds, binds him up and sends him back off into the battle. That's the role defined by this relationship that has enabled us to survive. The women are the ones who go to the funerals and bury these men and bear up under all of that, and provide them with the strength, whatever their battle is, to continue it. You have to have the Tonya character, because she's the flip side of the coin, she's part of the male. They would not be able to survive without her. So I wanted to give expression to that at the same time.

Oh, God, I love that. Everybody must tell you how much they love that speech. It's frightening, and it's absolutely perfect. When did you know you were doing a 10-play cycle?

After I'd written *Joe Turner* . . . because I'd written three plays that were all set in different decades. Why don't I continue to do that?

Was it like a red carpet unrolling? Was that a scary moment?

No, it kept me safe, in the sense that I was never finished. I never had to worry about what my next play was going to be and come up with an idea. I would just pick a decade and go: Okay, the '60s—and I would think about stuff from the '60s. Because I hadn't finished, I was never scared about anything, it was just: Okay, let's move on to the next one. It was all one work, and I hadn't finished, so I couldn't stop and rest on my laurels or be satisfied or wonder about where it's gone. I didn't know what was going to happen in the play, I just started with a line of dialogue or with a feeling. I work like this—in collages. I just write stuff down and pile it up, and when I get enough stuff I spread it out and look at it and figure out how to use it. You get enough stuff and you start to build the scene and you don't know where the scene's going, and you don't have any idea what's going to follow after that.

But once you get the first scene done (or it might be the fourth scene in the play), then you can sort of begin to see other possibilities. Just like working in collages, you shift it around and organize it: This doesn't go here; that speech doesn't really belong to that person, it belongs to this person. So, very much like Romare Bearden, you move your stuff around on the pages until you have a composition that satisfies you, that expresses the idea of something and then—bingo—you have a play.

I've never heard anyone say they work like that.

I didn't know what the hell I was doing, but I remained confident that it would all turn out.

Where does that confidence come from, man?

Well . . . I don't know. It comes from an interior life, and as Bearden said, "Art is born out of necessity." So the thing wills itself into being because it has to. Because this is part of your survival, the necessity, the urge to live. It's all part of all of that together. Confidence is a part of it, and you have to believe that you could dive off a cliff and that you'll be okay, that you'll sprout wings and you'll fly, otherwise you'll never dive off the cliff. So, once you do that the first time, and you do sprout wings, it becomes easier to do that the second time. There's no guarantee; it might be the end of it all. But unless you have confidence, you simply cannot do the work.

There's that line in *Radio Golf*, "You score too many points they'll change the rules." Do you ever feel like there are the rules of the game of theatre, and then there are the rules of writing—that after you write two plays, three plays, four plays, winning your Pulitzers, your Tony, being the great writer that you are, did you feel like you were scoring too many points, that the muse would change the rules up on you?

No, largely I was driven by things like this: I remember after I wrote *Piano Lesson*, I was doing an interview with a guy and he says, "Well, Mr. Wilson, now that you've written these four plays and exhausted the black experience, what are you going to write about next?"

(*Laughing.*) Sorry . . .

That's exactly what he said.

Oh, stop!

I said, "Wait a minute, the black experience is inexhaustible."

Oh, Lord have mercy. Did you hit him?

No, no. I didn't.

You were cool.

I just told him I would continue to explore the black experience, whether he thought it was exhausted or not. And then my goal was to prove that it was inexhaustible, that there was no idea that couldn't be contained by black life. That's part of the thing that drove me—I would go: Well, if that's all I have to do, then I'm confident I can do that. A lot of confidence was given to me by people negating the idea—what Albert Murray would call "antagonistic cooperation." They're cooperating with you in their antagonism. They are enabling you to do the work. I took that as fuel for confidence.

Sometimes I tell the younger kids to use shit for fuel, you know, because in the right package . . . .

Yeah. same idea.

You can explode something! It's like, who do you call him, the guy in *Gem of the Ocean* who collects the dog-doo?

Solly. They had dung collectors in Europe. There were guys that would go around and do that. I don't know what use it had . . . .

Fuel, right?

They would sell it.

I've been to India a couple of times. In some places they use cow dung for fuel—it makes a good fire.

And at the same time you keep the streets clean. Solly's part of a long European tradition.

What's great is you say there is no exhausting the African-American experience, and the architecture of your cycle of plays was never at odds with its subject. It's like Shakespeare's writing about kings in those great histories. You're writing about African Americans, and you're putting us in this brilliant cycle, suddenly we can see ourselves in the constellations. It's such an empowering thing you've done for so many people.

Well, thank you again. I'm glad it worked out that way; it didn't have to, but I was sure trying hard.

It did have to work out right, it was written in the *book*, man. It's a necessity. I wonder about the architecture, the renovation in the Hill District in *Radio Golf*, and the structure of the play. Were they ever at odds? Like, you've got the architecture of the play which has certain demands—and then there's that moment about bread pudding. It's this beautiful digression. That's not part of the traditional structure of a play, kind of like the house on Wylie Avenue, the remnant of something old and powerful. But somehow you have found a place for it. Was the subject matter of *Radio Golf* ever at odds with what the play has to do?

I hope not. I certainly don't think so. For me it had to have a certain smoothness, a different kind of language, like that of my characters Harmond and Roosevelt—but at the same time, we're talking about a 100-year history. So the bread pudding is simply representative of some of those houses that are still standing—the old way, the parts of the community that we're giving up. Miss Harriet, the fried chicken—these are all the things that were part of this Pittsburgh community that are being changed because of this slickness with the new building and Barnes & Noble and Whole Foods and Starbucks, simply to entice middle-class people to move back to the Hill, which is only a four-minute walk from downtown. That's prime real estate, and now what you've got is this slum sitting here. Now if we can get black and white people to move back into this area, we will have reclaimed this prime real estate for a better use. But the bread pudding is saying, "Wait a minute, there's a history here and it doesn't fit in with you guys' stuff." The bread pudding is not part of the traditional structure of the play, but it's part of the structure of this particular community backed up against change.

What's so great about you including this bread pudding in the play is that this is not a speech that would survive the test of a thousand dramaturgs! They'd say, "Cut the bread pudding." The renovation project says, "Tear down the house." Yet you let both live in the play and create this beautiful moment. I think that's radical dramaturgy; you're radical in ways that people aren't even hip to. People

think, "August Wilson, he's the great August Wilson and he's on Broadway" and shit, but you're not a Negro. I mean, in line with what Sterling Johnson says to Roosevelt Hicks, Mr. Wilson, you're not a Negro. You're totally not a Negro, and a lot of people think you are. A lot of people have got to get hip to the fact that you've got a lot of bread pudding going on, you know what I'm saying? It's thrilling.

Part of that is I saw my first professional play in 1976, and I didn't know much when I started writing plays in '79. I didn't even know what a play was. I had only seen two plays in my life; I had not read Arthur Miller and Tennessee Williams; I had not read the literature of playwriting. I sat down and questioned whether I could do that. And I thought: Yeah, man, do anything you want; do it your way. From the beginning I didn't pay attention to any rules—I just did whatever I thought was appropriate for a particular play. Of course, I immediately heard from all the people when I first went to the O'Neill, "This is not right, you should cut this, you should cut that, you can't have this speech there, it's got to follow a certain throughline." And I go, "Yeah, well, I see what you're saying, but this is the way I do it."

How did you survive?
Some things I changed because I was able to see where they were correct, but for the most part I would just say, "No, this is my play and this is the way I think it should go, and I trust the audience will sit for that speech—it may be long, but there's a lot of stuff in there and it's different than they're used to so they'll survive because there is a story." One of the things I discovered early on is that I was giving the audience too many things to hold on to at one time, so I started giving them less at the beginning of the play, because I could see where it was too much for them to digest and remember so that the rest of the play would pay off. I wasn't totally disregarding the stuff I had learned about traditional playwriting, but I was sort of mixing and matching them together.

That's being a revolutionary. If you had just followed the rule book—
I wasn't trying to start a revolution or anything. It was just the way I did it, and I didn't go around insisting this is the way it should be done. I just go, "This is me and that's you, and I like your play and the way you did it, that's cool, but this is the way I do it." So many people said I couldn't do it that way, but I just persisted. Like I say, it turned out good. It didn't have to turn out that way, but people saw a value in it.

It had to turn out good. It had to turn out great, man.
The reception of the plays emboldened me to continue to do it that way.

I heard this rumor that you don't go to the theatre much.
I don't go very often. I didn't grow up on theatre. Along with that, I always say that I don't go to the movies either. I'm not that kind of person—11 years, I didn't set foot in a movie theatre. I just simply wasn't interested. I'd rather read a book, but then again, I saw a lot of bad

movies when I did go. Even on a Saturday when the rest of the kids would go to the movies, I'd shoot marbles in my backyard instead of wasting all that time watching these cowboys and Indians or whatever—which all seemed to have the same storyline anyway.

Were you good at marbles?
I was excellent at marbles and those kinds of games, because I played a lot by myself. I enjoyed that. I got good at that kind of stuff, entertaining myself.

Did you have a lot of friends growing up? I would think you were really popular.
There were always the kids in the neighborhood. That was important in my life and growing up. I still remember all of them. Here again, I was sort of a loner, kept to myself, would rather read a book. I played basketball, I played baseball. I was the home run hitter on the team. I was good.

What position did you play?
I played left field.

Of course you played left field!
I wasn't a great fielder. I played prep league from ages 16 to 19. I was the only 16-year-old in the league who was on the starting team.

So you were good!
I had 11 home runs in 14 games—they weren't all over the fence, but all you had to do was hit it over the outfielder's head, and I was good at that, with one exception—I couldn't hit a curveball. Most of the guys couldn't throw curveballs anyway. My secret was to crowd the plate. They were scared to hit you, because that was a big no-no. So when they had to throw a strike, they were going to throw a fastball. I would step out of the batter's box, and when I got back in I didn't get quite as close as I had been before, and all you had to have was timing and reflexes and hit the ball. A lot of times I would just smash these long drives, and sometimes it went over the fence.

　　My career ended when the coach's son and I both struck out twice at a home game, because the pitcher could throw a curveball. Then the coach's son (who shouldn't even have been on the team, because this guy can't play at all) came up to me and said, "I'm batting for you, my dad said." And I go, "No, you're not." So we both went up to the plate at the same time, and I'm telling the pitcher to throw the ball. The coach is yelling, telling me to sit down, and the umpire is confused—and then my hometown fans, who came to see me hit these home runs, began telling me to sit down. I was absolutely going against the rules of the game and I knew it, but I couldn't stop myself. Then eventually I just dropped the bat and started walking toward the pitcher's mound, and I remember the pitcher running out of the way thinking I was coming to get him, but I couldn't even see the pitcher because I was crying. And I walked all the way through the field, and all the way home, crying. It was a long walk. And when I got there, my mom said, "The coach wants your uniform." And I said, "He can have it." That was the end of my baseball career.

I've got to say, I'm glad you didn't have a professional baseball career.
I was going to hit 756 home runs. It was going to be me and Hank Aaron.

Oh, that would've been cool.
If I did become a baseball player, I was going to have as spectacular a career as I had imagined in my mind. If I learned to hit a curveball.

I think you would've.
It's possible.

Look what you did instead! So, 1839 Wylie Avenue, is it always going to be standing?
Probably not. Matter of fact, I'm not even sure what's going to happen with it by the end of the play. I think that the bulldozer might come and the police will come to move all the people that are painting the house and tear it down. That's usually the way it goes. It's sort of a can't-win situation. Like the cat pissing on the sofa—he pisses on the sofa because he doesn't want you to sit there, but what happens is he gets snatched up and taken to the vet. Life goes on as usual, and the couch gets fumigated, and the cat has lost the battle. I figure it'll pretty much end up like that.

But, symbolically, 1839 will always be standing, as part of our repository of all our wisdom and knowledge that we as an African people have collected over the hundreds of years that we've been on the planet Earth. We haven't lost all of that stuff, because when we came here we did have a history, we did have customs, we did have a culture. And all that would have been lost, except they made a mistake by extending the slave trade over those hundreds of years. They were always bringing in fresh, new Africans who managed to keep that stuff alive.

And we managed to stay alive. I mean because, shoot, we make do and can do.
Well, it's the community. You can't survive by yourself. Look at the Eskimos. They live a very harsh life up there, and in order to survive they have to be a community. They have to share everything, even share their wives, because there's no way you can survive by yourself in that harsh environment. In order to survive you need a community of people who can support you. And we've always been those people that rise up in the face of adversity. And a lot of times it's the power of song that will get you through whatever situation. I've found that black Americans, whenever their back is pressed against the wall, so to speak, they always go to an interior light that connects to this African spiritual strength. They ultimately, in whatever way it comes out, sing a song, because when the old folks sing, "Everything's gonna be all right . . ."

it was all right—that's what made it all right. They braced up under whatever the conditions were and managed to survive them and move forward to the next experience. The more experience you have of survival and the more adversity, the stronger you become. Jane Hirshfield, who's a poet, said in one of her poems: "Flesh grows back across a wound more strong than the simple, untested surface before." It's a test; the flesh grows across the wound and is stronger than it was before, because you have managed to survive the test.

I just have one more question, sir, and I don't want to keep you too much longer. What are you writing these days?

I'm not writing anything now. I had a wonderful idea for a comedy about coffin-makers and undertakers, with cameo appearances by Queen Victoria and Fidel Castro and Benny Goodman. All of these things would come up on this coffin-maker's radio, and they would give discourses, like a discourse on British Imperialism given by Queen Victoria, and a discourse on socialism by Castro, a discourse on music by Benny Goodman. In the midst of this, these coffin-makers and undertakers have each hired guns to do battle in their disputes over the coffins. It was just a zany idea. I'm not going to be able to finish that. It's just one of those things that fell by the roadside. That would've been . . . that was my next project.

Suzan-Lori Parks's plays include *Topdog/Underdog*, which won the 2002 Pulitzer Prize for Drama, and the Pulitzer-nominated *In the Blood*, as well as *365 Days/365 Plays, Fucking A, Venus, The America Play* and *Imperceptible Mutabilities in the Third Kingdom*. She is also a screenwriter, novelist and MacArthur "genius" grantee.

HIP-HOP VISIONS OF AN ANCIENT WORLD

An interview with Will Power by Charles L. Mee

March 2006

Will Power is best known for his high-octane writing and performance in *Flow*, the widely toured hip-hop solo show produced by
New York City's Hip-Hop Theater Festival and New York Theatre
Workshop. But the kinetic performer and pioneer of the hip-hop theatre
movement has thrown something new—by way of the ancient—into
the mix. *The Seven*, Power's reworking of Aeschylus's *Seven Against
Thebes*, runs at New York Theatre Workshop through March 12. Originally commissioned by Tony Kelly of San Francisco's Thick Description and subsequently performed at the Hip-Hop Theater Festival in
2002, *The Seven* has been rewritten and expanded for this high-profile
outing, directed by Jo Bonney and choreographed by Bill T. Jones.
Charles L. Mee—himself a prolific adaptor of the Greeks—sat down
with Power at NYTW to talk about storytelling, myth and theatre.

**In the great tradition of Aeschylus, Sophocles, Euripides and Shakespeare,
you're taking a work from the culture that's been received as an inheritance, and
remaking it for your own time and in your own poetic language. I'd like to hear
what you feel the piece is—what it is you think we'll see.**
It's a retelling of another story—we're trying to flip it for today. For
me, hip-hop is all about flipping it. When I say flipping it, I mean you
take something and keep the essence and the quality and the feel of it,
but you make it something different. For example, a lot of black folks
in the '70s in New York either didn't have access to or couldn't afford
musical equipment, so they took their turntables and their record players and they flipped it. They turned them into musical instruments,
percussion instruments.

That's really what brought me to the piece. Jim [Nicola, artistic
director of New York Theatre Workshop] told me that, from what we
know of the way these plays were performed, they were in song. They
were chanted. The way Greek plays are performed today probably isn't

as true to the way they were written, but hip-hop is not so far from that. That was really interesting to me.

Can you say just what the story is?

Seven Against Thebes concerns itself with the sons of Oedipus. After Oedipus had his big fall, his two sons were embarrassed and they shunned him—they kicked him out. So Oedipus cursed them: "You will fight over the kingdom, the royal family, and eventually you're going to kill each other." And the sons were like, "Aw—we're not gonna do that. Let's make a deal: I'll rule for one year and then you rule for one year and we'll switch back and forth." But, in my opinion, a lack of faith in themselves, symbolized by lack of faith in each other, eventually does them in. They succumb to the belief that there's no way out—fate is fate. We're destined to repeat the mistakes of our forefathers. The reason it's called *Seven Against Thebes* is that once the two brothers start to fight, the one who doesn't rule the kingdom draws seven armies and they march on the city.

Some of my contemporaries might not agree, but I don't feel like there are any new stories. There are new characters, but the stories are really about the same issues human beings have always been struggling with. I was fascinated by this family. Oedipus was cursed; his father was cursed; and then after his sons kill each other, the sons of the sons come back and fight each other.

What's the curse, do you think?

We're trying to clarify that a little more in the script now, drawing parallels to hip-hop and African-American culture—but the curse is the belief in inevitable fate. Once you believe in that, it's a constant pull. Oedipus tried to control all this stuff—he tried to do the best he could, but he still fell to the curse. The question is: Do you have choice? Or are we destined to make the same mistakes?

Tell us a little more about how you flipped the story.

The opening monologue is by the DJ. A DJ can play a James Brown record from 1970, then mix it with a Jay-Z record that has that same James Brown sound. These two have a dialogue with each other. Do you know what a sample is? A sample is when you record a section of a song and you loop it in order to create an original song. You create an original song, but the foundation or the elements are from this older song. In some ways what hip-hop is doing is giving a nod to your elders and your ancestors. It's incorporating something old and adding something—like a DJ.

I'm trying to apply those principles of hip-hop to this play. This DJ, she finds a recording of the play *Seven Against Thebes* at a swap meet, and she starts playing it. The story is being told by these old-school, classic-voice types on the record, but then she interprets it. My play is not so much like *West Side Story*, which is a modern-day version of an old play; it's a fusion of both worlds. People ride chariots with hydraulics. They wear Phat Farm togas. They do Apollo at the Apollo. They can reference Shaft and Sophocles. They have both ends.

Who is Oedipus in our world? Who are Eteocles and Polynices, the two brothers? Who are the Seven? It reminds me of *The Wiz*, which was the first play I ever saw. It's different, but that was an example of taking this old play, *The Wizard of Oz*, and flipping it for the time—and that time was soul and funk. It pisses some people off. "Don't touch the classics." You don't have to do it the way I'm doing it, obviously—but if you can't make the connections to why it's important now, then it's not interesting.

I did a talk at the New School a few weeks ago, and someone asked me, "Are you going to stunt the language? The language of the Greeks is so high." I was like, hip-hop theatre is kind of new, but there are some hip-hop storytellers who have magnificently high language. He said, "Are you saying that's at the level of the Greeks?" Well, yeah, in some ways. Hip-hop pays a lot of attention to language, to rhythm. Jazz had scat. In hip-hop we have freestyling. Freestyling is when you're rapping, but it's improvisational rap—scatting, but with words. It's another level of scat. Hip-hop is thick with language. Some people might see that, someone else might not see it.

What you're doing is what Aeschylus and Sophocles and Euripides did—they took legends and stories and one another's plays and remade them.

As I've been working on this, I've been getting into the mythology. What is a myth? Part fiction, part fact. It's embellishing, but it's for a deep purpose—to keep people's history alive, people's culture alive. A message. And it's really great entertainment. As I've been studying Homer and these other writers, I've begun to think of my life in terms of the mythology I've grown up with: the West Coast, California, characters in my neighborhood that are larger than life. We had this bully in the neighborhood, for example, and there were stories about how he took advantage of this guy or fought with that guy. Most of it was true, but some of it was made up: "He beat up five guys! No, he beat up six guys!" It all comes out of Homer, right? We're pretty sure they were oral bards, storytellers spinning these tales to keep their history alive. There wasn't any writing. Homer had these stories, but then he had moments to improvise. That reminds me of hip-hop and the oral tradition of rhyming.

What drew you to this?

Partly the love of myth, flipping the story. It's also this idea, which I'm contemplating myself: Do you have a choice? Or are you destined to repeat the mistakes of the forefathers and mothers? I grew up in the Bay Area in the late '80s and '90s, and it was crazy. Now I go back home and the young people are still killing each other. Are we destined to repeat that? We have this president, George W. Bush. Ten years ago his father was president. Now I hear that they're trying to get Jeb Bush revved up. There's a good possibility that we could have a third Bush as president, not in '08, but 2012. So, are we destined to repeat?

We've been facing some exciting challenges about how to end the play. In the Greek tragedy, they kill each other. Aeschylus was, if I'm correct, one of the first playwrights to have the chorus debate the question: "You don't have to kill each other." "Yes we do. Yes we do." "No you don't. No you don't." But ultimately, it's a Greek tragedy, so they kill each other. In our play, do we want them to kill each other? And, if we do, do some characters leave the stage and say, "I'm not going to listen to this record anymore"? How do we negotiate that?

What's happening now in rehearsal?
This has been a really exciting, interesting process. There have been some big challenges. I'm in hip-hop theatre, I'm doing my thing. Jo Bonney is an excellent choice of director because she understands the world—she's worked with Danny Hoch and Universes. She's someone who's not from the culture, but still has that level of understanding of how to tell the story, the dramaturgy and stuff. Still, hip-hop theatre is a relatively new art form. The first generation of hip-hop theatre artists who came up, we were people who wrote our own material, directed it and performed it: Danny Hoch, Sarah Jones, Universes, in the dance-theatre world, Rennie Harris. Now, we write a play and pass it on, but that's incredibly difficult because the pool of performers who can do this kind of thing is still forming. If you want to do *West Side Story*, thousands of people can do, "When you're a Jet." That's already an established musical-theatre form. But with hip-hop theatre, you have to be able to rhyme, rhyme in character, handle the weight of the original text (because we sampled some of the original text), move with Bill T. Jones's choreography, and sing. It's challenging. We had people coming in who had worked on Broadway and Off Broadway, but just could not do it. We had rappers who could rhyme, but it was like, "Okay, remember: You're a 70-year-old psychic. You've got to rhyme like a 70-year-old psychic." The people we ended up getting are an amazing bunch of folks—young people who, in one way or another, have their pulse on this kind of thing.

Another challenge: My friend Will Hammond and I composed the music. But when I would hear it against Jay-Z or Erykah Badu, the composition was good, but the production was not. All my friends were like, "The music, man . . . ." So we needed to find our own hip-hop producer, someone who could take the song and "up it." But we needed someone who also had theatre sensibilities. That was really difficult to find. First I grabbed the CDs of people I like, and we started contacting people and they were like, "$20,000 a track." And we were like, "No." Or they were like, "Theatre . . . I don't understand. What is it? I don't get it." And the people who understood theatre—they didn't have the hip-hop sensibilities. We searched long and hard and we finally found one guy—in Atlanta. His name is Justin Ellington. He grew up with a youth ensemble in Atlanta, so he knows composing for theatre, but he's also a hip-hop producer. He's got a song on Ciara's album, but he also works at Alliance Theatre. We can talk about production on the level of Jay-Z, but we can also talk about the feeling of the character. We were so lucky to find him.

The last challenge was the DJ. She has to be able to act; she opens the whole play. What I wanted was someone like DJ Reborn, who worked with me in *Flow*. What we actually needed was a turntablist. But it was really difficult to find that person—I was kind of pulling for a DJ, and Jo was kind of pulling for an actor. So we said, let's get an actor who we can teach to be a DJ, someone who can spin around and cut in the air. She's telling a story, she can cut on this level. I really wanted a female for that role. [The part eventually went to Amber Efé.] The DJ finds the record. She digs the record, but as it goes on, she starts questioning it. Why does it have to be like this? I don't want to generalize, but I feel there's something about feminine energy as opposed to the masculine energy of the old, the conqueror. Also in hip-hop, there are not a lot of female DJs—there are some in New York, but not outside. With DJ Reborn for *Flow*—it's like a revelation in Iowa or in Minneapolis. I see young women's eyes just open right there. DJ Reborn is bad. That's something that can be a revelation and show people new ways into hip-hop culture. I think it's important, breaking down walls, breaking down stereotypes.

I've learned so much about the characters from the actors. These are seven heroes, and a lot of the actors who are playing them are very unique characters in themselves. Flaco Navaja—he's in Universes—is a character. As a person, he's a character. Edwin Lee Gibson, who plays Oedipus—he's strange, but in a beautiful way. Having strong personalities helps a lot. Oedipus is a personality and Edwin is a personality as well.

What to you is exciting about theatre that you couldn't do in some other form, or in some other way?
It comes down to a particular kind of storytelling that theatre involves—people in a room, you know? There was always something about that that excited me. I came up in a community theatre/activist/science-fiction type world. The theatre I knew as a kid was always about stretching the imagination. One of Sun Ra's dancers was my first drama teacher. She came into my community and created this Afro-centric, science-fiction, children's presentational theatre. You can still see that in my work today.

What happened between then and now?
When I was 14, I started to rhyme. Hip-hop hit the West Coast a little later. The first thing that got popular in my neighborhood was break-dancing. I tried to breakdance, but people would just blow me away. This was before the gang activity hit big-time. If you had beef with someone, you would break with them. I was getting taken out. I couldn't hang. So me and my friends, we switched to rhyming. At that point theatre or performance was about expressing yourself, more like a hobby, something to do, something fun. We didn't think hip-hop was something you could make a living from.

In my early twenties, in the neighborhoods there was some mad drama going on. Early '90s, people were dying, getting shot all the time. It was always around. Hip-hop theatre was like, how can we bring it back to telling stories? It wasn't that consciously thought out. Looking back now that I'm older, hip-hop theatre was really a response to the chaos that was going on. A lot of the hip-hop theatre pioneers were going through that at the same time I was. We created these artist collectives in London, New York. We didn't know each other.

Are you thinking about any other ideas for the theatre?

I have this idea about a teenage punk band in the early '70s. They're in high school. They practice in the garage. The Vietnam War is going on, people are getting drafted, people are coming back all jacked up. I think I'm going to develop it for the Children's Theatre Company in Minneapolis. The challenge is, it's a band. They don't have to rap because they didn't rap back then. But they have to sing, act and play instruments. The idea is that the bass player might be playing something and the drummer might jump from behind the drums and do a monologue about his father while the bass player is backing him. I want to see *Sweeney Todd* [directed by John Doyle on Broadway] because I hear they do stuff like that.

I'm 35 and for the first time in my life I'm looking forward to being on the road a little less. That's really how I've made my living, which I love, but I'm married. I have a dog. I have ideas for things that I need time to get out. It's a blessing to have this time to step back.

It will be interesting to see, in a number of years, how the story changes. It's really hard to live in cities now if you don't have a lot of money. A lot of poor people are moving out and some of the suburbs are getting rough. Up where I live, in Beacon, N.Y., it's okay, but Poughkeepsie or Peekskill—whoa. That's starting to be a trend. I don't know if that's going to affect me, affect where I live. I remember the cities of 1970s. It was a whole different world. In San Francisco you could rent half a Victorian as a single mother—and if you had a little more money, you could buy one. Not anymore. If you grow up poor in a city you still have more access to culture. There's more flavor: "I'm from Brooklyn." "I'm from Harlem." But if you live out in the middle of nowhere, and there's still violence—it's just strip mall, it's isolated. It's going to be interesting to see how that's eventually reflected, but we're in the middle of it right now. As a storyteller, you want to be contemporary, but you need a little time to reflect.

No more Greeks?

I'm going to be a Greek scholar after this! I've been reading so much Greek poetry, which is beautiful, but not for a while, man. You're a master playwright—you know how you get into the world. When I was doing *Flow*, I was into that world. Now I want to move to another world—the world of the early '70s. If Disney comes along and is like, "You want to do the *Iliad*?" I'll be like, "No, I'm good."

Charles L. Mee's plays inspired by the Greeks include *Iphigenia 2.0, Orestes, Trojan Women: A Love Story, Big Love* and *True Love*. He is the only playwright member of SITI Company, for whom he has written *bobrauschenbergamerica, Hotel Cassiopeia, Soot and Spit* and *Under Construction*. His complete works are available at *www.charlesmee.org*. His work is made possible by the support of Jeanne Donovan Fisher and Richard B. Fisher.

BILL RAUCH'S OREGON TRAIL

An interview by Rob Weinert-Kendt

October 2006

The first time Bill Rauch directed a play in Oregon, the venue was a cattle sale barn with a soil floor so dry that it had to be wet down before each performance so clouds of dust wouldn't get kicked up and blind the audience. The only bathroom facility was an outhouse a decorous distance away. That 1988 production, an adaptation of Brecht's *The Good Person of Setzuan*, retooled and re-titled for the farming town of Long Creek (pop. 230), featured a cast of local amateurs alongside Rauch's professional colleagues who, with Rauch as team leader, had logged thousands of miles bringing theatre to tiny, underserved communities throughout the U.S. under the upstart banner of the then two-year-old Cornerstone Theater Company.

Rauch will soon return to the Beaver State in a big way: Starting next month, he'll begin the process of taking over the reins of the Oregon Shakespeare Festival in Ashland, a $22.5-million repertory resident theatre powerhouse, succeeding Libby Appel to become only the fifth artistic director in the festival's 71-year history. The post, which will become his full-time job starting next June, takes Rauch a long way from the day in 1986 when he and 10 other founding members of Cornerstone piled into a blue van with a mission to remake American theatre from the grass roots up—and, pointedly, far away from what Rauch and company saw as the stultified, culturally homogeneous programming and audiences at most mainstream regional theatres.

In the nearly 20 years since that first trip to Oregon, Rauch and Cornerstone have both evolved, not so much away from their original mission as into an expanded understanding of the possibilities of theatrical dialogue and community. After five years on the road staging adapted classics in the nation's hinterlands, Cornerstone settled in multicultural Los Angeles and grew into an influential theatrical force with a budget edging toward $1 million (it's now $1.4 million) and an institute with an annual summer residency to pass on its methodology to new generations of theatremakers. It was from the company's unlikely West Coast home base that it began a rapprochement of sorts, mostly on its own terms, with the regional theatre establishment it had once opposed. Alternating with long-term playmaking residencies in L.A.'s far-flung communities (Watts, Pacoima, Boyle Heights and Beverly Hills, among others), Cornerstone mounted groundbreaking community collaborations with Arena Stage in Washington, D.C., Great Lakes Theater Festival in Cleveland, Long Wharf Theatre in New Haven, Conn., and even the nearby Mark Taper Forum.

Soon Rauch himself began to be lured away as a freelance director to such Southern California mainstays as the Taper and South Coast Repertory, as well as to Minnesota's Guthrie Theater and Connecticut's Yale Repertory Theatre; at the latter, he staged the premiere of Sarah Ruhl's *The Clean House* in 2004. Among the theatres that came calling was Oregon Shakes, starting with Robert Schenkkan's *Handler* in 2002. The company has invited Rauch back every year since.

In June, Rauch officially left Cornerstone as it hit its 20-year anniversary, with Alison Carey's contemporary update of *As You Like It*, presented at the Pasadena Playhouse, as his directorial send-off. This month at Lincoln Center Theater, he helms the starry New York premiere of *The Clean House*. His long-overdue Gotham splash proves that among the post-Cornerstone paths Rauch might have taken was a thriving freelance directing career. But as Ruhl herself puts it, "Directors are seen as hired guns, but Bill intuitively wants something larger. He wants to build an artistic home for himself and for the people he identifies with."

That's one impulse that's been clear from the beginning, says Carey, another Cornerstone founder.

"So much of the spirit of the company came from Bill's personality. I had a very populist and political motivation when we started out," says Carey. "But Bill's inclusiveness was more instinctive, I think—he was just always bringing people in. And nobody forced Bill to do administrative stuff; Bill's good at it and he enjoys it. He tends to bring administration into the art, and art into the administration. He's always had them integrated, in a way."

James Bundy observed this extraordinary balancing act up close: He served as Cornerstone's managing director for a crucial part of the rural years, and has invited the company both to Great Lakes Theater Festival and to Yale Rep, where he currently serves as artistic director.

"He makes a big difference to his community of collaborators in terms of how they do their job and how they see their roles," says Bundy of Rauch's work, both with Cornerstone and on his own. "I think it has a lot to do with his personal orientation to the world. Bill is genuinely interested in and open to every person he meets. That turns out to be to be a great orientation for somebody who is working with a first-time theatre artist, or for somebody coming into a theatre company where people have done things the same way for a long time."

But Rauch is no longer a post-collegiate revolutionary out to shake up theatrical business as usual, if he ever was. Artistic directors who've hired him repeatedly say they appreciate his leadership savvy as much as his boundary-breaking theatrical creativity.

"It's not as if bringing him in affects how we rehearse and mount plays," says David Emmes, founding co-artistic director of South Coast Repertory, where Rauch is an associate artist. "But I think his Cornerstone experience translates remarkably well into him being the kind of director who's really able to empower actors and designers, and allow them to be fully open to the journey of the play."

Says Libby Appel, who will retire as OSF's artistic director next year, "There is little ego but lots of vision with Bill. He has the leader's ability to value everyone in the room, but he still has the vision and strength of character to follow through on a decision." He's not been hired to shake up OSF, with its complex interlocking repertory schedule, she says: "This program has very severe structural demands, and he wouldn't be here if he hadn't worked beautifully over the last five years within the rules of the game. I can't imagine him not making innovative changes, but they will be within the general structure of the festival."

Nevertheless, Bundy thinks the theatrical landscape has changed since Cornerstone set out to map its own way—and that Rauch and Cornerstone themselves have had something to do with it. "I'm sure that Cornerstone has changed the game," Bundy says, calling Rauch "one of the five most influential people in American theatre, in terms of how we do our work," and citing the example of the Guthrie and Cornerstone's recent co-production of *The Falls*, Jeffrey Hatcher's new play inspired by Thornton Wilder's *The Long Christmas Dinner*.

Is Rauch poised to expand his influence from his powerful new post in Oregon? And can he keep his uniquely pacific blend of art and administration going? *American Theatre* sat down with him in L.A. to talk about his past as a path-breaker and community-builder and his future at the helm of a huge, lavishly budgeted resident theatre.

When you and your compatriots piled into a van in 1986 and headed for what we now call the red states, what did you think was ahead of you? Did you want to found a company that would one day have a home? Did you want to make a career?

We wanted to reach people who weren't being reached by the professional theatre. And we really did have this hunch, a very passionate hunch, that we would become better artists if we did work for people who weren't already going to theatre. When we first articulated it, in a letter to the Broadway producer Manny Azenberg, which is the first place we turned for money, we said, "If you just invest a couple hundred thousand dollars in us, we'll come back after two years with all these great new American plays that we will have created, and we'll bring them to some great theatre city." It was very naïve. But by the time we took off, on June 30, 1986, we were already thinking in much longer terms. I don't think any of us would have dared to say it would be around in 20 years. But it was all in service of trying to create something we believed in enough that we hoped it would have a long life.

The alternative was regional theatre, and that didn't interest you.
Well, 9 out of the 11 founding members went to Harvard/Radcliffe, so we were heavily exposed to the American Repertory Theatre. And one ART staff member gave us this advice: "You can get on an escalator that's swiftly moving up, or you can go try to reinvent the wheel for yourself." Of course, he meant, "Get on the escalator," but it felt crystal clear to us that we wanted to reinvent the wheel—that sounded much more exciting. The alternative, as we saw it, was regional theatre. Because we were young and we were arrogant, I don't think we fully appreciated the diversity of regional theatre; I don't think we appreciated how much regional theatre's roots were revolutionary, and that it was a proactive response to something that was frustrating in an earlier time. We just knew that the regional theatre largely served a small percentage of the population, and that frustrated us. We wanted to serve a wider segment of the American people.

It sounds like from the start your work was administrative as much as artistic—you had to build a company from scratch to do your art.
We were so open and free and easy about so many things, but there were certain things we were absolutely rigorous about. One was that we would never live as exchange students in other people's homes; that we would always have private bedrooms in otherwise unoccupied facilities. And two, that Cornerstone would be how we earned our paycheck. Those paychecks got mighty small in those early years, but it was never about getting a day job and doing Cornerstone on the side.

And we knew that if this was going to be how we made a living, we needed to build an infrastructure to make that possible. I think we also believed in the mission so passionately—believed in this dream of giving voice to community, creating art through community, collaborating with first-time artists, performing for first-time audience members—that we knew we needed to develop an infrastructure to make that possible because that infrastructure, as far as we knew, didn't exist.

But you were able to make room for yourself and other artists to make art in the midst of making a company?
The heart of it was the art, always. When I was a young director, I used to go to every performance of every play I directed, and continue to take notes and tinker. Cornerstone's early managing director, James Bundy, who's now at Yale, was like, "The play has opened. You've got all sorts of big-picture artistic director things that you should be doing." I was like, "I must be at every performance—they need me!" James is the one who really taught me that it's okay to let a show go after it's opened— and it's not only okay, it's actually healthier to let the actors own it and run with it. Of course, now the actors are protected by their union from my earlier impulses to continue to tinker, but in those early days, I used to just keep working on those shows until closing.

But you created a space, a headspace, where you could be an artist in the midst of all the logistics that had to happen.

Yes, because that was the reason we were creating the logistics. Also, I think we always thought of building the structure as a work of art unto itself.

You started Cornerstone in opposition to regional theatre. But now that the company has collaborated with major regional theatres, and you've directed there as a freelance artist, do you feel you've shifted the dialogue somewhat, so that you and the company come to these projects on your own terms?

I do think that when Cornerstone collaborates with a regional theatre, it's not business as usual for that regional theatre. Doug Wager deserves all the credit for being the first regional theatre artistic director, at Arena Stage, to bring Cornerstone in, for *A Community Carol* [1993]. When I first met with Doug, I went in thinking, "Oh, he wants to talk to me about doing a freelance show." My heart sank when I realized, three minutes into the conversation, that he wanted to talk about a Cornerstone show. I chafed at the idea that I'm not Bill, I'm Cornerstone, I have no separate identity. But within 10 minutes of that, I realized, what's a bigger event—that a regional theatre wants to hire me to direct a play, which would be a nice thing for me personally, or a regional theatre wants to completely shift its priorities, completely reshape how it does business, over the course of a year, in order to adopt Cornerstone's methodology and create a Cornerstone work of art? That was in fact a much bigger achievement, and a much more important thing for the company, for me personally, for American theatre—a much bigger deal.

Are you going to miss the community-based projects, working with nonprofessional or first-time community artists to develop and stage shows? Are there parts of that you won't miss?

I'll tell you what I won't miss—and this is very mundane but very real—is the scheduling, trying to work around the schedules of people who are shoving in being in the play on the side of the rest of our lives. You combine that with very large casts, and the logistical challenges but also the spiritual challenge of not having the freedom to have everybody in the room all the time you need them—I'm not going to miss that.

But there's so much that I already miss. I remember during the controversy over the representation of gay Muslims in *A Long Bridge Over Deep Waters* [2005's culminating "bridge show" of Cornerstone's "faith cycle" of plays], we had a meeting with about 25 members of the Muslim community representing multiple points of view about that issue. There were people inside and outside Cornerstone who said, "There are gay Muslims, and we want to represent them in our play. It's a non-issue." People were even insulted that we had to spend any time talking to anybody about it. And then there were people who said, "It's a non-issue—the majority of the community has said, 'This is offensive, this is against our religion, we don't want it in our play.' Why would Cornerstone even think about dragging a gay Muslim into the mix?" So you had these two completely contradictory worldviews, both of which were dismissive of the fact that the company would take the time to investigate both points of view.

Well, that meeting was scheduled for 90 minutes, and it was still going strong 4 hours and 15 minutes later. [Cornerstone ensemble member] Shishir Kurup walked me to my car afterwards, and he said, "You know, you're never going to have this give-and-take when you leave here. How do you feel about that?" I knew he was right. There's something about the purity of mission and the purity of heart at Cornerstone—the people that you meet and the conversations you end up having are extraordinary. I've tasted that for 20 years, so I'm going to try to create situations for myself where I'm having those conversations.

Were you happy with the way that controversy was resolved?
I'm very proud that the scene existed in the play. I am deeply proud of the fact that we had that dialogue with 25-plus members of the Muslim community. Were there costs? Of course. There were no straight Muslims in the cast by the time we opened; there were straight Muslims in the cast originally. That's a cost, but that's a cost we decided to bear.

Do you imagine that in professional situations you and the playwrights you're working with won't have to deal with this kind of concern?
Well, when I directed Jeff Whitty's *The Further Adventures of Hedda Gabler* at South Coast Rep [this past January], there was a series of characters that were different fictional renditions of Jesus in the piece. And we had some deep and meaningful discussions around the table about our responsibility for how we presented Jesus. Jeff made significant changes and was constantly grappling with trying to be responsible to people in the audience who might be Christian, and balancing that with what he wanted to say about how Christianity has been subverted and perverted by people who are perhaps not following its most profound teachings. That was a conversation I would have had in a Cornerstone rehearsal room.

If a theatre in this country decides to put on *Merchant of Venice*, and a local synagogue protests because of the anti-Semitism in the piece—these are issues that theatres have to grapple with all the time. How do you listen to the impulses of the artists working with you, how do you listen to community impulses, how do you respect it all and make decisions and move forward? And what are the ethical choices to be made in any given situation?

When you came to L.A., did you have a sense that you were coming to a theatre city, or to seek collaborations with local theatres?
No, we knew we were going to be attracted to working in neighborhoods that other professional theatres were not working with. We did know that the talent pool, in terms of professional artists, would be very different in this city. But the big part of why we picked L.A. was

cultural diversity. We were at the time still an all-white company, and we wanted to remake ourselves as a multi-ethnic company. And we very strategically chose Los Angeles because it looked like the United States of the 21st century.

There was skepticism among some of your supporters about your move to L.A.
Yeah, I was naïve about how intense the East Coast bias against Los Angeles is—the absolute fervor of that. When a little girl was killed by gang gunfire in Pacoima while we were working on a show there, we were told that we'd been rejected by our major foundation funder, and the quote from the foundation officer was, "The panel and I are disappointed that you've turned your backs on your mission, to seek the big time in Los Angeles." The juxtaposition of that little girl's death at our performance site and that quote just said it all. Or Peter Zeisler, who was running TCG at the time, invited me to be on the TCG board, but also expressed his displeasure about our move, saying, "Why did you leave America and move to L.A.?"

Do you think that you've turned around that perception or prejudice?
I think given the kind of work that we've done in Los Angeles, people get why we're in L.A. and what L.A.'s about. And the fact is, Cornerstone actors do work in film and TV, so all that stuff that we pooh-poohed, like, "That's not why we're moving here"—inevitably, when you hire professional actors in this city, the film and television industries are part of the mix for them. Including my own husband [Christopher Moore]. And I directed one episode of TV ["Judging Amy"]. I confess.

I'm wondering how your work with first-time, community-based performers has influenced your approach with professional actors. Are you the kind of director who wants to know about and use an actor's lived experience?
If Cornerstone has taught me nothing else, it has taught me that every human being is infinitely complex and beautiful. That lesson serves me as an artist wherever I'm working. Whatever I start to perceive as an actor's limitations—I'm able to remind myself very quickly to not start mythologizing that actor based on their limitations, but to remember that that actor has incredible untapped reserves, and the only limitation is actually my inadequacy as a director to help that actor tap those reserves. Whether it's somebody who's been acting for 45 years and is locked into crusty old habits, or whether it's somebody who's never set foot on stage before, they've got something in them that could move and dazzle audiences. Can I help them access it, within the limitations of time we have? That's the game, that's the joy. That's the steep mountain.

You could have a career as a freelance theatre director all over the country, but that's not the path you're choosing.
If I put enough energy into it, I could continue to make my living as a freelance director, moving from theatre to theatre. There are two problems with that being my long-term plan. One is artistic, and that

is that I think I'm an artistic director at heart. As seductive as only directing plays and not having to deal with the headaches of running an institution might be, even in this short time away from Cornerstone, I'm learning that I love the artwork of nurturing an institution and running an institution.

And the second one I would say is even more urgent, and that's my family. My husband of 22-plus years, and our two children, aged six and one—all four of us hate being apart. In what city in this country can you make a living as a freelance director without having to be on the road? It's not that viable.

Which brings us to OSF. Did you know from the first play you directed there that it was the place for you?

Handler was a turning point in my life. I do link it, frankly, to my leaving Cornerstone. It was a show about snake-handlers, low-income people in a rural community in the Southern United States. My Cornerstone M.O. would have been to create a show about that community with people from that community, and have a life-changing, frightening, thrilling experience. Well, there I was in Oregon, at a large theatre, working with all professional artists—and I had a life-changing, very sacred experience. The input was different; the people telling the story were not the people who had handled snakes, but we had as resources a bunch of documentaries, and Robert Schenkkan, the playwright, had lived for a week with snake-handlers and gone to services. It was really interesting to be using those different professional tools, and to be creating a sense of community with all professionals. As a very small but telling detail, many of us in the cast ended up calling each other Brother and Sister—I was Brother Bill to a lot of the cast members—just as the characters did.

There was something communal, and again I'll use the word sacred, about that entire experience. It was like going through a wormhole and suddenly being reconnected to the artist I was when I was 19, when I was 20, where suddenly I remembered what it was to create a work of art without the context of first-time actors and community-based methodology. And I was happy. I think maybe I'd fallen into a mental trap that community-based work was good, traditional professional work was bad. The *Handler* experience was so artistically and spiritually fulfilling that it opened up the possibility in my mind that while community-based work is good, professional work is also good, just in a different way.

Do you think that communal experience had something to do not just with where you were at that time, but also with the repertory acting company at OSF?

The fact that those actors were part of an ensemble, and knew each other, in the same way that Cornerstone works with an ensemble, in the same way the Wooster Group works with an ensemble, is not a coincidence. Resident acting companies in this country are an endangered species; they hardly exist anymore. And I do believe the best work in world drama comes out of company situations; I'm a passion-ate believer in company. You know, it's interesting, when you look at the places that have become my artistic homes of late: Cornerstone, ensemble; Oregon Shakespeare Festival, company; Yale Rep, not a company, but deeply connected to the Yale Drama School, so you have a group of students learning and working together over three years; South Coast Rep, run by founders, founding company members act in a majority of productions over the season; even the Guthrie, for many years an acting company. So I do think I'm attracted to places where company values are at the heart of the work.

What else draws to you Oregon Shakes?
I love the eclectic repertoire that the rotating repertory, and it being a destination theatre, demands. People come to see multiple plays, so there has to be a mix of Shakespeare and other classics, contemporary and commissioned work. That eclecticism appeals to me as an artist and as an artistic director. The legacy of the organization—that it was started in 1935, and to see the artistic bar just steadily rise and rise over those 70-plus years, is very moving to me. And how passionate and lit-erate and devoted and opinionated the audience is.

OSF has an extremely diverse company.
Diversity has been increasingly important to OSF over recent years. Obviously, given my experience at Cornerstone, a big part of what I bring to bear as artistic director is a commitment to diversity, on stage and off.

In what new directions do you hope to take the company?
I want to expand the commissioning of new work that has been so effec-tive at OSF. And to think about major multi-year artistic initiatives.

So after making plays everywhere but inside traditional theatres, you're realiz-ing that you can say what you want to say as an artist—even in a theatre.
Yes, that's right. You don't need to run away from the real theatre building to make exciting things happen. It's tricky to talk about this; obviously, Cornerstone was my life's work and it continues to be among the most vital theatre going on in this country. But for me as a director now, I'm excited to work in a space that was meant to be a theatre.

Rob Weinert-Kendt is a critic and arts journalist living in Brooklyn. He has written features and criticism for the *New York Times*, the *Los Angeles Times*, *Variety*, *Newsday*, the *Guardian* and the *San Francisco Chronicle*, among oth-ers, and was the founding editor of *Back Stage West*.

THE MANAGEMENT PUZZLE

A conversation with Steven Chaikelson, Debbie Chinn, Criss
Henderson, Melanie Joseph, Edward A. Martenson and
Susan Medak

By Joan Channick

January 2007

**Thirty years ago, there were few academic programs for theatre managers.
Today there are several dozen graduate training programs in theatre management and arts administration, which seem to be proliferating. As both a graduate of such a program myself and as a faculty member who has taught in a couple of programs, let me ask the heretical question: Is academic training
necessary? In a field where most people don't have formal training, what is the
purpose of your programs today?**

**STEVEN CHAIKELSON, chair of the theatre division at Columbia University
School of the Arts in New York City and head of its MFA program in theatre
management and producing:** Both as an educator and as someone who in
the real world outside the university employs people, I acknowledge
that formal academic training is not required; there are plenty of excellent people in the field who are working their way up and learning the
business, up the ladder, rung by rung. From an employer's perspective,
though, I find that graduates of MFA programs have a much greater
sense of the big picture—how very different areas of the industry have
impact on each other.

**So you'd characterize training programs as an efficient way to get broad experi-
ence in a brief period of time.**

CHAIKELSON: That would be the primary motivator. Secondarily, it's
also a great advantage in terms of building a network with the faculty
as well as the students with whom you're going through the program.

**EDWARD A. MARTENSON, chair of the theatre management program at the
Yale School of Drama, former executive director of the Guthrie Theater:** This
question has a very different answer if we're talking about the value of
the training from the students' perspective than it would if we're talking about the value of the training from the field's perspective. Appren-

ticeship always has been the primary mode of training for all disciplines in the theatre field and probably always will be. We look at the traditional content that comes in academic training as an add-on to that. Nothing can substitute for experience in our field. You have to be inculcated into the way things work through apprenticeship. In the context of our program and others I respect a lot, apprenticeship is at the center of what you would think of as an academic program, and the classroom work is in addition to that.

The answer to the question from the academic side is another question: What are the limitations to apprenticeship, and how can we fill them in? Apprenticeship is inevitably connected with the concept of best practices. You want to give students a clear idea of the way things are done best out in the field, so they can fast-track once they're out. If apprenticeship existed only on its own, if that's all there was, then best practices has the potential to become the thing you aspire to, as opposed to what would be more valuable for the field as a whole—which is viewing best practices as the platform that you stand on to innovate and raise the standard of practice. Academic training should be designed to give the students the tools—in addition to giving students best practices—that create the capacity for them to raise the standard of practice during their careers.

Criss, what was the impetus behind the creation of your new Arts Leadership Program? Why did Chicago Shakespeare Theater ally itself with the Theatre School at DePaul, and what distinguishes your program from those that already exist?

CRISS HENDERSON, executive director of Chicago Shakespeare Theater and director of the DePaul University/Chicago Shakespeare Theater MFA Arts Leadership Program: I had no formal arts management training other than the fact that I had this amazing theatre that gave me the opportunity to learn over 17 years, as we grew from a $100,000 budget to a $13.5-million budget. Building on some work that the Illinois Arts Alliance had done on succession planning (which raised the question of where the next round of leadership was coming from), we wanted to create a way for our organization to continue to serve as a laboratory for growth. The Arts Leadership Program is different from many of the established arts management programs. It is a very individually driven and determined educational/professional experience for only two fellows each year. The dual commitment as a Chicago Shakespeare Theater employee and DePaul graduate student creates a laboratory in which emerging leaders can experiment professionally and academically—honing and developing their skills and talents while finding or refining the direction they want to set out in as they enter what we hope will be a long and impactful life in art-making and arts management.

Susie, as president of the League of Resident Theatres, you've now taken on professional development of practicing managers as part of LORT's mission. What are the field needs that LORT is trying to address?

SUSAN MEDAK, managing director of Berkeley Repertory Theatre: There was a moment when it became clear that the organizations were becoming increasingly complex and that the management skills of people who were in the job pool were not up to those challenges. Our organizations are much more complicated than they were 20 years ago. So many of us realized that we would no longer hire ourselves to run these organizations. Many of us who have been managing for a long time came into the field with very little skill and a lot of good intentions and a great sense of idealism, and we were lucky enough to be able to apprentice ourselves to people who knew more and to be able to grow with the field.

The field and the world have become more complicated. I see a disconnect between the training programs and those of us who are hiring. While the training programs are producing young people who think of themselves as arts managers, they're not necessarily being hired in great numbers by the field. At the same time, the field is changing so quickly that most of us no longer have the skills that we need to be doing our jobs.

LORT has three groups of managers: There are the veterans who have decades of experience dealing with unknown things they haven't dealt with before and need to have new tools in their repertoires. There are midlevel or young managers who have never received formal training, or received it and then threw themselves into jobs, where they still don't feel completely equipped. And then there are people within our theatres who very much want to grow within the organization. While there isn't a natural mechanism within our theatres to be training them, there can be a mechanism within LORT for training them. Trying to address all three of those needs is a bit of a challenge, but it's what we're hoping to accomplish. If we do it right, I think we'll produce a generation of much more sophisticated managers.

MARTENSON: Whether we're talking about early-career training or executive education—that is, in-service training—the source of the problem is exactly the same: that is the high level of complexity of the organizations in the field. It's not only a matter of the environment that we inhabit being more complex, it's that the institutional form that we invented primarily for the nonprofit theatre is in and of itself a mechanism of much higher complexity than any mechanism that we've invented in the history of theatre. People need ways of being able to figure out new solutions. There are problems that they can't solve instinctively, and they need new ways to think about those things.

CHAIKELSON: I think that makes a really strong case for broad-based training programs that give a strong foundation in all aspects of the business of running theatres. I would make an analogy with a law school education, where it would be very rare for you to come out of law school and immediately become a partner in a law firm. You go to a law school, you get a very broad-based legal education that teaches you to think like a lawyer, then you can join a law firm, and from that base you then specialize and develop in your career.

MEDAK: The young people who have come out of training programs whom I have mentored have been among the most stimulating people that I have had the chance to work with. In addition to learning skills, they've also learned the rigor of how to think. We all have to be better thinkers. So I think the kind of graduate school training, the kind of intellectually engaged exercise that you're asking students to undertake, has the capacity to serve the field extremely well in the long run.

What are the kinds of skills or habits of mind that are needed to be successful managers or producers today?

DEBBIE CHINN, managing director of California Shakespeare Theater in Berkeley: The ability to converse with diverse constituents. We have about five generations of people that we now have to manage in different ways, from your older board members to your young interns, and we don't know quite how to move graciously or gracefully between some of those.

We need to learn how to deal with generations of people who speak very differently. I find I'm having to learn so many technical skills. I'm having to learn about how to communicate—I'm having to learn about MySpace, and all of these social networking things. It's mind-boggling to have to pick up those very basic skills. Then there are also people who don't respond to e-mails or text messages or IMs.

Where do you learn those things? Do you turn to the younger people in your organization, who are probably more technically adept than you are?

CHINN: I talk to my 21-year-old nephew. I learn some things through my colleagues, but I'm learning much more from people outside the profession, who are telling me that people don't respond to the ways in which I am communicating. We had an interesting session with a group of financial people from Clorox who helped us do a quick, down-and-dirty assessment of our business plan. They felt that we were still working out of an old business model, when people are communicating and expecting things in a different way. I'm learning from these 30-year-old MBAs, who don't read the paper but get all their news on their BlackBerrys. It's teaching me how to market in a different way. But I'm not learning marketing from my marketing colleagues, I'm learning from outside the profession. That, to me, was a big eye-opener, because I assumed I would learn about best practices marketing applications from marketing directors in the nonprofit sector.

MARTENSON: We have a profession that's built around conventions. An easy example is that if you know how to be a stage manager in one theatre, you know how to be a stage manager in another. If that weren't true, our whole structure would fall apart, because you'd have to spend five weeks training up a stage manager every time he or she came in. We have this huge volume of unstated "this is the way you do it" that can be transferred from gig to gig. That's our strength, and that's also our weakness. There comes a point where you bump up against the limitation of that and you have to look outside for new ways of thinking about the everyday problems.

MEDAK: Among the challenges right now is that the speed of change is such that as soon as you learn one way to solve a problem that solution is already obsolete and you have to start looking at the next way. The difficulty is that we can't afford to abandon completely all of the skills that we've accumulated, all of the practices that are in place to begin with. So what you're doing is accumulating new practices without being able to discard the old ones. You have to be able to absorb more information than we ever have before and to be able to process it quickly.

MARTENSON: I learned entirely through apprenticeship. I had no training. The first thing I learned was the rulebook. And the second thing that I learned was financial management. And the next thing that I learned was accounting, and then labor relations through participating in LORT, and so forth. By the time my career in managing theatres was drawing to a close, I had finally passed the point of knowing about H.R. from a kind of legal perspective, and I had finally gotten to the point of being interested in H.R. as how do you motivate groups of people and how do you mold organizational cultures and so forth. The apprentice way of learning these things is step-by-step. It's additive. We're like little libraries. We have to collect books, but you can't throw any of the old ones away. You have to keep expanding your capacity.

Melanie, you have defied the conventions of the field. You've created a new producing model, and you're also very thoughtful about developing the next generation of leadership within your own company. Talk about the challenge of developing a shared leadership model.

MELANIE JOSEPH, producing artistic director of the Foundry Theatre in New York City: I don't even like to think about the word "manager" because in some ways it's removing the person from the making of something. We make things. When I was structuring the Foundry, I didn't want to have a managing director and an artistic director. It didn't feel right to me. I always imagined that as the Foundry grew it would define itself as a collective (for lack of a better word). Imagine if there were five producers in the office and we were all producing projects and we shared some kind of aesthetic. I didn't know how to name it until I'd done it for a while, and then I realized what the word "producer" meant. The idea of an artistic producer is a person who is somehow still close to making things. Everybody learns pretty much everything. We tend to share the ownership so that when we have to negotiate a contract (which I hate to do most of all), all of us can do it. All of us can deal with an agent, all of us can deal with Equity, all of us can deal with a tour, all of us can deal with a presenter, all of us can deal with a technical rider, etc. It takes time for that to happen, but whenever an intern comes in here, they're literally exposed to everything, not confined to a department.

I'm soon going to be 51. I'm thinking about how I want to live the next chapter of my life. I was thinking at one point of succession, but I don't really want to leave the Foundry because there are so many things that I still want to do that the Foundry permits me to do. We got official about it. We now have three producing artistic directors who run the Foundry. We have a producer's chair where we are mentoring young producers. We give them a certain amount of money for a project, they have a chair in the office, and they have access to all our files and funders, and we mentor them through the production of that particular project.

One of the things that I find particularly surprising in the people who come out of the professional schools is their lack of connection to the art. I always feel so bad about it, because I don't know why they would be doing this if they didn't love art and artists. We were working with somebody out of a professional program—we were mentoring him through the production process—and we wanted to have a meeting with the whole company. He said, "Oh, we don't need to meet with the actors." And I said, "Oh, of course we have to meet with the actors. They're in the show. We're going forward on something together. How do we not meet?" He didn't understand even remotely what we were talking about.

CHAIKELSON: You've hit on a really crucial point. Most of these people who are coming in who want to have these ongoing careers in theatre as managers and producers have been acting or directing for years—they've gone back and forth between acting and directing and maybe writing as well. They get into these programs and, once they are compartmentalized in a management program or a producing program, they are somehow seen by the directors and actors they're in school with, and especially when they get out into the world and are working, as simply the paper-pushers and the check-writers. That has a really negative impact on their development.

MEDAK: I think there's a real discrimination. In many programs and in many organizations to be identified as an administrator means that you are not an artist—you're not somebody who thinks of herself or himself as having an artistic sensibility. Worse, I think you are perceived as being not creative.

JOSEPH: That's why I call myself an artistic producer. I don't mean that lightly. I think of myself as an artistic partner in every single show we do. I consider my opinion of that work as important as any director's. And I don't want to have to defend it. With any artist that we commission—we do all our work by commission—we make it really clear that if you work here, we are your collaborators. Period. We are not your producers.

CHAIKELSON: There's a feeling that the managers are not entitled to have an artistic opinion. Or that they're somehow in the way if they come out with something artistic in certain situations. At Columbia, at least once or twice over their training as an artist, directors and playwrights have a class with management and producing students so that they have more of an appreciation of them as individuals and what they bring to the table.

MARTENSON: Consciousness of this has to be foremost in our minds in the selection of the students and in the way that we orient them right from the beginning. It is so easy for those who put themselves on a management track to forget that it's necessary for us to be theatre people first and managers second. And if you ever lose sight of that as a profession then we're very likely, inch by inch by inch, to become like the symphony orchestras, where there's a wall between the artistic life of the institution and the management life of the institution.

MEDAK: I'm finding that even the smallest of companies is discovering that they need strong management skills. During the last two years, I've been asked to mentor three top leadership people from small, non-traditional organizations. None of them had envisioned becoming managers, and certainly not managers of anything that might be construed as institutions, and yet what each was experiencing was that as their organization grew, they needed to develop more refined administrative skills. If anything, each company was slowly and without intention moving toward a more institutional structure. I am increasingly convinced that form follows function in theatre as well as in anything else. Organizations develop institutional models, in part, because function drives the form. How an organization goes about attracting an audience is not separate from making theatre. It is about one aspect of making theatre, and it requires the same level of expertise as costume design—it's just a different kind of expertise.

HENDERSON: One of the things that we've tried to do with the Arts Leadership Fellows is to take a very far-reaching look at the structures. The Guthrie Theater's new structuring, where [artistic director] Joe Dowling dissolved the partnership and put this sort of cabinet beneath him, and the appointment of the three artistic directors at the Stratford Festival of Canada—these things signal new directions. I hope that there's a willingness on the part of institutions over the course of the next decade to let the leaders question those old forms. I think the spirit of the collective that Melanie talks about, and the semantic difference between art-making and art-managing, is essential, no matter what the size or scope of the work. As our organizations grow, it's valuable to go back to that sense of collective spirit that we had a decade ago.

I don't think we're giving our emerging leaders the voice. I don't think we're helping them find their voices to lead or steward or manage, or whatever their preferred direction may be. To some extent that may be a result of the proliferation of training programs. It may be that growing into a legitimate field we've created the separation.

CHINN: I like Melanie's idea about shared ownership, and I think what may be compounding the problem of the division of artistic and management is that we're held to different standards and benchmarks. I'm held to account for the financial results to our organization whereas my artistic director may not necessarily be so. There must be a way where we can start to craft a unification of both those top leadership positions so that we're held to the same objectives. A lot of artistic directors just assume that the financial piece of it will be taken care of by the managing director, and sometimes there's a great deal of tension when managers assume their positions in an organization. We're in survival mode, most of us.

I'm very fortunate that I have an artistic director [Jonathan Moscone] who is very, very creative and collaborative about reaching common financial goals and working within his artistic model to achieve those goals. I'm not entirely sure that students coming out of grad school understand that it takes both sides—that it's not "this is what a managing director does" and "that is what an artistic director does." You're successful artistically if you've had rave reviews, and you're successful from a management standpoint if you have a surplus. Seldom do we have a board that calls on both leaders to work together to come up with shared ownership of the organization.

How do you train future artistic and managing directors for their role in working with a board on the governance issues of a theatre? It's the one thing that can't be replicated within a training program.

MARTENSON: In our training program we're absolutely explicit that the reason that we exist is to raise the standard of practice in the field, and increasing the capacity of future leaders to do that is our method. Governance is the most important way in which these organizations we've created are more complex than anything that's gone before. I think this is our frontier. We can't get at a better sense of governance of our institutions just by looking around to see who's doing it best and emulating that. Governance isn't really about who is on the board and the relationships with the executives. Governance is about how you make decisions in the upper reaches of the organization, and that includes the artistic director and the managing director, with board members. Governance is really much more a shared function than the way in which we normally talk about it.

MEDAK: The two fundamental issues of management are managing process and managing people. The combination of those two drives all of those other decisions: how to draw good decision-making out, how to draw good observations out, how to move from thought to action are the fundamentals of the organization.

MARTENSON: Governance is a shared function. We're going to continue to be mired in dysfunction or borderline dysfunction as long we think about governance from the perspective of "Who gets to decide?" The real question about governance has to be, "How can we get the best decisions?" rather than drawing lines about who gets to decide.

CHAIKELSON: A large part of that is something that Ed's already touched on, which is how we address the thought process. We try to help build good collaboration, good leadership and good problem-solving skills. You start with the rules and regulations. You look at industry standards. You look at the conventional wisdom. You get all of that under your belt. Then, if you're dealing with a not-for-profit, you look at the commercial models. If you're dealing with the commercial, you look at the not-for-profit models. And you look at other areas of entertainment or industries to explore other ways that people are solving problems.

JOSEPH: And you look outside the United States as well, because there are really interesting things going on in the rest of the world.

Steven, we've been focusing on the not-for-profit theatre, but one of the distinctive things about Columbia's program is that you give equal emphasis to the commercial and not-for-profit worlds. How do you use the interaction between those two sectors? Are they separate tracks?

CHAIKELSON: No, they're completely complementary. In some cases the focus of an individual course may be more not-for-profit or more commercial. In other classes, one lecture may encompass both not-for-profit and commercial and the way that they have similarities and differences, or the way they work together in respect to particular issues. The faculty are people who move rather seamlessly between commercial and not-for-profit worlds. You can be a leader in a not-for-profit theatre and have to deal with the commercial producer in terms of enhancement. You may be self-producing in more of a commercial arena, especially if you're at a Roundabout or a Manhattan Theatre Club or a Lincoln Center on Broadway. A lot of our alums tend to move back and forth between the commercial world and the not-for-profit world and bring the practices from one to the other.

So an important skill that one needs to have today, which perhaps wasn't necessary 30 years ago, is to be able to operate in both the not-for-profit and commercial sectors, because there's so much greater interaction between the two worlds.

MEDAK: I think to say "both worlds" is too narrow, because there are multiple commercial structures and multiple nonprofit structures. We have to have a comfort level with a fluidity of styles.

So much of management is about human relationships. The strength of a manager, the strength of the management process, the strength of the decision-making process, always comes down to the capacity of people of goodwill to interact with each other. And I have yet to figure out how you train people for that skill set. I'd love to hear how you try to integrate that into your programs.

CHAIKELSON: Well, certainly coming in with a degree in psychology wouldn't hurt. One of the things we try to do is complement the pure management-type classes with courses that are producing and management oriented, but where you're sitting around the table with your directing colleagues, or with playwrights, or with dramaturgs, or, in some cases, students from other areas of Columbia University. Bringing other people into the room, seeing how they perceive a certain area of the business and getting the issues out on the table is a very important part of the program.

HENDERSON: One of the things that the full-time employment component of our training program allows for is that every fellow has projects that are based with the senior staff of the organization. The program requires that the fellows work through the different leaders with their different styles and their different objectives. Each fellow also produces our annual corporate gala and is the key person who sits with the gala committee and the gala chair, who represent leaders in the community. It has turned out to be a great opportunity for the fellows to sit with major CEOs of companies, one on one, and work on a specific project. The understanding on the part of the board member or the CEO that this is an emerging leader, an arts manager in training, has made for a really interesting dynamic on both sides.

MARTENSON: Working effectively with others is an indispensable skill. At the Yale School of Drama we don't isolate that into a course or into a little program element. It permeates everything that we do. In order to graduate from our program, you have to have demonstrated that you can go out and work with people in order to get things done without having the formal authority to do it.

How are artistic leaders being trained? Most of these academic programs tend to be focused on what we'd consider traditional managerial roles, although there is some looseness about that. People being trained as directors may aspire to lead theatres as artistic directors, but there's not the same kind of attention being paid to leadership training for artists. National Arts Strategies, TCG and other service organizations have begun to try to fill that gap.

MARTENSON: A few years ago Greg Kandel and I put together an executive program for artistic directors under National Arts Strategies and TCG and Dance/USA, and the response to that has been overwhelming. It certainly is part of my agenda that I've carried with me into my new job at Yale, to try to explore whether we should be more formal about a description of a leadership training track for artistic directors.

JOSEPH: It's kind of interesting to think of the divisions of labor that are articulated even at the school level—the management program, the directing program. It's interesting to think of how it gets perpetuated by those divisions.

MARTENSON: Certainly it's a widespread assumption in the field that the primary training to be an artistic director is to be a director. I think that there's no reason at all to shy away from questioning the validity of that assumption. There's no reason why if a young playwright has a serious interest at some point in his or her career in directing a theatre, he or she shouldn't take advantage of a training track.

CHAIKELSON: At Columbia, while we don't have a formal training program specifically for artistic directors, we have this philosophy of not just wanting to turn out a bunch of quote-unquote "managers," but more creative managers, creative producers and producing artistic directors. We have classes in which the students are working to create new non-profit theatres and build those models within a classroom setting, where they can wear an artistic hat. We have courses on planning your season where, again, people who are interested in much more of the producing and artistic direction side can learn those skills, take what they know about dramatic literature and the development of new work and apply it to setting your season, impacting audiences, budgeting.

How do we keep talented people engaged over the arc of a long career? How do we create a learning culture in our field? Where is knowledge developed? In the university-based programs, do you see yourselves as the place where research and development happens in this field? And how do you then share that learning with the broader field?

CHINN: Executive coaching is critical for people who have been in the field for a long time. There comes a point where we tend to feel very isolated, or sort of stuck. We need to be able to fine-tune our leadership skills as we get deeper into our careers, to help prevent burnout. It can be helpful to talk with a coach—who isn't a professional colleague—about a certain conflict issue that you might have with an actor or the union rep or the artistic director or whatever, and to learn how to speak differently so that it's not confrontational. Many of us could benefit from renewed learning.

MARTENSON: We've graduated about 40 classes, about 260 graduates, from the management program at the Yale School of Drama. About three-quarters of our graduates remain in the arts and entertainment field, but only about half of those, a little more than a third of the total, are in the theatre. That would put us somewhere in the vicinity of 90 people who have had the kind of leadership impact in the theatre field that we train for. And you can look at that as half empty or half full.

The ultimate value of all of the training activities that we're talking about is really limited by the value that the field places on them.

The practicing leaders in the field are the ones who determine whether they have a hunger to make themselves better. The practicing leaders in the field are the gatekeepers who decide what young people they hire and choose to bring along. So, in a kind of marketplace way, they are assigning a value to training that I think that all of us would prefer to be higher. People in the field tend to think that the reason more people coming out of the training programs don't commit themselves to the theatre field is that they choose not to—whereas from the point of view of the students, it's a choice that the gatekeepers in the field are making. They have to go where the jobs are.

CHINN: Does compensation play into that?

MARTENSON: It plays into it a lot, because all of these training programs are very expensive and you come out of them with loans. Those economic realities are forceful.

MEDAK: It would be glorious if we could create better linkages between the graduate programs that are training people and the theatres that are hiring people. If there were a perception that there was a more natural link between the two—if there were a perception that your graduate school training program was actually going to help you attract a job—I think there would be greater incentive for people to become well-educated.

JOSEPH: Most of our politics are determined by the market, by economics. How you keep people in the field, or don't keep them, or attract them into the field, has to do with how the field exists in the continuum of the world that we live in. There's perhaps a sanctity to art being a public institution and not necessarily financially sensible. I don't think we can separate ourselves from the context that we exist in and the kind of rabid appetite of the way the market governs our world.

MARTENSON: The economic realities can't be divorced from it altogether, but it seems to me that they're minor in comparison to things more in the realm of social relations. I've been very interested in the question of why is it that in our field the employers, that is the theatres, aren't beating down the door to hire all of our graduates the moment that they graduate, while in other fields that happens as a matter of course. As near as I can tell, the single reason that separates fields that do that from fields that don't is that in our field the people who are doing the hiring weren't educated in that way. They came up through apprenticeship. But, for example, in the field of consulting, nobody gets to work unless they've had the training to begin with, so they automatically assume that the new people that they bring in are going to have to be well trained. That's almost a cultural assumption, and not an economic matter.

MEDAK: There's a real prejudice in the field among those many people who didn't go to graduate school against the students who come out of graduate school. It's an unpleasant thing to say, but we know that it exists, whether it's based on insecurity or on the idea that I learned in a certain way and therefore you should, too. We don't operate the way medical and law schools do. It's a terrible waste that we don't think about the graduate schools being a point of entry for most of our organizations. This may be a time where people are more open to that than they've been.

HENDERSON: I hope that our program in Chicago can serve as a model for theatres across the country, encouraging them to engage more deeply in professional training through strategic partnerships within their own communities. Each of our organizations has people, energies and expertise to share. If theatres could formalize those core educational competencies and make them available in various forms to the next generation of arts leaders, it would be a win-win proposition for the theatre, the students and the field.

In fact, our Arts Leadership Program has as much positive impact on our theatre as it has on the fellows themselves. The fellows have challenged many of the modes of operation and institutional conventions here at the theatre in a way that only a student can. That wide-eyed curiosity cuts through a lot of old-school theatrical thinking. The program allows us to draw from a national pool of candidates and keep our young staff among the best and brightest in the field. It has created a greater sense of responsibility among our senior staff to mentor and coach—and not simply supervise. It has also inspired staff throughout the organization to look at professional development opportunities, and many more are requesting to attend seminars and conferences than did before.

All in all, there is a culture of learning that helps everyone stay connected to the work. I believe that the spirit of questioning and curiosity that results will help us keep our work under the microscope of this learning laboratory and challenge us always to make what we see through its lens better.

Joan Channick is associate dean of Yale School of Drama in New Haven, Conn. She spent three seasons as the managing director of Long Wharf Theatre, also in New Haven, and has taught in Goucher College's distance learning arts administration program. From 1998 to 2006 she was deputy and managing director of TCG.

LOOKING BOTH WAYS

A conversation with Gina Gionfriddo, Rolin Jones and Adam Rapp

By Sarah Hart

July/August 2008

The siren song of film and television—leeching the theatre's best and brightest—has generated quite a bit of hand-wringing, especially when it comes to playwriting. Theresa Rebeck famously threw down the gauntlet in 1995, issuing her opinion in the Dramatists Guild newsletter that there should be space for writers to lend their talents to both stage and screen—which earned her a hefty share of field-wide scorn. The writers' strike this past winter led Charles Isherwood of the *New York Times* to beseech prodigal playwrights—tongue only somewhat in cheek—"Return to the fold! Fate has given you another shot at artistic redemption. Don't let it slip away." But even as the theatre community convenes panel discussions to cope with ominous talent drain, a growing number of writers (and actors, directors, etc.) are making a dual- or tri-media lifestyle work—*without* abandoning the theatre.

So if the boundaries are more porous than they used to be—or are at least becoming that way—does it change the way writers are creating theatre? Does it—perhaps more subversively—change accepted forms in television and film? For its 32nd Humana Festival of New American Plays, Kentucky's Actors Theatre of Louisville and *American Theatre* convened playwrights Gina Gionfriddo, Rolin Jones and Adam Rapp to delve into the culture and aesthetics of crossing media, setting aside—for the most part—the issue of financial disparity (though, insists Gionfriddo, "it's something we should *never* stop talking about").

For Showtime's "Weeds," starring Mary-Louise Parker, Jones is bemused to receive all the serious scenes for rewrites. "I'm the serious guy over there. That's not necessarily my wheelhouse in the theatre world," says the writer, who dreamed up an emotionally stunted 20-year-old agoraphobic robotics expert bent on discovering her Chinese birth mother via an android doppelgänger for *The Intelligent Design of Jenny Chow*. "'Law & Order' is about resolution," notes Gionfriddo of her work for NBC's procedural shows. "I think my plays are about no resolution." Indeed, her *Becky Shaw*, at Humana this year, is a crackling tale of relationships unraveling, with no final answers. Rapp has found more artistic space in his film work—including 2005's *Winter Passing* and a screen adaptation of his play *Blackbird* in 2007—than in his stint as a writer for "The L Word," also on Showtime, in 2006, but both diverge from his stage work, in which he prefers to keep his characters in one room.

No matter the venue or form, it is—as Jones points out—all story-telling, and any chance to hone craft feeds the theatre.

Can you talk first about writing for television? What is the process? What is the room like?

GINA GIONFRIDDO: The "Law & Order" shows are a little bit atypical in that we don't have a room [for collaborative writing]. They tend to be run more like benign dictatorships—you work with one other person, then the two of you go up against the big boss.

ROLIN JONES: For "Weeds," we get together at the start of the year. We've got boards all over the place, then a couple of slaves to write things on the boards. We plot out the entire season—events, character arcs, how we're going to try not to piss off Mary-Louise. It's very col-legial—the non-loneliest writing job ever. You're just bouncing each other back and forth. Then we're handed out individual stories or episodes. You're delivered your plot, so you're just coming up with bull-shit dialogue. Then it goes up to network, and they give you strange dra-maturgy, and you kind of ignore it. And then you've got five days to shoot it. If you can't get it in, you have to rewrite a little bit because it's money and time, and then we edit it, so by the time you guys see it, it's this watered-down, horrible, sad thing that was once something beautiful. And occasionally there's something lovely that actually ends up there.

ADAM RAPP: "The L Word" was a room with catered food and occa-sional yoga and me and six wonderful lesbians. There was a woman from a lesbian rock band called BETTY; a young Bay Area graphic novelist; A.M. Homes, the novelist; Rose Troche, who wrote and directed *Go Fish*; I was the playwright; and the showrunner, Ilene Chaiken, was a TV person. She was the queen and we were the sort of smart minions. We were the band jamming, and she was like, "I like that section." I was expecting it to be adversarial. I was the only male voice in the room. I didn't know television very well. I was expecting the four-act structure or the six-act structure of cliff-hanging, all that stuff that people have to do on network. But there was no pressure for that because we're not trying to sell Kit Kat bars every 12 minutes.

GIONFRIDDO: That's a major difference. On "Law & Order," we have to structurally build in act ends that will bring people back after the com-mercial break. Also, we don't do the beginning-of-the-season arcs because our shows are designed to make money in syndication. They don't want a serial component. They want self-contained stories.

Being the playwright, do you feel like your job is different than the other TV writers? Are you more focused on structure?

GIONFRIDDO: Because procedurals can become a little like machines, I tend to be the character person: "You just told her her son was murdered. She needs to have more of a reaction." "Law & Order" is like working with a poetic form. The challenge is getting a compelling story told within this rigorous little formula. The danger is that it becomes all about the trick and the clue—unless you have character. When I did "Criminal Intent," we were almost all playwrights, but I'm on the original "Law & Order" staff now, and half the writers are lawyers, some of whom began with the show in an advisory capacity. I think we complement each other. They can do the procedural nuts-and-bolts, the inspired legal strategies. Writers who are coming from playwriting or short-story writing will focus more on character.

JONES: We've had four playwrights: me, Rinne Groff, Blair Singer and Ron Fitzgerald. There are a lot of frustrated sitcom writers who were tired of doing network television, who wanted to be free and tell different kinds of stories. You want a cacophony for an effective room. I did come from a very different perspective, but four years into it I'm flexing a different muscle. My writing is much more event-oriented, especially having to deal with terrific but demanding actors. You have to find real wants and needs for them.

What has your work in other media brought back to your playwriting?

RAPP: A lot more economy. The compression of scenes and getting in and out of the room is really important in television and film. The mood is more important than dialogue. You can show more in a reaction shot than you can in four exchanges of dialogue. Learning how to compress has made me a better editor and a better first-draft writer. My theatre scripts are a little leaner now. I generally write a very sprawling first draft. I think I'm a little closer now to what it becomes in a second draft because of the muscle I've been developing in film and TV.

GIONFRIDDO: When I was in college, I took a class with Romulus Linney and he used to try to hammer home that worse than being overly explicit in a play was being willfully obscure. I sort of couldn't hear that. When I started writing "Law & Order," I would talk about a character having four underlying motives that were competing. They said to me, "We can't do *Scenes from a Marriage*. This is a 42-minute teleplay. If you want the audience to know those things are going on, you need to show it." So it has helped me to be a little more disciplined about putting in the play what was in the head.

In terms of pace, you have it at both ends: It's a 42-minute teleplay, which is much shorter than anything you would write for the theatre, but at the same

time you stretch the story over a season or several seasons. Does dealing with that fuller, longer storyline affect your playwriting also?

JONES: We're on season four, so this is the 19th hour of Mary-Louise's drug-dealing mom. *The Godfather* was six hours, for crying out loud. What's left to do? And if anybody watches our show, you know we're horrible with time. It's supposed to have taken three years—but if you look at the stories, it's been like three weeks. You're still only writing those very encapsulated, Aristotelian, three-day, pressure-packed things. There's a lot of baton-writing to the next episode. It's a challenge to go back into a play in that you've got breadth and time to get your story encapsulated. It's like writing a season. We break a season into three acts—episode 5 is the end of Act 1, episode 10 is the end of Act 2.

RAPP: I can talk about it from the film-making point of view. I only got about three days of rehearsal with the principals in my first film. The actors fly in and they go to their trailer, and you meet them and you discuss the scene for like 16 minutes, then you go block it, they're setting up, and then you're shooting a rehearsal. You're giving them notes based on a rehearsal. It's like learning how to build a fire without any instruments. Then you're in the editing room and it's a kind of rewriting process. I realized, six months after we shot it and I'm still in the editing room, that it's a superficial, manipulative form. I was so starving to get back in an organic process in the theatre where you're actually dealing with people—where you're in a five-week rehearsal and having more than a five-minute conversation.

Generally in my stuff, especially in the theatre, people get in one room and they stay there until someone has to leave. The film and TV stuff is one scene and the next. I was getting notes from producers like, "This is a six-page scene." I was like, "I generally write 40-page scenes." "How are you going to shoot this?" I learned that the information the audience had to know had to come on page point-five in order for it to actually work in this medium. I was happy to get back to writing real-time scenes in rooms.

Do you find yourself writing into your plays things you could never do in television or film?

JONES: I don't put that private part of myself in the TV stuff. You've got to save it. If there's a great idea that's come up in the room, something for me, I will squirrel it away like a little nut.

RAPP: They own us. They own our copyright.

GIONFRIDDO: That's a big deal for me. Until you're a showrunner, your scripts are to some extent rewritten. I've had to learn not to invest so much that I'm heartbroken when something is cut.

RAPP: I wrote a pilot for 20th Century Fox. They came after me, saying, "We love your theatre, we love your characters, we love your dialogue, and we love how unique your voice is." So I wrote this thing set in the barrio in New York, an apartment building that was being gentrified. There were all these variously aged people—a little girl who was stealing soap from everybody's apartment, and an old couple in their senior years, and a weird loner guy and a band in the basement. I was really excited about it. And they said, "Can we make the 35-year-old woman who has the shaky hands like 22 and really sexy?" They think I have a good voice, but ultimately they just want to water it down like everything else. I don't understand why they keep coming after people like us—but I guess it's the skill or the craft that we learn in the theatre. It's really hard to hold an audience for two hours when you don't have quadraphonic surround sound and commercials that move like music videos. We have to develop skills in the theatre that are really difficult. It's interesting to me that they go after the playwrights—and it's a sexy thing to have a playwright on your staff—but when you actually come up with a complex character or something you've learned to deal with in the theatre, they don't want to use that skill. It may not be across the board, but it seems like there's a dumbing down.

JONES: You'd be hard-pressed to find better writing in the theatre or in movies than was done on "The Wire," which just ended on HBO. HBO has really opened up television to be able to tell adult stories. That's changed things. That's why I think this line, this separation between theatre and TV, can be starting to blur to the extent that we can just talk about it as storytelling. They do, on HBO, want your shaky-hand thing, I think.

GIONFRIDDO: The fantasy for those of us writing for network is that at a place like HBO or Showtime you won't get the stupid network notes. Network television is in a very, very dire place right now. The fall season tanked. It tanked because the shows weren't good—and the reason the shows weren't good, I'm convinced, is because there are too many people on salary to give notes. We're somewhat insulated at "Law & Order" because of Wolf Films's track record. But new shows can really be ruined by the network notes process, I think. You get 15 sets of notes from executives who need to justify their salaries, and you may have had an interesting product at the beginning, but you don't at the end. That happens because the notes are generally about the "relatability" and likability of the characters. The goal is not to offend. I don't know if we're giving network audiences enough credit. I grew up on Norman Lear's stuff, which was about poverty and racism, and that was all done on network.

JONES: Well, "All in the Family" would be on HBO now.

GIONFRIDDO: I watched "Sanford and Son" the other day. I don't know where that show would be. It is a one-set show set in a junkyard. They would never let you put that on.

Do you consider your audiences for film and television differently than you would for theatre?

RAPP: I'd like to believe that, in New York at least, we try to bring the younger audiences in, and I think we do succeed in some cases. But generally in the theatre we're writing for older and older people, and that's really frustrating. Jim Ryan is a playwright who now teaches at the New School and doesn't write very many plays anymore. He wrote and directed a film called *The Young Girl and the Monsoon*, which was originally a play at Playwrights Horizons. I was on a panel with him, and he was saying that the new Off Broadway is independent film. The price to see an independent film is what it used to be to see an Off-Broadway play. That's the kind of storytelling you used to get when you'd see *American Buffalo* Off Broadway.

JONES: I don't know if it was any different when I was going to theatre. The Mark Taper Forum was sort of my home when I was a kid. I'd go and be the only young guy. I'm still writing for the 20 kids that are there—for myself, when I was sitting there.

GIONFRIDDO: When I lived in Rhode Island, straight out of college, this was the bane of my existence. I had all of these friends who would drop enormous amounts of money on martinis and food, and then you'd say, "Do you want to go see this play? It's $35," and they'd say, "That's a little rich for my taste."

JONES: Martinis are delicious.

GIONFRIDDO: They're delicious, and you always know what you're getting.

JONES: A bad play is a lot worse than a bad martini. Bad theatre is brutal. But watching Gina's play yesterday, the guy playing the lead [David Wilson Barnes] was just nailing everything. The rhythm with that laughing—you can't have that thing that goes back and forth between the audience and the play, riding that wave, in TV or film. If you wrote the movie version of *Becky Shaw*, there would be different rhythms and it would have to be edited in a way to replicate what happened last night.

GIONFRIDDO: It's why I haven't successfully written a screenplay. You can't have that much dialogue in a movie.

JONES: I think you can do it. All the screwball comedies, like the Cary Grant movies, are at your pace. There's still the walk-and-talk in "The West Wing." You just have to edit it to re-create what you're doing with two people conversing on the couch. Remember *Six Degrees of Separation?* That was a play that kind of existed on couches. In the film, they just put that on its feet, so everyone was moving constantly to try to get that energy that was in that Lincoln Center production. Not that that was necessarily the most successful adaptation ever—but in terms of audience, all you're doing is moving these seats over and over again.

RAPP: It's fascinating to watch Woody Allen films because they are just master shots. What he does is so theatrical. I worked with Will Ferrell on my first film [*Winter Passing*], and he was in *Melinda and Melinda* just before. He said Woody Allen will shoot a scene 40 times. We were doing three takes on my little indie film. I said, "Does he give you notes?" He said, "Well, he kind of just says, 'Let's do it again.'" But you would get into this rhythm, and what you're doing is rehearsing. You're rehearsing a stage scene.

GIONFRIDDO: David Fincher does that, too.

RAPP: Ultimately he's shooting a master shot—and it goes master shot to master shot to master shot. He's essentially using theatrical techniques as a filmmaker. You look at a two-person scene in most movies and when they go into the over-the-shoulder, you know it was a four-page scene that got cut down. That's what going in close does. It gives them the ability in the editing room to completely re-create and condense a scene.

JONES: Well, it's hard to pop out. Once you go in, you've got to have a reason in your scene to break. This big moment will happen, and there's nothing left to say, and then you go out to this master and sit there. It's kind of like a theatre beat. That's how that language works. It's interesting what great training theatre is for this, if you kind of unlock your mind. You're at a competitive advantage, I think, if you've had to make it work like this.

RAPP: We control the eye in the theatre by doing really good staging and really great acting and great lighting. But still, it's a big master shot, and anybody over there can look anywhere they want. So every moment has to be valued, whereas I think in the film world, we can be sloppy and then re-create it in the editing room.

JONES: You actually want slop. You want options so you can try to get that spontaneity back in. Because otherwise film can be really canned and dead.

With the blurring of the lines between all of these media—for writers, actors and other artists—do you see a shift in the way theatre is made?

RAPP: Alex Cunningham, who had a play at Humana [in 2000], *No. 11 (Blue and White)*, and writes for "Desperate Housewives" now, was at

Juilliard with me in 1999 and 2000. What she was writing were definitely plays, but they were plays with 72 scenes. She never said anything but "I want to write film and TV." She was working on her technique through the theatre. During that time in New York there were all these plays with so many scenes and so much furniture being shuffled on and off. It was like watching a banquet. I love getting people in a room and leaving them there. I love *The Heiress*. I love watching people sit in a chair and wait. So I was wondering, "What's going on? Are we becoming more like film and TV?" But I don't think that's the case anymore. I think there might have been a reaction to that, and people putting on plays now in New York are valuing the room more than they were.

GIONFRIDDO: I agree. It's such a different landscape now that you have networks like HBO, Showtime and FX, because writers have an outlet for complex storytelling there. So I think who *stays* writing for theatre is interesting. I'm fascinated by who keeps coming to see theatre. I could get the DVDs of "Six Feet Under" and "The Sopranos" and stay in my apartment and watch really great, complicated storytelling. So if I keep going out to the theatre—why do I do that? I get a little Pollyanna about it. To go to the theatre when you've got all this good stuff at home—you're looking for something big.

JONES: Big is totally the word. No more fucking plays about looking for an apartment in New York City. Wrestle with some big shit here. You do have to pay more for it. And you do have live actors working their fucking asses off, and you have people coming who can see a different version of it on TV. Save your big ideas. Be big.

GIONFRIDDO: You can't put "Law & Order" on stage because "Law & Order" is at home, and it's free. So I don't want to see a procedural play.

RAPP: My first year at the O'Neill [Playwrights Conference], in 1996, Lloyd Richards asked, "Who knows what the definition of a playwright is?" There were 11 playwrights, and I was the youngest and Lee Blessing was the oldest. No one said anything, and he said, "The definition of a playwright is: You're walking down the street in the middle of Manhattan, and somebody taps you on the shoulder, and it's a busy street and there's traffic, and they say, 'I have something really, really important to say. It happens at 8:00. You have to drop all of the things you were supposed to do tonight. You have to pay about $40 to $80. You have to get on a subway.' That's what a playwright is." I think when we write, we aspire to ask big questions, and when we don't it just becomes an exercise. To go to the theatre and sit among people you don't know in the dark and await something magical to happen—it had better be really, really powerful.

JONES: Plus, all the people who are working on your play, who have completely screwed their quality of life to do this thing—don't bring limp-dick writing. I haven't written a full-length play in three years. I'm not going to waste anybody's time, or mine, if it's not big. There's a level of pressure that's sometimes not necessarily helpful, but you do have to check yourself about that. All this conversation about losing playwrights to TV—if you're a real playwright and you really love the theatre, it ain't ever going to happen. You're never competing with film and TV for our hearts and the best of our work. It's already fixed. It's a crack addiction. None of us is going to make any money at it. So we're doing it for this other reason.

RAPP: I left "The L Word" in the middle of the season to take a play to the Edinburgh Festival that I got no money for. I got on a plane. I'd just had back surgery. My friends said, "What are you doing? You're giving up your salary." I actually enjoyed writing "The L Word." I enjoyed all the stuff that it did for me. I loved the people I worked with. But it was the crack of the theatre.

If it weren't for the money, would you still go to write for television? Do you feel like there's a value in the form?

JONES: It's fun storytelling—it's all storytelling. There's stuff you cannot do on stage that you can do on TV. The visual aspect of it is lovely. I think it can be artful. If the MacArthur "genius" grant dropped in my lap, yeah, maybe I would take eight years and do nothing but theatre. Poverty doesn't help your theatre career. It doesn't make you a better playwright because you have to go wait tables or cater. That takes just as much of your energy away as your "soul-sucking TV job."

RAPP: I won't do TV anymore. It's not because I don't want to be paid—it's because I don't want to interrupt my life in the way that I had to. I want to have as many good experiences as I can in the theatre, fiction, maybe some films. But I'll tell you: The TV thing really, really helped me get on my feet financially and finally get out of a hole. Writing for theatre is a third-class citizenship. I had two plays at Rattlestick [Playwrights Theater in New York City] in the past few years, and they're a great company that I have great respect for. They pay you a thousand dollars. If you write one play a year and that gets done—that's worse than working at McDonald's. There's no health in that. The Dramatists Guild doesn't have benefits. That's another thing we have to think about.

GIONFRIDDO: TV has been a much better adjunct to playwriting than what I was doing before—teaching freshman composition, catering. All of that really sucked the energy out of me in a way that TV doesn't.

JONES: One of the other seductive things that doesn't come in your personal pocketbook is that you can finally cast your actor friends. In the TV world, you're producer. You can give them jobs. You have no idea the great pleasure and the great joy it is to be able to deliver for your friends in that way.

GIONFRIDDO: It's one of the greater joys of my life.

RAPP: I've become friends with Craig Wright. He was on "Six Feet Under," then "Lost" for a while, and now he has his own show, "Dirty Sexy Money." I talk to him all the time about how much he loves the theatre. We did *Orange Flower Water* at Edge Theatre Company [in New York City] a few years ago and he came and he was having this kind of religious experience. But I do think there is the danger—we go from making no money to making six-figure incomes, and suddenly we get a taste of a car and a decent meal three times a week.

GIONFRIDDO: But—and this sticks in my craw—I don't know any playwrights who stopped writing plays because they wanted a personal jet and a vacation home. What I see is people like Diana Son, who has three kids and is looking ahead to three college tuitions. None of us have kids. Once you have children with tuitions, with needs, I think that's the "lifestyle" that keeps writers in television rather than theatre.

JONES: In the theatre, though, as a writer, you're treated like a rock star—and you'll never get that in TV and film. You might be able to call your parents and not be ashamed anymore because you're actually making a living. But god bless Humana, for keeping me alive and bringing me here for these 10-minute plays for the past three years. My self-worth as a writer is all about what I do in the theatre.

Sarah Hart is the managing editor of *American Theatre*.

INDEX

Notes on the cover images from *American Theatre*

On the front cover, from top left, Johannes Leiacker's set design for *Tosca* at Austria's Bregenz Festival (May/June '08); Lorraine Hansberry (photo by David Attie/courtesy of Robert Nemiroff, Nov. '84); Nina Hellman in Ruth Margraff's *Red Frogs* at P.S. 122 (photo by Bob Handelman, Nov. '02); Joseph Papp (photo by Eric Knoll, Sept. '86); the Broadway cast of *Spring Awakening* (photo by Joan Marcus, July/Aug. '07); Robert Lepage in *Vinci* (photo by Robert Laliberte, Nov. '91); Tony Kushner, Naomi Wallace and Carl Hancock Rux (photo by Susan Johann, Oct. '01); August Wilson (photo by Dana Lixenberg, Nov. '05); illustration for Yale Repertory Theatre's *The Psychic Life of Savages* by Amy Freed (photo by David Cooper, April '03); Socorro Valdez in El Teatro Campesino's *La Carpa de los Rasquachis* by Luis Valdez (Jan. '88); David Henry Hwang (photo by Susan Johann, April '98); Fiona Shaw (photo by Neil Libbert, March '97); Adam Pascal and Anthony Rapp in *Rent* (photo by Joan Marcus, July/Aug. '96); Philip Kan Gotanda (photo by Diane Takei, March '07); Culture Clash in *The Birds* at South Coast Repertory (photo by Charlaine Brown, March '98); Mabou Mines's *The Red Horse Animation* (Jan. '96); Martha Plimpton in *Hedda Gabler* at Steppenwolf Theatre Company (photo by Michael Brosilow, Dec. '01); Peter Brook (May '84); Reggie Montgomery in Suzan-Lori Parks's *The America Play* at Yale Repertory Theatre (photo by Marianne Bernstein, March '94); Tony Kushner's *Angels in America: Millennium Approaches* at the Royal National Theatre (photo by John Haynes, June '92).

On the spine, from top, Sam Shepard (photo by Melinda Wickman/Gamma Liaison, April '84); Taylor Mac in *The Face of Liberalism* (photo by Derrick Little; Nov. '08).

On the back cover, from top left, Carla Gugino and Brian Dennehy in *Desire Under the Elms* at the Goodman Theatre (photo by Eric Y. Exit; Feb. '09); Michael Sullivan, Rebecca Klinger and Isa Nidal Totah in the San Francisco Mime Troupe's *Seeing Double* (photo by Donna Gray, Jan. '90); John Kelly (photo by Paula Court, Nov. '93); Erin Craney in Peter Sellars's *Nixon in China* (photo by Jim Caldwell, Dec. '87); Birgitte Larson in *The Wild Duck* by the National Theatre of Norway (photo by LP Lorenz, May/June '06); Lincoln Center Theater's *Sarafina!* (photo by Brigitte Lacombe, Nov. '88), Steven Epp and Sarah Agnew in *The Miser*, co-produced by Theatre de la Jeune Lune, American Repertory Theatre and Actors Theatre of Louisville (photo by Richard Feldman, Oct. '04).